Taxation

Taxation

Finance Act 2022

Twenty-eighth edition

Alan Melville
FCA, BSc, Cert. Ed.

Pearson

Harlow, England • London • New York • Boston • San Francisco • Toronto • Sydney • Dubai • Singapore • Hong Kong
Tokyo • Seoul • Taipei • New Delhi • Cape Town • São Paulo • Mexico City • Madrid • Amsterdam • Munich • Paris • Milan

PEARSON EDUCATION LIMITED
KAO Two
KAO Park
Harlow
CM17 9NA
United Kingdom
Tel: +44 (0)1279 623623
Web: www.pearson.com/uk

First published 1995 (print)
Twenty-eighth edition published 2023 (print and electronic)

ISBN: 978-1-292-43953-2 (print)
          978-1-292-43949-5 (PDF)
          978-1-292-43948-8 (ePub)

10 9 8 7 6 5 4 3 2 1
26 25 24 23 22

Front cover image © Cubankite/Shutterstock
Cover design by Kelly Miller

Print edition printed by Ashford Colour Press Ltd, Gosport

NOTE THAT ANY PAGE CROSS REFERENCES REFER TO THE PRINT EDITION

Contents

Part 4 Miscellaneous

Part 5 Answers

Preface

The main aim of this textbook is to describe the UK taxation system in sufficient depth and with sufficient clarity to meet the needs of those undertaking a first course of study in taxation. The book has not been written with any specific syllabus in mind but should be useful to anyone who is studying taxation as part of a university or college course in accounting, finance or business studies. The book should also be of value to students who are preparing for the taxation examinations of the professional accounting bodies. A list of relevant examinations is given on the back cover of the book.

Every effort has been made to explain the tax system as clearly as possible. There are numerous worked examples and each chapter (except Chapter 1) concludes with a set of exercises which thoroughly test the reader's grasp of the new topics introduced in that chapter. The book also contains four sets of review questions, drawn mainly from the past examination papers of the professional accounting bodies. The solutions to most of these exercises and questions are located at the back of the book but solutions to those exercises and questions marked with an asterisk (*) are provided in a separate Instructor's Manual.

This twenty-eighth edition is up-to-date in accordance with the provisions of Finance Act 2022, which is based upon the October 2021 Budget proposals. The book also takes into account the Spring Statement which took place in March 2022.

Alan Melville
May 2022

Acknowledgements

I would like to thank the following accounting bodies for granting me permission to use their past examination questions:

▸ Association of Chartered Certified Accountants (ACCA)

▸ Chartered Institute of Public Finance and Accountancy (CIPFA)

▸ Association of Accounting Technicians (AAT).

I must emphasise that the answers provided to these questions are entirely my own and are not the responsibility of the accounting body concerned. I should also point out that the questions which are printed in this textbook have been amended (in some cases) so as to reflect changes in taxation law which have occurred since those questions were originally published by the accounting body concerned.

I would also like to thank the Office for National Statistics for granting me permission to reproduce the table of Retail Price Indices given in Chapter 24.

Please note that, unless material is specifically cited with a source, any company names used within this text have been created by me and are intended to be fictitious.

Alan Melville
May 2022

Summary of Tax Data

Income Tax

	2022-23	2021-22
TAX RATES AND BANDS[†]		
Basic rate	20%	20%
Higher rate	40%	40%
Additional rate	45%	45%
Basic rate limit[‡]	£37,700	£37,700
Higher rate limit	£150,000	£150,000

[†] *Different tax rates and bands apply to the non-savings income of Scottish taxpayers (see below)*
[‡] *Basic rate limit frozen at £37,700 until the end of tax year 2025-26*

	2022-23	2021-22
Starting rate for savings	0%	0%
Starting rate limit for savings	£5,000	£5,000
Personal savings allowance (basic rate taxpayer)	£1,000	£1,000
Personal savings allowance (higher rate taxpayer)	£500	£500
Dividend ordinary rate	8.75%	7.5%
Dividend upper rate	33.75%	32.5%
Dividend additional rate	39.35%	38.1%
Dividend allowance	£2,000	£2,000

	2022-23	2021-22
SCOTTISH TAX RATES AND BANDS[†]		
Starter rate	19%	19%
Basic rate	20%	20%
Intermediate rate	21%	21%
Higher rate	41%	41%
Top rate	46%	46%
Starter rate limit	£2,162	£2,097
Basic rate limit	£13,118	£12,726
Intermediate rate limit	£31,092	£31,092
Higher rate limit	£150,000	£150,000

[†] *These tax rates and bands apply only to the non-savings income of Scottish taxpayers*

PERSONAL ALLOWANCES

	2022-23	2021-22
Personal allowance†	£12,570	£12,570
Marriage allowance	£1,260	£1,260
Blind person's allowance	£2,600	£2,520
Married couple's allowance:		
Born before 6 April 1935	£9,415	£9,125
Minimum amount	£3,640	£3,530
Income limit for basic personal allowance	£100,000	£100,000
Income limit for married couple's allowance	£31,400	£30,400

† *Personal allowance frozen at £12,570 until the end of tax year 2025-26*

CAR AND FUEL BENEFIT

	2022-23	2021-22
Zero emissions	2%	1%
*1-50 g/km (depending upon electric range)	2%-14%	2%-14%
*51g/km to 54g/km	15%	15%
*55g/km to 59g/km	16%	16%
*60g/km to 64g/km	17%	17%
*65g/km to 69g/km	18%	18%
*70g/km to 74g/km	19%	19%
*75g/km	20%	20%
Each additional 5g/km	+1%	+1%
Maximum charge	37%	37%
Amount used in car fuel benefit calculation	£25,300	£24,600

* *These percentages were 1% lower in 2021-22 if the car was registered on or after 6 April 2020*

CAPITAL ALLOWANCES

	2022-23	2021-22
Writing Down Allowance (WDA)		
Main pool of plant and machinery	18%	18%
Special rate pool of plant and machinery	6%	6%
Annual Investment Allowance (AIA)	100%	100%
AIA annual limit from 1 January 2016†	£200,000	£200,000
First Year Allowances (FYAs)	100%	100%
Structures and Buildings Allowances (SBAs)	3%	3%

† *AIA annual limit temporarily raised to £1m between 1 January 2019 and 31 March 2023*

PENSION SCHEMES

	2022-23	2021-22
Annual allowance	£40,000	£40,000
Lifetime allowance†	£1,073,100	£1,073,100

† *Lifetime allowance frozen at £1,073,100 until the end of tax year 2025-26*

National Insurance Contributions

	2022-23	2021-22
CLASS 1 _(Employer + Employees)_		
Lower earnings limit (weekly)	£123	£120
Primary threshold (weekly) (_£190 until 6 July 2022_)	£242	£184
Upper earnings limit (weekly)	£967	£967
Secondary threshold (weekly)	£175	£170
Upper secondary threshold (weekly)	£967	£967
Employee contributions		
Rate on earnings between primary threshold and UEL	13.25%	12%
Rate on earnings beyond UEL	3.25%	2%
Employer contributions		
Rate on earnings beyond secondary threshold	15.05%	13.8%
Employment allowance	£5,000	£4,000
CLASS 1A _- Employeers_		
Rate _on BIK_	15.05%	13.8%
CLASS 2		
Weekly contribution	£3.15	£3.05
Small profits threshold	£6,725	£6,515
CLASS 3		
Weekly contribution	£15.85	£15.40
CLASS 4		
Lower profits limit	£11,908	£9,568
Upper profits limit	£50,270	£50,270
Rate on profits between lower and upper limit	10.25%	9%
Rate on profits beyond upper limit	3.25%	2%

Capital Gains Tax

	2022-23	2021-22
Standard rate[†]	10%	10%
Higher rate[†]	20%	20%
Business asset disposal relief rate	10%	10%
Business asset disposal relief lifetime limit	£1,000,000	£1,000,000
Annual exempt amount[‡]	£12,300	£12,300

[†] _Taxable gains on the disposal of residential property are taxed at 18% and 28%_
[‡] _Annual exempt amount frozen at £12,300 until the end of tax year 2025-26_

Corporation Tax

Financial Year	FY2022	FY2021	FY2020	FY2019	FY2018
Main rate†	19%	19%	19%	19%	19%
Patent box (effective rate)	10%	10%	10%	10%	10%
R&D SMEs payable credit	14.5%	14.5%	14.5%	14.5%	14.5%
R&D expenditure credit	13%	13%	13%	12%	12%

† *The main rate for FY2023 will be 25%. However, a "small profits rate" of 19% will apply to companies with profits not exceeding £50,000. Companies with profits between £50,000 and £250,000 will be subject to the main rate, but reduced by a marginal relief.*

Inheritance Tax

Date of transfer	Nil rate band†‡	Rate on life-time transfers	Rate on death	Lower rate
6 April 2006 to 5 April 2007	0 - £285,000	20%	40%	-
6 April 2007 to 5 April 2008	0 - £300,000	20%	40%	-
6 April 2008 to 5 April 2009	0 - £312,000	20%	40%	-
6 April 2009 to 5 April 2012	0 - £325,000	20%	40%	-
6 April 2012 to 5 April 2023	0 - £325,000	20%	40%	36%

† *Residence nil rate band for 2022-23 is £175,000*
‡ *Nil rate band and residence nil rate band both frozen until the end of tax year 2025-26*

Value Added Tax

Standard rate	20%	(from 4 January 2011)
Reduced rate	5%	
Registration threshold†	£85,000	(from 1 April 2017)
Deregistration threshold†	£83,000	(from 1 April 2017)

† *Thresholds frozen until April 2024*

Part 1

INCOME TAX AND NATIONAL INSURANCE

Chapter 1

Introduction to the UK tax system

Introduction

The purpose of this first chapter is to provide an overview of the UK tax system. The principal UK taxes are introduced and classified and the main sources of taxation law are explained. This chapter also deals with:

(a) the structure and functions of Her Majesty's Revenue and Customs (HMRC) which is the organisation responsible for the administration of the UK tax system

(b) the annual procedure which is used to determine the tax liability of an individual.

The chapter concludes by distinguishing between tax avoidance and tax evasion.

UK taxes

The UK taxation system is composed of a number of different taxes, some of which are *direct* taxes and some of which are *indirect* taxes:

(a) Direct taxes are charged on income, profits or other gains and are either deducted at source or paid directly to the tax authorities. The main direct taxes which are payable by individuals are income tax, capital gains tax and inheritance tax. The main direct tax payable by companies is corporation tax. All of these direct taxes are administered by HM Revenue and Customs (HMRC), which was formed in April 2005 when the Inland Revenue and HM Customs and Excise were merged together.

National Insurance contributions, which can also be regarded as a form of direct taxation, are administered by the NICs and Employer Office of HMRC.

(b) Indirect taxes are taxes on spending. They are charged when a taxpayer buys an item and are paid to the vendor as part of the purchase price of that item. It is then the vendor's duty to pass the tax on to the tax authorities. The indirect taxes include value added tax (VAT), stamp duty, customs duties and the excise duties levied on alcohol, tobacco and petrol. The only indirect tax considered in this book is VAT, which is also administered by HM Revenue and Customs.

Sources of tax law

There is no single source of UK taxation law. The basic rules are laid down in Acts of Parliament but it is left to the courts to interpret these Acts and to provide much of the detail of the tax system. In addition, HMRC issues a variety of statements which explain how the law is implemented in practice. These statements explain the tax authorities' interpretation of the law and will be adhered to unless successfully challenged in the courts.

Statute law

The basic rules of the UK tax system are embodied in a number of tax *statutes* or Acts of Parliament. The main statutes currently in force for each tax are as follows:

Tax	Statute	Abbreviation
Income tax	Capital Allowances Act 2001	CAA 2001
	Income Tax (Earnings and Pensions) Act 2003	ITEPA 2003
	Income Tax (Trading and Other Income) Act 2005	ITTOIA 2005
	Income Tax Act 2007	ITA 2007
National Insurance	Social Security Contributions and Benefits Act 1992	SSCBA 1992
Capital gains tax	Taxation of Chargeable Gains Act 1992	TCGA 1992
Inheritance tax	Inheritance Tax Act 1984	IHTA 1984
Corporation tax	Taxation of Chargeable Gains Act 1992	TCGA 1992
	Capital Allowances Act 2001	CAA 2001
	Corporation Tax Act 2009	CTA 2009
	Corporation Tax Act 2010	CTA 2010
Overseas aspects of tax	Taxation (International and Other Provisions) Act 2010	TIOPA 2010
Value added tax	Value Added Tax Act 1994	VATA 1994
Administration of }	Taxes Management Act 1970	TMA 1970
the tax system }	Customs and Excise Management Act 1979	CEMA 1979

These statutes are amended each year by the annual Finance Act, which is based upon the Budget proposals put forward by the Chancellor of the Exchequer. Some of the tax statutes provide for the making of detailed regulations by *statutory instrument*. A statutory instrument (SI) is a document which is laid before Parliament and (in most cases) automatically becomes law within a stated period unless any objections are raised to it.

European Union law

Until 1 February 2020, the UK was a member of the European Union (EU) and was required to comply with EU law. Member states of the EU do not adopt a common tax system but must implement EU Directives, some of which are concerned with taxation (principally VAT). As from 1 February 2020, the UK entered a transition period during which EU law continued to apply. But this period came to an end on 31 December 2020 and EU law ceased to have effect in the UK as from 1 January 2021.

Although the UK has now left the EU, some aspects of the UK tax system were originally devised so as to comply with EU Directives and these will continue unless amended or repealed by subsequent legislation. Much of the UK VAT law falls into this category.

Furthermore, when the UK was a member of the EU, it was necessary to seek EU "State aid" approval for UK tax-advantaged schemes such as the Enterprise Investment Scheme (see Chapter 6) or the R&D tax credits scheme (see Chapter 23). These schemes had to be designed within the constraints of EU law, but the UK is now at liberty to amend such schemes or to introduce new ones as it sees fit.

Case law

Over the years, taxpayers and the tax authorities have frequently disagreed over the interpretation of the tax Acts. As a result, many thousands of tax cases have been brought before the courts. The decisions made by judges in these cases form an important part of the tax law of the UK and some of the more significant cases are referred to in this book.

Statements made by the tax authorities

The main statements and other documents produced by HM Revenue and Customs as a guide to the law on taxation are as follows:

(a) **Statements of Practice**. An HMRC Statement of Practice (SP) sets out the HMRC interpretation of tax legislation and clarifies the way in which the law will be applied in practice. For example, SP 4/97 (the fourth SP issued in 1997) deals with the taxation treatment of commissions, cashbacks and discounts.

(b) **Extra-Statutory Concessions**. An Extra-Statutory Concession (ESC) consists of a relaxation which gives taxpayers a reduction in liability to which they are not entitled under the strict letter of the law. In general, concessions are made so as to resolve anomalies or to relieve hardship. For example, ESC A91 deals with the taxation treatment of living accommodation provided by reason of employment.

A process of giving statutory effect to certain ESCs is currently underway. This is generally being done by means of statutory instruments.

(c) **Announcements**. Announcements are issued by HMRC throughout the year on a wide variety of tax-related subjects. Of especial interest are the documents issued on Budget day, which provide a detailed explanation of the Budget proposals.

(d) **Internal Guidance Manuals**. HMRC produces a comprehensive set of internal tax manuals for the guidance of its own officers. These manuals may be accessed on the HMRC website (see below).

(e) **Explanatory publications**. Leaflets, factsheets and booklets are aimed at the general public and explain the tax system in non-technical language. These can usually be accessed online, though some are still available in printed form.

Most of the above information is now available on the HMRC website, the address of which is www.gov.uk/government/organisations/hm-revenue-customs.

The tax year

The changes to the tax system that are proposed in the annual Budget speech are usually intended to take effect as from the start of the next *tax year*. Tax years for individuals and for companies are identified as follows:

(a) For individuals, a tax year runs from 6 April to the following 5 April. For instance, tax year 2021-22 began on 6 April 2021 and ended on 5 April 2022. Tax years are also referred to as *fiscal years* or *years of assessment*.

(b) For companies, a corporation tax *financial year* runs from 1 April to the following 31 March and is identified by the year in which it begins. For instance, the financial year referred to as FY2021 began on 1 April 2021 and ended on 31 March 2022.

This book takes into account the provisions of Finance Act 2022[‡] (which is based upon the October 2021 Budget[†]) and describes the UK taxation system for fiscal year 2022-23 and corporation tax financial year FY2022.

[†] *The annual Budget (which used to take place in March each year) now takes place in the preceding October. This gives individuals and businesses more time to digest the tax changes before they take effect at the start of the next tax year. However, there is also a Spring Statement in March. This is largely concerned with public spending plans but may introduce further tax changes.*

[‡] *Finance Act 2022 (which implements the October 2021 Budget proposals) received Royal Assent on 24 February 2022. Further tax changes were introduced by the Spring Statement on 23 March 2022 and these are also explained in this book.*

Structure of HM Revenue and Customs

Her Majesty's Revenue and Customs (HMRC) consists of a large body of civil servants which is headed by the *Commissioners for Revenue and Customs*. The Commissioners are appointed by Her Majesty The Queen in accordance with recommendations made by the *Treasury*. This Government department has overall responsibility for the public finances of the UK and is directed by the *Chancellor of the Exchequer*. The principal functions of the Commissioners for Revenue and Customs are as follows:

(a) to implement the law relating to direct and indirect taxation

(b) to provide advice to the Chancellor of the Exchequer on taxation matters

(c) to administer the divisions and offices into which HMRC is organised.

The routine work of HMRC is carried out by officials known as *Officers of Revenue and Customs*. With regard to direct taxation, the main function of these officials is generally to check a taxpayer's own self-assessment of the tax liability (see below) and then to ensure that the correct amount of tax is paid. The functions of HMRC with regard to indirect taxation (and VAT in particular) are explained later in this book (see Chapter 30).

HMRC has specialist offices which deal with such matters as pension schemes, charities and so forth but most of the day-to-day work relating to direct taxation takes place in local area offices. These offices are responsible for routine assessment and collection of tax and for ensuring that taxpayers comply with tax regulations. Until recently, HMRC had 170 local offices but these are being consolidated into 13 regional centres.

Support for taxpayers who need help with their tax affairs is provided by means of specialist expert advice either given over the telephone (or online) or delivered by mobile advisors at convenient locations in the community.

Administration of the tax system

The remainder of this chapter describes the administration system which is used to assess an individual's liability to income tax and capital gains tax in each tax year. This system is referred to as "Self Assessment". Under this system, the taxpayer (*not* HMRC) is primarily responsible for ensuring that:

(a)   the tax liability for each tax year is properly assessed, and

(b)   the correct amount of tax is paid on the due date or dates.

Subsequent chapters of this book explain the administration systems which are used for the purposes of corporation tax, inheritance tax and VAT.

Self Assessment

If an individual's tax liability for a tax year cannot be collected entirely by deduction at source (see Chapter 2) or via the PAYE system (see Chapter 7), then the liability must be formally assessed. The starting point in the assessment process is usually the completion of a *self assessment tax return*[†][‡]. The annual procedure is as follows:

(a)   At the end of every tax year, a statutory "notice to file" is normally issued to each taxpayer who is required to submit a self assessment tax return. Such a notice requires that a return is made and delivered to HMRC either on paper or electronically. Paper tax return forms (for those taxpayers who need them) can be downloaded and printed from the HMRC website or may be obtained by telephoning HMRC. Voluntary tax returns (i.e. returns submitted without a notice to file) are accepted and valid.

[†] *In certain circumstances, HMRC is empowered to make an assessment of an individual's income tax or capital gains tax liability without that person being first required to complete a tax return. This "simple assessment" procedure may be used in straightforward cases where HMRC already has sufficient information about the individual to make the assessment.*

[‡] *The Government intends to replace tax returns with online "digital tax accounts" as part of the "Making Tax Digital" project (see later in this chapter).*

(b) The main paper tax return consists of a basic eight-page form. There are also several sets of supplementary pages, each of which deals with a different type of income or gains (e.g. income from self-employment). Taxpayers are required to complete only those supplementary pages that are relevant to their circumstances.

(c) A short tax return (STR) is available for taxpayers with less complex tax affairs.

(d) Rather than completing a paper tax return, taxpayers can file returns electronically by means of the internet and are encouraged to do so. Over 95% of self assessment tax returns are in fact filed electronically.

(e) The information requested in a tax return relates to the tax year that has just ended. For instance, the tax return notices issued in April 2022 required taxpayers to declare their income and gains for tax year 2021-22.

(f) A tax return must be completed in full. It is not permissible to omit figures or to make entries such as "see accounts" or "as submitted by employer". Unless asked to submit accounts or other supporting documentation with the return, a taxpayer is under no obligation to do so. However, it is necessary to retain all supporting documentation in case HMRC enquires into the accuracy of a return.

(g) If a main tax return is submitted on paper, the taxpayer has the option of calculating his or her own tax liability (using "tax calculation summary" pages) and submitting this calculation to HMRC as part of the return. HMRC will calculate the tax liability for taxpayers who do not take up this option or for those who submit the short tax return (which does not include a self-calculation facility). However, if a paper return is submitted late (see below), HMRC does not guarantee to advise the taxpayer of the liability in time for the correct amount of tax to be paid on the correct date.

   If a tax return is filed electronically, the tax liability is calculated by computer software. In all cases, the resulting assessment is referred to as a "self-assessment".

(h) Self assessment tax returns must normally be filed (i.e. submitted to HMRC) on or before the following dates:
   - for paper returns, 31 October following the end of the tax year
   - for returns filed electronically, 31 January† following the end of the tax year.

   However, if the return notice is issued after 31 July following the end of the tax year (but not after 31 October) the taxpayer has three months from the date of the notice to submit a paper return. The deadline for electronic filing in such a case remains at 31 January. If the notice is issued after 31 October, the taxpayer has three months from the date of the notice to submit the return either on paper or electronically.

   † *Extended to 28 February 2022 for 2020-21 tax returns, in view of the Covid-19 situation.*

(i) Penalties are imposed if a return is filed late. Furthermore, the submission of a late return may mean that the tax liability for the year is not determined until after the due date of payment (see below). A taxpayer who pays tax late will incur interest and may also incur a late-payment penalty (see Chapter 15).

(j)   The 31 January which follows the end of a tax year is known as the "filing date" for that year. For example, the filing date for tax year 2022-23 is normally 31 January 2024. However, if a return notice is issued after 31 October, the filing date becomes the date which falls three months after the issue date of the notice.

(k)   HMRC is empowered to correct a tax return (so as to rectify any obvious errors or omissions or anything else that is believed to be incorrect) within nine months of the date on which the return is filed. Similarly, the taxpayer has the right to amend his or her tax return within 12 months of the filing date for that return.

(l)   A taxpayer who has paid an amount of tax but now believes that this tax should not have been paid (a situation that could be caused by an error in a tax return) may make a claim for recovery of the overpaid tax. Such a claim must be made within four years of the end of the tax year to which it relates. Depending upon the circumstances of the case, HMRC may or may not accept the claim.

(m)   The tax due in relation to a self-assessment is normally payable as follows:

    (i)   A first payment on account (POA) is due on 31 January in the tax year to which the self-assessment relates.

    (ii)   A second POA is due on the following 31 July.

    (iii) A final balancing payment is due on the following 31 January.

    For example, the tax due in relation to a 2022-23 self-assessment would normally be payable on 31 January 2023 (first POA), 31 July 2023 (second POA) and 31 January 2024 (balancing payment). Further information is given in Chapter 15 of this book.

(n)   An employed taxpayer whose balancing payment does not exceed £3,000 may require that this should be collected via the PAYE system (see Chapter 7). In such a case, taxpayers who file their tax returns electronically must do so by 30 December so as to give HMRC sufficient time to make the necessary arrangements.

Notification of chargeability to tax

An individual who has not received a notice to submit a tax return, but has taxable income (or gains) of which HMRC is not aware, must notify HMRC of his or her chargeability to tax within six months of the end of the tax year in which the income arises. However, notification of chargeability is *not* required if *all* of the following conditions are satisfied:

(a)   the individual has no capital gains

(b)   the individual is not liable to tax at a rate which exceeds basic rate (see Chapter 2)

(c)   all of the individual's income has been subject to deduction of income tax at source (see Chapter 2) or has been dealt with via the PAYE system (see Chapter 7)

(d)   the individual is not liable to a high income child benefit charge (see Chapter 7).

An individual who fails to notify chargeability within the permitted six-month period will incur a penalty (see Chapter 15).

Determinations

If an individual fails to submit a tax return by the required date, an Officer of Revenue and Customs may make a determination of the tax due, calculated according to "the best of his information and belief". There is no right of appeal against a determination and the tax due cannot be postponed. A determination can be displaced only if the return is filed.

Enquiries

HMRC may "enquire" into any tax return. The usual reason for opening an enquiry is the suspicion that something is wrong with the return. However, some enquiry cases may be selected at random and HMRC is under no obligation to justify the opening of an enquiry or to state whether or not the case has been chosen randomly. Note that:

(a) If a tax return is filed by the due date, an enquiry cannot usually begin more than 12 months after the date on which the return was filed. This means that the "enquiry window" for a return which is filed early closes correspondingly early.

(b) If a return is filed late or is amended after the date on which the return was due to be filed, the enquiry window is extended until the quarter day which follows the first anniversary of the date on which the return or amendment was filed. For this purpose, the quarter days are 31 January, 30 April, 31 July and 31 October.

EXAMPLE

In April 2022, HMRC issues a notice requiring an individual to submit a tax return for the year 2021-22. The return is submitted electronically to HMRC on 8 December 2022.

(a) State the date by which any enquiry into the above return must begin.

(b) How would the situation differ if the return was submitted on 17 March 2023?

Solution

(a) The return is filed before the due date (31 January 2023). So any enquiry must begin within 12 months of the date that the return is filed (i.e. by 8 December 2023).

(b) The return is filed late. Any enquiry must begin by the quarter day which follows the first anniversary of the date that the return is filed (i.e. by 30 April 2024).

Discovery assessments

HMRC may raise a "discovery assessment" if it is discovered that full disclosure has not been made in a tax return and tax has been lost as a result.

The time limit for making a discovery assessment is normally four years after the end of the tax year concerned. This increases to six years if the taxpayer has been negligent and 20 years if the taxpayer has been dishonest. But the normal time limit is 12 years if an offshore matter is involved, increasing to 20 years in the case of dishonesty.

Record keeping

Taxpayers are required to keep proper records so that they can make an accurate tax return and (if necessary) substantiate the figures entered on the return. A taxpayer who is in business or who lets property must normally preserve these records for five years after the 31 January which follows the end of the tax year concerned. Otherwise, records must be preserved for 12 months after the 31 January which follows the end of the tax year. For example, records for tax year 2022-23 must normally be retained until 31 January 2029 by a taxpayer who is in business or who lets property and until 31 January 2025 otherwise.

Appeals

Taxpayers have the right of appeal against many HMRC decisions. For example, a taxpayer may appeal against a discovery assessment or against an HMRC amendment to a self-assessment. The main features of the appeals system are as follows:

(a) An appeal must be sent to HMRC in writing within 30 days of the disputed decision.

(b) The taxpayer may also apply to postpone payment of all or part of any tax which is payable as a result of the decision, though interest will continue to accrue on the postponed amount until the appeal is settled. However, postponement is generally not available if the appeal relates to the use of a tax avoidance scheme covered by the DOTAS rules (see below) or arises in connection with arrangements which have been counteracted by HMRC under the GAAR (see below).

(c) On receiving an appeal, HMRC considers the taxpayer's reasons for disputing the decision. Most appeals are settled by discussion and agreement at this stage.

(d) If the taxpayer and HMRC are unable to agree, the taxpayer will usually be offered an internal review of the decision. A taxpayer who wishes to accept this offer must normally do so within 30 days. An internal review is carried out by an HMRC officer who has not previously been involved with the disputed decision and is usually completed within 45 days. The review officer then writes to the taxpayer to inform him or her of the review's conclusions.

(e) A taxpayer who rejects the offer of an internal review may appeal to a tribunal within 30 days of the date of the offer letter. Otherwise, an appeal to a tribunal may be made within 30 days of the date of the review conclusion letter.

(f) Most appeals are dealt with by the Tax Chamber of the First-tier Tribunal. However, more complex appeals may be heard by the Tax and Chancery Chamber of the Upper Tribunal. The Upper Tribunal also hears appeals against First-tier Tribunal decisions.

(g) If either HMRC or the person concerned is dissatisfied with a decision made by the Upper Tribunal, a dispute on a point of law may be referred to the Court of Appeal.

(h) The costs of bringing an appeal before the First-tier Tribunal are usually fairly modest. Parties to the appeal bear their own costs and so a taxpayer who loses an appeal is not normally required to pay HMRC's costs (unless the taxpayer has acted wholly unreasonably). The costs of taking an appeal to higher authority can be very high and an unsuccessful taxpayer may be required to pay HMRC's costs in defending the appeal as well as his or her own costs.

Tax evasion

Taxpayers are required to provide information which is correct and complete. Dishonest behaviour (e.g. concealing a source of income) is known as *tax evasion* and is against the law. On summary conviction in a magistrates' court, an offender may be imprisoned for up to six months. If the conviction is obtained on indictment in a higher court, the maximum prison term is seven years. In either case, a fine of any amount may also be imposed.

Tax avoidance

Taxpayers are entitled to organise their financial affairs in such a way that their tax burden is minimised. This perfectly legal activity is known as *tax avoidance*. For example, a tax-payer might legally avoid income tax and/or capital gains tax by moving funds into a tax-efficient investment (see Chapter 6). Tax avoidance (which is legal) should be sharply contrasted with tax evasion (which is not).

Tax avoidance is acceptable within limits but, over the years, tax advisors have shown great ingenuity in devising very complex and highly artificial tax avoidance schemes to exploit "loopholes" in the tax system. These schemes often result in a significant loss of tax revenue until eventually blocked by specific anti-avoidance legislation. So as to limit the effectiveness of tax avoidance schemes, a regime known as DOTAS (Disclosure of Tax Avoidance Schemes) has been introduced which requires certain disclosures by those who devise such schemes or use them. A brief summary of the requirements is as follows:

(a) Those who promote and market schemes which bear certain "hallmarks" of tax avoidance are required to provide HMRC with details of each scheme. Promoters must provide a description of the scheme, including details of its tax consequences and the statutory provisions on which it relies. The scheme is then registered by HMRC and is allocated a reference number.

(b) Taxpayers using such a scheme are required to quote the reference number of the relevant scheme in their tax returns. Taxpayers who develop their own "in-house" tax avoidance schemes must provide details of each scheme directly to HMRC.

The DOTAS rules are intended to provide HMRC with advance warning of tax avoidance schemes, so enabling swifter and more effective investigation and counteraction.

General anti-abuse rule (GAAR)

Finance Act 2013 introduced a "general anti-abuse rule" (GAAR) into UK tax law. This rule applies to income tax, capital gains tax, inheritance tax, corporation tax and certain indirect taxes. The aim of the GAAR is to counteract tax advantages arising from abusive tax arrangements. Tax arrangements are defined as "abusive" if they cannot be regarded as reasonable in relation to the relevant tax law, having regard to whether the arrangements:

(a)   are consistent with the principles on which the relevant tax law is based
(b)   involve any contrived or abnormal steps
(c)   are intended to exploit any shortcomings in the tax law.

The GAAR empowers HMRC to make "just and reasonable" adjustments to counteract the tax advantages that would otherwise arise from tax arrangements that are deemed to be abusive. These adjustments may involve increasing a taxpayer's tax liability or imposing a tax liability where otherwise there would be none. However, before making any such adjustments, HMRC must comply with the following procedure:

(a)   If an officer of HMRC considers that a tax advantage has arisen as a result of abusive tax arrangements, the taxpayer concerned must be provided with a written notice to that effect. The notice must explain why HMRC considers the arrangements to be abusive and must set out the proposed counteraction. The taxpayer then has 45 days in which to make written representations in response to this notice.

(b)   If, after considering any representations received from the taxpayer, HMRC still believes that counteraction should be taken, the matter must then be referred to the GAAR Advisory Panel (an independent panel established for this purpose). The taxpayer must be notified that the matter is being referred in this way and then has 21 days in which to make written representations to the Advisory Panel.

(c)   The GAAR Advisory Panel considers the tax arrangements concerned and produces an opinion notice, stating whether or not (in the opinion of the Panel members) the arrangements are abusive. HMRC must then issue a notice to the taxpayer, setting out whether the tax arrangements are to be counteracted.

(d)   A penalty[†] will generally apply in cases where abusive tax arrangements have been successfully counteracted by means of the GAAR. The penalty is equal to 60% of the additional tax payable as a result of the counteraction (see Chapter 15).

Taxpayers may appeal against an HMRC decision to counteract tax arrangements. When considering such an appeal, the tribunal or court must take into account the opinion expressed by the GAAR Advisory Panel.

[†] *The Government has also introduced a penalty for the "enablers" of abusive tax arrangements which are defeated by HMRC. An enabler is typically someone who designs abusive tax arrangements and markets them to clients The amount of the penalty is equal to 100% of the fees charged by the enabler to clients who use the arrangements in the hope of gaining a tax advantage.*

Making Tax Digital (MTD) for income tax

In 2015, it was announced that self assessment tax returns would be replaced by "digital tax accounts". Over 20 million individuals now have these accounts, which are pre-populated with information already held by HMRC (e.g. employment income, interest received etc).

The next step in the phasing-in of "Making Tax Digital" for income tax self assessment (MTD ITSA) will be implemented on 6 April 2024. As from that date, most self-employed taxpayers and landlords will be required to maintain digital accounting records and submit information to HMRC digitally†. The main features of the system are as follows:

(a) In general, taxpayers who are self-employed or have income from property will be required to keep digital records of their transactions (e.g. income and expenses) using "functionally compatible software" which complies with HMRC specifications.

(b) Every three months, taxpayers must use this software to provide a quarterly update to HMRC. The standard quarters for a tax year are the three-month periods ending on 5 July, 5 October, 5 January and 5 April. However, taxpayers may elect instead to use quarters ending on 30 June, 30 September, 31 December and 31 March.

(c) In all cases, the deadlines for filing the quarterly updates fall one month after the end of the standard quarters i.e. 5 August, 5 November, 5 February and 5 May. There are penalties for making a late submission or for submitting a late EOPS (see below).

(d) Taxpayers must also provide HMRC with an "end of period statement" (EOPS) at the end of each tax year. Presumably taxpayers with both income from self-employment and income from property will need to supply two such statements.

(e) The EOPS is used to make any necessary accounting adjustments and to claim reliefs such as capital allowances (see Chapter 11). It must be submitted using MTD software. The deadline for submission is 31 January following the end of the tax year.

(f) Lastly, taxpayers must make a "final declaration" at the end of each tax year. This replaces the self assessment tax return and is used to declare any personal income and to submit claims for further reliefs (if any). This must be submitted by 31 January following the end of the tax year. Once again, there are penalties for filing late.

Taxpayers with qualifying income not exceeding £10,000 (before deducting expenses) are exempt from MTD ITSA. Qualifying income is the sum of the person's income from self-employment and income from property for the year concerned. Taxpayers whose income does not exceed the limit may nonetheless join MTD ITSA if they so wish. There is also an exemption for taxpayers who are "digitally excluded", either on religious grounds or because of their age, disability or location.

† *MTD for VAT was introduced for larger businesses on 1 April 2019 and was extended to all VAT-registered businesses (with a few exceptions) on 1 April 2022 (see Chapter 30). MTD will also be extended to corporation tax in due course, but not until April 2026 at the earliest.*

The HMRC Charter

The HMRC Charter sets out the service and standards of behaviour that taxpayers should expect when dealing with HMRC. In brief, a taxpayer can expect that HMRC will:

- provide services that are accessible, easy and quick to use, at minimum cost
- provide accurate, consistent and clear information
- be responsive, answer questions quickly and rectify any mistakes as soon as possible
- work to make sure that everyone pays the right amount of tax
- assume that taxpayers are telling the truth, unless there is evidence to the contrary
- take firm action against those who bend or break the law
- be aware of the taxpayer's personal situation and provide support if necessary
- protect taxpayer information and use that information fairly and lawfully
- treat the taxpayer with respect.

In return, HMRC expects taxpayers to give full, accurate and timely answers when asked for information and to treat HMRC staff with respect.

The Adjudicator

An independent and impartial Adjudicator considers complaints received from taxpayers who are not satisfied with the quality of the service they have received from HMRC. The Adjudicator writes an annual report and makes recommendations for improvements to HMRC procedures and practices. The Adjudicator is not empowered to hear tax appeals.

Summary

▶ The main direct taxes comprise income tax, capital gains tax (CGT), inheritance tax and corporation tax. National Insurance Contributions (NICs) can also be regarded as a form of direct taxation. Indirect taxes include VAT, stamp duty and excise duties.

▶ Taxation law is a combination of both statute law and case law. Statements made by the tax authorities provide information on the authorities' interpretation of the law.

▶ The tax year for individuals runs from 6 April to the following 5 April. The corporation tax financial year runs from 1 April to the following 31 March.

▶ Individuals who fall within Self Assessment are normally required to submit an annual tax return. Paper returns must be filed by 31 October following the end of the tax year. Returns submitted electronically must be filed by the following 31 January.

▶ Taxpayers who submit a paper tax return have the option of calculating their own tax liability. If a return is submitted electronically, the liability is calculated by HMRC's computer software. The resulting assessment is referred to as a "self-assessment".

▸ The tax due in relation to a self-assessment is normally satisfied by making two payments on account (which fall due on 31 January in the tax year concerned and on the following 31 July) and then a balancing payment on the following 31 January.

▸ A taxpayer who has not received a tax return notice, but has taxable income or gains of which HMRC is not aware, must notify HMRC of his or her chargeability to tax within six months of the end of the tax year in which the income arises.

▸ If a tax return is submitted by the required filing date, HMRC cannot usually initiate an enquiry into the return more than 12 months after the date on which the return is submitted. Discovery assessments may be made after the enquiry window has closed if it is discovered that the taxpayer has not made full disclosure of all relevant facts.

▸ Tax appeals which cannot be settled by agreement between the taxpayer and HMRC are dealt with by a two-tier tribunals system. Disputes on a point of law may be further referred to the Court of Appeal.

▸ Tax evasion involves dishonest conduct by the taxpayer and is illegal. Tax avoidance involves the sensible arrangement of the taxpayer's affairs so as to minimise the tax liability and is legal. However, abusive tax avoidance schemes may fall foul of the general anti-abuse rule (GAAR) and be counteracted by HMRC.

▸ Making Tax Digital (MTD) for income tax will be implemented as from 6 April 2024. Most self-employed taxpayers and landlords will be required to use MTD-compliant software to keep digital records of their income and expenses and to submit quarterly updates to HMRC. It will also be necessary to provide HMRC with an annual end of period statement (EOPS) and this must also be submitted digitally.

▸ Taxpayers with gross income from self-employment and gross income from property not exceeding a total of £10,000 per annum will be exempt from MTD but may join if they so wish. Digitally excluded taxpayers will also be exempt.

Multiple choice questions

A set of multiple choice questions for this chapter is available on the website which accompanies this book. The website can be accessed at go.pearson.com/uk/he/resources.

Chapter 2

Introduction to income tax

Introduction

Income tax assessments are computed for each tax year (or "year of assessment") and are based upon the taxpayer's total income for the year from all sources, ignoring any income which is exempted from income tax. This chapter explains the main features of an income tax computation, in preparation for the much more detailed information which is provided in subsequent chapters.

Most of the primary legislation relating to income tax used to be located in the Income and Corporation Taxes Act 1988, but this legislation has now been mostly rewritten and moved to more recent statutes. Income tax legislation can now be found mainly in the Income Tax (Earnings and Pensions) Act 2003, the Income Tax (Trading and Other Income) Act 2005 and the Income Tax Act 2007, as amended by subsequent Finance Acts.

Taxable persons

Individuals who are resident in the UK for a tax year are generally chargeable to income tax on all of their income for that year, including both income arising in the UK and income arising overseas. However, there are two main exceptions to this general rule:

(a) Some forms of income are exempt from income tax altogether (see below).

(b) UK residents who are not UK-domiciled (i.e. whose permanent home is not the UK) may claim that their overseas income should be subject to UK income tax only to the extent that the income is remitted to the UK. However, this may lead to an additional tax charge of £30,000 or more in some cases (see Chapter 32).

Individuals who are not resident in the UK are liable to pay income tax on their UK income only (see Chapter 32). Income tax is payable by:

(a) adults, on their own income and on their share of the income of a partnership

(b) children, if they have sufficient income to pay tax (see below)

(c) trustees, on the income of a trust or settlement

(d) personal representatives, on income arising from the estate of a deceased person.

Child's income derived from parent

If an unmarried minor child receives investment income which is derived from a parent, this income is treated for tax purposes as the income of the parent, not the child, unless the amount involved does not exceed £100 (per parent per child) in the tax year. This prevents parents from transferring income-bearing assets to a child so as to take advantage of the child's personal allowance (see Chapter 3).

However, income which is derived from parental contributions to a Child Trust Fund account or a Junior ISA (see Chapter 6) does not count towards the £100 limit.

Exempt organisations and individuals

Most organisations are generally exempt from income tax, subject to various restrictions and exceptions. Certain individuals are also exempt. Exempt organisations and individuals include the following:

(a) companies, which are liable to corporation tax rather than income tax

(b) clubs and societies, which are also liable to corporation tax

(c) registered pension schemes

(d) registered charities (on income used for charitable purposes)

(e) representatives of foreign countries (e.g. ambassadors)

(f) visiting members of foreign armed forces (on their service pay and on income arising from a source outside the UK).

Classification of income

Income is classified for income tax purposes into a number of types or categories, each with its own set of rules for calculating the amount of income of that type which arises in a tax year. These rules are located in the Income Tax (Earnings and Pensions) Act 2003 and in the Income Tax (Trading and Other Income) Act 2005. The main classes of income which are subject to income tax are as follows:

Statute	Type of income	Chapter of this book
ITEPA 2003	Employment income	Chapters 7-8
	Pensions	Chapter 7
	Social security income	Chapter 7
ITTOIA 2005	Trading income	Chapters 9-13
	Property income	Chapter 5
	Interest	Chapter 6
	Dividends	Chapter 6
	Miscellaneous income	Chapter 6

Each of these classes of income is considered in some detail in later chapters of this book.

Exempt income

Certain types of income are specifically exempt from income tax and should therefore be completely ignored when preparing income tax computations. Some of the more important sources of exempt income are as follows:

(a) Exempt savings and investment income (see Chapter 6):

- income from Individual Savings Accounts

- income from National Savings Certificates

- interest arising from a Save As You Earn arrangement linked to a tax-advantaged employee share option scheme (see Chapter 7)

- income from investments held in a Child Trust Fund account

- dividends on shares held in a Venture Capital Trust (subject to conditions)

(b) Exempt employment income (see Chapter 7):

- certain minor benefits provided by employers for their employees

- bonus payments of up to £3,600 per annum received by employees of companies controlled by an employee ownership trust

- the first £30,000 of "ex gratia" compensation received for loss of employment

- certain lump sums payable under registered pension schemes (e.g. a lump sum payable at the commencement of a pension)

- the operational allowance paid to UK armed forces serving in specified locations

(c) Exempt property income (see Chapter 5):

- gross property income of up to £1,000 per annum

- income of up to £7,500 per annum received under the "rent-a-room" scheme

(d) Other exempt income:

- gross trading income of up to £1,000 per annum (see Chapter 9)

- winnings from betting, competition prizes and premium bond prizes

- maintenance payments (see Chapter 4)

- income from scholarships

- wound and disability pensions

- certain social security benefits (e.g. child benefit[†] and housing benefit)

- income from the sale of electricity generated by home microgeneration systems

- most commissions, discounts and cashbacks received by ordinary retail customers

- damages or compensation received for personal or professional injury

- certain payments made to individuals who foster or adopt children.

[†] *Although child benefit is exempt from income tax, a taxpayer who receives child benefit and has an income exceeding £50,000 p.a. may be subject to an income tax charge known as the "high income child benefit charge" (see Chapter 7).*

Structure of an income tax computation

In order to calculate a taxpayer's income tax liability for a tax year it is necessary to bring together *all* of the taxpayer's income into a single income tax computation. The structure of this computation is specified in the Income Tax Act 2007. A typical computation for the year 2022-23 might appear as follows:

	£
Business profits	59,230
Loan interest taxed at source (pre-tax equivalent)	640
Bank interest received	60
Total income	59,930
<u>Less</u>: Tax reliefs	750
Net income	59,180
<u>Less</u>: Personal allowance	12,570
Taxable Income	46,610

Income tax[†]

37,700	@ 20%	7,540.00
8,210	@ 40%	3,284.00
500	@ 0%	0.00
200	@ 40%	80.00
46,610		10,904.00
<u>Less</u>: Tax reductions		0.00
Tax borne		10,904.00
<u>Add</u>: Tax withheld on payments		0.00
Tax liability for the year		10,904.00
<u>Less</u>: Tax paid by deduction at source		128.00
Tax payable		10,776.00

[†] *This section of the computation would be different for a Scottish taxpayer (see below).*

All of the terms used in this computation are explained in detail in this chapter and in later chapters. For now, the main features of the computation are as follows:

(a) The taxpayer's "total income" for the tax year is calculated by adding together income from all sources, including the pre-tax equivalent of any income from which tax has been deducted at source but excluding income which is exempt from income tax.

(b) Relief for certain payments made by the taxpayer (see Chapter 4) together with certain loss reliefs (see Chapters 5 and 12) and relief for certain pension contributions (see Chapter 14) are deducted from total income, giving "net income".

(c) Any personal allowance available to the taxpayer is deducted from net income to give "taxable income". The personal allowance for tax year 2022-23 is usually £12,570, ensuring that those on very low incomes are not liable to income tax. However, the allowance is reduced (possibly to zero) for those on high incomes (see Chapter 3).

(d) Income tax is charged on the taxable income figure, using the rates of tax in force for the year. The amount of tax calculated in this way is then subject to a number of adjustments and the result is the tax payable to HM Revenue and Customs.

(e) The *tax borne* by the taxpayer is the amount of income tax suffered for the year. This may be different from the *tax liability*, which is the amount of tax which must be accounted for to HMRC and the *tax payable* which is the income tax remaining to be paid after deducting any tax already paid for the year. These distinctions will become clearer in the course of the next two chapters.

A formal tax computation is not required for every taxpayer. For example, a tax computation is generally not required for an individual whose income is derived entirely from employment, since the correct amount of tax is normally deducted automatically by the PAYE system (see Chapter 7). However, the only way to calculate the income tax liability in more complex cases is to prepare a tax computation.

Married couples and civil partners

Married couples are taxed independently, which means that the husband's income and the wife's income are taxed completely separately. This is also the case for civil partners who have entered into a legally-recognised civil partnership.

If a married couple (or civil partners) have income which is derived from an asset held in their joint names, such as interest on a joint bank account, the amount of that income will normally be divided between them equally for tax purposes. But if the source of income is genuinely held between them in some other proportion, the couple may make a declaration to that effect and the income will then be divided between them as appropriate.

Rates of income tax for 2022-23

An individual's taxable income is taxed according to the rates of income tax in force for the year in question. *For non-Scottish taxpayers*, the main income tax rates and thresholds for tax year 2022-23 are as follows:

Band	*Rate*
First £37,700 of taxable income	20% (the "basic rate")
Next £112,300 of taxable income (up to £150,000)	40% (the "higher rate")
Remaining taxable income after the first £150,000	45% (the "additional rate")

Note that:

(a) The point at which basic rate tax gives way to higher rate tax is known as the "basic rate limit". For non-Scottish taxpayers in 2022-23, this limit is £37,700[†] and the first £37,700 of taxable income is referred to as the "basic rate band". Similarly, the figure of £150,000 is known as the "higher rate limit" and taxable income lying between £37,700 and £150,000 may be referred to as the "higher rate band".

(b) Savings income and dividend income are treated specially, as explained below.

(c) Calculations are made to the nearest pound when calculating taxable income. The amount of tax due on that income is calculated to the nearest penny in this book but HMRC will generally accept calculations made to the nearest pound.

[†] *Finance Act 2021 freezes the basic rate limit at £37,700 until the end of tax year 2025-26.*

Scottish taxpayers

Scotland Act 2016 gives the Scottish Parliament full control over the income tax rates and thresholds which should apply to the non-savings income of Scottish taxpayers[†]. The term "non-savings income" refers to taxable income which is neither savings income nor dividends (see later in this chapter) and encompasses mainly income from employment or self-employment and income from property. For 2022-23, the income tax bands and rates which apply to the non-savings income of Scottish taxpayers are as follows:

Band	Rate
First £2,162 of taxable non-savings income	19% (the "starter rate")
Next £10,956 (up to £13,118)	20% (the "basic rate")
Next £17,974 (up to £31,092)	21% (the "intermediate rate")
Next £118,908 (up to £150,000)	41% (the "higher rate")
Remainder after the first £150,000	46% (the "top rate")

Therefore the starter rate limit for 2022-23 is £2,162, the basic rate limit is £13,118, the intermediate rate limit is £31,092 and the higher rate limit is £150,000.

[†] *Scottish taxpayers are broadly defined as those who live in Scotland. Please see the Appendix at the end of this chapter for more information.*

EXAMPLE 1

Calculate the 2022-23 income tax liability of a non-Scottish taxpayer with taxable income (i.e. income remaining after deducting any available personal allowance) of:

(a) £11,730   (b) £15,280   (c) £30,000

(d) £33,150   (e) £58,800   (f) £231,400

Assume that none of the income is derived from savings or dividends. How would these income tax liabilities differ in the case of a Scottish taxpayer?

Solution

Non-Scottish taxpayer:

(a)   £11,730 @ 20% = **£2,346.00**

(b)   £15,280 @ 20% = **£3,056.00**

(c)   £30,000 @ 20% = **£6,000.00**

(d)   £33,150 @ 20% = **£6,630.00**

(e)   £37,700 @ 20% + £21,100 @ 40% = **£15,980.00**

(f)   £37,700 @ 20% + £112,300 @ 40% + £81,400 @ 45% = **£89,090.00**

Scottish taxpayer:

(a)   £2,162 @ 19% + £9,568 @ 20% = **£2,324.38**

(b)   £2,162 @ 19% + £10,956 @ 20% + £2,162 @ 21% = **£3,056.00**

(c)   £2,162 @ 19% + £10,956 @ 20% + £16,882 @ 21% = **£6,147.20**

(d)   £2,162 @ 19% + £10,956 @ 20% + £17,974 @ 21% + £2,058 @ 41% = **£7,220.30**

(e)   £2,162 @ 19% + £10,956 @ 20% + £17,974 @ 21% + £27,708 @ 41% = **£17,736.80**

(f)   £2,162 @ 19% + £10,956 @ 20% + £17,974 @ 21% + £118,908 @ 41% +
      £81,400 @ 46% = **£92,572.80**

Note that a Scottish taxpayer pays less income tax (on non-savings income) than a non-Scottish taxpayer in 2022-23 until taxable income reaches £15,280. At this point the tax liabilities are equal. But if taxable income exceeds £15,280, a Scottish taxpayer will pay more income tax than a non-Scottish taxpayer.

Welsh taxpayers

Wales Act 2014 gives the National Assembly for Wales the right to set Welsh rates of income tax. The rates of income tax which apply to the non-savings income of Welsh taxpayers[†] are derived by subtracting 10p in the pound from the basic rate, the higher rate and the additional rate which apply in the remainder of the UK (other than Scotland) and then adding on the Welsh rates set for that year for the purpose of calculating the Welsh basic rate, the Welsh higher rate and the Welsh additional rate.

However, the three Welsh rates for tax year 2022-23 have all been set at 10%. Therefore the rates of income tax payable by Welsh taxpayers for 2022-23 are the same as those paid elsewhere in the UK (apart from in Scotland). For instance, the Welsh basic rate is (20% − 10% + 10%) = 20%.

[†] *Welsh taxpayers are broadly defined as those who live in Wales and the definition of a Welsh taxpayer is very similar in principle to the definition of a Scottish taxpayer (see the Appendix at the end of this chapter).*

Income taxed at source

Certain types of income are *taxed at source*, which means that basic rate income tax is deducted from the income before the taxpayer receives it. In tax year 2022-23, the main types of income normally received net of basic rate tax are:

(a) debenture and other loan interest[†] paid by UK companies

(b) interest on UK government securities ("gilt-edged" securities) if the taxpayer applies to receive this interest with tax deducted at source

(c) the income element of a purchased life annuity (as long as the annuity has not been purchased with assets held under a registered pension scheme)

(d) patent royalties.

[†] *Bank and building society interest is paid gross (i.e. without deduction of tax at source).*

Income which has been taxed at source must still be included in the taxpayer's income tax computation, despite the fact that tax has already been paid. This may seem unnecessary but there are two good reasons for including such income in the tax computation:

(a) It is important to derive correct figures for the taxpayer's "total income" and "net income", as will become clearer in later chapters.

(b) The basic rate tax which has been deducted at source might be inadequate or might be excessive, depending upon the taxpayer's individual circumstances. The only way to check this is to aggregate the income concerned with all of the taxpayer's other income in a single tax computation.

In a tax computation, all income must be shown "gross". In other words, the amount of income shown must be the amount of the income *before* any income tax was deducted at source. When the tax liability has been calculated, tax paid by deduction at source is subtracted and the taxpayer is then required to pay only the balance of the liability. A tax refund is given if tax deducted at source exceeds the tax liability for the year.

If income is taxed at source, the amount received by the taxpayer is often referred to as the "net" amount of the income. This usage of the term "net" must be distinguished from the entirely different usage of the same term in the Income Tax Act 2007, which defines "net income" as being equal to a taxpayer's total income less tax reliefs.

Grossing up

If income has been received net of basic rate (20%) income tax, the gross amount of the income can be ascertained by multiplying the amount received by 100/80. This calculation is often referred to as "grossing up". When wages and salaries are received net of income tax, the gross pay and the amount of tax deducted can be ascertained by examining the end-of-year certificate supplied by the taxpayer's employer (see Chapter 7).

Savings income

The tax liability on a taxpayer's "savings income" is calculated differently from the tax liability on non-savings income. The main categories of savings income are:

(a) interest received from banks, building societies and NS&I, plus interest received on gilt-edged securities and corporate bonds (e.g. debentures and loan stocks)

(b) the income element of purchased life annuities (other than annuities from registered pension schemes, which are treated as non-savings income)

(c) certain foreign income (see Chapter 32).

But savings income does *not* include dividends received. The tax regime which applies to dividends is explained later in this chapter.

An important difference between the taxation of savings income and non-savings income is that savings income which falls into the first £5,000 (for 2022-23) of taxable income is taxed at the *starting rate for savings* of 0%, so that such income is effectively tax-free. If a taxpayer has both savings income and non-savings income, it is necessary to split taxable income between these two categories before the tax liability can be calculated. Note that:

(a) Non-savings income is regarded as the bottom layer or "slice" of taxable income and savings income is regarded as a higher layer. This means that the starting rate will not be available (in 2022-23) if taxable income includes non-savings income of at least £5,000. Otherwise, some or all of the taxpayer's savings income (if any) will fall into the first £5,000 of taxable income and will be taxed at the starting rate of 0%.

(b) Tax reliefs and the personal allowance are set against income in the way which gives the lowest tax liability. In general, these deductions should be made from non-savings income in priority to savings income, since non-savings income cannot benefit from the 0% rate. However, there are exceptions to this rule (see later in this chapter).

(c) The figure of £5,000 (for 2022-23) is known as the *starting rate limit for savings*.

A further difference between the taxation of savings income and non-savings income is that the income tax liability on a taxpayer's savings income is unaffected by whether or not the taxpayer is Scottish (or Welsh). The Scottish tax rates and limits (and the Welsh rates) listed earlier do not apply to savings income, which is always taxed using the rates and limits that apply throughout the remainder of the UK (see examples below).

Personal savings allowance

ITA 2007 provides that taxpayers are entitled to a personal "savings allowance" (PSA) of up to £1,000 per tax year. In general, this means that the first £1,000 of savings income included in taxable income is taxed at the "savings nil rate" of 0%. However, the PSA is lower than £1,000 in some cases (see below).

It is important to realise that the PSA is *not* used against any savings income which falls within the first £5,000 of taxable income and so already benefits from the starting rate for savings. The PSA is used only against savings income which falls beyond the first £5,000 of taxable income. So a taxpayer with taxable non-savings income of £nil in 2022-23 and a PSA of £1,000 will pay 0% income tax on the first £6,000 of taxable savings income. Note the following important points relating to the PSA:

(a) A taxpayer's PSA for 2022-23 is £1,000 unless:

    (i) taxable income for the year exceeds the non-Scottish[†] basic rate limit (but does not exceed the higher rate limit) in which case the PSA is £500

    (ii) taxable income for the year exceeds the higher rate limit, in which case the PSA for the year is £nil.

The non-Scottish basic rate limit for 2022-23 is normally £37,700 (see above) and the higher rate limit is normally £150,000. However, these figures are both increased if the taxpayer makes Gift Aid donations in the year (see Chapter 4) or makes pension contributions that are "relieved at source" (see Chapter 14).

    [†] *In the case of Scottish taxpayers, the non-Scottish basic rate limit of £37,700 is used both for the purpose of determining the amount of the PSA to which the taxpayer is entitled and when calculating the amount of income tax due on savings income. This ensures that the amount of income tax payable on the savings income of a Scottish taxpayer is exactly the same as would be payable if he or she were not a Scottish taxpayer.*

(b) Although savings income falling within the PSA is effectively tax-free, the income concerned is still part of the taxpayer's taxable income for the year. This is significant when determining whether taxable income exceeds the basic rate limit or higher rate limit (see above) and may also be significant when calculating the taxpayer's entitlement to personal allowances (see Chapter 3). The same point applies to savings income which is taxed at the starting rate for savings.

EXAMPLE 2

Calculate the personal savings allowance available in 2022-23 to a taxpayer with taxable income for the year (i.e. net income less any available personal allowance) of:

(a) £20,000   (b) £37,701   (c) £63,000   (d) £375,000

Assume that there are no Gift Aid donations or pension contributions during the year.

Solution

(a) Taxable income does not exceed £37,700, therefore the PSA is £1,000.

(b) Taxable income exceeds £37,700 but does not exceed £150,000. Therefore the PSA is £500. Exceeding the basic rate limit by £1 has reduced the PSA by £500.

(c) Taxable income exceeds £37,700 but does not exceed £150,000. The PSA is £500.

(d) Taxable income exceeds £150,000, therefore the PSA is £nil.

Note: These PSA figures are the same whether or not the taxpayer is Scottish.

EXAMPLE 3

In 2022-23, Robert (who is not a Scottish taxpayer) has business profits of £40,000 and receives bank interest of £1,250. His personal allowance is £12,570. Calculate Robert's income tax liability for the year. How would this differ for a Scottish taxpayer?

Solution

	Total £	Non-savings £	Savings £
Business profits	40,000	40,000	
Bank interest	1,250		1,250
Total income	41,250	40,000	1,250
Less: Personal allowance	12,570	12,570	
Taxable income	28,680	27,430	1,250

Income tax due

Non-savings income	: Basic rate	27,430	@ 20%	5,486.00
Savings income	: Nil rate	1,000	@ 0%	0.00
	: Basic rate	250	@ 20%	50.00
		28,680		
Tax liability				5,536.00

Notes:

(i)   Taxable income includes non-savings income of more than £5,000. Therefore the starting rate for savings is not available.

(ii) Taxable income does not exceed £37,700, so the PSA is £1,000. Savings income of £1,000 is taxed at the savings nil rate.

(iii) Non-savings income occupies the first £27,430 of the basic rate band, so there is £10,270 (£37,700 – £27,430) of this band remaining. Savings income is less than this and is therefore taxed at 20% (apart from the first £1,000 covered by the PSA).

Scottish taxpayers

If Robert were a Scottish taxpayer, the income tax on his non-savings income would be calculated using Scottish rates and limits. Taxable non-savings income is £27,430 so the tax due on this income would be (£2,162 × 19%) + (£10,956 × 20%) + (£14,312 × 21%) = £5,607.50. This would increase his total tax liability by £121.50 to £5,657.50.

It is important to appreciate that the tax due on savings income would be unaffected. The PSA would still be determined by comparing taxable income (£28,680) with £37,700. And the tax due on savings income would be calculated as above, using non-Scottish income tax rates and limits.

EXAMPLE 4

In 2022-23, Roberta (who is not a Scottish taxpayer) has rental income of £16,770 and receives building society interest of £1,100. Her personal allowance is £12,570. Calculate the income tax liability for the year. How would this differ for a Scottish taxpayer?

Solution

			Total £	Non-savings £	Savings £
Income from property			16,770	16,770	
Building society interest			1,100		1,100
Total income			17,870	16,770	1,100
Less: Personal allowance			12,570	12,570	
Taxable income			5,300	4,200	1,100

Income tax due					
Non-savings income	: Basic rate	4,200	@ 20%	840.00	
Savings income	: Starting rate	800	@ 0%	0.00	
	: Nil rate	300	@ 0%	0.00	
		5,300			
Tax liability				840.00	

Notes:

(i) The non-savings income occupies £4,200 of the basic rate band. This allows £800 (£5,000 – £4,200) of the savings income to be taxed at the starting rate of 0%.

(ii) Taxable income does not exceed £37,700, so the PSA is £1,000.

(iii) The remaining £300 of savings income (£1,100 – £800) does not exceed £1,000, so this is taxed at the savings nil rate.

Scottish taxpayers

If Roberta were a Scottish taxpayer, the income tax on her non-savings income would be calculated using Scottish rates and limits. Taxable non-savings income is £4,200 so the tax due on this income would be (£2,162 × 19%) + (£2,038 × 20%) = £818.38. This would reduce her total liability by £21.62. The tax due on savings income would be unaffected.

EXAMPLE 5

In 2022-23, Kenneth (who is not a Scottish taxpayer) has business profits of £59,120 and bank interest of £980. His personal allowance for the year is £12,570. He makes no Gift Aid donations or pension contributions during 2022-23. Calculate Kenneth's income tax liability for the year. Also explain how this liability would differ for a Scottish taxpayer.

Solution

	Total £	Non-savings £	Savings £
Business profits	59,120	59,120	
Bank interest	980		980
Total income	60,100	59,120	980
Less: Personal allowance	12,570	12,570	
Taxable income	47,530	46,550	980

Income tax due

Non-savings income	: Basic rate	37,700 @ 20%	7,540.00
	: Higher rate	8,850 @ 40%	3,540.00
Savings income	: Nil rate	500 @ 0%	0.00
	: Higher rate	480 @ 40%	192.00
		47,530	
Tax liability			11,272.00

Notes:

(i) Taxable income includes non-savings income of more than £5,000. Therefore the starting rate for savings is not available.

(ii) Taxable income exceeds £37,700, so the PSA is £500 and the first £500 of savings income is taxed at the savings nil rate.

(iii) Non-savings income occupies the whole of the basic rate band. Therefore savings income is taxed at 40% (apart from the first £500 which is covered by the PSA).

Scottish taxpayers

If Kenneth were a Scottish taxpayer, the income tax on his non-savings income would be calculated using Scottish rates and limits. Taxable non-savings income is £46,550 so the tax due on this income would be (£2,162 × 19%) + (£10,956 × 20%) + (£17,974 × 21%) + (£15,458 × 41%) = £12,714.30. This would increase his total tax liability by £1,634.30 to £12,906.30. The tax due on his savings income would be unaffected.

EXAMPLE 6

In 2022-23, Philip (who is not a Scottish taxpayer) has business profits of £240,235 and building society interest of £1,600. His personal allowance for the year is zero. He makes no Gift Aid donations or pension contributions during 2022-23. Calculate his income tax liability for the year. Also explain how this liability would differ for a Scottish taxpayer.

Solution

	Total £	Non-savings £	Savings £
Business profits	240,235	240,235	
Building society interest	1,600		1,600
Total income	241,835	240,235	1,600
Less: Personal allowance	0	0	
Taxable income	241,835	240,235	1,600

Income tax due

Non-savings income	: Basic rate	37,700	@ 20%	7,540.00
	: Higher rate	112,300	@ 40%	44,920.00
	: Additional rate	90,235	@ 45%	40,605.75
Savings income	: Additional rate	1,600	@ 45%	720.00
		241,835		
Tax liability				93,785.75

Notes:

(i)   Taxable income includes non-savings income of more than £5,000. Therefore the starting rate for savings is not available.

(ii) Taxable income exceeds the higher rate limit, so the PSA is £nil.

(iii) Non-savings income occupies the whole of the basic rate and higher rate bands, so the bank interest is taxed at the additional rate of 45%.

Scottish taxpayers

If Philip were a Scottish taxpayer, the income tax on his non-savings income would be calculated using Scottish rates and limits. Taxable non-savings income is £240,235 so the tax due on this income would be (£2,162 × 19%) + (£10,956 × 20%) + (£17,974 × 21%) + (£118,908 × 41%) + (£90,235 × 46%) = £96,636.90. This would increase his total liability by £3,571.15 to £97,356.90. The tax due on savings income would be unaffected.

EXAMPLE 7

In 2022-23, Philippa has business profits of £10,000. She also receives bank interest of £3,450 and <u>net</u> loan interest of £36,680. Her personal allowance is £12,570 and she makes no Gift Aid donations or pension contributions during 2022-23.

Calculate the income tax payable by Philippa for the year. Does it matter whether or not she is a Scottish taxpayer?

Solution

	Total £	Non-savings £	Savings £
Business profits	10,000	10,000	
Bank interest	3,450		3,450
Loan interest £36,680 x 100/80	45,850		45,850
Total income	59,300	10,000	49,300
<u>Less</u>: Personal allowance	12,570	10,000	2,570
Taxable income	46,730	nil	46,730

Income tax due

Savings income	: Starting rate	5,000	@ 0%	0.00
	: Nil rate	500	@ 0%	0.00
	: Basic rate	32,200	@ 20%	6,440.00
	: Higher rate	9,030	@ 40%	3,612.00
		46,730		

Tax liability		10,052.00
<u>Less</u>: Tax deducted at source (£45,850 – £36,680)		9,170.00
Tax payable		882.00

Notes:

(i) Taxable income does not include any non-savings income. Therefore the first £5,000 of savings income is taxed at the starting rate.

(ii) Taxable income exceeds the basic rate limit (but not the higher rate limit) so the PSA is £500 and the next £500 of savings income is taxed at the savings nil rate.

(iii) The next £32,200 (£37,700 – £5,500) of the savings income is taxed at the basic rate and the remaining £9,030 is taxed at the higher rate.

Scottish taxpayers

Taxable income does not include any non-savings income. So the income tax computation is the same, whether or not Philippa is a Scottish taxpayer.

Dividend income

The income tax liability on a taxpayer's dividend income is calculated differently from the liability on non-savings income or savings income. The main points are as follows:

(a) Dividends are treated as the top slice of taxable income, ranking above both non-savings and savings income.

(b) In 2022-23[†], dividends which fall into the basic rate band[‡] are generally taxed at the "dividend ordinary rate" of 8.75%. Dividends which fall into the higher rate band are generally taxed at the "dividend upper rate" of 33.75%. Any dividends which lie above the higher rate limit are generally taxed at the "dividend additional rate" of 39.35%.

(c) However, taxpayers are entitled to a tax-free "dividend allowance" of £2,000 (in tax year 2022-23) so that the first £2,000 of any dividends included in taxable income are taxed at the "dividend nil rate" of 0%. Unlike the personal savings allowance (see above) which is reduced for higher-rate and additional-rate taxpayers, the dividend allowance is £2,000 in all cases.

(d) As stated earlier in this chapter, tax reliefs and the personal allowance are set against income in the way which gives the lowest income tax liability. In general, these deductions should be made against non-savings income in priority to savings income and against savings income in priority to dividends. However, there are exceptions to this general rule (see later in this chapter).

(e) Although dividend income falling within the £2,000 dividend allowance is tax-free, the income concerned is still part of the taxpayer's taxable income for the year. This may be significant when determining whether a taxpayer's taxable income exceeds the basic rate limit or higher rate limit (which affects entitlement to the PSA) and when calculating the taxpayer's entitlement to personal allowances (see Chapter 3).

[†] *The three dividend rates for tax year 2022-23 (and subsequent years) are each 1.25% higher than in 2021-22. This increase will be used to provide extra funding for health and social care.*

[‡] *In the case of Scottish taxpayers, the non-Scottish tax bands and limits are used when calculating the amount of income tax due on dividend income. This ensures that the amount of income tax payable on the dividend income of a Scottish taxpayer is exactly the same as would be payable if he or she were not a Scottish taxpayer.*

Dividends from UK-REITs

A UK company which is a property investment company may elect to become a UK Real Estate Investment Trust (UK-REIT). Dividends received from a UK-REIT, to the extent that they derive from the company's tax-exempt property income or gains (see Chapter 23) are subject to a different tax regime than the one which is described above. Such dividends are received net of basic rate (20%) income tax and are treated as property income.

The examples and exercises in this book all assume that any dividends received are received from companies other than UK-REITs.

EXAMPLE 8

In 2022-23, Christopher (who is not a Scottish taxpayer) has rental income of £28,790. He also has bank interest of £1,050 and dividends of £204,100. His personal allowance for the year is zero and he makes no Gift Aid donations or pension contributions. Calculate his income tax liability for the year. How would this differ for a Scottish taxpayer?

Solution

	Total	Non-savings	Savings	Dividends
	£	£	£	£
Income from property	28,790	28,790		
Bank interest	1,050		1,050	
Dividends	204,100			204,100
Total income	233,940	28,790	1,050	204,100
Less: Personal allowance	0	0		
Taxable income	233,940	28,790	1,050	204,100

Income tax due

Non-savings income	: Basic rate	28,790	@ 20%	5,758.00
Savings income	: Basic rate	1,050	@ 20%	210.00
Dividend income	: Nil rate	2,000	@ 0%	0.00
	: Ordinary rate	5,860	@ 8.75%	512.75
	: Upper rate	112,300	@ 33.75%	37,901.25
	: Additional rate	83,940	@ 39.35%	33,030.39
		233,940		
Tax liability				77,412.39

Notes:

(i) Taxable income includes non-savings income of more than £5,000, so the starting rate for savings is not available. Taxable income exceeds the higher rate limit so the PSA is £nil. The available basic rate band of £8,910 (£37,700 − £28,790) exceeds the savings income of £1,050 so the whole of the savings income is taxed at 20%.

(ii) The first £2,000 of the dividends are taxed at the nil rate. There is now £5,860 of the basic rate band remaining (£37,700 − £28,790 − £1,050 − £2,000) and therefore the next £5,860 of the dividends are taxed at the dividend ordinary rate of 8.75%.

(iii) Dividends of £112,300 are taxed at the dividend upper rate of 33.75% and the final £83,940 of the dividends are taxed at the dividend additional rate of 39.35%.

Scottish taxpayers

For a Scottish taxpayer, the income tax on non-savings income would be (£2,162 × 19%) + (£10,956 × 20%) + (£15,672 × 21%) = £5,893.10. This would increase the total liability by £135.10. The tax due on savings income and dividends would be unaffected.

EXAMPLE 9

In 2022-23, Charlie (who is not a Scottish taxpayer) receives a pension of £17,820, bank interest of £195 and dividends of £1,600. His personal allowance is £12,570. Calculate his income tax liability for the year. How would this differ for a Scottish taxpayer?

Solution

	Total	Non-savings	Savings	Dividends
	£	£	£	£
Pension	17,820	17,820		
Bank interest	195		195	
Dividends	1,600			1,600
Total income	19,615	17,820	195	1,600
Less: Personal allowance	12,570	12,570		
Taxable income	7,045	5,250	195	1,600

Income tax due

Non-savings income	: Basic rate	5,250 @ 20%	1,050.00
Savings income	: Nil rate	195 @ 0%	0.00
Dividend income	: Nil rate	1,600 @ 0%	0.00
		7,045	
Tax liability			1,050.00

Notes:

(i)   Taxable income includes non-savings income of more than £5,000. Therefore the starting rate for savings is not available. However, taxable income does not exceed the basic rate limit so the PSA is £1,000. Since savings income is only £195, this is all taxed at the savings nil rate of 0%.

(ii) The dividends of £1,600 fall within the dividend allowance of £2,000 and are all taxed at the dividend nil rate of 0%.

Scottish taxpayers

For a Scottish taxpayer, the income tax on non-savings income would be (£2,162 × 19%) + (£3,088 × 20%) = £1,028.38. This would reduce the total liability by £21.62. The tax due on savings income and dividends would be unaffected.

Allocation of the personal allowance

Section 25 of ITA2007 states that the personal allowance[†] should be deducted from total income "*in the way which will result in the greatest reduction in the taxpayer's liability to income tax*". Until recently, the best approach was to deduct the personal allowance first from non-savings income, then from savings income and finally from dividends.

However, the problem of identifying the most beneficial way of allocating the personal allowance has become more complex in recent years, with the introduction of the personal savings allowance and the dividend allowance (as well as the starting rate for savings). A number of points should be borne in mind when making this allocation:

(a) In general terms, the approach should be to deduct the personal allowance from income which would otherwise be taxed at higher rates rather than income which would be taxed at lower rates.

(b) The personal allowance will be wasted if it is deducted from income which would otherwise be taxed at 0%. This applies to savings income taxable at the starting rate, savings income within the PSA and dividends within the dividend allowance.

(c) The income tax liability will be reduced if income taxed at either the savings nil rate or the dividend nil rate is income which would otherwise be taxed at higher rates rather than lower rates.

[†] *This also applies to other reliefs that are deductible from total income.*

EXAMPLE 10

In 2022-23, Kim (who is not a Scottish taxpayer) has business profits of £48,920 and bank interest of £2,000. Her personal allowance for the year is £12,570 and she makes no Gift Aid donations or pension contributions. Calculate her income tax liability for the year if the personal allowance is set against non-savings income.

Show how the income tax liability changes if only £11,220 of the personal allowance is set against non-savings income and the remaining £1,350 is set against savings income.

Solution

	Total £	Non-savings £	Savings £
Business profits	48,920	48,920	
Bank interest	2,000		2,000
Total income	50,920	48,920	2,000
Less: Personal allowance	12,570	12,570	
Taxable income	38,350	36,350	2,000

Income tax due

Non-savings income	: Basic rate	36,350	@ 20%	7,270.00
Savings income	: Nil rate	500	@ 0%	0.00
	: Basic rate	850	@ 20%	170.00
	: Higher rate	650	@ 40%	260.00
		38,350		
Tax liability				7,700.00

If only £11,220 of the personal allowance is set against non-savings income and £1,350 is set against savings income, taxable non-savings income becomes £37,700 and taxable savings income becomes £650. The tax liability is then (£37,700 × 20%) + (£500 × 0%) + (£150 × 40%) = £7,600. The tax saving is £100.

With this approach, the savings income of £500 which is taxed at the nil rate is income which would otherwise be taxed at 40% (not 20%), saving (£500 x (40% − 20%)) = £100.

Summary

▸ In general, income tax is chargeable on all of the income of UK residents and on the UK income of non-residents.

▸ Income is classified into a number of categories, each of which has its own rules for determining the amount of assessable income in a tax year. However, certain types of income are specifically exempt from income tax.

▸ To calculate a taxpayer's income tax liability it is necessary to bring together all of the taxpayer's income into a single computation. The gross equivalent of any income received net of income tax must be included in the computation.

▸ Husbands, wives and civil partners are assessed to income tax independently.

▸ In 2022-23, the main rates of income tax are the basic rate of 20%, the higher rate of 40% and the additional rate of 45%. Savings income which occupies the first £5,000 of the basic rate band is taxed at the starting rate for savings of 0%.

▸ In 2022-23, basic rate taxpayers are entitled to a personal savings allowance (PSA) of £1,000. The PSA is £500 for higher rate taxpayers and is £nil for additional rate tax-payers. Savings income falling within the PSA is taxed at the savings nil rate.

▸ In 2022-23, the first £2,000 of dividends included in taxable income are taxed at the dividend nil rate. Dividends after the first £2,000 are taxed at 8.75% in the basic rate band, 33.75% in the higher rate band and 39.35% otherwise.

▸ *For Scottish taxpayers*, the income tax liability on non-savings income is calculated using different tax rates and limits than elsewhere in the UK.

Appendix

Definition of a Scottish taxpayer

In general terms, a Scottish taxpayer is an individual who lives in Scotland. Whether the individual identifies as Scottish is irrelevant. Nor does it matter whether he or she works in Scotland. This means that employers elsewhere in the UK must apply Scottish rates of income tax to any of their employees who live in Scotland (see Chapter 7).

It will usually be obvious whether or not an individual is a Scottish taxpayer. But it may be necessary to apply a number of tests in more complex cases. An individual is treated as a Scottish taxpayer for a tax year if he or she is UK resident in that year (see Chapter 32) and satisfies <u>any</u> of the following criteria:

(a)   the individual has a "close connection" with Scotland, usually through having only a single UK place of residence (which is in Scotland) and living there for at least part of the tax year in question, or

(b)   the individual does not have a close connection with any other part of the UK and spends more days of the tax year in Scotland than in any other part of the UK, or

(c)   the individual is a Scottish Parliamentarian (e.g. an MP for a Scottish constituency or a member of the Scottish Parliament).

Note that the status of the individual has to be determined for whole tax years and it is not possible to be a Scottish taxpayer for only part of the tax year. Furthermore, it is quite feasible that an individual could be a Scottish taxpayer in one tax year but not in the next tax year (e.g. by moving away from Scotland).

Exercises

It should be assumed in all of these exercises that the taxpayer makes no Gift Aid donations or pension contributions during tax year 2022-23. A set of multiple choice questions for this chapter is available on the accompanying website.

2.1   Calculate the income tax liability for 2022-23 of a non-Scottish taxpayer with a taxable income (after deducting any available personal allowance) of:

(a)   £1,830   (b)   £32,300   (c)   £72,033   (d)   £320,000.

Assume that none of the income is derived from savings or dividends. How would these liabilities differ in the case of a Scottish taxpayer?

2.2   Calculate the 2022-23 income tax liability of a non-Scottish taxpayer with income for the year as follows:

(a)   Business profits of £28,175 and bank interest of £720.

(b)   Business profits £50,420, building society interest £930 and bank interest £570.

(c)   Net loan interest of £130,604.

Assume a personal allowance of £12,570 in cases (a) and (b) and £nil in case (c). How would these liabilities differ in the case of Scottish taxpayers?

2.3   Stephanie (who is not a Scottish taxpayer) has the following income in 2022-23:

	£
Income from self-employment	29,950
Rents received	15,730
Bank interest	200
Dividends	250

Compute Stephanie's income tax liability for the year, assuming that the rents received are not within the "rent-a-room" scheme and that Stephanie is entitled to the personal allowance of £12,570. How would this differ for a Scottish taxpayer?

2.4   Ernest (who is not a Scottish taxpayer) has a retirement pension in 2022-23 of £57,160 and bank interest of £620. His personal allowance for the year is £12,570. Compute Ernest's income tax liability for the year. What difference would it make if Ernest had received dividends of £620 instead of the bank interest?

*2.5   Ivan (who is not a Scottish taxpayer) has the following income for tax year 2022-23:

	£
Part-time salary	17,055
Net interest on gilt-edged securities	1,360
Premium bond prize	50
Dividends	15,560

His personal allowance for 2022-23 is £12,570. Compute the income tax payable by Ivan for the year. How would this differ for a Scottish taxpayer?

*2.6   Mary's income for tax year 2022-23 consists of business profits of £26,930, dividends received of £124,460 and rents received of £3,750. She is not a Scottish taxpayer and her personal allowance for the year is £nil. Calculate Mary's income tax liability for 2022-23, assuming that the rents received are not within the "rent-a-room" scheme.

Chapter 3

Personal allowances

Introduction

One of the factors which must be taken into account when preparing an income tax computation is the taxpayer's entitlement to any *personal allowances*. Most taxpayers can claim only the basic personal allowance but there are extra allowances for blind taxpayers and for older married couples. The purpose of this chapter is to identify the allowances that are available in tax year 2022-23 and to explain the way in which each allowance is dealt with in an income tax computation.

It is important to appreciate that personal allowances are indeed "personal". If all or part of a personal allowance cannot be used by the person to whom it is available, then any unused part of the allowance is generally lost. Excess allowances cannot normally be transferred to anyone else and cannot be carried back to previous years or carried forward to future years. However, some limited provisions exist for transferring allowances between spouses or civil partners (see later in this chapter).

Personal allowances for 2022-23

The personal allowances for tax year 2022-23 are as follows:

Allowances which are deducted from income	£
Personal allowance	12,570
Blind person's allowance	2,600
Allowances which are "tax reducers"	
Married couple's allowance:	
Born before 6 April 1935	9,415
Minimum amount	3,640
Marriage allowance	1,260
Income limit for basic personal allowance	100,000
Income limit for married couple's allowance	31,400

The circumstances in which each of these allowances may be claimed (and the way in which each allowance is given effect in an income tax computation) are explained below.

Personal allowances may be claimed by UK residents and by certain non-residents. The main classes of non-resident who may claim personal allowances (and so reduce their UK income tax liability in relation to any UK income) are as follows:

(a) nationals of the UK or the European Economic Area (EEA), which comprises all EU states plus Norway, Iceland and Liechtenstein

(b) residents in the Isle of Man or the Channel Islands

(c) persons who used to reside in the UK but now reside abroad for health reasons

(d) Crown servants and ex-Crown servants

(e) widows or widowers of Crown servants (or their surviving civil partners)

(f) missionaries.

The personal allowance (PA)

Anyone who is entitled to claim personal allowances may claim at least the basic personal allowance. This allowance is deducted from the taxpayer's income when computing his or her income tax liability. The basic personal allowance for 2022-23 is £12,570[†] but this is reduced (possibly to zero) if the taxpayer has income exceeding £100,000 (see below).

The personal allowance is fully available in the tax year in which a taxpayer is born or dies, apart from being reduced as usual if income for that year exceeds £100,000.

[†] *Finance Act 2021 freezes the personal allowance at £12,570 until the end of tax year 2025-26.*

Reduction in the basic personal allowance

The amount of the basic personal allowance for a tax year is reduced if the taxpayer's "adjusted net income" for the year exceeds £100,000. Adjusted net income is defined as the taxpayer's net income less the grossed-up amount of any Gift Aid donations made during the year (see Chapter 4) and less the gross amount of any pension contributions relieved at source during the year (see Chapter 14).

If adjusted net income exceeds £100,000, the basic personal allowance is reduced by one-half of the excess. Therefore the allowance is reduced to zero in 2022-23 if adjusted net income is £125,140 (£100,000 + (2 × £12,570)) or more.

Note that the gradual withdrawal of the personal allowance means that a taxpayer with income in the range £100,000 to £125,140 can be subject to a marginal rate of income tax of 60% (*61.5% for a Scottish taxpayer*). This surprising result is illustrated below.

EXAMPLE 1

Ben (who is not a Scottish taxpayer) has business profits of £110,520 in 2022-23. He has no other income and makes no Gift Aid donations or pension contributions. Calculate the amount of his 2022-23 personal allowance and show that a £100 increase in his business profits would result in a £60 increase in his income tax liability for the year.

Solution

	Profits £110,520	Profits £110,620
	£	£
Business profits	110,520	110,620
Less: Personal allowance (see below)	7,310	7,260
Taxable income	103,210	103,360
Income tax due		
£37,700 @ 20%	7,540.00	7,540.00
£65,510 @ 40%	26,204.00	
£65,660 @ 40%		26,264.00
Tax liability	33,744.00	33,804.00

Notes:

(i) With adjusted net income of £110,520, the personal allowance for the year is £7,310 (£12,570 − 1/2 x £10,520). If profits increase by £100, adjusted net income becomes £110,620 and the personal allowance is £7,260 (£12,570 − 1/2 x £10,620).

(ii) A £100 increase in Ben's business profits causes a £50 reduction in his personal allowance. So taxable income increases by £150 and his income tax liability rises by (£33,804 − £33,744) = £60, which is 60% of the £100 increase in income.

(iii) *For a Scottish taxpayer*, the marginal rate of tax would be 41% and so the tax liability would rise by (£150 × 41%) = £61.50, which is 61.5% of the increase in income.

Marriage allowance

Subject to certain conditions, an individual may elect to transfer part of his or her personal allowance to a spouse or civil partner. The "transferable amount" is equal to 10% of the basic personal allowance for the year. If this amount is not an exact multiple of £10 it is rounded up to the next multiple of £10, so the transferable amount for 2022-23 is £1,260. HMRC refers to this amount as the "marriage allowance", although this term is not used in the legislation. The main conditions which must be satisfied are as follows:

(a) The transferor is entitled to the basic personal allowance for the year.

(b) Neither the transferor nor the transferee is liable to income tax for the year at the higher rate, the additional rate, the dividend upper rate, the dividend additional rate or any Scottish rate above the intermediate rate[†]. Furthermore, this will remain the case after the transfer has been made.

(c) Neither party claims married couple's allowance (MCA) for the year (see below).

[†] *A non-Scottish taxpayer may elect to make this transfer for 2022-23 if his or her net income (and the net income of the other party) does not exceed £50,270 (£12,570 + £37,700). But for a Scottish taxpayer with non-savings income only, the limit is just £43,662 (£12,570 + £31,092).*

A marriage allowance election must be made within four years of the end of the tax year to which it relates†. If such an election is made, the personal allowance of the transferor is reduced by the transferable amount but the personal allowance of the spouse or partner is *not* increased. Instead, the income tax liability of the spouse or civil partner is reduced by the transferable amount multiplied by the basic rate‡ of income tax (20% for 2022-23). In other words, the marriage allowance acts as a "tax reducer" (see below).

It is important to note that the marriage allowance is *not* an extra allowance. It is merely an opportunity to transfer part of the personal allowance to a spouse or civil partner. This may be of benefit to those taxpayers with a low income who cannot use the whole of their personal allowance. It is also important not to confuse the marriage allowance with the married couple's allowance (MCA) which is available to older couples (see below).

† *A marriage allowance election may be made after one (or both) of the parties to a marriage or civil partnership has died, either by a surviving spouse or civil partner or by the personal representatives of a deceased spouse or civil partner.*

‡ *In the case of Scottish taxpayers, the tax reduction is calculated at the Scottish basic rate.*

EXAMPLE 2

In 2022-23, a husband has a pension of £11,360 and his wife has a pension of £20,000. They have no other income and they are not Scottish taxpayers. Calculate the combined tax liability of the couple for the year if:

(a)   no marriage allowance election is made

(b)   the husband elects to transfer part of his personal allowance to his wife.

Solution

(a)   The husband's income is exceeded by his personal allowance of £12,570 so his tax liability is £nil. His wife's liability is (£20,000 – £12,570) × 20% = £1,486.

(b)

	Husband	Wife
	£	£
Total income	11,360	20,000
Less: PA (Husband £12,570 – £1,260)	11,310	12,570
Taxable income	50	7,430
Income tax at 20%	10.00	1,486.00
Less: Marriage allowance £1,260 @ 20%		252.00
Tax liability	10.00	1,234.00

The combined tax liability is £1,244, a saving of £242. *For Scottish taxpayers,* the first £2,162 of taxable income would be taxed at the starter rate of 19%. Therefore the wife's tax liability would be £21.62 lower both before and after the transfer and the husband's liability after the transfer would be £9.50, giving a tax saving of £242.50.

Blind person's allowance (BPA)

The blind person's allowance (£2,600 in 2022-23) may be claimed by registered blind persons. This allowance is deducted from income and is given in full for the tax year in which the taxpayer is first registered as a blind person.

Any unused part of the BPA can be transferred to the taxpayer's spouse or civil partner, even if that spouse or partner is not a registered blind person.

Tax reducers

The personal allowance and the blind person's allowance are deducted from net income when calculating taxable income. By contrast, the "marriage allowance" (see above) acts as a "tax reducer". The transferred allowance is ignored until the amount of tax due on the spouse's or civil partner's income has been calculated but then this liability is reduced by 20% of the transferred amount. Similarly, the married couple's allowance (the only other allowance available in 2022-23) is a tax reducer. If MCA is claimed, the taxpayer's income tax liability is reduced by *10% of the amount of the allowance*. Note that:

(a) Certain payments and some types of investments made by a taxpayer also act as tax reducers (see Chapters 4 and 6).

(b) The amount of tax borne can never be reduced to less than zero as a result of the tax reduction process. If available tax reductions exceed the tax due on taxable income, there is no repayment of the excess. Any unused part of a tax reduction is generally lost. However, the tax reduction relating to the MCA may be transferred between spouses or civil partners in certain cases (see below).

Married couple's allowance (MCA)

The married couple's allowance is available to a legally married couple who live together for at least part of the tax year, *so long as at least one of the two spouses was born before 6 April 1935*. MCA is also available to civil partners, so long as at least one of the partners was born before 6 April 1935. Note the following points:

(a) MCA is not available to a couple who are separated for the whole of the tax year.

(b) The amount of the MCA for 2022-23 is £9,415, giving a maximum tax reduction of £941.50 (£9,415 @ 10%).

(c) In the case of marriages which took place before 5 December 2005, MCA is generally claimed by the husband. However, the couple may elect that the MCA should instead be claimed by the spouse with the higher net income. Such an election must be made before the start of the first tax year in which it is to have effect and then applies to all subsequent tax years. The election is irrevocable.

(d) For couples who marry on or after 5 December 2005 (and for civil partners) the MCA is claimed by the spouse or partner with the higher net income.

(e) The MCA is reduced if the *claimant's* adjusted net income exceeds a specified limit (£31,400 in 2022-23). If adjusted net income exceeds this limit, the MCA is reduced by one-half of the excess. But the MCA is never reduced to less than a specified minimum amount (£3,640 in 2022-23).

It is noteworthy that the other spouse's (or other partner's) income is not taken into account for this purpose, even if the MCA is available because of that spouse's or partner's age rather than because of the claimant's age.

EXAMPLE 3

Calculate the MCA available for 2022-23 in the following situations:

Husband	*Wife*
(a) Born 5 July 1938, income £19,700	Born 1 March 1935, income £12,450.
(b) Born 3 May 1933, income £31,510	Born 7 September 1938, income £nil.
(c) Born 4 June 1934, income £43,880	Born 8 October 1934, income £13,950.
(d) Born 16 November 1939, income £nil	Born 9 July 1934, income £49,300.

In each case, MCA is claimed and the stated income figure is the adjusted net income. All of the couples were married before 5 December 2005 and none of them have elected that MCA should be claimed by the spouse with the higher net income.

Solution

(a) The husband is entitled to claim an MCA of £9,415 because his wife was born before 6 April 1935. The MCA is available in full because his income does not exceed the £31,400 limit.

(b) The husband is entitled to claim MCA because he was born before 6 April 1935. But his income exceeds £31,400 by £110, so the MCA is reduced by £55 (1/2 × £110) to £9,360 (£9,415 – £55).

(c) The husband is entitled to claim MCA because he and his wife were both born before 6 April 1935. His income exceeds £31,400 by £12,480. A reduction of £6,240 (1/2 × £12,480) would give an MCA of only £3,175 (£9,415 – £6,240) but the MCA is never reduced to less than the minimum amount of £3,640. Therefore the MCA is £3,640.

(d) The husband is entitled to an MCA of £9,415 because his wife was born before 6 April 1935. His income does not exceed the £31,400 limit so the MCA is available in full. Since the husband is the claimant, his wife's income is not taken into account at all when calculating the MCA, even though (in this case) the MCA is available only by virtue of her age (not his).

Allocation of the MCA

The tax reduction relating to the MCA is normally set against the income tax liability of the *claimant*, but note that:

(a) The couple may elect jointly that the tax reduction relating to the MCA minimum amount (£3,640 for 2022-23) should be set against the tax liability of the claimant's spouse or civil partner.

(b) The claimant's spouse or civil partner may elect unilaterally that the tax reduction relating to 50% of the MCA minimum amount (£1,820 for 2022-23) should be set against his or her tax liability.

(c) If either spouse or partner is unable to use their MCA-related tax reduction in full or in part, the unused part may be transferred to the other spouse or partner.

The elections described in (a) and (b) above must normally be made before the start of the tax year to which they relate, but they can be made during the tax year if this is the year of marriage or the year in which a civil partnership is registered. If either of these elections is made, any remaining part of the MCA is dealt with in the claimant's tax computation.

The transfer described in (c) must be claimed within four years of the end of the tax year to which it relates.

Year of marriage and year of separation or death

In a tax year in which a marriage occurs (or a civil partnership is registered) and at least one of the parties was born before 6 April 1935, MCA is calculated as usual but is then reduced by 1/12th for each full tax month which elapses between the start of the year and the date of the marriage or registration†. An election to transfer all or 50% of the MCA minimum amount to the claimant's spouse or civil partner in the year of marriage or registration applies to that amount reduced in the same proportion as the MCA itself.

MCA is available in full in the tax year in which a couple separate or in which one of them dies (subject to the usual restriction if the claimant's income exceeds the limit).

† *In 2022-23, this situation would arise only if one or both of the parties concerned was at least 87 years old on the date of the marriage or civil partnership.*

EXAMPLE 4

Calculate the MCA available in 2022-23 to a couple (both born in August 1934) who each have an adjusted net income not exceeding £31,400 and who form a civil partnership on 23 June 2022.

Solution

Two full tax months have elapsed since the start of the tax year (6 April 2022 to 5 May 2022 and 6 May 2022 to 5 June 2022). So the MCA is £9,415 x 10/12 = £7,846.

EXAMPLE 5

Calculate the income tax liability for 2022-23 of a husband and wife (both born in March 1935) given the information shown below. They were married in 1961 and have not elected that MCA should be claimed by the spouse with the higher net income. None of their income is derived from savings or dividends and they are not Scottish taxpayers.

(a) Husband's income £16,330, wife's income £23,320. The couple have jointly elected that the tax reduction relating to the MCA minimum amount should be set against the wife's income tax liability.

(b) Husband's income £31,460, wife's income £17,765. The wife has elected that the tax reduction relating to 50% of the MCA minimum amount should be set against her income tax liability.

(c) Husband's income £15,155, wife's income £24,325. Husband dies on 12 May 2022.

In each case, the stated income figure is the taxpayer's net income (i.e. total income less tax reliefs) and adjusted net income is the same as net income.

Solution

	(a) £	(b) £	(c) £
HUSBAND			
Net income	16,330	31,460	15,155
Less: Personal allowance	12,570	12,570	12,570
Taxable income	3,760	18,890	2,585
Income tax due @ 20%	752.00	3,778.00	517.00
Less: MCA £5,775 @ 10%	577.50		
MCA £7,565 @ 10%		756.50	
MCA £9,415 @ 10% = £941.50			517.00
Tax liability	174.50	3,021.50	nil
WIFE			
Net income	23,320	17,765	24,325
Less: Personal allowance	12,570	12,570	12,570
Taxable income	10,750	5,195	11,755
Income tax due @ 20%	2,150.00	1,039.00	2,351.00
Less: MCA £3,640 @ 10%	364.00		
MCA £1,820 @ 10%		182.00	
MCA £941.50 – £517.00			424.50
Tax liability	1,786.00	857.00	1,926.50

Notes:

(i)   In case (a), the husband's income does not exceed the income limit, so an MCA of £9,415 is available. They have elected for the wife to receive MCA of £3,640, so the husband's MCA is £5,775 (£9,415 – £3,640).

For Scottish taxpayers, the tax liability of each spouse would be £21.62 lower.

(ii) In case (b), the husband's income is £60 over the income limit, so the MCA is reduced to £9,385 (£9,415 – 1/2 x £60). MCA of £1,820 (one-half of the minimum amount) is claimed by the wife, leaving £7,565 for the husband.

For Scottish taxpayers, his tax liability would be (£2,162 × 19%) + (£10,956 × 20%) + (£5,772 × 21%) less MCA £756.50 = £3,057.60. Her liability would fall by £21.62.

(iii) In case (c), the MCA is available in full in the year of the husband's death. The tax reduction that he cannot use (£424.50) is transferred to his wife.

For Scottish taxpayers, his liability (before MCA) would be £21.62 lower so he would use only £495.38 of the tax reduction, transferring £446.12 to his wife. Her tax liability (before MCA) would also fall by £21.62, so her final liability would be £43.24 lower.

Summary

▸   UK residents and certain non-residents are entitled to claim at least the basic personal allowance. But this allowance is reduced (possibly to zero) if the taxpayer's adjusted net income for the year exceeds £100,000.

▸   Subject to conditions, an individual may transfer 10% of the basic personal allowance to a spouse or civil partner. The tax liability of the transferee is reduced by 20% of the amount transferred.

▸   The blind person's allowance is granted to registered blind persons. Any unused part of this allowance can be transferred to the person's spouse or civil partner.

▸   The married couple's allowance is available to a legally married couple who live together for at least part of the tax year, so long as at least one of the spouses was born before 6 April 1935. MCA is also available to civil partners.

▸   MCA is reduced if the claimant's adjusted net income exceeds a specified limit for the year. But the MCA is never reduced to less than a specified minimum amount.

▸   In certain circumstances, all or part of the MCA may be transferred to the claimant's spouse or partner if an appropriate claim or election is made.

▸   The personal allowance and the blind person's allowance are deducted from the taxpayer's net income when computing taxable income. The MCA reduces tax borne by 10% of the amount of the allowance.

▸   Personal allowances which cannot be used in the tax year to which they relate are lost. There is no provision for carrying unused allowances backwards or forwards.

Exercises

It should be assumed in these exercises that the taxpayers concerned made no Gift Aid donations or pension contributions during tax year 2022-23. It may also be assumed that the taxpayers are not Scottish taxpayers. However, an alternative solution is provided (where necessary) to indicate how the income tax liability would differ for a Scottish taxpayer.

A set of multiple choice questions for this chapter is available on the accompanying website.

3.1 Calculate the basic personal allowance available in 2022-23 to a taxpayer with adjusted net income of:

(a) £90,000   (b) £108,000   (c) £140,000.

3.2 Alisha's salary in 2022-23 is £105,000. She has no other income.

(a) Calculate her income tax liability for 2022-23.

(b) Re-calculate her income tax liability as it would have been if her salary for the year had been £25,000 higher.

(c) Explain how the difference between these two tax liabilities arises.

3.3 Calculate the married couple's allowance available to the following couples in 2022-23, assuming that they were married before 5 December 2005 and that they have not elected for MCA to be claimed by the spouse with the higher net income:

(a) Husband born 1931, income £19,900; wife born 1932, income £29,500

(b) Husband born 1929, income £31,440; wife born 1934, income £10,070

(c) Husband born 1934, income £37,800; wife born 1939, income £20,000

(d) Husband born 1936, income £18,600; wife born 1933, income £46,700.

In each case, the stated income figure is the adjusted net income.

3.4 Calculate the tax liability for 2022-23 of a husband and wife (both born in 1933), using the information below. No elections have been made in relation to the MCA and none of the income is derived from savings or dividends.

(a) Married in 1956; husband's income £19,210, wife's income £20,510

(b) Married in 2006; husband's income £11,300, wife's income £21,445

(c) Married in 1956 but husband dies on 16 September 2022; husband's income to date of death £12,905, wife's income for the year £20,375.

In each case, the stated income figure is the taxpayer's net income (i.e. total income less tax reliefs), MCA is claimed and adjusted net income is the same as net income.

3.5 Toby is a widower. He was born in August 1933. His wife was born in June 1934 but she died in March 2022. Toby's income for 2022-23 is as follows:

	£
Retirement pension	11,550
Income from purchased life annuity (net)	912

Calculate the amount of income tax repayable to Toby for 2022-23.

3.6 Brian and Daniel are civil partners. They were both born in 1978. Brian's total income for 2022-23 is £30,000 and Daniel's total income for the year is £10,000. None of their income is derived from savings or dividends.

(a) Calculate their income tax liabilities if Daniel does not make an election to transfer part of his personal allowance to Brian.

(b) Calculate their income tax liabilities if Daniel does make the election.

(c) How would the situation change if Brian's total income were £60,000?

3.7 Richard was born on 5 April 1935. His wife, Patricia, was born on 7 October 1938. They were married in 1968. Their income for tax year 2022-23 is as follows:

	£
Richard:	
Business profits	35,410
Patricia:	
Dividends received	3,600

Calculate their income tax liabilities for 2022-23.

*3.8 A married man (born 3 November 1934) died on 8 July 2022. He received a retirement pension of £15,000 between 6 April 2022 and the date of his death. His wife (born 12 August 1940) had no income whilst her husband was alive but received a pension of £19,955 between 8 July 2022 and 5 April 2023. They were married in 1970 and made no elections in relation to the married couple's allowance.

Calculate their income tax liabilities for 2022-23.

*3.9 Bill was born in 1983. He is married to Hazel who was born in 1987. In 2022-23, Bill had business profits of £52,820 and received dividends of £2,200. Hazel received a salary of £220,570 and bank interest of £3,040.

Calculate their income tax liabilities for the year.

Chapter 4

Payments and gifts eligible for tax relief

Introduction

Certain payments and gifts made by a taxpayer are eligible for tax relief. Some of these are subtracted from the taxpayer's total income when computing his or her tax liability. Others act as tax reducers and are relieved by reducing the amount of income tax payable on the taxpayer's taxable income. A special tax regime applies to charitable donations which fall within the "Gift Aid" scheme.

The purpose of this chapter is to identify the main classes of payments and gifts which attract tax relief in these ways and to explain how relief is given for each. However, this chapter does *not* deal with:

(a) payments and gifts which are deductible when computing a taxpayer's income from either employment (see Chapter 7) or self-employment (see Chapter 9)

(b) pension contributions (see Chapter 14).

Payments and gifts deductible from total income

The following payments and gifts are deductible from a taxpayer's total income for the tax year in which the payment or gift is made:

(a) eligible interest payments

(b) certain "annual payments"

(c) gifts of listed shares or securities to a charity

(d) gifts of land or buildings to a charity.

Each of these is explained later in this chapter. As stated in Chapter 2, the income which remains after these items (and certain other reliefs) have been subtracted from total income is referred to by Income Tax Act 2007 as the taxpayer's "net income".

Tax relief for these payments and gifts is given at "marginal rate" (i.e. at the highest rates of income tax to which the taxpayer is liable). Deducting them from total income will automatically give the right amount of relief, since the effect of the deduction is to reduce the amount of taxable income which falls into the upper tax bands.

Payments made gross or net

Most of the payments which are deductible from total income are made gross (without deduction of income tax). However, certain payments are required by law to be paid net, after deduction of basic rate income tax (see later in this chapter).

Payments made gross are deducted from the taxpayer's total income when computing his or her income tax liability, but it is tempting to ignore any payments made net since the taxpayer has already taken tax relief at source. However, the income tax deducted at source is always calculated at the basic rate (20% for 2022-23) and this will not give the right amount of relief to a taxpayer whose highest rate of tax is not the basic rate. The only way to be sure that the right amount of tax relief is given for a payment made net is to:

(a)   calculate the gross amount of the payment (net payment × 100/80)

(b)   subtract the gross figure from the taxpayer's total income

(c)   increase the taxpayer's income tax liability by the amount of basic rate tax which was deducted from the payment when it was made.

In effect, the person making the payment is regarded as having collected basic rate income tax from the recipient on behalf of HM Revenue and Customs and must therefore account to HMRC for this tax as part of his or her income tax liability. Note the following points:

(a)   This treatment of payments made net of tax is entirely consistent with the treatment of income received net of tax (see Chapter 2). Income received net is shown gross in the taxpayer's income tax computation and the amount of tax deducted at source is subtracted when calculating tax payable. Similarly, any payments made net are shown gross in the taxpayer's income tax computation and the amount of tax deducted at source is added when calculating tax payable.

(b)   Basic rate tax must be deducted at source from certain payments which are allowable when computing a taxpayer's income from self-employment (see Chapter 9). In this case, to ensure that tax relief is not given twice, these payments are not also deducted from total income. However, the amount of tax deducted at source must still be accounted for to HMRC and this is achieved by adding this amount to the taxpayer's income tax liability for the year.

EXAMPLE 1

(a)   Bob (who is not a Scottish taxpayer) has total income of £22,515 in 2022-23. None of his income is derived from savings or dividends. During the year he makes a payment which is deductible from total income of £200 (paid gross).

(b)   Cathy's circumstances are precisely the same as Bob's except that her payment is required by law to be made net of basic rate tax, so she pays a net amount of £160.

Compute Bob and Cathy's income tax liabilities for 2022-23. Does it seem to make any difference whether a deductible payment is made gross or net?

Solution

	Bob	Cathy
	£	£
Total income	22,515	22,515
Less: Payment	200	
Payment £160 x 100/80		200
Net income	22,315	22,315
Less: Personal allowance	12,570	12,570
Taxable income	9,745	9,745
Income tax		
£9,745 @ 20%	1,949.00	
£9,745 @ 20%		1,949.00
Tax borne	1,949.00	1,949.00
Add: Tax deducted from payment	0.00	40.00
Tax liability	1,949.00	1,989.00

Bob has made a payment of £200 and has a tax liability of £1,949.00, a total of £2,149.00. Cathy has made a payment of £160 and has a tax liability of £1,989.00, again a total of £2,149.00. Apart from the timing of the cash flows involved, it makes no difference whether a deductible payment is made gross or net and this is evidenced by the fact that tax borne is the same for both taxpayers.

For Scottish taxpayers, the first £2,162 of taxable income would be taxed at 19%, reducing tax borne and the liability by £21.62 in each case.

Taxpayers whose marginal rate is higher than the basic rate

If a taxpayer is chargeable to income tax at a rate above the basic rate, a payment or gift which is deductible from total income will effectively cost the taxpayer less than it would cost a basic rate taxpayer. This is because tax relief is given at marginal rate. The method of computation described above will ensure that the correct amount of tax relief is given.

EXAMPLE 2

Derek's total income for 2022-23 is £68,310 (entirely non-savings) and he makes a gross deductible payment of £3,000 in the year. He is not a Scottish taxpayer and he makes no Gift Aid donations or pension contributions. Show his income tax computation:

(a) with the deductible payment   (b) as it would have been without the payment.

How much has the payment effectively cost him? How much would it have cost him if his total income for the year had been £168,310? And in what ways would the situation have differed if his total income for the year had been £115,000?

Solution

			Income £68,310		Income £168,310	
			(a)	(b)	(a)	(b)
			£	£	£	£
Total income			68,310	68,310	168,310	168,310
Less: Payment			3,000		3,000	
Net income			65,310	68,310	165,310	168,310
Less: Personal allowance			12,570	12,570	0	0
Taxable income			52,740	55,740	165,310	168,310

Income tax

37,700	37,700	@ 20%	7,540.00	7,540.00		
15,040	18,040	@ 40%	6,016.00	7,216.00		
52,740	55,740					
37,700	37,700	@ 20%			7,540.00	7,540.00
112,300	112,300	@ 40%			44,920.00	44,920.00
15,310	18,310	@ 45%			6,889.50	8,239.50
165,310	168,310					
Tax liability			13,556.00	14,756.00	59,349.50	60,699.50

Notes:

(i) With total income of £68,310, Derek's income tax liability for the year is reduced by £1,200 if he makes the £3,000 payment, so in fact it costs him only £1,800. In effect, tax relief has been given at 40%, which is Derek's highest rate of tax.

(ii) With total income of £168,310, Derek's tax liability is reduced by £1,350 if he makes the £3,000 payment, so it now costs him only £1,650. Tax relief has been given at 45%, which is Derek's highest rate of tax. The personal allowance is zero in this case because adjusted net income greatly exceeds £100,000 (see Chapter 3).

(iii) With total income of £115,000, the £3,000 payment reduces Derek's net income to £112,000 so his PA is £6,570 (£12,570 – 1/2 x £12,000). Without the payment, the PA is only £5,070 (£12,570 – 1/2 x £15,000). So the combination of the £3,000 payment and the extra PA of £1,500 reduces taxable income by £4,500.

Since marginal rate in this case is 40%, tax saved is £1,800 (40% of £4,500). A tax saving of £1,800 on a payment of £3,000 amounts to an effective rate of tax relief of 60%. This exceptionally high rate of relief will always occur in 2022-23 if adjusted net income lies between £100,000 and £125,140 (see Chapter 3).

For a Scottish taxpayer with income of £68,310, tax relief on the £3,000 payment would be (£3,000 × 41%) = £1,230. With income of £168,310, tax relief would be (£3,000 × 46%) = £1,380. With income of £115,000, the effective rate of relief would be 61.5% and tax relief on the payment would be (£3,000 × 61.5%) = £1,845 (see Chapter 3).

Taxpayers with marginal rate less than basic rate (and non-taxpayers)

Since tax relief on deductible payments and gifts is given at marginal rate, a taxpayer whose highest rate of tax is lower than basic rate will be entitled to less tax relief on such payments and gifts than a basic rate taxpayer. Similarly, a non-taxpayer or a taxpayer whose highest rate of tax is either the starting rate for savings, the savings nil rate or the dividend nil rate (all of which are 0% in 2022-23) is not entitled to any tax relief at all. But the method described above will ensure that tax relief (if any) is given at the correct rate.

EXAMPLE 3

Esmé receives dividends of £15,230 in tax year 2022-23 and has no other income for tax purposes. She makes a gross deductible payment of £100 during the year. Calculate her income tax liability for 2022-23:

(a) with the deductible payment   (b) as it would have been without the payment.

How would the situation differ if her dividend income had been £1,000 lower?

Solution

				Dividends £15,230 (a) £	Dividends £15,230 (b) £	Dividends £14,230 (a) £	Dividends £14,230 (b) £
Dividends received				15,230	15,230	14,230	14,230
Less: Payment				100		100	
Net income				15,130	15,230	14,130	14,230
Less: Personal allowance				12,570	12,570	12,570	12,570
Taxable income				2,560	2,660	1,560	1,660
Income tax							
2,000	2,000	@ 0%		0.00	0.00		
560	660	@ 8.75%		49.00	57.75		
2,560	2,660						
1,560	1,660	@ 0%				0.00	0.00
Tax liability				49.00	57.75	0.00	0.00

Notes:

(i) With dividends of £15,230, Esmé's highest rate of tax is the dividend ordinary rate. If she makes the payment, her tax liability is reduced by £8.75 (8.75% of £100).

(ii) With dividends of £14,230, Esmé's highest rate of tax is the dividend nil rate and her tax liability is zero with or without the payment. She is entitled to tax relief at 0% (i.e. no tax relief at all) and so the payment costs her the full £100.

Eligible interest payments

The interest paid on certain loans is deductible from a taxpayer's total income. This interest is generally paid gross. The main types of eligible loan are:

(a) A loan to purchase plant or machinery which is necessarily acquired for use in the taxpayer's employment. Interest on such a loan is eligible for relief in the tax year in which the loan is taken out and the next three years. This relief is not available in relation to the purchase of a mechanically propelled vehicle or a cycle.

(b) A loan to purchase plant or machinery for use in the business of a partnership in which the taxpayer concerned is a partner. Interest on such a loan is eligible for tax relief if it is paid no later than three years after the end of the period of account in which the loan was made.

(c) A loan to purchase ordinary shares in a close company (see Chapter 27), so long as the taxpayer owns at least 5% of the company's ordinary share capital or works for the greater part of his or her time in the management of the company.

   This relief also applies to the purchase of shares in companies which are resident in the European Economic Area (EEA) and which would have been regarded as close companies if they had been resident in the UK.

(d) A loan to purchase shares in an employee-controlled company that is resident in the UK or in the EEA, or to purchase an interest in a partnership.

(e) A loan to pay inheritance tax. The interest on such a loan is eligible for tax relief if it relates to a period ending within 12 months of the date that the loan was made.

Note that interest which is paid wholly and exclusively for business purposes is treated as a business expense and is deducted when calculating the business profits which are charged to income tax as trading income (see Chapter 9). In this case, the interest is not deductible from total income.

Limit on income tax reliefs

ITA 2007 imposes a limit on the aggregate amount of the tax reliefs that may be deducted from a taxpayer's total income when calculating his or her net income. This limit applies only to specified tax reliefs and is mainly concerned with reliefs available in relation to trading losses (see Chapter 12). However, the eligible interest payments listed above also fall within the scope of this rule.

   In general terms, the total of the tax reliefs to which this limit applies cannot exceed the greater of £50,000 and 25% of the taxpayer's total income. A more detailed explanation of the limit on income tax reliefs is given in Chapter 12 of this book.

Annual payments

ITA 2007 requires that certain "annual payments" made by an individual should be made net of basic rate income tax. One example of this is the payment of royalties to a person who holds intellectual property as an investment. Tax relief on a qualifying annual payment may be obtained in one of two ways. Either:

(a) the gross amount of the payment may be deductible when calculating the taxpayer's trading profits for income tax purposes (see Chapter 9), or

(b) if the payment is not deductible when calculating trading profits, the gross amount of the payment is relieved instead by deduction from the taxpayer's total income[†].

In either case, the amount of tax deducted at source from the payment must be accounted for to HMRC by being added to the taxpayer's income tax liability for the year concerned.

[†] *Patent royalties can no longer be relieved by deduction from total income. So if patent royalties are not deductible when calculating trading profits, they will not be relieved at all.*

Gifts of shares or property to charity

A gift of listed shares or securities made to a charity attracts tax relief in the same way as a deductible payment. The amount of the gift is taken to be the market value of the shares on the date of the gift, plus any incidental costs borne by the donor and less the value of any benefits that are received by the donor in consequence of making the gift. Gifts of land or buildings to a charity are also eligible for relief.

This income tax relief is in addition to the relief from capital gains tax which arises when assets are given to charities (see Chapter 17).

EXAMPLE 4

In 2022-23, a taxpayer whose marginal rate of income tax is 45% (and who pays capital gains tax at 20%) gives listed shares worth £20,000 to a charity. A capital gain of £12,000 would have arisen if the shares had been sold instead. How much does it cost the taxpayer to make this gift rather than selling the shares?

Solution

Assuming that 45% income tax would have been payable on at least £20,000 of taxable income if the gift had not been made, income tax saved is £9,000 (45% of £20,000). CGT of £2,400 (20% of £12,000) is also saved. The total tax saving is £11,400. This amounts to tax relief at a total rate of 57% and the gift has effectively cost the taxpayer only £8,600.

For a Scottish taxpayer, income tax relief would be (£20,000 × 46%) = £9,200, so the total tax saving would be £11,600 and the effective cost of the gift would be £8,400.

Payments which are tax reducers

The following payments are granted tax relief by means of a reduction in the income tax liability of the taxpayer who makes the payment:

(a) certain alimony or maintenance payments (as long as either the payer or the recipient was born before 6 April 1935)

(b) interest on a loan secured on the taxpayer's main residence and used to purchase a life annuity (so long as the loan was taken out before 9 March 1999).

If such a payment is made gross, a tax reduction at the relevant rate (see below) is given in the payer's income tax computation. This tax reduction takes priority over tax reductions for the marriage allowance or the married couple's allowance (see Chapter 3). No refund is available if available tax reductions exceed the tax due on the payer's taxable income.

If such a payment is made net, it should be *entirely omitted* from the taxpayer's income tax computation, since precisely the right amount of tax relief has already been given at source and there is nothing more to be done.

Maintenance payments

Maintenance payments consist of periodical payments made:

(a) by one of the parties to a marriage or civil partnership (or a former marriage or civil partnership) for the maintenance of the other party, at a time when:

    (i) the couple are no longer living together, and

    (ii) the party for whose benefit the payment is made has not entered into a new marriage (or civil partnership)

(b) by one parent of a child to the other parent, made for the child's maintenance and at a time when the two parents are not living together.

Tax relief is available to a person who makes maintenance payments if at least one of the parties or parents was born before 6 April 1935 and the payments are made under either a court order, a legally binding agreement or an assessment made under the Child Support Act 1991. The income tax regime which applies to such payments is as follows:

(a) Maintenance payments are made gross, without any deduction of tax at source.

(b) In 2022-23, a taxpayer making qualifying maintenance payments is entitled to a tax reduction equal to 10% of the *lower* of:

    (i) the payments made by the taxpayer which fall due in the tax year, and

    (ii) the minimum married couple's allowance (£3,640).

(c) The recipient of maintenance payments is not liable to pay income tax on them.

Loans used to purchase a life annuity

Tax relief is available[†] in relation to the interest payable on the first £30,000 of a loan taken out *before 9 March 1999* and which was:

(a) made to a taxpayer aged 65 or over at the time that the loan was made, and

(b) used to purchase a life annuity, and

(c) secured on the taxpayer's main residence.

Such arrangements are often referred to as *home income plans*.

Tax relief takes the form of a tax reduction equal to 23% of the qualifying interest. This rate of tax relief remains at 23% (the basic rate of income tax for tax year 1998-99) even though the basic rate has now fallen to only 20%. If the interest is paid gross, relief is given in the taxpayer's income tax computation. If the interest is paid net it should be entirely omitted from the tax computation, as explained above.

[†] *The Government has decided not to withdraw this tax relief (as had originally been intended).*

Gifts of pre-eminent property to the nation

Subject to certain conditions, an individual who makes a gift of "pre-eminent property" to the nation (e.g. a work of art) is entitled to a total tax reduction equal to 30% of the agreed value of that property. This total tax reduction may be split between the tax year in which the gift is made and the following four tax years in any way that the individual wishes. For instance, the total tax reduction of £300,000 relating to a gift with an agreed value of £1m made in tax year 2022-23 could be allocated as follows:

(a) the entire £300,000 could be allocated to 2022-23, or

(b) £60,000 could be allocated to each tax year from 2022-23 to 2026-27 inclusive, or

(c) the £300,000 could be allocated to the five tax years in any other way at all (including a nil allocation in some years).

The tax reduction that is allocated to a tax year is normally set first against the individual's income tax liability for the year. If this liability is less than the tax reduction, the balance is then set against the individual's capital gains tax liability[†] for the year. However, the individual may choose to reverse this order if he or she so wishes.

Note that tax relief is also available to *companies* which make a gift of pre-eminent property to the nation (see Chapter 23).

[†] *A qualifying gift of pre-eminent property to the nation is exempt from capital gains tax and so does not itself result in a CGT liability (see Chapter 17). However, such a liability might arise as a consequence of other disposals made by the individual during the tax year.*

Gift Aid

The Gift Aid scheme provides a tax incentive for individuals and companies to make charitable donations. The way in which the scheme applies to individuals is explained here. The way in which the scheme applies to companies is explained in Chapter 23.

This scheme applies to any charitable donation (including donations made to community amateur sports clubs) so long as:

(a) The donor is a UK resident or a non-resident with income or gains charged to UK tax.

(b) The donation takes the form of a gift of money and this gift is not repayable to the donor, is not relieved under the payroll giving scheme (see Chapter 7) and is not deductible when computing the donor's income from any source.

(c) The donor receives no benefit at all from making the gift, or receives a benefit which does not exceed the following limits:

    (i)   for a gift which does not exceed £100, 25% of the amount of the gift

    (ii) for a gift which exceeds £100, the sum of £25 plus 5% of the amount by which the gift exceeds £100

    subject to a limit of £2,500 on the value of the benefits which the donor may receive in any one tax year as a consequence of donations to any one charity.

(d) The donor makes a Gift Aid declaration with regard to the donation.

If all of these conditions are satisfied, the gift is treated as if made net of basic rate tax and the charity can recover the tax deemed to have been deducted at source. For instance, a £20 gift would be treated as a gross gift of £25 (£20 × 100/80) less tax deducted of £5. In this case, the charity would receive £20 from the donor and a further £5 from HMRC.

Gift Aid relief for donors

The following provisions apply:

(a) The donor must pay total income tax and capital gains tax equal to at least the amount of tax deemed to have been deducted from the gift. If this is not the case, the donor's personal allowance is restricted to ensure that sufficient tax is paid. If this restriction does not give the required result, the donor is charged to income tax at the basic rate on as much of the gift as necessary to ensure that the required amount of tax is paid.

(b) The donor's basic rate and higher rate limits are both increased by the gross amount of the gift, so giving further relief to higher rate and additional rate taxpayers[†].

[†] *For Scottish taxpayers, the intermediate rate limit is also increased.*

Carry-back of Gift Aid relief

A donor may elect that a Gift Aid donation should be treated as if paid in the previous tax year. Such an election must be made by the date that the tax return for the previous tax year is submitted and no later than the 31 January which follows the end of that year.

EXAMPLE 5

In 2022-23, Owen (who is not a Scottish taxpayer) makes qualifying Gift Aid donations totalling £760. He has no capital gains tax liability for the year. Show his income tax computation if his only income for the year consists of business profits of:

(a) £28,895   (b) £12,785   (c) £246,590.

Solution

	(a) £	(b) £	(c) £
Business profits	28,895	12,785	246,590
Less: Personal allowance	12,570	11,835	0
Taxable income	16,325	950	246,590

Income tax

(a)	(b)	(c)				
16,325	950	38,650	@ 20%	3,265.00	190.00	7,730.00
		112,300	@ 40%			44,920.00
		95,640	@ 45%			43,038.00
16,325	950	246,590				

Tax liability	3,265.00	190.00	95,688.00

Notes:

(i)   Gross donations are £950 (£760 x 100/80). Deemed tax deducted is £190.

(ii)   In case (a), the tax liability exceeds £190 so there is no more to be done.

(iii) In case (b), the tax liability will be only £43 if the full personal allowance is given i.e. (£12,785 − £12,570) = £215 x 20% = £43. So Owen must pay further income tax of (£190 − £43) = £147. This is achieved by reducing his PA by £735 to £11,835.

(iv)   In case (c), the basic rate and higher rate limits are both increased by £950. This moves £950 of taxable income from additional rate to basic rate and saves tax of £237.50 (£950 x 25%). The charity receives £950 but the cost to Owen is only £522.50 (£760 − £237.50). Total tax relief is therefore £427.50 (i.e. £950 x 45%).

For a Scottish taxpayer, the tax liability in (a) would be (£2,162 × 19%) + (£10,956 × 20%) + (£3,207 × 21%) = £3,275.45. In (b), the PA would be restricted to £11,785, giving a tax liability of (£1,000 × 19%) = £190. In (c), the basic rate limit, the intermediate rate limit and the higher rate limit would all increase by £950, moving £950 of taxable income from top rate to basic rate and saving tax of £247 (£950 × 26%).

Summary

▸ Certain payments and gifts made by a taxpayer are either deducted from total income or act as tax reducers. Payments which are deducted from total income must always be shown gross in the payer's income tax computation. Any tax which was deducted when the payment was made is added to the tax liability of the payer.

▸ If a payment which ranks as a tax reducer is made gross, the appropriate tax reduction is given in the payer's tax computation. But payments of this type that are made net should be omitted from the computation entirely.

▸ The main deductible payments are eligible interest payments and certain annual payments. A charitable gift consisting of listed shares or securities or comprising land and buildings may also be deducted from total income.

▸ Qualifying maintenance payments of up to the minimum MCA are relieved at 10%. Interest on qualifying loans used to buy a life annuity is relieved at 23%.

▸ Qualifying Gift Aid donations are deemed to have been made net of basic rate tax.

▸ A Gift Aid donor must pay income tax and CGT of at least the amount of tax deemed to have been deducted from the donation. Further tax relief is available to Gift Aid donors who pay tax at a rate higher than basic rate.

Exercises

It should be assumed in the following exercises that the taxpayers concerned are not Scottish taxpayers. However, an alternative solution is provided (where necessary) to indicate how the tax liability would differ for a Scottish taxpayer. A set of multiple choice questions for this chapter is available on the accompanying website.

4.1   Mabel has total income of £24,275 in 2022-23, none of which is derived from savings or dividends. During the year she makes a net deductible payment of £200. Show her income tax computation for the year.

4.2   Paul has total income of £54,160 in 2022-23, none of which is derived from savings or from dividends. During the year he pays gross eligible interest of £1,600. Show his income tax computation:

(a) with the interest payment   (b) as it would be without the interest payment.

How much has the interest effectively cost him?

4.3   Rose is single and has total income of £12,300 in 2022-23. She makes a gross deductible payment of £25 during the year. Show her income tax computation for the year and determine the amount of tax relief given in relation to the payment.

4.4   At what rate of income tax is each of the following types of payment relieved in tax year 2022-23?

(a)   a gift of listed shares to a charity

(b)   interest on a loan used to buy an interest in a partnership

(c)   qualifying maintenance payments

(d)   a gift of pre-eminent property to the nation.

4.5   A taxpayer with no capital gains tax liability makes a qualifying Gift Aid donation of £960 in tax year 2022-23. Explain:

(a)   why this donation is worth more than £960 to the charity which receives it

(b)   why this donation might cost the taxpayer more than £960

(c)   why this donation might cost the taxpayer less than £960.

4.6   In 2022-23, Raj has dividend income of £63,670. He has no other income. He makes a qualifying Gift Aid donation of £440 during the year. Show his 2022-23 income tax computation.

4.7   Matthew (who was born on 1 October 1934) dies on 23 December 2022. His only income in tax year 2022-23 is a retirement pension of £31,930. He made a Gift Aid donation of £200 in July 2022. His wife has income from property of £21,965 and no other income. In August 2022 she gave listed shares to charity with a market value of £500.

They were married for many years and made no elections with regard to the married couple's allowance. Calculate their tax liabilities for 2022-23.

*4.8   Pauline (born August 1974) married Adrian (born March 1975) on 17 October 2022. Their income for 2022-23 is as follows:

	£
Pauline:	
Share of partnership profit	17,920
Building society interest	1,125
Adrian:	
Income from property	53,870
Dividends received	3,760

During 2022-23, Pauline paid interest of £450 on a loan which she used to buy a share in the business partnership of which she is now a member. Adrian paid maintenance of £4,000 to his former wife, as required by a court order. She was born in 1977 and has not remarried. He also made Gift Aid donations of £680.

Show Pauline's and Adrian's income tax computations for 2022-23.

*4.9   Geoffrey's income for 2022-23 comprises a salary of £114,600 and dividends received of £4,400. He makes qualifying Gift Aid donations of £7,200 during the year. Calculate his 2022-23 income tax liability.

Chapter 5

Income from property

Introduction

An individual's income from property is charged to income tax in accordance with the rules of the Income Tax (Trading and Other Income) Act 2005. The main purpose of this chapter is to explain those rules and to show how a taxpayer's UK property income is calculated. Income from overseas property is considered separately in Chapter 32.

Definition of property income

ITTOIA 2005 states that income tax is charged on the profits of a property business. This statute also states that a UK property business consists of a business which is carried on for the purpose of generating income from land which is situated in the UK and that "generating income from land" means *"exploiting an estate, interest or right in or over land as a source of rents or other receipts"*. This is a fairly broad definition but, in practice, the main classes of property income are:

(a)   rents

(b)   lease premiums (if the length of the lease does not exceed 50 years)

(c)   amounts receivable in respect of rights of way, sporting rights etc.

(d)   income from the letting of fixed caravans or permanently moored houseboats.

Dividends received from a UK Real Estate Investment Trust (UK-REIT) are also treated as property income to the extent that they are derived from the company's tax-exempt property income or gains (see Chapter 23). Such dividends are received net of basic rate income tax and rank as non-savings income (see Chapter 2).

Despite the use of the word "business" above, income from property is almost always treated as *unearned* income. The only occasion on which property income is treated as earned income is when the income derives from the commercial letting of furnished holiday accommodation (see later in this chapter). The distinction between earned and unearned income may be especially important if the taxpayer is hoping to obtain tax relief on pension contributions (see Chapter 14).

Basis of assessment and allowable expenditure

For income tax purposes, the profit of a property business is usually calculated on the cash basis[†]. Income is taxed in the tax year[‡] in which it is received and expenditure is deducted in the tax year in which it is paid, with no adjustments for receivables, payables etc. But the cash basis does not apply to property businesses with receipts for the tax year which exceed £150,000 (in which case the accruals basis applies). Furthermore, landlords with receipts which do not exceed £150,000 may elect for the accruals basis if they so wish.

Expenditure incurred "wholly and exclusively" for the purposes of a property business is deducted when computing property income. The types of expenditure which are likely to be deductible include the following:

(a)   repairs and maintenance (excluding improvements) and insurances

(b)   the cost of providing services to tenants

(c)   administrative and management costs[†] (including bad debts if cash basis not used)

(d)   rent paid to a superior landlord (if the property is sub-let)

(e)   any business rates, water rates or council tax paid by the landlord.

If a property is partly let and partly owner-occupied, the proportion of the expenditure which relates to the letting of the property is deductible when computing property income, as long as this proportion can be determined with reasonable accuracy.

If a taxpayer rents out more than one property, total property expenditure is deducted from total rental income, giving a single profit (or loss) figure for the year.

[†] *The cash basis for property income operates in much the same way as the cash basis for trading income (see Chapter 9). Whether or not the cash basis is used, motor expenses may be calculated by reference to specified mileage rates under the "fixed rate deduction scheme" (see Chapter 9).*

[‡] *Since property business profits are taxed by reference to tax years, it is expected that most property businesses will prepare accounts to 5 April each year. But if accounts are prepared to some other date, it will be necessary to apportion profits between tax years (usually on a time basis). The basis period rules which apply to trading income (see Chapter 10) do not apply to property income.*

Tax relief for interest paid

Loan interest[†] paid in connection with the letting of residential property is not a deductible expense and so cannot be deducted when computing property income. Instead, such interest is treated as a tax reducer (see Chapters 3 and 4) and is relieved at basic rate. This restriction applies to interest and other finance costs incurred in relation to "dwelling-related loans", including mortgage interest, interest on loans to buy furniture and the incidental costs of obtaining such loan finance. However, the restriction does not apply to interest etc paid in connection with the letting of commercial property such as office accommodation. Nor does it apply to furnished holiday lettings (see later in this chapter).

[†] *The £500 per annum restriction on the loan interest eligible for tax relief in the case of businesses which operate the cash basis (see Chapter 9) does not apply to property businesses.*

Note, however, that the tax reduction for interest (and finance costs) incurred when letting residential property is limited in any tax year to basic rate income tax on the *lower* of:

(a)   the amount of the loan interest and other finance costs for the year concerned

(b)   the taxpayer's property income for the year, less any losses brought forward

(c)   the taxpayer's "adjusted total income" for the year, which is defined for this purpose as net income (excluding savings and dividend income) less the personal allowance and the blind person's allowance (if any).

If the available tax reduction for a year is based upon either (b) or (c) above, then the excess of (a) over the amount on which the tax reduction is based is carried forward to the following tax year and is included in (a) for that year.

Capital expenditure

Under the cash basis, capital expenditure on plant and machinery acquired for use in the repair, maintenance or management of let property is generally deductible as an expense in the year of payment. Under the accruals basis, such expenditure will generally be the subject of a claim for capital allowances (see Chapter 11). But note that:

(a)   Under either basis, if fixed rate deductions (using mileage rates) are made in relation to a vehicle, no other deductions are available for that vehicle.

(b)   Under the cash basis, expenditure on a motor car is not a deductible expense. But capital allowances are available unless fixed rate deductions are claimed.

Replacement domestic items relief

A relief known as "replacement domestic items relief" is available for the cost of replacing certain items provided for domestic use in let residential property, including furniture and furnishings, household appliances and kitchenware. Note that:

(i)   Relief is available only when an "old item" is replaced by a "new item". There is no relief for the original cost of acquiring the very first item in a chain of items.

(ii)   If the new item is substantially the same as the old item which it replaces, the full cost of the new item is deductible. Otherwise, the deduction from property income is restricted to that part of the cost of the new item that does not exceed the expenditure which would have been incurred on an item substantially the same as the old item.

(iii)   The deductible cost of the new item is increased by any disposal costs relating to the old item but reduced by any disposal proceeds of the old item.

(iv)   Replacement domestic items relief is not available if "rent-a-room" relief applies or in the case of furnished holiday lettings (see later in this chapter).

Capital allowances are <u>not</u> available in relation to plant and machinery provided for use by tenants in let residential property.

EXAMPLE 1

Ryan owns a dwelling house which he lets to a tenant. Rent is payable monthly in advance on the first day of each month. The rent was £600 per month until 1 January 2023, when it was increased to £650. All rent due during 2022-23 was paid by the tenant on the due date except that the rent due on 1 April 2023 was not paid until 7 April 2023.

Ryan spent £1,130 on property repairs in 2022-23 and he paid mortgage interest of £3,200. Compute his property income for the year (assuming no election for the accruals basis).

Solution

On the cash basis, rents for the year are (£600 x 8) + (£650 x 3) = £6,750. The mortgage interest (which relates to residential property) is not deductible. Therefore property income is £5,620 (£6,750 – £1,130). The interest of £3,200 is relieved as a tax reducer at 20% (as long as Ryan has adjusted total income for the year of at least £3,200).

EXAMPLE 2

Ursula owns a flat which was let to a tenant throughout tax year 2022-23. Rents received during the year were £10,500. Expenditure during the year was as follows:

	£
Insurance for the year to 30 June 2023	380
Repairs and maintenance	1,150
Replacement of sofa	729

The new sofa is superior to the sofa it replaced (and which was scrapped). It would have cost only £399 to have bought a new sofa which was equivalent in quality to the old one. Compute property income for 2022-23 (assuming no election for the accruals basis).

Solution

	£	£
Rents for the year		10,500
Less: Insurance	380	
Repairs and maintenance	1,150	
Replacement of domestic item	399	1,929
Property income		8,571

Property income allowance

Gross property income of up to £1,000 p.a. (before deduction of expenses) is exempt from income tax. If this figure is exceeded, the taxpayer may elect to be taxed on the excess of gross income over £1,000. Otherwise, property income is calculated by deducting expenses from gross income in the usual way. The details of this "property income allowance" are similar to those of the trading income allowance (see Chapter 9).

Losses

If a taxpayer's gross property income for a tax year is exceeded by the allowable expenditure, then the taxpayer has incurred a loss and taxable property income for the year is £nil. The loss is carried forward and relieved against the first available property income arising in subsequent tax years. Strictly speaking, relief is given by deduction from the taxpayer's total income (see Chapter 2), but the amount of relief given in any tax year cannot exceed the property income for that year.

Any loss incurred on an individual property in a tax year will automatically be set against profits arising on other properties in the same year, since property income and expenditure is generally pooled to give an overall profit or loss for the year.

EXAMPLE 3

Sandra's entire income is derived from the letting of property. Her income and expenditure in tax years 2020-21 through to 2022-23 are as follows:

	2020-21 £	2021-22 £	2022-23 £
Total rental income	49,320	51,400	76,100
Total allowable expenditure	78,510	25,430	17,540

Compute her net income for each year.

Solution

	2020-21 £	2021-22 £	2022-23 £
Total rental income	49,320	51,400	76,100
Total allowable expenditure	78,510	25,430	17,540
Property income/(loss)	(29,190)	25,970	58,560
Total income	0	25,970	58,560
Less: Losses b/f	-	(25,970)	(3,220)
Net income	0	0	55,340

Note:

The 2020-21 loss must be set against the first available property income in subsequent years. This means that Sandra's net income for 2021-22 is reduced to £nil and that her personal allowance for that year is unused. However, it may be possible to transfer 10% of her 2021-22 personal allowance to a spouse or civil partner (see Chapter 3).

Lease premiums

A premium is a lump sum paid by a tenant to a landlord on the grant of a lease. The income tax treatment of lease premiums is as follows:

(a) Premiums arising on the grant of a "long lease" (a lease of more than 50 years) are not charged to income tax at all.

(b) Premiums arising on the grant of a "short lease" (a lease of 50 years or less) are charged to income tax in the tax year in which the lease is granted. However, the amount of the premium is reduced for this purpose by 2% for each year of the lease except for the first year.

Note that these provisions apply only to the *grant* of a new lease, not to the *assignment* of an existing lease. Note also that lease premiums arising on the grant of a lease may give rise to a capital gains tax liability (see Chapter 19).

EXAMPLE 4

In tax year 2022-23, a landlord receives a premium of £36,000 when granting a 25-year lease to a tenant. How much of this premium is chargeable to income tax?

Solution

£36,000 − (24 × 2% × £36,000) = £18,720.

Relief for premiums paid

A tenant who pays a premium on being granted a short lease may obtain tax relief on the premium paid in one of two ways:

(a) If the tenant uses the property for business purposes, he or she may claim an annual deduction from trading profits. This is equal to the amount of the premium on which the landlord is charged to income tax, divided by the lease duration (see Chapter 9).

(b) If the tenant sub-lets the property and receives a premium from the sub-lessee, then the assessable amount of the premium received is reduced by:

$$\text{Landlord's income tax assessment on premium paid} \times \frac{\text{Duration of sub-lease}}{\text{Duration of head-lease}}$$

If this reduction cannot be made in full (either because the premium received is too small or because no premium was received at all) the excess is spread evenly over the period of the sub-lease and set against the rents[†] receivable from the sub-lessee.

[†] *This deduction from rental income is not available under the cash basis. However, the deduction could be obtained by opting for the accruals basis.*

EXAMPLE 5

Susan is granted a 20-year lease on a property, paying a premium of £76,000. Explain how tax relief will be given in relation to this premium if:

(a)   she uses the property for trading purposes, or

(b)   she grants a sub-lease to Timothy for five years, receiving a premium of *either*:

      (i)   £25,000

or (ii)   £10,000.

Solution

(a)   The amount assessable to income tax on Susan's landlord is £47,120 (£76,000 less 38% of £76,000). If Susan uses the premises for trading purposes she will be able to claim an annual deduction of £2,356 from her trading profits for each of the next 20 years (£47,120 divided by 20 = £2,356).

(b)

	(i) £	(ii) £
Premium received	25,000	10,000
Less: 2% x 4 x £25,000	2,000	
2% x 4 x £10,000		800
	23,000	9,200
Less: Premium paid £47,120 x $\dfrac{5}{20}$ = £11,780	11,780	9,200
Assessable premium	11,220	nil

In case (ii), the reduction available in relation to the premium paid cannot be made in full. The amount unrelieved is £2,580 (£11,780 – £9,200). There will be no income tax assessment on the premium received in this case. And if Susan applies the accruals basis, a deduction of £516 will be made from her property income for each of the five years of the sub-lease (£2,580 divided by 5 = £516).

Reverse premiums

A "reverse premium" is a premium paid by a landlord to a potential tenant so as to induce that tenant to take out a lease. From the point of view of the tenant[†], a reverse premium is chargeable to income tax unless the rented premises are used by the tenant as his or her only or main residence. If the rented premises are used for business purposes, the amount received is treated as trading income (see Chapter 9). Otherwise the amount received is treated as property income.

[†] *As regards the landlord, the payment of a reverse premium is usually treated as enhancement expenditure for capital gains tax purposes (see Chapter 18).*

"Rent-a-room" relief

If a taxpayer lets furnished accommodation which forms part of his or her main residence, gross annual rents not exceeding a specified limit (£7,500 for 2022-23) are exempt from income tax. However, the taxpayer may elect to ignore this exemption and apply the usual property income rules[†] instead. This might be beneficial if the rents were exceeded by expenses, so that a loss could be claimed.

If gross rents for a tax year exceed the limit, rents less expenses are assessed to income tax in the normal way. However, the taxpayer may elect to be assessed instead on the excess of gross rents over the limit, without deducting expenses of any kind.

Both of the elections referred to above must be made by 31 January in the second tax year following the tax year to which the election relates. The first election applies only to the year for which it is made. The second election applies to all subsequent tax years until a year arises in which gross rents do not exceed the limit (or the election is withdrawn).

[†] *Note that the £1,000 property allowance (see earlier in this chapter) does not apply if a property letting is eligible for rent-a-room relief.*

EXAMPLE 6

In 2022-23, Victor rents out a room in his home and receives rents of £8,150. He incurs allowable expenses of £820. What "rent-a-room" elections (if any) should he make?

Solution

The rent-a-room exemption does not apply since gross rents exceed £7,500. If Victor does nothing, he will be charged to income tax on property income of £7,330 (£8,150 − £820).

If he elects to be assessed on the excess of gross rents over the rent-a-room relief limit, his property income for tax purposes will be only £650 (£8,150 − £7,500). He should make this election and he has until 31 January 2025 to do so.

Furnished holiday lettings (FHL)

Income from "*the commercial letting of furnished holiday accommodation*" is treated for certain tax purposes as if it were trading income, with the following beneficial effects:

(a) The income is regarded as earned income when determining the extent to which tax relief is available in relation to pension contributions (see Chapter 14).

(b) Capital allowances may be claimed in relation to plant and machinery (including furniture) provided for use by tenants (see Chapter 11).

(c) Business-related capital gains tax reliefs may be available (see Chapter 22).

Furthermore, the rules which restrict tax relief for loan interest incurred in connection with residential lettings (see earlier in this chapter) do not apply to furnished holiday lettings.

FHL conditions

Letting qualifies as the commercial letting of furnished holiday accommodation if *all* of the following conditions are satisfied:

(a) The property concerned is situated in the UK or in the European Economic Area (EEA) (see Chapter 3) and is let furnished with a view to profit.

(b) The property is available for letting to the general public as holiday accommodation for at least 210 days in the tax year and is actually let for at least 105 days, ignoring any periods of "longer-term occupation" (i.e. periods of more than 31 consecutive days during which the accommodation is in the same occupation).

(c) The property is not in longer-term occupation for more than 155 days in the tax year.

A taxpayer who has furnished holiday lettings both in the UK and in the EEA is treated as having two separate FHL businesses. All of the qualifying property in the UK forms one FHL business. All of the qualifying property in the EEA forms a separate FHL business. A loss incurred in either of these FHL businesses may be set only against income arising from the same FHL business.

If a property qualifies as furnished holiday accommodation in one tax year, the taxpayer who owns the property may elect to treat the property as continuing to qualify for up to two further tax years (the "period of grace") even though it does not satisfy the 105-day condition in those years. An averaging election (see below) cannot be made in respect of a property which qualifies for FHL purposes only because of this period of grace rule.

Averaging

A taxpayer who owns two or more properties, each of which qualifies for FHL purposes except that at least one property does not satisfy the 105-day condition, may claim that any or all of these properties should be treated as furnished holiday accommodation as long as their average number of days let is at least 105 days.

An averaging claim must be made by 31 January in the second tax year following the tax year to which the election relates.

EXAMPLE 7

Yvonne owns four cottages, all let furnished with a view to profit. None of the cottages is ever let to the same tenant for more than 31 consecutive days. In 2022-23 the number of days each cottage was available for letting and the number of days actually let were:

	Days available	Days actually let
Cottage A	220	115
Cottage B	240	85
Cottage C	190	148
Cottage D	250	103

Show Yvonne's potential averaging claims.

Solution

Cottage C cannot be treated as furnished holiday accommodation since it does not pass the 210-day test. Cottages A, B and D all pass this test but only Cottage A also passes the 105-day test. Without any averaging claims, therefore, only Cottage A will be regarded as furnished holiday accommodation. Possible averaging claims are:

(a) Average Cottage A with Cottage B. This is no use since the average number of days let is only 100.

(b) Average Cottage A with Cottage D. This would be beneficial since the average number of days let is 109.

(c) Average Cottage A with Cottage B and Cottage D. This is no use since the average number of days let is only 101.

Therefore, Yvonne should claim that Cottage A should be averaged with Cottage D, in which case both cottages would qualify as furnished holiday accommodation.

Summary

▸ Income tax is charged on the profits of a business which is carried on for the purpose of generating income from land situated in the UK.

▸ For income tax purposes, property income is generally calculated on the cash basis. However, the cash basis does not apply to property businesses with receipts for the tax year which exceed £150,000. Expenditure that is incurred wholly and exclusively for the purposes of a property business is deducted when computing property income.

▸ Loan interest incurred in connection with residential property lettings is not deductible when computing property income. Such interest is relieved at basic rate instead.

▸ Under the cash basis, the cost of plant and machinery used in the repair, maintenance or management of let property is a deductible expense. Capital allowances may be claimed if the accruals basis applies. Tax relief is also available in relation to the cost of replacing domestic items provided for use by tenants.

▸ Losses incurred by a property business are carried forward and set against the first available property income arising in subsequent years.

▸ A premium received on the grant of a lease is charged to income tax if the lease does not exceed 50 years. The assessable amount is the amount of the premium less 2% for each year of the lease except the first.

▸ Rent-a-room relief is available if a taxpayer receives rents of up to £7,500 per annum from the letting of furnished rooms in his or her main residence.

▸ Under certain conditions, letting of furnished property qualifies as the commercial letting of furnished holiday accommodation. This offers a number of tax benefits.

Exercises

Unless stated otherwise, it may be assumed in each of the following exercises that the taxpayer concerned has <u>not</u> made an election for the accruals basis to apply. A set of multiple choice questions for this chapter is available on the accompanying website.

5.1   Andrew owns a dwelling which he lets to tenants. Rent is payable quarterly in advance on 1 January, 1 April, 1 July and 1 October. The rent was £8,000 per annum until it was increased to £8,800 per annum with effect from 1 January 2023. Rents received by Andrew during 2022-23 were as follows:

	£
2 July 2022	2,000
30 September 2022	2,000
3 January 2023	2,200
	6,200

Andrew did not receive the rent due on 1 April 2023 until 6 April 2023. Compute his property income for 2022-23, assuming that the only expenditure incurred during the year comprised repairs and insurances of £1,300 and buy-to-let mortgage interest of £4,100.

5.2   Simon owns an apartment which he lets to tenants. The apartment was let throughout tax year 2022-23 and rents received during the year were £16,640. The expenses incurred by Simon in relation to this apartment during 2022-23 were as follows:

	£
Advertising for new tenant	135
Repairs and maintenance	590
Insurance costs	730
Replacement of refrigerator	325
Interest on buy-to-let mortgage	3,120
Capital repayments on buy-to-let mortgage	2,160

The new refrigerator is very similar in all respects to the old one which was provided at a cost of £270 several years previously and has now been scrapped. Costs of £10 were incurred in order to transport the old refrigerator to the local recycling centre.

Compute Simon's property income for 2022-23. Also explain how the computation would differ if Simon had decided to buy a superior refrigerator (costing £575) instead of the one which cost him £325.

5.3   In 2022-23, a landlord receives a premium of £12,000 when granting a lease to a tenant. Compute the amount of this premium which is chargeable to income tax if the length of the lease is:

(a)   60 years

(b)   50 years

(c)   20 years.

5.4   In 2022-23, Rashid is granted a 10-year lease on a property, paying a premium of £15,000. He uses the property for trading purposes. Compute the tax relief which he will be allowed in respect of the lease premium.

5.5   Georgina owns three holiday flats, all of which she lets furnished with a view to profit. None of the flats is ever let to the same tenant for more than 31 consecutive days. The number of days for which each flat was available for letting during tax year 2022-23, and the number of days actually let, were:

	Days available	Days actually let
Flat 1	210	99
Flat 2	220	107
Flat 3	252	109

Show Georgina's potential averaging claims.

*5.6   In 2022-23, Peter is granted a 12-year lease on a property, paying a premium of £40,000 to his landlord. He immediately grants a 4-year sub-lease to Paula, receiving a premium from her of £14,000. Calculate the income tax assessment on this premium.

*5.7   Melissa (who is not a Scottish taxpayer) owns a house which she lets to tenants. The house was let throughout 2022-23 and the total rents received during the year were £7,300. Her deductible expenditure for the year was £900. She had property losses brought forward from 2021-22 of £6,550. Her other income in 2022-23 was as follows:

	£
Retirement pension	17,050
Building society interest	1,730

Compute Melissa's income tax liability for the year, assuming that she makes any beneficial elections. How would this differ for a Scottish taxpayer?

Chapter 6

Income from savings and investments

Introduction

The main purpose of this chapter is to explain the tax treatment of income arising from savings and investments. The main options available to a taxpayer who wishes to save or invest are to deposit money in bank and building society accounts or to invest in shares and securities. Each of these courses of action has its taxation implications and this chapter explains those implications.

This chapter also briefly considers the taxation of income from trusts and settlements and the tax treatment of certain miscellaneous sources of income.

Interest received

Interest received by a taxpayer is charged to income tax by the Income Tax (Trading and Other Income) Act 2005. This Act states that tax is charged on the full amount of interest arising in the tax year and that interest "arises" when it is paid to the taxpayer or when it is credited to the taxpayer's account. Accrued interest is ignored when computing the amount of interest arising in a tax year. Note that:

(a) Interest ranks as savings income and so any interest which falls into the first £5,000 of taxable income (in 2022-23) is taxed at the starting rate for savings of 0%. Most taxpayers are also entitled to a personal savings allowance (PSA) of £1,000. This is reduced to £500 if taxable income exceeds the non-Scottish basic rate limit and to £nil if taxable income exceeds the higher rate limit. Interest which falls within the PSA in 2022-23 is taxed at the savings nil rate of 0% (see Chapter 2).

(b) In general, no expenses are allowed against this form of income. However, taxpayers who make loans through "peer-to-peer" platforms may offset any bad debts incurred on such loans against the interest received.

Interest from banks and building societies (and from NS&I) is received gross, with no tax deducted at source. Interest received from unit trusts and investment trusts and interest on peer-to-peer loans is also received gross. But certain other types of interest are received net of basic rate tax (see Chapter 2). When preparing an income tax computation, the gross equivalent of any interest received net of tax should be included in total income. The tax suffered by deduction at source is then subtracted from the income tax liability when calculating the amount of tax payable for the year.

Self-certification

Basic rate income tax is still deducted at source from the income element of purchased life annuities (see Chapter 2). However, a UK-resident individual who is unlikely to be liable to income tax for a tax year may supply a certificate to this effect (form R89) to the payer of the annuity. Such individuals then receive their interest gross. This avoids the need to claim a repayment of overpaid tax from HMRC at the end of the tax year.

EXAMPLE 1

In 2022-23, Alfred (not a Scottish taxpayer) had business profits of £16,940 and received net debenture interest of £1,520. He acquired the debentures on 1 July 2022 and accrued interest (gross) on 5 April 2023 was £950. Calculate the income tax payable for the year.

Solution

	Total £	Non-savings £	Savings £
Business profits	16,940	16,940	
Debenture interest £1,520 x 100/80	1,900		1,900
Total income	18,840	16,940	1,900
Less: Personal allowance	12,570	12,570	
Taxable income	6,270	4,370	1,900

Income tax due

Non-savings income	: Basic rate	4,370	@ 20%	874.00
Savings income	: Starting rate	630	@ 0%	0.00
	: Nil rate	1,000	@ 0%	0.00
	: Basic rate	270	@ 20%	54.00
		6,270		

Tax liability		928.00
Less: Tax deducted at source (£1,900 – £1,520)		380.00
Tax payable		548.00

Note:

Taxable income does not exceed the basic rate limit, so the PSA is £1,000. Accrued debenture interest is ignored. *For a Scottish taxpayer*, the first £2,162 of taxable non-savings income would be taxed at the 19% starter rate, reducing the liability by £21.62.

Accrued income scheme

The accrued income scheme exists in order to prevent a form of tax avoidance known as "bondwashing". Bondwashing involves selling securities "cum interest" (so that the buyer of the securities will receive the next interest payment) just before an interest payment is due. The price paid by the buyer reflects the fact that the sale is made cum interest and so the seller of the securities is not disadvantaged. However, the effect of the transaction from the tax point of view is that the seller has converted what would have been income into a capital gain. Since gains arising on the disposal of certain securities are exempt from capital gains tax (see Chapter 20) the seller appears to have avoided tax.

The accrued income scheme overcomes this potential loss of tax by charging the seller income tax on the interest which has accrued up to the date of the sale. The buyer of the securities is entitled to tax relief on the same amount and this is given by deduction from the next interest payment the buyer receives. Similar arrangements apply if securities are transferred "ex interest" (so that the seller will receive the next interest payment). In this case, the buyer is taxed on the interest accruing from the date of the sale to the date of the next interest payment and the seller is entitled to tax relief on the same amount.

The accrued income scheme applies to securities such as gilts, local authority bonds and company debentures. It does not apply to ordinary or preference shares. Transfers made by individuals who have not held securities with a total nominal value exceeding £5,000 in the current tax year or in the preceding tax year are excluded from the scheme.

Dividends received

Dividends received are charged to tax by the Income Tax (Trading and Other Income) Act 2005. Income tax is charged on the amount of dividends received in the tax year, with no adjustment for any accrued dividends. No expenses are allowed against dividend income.

For 2022-23, the first £2,000 of dividends included in taxable income are taxed at the dividend nil rate. Any further dividends are taxed at the dividend ordinary rate (8.75%), the dividend upper rate (33.75%) or the dividend additional rate (39.35%). Note that:

(a) The "dividend allowance" of £2,000 also applies to dividends received from overseas companies (see Chapter 32).

(b) Any capital gain which arises on a disposal of shares is generally subject to capital gains tax (see Chapter 20).

Tax-efficient investments

A taxpayer who is seeking a tax-efficient means of investing in an interest-bearing account or in shares and securities may invest in any of the following:

(a) an Individual Savings Account (ISA)

(b) the Enterprise Investment Scheme (EIS)

(c) a Venture Capital Trust (VCT)

(d) a Child Trust Fund (CTF).

Each of these forms of investment is considered below. Further tax-efficient investment opportunities are offered by the Community Investment Tax Credits (CITC) scheme and by investments which qualify for Social Investment Tax Relief (SITR). The main features of each of these schemes are explained on the website which accompanies this book. The website can be accessed at go.pearson.com/uk/he/resources.

Individual Savings Accounts

Individual Savings Accounts (ISAs) may be held by individuals who are at least 16 years old and resident in the UK. The residence requirement is waived in the case of Crown servants serving overseas and their spouses (or civil partners). The main features of these tax-free accounts are as follows:

(a) ISAs are of two main types[†]. These are "cash ISAs" and "stocks and shares ISAs". Money which is invested in a cash ISA is held in a savings account. Money invested in a stocks and shares ISA is used by the ISA provider to acquire stocks and shares on the saver's behalf. These stocks and shares may be listed on a stock exchange anywhere in the world. However, it is now permissible for a stocks and shares ISA to hold some cash on deposit. Savers under the age of 18 may invest in a cash ISA only.

> [†] *There is also a third type of ISA (the "innovative finance ISA"). Money invested in such an ISA is used to make peer-to-peer loans.*

(b) Each tax year, a saver may invest in only one ISA of each type. Savers may start fresh ISAs each year or may invest in ISAs started in previous years.

(c) The maximum amount ("subscription limit") which a saver may invest in ISAs during tax year 2022-23 is £20,000. This may be allocated in any way between the different types of ISA. There is no lifetime limit on the amount that may be saved in ISAs, nor is there a minimum level of saving.

(d) Some or all of the money saved in cash ISAs in previous tax years may be transferred to stocks and shares ISAs (or vice versa). Savers may also transfer *all* of the money saved in a cash ISA in the current year to a stocks and shares ISA (or vice versa). Such transfers do not count towards the £20,000 annual subscription limit.

(e) Interest and dividends arising from ISAs are exempt from income tax. Capital gains (and losses) arising from ISAs are exempt from capital gains tax.

(f) Withdrawals may be made from an ISA without loss of tax relief. ISA providers are now able to offer savers the flexibility of withdrawing cash from an ISA and then replacing it later in the same tax year, without this replacement counting towards the subscription limit for the year concerned.

(g)   The surviving spouse or civil partner of an ISA saver who dies is granted an extra ISA allowance equal to the value of the deceased person's ISA savings on death. This allowance must be used within a specified time period.

(h)   "Help to Buy" ISAs provide a tax-free bonus of up to £3,000 to savers who use the amount saved to buy their first home[†]. "Lifetime" ISAs are available to savers under the age of 40. Up to £4,000 p.a. can be saved in such an ISA until the age of 50 and a bonus of 25% is added to the amount saved. However, withdrawals before the age of 60 incur a withdrawal charge of 25% unless the funds are used to buy a first home.

[†] *Help to Buy ISAs were closed to new applicants on 30 November 2019. However, existing accounts may remain open until Autumn 2029 and are still eligible for the bonus if used to buy a first home.*

EXAMPLE 2

For each of the following savers, identify the further ISA investments that may be made during tax year 2022-23:

(a)   Umar saves £500 in a cash ISA on 26 April 2022.

(b)   Bianca saves £6,000 in a stocks and shares ISA on 21 May 2022.

(c)   Jon saves £1,000 in a cash ISA on 17 June 2022 and £8,000 in a stocks and shares ISA on 4 August 2022.

Solution

(a)   £19,500 (£20,000 – £500) may be saved, in either the same cash ISA or a stocks and shares ISA or an innovative finance ISA (or in a combination of these).

(b)   £14,000 (£20,000 – £6,000) may be saved, in either the same stocks and shares ISA or a cash ISA or an innovative finance ISA (or in a combination of these).

(c)   £11,000 (£20,000 – £9,000) may be saved, in either the same cash ISA or the same stocks and shares ISA or an innovative finance ISA (or in a combination of these).

Junior ISAs

Junior ISAs (JISAs) are available to children under 18 who are UK resident and do not have a Child Trust Fund account (see below). JISAs are tax-free and investments may be made in cash or in stocks and shares. Funds invested in a JISA are owned by the child but are locked in until he or she reaches the age of 18.

The maximum amount that can be invested in a JISA in 2022-23 is £9,000. Note that:

(a)   The fact that a child has a JISA does not prevent that child from also having an adult ISA as from the age of 16, in which case the existence of the JISA has no impact upon the adult ISA subscription limits.

(b)   Any income derived from parental contributions to a JISA does not count towards the £100 limit relating to income derived from a parent (see Chapter 2).

Enterprise Investment Scheme

The Enterprise Investment Scheme (EIS) is a tax-advantaged scheme which encourages taxpayers to invest in unlisted trading companies. The main features of the EIS are as follows:

(a) Income tax relief is available to taxpayers who subscribe for newly-issued ordinary shares in certain qualifying companies. Broadly, these are unlisted trading companies with less than 250 employees (500 for "knowledge-intensive" companies) which have a permanent establishment in the UK and gross assets not exceeding £15m immediately before the issue and £16m immediately after it. The company must normally have been trading for no more than seven years (ten for knowledge-intensive companies) and the total raised under the EIS and other venture capital schemes must not exceed £5m per annum (£10m for knowledge-intensive companies).

(b) The total amount of the tax-advantaged investments which a company may receive under the EIS and under other venture capital schemes such as the SEIS and the VCTs scheme (see below) is capped at £12m (£20m for knowledge intensive companies).

(c) Income tax relief takes the form of a reduction in the amount of tax due on the taxpayer's taxable income. This tax reduction is equal to 30% of the amount invested in qualifying companies during the tax year and takes priority over the tax reductions relating to certain payments (see Chapter 4) and the MCA (see Chapter 3).

(d) A taxpayer's EIS investments of up to £2m in each tax year are eligible for tax relief, as long as any amount over £1m is invested in knowledge-intensive companies. Any of the EIS investments made in a tax year may be carried back and treated as if made in the previous year, but the total EIS investment that can attract income tax relief in any one tax year is subject to the £2m limit.

(e) The taxpayer must not be connected with the company at any time during the two years prior to the date of the investment and the three years following that date. Broadly speaking, an individual is connected with a company for this purpose if he or she is an employee of the company or, together with associates, owns more than 30% of the company's ordinary shares.

(f) Dividends received on the shares are subject to income tax in the usual way.

(g) Any capital gain arising on the eventual disposal of EIS shares is exempt from CGT but any loss on the disposal is eligible for relief. When calculating the loss, the shares are deemed to have been acquired for their issue price, less the tax reduction obtained when the shares were purchased. A loss may be relieved as a capital loss, in the usual way (see Chapter 17) or against the taxpayer's total income (see Chapter 12).

Furthermore, the capital gain arising on the disposal of *any* asset may be deferred if an amount of money equal to the gain is invested in EIS shares (see Chapter 22).

The taxpayer must retain the shares for a minimum holding period of at least three years or both the income tax and capital gains tax reliefs are lost.

Seed Enterprise Investment Scheme

The Seed Enterprise Investment Scheme (SEIS) is a tax-advantaged scheme which encourages taxpayers to invest in start-up companies. The main features of the scheme are:

(a) Subject to certain conditions, tax relief is available to investors who subscribe for ordinary shares in a company which is carrying on a new business. A new business is one which started no more than two years before the share issue.

(b) The company concerned must be an unlisted trading company with a permanent establishment in the UK. The company must have fewer than 25 employees and its total assets must not exceed £200,000 before the SEIS investment is made. Also, the amount of all SEIS investment received by the company in the three years to the date of the latest investment must not exceed £150,000.

(c) During the period from the company's incorporation until the third anniversary of the share issue, the investor must not own 30% or more of the company's share capital. Also, the investor cannot be an employee of the company (other than a director).

(d) Tax relief takes the form of an income tax reduction equal to 50% of the amount invested up to a limit of £100,000 per annum. Relief is withdrawn if the shares are disposed of within three years. As with the main EIS, any SEIS investments made during a tax year may be carried back and treated as if made in the previous year.

(e) Any capital gain arising on the eventual disposal of the shares is exempt from CGT but any loss on the disposal is eligible for relief. Furthermore, the gain arising on the disposal of *any* asset may be reduced for tax purposes by 50% of the amount invested through the seed EIS during the year in which the disposal occurs (see Chapter 22).

The scheme was scheduled to end on 5 April 2017 but has now been extended indefinitely.

Venture Capital Trusts

Venture Capital Trusts (VCTs) offer taxpayers a further tax-advantaged encouragement to invest in unlisted trading companies. A VCT is a company which is approved as such by HMRC. The main conditions which must be satisfied to gain approval are as follows:

(a) The company's ordinary shares must be traded on a UK or EU regulated market.

(b) Its income must be derived wholly or mainly from shares or securities and no more than 15% of this income may be retained by the company.

(c) At least 80% of its total investments must be "qualifying holdings" and at least 70% of these holdings must be "eligible" shares. Broadly, shares or securities owned by a VCT rank as qualifying holdings if they were newly issued to the VCT and are shares or securities of a company which would be a qualifying company for the purposes of the EIS (see above). Eligible shares exclude redeemable shares.

(d) No holding in any one company (other than in another VCT) can represent more than 15% of a VCT's investments. At least 10% of a VCT's investment in a company must be held in the form of eligible shares.

(e) At least 30% of the funds that are raised by a VCT during an accounting period must be invested in qualifying holdings within 12 months of the end of that period.

Income tax relief is available to taxpayers who subscribe for newly-issued ordinary shares of a VCT. This relief takes the form of a tax reduction equal to 30% of the amount invested, subject to an investment limit of £200,000 per tax year. This reduction takes priority over the tax reductions relating to certain payments made by the taxpayer (see Chapter 4) and the tax reduction relating to the MCA (see Chapter 3). To qualify for income tax relief, the taxpayer must hold the shares for a minimum holding period of at least five years.

Dividends on the first £200,000 of VCT shares acquired in each tax year are exempt from income tax and any capital gain or loss arising on the disposal of these shares is exempt from capital gains tax, regardless of whether or not the shares have been held for the minimum holding period.

Child Trust Funds

Child Trust Fund accounts were introduced in 2005 as a tax-efficient means of building up a fund of assets for a young person to use (or re-invest) at the age of 18. This scheme involved the establishment of a CTF account for each child born on or after 1 September 2002[†]. The Government would contribute funds into each CTF account and additional contributions could be made by the child and by his/her family and friends.

However, the Child Trust Funds scheme has now been wound down. Children born after 2 January 2011 do not qualify for CTF accounts and all Government contributions to existing accounts have ceased. But existing CTF accounts remain open and these accounts continue to offer the following tax advantages:

(a) Additional contributions may still be made into a CTF account. These contributions do not attract tax relief in themselves. But any income and gains arising from CTF investments are tax-free and no tax liability arises when a CTF account reaches maturity on the child's 18th birthday.

The maximum amount (the "subscription limit") that may be invested in a CTF in tax year 2022-23 is £9,000.

(b) Any income derived from parental contributions to a CTF account does not count towards the £100 limit relating to income derived from a parent (see Chapter 2).

Note, however, that no funds may be withdrawn from a CTF account until maturity.

† *CTF accounts began to mature as from 1 September 2020 (i.e. on the 18th birthday of children born on 1 September 2002). Maturing CTFs are transferred to an ISA or other tax-free account unless instructions to the contrary are received from the account holder.*

Income from trusts and settlements

A trust or settlement is an arrangement whereby property is held by persons known as *trustees*, for the benefit of other persons known as *beneficiaries*. Trusts fall into two main categories, as follows:

(a) If one or more persons are entitled to receive all of the income which is generated by the trust property, then those persons are "life tenants" and the trust is a "trust with an interest in possession".

(b) If there are no life tenants and the trustees have the discretion to distribute as much or as little of the trust income to the beneficiaries as they see fit, the trust is referred to as a "discretionary trust".

Trust taxation is a very complex matter and a full study of the subject is beyond the scope of this book. However, an introduction to trust taxation is given below.

Trusts with an interest in possession

For tax year 2022-23, the trustees of a trust with an interest in possession are chargeable to income tax at the dividend ordinary rate (8.75%) on the trust's dividend income and at the basic rate (20%) on all of its other income. Note that:

(a) The tax liability of the trustees is never calculated at the starting rate for savings, the higher rate, the additional rate or the dividend upper and additional rates. Trustees are not entitled to either the personal savings allowance or the dividend allowance, so the savings nil rate and dividend nil rate (see Chapter 2) are both unavailable[†].

(b) The general expenses of administering the trust are *not* allowed when computing the income tax liability of the trustees. However, expenses which relate to specific items of trust income (e.g. expenses normally deductible from property income) are set against that income.

(c) The trustees' tax liability is calculated without deduction of personal allowances.

(d) Relief is given for income tax deducted at source (if any).

[†] *Scottish income tax rates do not apply to trusts.*

The income which remains after income tax and all expenses have been deducted (including general administration expenses) is paid to the life tenants and is then dealt with in their personal tax computations. In those computations:

(a) trust non-savings income and trust savings income are treated as income received net of basic rate tax

(b) trust dividend income is treated as dividend income received net of tax calculated at the dividend ordinary rate.

The general administration expenses of the trust are deemed to have been paid first out of dividend income, then out of savings income and then out of non-savings income.

EXAMPLE 3

An interest in possession trust with one life tenant has the following income in 2022-23:

	£
Rents receivable	30,200
Loan interest received (net)	7,200
Dividends received	1,600

Expenses were incurred in the year as follows:

	£
Property expenses	6,900
Administration expenses	2,100

(a) Compute the trustees' income tax liability for 2022-23.

(b) How much income does the life tenant receive from the trust in 2022-23 and how will this be treated in his or her personal tax computation?

Solution

	Total £	Non-Savings £	Savings £	Dividends £
Property income £30,200 – £6,900	23,300	23,300		
Interest received £7,200 x 100/80	9,000		9,000	
Dividends received	1,600			1,600
	33,900	23,300	9,000	1,600
Income tax @ 20%	(4,660)	(4,660)		
Income tax @ 20%	(1,800)		(1,800)	
Income tax @ 8.75%	(140)			(140)
Income after tax	27,300	18,640	7,200	1,460
Administration expenses	(2,100)		(640)	(1,460)
Income after tax and expenses	25,200	18,640	6,560	0

(a) The trustees' tax liability for the year is £6,600 (£4,660 + £1,800 + £140). The £1,800 of tax deducted at source (£9,000 – £7,200) is deducted, leaving tax payable by the trustees of £4,800.

(b) The income of the life tenant is:

	Gross £	Tax deducted £
Non-savings £18,640 x 100/80	23,300	4,660
Savings £6,560 x 100/80	8,200	1,640
Total	31,500	6,300

The gross income will be included in the life tenant's computation for 2022-23. The tax deducted at source will be subtracted when computing tax payable for the year.

Discretionary trusts

The income tax liability of the trustees of a discretionary trust is normally calculated at the "dividend trust rate" on dividend income and at the "trust rate" on all other income. For tax year 2022-23, these rates are 39.35% and 45% respectively. But these rates do not apply to income which has been used to fund the expenses of administering the trust. Such income is taxed at either the dividend ordinary rate (8.75%) or the basic rate (20%), depending upon the type of income involved.

Furthermore, the first £1,000 of the income of a discretionary trust is not charged to tax at the special trust rates but is taxed instead at the income tax rate which applies generally to the class of income concerned (i.e. the dividend ordinary rate or the basic rate). When identifying the first £1,000 of a trust's income, non-savings income is considered first, then savings income, then dividends.

Any payments which are made to beneficiaries are deemed to have been made net of tax at the trust rate (45%) and must therefore be grossed-up at 100/55 in their personal income tax computations. The amount of tax which is deemed to have been deducted from such payments is assessable on the trustees, but only to the extent (if any) that it exceeds the trustees' "tax pool". Broadly, this comprises the sum of:

(a) the pool balance brought forward (if any) from the previous tax year

(b) any tax suffered by the trustees for the current tax year at the trust rate (45%) or the dividend trust rate (39.35%), plus any tax suffered on the first £1,000 of trust income, calculated at the basic rate (20%) or the dividend ordinary rate (8.75%).

If the total in the tax pool exceeds the amount of tax treated as deducted from payments made to beneficiaries during the year, the balance is carried forward to the next tax year and forms the opening balance of the tax pool for that year (see (a) above).

Trusts with vulnerable beneficiary

A special tax regime applies to certain trusts with a "vulnerable beneficiary" (generally a disabled person or an orphan). This tax regime (if opted for) ensures that the tax liability of the trust is reduced to the amount of tax that would have been payable if the trust income and gains had accrued directly to the beneficiary concerned.

EXAMPLE 4

Assume that a discretionary trust has the same income and expenses in 2022-23 as the trust described in the above example. Assume also that a payment of £5,500 was made to a beneficiary during the year.

(a) Compute the trustees' income tax liability for 2022-23.

(b) Show how the £5,500 received by the beneficiary will be treated in his or her personal tax computation.

Solution

	Total	Non-Savings	Savings	Dividends
	£	£	£	£
Property income £30,200 – £6,900	23,300	23,300		
Interest received £7,200 x 100/80	9,000		9,000	
Dividends received	1,600			1,600
	33,900	23,300	9,000	1,600
First £1,000 of trust income:				
Income tax at 20% on £1,000	(200)	(200)		
Remainder of trust income:				
Income tax @ 8.75% on £1,600	(140)			(140)
Income tax @ 20% on £800	(160)		(160)	
Income tax @ 45% on £8,200	(3,690)		(3,690)	
Income tax @ 45% on £22,300	(10,035)	(10,035)		
Income after tax	19,675	13,065	5,150	1,460
Administration expenses	(2,100)		(640)	(1,460)
Income after tax and expenses	17,575	13,065	4,510	0

Note:

The administration expenses of £2,100 are deemed to have been paid out of the trust's after-tax income, first out of dividends (£1,460) and then out of savings income (£640). As £640 of net savings income has been used for this purpose, gross savings income of £800 is taxed at only 20% and not at the special rate of 45%.

(a) The trustees' tax liability is £14,225 (£200 + £140 + £160 + £3,690 + £10,035). The tax deducted at source of £1,800 is subtracted, leaving tax payable by the trustees of £12,425. This consists of £10,235 payable on the non-savings income, an extra 25% (45% – 20%) on the £8,200 of savings income which is taxed at the trust rate (25% × £8,200 = £2,050) and £140 on the dividend income.

(b) Gross trust income of £10,000 (£5,500 × 100/55) is included in the beneficiary's tax computation for 2022-23 and the £4,500 of tax deducted at source is subtracted when computing tax payable. The trustees' tax pool is £13,925 (£10,235 + £3,690) plus any balance brought forward from 2021-22. This exceeds £4,500, so there is no further assessment on the trustees in relation to this payment.

Miscellaneous income

ITTOIA 2005 charges income tax on certain types of miscellaneous income to the extent that this income is not already taxed under another heading. Relevant categories include income from intellectual property, income from films or sound recordings, income from telecommunications rights and any other income which is not otherwise charged to tax.

A loss arising under one of these categories during a tax year is relieved against the first available miscellaneous income of the same type in that year or in future years.

Summary

‣ Income tax is payable on the interest actually received by a taxpayer during the tax year. Most interest is now received gross but any interest received net is grossed up in the tax computation. Tax deducted at source is then subtracted from the income tax liability. Income tax is also payable on dividends received.

‣ Individual Savings Accounts (ISAs) provide a tax-free means of either saving cash, investing in stocks and shares or making peer-to-peer loans. Junior ISAs are available to children and Lifetime ISAs are available to savers under the age of 40.

‣ The Enterprise Investment Scheme (EIS) provides tax reliefs to those who subscribe for the newly-issued ordinary shares of qualifying unlisted UK trading companies. The Seed Enterprise Investment Scheme (SEIS) provides tax reliefs to investors who subscribe for newly-issued ordinary shares in start-up companies.

‣ Subject to certain conditions, tax relief is available in relation to an investment in a Venture Capital Trust (VCT).

‣ Child Trust Fund (CTF) accounts provide a tax-free means of building up a fund of assets for a young person born between 1 September 2002 and 2 January 2011.

‣ Trustees must account for income tax on the income of a trust. The general administration expenses of the trust are not allowed when computing the trustees' income tax liability. Special rates of tax apply to the income of a discretionary trust.

‣ Certain forms of miscellaneous income are charged to income tax.

Exercises

A set of multiple choice questions for this chapter is available on the accompanying website.

6.1 Edward has the following income in 2022-23:

	£
Bank interest	520
Loan stock interest (net)	17,720
Dividends received	53,600

He makes a total of £800 of Gift Aid donations during 2022-23. Compute the amount of income tax payable for the year.

6.2   Anne's income for 2022-23 is as follows:

	£
Bank interest:	
Interest on deposit account	480
Interest credited to cash ISA	83
Dividends received	650
Retirement pension	11,956

Compute her income tax liability for the year.

6.3   Outline the income tax advantages of investing in:

(a)   the Enterprise Investment Scheme

(b)   the Seed Enterprise Investment Scheme

(c)   a Venture Capital Trust.

6.4   Outline the main features of Individual Savings Accounts.

6.5   Bernice (who is not a Scottish taxpayer) has the following income in 2022-23:

	£
Business profits	102,850
Building society interest	410
Dividends received	7,240

She makes a qualifying EIS investment of £20,000 in August 2022. Compute her income tax liability for 2022-23, assuming that there are no Gift Aid donations or pension contributions during the year.

*6.6   An interest in possession trust with two life tenants has the following income in tax year 2022-23:

	£
Rents received	12,620
Bank deposit interest	1,240
Gilts interest received gross	1,800
Dividends received	14,480

Property expenses incurred in the year were £2,220 and general administration expenses amounted to £1,825.

(a)   Compute the trustees' income tax liability for 2022-23.

(b)   Assuming that the trust income is divided equally between the two life tenants, calculate each life tenant's income from the trust in 2022-23.

Chapter 7

Income from employment (1)

Introduction

Income from employment is charged to tax in accordance with the rules of the Income Tax (Earnings and Pensions) Act 2003. The main purpose of the next two chapters of this book is to introduce these rules and to explain how an individual's income from employment is calculated for tax purposes.

This chapter begins by distinguishing between employment and self-employment and then deals with various aspects of the taxation of employment income, including the basis of assessment, non-taxable employment income and deductible expenses. There is also a brief description of the Pay As You Earn (PAYE) system which is used to collect both income tax and National Insurance contributions (NICs) from employees. The chapter concludes by outlining the features of a number of tax-efficient employee incentive schemes. The tax treatment of benefits in kind is explained in the next chapter.

These two chapters are concerned with employees whose duties are performed wholly within the UK. The taxation of overseas earnings is considered in Chapter 32.

Employment and self-employment

As will become clear in subsequent chapters, self-employed people enjoy tax advantages in comparison with employees. Two of the main advantages of being self-employed are:

(a) A much wider range of expenses is allowed against the income of self-employed people than against the income of employees (see Chapter 9).

(b) Self-employed people (see Chapter 15) generally pay their income tax much later than employees, who pay income tax under the Pay As You Earn system.

It is usually quite obvious whether someone is employed or self-employed but sometimes there are borderline cases. For example, it may be extremely difficult to distinguish between an employee with a number of part-time jobs and a self-employed person with a number of clients. In such cases, the taxpayer will usually wish to claim self-employed status, whilst HMRC will often insist that the taxpayer should be treated as an employee.

The key test to be applied when trying to establish a taxpayer's status in cases such as these is concerned with the nature of the contract between the taxpayer and the person who is paying for the work done by that taxpayer. There are two possibilities:

(a) If it can be shown that a *contract of service* exists, then the taxpayer is regarded as an employee who is in service to an employer. This requires a "mutuality of obligation" between the employee (who is obliged to work) and the employer (who is obliged to pay the employee and to make work available for the duration of the contract).

(b) If it can be shown that a *contract for services* exists, then the taxpayer is regarded as a self-employed person who is rendering services to a client.

A great deal of case law has accumulated on this subject over the years and several criteria have been established which may be used to distinguish between the two types of contract. The main criteria are as follows:

(a) **Control**. The more control that the person who is paying for the work has over the person who is doing the work, the more likely it is that a contract of service exists. Employees are usually unable to choose whether or not to do certain work, how to do the work, when to do the work or where to do the work. Self-employed people are usually able to decide these matters for themselves.

(b) **Remuneration and financial risk**. Employees usually receive a regular wage or salary; they are paid whether or not their employer is making a profit and do not risk their own capital in the business. Self-employed people are normally paid a separate fee for each job they do; they may make losses as well as profits and may lose their capital if their business fails.

(c) **Equipment**. In general, employees do not provide their own equipment but self-employed people do.

(d) **Work performance and correction**. Employees are normally expected to do their work themselves. If they make mistakes they will correct the work during working hours and so get paid for both the original work and the corrections. Self-employed people often delegate their work to staff or subcontractors. If the work done is unsatisfactory, the client will not expect to pay for it to be corrected.

(e) **Holidays and sickness**. Employees are likely to receive holiday pay and sick pay from their employers. Self-employed people are paid by their clients only for the work that they do and do not get paid when on holiday or when ill.

(f) **Exclusivity**. In general, an employee is employed by just one employer and is an integral part of that employer's business. Self-employed people normally have a number of clients and are not integral to any of their clients' businesses.

However, there are exceptions to each of the above statements and it is very important to consider the facts of each case as a whole[†] and not to rely upon just one criterion when determining whether a taxpayer should be regarded as employed or self-employed.

† *See the leading case of Hall v Lorimer (1993) in Exercise 7.6 at the end of this chapter.*

Personal service companies

An individual might seek to avoid being classed as an employee by forming a "personal service company" and then hiring out his or her services in the name of that company. The IR35† legislation exists to thwart this kind of disguised employment, which is referred to as "off-payroll working". The main features of this legislation are as follows:

(a) The legislation applies to "relevant engagements" where a worker provides services to a client through an intermediary (usually a company) in circumstances such that the income arising from the engagement would have been treated as income from employment if it had not been for the presence of the intermediary.

(b) If the client is a public sector organisation or a medium or large-sized private sector organisation, it is the *client's* responsibility to determine whether the IR35 rules apply and to account for income tax and NICs accordingly. If the rules do apply, the client is treated as making a "deemed direct payment" to the worker, comprising the amount paid to the intermediary for the worker's services, less expenses. These include the cost to the intermediary of any materials used in performance of the services, plus expenses incurred by the intermediary which would be deductible as employment expenses if incurred by the worker directly. The 5% deduction (see below) is not available.

(c) If the client is a small private sector organisation, it is the *intermediary's* responsibility to determine whether the IR35 rules apply. If these rules apply and the intermediary's income from relevant engagements for a tax year (less expenses) exceeds the worker's employment income from the intermediary in that year, then the excess is treated as a "deemed employment payment" made to the worker on the last day of the year. This deemed payment is subject to both income tax and NICs, collected via PAYE.

   The expenses referred to above include expenses incurred by the intermediary which would have been deductible if incurred by the worker directly, plus employer's pension contributions and employer's NICs paid by the intermediary, plus a further 5% of the income from engagements (to cover the costs of administering the IR35 rules).

(d) In all cases, provisions are in place so as to avoid double taxation if the worker is taxed on both a deemed payment and income actually received from the intermediary.

Similarly, if an individual has a contract with an agency, under which the individual renders services to a client, and these services are subject to "supervision, direction or control" by any person, the worker will generally be treated as an employee.

† *The off-payroll rules were introduced in Budget Press Release IR35 on 9 March 1999.*

Managed service companies

A "managed service company" (MSC) is a service company set up by an MSC provider. A number of workers (typically ten to twenty) may become shareholders in an MSC, which then offers their services to clients. Anti-avoidance legislation has been introduced to ensure that the income received by individuals who provide their services through MSCs is treated as employment income and that income tax and NICs are collected via PAYE.

Basis of assessment

An individual's employment income for a tax year is the income actually received in that tax year (the "receipts basis"). This is not necessarily the same as the income *earned* during the year. Employment income is deemed to be received on the *earliest* of:

(a) the date that the income is actually received by the employee

(b) the date that the employee becomes entitled to receive the income

and, for a company director only:

(c) the date that the income is credited to the director in the company's records

(d) the end of a period of account, if the amount of the director's income for that period is determined before it ends

(e) the date that the amount of the director's income for a period of account is determined, if this falls after the end of that period.

EXAMPLE 1

Barry (who is not a director) receives an annual salary of £45,000. His bonus for the year to 31 March 2022 was £7,350, received in May 2022. His bonus for the year to 31 March 2023 is £7,900, received in May 2023. Compute his employment income for 2022-23.

Solution

Employment income for 2022-23 is £52,350 (£45,000 + £7,350). The bonus received in May 2022 is taxed in 2022-23, even though it was earned before the year began.

Employment income

The term "employment income" includes practically anything that could be received by an employee in respect of an employment (e.g. wages, salaries, bonuses, commissions, fees, expense allowances, benefits in kind, payments on the termination of employment and pensions arising from an employment). Also, certain social security benefits[†] are taxed in the same way as employment income, including:

(a) the state retirement pension

(b) the job seeker's allowance (up to a specified maximum amount)

(c) statutory sick pay, maternity pay and paternity pay.

Note that it is not necessary for the employee to receive the income directly from the employer. As long as the income in question is received as a result of employment it is taxable as employment income, no matter who has paid it. For example, a waiter's tips are taxable, even though these are paid by customers rather than by the employer.

[†] *A special tax treatment applies to child benefit (see later in this chapter).*

Non-taxable employment income

Certain forms of income from employment are exempt from income tax. These include:

(a) trivial benefits in kind costing £50 or less (see Chapter 8)

(b) free or subsidised meals in a staff canteen, if available to all employees

(c) a party or similar function paid for by the employer, so long as the function is open to staff generally and the cost does not exceed £150 per head, but note that:

    (i) if a function costs over £150 per head, the whole cost is taxable

    (ii) if there is more than one function in the tax year and their total cost exceeds £150 per head, functions totalling £150 or less per head are exempt but any other functions are taxed in full (unless covered by the trivial benefits exemption)

(d) the provision of a parking space at or near the employee's place of work

(e) the provision of a taxi home for an employee who is occasionally required to work later than usual and until at least 9pm (but no more than 60 journeys per year)

(f) the payment by an employer of the costs of an employee's journey home if the employee regularly travels to work in a shared car, but is prevented from travelling home in the shared car because of unforeseen and exceptional circumstances

(g) "green commuting" benefits paid for by the employer and used by employees for travel between home and work, including the provision of:

    - bicycles and cycling safety equipment loaned to employees[†]
    - works buses with a seating capacity for nine or more passengers
    - subsidies to public bus services

(h) contributions by an employer towards the additional household costs incurred by an employee who works at home[†] (supporting evidence of these costs being required only if the contributions exceed £6 per week)

(i) approved mileage allowances (see below)

(j) payment of an employee's "incidental overnight expenses" (e.g. the cost of telephone calls home) when the employee is away from home overnight on business, of up to £5 per night for stays within the UK or up to £10 per night for stays outside the UK

(k) reasonable removal expenses (up to £8,000) paid by an employer when an employee first takes up an employment or transfers to a new location within the organisation

(l) awards of up to £5,000 made under a staff suggestion scheme

(m) reasonable gifts made by employer to employee in a personal capacity rather than as remuneration for services rendered (e.g. a wedding present)

(n) non-cash gifts received by virtue of the employment from someone other than the employer, so long as the value of the gifts from any one source amounts to no more than £250 in the tax year and the gifts are not made in recognition of the performance of particular services in the course of the employment

[†] *See the accompanying website for temporary Covid-19 easements made in relation to these items.*

(o) non-cash long-service awards, so long as the award is in respect of at least 20 years of service, does not cost the employer more than £50 per year of service and no such award has been made to the employee in the previous ten years

(p) the provision of work-related training courses for an employee and payments of up to £15,480 p.a. made to an employee who is attending a full-time academic course

(q) the provision of retraining courses for employees who will be leaving within the next two years or for past employees who have left within the previous 12 months

(r) the provision of one mobile telephone (or smartphone) for an employee's use

(s) the provision of job-related living accommodation (see Chapter 8)

(t) the provision of workplace childcare, sports or recreation facilities

(u) up to £55 per week of childcare if the employer contracts directly with an approved childminder or provides childcare vouchers (*reduced to only £28 per week for higher-rate taxpayers and £25 per week for additional-rate taxpayers who joined employer-supported childcare schemes after 5 April 2011*) but only if the employee joined the childcare scheme before 4 October 2018

(v) welfare counselling, eye tests and spectacles for VDU use, one health screening and one medical check-up[†] per year and up to £500 per year of medical treatment to help an employee return to work after a period of absence caused by illness or injury

(w) bonus payments of up to £3,600 per year received by the employees of a company controlled by an employee ownership trust

(x) employer-provided pensions advice of up to £500 per tax year

(y) an employer's contributions to a registered pension scheme (see Chapter 14)

(z) electricity provided in workplace charging points for electric or hybrid vehicles used by employees (if available to all employees).

[†] *See the accompanying website for a temporary Covid-19 extension to this item.*

Approved mileage allowances

Employees who use their own vehicles on business may receive mileage allowances from their employers. These allowances are tax-free so long as they do not exceed the HMRC approved mileage allowance payment (AMAP) which is calculated by reference to a table of approved mileage rates. For 2022-23, these rates are:

	first 10,000 miles in tax year	*each mile over 10,000 miles*
Motor cars and vans	45p per mile	25p per mile
Motor cycles	24p per mile	24p per mile
Bicycles	20p per mile	20p per mile

If the mileage allowances paid to an employee exceed the amount calculated using these rates, then the excess is taxable. On the other hand, if the mileage allowances paid to an employee are less than the amount calculated using these rates, the deficit is a deductible expense. Tax relief cannot be claimed for any costs above the AMAP rate.

Employers may also pay employees up to 5p per mile tax-free for each passenger carried on a business trip. However, employees cannot claim tax relief if the employer pays less than this (or pays nothing at all).

EXAMPLE 2

Julie uses her own car when travelling on her employer's business. In 2022-23 she drives 12,000 business miles. Explain the taxation implications if her employer pays her:

(a) 47p per mile   (b) 37p per mile   (c) None.

Solution

(a) Having driven 12,000 business miles in the year, Julie may receive a tax-free mileage allowance of up to £5,000 ((10,000 × 45p) + (2,000 × 25p)). She actually receives £5,640 (12,000 × 47p) so her taxable mileage allowance is £640.

(b) Julie receives £4,440 (12,000 × 37p) and therefore she has a deductible expense of £560 (£5,000 – £4,440) which may be set against her income from employment.

(c) If Julie receives nothing, she has a deductible expense of £5,000.

Deductible expenses

If an employee incurs an expense in connection with his or her employment, then one of two situations may arise:

(a) The employee pays the expense and is not reimbursed by the employer. In this case, as long as the expense is deductible (see below), the amount of the expense will be subtracted from the employee's income for tax purposes.

(b) The employer reimburses the employee or pays the expense directly. In this case, as long as the expense is either:

(i) an expense that would have been deductible if it had been paid by the employee without reimbursement, or

(ii) an expense which has been calculated in an "approved way"

then the amount paid by the employer is exempt from income tax and is not treated as part of the employee's income from employment. Otherwise, the amount paid by the employer is treated as employment income for tax purposes. The employee may then try to claim a deduction (if possible) for the expense concerned.

An expense is calculated in an "approved way" if it has been calculated in accordance with HMRC regulations. One example of such an expense is a meal allowance paid to an employee who is required to travel for business purposes. Regulations stipulate that such meal allowances are approved if they do not exceed specified amounts varying from £5 to £25 per day, depending upon the duration and timing of the business travel on that day.

Expenses incurred by an employee are deductible (or "allowable") for tax purposes only if they fall into one of the following categories:

(a) contributions to an occupational pension scheme, if these contributions are deducted from the employee's pay by the employer (see Chapter 14)

(b) subscriptions to relevant professional bodies

(c) donations made under a payroll giving scheme (see later in this chapter)

(d) travel and subsistence expenses necessarily incurred in the performance of the duties of the employment (see below)

(e) other expenses incurred wholly, exclusively and necessarily in the performance of the duties of the employment.

The "wholly, exclusively and necessarily" rule is applied very stringently. In particular, the "necessarily" part of the rule means that an expense will not be allowed unless it can be shown that the duties of the employment concerned could not be performed (by anyone) if the expense were not incurred.

Travel between home and work

As stated above, travel and subsistence expenses are allowable for tax purposes only if they are necessarily incurred in the performance of the duties of the employment. This means that the cost of travel between home and work is normally disallowed on the grounds that the duties of the employment do not begin until the employee arrives at work. However, the following costs of travel between home and work are allowable:

(a) travel and subsistence costs incurred by a "site-based" employee (i.e. an employee who has no normal place of work) when travelling between home and the site

(b) travel and subsistence costs incurred by an employee who has a normal place of work, when undertaking business journeys which start from home

(c) travel and subsistence costs incurred by an employee who is seconded to a temporary place of work, so long as it is expected that he or she will return to the normal place of work within 24 months.

EXAMPLE 3

In which of the following cases would the expenses described be deductible from the employee's income for tax purposes?

(a) A bank manager voluntarily pays an annual subscription to a London club. He uses the club only for the purpose of meeting the bank's clients.

(b) The finance director of a company pays an annual subscription to the Institute of Chartered Accountants.

(c) A clerk pays fees to attend a college course in the evenings, so as to gain qualifications and improve her career prospects.

(d) A workman is required to provide his own tools and protective clothing.

(e) A barrister living and practising in London is appointed as Recorder of Portsmouth. He pays his own train fares between London and Portsmouth.

Solution

(a) The bank manager uses the club wholly and exclusively for business purposes, but it is not necessary for him to be a member of the club in order to perform his duties. Therefore the cost of the subscription will be disallowed. The facts of this case are similar to those of *Brown* v *Bullock* (1961).

(b) Relevant professional subscriptions of this nature are specifically allowed by statute. Therefore the cost of the subscription will be allowed.

(c) Whilst attending college, the clerk is not performing the duties of her employment. Therefore the cost of the college course will be disallowed. The facts of this case are similar to those of *Blackwell* v *Mills* (1945).

(d) The cost of necessary tools and protective clothing will be allowed. In some cases, HMRC has agreed flat-rate allowances with the relevant trade union or association for expenses such as tools, protective clothing, uniforms and laundry costs.

(e) The duties of the employment are carried out entirely in Portsmouth. Whilst travelling from London, the barrister is not performing those duties so the expense will be disallowed. The facts of this case are similar to those of *Ricketts* v *Colquhoun* (1925).

Entertaining expenses

In general, entertaining expenses are not allowable against employment income and an employee who is obliged to defray such expenses personally cannot claim a deduction for them. However, if an employer either:

(a) reimburses an employee for entertaining expenses incurred, or

(b) pays the employee a specific entertaining allowance

then the entertaining expenses incurred by the employee (if incurred wholly, exclusively and necessarily in the performance of the duties of the employment) may be set against the sums received from the employer. But these sums are <u>not</u> allowable when calculating the employer's profit for tax purposes (see Chapter 9).

Payroll giving scheme

Employees whose employers operate an approved "payroll giving scheme" may make charitable donations by requesting that the donations should be deducted from their gross earnings. Income tax is then payable on the earnings which remain *after* the donations have been deducted, thus providing tax relief. The employer passes the donations on to an approved charity.

Termination payments

Payments which are received by an employee on the termination of employment fall into three distinct categories:

(a) **Fully exempt**. The following termination payments are exempt from income tax:

    (i)   payments made on the death of the employee

    (ii) payments made to the employee because of injury or disability

    (iii) lump sum payments under registered pension schemes.

(b) **Fully taxable**. If an employee receives a termination payment which does not fall into any of the above categories and which is made by way of reward for the employee's services, then the payment is fully taxable in the year in which it is received. This applies if the employee was contractually entitled to the payment or if there was a reasonable expectation that the payment would be made.

    Payments in lieu of notice (PILONs) are also fully taxable, whether or not they are described as such and whether or not there is a contractual entitlement. Employers are required to calculate the amount of any "post-employment notice pay" included in a termination payment and this amount is fully taxable.

(c) **Partially exempt**. Payments (other than PILONs) made at an employer's discretion to compensate an employee for loss of employment ("ex gratia" payments) are exempt from income tax if the amount received does not exceed £30,000. Any excess over £30,000 is taxed in the year in which it is received. However, the £30,000 threshold is reduced by any statutory redundancy pay (SRP) that the employee also receives, even though SRP is itself exempt from income tax.

The taxable part of a partially exempt termination payment is treated as the top slice of income, ranking above both savings income and dividends. This rule ensures that savings and dividend income are not moved into higher tax bands and was originally intended to reduce the total tax liability. But subsequent changes to the way in which savings income and dividends are taxed mean that this rule may now have the opposite effect.

EXAMPLE 4

Priyanka (who is not a Scottish taxpayer) is made redundant in March 2023. She receives statutory redundancy pay of £4,500 and an ex gratia compensation payment from her employer of £40,000, none of which ranks as a payment in lieu of notice.

Her only other income in 2022-23 comprises her salary of £40,450 and dividends of £9,400. Calculate her income tax liability for the year.

Solution

The exempt part of the ex gratia payment is £25,500 (£30,000 − £4,500). The remaining £14,500 is treated as the top slice of income. The income tax computation is as follows:

	Total £	Non-savings £	Dividends £	Compensation £
Salary	40,450	40,450		
Dividends received	9,400		9,400	
Compensation £40,000 – £25,500	14,500			14,500
Total income	64,350	40,450	9,400	14,500
Less: Personal allowance	12,570	2,750		9,820
Taxable income	51,780	37,700	9,400	4,680

Income tax due

Non-savings income	: Basic rate	37,700	@ 20%	7,540.00
Dividend income	: Nil rate	2,000	@ 0%	0.00
	: Upper rate	7,400	@ 33.75%	2,497.50
Compensation	: Higher rate	4,680	@ 40%	1,872.00
		51,780		
Tax liability				11,909.50

Notes:

(i) The personal allowance has been allocated so as to minimise the tax liability. If the whole allowance had been set against the salary, taxable non-savings income (other than compensation) would have been (£40,450 – £12,570) = £27,880 and the tax liability would have been (£27,880 × 20%) + (£2,000 × 0%) + (£7,400 × 8.75%) + (£420 × 20%) + (£14,080 × 40%) = £11,939.50. In fact, the above effect could be achieved by simply setting the whole personal allowance against the compensation.

(ii) Any tax paid by means of PAYE would be deducted when computing tax payable.

For a Scottish taxpayer, the way in which the "top-slice" rule interacts with Scottish tax limits is not clear. However, the lowest tax liability may be achieved by setting £12,150 of the PA against the salary (so that the dividends fall into the basic rate band) and £420 against the compensation. The tax liability is then (£2,162 × 19%) + (£10,956 × 20%) + (£15,182 × 21%) + (£2,000 × 0%) + (£7,400 × 8.75%) + (£14,080 × 41%) = £12,210.50.

High income child benefit charge

Child benefit is a social security benefit which is not taxable. However, a taxpayer who has adjusted net income (see Chapter 3) in excess of £50,000 per annum and receives child benefit (or whose partner receives child benefit) may be subject to the "high income child benefit charge". This income tax charge is equal to 1% of the child benefit award for each £100 of income between £50,000 and £60,000. The tax charge for taxpayers with income of £60,000 or more is 100% of the child benefit award.

This charge applies only to taxpayers whose income exceeds £50,000 for the tax year. If both of the partners to a domestic partnership have income exceeding £50,000, the charge applies only to the partner with the higher income.

The PAYE system

Under the Pay As You Earn (PAYE) system, employers are required to deduct income tax and National Insurance contributions from their employees when paying them their wages and salaries. The amounts deducted from employees, together with the secondary National Insurance contributions payable by the employer (see Chapter 16) must be paid to HMRC within 14 days of the end of the tax month in which the employees are paid (or 17 days if payment to HMRC is made electronically). A tax month runs from the 6th of one month to the 5th of the next month. Therefore employers generally make a payment to HMRC on or before the 19th (or 22nd) of each month. However, employers whose payments to HMRC do not exceed an average of £1,500 per month are allowed to make quarterly payments.

The PAYE system applies to all payments which are assessable as employment income, including wages, salaries, bonuses, commissions etc. The system also covers:

(a) payments consisting of assets which are readily convertible into cash, such as shares or other commodities, but excluding "own company" shares which are provided by the employer under an approved share scheme (see later in this chapter)

(b) vouchers exchangeable either for cash or for readily convertible assets

(c) remuneration schemes involving trade debts, whereby employers assign trade debts to employees, who then receive cash when the debts are settled.

Benefits in kind (see Chapter 8) are usually brought within the scope of PAYE by making an adjustment to the employee's tax code (see below).

Tax codes

The PAYE system is based upon the concept of "tax codes". HMRC issues a tax code for each employee for each tax year, representing the amount which the employee may earn in that year before becoming liable to income tax. The tax code takes into account a number of factors which may affect an employee's income tax liability, including:

(a) the personal allowances to which the employee is entitled

(b) the employee's expenses and tax reliefs (e.g. payments deductible from total income)

(c) adjustments made in order to collect tax on benefits in kind[†]

(d) adjustments for tax overpaid or underpaid in previous years, including tax debts of up to £17,000 (with or without the taxpayer's consent) and self assessment balancing payments of up to £3,000 (see Chapter 15).

The tax code allocated to an employee is equal to one-tenth of the aggregate of the above items, rounded down to a whole number.

† *Until 2016-17, HMRC could not determine the amount of an employee's benefits in kind until these were reported by the employer on form P11D at the end of the year (see below). However, employers are now able (voluntarily) to quantify certain benefits in kind themselves and then collect tax on these benefits in real time through the PAYE RTI system (see later in this chapter).*

EXAMPLE 5

Henry is single and claims only the basic personal allowance. He makes a deductible payment of £100 per annum and pays an allowable subscription of £85 per annum. His taxable benefits in kind for 2022-23 are expected to be £500. Determine his tax code for 2022-23, assuming that his income for the year is not expected to exceed £100,000.

Solution

By virtue of his personal allowance, deductible payment and allowable expenses, Henry is entitled to earn £12,755 (£12,570 + £100 + £85) in the year before paying tax. But some of this will be set against his benefits in kind of £500, leaving only £12,255 to set against his salary. So his tax code for the year is "1225" (i.e. one-tenth of £12,255, rounded down to a whole number).

The same result would be obtained if the aggregate figure (£12,255) were anywhere in the range £12,250 to £12,259, so tax codes are not precise. But dividing the aggregate figure by ten results in only one-tenth as many different tax codes as would be obtained otherwise and cuts down the size of the tax tables used by employers (see below).

Tax code suffixes

A tax code may also have a suffix comprising a letter of the alphabet. The most common suffix is L which stands for "low" and indicates that the employee is entitled to the basic personal allowance (currently £12,570). So Henry's full tax code in the above example would actually be "1225L". Other suffixes include:

M - the employee's spouse or civil partner has elected to transfer part of his/her personal allowance to the employee

N - the employee has elected to transfer part of his/her personal allowance to a spouse or civil partner.

Code BR instructs the employer to deduct basic rate tax from all payments made to the employee. Code NT instructs the employer not to deduct any tax from the employee at all. Codes prefixed[†] with the letter K are negative codes, used mainly for employees whose taxable benefits in kind exceed their allowances. Tax on the excess benefits is collected by increasing the amount of tax charged on the employee's wage or salary.

One purpose of tax code suffixes is to facilitate the recoding exercise which is needed whenever personal allowances increase. When this happens, HMRC may (for example) simply instruct employers to increase all L codes by the amount required to reflect the increase in the basic personal allowance, so avoiding the need to recode every employee in the country individually.

† *The tax codes of Scottish employees are prefixed with the letter S and employers are required to apply Scottish rates of income tax to such employees, whether or not the employer is located in Scotland (see Chapter 2). Similarly, the tax codes of Welsh employees are prefixed C (Cymru).*

Operation of the PAYE system

Employers who operate manual payroll systems (now rare) are issued with sets of tax tables which enable them to calculate the amount of income tax that should be deducted from an employee in a given week or month. The main tables used are:

Table A   This table (also known as the Pay Adjustment Table) contains pages for each week or month of the year and shows, for each tax code, the amount of tax-free pay to which the employee is entitled for the year to date. In effect, the table spreads an employee's allowances evenly over the year, giving 1/12th of the allowances per month or 1/52th of the allowances per week.

Table B   This table (also known as the Taxable Pay Table) is used to look up an employee's income tax liability for the year to date, after the entitlement to tax-free pay has been taken into account.

In outline, the procedure followed for each employee in each week or month is:

(a)   The employee's tax code is looked up in Table A, which shows the amount of tax-free pay to which the employee is entitled for the year to date.

(b)   This is then subtracted from the employee's gross pay for the year to date giving the employee's taxable pay for the year to date.

(c)   The employee's taxable pay for the year to date is then looked up in Table B, which shows the tax due for the year to date. Further tables are used if the employee is a higher rate taxpayer.

(d)   Finally, the tax paid to date by the employee in previous weeks or months is subtracted from the tax due for the year to date, giving the employee's income tax liability for the current week or month.

The entire system is cumulative and requires employers to keep track of each of their employees' gross pay and income tax paid to date (i.e. since the beginning of the tax year on 6 April). Employers are provided with deductions working sheets (form P11) which facilitate the accumulation of the necessary "to date" figures.

In computer-based payroll systems (which are now used by nearly all employers) the tax tables become computer files and the weekly or monthly procedure is carried out by computer software. However, the operation of the PAYE system does not change in principle when a manual payroll system is replaced by a computer-based system.

PAYE forms

P2   A notice of coding, sent by HMRC to both the employer and the employee.

P11   Deductions working sheet (see above).

P11D   An end-of-year return showing an employee's benefits in kind and expenses for the year. Forms P11D must be submitted to HMRC by 6 July following the end of the tax year. Employees must be provided with copies by the same date.

P45 A four-part form used when an employee leaves an employment, showing the employee's tax code, gross pay to date and tax paid to date. Part 1 of the form is sent to HMRC and the other three parts are given to the leaving employee. The employee gives parts 2 and 3 to his or her new employer who retains part 2 and sends part 3 to HMRC. The employee retains part 1A.

P46 A form providing details of a new employee who does not have a P45 from a previous employment. Sent to HMRC by the employer.

P60 Certificate of gross pay and tax deducted, given to employees by employers at the end of the tax year. Forms P60 must be provided to employees by 31 May following the end of the tax year.

Notes:

(a) Online filing of "in-year" forms P45 and P46 via the RTI system (see below) is now mandatory. End-of-year P11Ds may also be filed online.

(b) Employers are allowed to provide P60s to their employees by electronic means, as long as the employees concerned are able to access their P60s easily and securely.

(c) Employers with 250 or more employees are required to make their PAYE payments to HMRC by electronic means.

Real Time Information

The PAYE Real Time Information (RTI) system was introduced during tax year 2013-14 and is now in use by virtually all employers. This system requires employers to send data about their employees' pay and deductions (income tax and NICs) to HMRC at the time that the employees are paid. Online data transmission is mandatory.

Before the advent of RTI, it was necessary for employers to send end-of-year forms to HMRC showing each employee's gross pay, tax paid and NICs for the year. RTI removes the need for these forms, since the necessary data is automatically submitted to HMRC during the tax year each time that the employee is paid. Furthermore, information about starters and leavers is transmitted as part of the RTI process, so there is no longer any need for employers to submit forms P45 and P46 to HMRC separately.

Employers may also deal with most[†] benefits in kind through the PAYE RTI system. An employer who chooses to do so (and is authorised by HMRC) computes the taxable amount of each benefit in kind to be received by an employee during the tax year and spreads this evenly over the payment periods (months or weeks) which fall into that year. The amount allocated to each period is then treated as extra pay and is taxed accordingly. Information about the employee's benefits in kind is submitted to HMRC in real time, so there is no need to supply form P11D at the end of the tax year.

[†] *Voluntary "payrolling" of benefits in kind is not applicable to living accommodation or beneficial loans (see Chapter 8) so P11Ds are still required for employees who receive these benefits.*

Construction industry scheme

The construction industry scheme (CIS) may apply when a contractor makes payments to a subcontractor under a contract which relates to construction operations. Subcontractors who rank as employees are dealt with via the PAYE system in the usual way, but it has proved necessary to introduce a special scheme in relation to subcontractors who do not rank as employees, so as to counter tax evasion. The main features of the CIS are as follows:

(a) Subcontractors are encouraged to register as such with HMRC. They may apply to be paid gross by the contractors for whom they work or they may register to be paid under deduction of tax instead. In order to qualify for gross payment, a subcontractor must be running a business which:

    (i) is carried on in the UK and has a bank account (the "business test")
    (ii) has a construction turnover of at least a specified amount (the "turnover test")
    (iii) has complied with all of its tax obligations (the "compliance test").

For sole traders, the "specified amount" referred to above is £30,000 per annum. For partnerships and companies, the specified amount is the *lower* of £100,000 and the figure obtained by multiplying £30,000 by the number of partners or directors.

(b) Subcontractors must give contractors their name, unique taxpayer reference (UTR) and National Insurance number (in the case of a sole trader) when entering into a contract. The contractor then contacts HMRC to check on the subcontractor's status. This process is known as "verification".

(c) If the subcontractor is registered with HMRC, the contractor will be told either to pay the subcontractor gross or to apply the standard rate of deduction (20%). However, any payment which represents a reimbursement of the cost of materials supplied by the subcontractor is excluded from the amount which is subject to deduction of tax.

(d) If the subcontractor is not registered with HMRC, the contractor will be told to apply a higher rate of deduction (30%) when making payments to that subcontractor.

(e) Within 14 days of the end of each tax month, contractors must provide a statement to each subcontractor from whom a tax deduction has been made, showing details of the payments made and the amounts deducted.

(f) Also within 14 days of the end of each tax month, contractors must send a return to HMRC showing all of the payments made to subcontractors during the month, whether paid gross or paid under deduction of tax. Online filing of these CIS returns is now mandatory.

(g) All deductions made from subcontractors during a tax month must be paid over to HMRC within 14 days of the end of the tax month. Three further days are allowed if payment is made electronically.

Employee incentive schemes

An employee incentive scheme provides financial incentives for employees to improve their work performance. The main schemes which currently have income tax implications are:

(a) share incentive plans (SIPs)

(b) approved share option schemes

(c) enterprise management incentives (EMIs).

A brief description of each of these types of scheme is given below.

Share incentive plans

Share incentive plans (SIPs) offer employees a tax-efficient way of acquiring shares in the companies for which they work. SIPs were originally known as all-employee share ownership plans (AESOPs). The main features of these plans are as follows:

(a) Companies which set up a SIP may offer their employees:

   (i) *free shares* in the company worth up to £3,600 per annum per employee

   (ii) the opportunity to use salary of up to £1,800 per annum to buy *partnership shares* in the company (without having to pay either income tax or NICs on the salary used for this purpose)

   (iii) up to two free *matching shares* for each partnership share.

   This means that (in 2022-23) a non-Scottish† employee paying income tax at basic rate could acquire up to £9,000 worth of shares at a cost of £1,440 (80% × £1,800). The cost would be £1,080 (60% × £1,800) for an employee paying tax at the higher rate and only £990 (55% × £1,800) for an employee paying tax at the additional rate. There would also be a saving in National Insurance contributions (see Chapter 16).

   † *A Scottish taxpayer paying income tax at intermediate rate, higher rate or top rate would save tax on £1,800 at 21%, 41% or 46% respectively.*

(b) The company may offer free shares only, partnership shares only, free shares and partnership shares only, partnership shares and matching shares only, or all three of these types of shares.

(c) Subject to certain conditions, the plan may link the provision of free shares to the achievement of employee performance targets.

(d) In general, all employees must be eligible to participate in the plan. However, the plan may specify that employees do not become eligible until they have been employed by the company (or employed by the group, in the case of a group of companies) for a qualifying period of not more than 18 months.

(e) The plan may allow (or may compel) dividends arising on an employee's shares to be reinvested tax-free in further *dividend shares*.

(f) All of an employee's shares leave the plan when he or she ceases to be employed by the company (or group). The plan rules may specify that employees who leave within three years should forfeit their free and matching shares. Additionally, employees may take some or all of their shares out of the plan as follows:

Free/matching shares : at any time after the end of the holding period specified by the plan, which must be between three and five years

Partnership shares : at any time (though any related matching shares may be forfeited if this occurs within three years)

Dividend shares : at any time after three years.

(g) If free, matching or partnership shares leave the plan within three years, a charge to income tax and NICs arises based on the market value of the shares when leaving the plan. If the shares leave the plan after three years but in less than five years, this charge is based upon the *lower* of the market value of the shares when originally awarded and the market value of the shares when leaving the plan.

(h) If dividend shares leave the plan within three years, a tax charge arises on a *notional dividend* equal to the cash dividend which was used to acquire the shares.

(i) No tax charge arises if shares of any type leave the plan after five years (or earlier if caused by the employee's retirement or by death, injury, disability or redundancy).

(j) Employees who keep their shares in the plan until they sell them incur no liability to capital gains tax. Employees who take their shares out of the plan and sell them later pay CGT on any increase in value since the shares were taken out.

Approved share option schemes

In general, a charge to income tax (and NICs) may arise if an employee who works for a company is granted an option to buy shares in that company. The charge arises when the option is exercised and is based upon the market value of the shares obtained, less the amount paid for the shares and less the amount (if any) which was paid to acquire the option. However, this charge can be avoided if the option falls within an approved share option scheme. Approved schemes are of two main types:

(a) **Savings-related share option schemes**. Under a savings-related scheme, employees are granted an option to buy shares and then save through a tax-free savings scheme in order to raise funds to exercise the option. The amount saved must be no more than £500 a month and the savings contract may last for three or five years. The scheme must be open to all employees who have worked for the company for a specified qualifying period (which cannot exceed five years). The price at which employees are given the option to buy shares must be at least 80% of the shares' market value at the time that the option is granted.

(b) **Company share option plans (CSOPs)**. These schemes are less restrictive than the savings-related schemes. The company can select the employees to whom it would like to offer share options and can set these employees performance targets which must be achieved before the options will be made available. The price at which an option may be exercised must not be manifestly less than the market value of the shares at the time that the option is granted and options must normally be exercised no earlier than three years and no later than ten years after they are granted. However, options may be exercised within three years of being granted if an employee's participation in the scheme ends through injury, disability, redundancy or retirement. There is an upper limit of £30,000 on the value of the shares (at the time of the grant) for which an employee may hold options at any one time.

If a share option is granted under an approved scheme of either type and all necessary conditions are satisfied, then no income tax or NICs are payable on either the grant of the option or the exercise of the option. For capital gains tax purposes (see Chapter 18) the allowable cost of shares acquired under an approved share option scheme is the price actually paid for the shares by the employee.

Enterprise management incentives

Enterprise management incentives (EMIs) offer trading companies that have a permanent establishment in the UK the chance to reward selected employees with tax-free share options. In order to be eligible, a company must have fewer than 250 employees and gross assets not exceeding £30 million. The main features of the EMIs scheme are:

(a) The scheme allows a qualifying company to grant share options to any employee who works at least 25 hours per week for the company, or (if less) for at least 75% of his or her working time[†]. The company may select the employees to whom it wishes to grant options and may award different amounts to different employees.

(b) Employees who own more than 30% of the company's ordinary share capital are excluded from the scheme.

(c) If the company so wishes, options may be granted to acquire shares at less than their market value at the time of grant or even at nil cost.

(d) No charge to either income tax or NICs arises when an option is granted under the EMIs scheme. When the option is exercised, no charge arises if the shares are acquired at not less than their market value at the time of grant. Otherwise, a tax charge arises based on the *lower* of:

   (i) the excess of the market value of the shares at the time that the option was granted over the amount (if any) paid to acquire them

   (ii) the excess of the market value of the shares at the time that the option is exercised over the amount (if any) paid to acquire them.

[†] *See the accompanying website for a temporary Covid-19 relaxation to this working time rule.*

(e) There is an upper limit of £250,000 on the value of the shares (at the time of grant) for which an employee may hold unexercised options that have been granted under the EMIs scheme. At any time, the total value of the shares for which options have been granted, but not yet exercised, cannot exceed £3 million.

(f) The sale of shares which were acquired under the scheme is a chargeable disposal for capital gains tax purposes, but such a disposal is generally eligible for business asset disposal relief (see Chapter 22).

EMIs were originally established under EU "State Aid" rules and were extended until the end of the EU departure transition period, but now continue under UK law.

Summary

‣ It is important to distinguish employment from self-employment. Several criteria have been established which help to make this distinction.

‣ The aim of the "IR35" legislation is to ensure that those individuals who provide their services through a personal service company are classed as employees.

‣ Employment income is taxed on the receipts basis.

‣ Income tax is payable on practically all of the income received by an individual in respect of an employment, including benefits in kind. However, some minor items of employment income are exempt from income tax.

‣ In general, an employee's expenses are deductible for tax purposes only if incurred wholly, exclusively and necessarily in performing the duties of the employment.

‣ Certain termination payments (e.g. on death or injury) are fully exempt from income tax. Otherwise, any amounts to which an employee is contractually entitled on the termination of employment are fully taxable. Ex gratia termination payments (other than payments in lieu of notice) are partially exempt.

‣ The PAYE system is used to deduct both income tax and NICs from employees' wages and salaries. The system now operates in real time, so it is no longer necessary for employers to submit end-of-year returns to HMRC,

‣ The construction industry scheme (CIS) rules may apply when payments are made by a contractor to a sub-contractor in connection with a construction contract.

‣ Certain employee incentive schemes offer tax advantages. Share incentive plans provide employees with a tax-efficient means of acquiring shares in the companies for which they work. Share options may be granted tax-efficiently to employees by means of approved share option schemes and enterprise management incentives.

Exercises

A set of multiple choice questions for this chapter is available on the accompanying website.

7.1   List the criteria which might be used to distinguish employment from self-employment.

7.2   Malcolm's gross annual salary is £57,500. He is also entitled to an annual bonus which is based on his employer's profits for the previous calendar year. His bonus for the year to 31 December 2021 was £8,350 (which he received on 9 April 2022). His bonus for the year to 31 December 2022 is £9,570 (which he receives on 18 April 2023). Malcolm is not a company director. Calculate his employment income for 2022-23.

7.3   Which of the following forms of income from employment would be exempt from income tax in tax year 2022-23?

(a)   Free meals in the company canteen.

(b)   Removal expenses of £4,500.

(c)   £1,000 given to an employee on reaching 25 years of service with his employer.

(d)   A canteen of cutlery given to an employee on his marriage.

(e)   A mileage allowance of 35p per mile given to an employee who drives her own motor car for 2,500 business miles per year.

(f)   A payment of £10 per week made to a homeworker to cover the additional costs of working from home.

7.4   Which of the following expenses incurred by an employee would be deductible when computing employment income for tax purposes?

(a)   Travel between work and home.   (b)   Travel between work sites.

(c)   Professional subscriptions.   (d)   Protective clothing.

(e)   A suit to wear at the office.   (f)   Entertaining expenses.

*7.5   On 21 March 2023, Penny is made redundant by her employer. She receives statutory redundancy pay of £4,750 and an ex gratia compensation payment of £32,000 (none of which ranks as a PILON). Her only other income in tax year 2022-23 is her salary of £46,685 and building society interest of £1,000. She is not a Scottish taxpayer.

Calculate Penny's income tax liability for 2022-23.

*7.6   Ian is a freelance television technician. In a typical tax year he works for approximately 20 separate TV companies. None of his engagements with any of these companies lasts for more than 10 days at a time. All of his work is performed at studios owned by the TV companies, using very expensive equipment also owned by these companies.

The TV companies initially book his services by telephoning him at his home (where he has an office) and then send a confirmation letter giving the dates of the engagement and the amount of the agreed fee. Ian's work is very skillful and he is required to do this work himself. He is not allowed to subcontract the work to anyone else.

Is Ian employed or self-employed?

Chapter 8

Income from employment (2)

Introduction

As explained in Chapter 7, the term "employment income" includes any benefits in kind which an employee might receive. Benefits in kind consist of income received in the form of goods or services (rather than money) and include items such as living accommodation, company cars and interest-free loans. The purpose of this chapter is to explain how an employee's benefits in kind are calculated for tax purposes.

Benefits in kind

As a general rule, employees are charged to income tax on the cost to their employer of providing benefits in kind. The cost of providing a benefit is normally the additional cost borne by the employer as a consequence of providing that benefit. This rule was established in the case of *Pepper* v *Hart* (1992) which concerned the provision of school places for the children of masters at the school. It was held that the cost of each such place for tax purposes should consist of only the additional costs borne by the school (e.g. extra food) rather than the figure obtained by dividing the total running costs of the school by the total number of pupils. However, there are special rules for calculating the taxable benefit in relation to:

(a) living accommodation provided for an employee's use

(b) assets loaned to the employee for private use

(c) ancillary services connected with living accommodation

(d) cars and fuel provided for private use

(e) vans provided for private use

(f) beneficial loans.

These special rules are explained later in this chapter.

Note that no taxable benefit arises if an employer provides an employee with a benefit in kind and the cost of this benefit would have been a deductible expense if the employee had met this cost personally (see Chapter 7). Note also that any financial contribution made by an employee towards the cost of a benefit is not taken into account for tax purposes unless the contribution is made by 6 July following the end of the tax year concerned.

Trivial benefits

There is an exemption from income tax (and NICs) for so-called "trivial" benefits in kind which satisfy certain conditions. The main conditions are:

(a)   the cost of providing the benefit does not exceed £50

(b)   the benefit is not cash or a cash voucher

(c)   the employee is not contractually entitled to the benefit[†] and it is not provided in recognition of particular services performed in the course of the employment.

If trivial benefits are provided to the directors of a close company (see Chapter 27), the exemption is capped at £300 per director per tax year. Note also that:

(a)   If the cost of a benefit in kind exceeds £50, the full amount of the benefit is taxable (not just the excess over £50).

(b)   Non-cash vouchers (e.g. gift vouchers which can be exchanged for goods) are eligible for the trivial benefits exemption if all of the necessary conditions are satisfied.

(c)   If a benefit is eligible for another exemption, that exemption and the trivial benefits exemption are applied in the way that is most favourable to the employee. However, if another exemption exempts only *part* of the cost of a benefit, the excess cost is not eligible for the trivial benefits treatment, even if that excess is less than £50.

[†] *Trivial benefits are generally irregular or infrequent and are typically provided for staff welfare purposes. Benefits provided on a regular basis are likely to be linked to the employee's services and are therefore unlikely to qualify as trivial benefits.*

EXAMPLE 1

In tax year 2022-23, an employer provides employees with a party at Christmas and a dinner dance in the summer. Calculate the taxable benefit if the cost to the employer of these two functions (per employee) is:

(a)   £60 and £80.   (b)   £45 and £120   (c)   £75 and £100.

What would the tax situation be if there had been only one function during the tax year costing £200 per employee?

Solution

(a)   The total cost does not exceed £150 (see Chapter 7) so there is no taxable benefit.

(b)   The total cost exceeds £150. The most favourable treatment is to use the £150 rule to exempt the £120 function and then use the trivial benefits rule to exempt the £45.

(c)   The £150 rule can be used to exempt the £100 function. But the remaining £75 is not trivial and is a taxable benefit.

If there had been only one function costing £200, this would not be exempt under either the functions rule or the trivial benefits rule and so the entire £200 would be taxable.

Vouchers for goods or services

Employees are charged to tax on the cost to their employer of providing vouchers which may be exchanged for goods or services. But no tax liability arises if a voucher is used to provide a benefit that would otherwise be exempt from tax. Note that:

(a) Entertainment and hospitality vouchers provided by a person other than the employer or someone connected with the employer are exempt from income tax unless provided as a reward for specific services rendered by the employee.

(b) The provision of a cash voucher results in a taxable benefit equal to the amount of cash into which the voucher can be converted.

Fair bargain rule

In general, no taxable benefit arises if an employee acquires goods or services from his or her employer at the same price (and on the same terms) as would apply if those goods or services were sold to a member of the public. This is known as the "fair bargain" rule.

However, this rule does *not* apply to living accommodation, cars and vans provided for private use and beneficial loans. In each of these cases, the taxable benefit is calculated according to special rules set out in ITEPA 2003 and these rules take into account any payment made by the employee. This may result in a charge to tax even if the employee pays the same price for the item concerned as would be paid by a member of the public.

Living accommodation

In general, a taxable benefit arises if an employer provides living accommodation for an employee. The rules are as follows:

(a) In the case of accommodation which is owned by the employer, the employee is taxed on the "annual value" of the accommodation concerned. In practice, this is taken to be the accommodation's rateable value, which was used in the calculation of domestic rates before these were abolished. The rateable value of properties constructed since the abolition of domestic rates has to be estimated.

(b) In the case of accommodation rented by the employer, the employee is taxed on the greater of the rent paid by the employer and the accommodation's annual value.

In either case, the taxable benefit is reduced by any contribution made by the employee (*if made by 6 July following the tax year*). Accommodation costing the employer more than £75,000 is regarded as "expensive" and gives rise to an increase in the taxable benefit. This increase is calculated by applying an appropriate percentage to the amount by which the cost of the accommodation exceeds £75,000. Note the following points:

(a) The "appropriate percentage" used for this purpose is the same as the official rate of interest used in beneficial loan calculations (see later in this chapter) as that rate stood at the beginning of the tax year for which the benefit is being calculated.

(b) The cost of providing accommodation is generally equal to the purchase price of the property, *plus* the cost of any improvements made to the property before the start of the tax year concerned, *less* any capital contribution made by the employee.

(c) But if the property was acquired by the employer more than six years before it was made available to the employee, the cost of providing the accommodation is taken to be its market value on the date when it was first occupied by the employee, *plus* the cost of any improvements made since that date but before the start of the tax year concerned, *less* any capital contribution made by the employee.

EXAMPLE 2

As from 1 January 2022, an employee is provided by his employer with the use of a house which has an annual value of £5,300. The following information is relevant:

(a) The employer bought the house in 2019 at a cost of £270,000 and spent £35,000 on improvements in 2020. A further £10,000 was spent on improvements in July 2022.

(b) The employee pays £3,000 per annum to his employer in relation to this benefit.

Calculate the taxable benefit in 2022-23, assuming that the official rate of interest as at 6 April 2022 was 2% per annum.

Solution

	£
Annual value	5,300
Add: 2% x (£270,000 + £35,000 – £75,000)	4,600
	9,900
Less: Employee contribution (if made by 6 July 2023)	3,000
Taxable benefit	6,900

Job-related accommodation

If accommodation provided by an employer for an employee's use is "job-related", then no taxable benefit arises. Accommodation is job-related if:

(a) it is necessary for the employee to reside in the accommodation so that he or she can properly perform the duties of the employment (e.g. a caretaker who is required to live in a caretaker's flat on an employer's premises)

(b) the accommodation is provided for the better performance of the employee's duties and it is customary for such accommodation to be provided (e.g. a clergyman who lives in a vicarage provided by an employer)

(c) there is a special threat to the employee's security and the accommodation is provided as part of security arrangements.

Assets loaned to the employee for private use

If an employer lends an asset to an employee for private use, the employee is taxed each year on 20% of the market value of the asset on the date of the loan. If the asset is subsequently sold or given to the employee, tax is also charged on the *greater* of:

(a) the market value of the asset when sold or given to the employee, less any amount paid for the asset by the employee, and

(b) the market value of the asset when first loaned to the employee, less the amounts already assessed to tax during the period of the loan, less any amount paid for the asset by the employee.

The loan of a bicycle and cycling safety equipment is exempt from tax if used wholly or mainly for travel between home and work.

EXAMPLE 3

On 6 April 2020, an employer purchases a music system for £800 and immediately lends the system to an employee for his private use. The system remains in the employee's possession until 6 October 2022 when the employee buys it from his employer for £100, its market value on that day being £240. Calculate the taxable benefit in kind for tax years 2020-21 to 2022-23 inclusive.

Solution

			£
2020-21	20% of £800		160
2021-22	20% of £800		160
2022-23	20% of £800 x 6/12	80	
	plus, the greater of:		
	(i) £240 – £100 = £140		
	(ii) £800 – £160 – £160 – £80 – £100 = £300	300	380
Total benefit assessed to tax over period of the loan			700

Ancillary services connected with living accommodation

An employee who is provided with living accommodation is charged to tax not only on the accommodation itself but also on the cost to the employer of providing any "ancillary services" in connection with that accommodation. Ancillary services include such items as heating and lighting, repairs and maintenance and cleaning. The provision of furniture for the employee's use is also included under the heading of ancillary services and is taxed as a loaned asset (see above). Note that:

(a) The taxable benefit in relation to ancillary services is reduced by any contribution made by the employee towards their cost (*if made by 6 July following the tax year*).

(b) In the case of job-related accommodation, the taxable benefit with regard to ancillary services cannot exceed 10% of the employee's net earnings for the year, less any contribution made by the employee. Net earnings are defined for this purpose as total earnings for the year (apart from the ancillary services) less allowable expenses.

EXAMPLE 4

In 2022-23, an employer provides living accommodation for an employee. The employer also provides the following services in connection with this accommodation:

	£
Heating, lighting and cleaning	1,890
Repairs and maintenance	1,235
Loan of furniture, cost to the employer	13,000

The employee contributes £100 each month towards these services and has net earnings for the year (excluding the ancillary services) of £42,500. Compute the taxable benefit.

Solution

If the accommodation is not job-related, the taxable benefit is £4,525 (£1,890 + £1,235 + 20% of £13,000, less £1,200). If the accommodation is job-related, the taxable benefit is limited to 10% of £42,500, less £1,200 = £3,050.

Cars provided for private use

An employee is taxed on the provision of a motor car unless the car is totally unavailable for the employee's private use. The taxable benefit is based upon the list price of the car when new (even if the employer bought the car for less than list price or bought it second-hand) and is adjusted according to the car's level of carbon dioxide emissions. The main features of the method of computation are as follows:

(a) The price of the car for the purpose of calculating the benefit in kind is the sum of:

   (i) the list price of the car when new, including standard accessories

   (ii) the cost of all optional accessories (other than mobile telephones) fitted to the car before it is made available to the employee

   (iii) the cost of any optional accessories (other than mobile telephones) costing £100 or more and fitted to the car after it is made available to the employee.

   Accessories acquired to enable a disabled person to use the car are excluded, as are security features (e.g. armour plating) for employees who can demonstrate that their employment creates a threat to their personal security.

(b) The taxable benefit is based upon the price of the car, less any capital contribution (up to a maximum of £5,000) made by the employee towards the car's cost.

(c) If the car is a "classic car", the car's market value at the end of the tax year is used instead of list price when calculating the taxable benefit. A classic car is one which is over 15 years old at the end of the tax year and has a market value at the end of the year exceeding £15,000 and exceeding the price calculated at (a) above.

(d) The taxable benefit for a tax year is calculated by applying a percentage to the figure calculated at (b) above. The appropriate percentage depends upon the car's level of carbon dioxide emissions (rounded down to the nearest 5g/km if over 75g/km). For tax year 2022-23 this percentage is computed in accordance with the table below:

Carbon dioxide emissions (grams per kilometre)	Applicable percentage
Zero emissions	2%
1-50g/km:	
electric range[†] 130 miles or more	2%
electric range 70-129 miles	5%
electric range 40-69 miles	8%
electric range 30-39 miles	12%
electric range less than 30 miles	14%
51g/km to 54g/km	15%
55g/km to 59g/km	16%
60g/km to 64g/km	17%
65g/km to 69g/km	18%
70g/km to 74g/km	19%
75g/km	20%
each additional 5g/km	1% increase

The <u>maximum</u> applicable percentage is 37% in all cases.

[†] *The "electric range" of a motor car is defined as the furthest distance for which the car can be driven in electric mode without recharging the battery.*

(e) The applicable percentage is generally increased by a further 4% for cars propelled solely by diesel fuel, unless the car meets the Real Driving Emissions Step 2 standard. But the maximum applicable percentage remains at 37% regardless.

(f) If a disabled employee is obliged by his or her disability to drive a car with automatic transmission, the taxable benefit is based upon the price (if lower) and emission rating (if lower) of the equivalent car with manual transmission.

(g) If a car is made available to the employee for only part of the year, the benefit in that year is reduced proportionately, depending upon the number of days for which the car is made available. This also applies if the car is unusable for a continuous period of at least 30 days in the year.

(h) Finally, the taxable benefit is reduced by any contribution made by the employee to the employer for private use of the car (*as long as this contribution is paid by 6 July following the end of the tax year to which it relates*).

EXAMPLE 5

(a) Throughout the whole of tax year 2022-23, Lucy is provided by her employer with a motor car with a list price of £27,400. The car does not use diesel fuel. Lucy contributed £4,000 towards the car's purchase price and she pays her employer £100 per month for her private use of the car. Calculate the taxable benefit arising in 2022-23 if the car has an emission rating of:

(i) 43g/km (electric range 35 miles)
(ii) 52g/km (iii) 91g/km (iv) 148g/km (v) 174g/km

Also re-calculate the taxable benefits in cases (ii), (iii), (iv) and (v) as they would be if the car ran solely on diesel fuel and did not comply with the RDE2 standard.

(b) During 2022-23, Luke is provided by his employer with the use of a petrol-driven car first registered in 2019 with a list price at that time of £21,000. His employer bought the car for £16,700 in 2021. The car's emission rating is 116g/km. Calculate the taxable benefit in 2022-23 if:

(i) the car is available to Luke throughout the entire year
(ii) the car is made available to Luke only from 6 November 2022.

Solution

(a) The capital contribution reduces the price of the car to £23,400. If the car is not diesel-driven, the taxable benefit in each case is as follows:

(i) 12% x £23,400 = £2,808, less £1,200 = £1,608.

(ii) 15% x £23,400 = £3,510, less £1,200 = £2,310.
(Note that 52g/km is not rounded down to 50g/km.)

(iii) 20% + 3% = 23% x £23,400 = £5,382, less £1,200 = £4,182.
(The car's emission rating is rounded down to 90g/km. This exceeds 75g/km by 15g/km, which is three multiples of 5g/km.)

(iv) 20% + 14% = 34% x £23,400 = £7,956, less £1,200 = £6,756.

(v) 37% x £23,400 = £8,658, less £1,200 = £7,458.

In cases (ii) to (v), if the car is diesel-driven and does not meet standard RDE2, the percentage is increased by 4% (but cannot exceed 37%). The taxable benefits are:

(ii) 15% + 4% = 19% × £23,400 = £4,446, less £1,200 = £3,246.

(iii) 23% + 4% = 27% x £23,400 = £6,318, less £1,200 = £5,118.

(iv) 37% x £23,400 = £8,658, less £1,200 = £7,458.

(v) 37% x £23,400 = £8,658, less £1,200 = £7,458.

(b) The fact that Luke's employer bought the car for £16,700 is irrelevant. The benefit is based on the list price of the car and the applicable percentage is 28% (20% + 8%).

(i) 28% x £21,000 = £5,880.

(ii) 28% x £21,000 = £5,880 x 5/12 = £2,450.

Pool cars

A "pool car" is one which satisfies all of the following criteria:

(a) it is not used by one employee exclusively,

(b) it is not normally kept at an employee's residence overnight,

(c) any private use by an employee is merely incidental to its use for business purposes.

If all these criteria are satisfied, no taxable benefit will arise in relation to the car.

Car fuel provided for private use

The taxable benefit described above covers the cost of providing the car itself, together with the costs of vehicle excise duty, insurance and maintenance. But a separate taxable benefit arises if the employer also provides the employee with fuel for private motoring[†]. Fuel benefit for a tax year is calculated by applying the same percentage as was used in the calculation of the car benefit to a fixed amount set by the Government for that tax year. *For 2022-23 this amount is £25,300.* The tax charge is reduced proportionately if the car is not made available to the employee for the whole of the tax year and is normally reduced if the employee receives fuel for private use for only part of the year. However, a full year's tax charge arises if fuel for private use ceases to be provided at some point during the tax year but is then provided again later in that same year.

It is important to appreciate that the taxable fuel benefit is <u>not</u> reduced by any partial contribution made by the employee towards the cost of private fuel. There is no taxable benefit if the employee pays the full cost of all private fuel (*as long as payment is made by 6 July following the tax year*). Otherwise, the benefit is calculated as above, ignoring any partial contribution towards fuel costs.

[†] *For these purposes, the word "fuel" does not include electricity. Nor does it include any form of energy supplied for a car which cannot in any circumstances emit carbon dioxide.*

EXAMPLE 6

Throughout 2022-23, Deepika is provided with a petrol-engined motor car (113g/km) for business and private use. Her employer pays all running costs. The cost of the petrol used for private motoring is £1,795. Calculate the taxable fuel benefit arising in 2022-23 if the amount that Deepika reimburses to her employer for the cost of private fuel is:

(a) £nil   (b) £1,795   (c) £1,750

Solution

(a) 20% + 7% = 27% x £25,300 = £6,831.

(b) £nil, since Deepika pays the full cost of private fuel (presumably by 6 July 2023)

(c) Deepika's contribution is less than 100% and so the taxable benefit is £6,831.

Vans provided for private use

No taxable benefit arises if a motor van is made available to an employee mainly for business use and the employee is not allowed to use the van for private journeys other than ordinary commuting between home and work. But if a motor van is made available with no restrictions as to private use, the employee is normally liable to income tax on a taxable benefit (for 2022-23) of £3,600. Note that:

(a) The taxable benefit is reduced proportionately if the van is made available to the employee for only part of the tax year and is also reduced by any amount which the employee pays to the employer for private use of the van (*if paid by 6 July following the end of the tax year concerned*).

(b) A further taxable benefit arises if the employer provides fuel for unrestricted private use, with no reduction for any partial contribution made by the employee towards the cost of such fuel. The amount of this taxable benefit for 2022-23 is £688.

(c) No taxable benefit arises in relation to a heavy goods vehicle (a van weighing more than 3,500kg) unless the vehicle is used wholly or mainly for private purposes.

However, the taxable benefit arising in relation to a "zero-emission" van in 2022-23 is £nil. For this purpose, a zero-emission van is defined by ITEPA 2003 as one which "*cannot in any circumstances emit CO_2 by being driven*".

Beneficial loans

A beneficial loan is one that is granted by an employer to an employee (or to a relative of the employee) either interest-free or at a rate of interest which is less than the "official rate". Employees are taxed on the difference between the interest actually payable to the employer and the interest that would have been payable at the official rate. Note that:

(a) Loans made in the ordinary course of an employer's money-lending business and made on the same terms and conditions as loans made to the general public are ignored. Loans which qualify for tax relief (see Chapter 4) are also ignored. A loan made to a relative of an employee is ignored if the employee derives no personal benefit from the loan.

(b) No taxable benefit arises in connection with a loan made in the normal course of the employer's domestic, family or personal relationships.

(c) No taxable benefit arises if the total amount outstanding on all beneficial loans made to an employee, apart from those covered by (a) and (b) above, does not exceed £10,000 at any time during the tax year.

If a loan made by an employer to an employee (by reason of the employment) is wholly or partly written off, the amount written off is generally charged to income tax in the tax year in which the write-off takes place. This applies whether or not the loan is a beneficial loan. However, no taxable benefit arises if a loan is written off on the death of the employee.

EXAMPLE 7

Adam has the following four loans from his employer:

(a) A £96,000 loan at interest of 1% p.a. to enable Adam to buy his own home.

(b) An interest-free season ticket loan of £10,000.

(c) A £15,000 personal loan at interest of 1.5% p.a.

(d) A £4,000 loan to buy necessary equipment for use in his employment.

The full amount of each loan was outstanding at 6 April 2022 and no repayments were made during 2022-23. Calculate Adam's taxable benefit in 2022-23 (assuming an official rate of interest of 2% per annum).

Solution

The £4,000 loan is a qualifying loan and is ignored. The remaining loans total more than £10,000 and so give rise to taxable benefits. The amount assessed to tax is:

	£
£96,000 x (2% – 1%)	960
£10,000 x 2%	200
£15,000 x (2% – 1.5%)	75
	1,235

Beneficial loans which vary during the year

In the above example, it was assumed that the amount of the loans did not vary during the tax year. However, if the amount of a beneficial loan does vary during the year, the taxable benefit can be calculated in one of two ways:

(a) **Normal method**. The amount of the loan at the start of the tax year (or when the loan began, if later) and at the end of the tax year (or when the loan ended, if earlier) are averaged and multiplied by the average official rate for the year. If the loan began or ended during the year, the result of this calculation is multiplied by the number of months for which the loan was outstanding in the year and divided by 12.

Interest actually paid by the employee (if any) is then subtracted, giving the taxable benefit.

(b) **Alternative method**. Interest at the official rate is calculated precisely on the day-to-day outstanding balance. Any interest paid by the employee is then subtracted, giving the taxable benefit.

The first method is easier and is generally used. However, either the employee concerned or HMRC may insist that the alternative method should be used. The employee will presumably do so if this results in a lower taxable benefit. HMRC may do so if it appears that the normal method is being deliberately exploited for tax avoidance purposes.

Salary sacrifice

An optional remuneration (or "salary sacrifice") agreement allows employees to give up part of their salary in exchange for benefits in kind. Until 6 April 2017, such an agreement could generate a tax saving if the benefits concerned were exempt from tax or if the value of the benefits for tax purposes was less than the amount of salary foregone.

However, as from 6 April 2017, the taxable value of benefits in kind provided through salary sacrifice agreements is fixed at the *greater* of:

(a) the value of those benefits calculated in the normal way, and

(b) the amount of salary which has been sacrificed.

This rule applies even if the benefits in question are normally exempt from tax. But certain benefits are specifically excluded from the rule, including employer-provided pensions and pensions advice, childcare, cycle to work benefits and the provision of cars with emissions not exceeding 75g/km.

Summary

▶ Employees are taxed on the cost of employer-provided benefits in kind. But benefits costing no more than £50 (and satisfying certain criteria) are regarded as "trivial" and are exempt from income tax.

▶ The taxable benefit arising in relation to living accommodation is generally based on the annual value of the property concerned. The benefit increases if the property cost more than £75,000. No benefit arises if the accommodation is job-related.

▶ An asset loaned to an employee gives rise to an annual taxable benefit equal to 20% of the value of the asset on the date of the loan. A further benefit may arise if the asset is subsequently sold or given to the employee.

▶ Employees are taxed on any ancillary services provided in connection with living accommodation. The tax charge is capped if the accommodation is job-related.

▶ The amount of the taxable benefit arising in relation to a motor car provided to an employee for private use depends primarily on the car's list price and its carbon dioxide emissions. A further benefit will arise if the employee is provided with fuel for private motoring and does not fully reimburse the employer for the cost of this fuel.

▶ Taxable benefits may also arise in connection with the provision by an employer of motor vans and fuel for private use by employees.

▶ If an employee is provided with a beneficial loan, the employee is generally taxed on the difference between the loan interest actually payable (if any) and the interest that would have been payable at the official rate.

Exercises

A set of multiple choice questions for this chapter is available on the accompanying website.

8.1   Kim lives in a house provided by her employer. The house cost her employer £246,500 in 2020 and a further £28,500 was spent on improvements in 2021. The house has a gross rateable value of £4,200 and it has been agreed with HMRC that there is 12% business use. Kim pays rent of £400 per month to her employer for her private use of the house. Compute the taxable benefit in 2022-23 (the official rate of interest is 2% p.a.).

8.2   Throughout 2022-23, Niall is provided by his employer with a diesel-engined motor car which had a list price when new of £54,200. The car has an emission rating of 129g/km. Niall's employer pays all of the car's running expenses including fuel for private use. Compute the taxable benefit in 2022-23.

8.3   On 1 July 2022, Alexander was provided by his employer with an interest-free loan of £20,000. He repays £5,000 of this loan on 1 January 2023 and repays another £3,000 on 1 March 2023. Compute the taxable benefit in 2022-23 using:

(a)   the normal method   (b)   the alternative method.

Assume that the official rate of interest is 2% per annum. Perform all calculations to the nearest month and to the nearest pound.

*8.4   Emma is the sales director of a company. She earns an annual salary of £95,000 together with a bonus (received in September each year) based on the company's profits for the accounting year ending on the previous 30 June. She also receives a general expenses allowance of £8,000 per annum, which she uses for business travel and entertaining. The company provides her with a new BMW motor car every two years and pays all running costs. She has an interest-free loan from the company of £20,000 and the company pays her annual subscription to a private medical insurance scheme, costing £1,850. Explain the taxation implications of each of the elements of Emma's remuneration package.

*8.5   Jim is the managing director of a company and earns a basic salary in 2022-23 of £225,000. He receives benefits from the company during the year as follows:

(a)   He is provided with the use of a company house which has an annual value of £9,750 and which cost his employer £445,000 in 2019. Jim makes no contribution towards the cost of the house or towards its running costs which cost the company £5,450 in 2022-23. The company has also furnished the house at a cost of £38,500. Jim's occupation of the house is not job-related.

(b)   He is provided with a petrol-engined company car which had a list price when new of £45,000. The car has an emission rating of 103g/km and the company pays all running costs.

(c)   He is provided with a company loan of £50,000 on which he is charged interest at 0.5% per annum.

Calculate Jim's taxable benefits in 2022-23 (the official rate of interest is 2% p.a.).

Chapter 9

Income from self-employment: Computation of income

Introduction

This is the first of five chapters which deal with income from self-employment. The profits of a self-employed person are charged to income tax by the Income Tax (Trading and Other Income) Act 2005 and the main purpose of this chapter is to show how those profits are calculated for tax purposes. Subsequent chapters deal with related topics such as tax relief for capital expenditure, the tax treatment of trading losses and partnerships.

A self-employed person may be conducting a trade or may be exercising a profession or vocation. However, the profits of trades, professions and vocations are all taxed in accordance with the same set of rules. Therefore, both in this chapter and in subsequent chapters, references to "trades" and "trading" should be assumed to include professions and vocations. Similarly, the terms "trader" and "sole trader" will be used to refer to any self-employed person, regardless of whether that person is actually conducting a trade or is in fact exercising a profession or vocation.

The badges of trade

ITTOIA 2005 states that the trading profits of a person who is resident in the UK are chargeable to income tax wherever the trade is carried on. The trading profits of a non-UK resident are generally chargeable to income tax only if the trade is carried on wholly or partly in the UK (see Chapter 32). When deciding whether or not a person is trading it is necessary to make two important distinctions:

(a) the distinction between employment and self-employment (see Chapter 7)

(b) in the case of a person who sells goods or other assets, the distinction between trading activities (which give rise to trading profits) and non-trading activities (which will usually fall within the scope of capital gains tax).

Section 989 of the Income Tax Act 2007 states that a "trade" includes "*any venture in the nature of trade*". This circular definition is of little real help and therefore it has been left largely to the courts to decide whether or not a given activity constitutes trading.

The main criteria which have arisen from case law decisions and which may be used to distinguish between trading and non-trading activities are known as the "badges of trade". They are as follows:

(a) **Subject matter of the transaction**

If a taxpayer sells assets of a type which might normally be acquired for personal enjoyment or held as a source of income, this may suggest that any profit arising on their sale should be treated as a capital gain rather than a trading profit.

But if the assets concerned do not provide personal enjoyment and do not yield income, it would seem that the only way in which they could be turned to advantage is by selling them. In these circumstances, any profit arising on their sale might be treated as a trading profit. In *Martin* v *Lowry* (1926), the taxpayer bought and sold a huge quantity of war surplus linen. In *Rutledge* v *CIR* (1929), the taxpayer bought and sold one million toilet rolls. In both of these cases, it was held that the subject matter of the transaction was such that the activity must be construed as trading.

(b) **Length of the period of ownership**

Trading stocks are normally retained for only a short period before being sold, whereas assets acquired for personal use or as a source of income are generally retained for longer. Therefore, if assets are bought and sold within a short space of time it is more likely that any profit made will be treated as a trading profit.

(c) **Frequency of transactions**

The more often that a taxpayer repeats a certain type of transaction, the more likely it is that the activity will be construed as trading. In *Pickford* v *Quirke* (1927), the taxpayer bought a cotton mill and then sold off its assets at a profit. This was the fourth time that the taxpayer had carried out this particular type of transaction and therefore he was held to be trading.

(d) **Supplementary work**

A taxpayer who buys an asset, performs some work on the asset so as to make it more saleable and then sells the asset is more likely to be regarded as trading than someone who simply buys and sells an asset without performing any supplementary work. In *Cape Brandy Syndicate* v *CIR* (1921), a group of individuals bought a large quantity of brandy which they first blended and then sold. They were held to be trading.

(e) **Reason for the sale**

The circumstances which have prompted the sale of an asset might be taken into account when deciding whether trading has occurred. A sale necessitated by a sudden urgent need for cash is less likely to be regarded as a trading activity than a sale made in the normal course of events.

(f) **Motive**

The presence of a profit motive in the mind of the taxpayer when acquiring an asset provides strong evidence of trading. In *Wisdom* v *Chamberlain* (1969), the taxpayer acquired silver bullion to counter the effects of a possible devaluation of the pound. His only motive was to sell the silver at a profit. He was held to be trading.

However, this test is not always conclusive. After all, many investments are bought at least partially with a view to their eventual sale at a profit and yet such profits are generally treated as capital gains. This point emphasises the need to consider the evidence provided by *all* of the badges of trade (not just one) when trying to decide whether or not trading has occurred.

Since trading requires the presence of a profit motive when the asset was acquired, the sale of an asset which was originally acquired by inheritance or gift (or in any way otherwise than by purchase) is very unlikely to be construed as trading.

The calculation of trading profits

The computation of a self-employed person's trading profit should begin with the net profit shown by that person's accounts. For tax purposes, trading profits are normally calculated in accordance with generally accepted accounting practice, which means that income and expenditure should be measured on the accruals basis[†].

It is usually necessary to make a number of adjustments to the net profit shown by the accounts in order to arrive at the trading profit for tax purposes These adjustments can be summarised as follows:

	£	£
Net profit shown by the accounts		xxx
Add: Expenditure shown in the accounts but not deductible for tax purposes	xxx	
Trading income not shown in the accounts	xxx	xxx
		xxx
Less: Expenditure deductible for tax purposes but not shown in the accounts	xxx	
Non-trading income shown in the accounts	xxx	xxx
Trading profit adjusted for tax purposes		xxx

Each of these adjustments is explained in this chapter.

[†] *Small businesses (with receipts not exceeding a stipulated threshold) may now choose to adopt the cash basis when calculating their profits for tax purposes. Furthermore, all businesses have the option of using simplified "fixed rate deductions" to calculate some of their expenses (whether or not the cash basis is adopted). An explanation of the cash basis rules and the rules relating to simplified expenses is given at the end of this chapter.*

Deductibility of expenditure

In general, expenditure is deductible (allowable) when computing trading profits only if it is incurred *wholly and exclusively for the purposes of the trade*. This rule is much less restrictive than the "wholly, exclusively and necessarily" rule applied to the expenses of an employee (see Chapter 7) but it does have the following implications:

(a) Expenditure which has no connection with the trade is disallowed (the "remoteness test"). In *Strong & Co of Romsey Ltd* v *Woodifield* (1906), damages paid by a brewery to a hotel guest injured by a falling chimney were disallowed. These damages were incurred by the brewery in its capacity as a property owner, not in its capacity as a trader, and therefore failed the remoteness test.

(b) Expenditure which serves both a business purpose and a private purpose cannot be allowed in full (the "duality test"). If the expenditure can be apportioned with reasonable accuracy, then the private element is disallowed. However, in *Mallalieu* v *Drummond* (1983), the cost of sober clothing worn in court by a lady barrister was wholly disallowed, since it was not possible to apportion the cost of the clothing between the part which satisfied professional standards of dress and the part which simply provided warmth and decency.

Even if expenditure passes both of these tests it may still be disallowed by statute.

Disallowed expenditure

Certain classes of expenditure are disallowed (either by statute or by case law) when computing trading profits. If any of these types of expenditure have been deducted in the accounts of a self-employed person, then the amount of the expenditure must be "added back" to the profit shown by the accounts in order to arrive at the trading profit for tax purposes. The main classes of disallowed expenditure are identified below.

Capital expenditure

Capital expenditure is specifically disallowed by ITTOIA 2005. However, the Act does not provide a definition of the term "capital". Consequently, there is a great deal of case law on this subject, much of which is concerned with distinguishing between repairs (which are allowable) and improvements (disallowed as capital expenditure). In *Atherton* v *British Insulated & Helsby Cables Ltd* (1926), it was stated that capital expenditure is such that it brings an "enduring benefit" to the business, and this test is still widely used. The following capital-related expenses are also disallowed:

(a) legal or professional fees incurred in relation to an item of capital expenditure

(b) depreciation and amortisation charges (and losses on disposal of non-current assets) although capital allowances may be available instead (see Chapter 11).

Even repairs may be disallowed if they relate to a newly acquired asset and the repairs are required in order to put the asset into usable condition. In the case of *Law Shipping Co Ltd v CIR* (1923), the costs of putting a newly acquired ship into seaworthy condition were disallowed for this reason. However, repairs to a newly acquired asset which was usable before the repairs were carried out are generally allowed. In the case of *Odeon Associated Theatres Ltd v Jones* (1971), repairs to cinemas which had been purchased in a state of disrepair (but were nonetheless usable) were allowed.

In general, a repair restores an asset to its original condition, whereas an improvement makes the asset better than it was originally. The use of modern materials in the course of a repair may give the impression of an improvement, but the work will still be classed as a repair unless the asset's functionality has been enhanced. On these grounds, HMRC now takes the view that the replacement of old windows by modern double-glazed windows should normally be classed as a repair rather than an improvement.

Appropriations of profit

Appropriations of profit made by the owner of a business (whether these are described as drawings, owner's salary or anything else) are disallowed. The owner's personal income tax payments and personal National Insurance contributions are also disallowed.

Provisions

Provisions are allowed so long as they are in respect of revenue expenditure and are made in accordance with generally accepted accounting practice. However, a provision will be disallowed if it cannot be estimated with sufficient accuracy.

Transfers to a *general* provision for doubtful debts (which is perhaps more correctly referred to as an "allowance" rather than a "provision") are disallowed when computing trading profits, since the amount involved is insufficiently accurate. The same is true of transfers to other general provisions (e.g. a general stock provision). However, transfers to *specific* provisions are normally allowable.

Entertainment and gifts

The cost of business entertainment (e.g. customer entertaining) is disallowed. The cost of staff entertaining (e.g. a staff party) is allowable but the employees concerned may incur an income tax liability on a benefit in kind if the amount involved exceeds specified limits (see Chapter 7). The cost of gifts is also disallowed, other than:

(a) gifts to employees, if made wholly and exclusively for trade purposes

(b) samples of trading stock given to the public so as to advertise the business

(c) gifts to customers which display a conspicuous advertisement for the business, cost no more than £50 per customer per year and do not consist of food, drink or tobacco

(d) gifts of trading stock (or inventory) or used plant and machinery to designated UK educational establishments, charities or community amateur sports clubs

(e)   reasonable gifts made by an employer for the benefit of employees (e.g. a gift to a local general hospital, or a gift to a trade charity which exists primarily for the purpose of helping workers in the employer's trade category).

Charitable donations made within the Gift Aid scheme are given tax relief under the Gift Aid rules and are disallowed when computing trading profits (see Chapter 4).

Political donations

Political donations and subscriptions are usually disallowed. But political donations which result in a definite benefit to the trade may be allowed. In *Morgan* v *Tate & Lyle Ltd* (1954), the costs of a political campaign against nationalisation were allowed on the grounds that the campaign was waged for the survival of the trade.

Non-trade bad debts

Bad debts incurred in the course of trade are allowable. But loans written off are generally not allowable unless:

(a)   the taxpayer is in the business of lending money and the loan concerned was made in the course of trade, or

(b)   the loan was to an employee and was made by reason of the employment and for trade purposes; in this case, the amount of the written-off loan will usually be taxable on the employee as income from employment (see Chapter 8).

Transfers to a *specific* bad debts provision (or allowance) are allowable but transfers to a *general* provision are usually disallowed, as stated earlier. Bad debts recovered and reductions in a specific bad debts provision are both treated as trading income.

EXAMPLE

A sole trader's income statement for the year to 30 June 2022 shows an expense of £923 in relation to bad and doubtful debts. This expense comprises:

	£
Trade debts written off	812
Trade debts previously written off, now recovered	(42)
Staff loan written off	50
Increase in general allowance for doubtful debts	103
	923

The staff loan written off was not made for trade purposes.

(a)   How much of the £923 charged to the income statement for the year should be added back when computing trading profits for tax purposes?

(b)   How would this differ if the allowance for doubtful debts was a specific allowance rather than a general allowance?

Solution

(a) The staff loan written off (non-trade) of £50 and the increase of £103 in the general allowance for doubtful debts are disallowed, so a total of £153 should be added back when calculating the trading profits for tax purposes.

(b) If the allowance for doubtful debts was specific (rather than general) the increase of £103 would be allowable, so only £50 would be added back when calculating the trading profits for tax purposes.

Fines and penalties

Fines or penalties incurred because of infringements of the law are generally disallowed. But an exception occurs if an employer pays parking fines incurred by employees whilst on their employer's business. Such payments are usually allowed when computing trading profits but may then be assessed on the employees as income from employment.

Criminal payments

A payment is disallowed if the making of the payment constitutes a criminal offence (e.g. a bribe). Payments to blackmailers or extortionists are also disallowed.

Allowable expenditure

As explained earlier in this chapter, expenditure is generally allowable when computing trading profits if it has been incurred wholly and exclusively for trade purposes and is not specifically disallowed by statute. Apart from the disallowed items listed above, most of the expenditure shown in a typical income statement (or profit and loss account) will probably be allowable but the following points should be noted:

(a) **Interest**. Interest, including credit card and overdraft interest, is allowable if it is incurred for trade purposes. But interest paid on overdue tax is disallowed.

(b) **Legal and professional fees**. Legal and professional fees relating to items of capital expenditure are specifically disallowed (see above), but fees incurred for other trade purposes are normally allowable. For example, fees are allowed if incurred in connection with such matters as the collection of trade debts, obtaining loan finance, the renewal of a short lease (a lease of up to 50 years), a legal action for breach of contract or the preservation of trading rights.

Audit and accountancy fees incurred in relation to the preparation of accounts and the agreement of tax liabilities are normally allowed. Fees incurred in relation to a tax investigation by HMRC are incurred in the role of taxpayer rather than trader and are generally disallowed unless no profit adjustment arises from the investigation. The cost of tax appeals is disallowed, even if successful.

(c) **Short lease premiums**. A premium paid for the grant of a short lease of business premises (i.e. 50 years or less) is discounted according to the length of the lease and is then deductible† in equal annual instalments over the lease term (see Chapter 5).

A reverse premium received by a tenant using premises for business purposes is taxable as trading income.

† *This deduction is not available if the cash basis is adopted (see later in this chapter).*

(d) **Damages**. The costs of civil damages paid for injury to others are allowable if caused by trading operations. But penalties for breaches of the law are not allowed.

(e) **Value added tax**. If a trader pays VAT in relation to an item of expenditure and is unable to reclaim that VAT (see Chapter 30), the amount of VAT suffered will be allowable so long as the item of expenditure is itself allowable.

(f) **Trade subscriptions**. Subscriptions payable to professional and trade associations are generally regarded as having been incurred for the purposes of the trade and are allowable. Political subscriptions are generally disallowed.

(g) **Employees' remuneration**. Employees' remuneration is allowable if it is genuinely expended for business purposes. In *Copeman v Flood (William) & Sons Ltd* (1941), it was held that large fees paid to family members could be allowed only to the extent that they were reasonable in relation to the duties performed. Employer's National Insurance contributions (see Chapter 16) are also allowable.

Remuneration which is not actually paid to employees within nine months of the end of the period of account in which it is accrued is disallowed in that period but allowed in the period of payment.

Employers' contributions to registered pension schemes (see Chapter 14) are allowed in the *period of account in which they are paid*.

Redundancy payments and compensation payments made for loss of employment are generally allowable. On a cessation of trade, contractual redundancy payments, statutory redundancy payments and non-contractual redundancy payments of up to three times the statutory amount are all allowed.

The cost of educational courses provided for employees is allowable if incurred for trade purposes. The cost of retraining employees who are about to leave (or have recently left) is allowed subject to certain conditions. The cost of temporarily seconding an employee to a charity or educational establishment is allowable.

(h) **Staff defalcations**. Losses caused by the dishonesty of an employee are normally allowable. But, following the decision in *Curtis v J & G Oldfield Ltd* (1925), the defalcations of a person having control over the business (e.g. a business partner) are not allowed.

(i) **Travel expenses**. The cost of business travel is allowable but the cost of travelling between home and work is generally disallowed. In *Newsom v Robertson* (1952), the travelling expenses of a barrister between his home and his legal chambers were disallowed. But in *Horton v Young* (1971), the travelling expenses of a self-employed bricklayer between his home and the sites at which he worked was allowed, on the grounds that his business was conducted from his home.

As explained at the end of this chapter, unincorporated businesses may choose to use the "fixed rate deduction scheme" to calculate the expenses allowed in relation to a motor vehicle. No other motor expenses or capital allowances may then be claimed in relation to the vehicle concerned.

(j) **Leased cars**. The amount of the lease rental payments allowed in relation to a leased car is restricted if the car has emissions exceeding 50g/km (*110g/km if the lease began before 6 April 2021*). The restriction takes the form of a disallowance of 15% of the lease payments, but does not apply if the car is leased for no more than 45 days.

(k) **Patent royalties**. Patent royalties that are paid for trade purposes are allowable. The cost of registering a patent (or trademark) is also allowable.

(l) **Pre-trading expenditure**. Expenditure incurred during the seven years before starting to trade is treated as if incurred on the first day of trading and is allowable so long as the expenditure is of a type which would normally be allowable.

Expenditure not shown in the accounts

The most common example of allowable expenditure not being shown in the accounts of a business is the trader's claim (if any) to capital allowances (see Chapter 11).

Another instance of allowable expenditure not shown in the accounts is a premium paid for the grant of a short lease. As explained earlier, part of such a premium is deductible from trading income in equal annual instalments over the lease period. If the premium is being amortised in the accounts, the amortisation charges are added back and the allowable amount of the premium (see Chapter 5) is deducted instead.

Adjustments relating to income

Most of the adjustments required when calculating trading profits for tax purposes are concerned with business expenditure. But further adjustments might be needed in relation to the income of the business. These adjustments are as follows:

(a) **Non-trading income shown in the accounts**. Any non-trading income which is shown in the accounts of a business must be deducted from the net profit figure when computing trading profits. The main categories of non-trading income which might be found in the accounts of a business are:

(i) income which is taxed under another heading (e.g. interest, property income)

(ii) profits on the disposal of non-current assets; these are normally depreciation adjustments but a genuine gain may be chargeable to capital gains tax

(iii) decreases in general provisions or allowances.

(b) **Trading income not shown in the accounts**. A common example of trading income not being shown in the accounts of a business occurs when the owner appropriates trading stock (inventory) for personal use. This is referred to as "own consumption".

In this situation, generally accepted accounting practice (GAAP) would suggest that the cost of the goods concerned, less any contribution made by the owner, should be credited to the income statement. But ITTOIA 2005 requires that own consumption of trading stock is accounted for at *market value*. This means that the trading profit of the business for tax purposes should be increased by the *selling price* of the goods, less any contribution made by the owner. For this purpose, "trading stock" consists of goods that are sold in the ordinary course of trade (including partially manufactured stock) but does not include raw materials (which are accounted for at cost).

This rule puts onto a statutory basis the view that was originally expressed in the famous case of *Sharkey* v *Wernher* (1955). In this case, horses were transferred from a farm to the owner's private stables and it was held that the profits of the farm should be increased, for tax purposes, by the full market value of those horses.

Post-cessation receipts

Post-cessation receipts are sums received after a person permanently ceases trading and which arise from the carrying on of the trade prior to cessation. Such receipts fall within the scope of ITTOIA 2005 and are chargeable to income tax.

Deductions are allowed for any expenses incurred which would have been deductible in calculating the profits of the trade if it had not ceased.

Trading income allowance

Gross trading income of up to £1,000 per annum (before deduction of expenses) is automatically exempt from income tax and the profit or loss for the tax year concerned is treated as £nil. Note, however, that a self-employed person may elect to disapply this exemption and presumably will do so if a trading loss has been incurred in the year and tax relief is sought for this loss (see Chapter 12).

If gross trading income for the tax year exceeds £1,000, the person may elect to be taxed on the excess of gross income over £1,000 (with no deduction for expenses). Otherwise, trading income is calculated by deducting expenses from gross income in the usual way.

This "trading income allowance" is primarily of benefit to "micro-entrepreneurs" with very low amounts of trading income[†]. If an individual's gross trading income for a tax year does not exceed £1,000, there is no need to declare this income to HMRC or to pay tax on it. Individuals with gross trading income which exceeds the allowance may calculate their trading profit by simply deducting £1,000 from the gross figure.

Both of the elections referred to above must be made by 31 January in the second tax year following the tax year to which the election relates.

[†] *A similar allowance is available in relation to property income (see Chapter 5).*

Cash basis and simplified expenses

As stated earlier in this chapter, small unincorporated businesses may choose to calculate their profits for tax purposes on the cash basis. If this basis is applied, taxable profits for an accounting period are simply the difference between income actually received in the period and expenses actually paid. There is no need to adjust for receivables, payables or inventories. Nor is there any need to distinguish between capital expenditure and revenue expenditure. The main features of the cash basis are as follows:

(a) A self-employed person may use the cash basis in a tax year if his or her total trading receipts for that year do not exceed a stipulated threshold. Trading receipts for a tax year are the receipts of the basis period for that year (see Chapter 10). The threshold is currently £150,000, reduced proportionately for periods of less than 12 months.

(b) A person who starts to use the cash basis may continue on this basis in subsequent years even if trading receipts exceed the threshold in those years. However, the cash basis cannot be used if receipts exceed twice the threshold. A person may also voluntarily leave the cash basis and might do so if (for example) he/she wishes to claim "sideways relief" in relation to trading losses or if loan interest exceeds £500 p.a. (see below).

(c) Receipts are defined as all amounts received in connection with the business during the accounting period, including disposal proceeds of non-current assets.

(d) Expenses are defined as any payments made during the accounting period wholly and exclusively for business purposes, including capital expenditure. However, there are special rules relating to certain types of expenses. In particular:

   (i) Expenditure on buying a motor car is not deductible as an expense. Businesses may choose to claim fixed rate deductions in relation to their motoring expenses (see below) and these include an element of depreciation. But if the fixed rate deductions are not claimed, the business may claim capital allowances in relation to the purchase of a motor car (see Chapter 11).

   (ii) No deduction is allowed for capital expenditure on land and buildings or on non-depreciating assets. A depreciating asset is one with a useful life not exceeding 20 years or one which will decline in value by at least 90% in 20 years.

   (iii) Loan interest is allowable up to a maximum of £500.

(e) In the case of a VAT-registered business (see Chapter 29) receipts and expenses may be recorded either including or excluding VAT. If VAT is included, any payments of VAT to HMRC are treated as expenses and any VAT refunds are treated as receipts.

(f) Businesses which choose to adopt the cash basis are prohibited from claiming capital allowances (see Chapter 11) except in relation to motor cars.

(g) If a business which is using the cash basis incurs a trading loss, that loss can only be carried forward and set against any profits arising from the same trade in subsequent years. "Sideways relief" (see Chapter 12) is not available.

Simplified expenses

As stated earlier in this chapter, *any* unincorporated business may choose to use the "fixed rate deduction scheme" when calculating certain expenses for tax purposes. This scheme is available whether or not the business is small and whether or not it has adopted the cash basis. The expenses concerned are as follows:

(a) **Motor expenses**. Motor expenses in relation to a car, a goods vehicle or a motor cycle may be calculated with reference to specified mileage rates. At present, these are the same as the employee AMAP rates (see Chapter 7). If a fixed rate deduction is made in relation to a vehicle, no other expenses (or capital allowances) may be claimed in relation to the vehicle and use of the fixed rate deduction scheme is then compulsory for that vehicle in all future periods.

(b) **Use of home for business purposes**. A self-employed person who uses his or her home for business purposes may claim standard deductions based upon the number of hours spent working at home. These vary from £10 per month to £26 per month and cover expenses such as heat, light and power. A separate deduction may be claimed for the business proportion of telephone and broadband/internet costs.

(c) **Business premises used partly as a home**. If business premises are used partly as a home, the private proportion of expenses incurred in relation to the premises may be calculated as a fixed amount based upon the number of occupants. For instance, if there are two occupants, the private element is a standard £500 per month.

Summary

▸ A set of criteria known as the "badges of trade" may be used to distinguish between trading activities and non-trading activities.

▸ Expenditure is deductible when computing trading profits only if it is incurred wholly and exclusively for the purposes of the trade. Expenditure which is not so incurred is disallowed. Certain categories of expenditure are disallowed by statute.

▸ Any disallowed expenditure shown in a trader's accounts must be added back to the profit shown by those accounts when computing the trading profit for tax purposes.

▸ If the owner of a business takes trading stock for personal use, the full market value of that stock (less any amount paid by the owner) must be added to the net profit shown by the accounts when computing the trading profit.

▸ Non-trading income included in the accounts of a business must be deducted from the net profit shown by those accounts when computing the trading profit.

▸ Certain small businesses may choose to adopt the cash basis when calculating their profits for tax purposes. Unincorporated businesses may also apply simplified fixed rate deductions in relation to some of their expenses.

Exercises

It may be assumed in these exercises that (unless stated otherwise) the businesses concerned have not adopted the cash basis and do not use fixed rate deductions to calculate any of their expenses. A set of multiple choice questions for this chapter is available on the accompanying website.

9.1   List and explain the six badges of trade.

9.2   (a)   State the general rule which governs whether or not expenditure is deductible when computing trading profits.

(b)   Explain the "remoteness" test and the "duality" test and the consequences which ensue if an item of expenditure fails either of these tests.

9.3   Which of the following items of expenditure would be allowed when computing trading profits?

(a)   the salary paid to a sole trader's wife

(b)   a Gift Aid donation

(c)   a new machine bought for use by an engineering business

(d)   diaries costing £3 each given to customers

(e)   the cost of the annual staff outing to Blackpool

(f)   the black suit worn at work by a self-employed undertaker

(g)   the legal costs of acquiring new freehold premises

(h)   a subscription to the local chamber of commerce

(i)   cases of wine costing £49.99 each given to customers at Christmas

(j)   the legal costs of suing a trade debtor for non-payment.

9.4   Julian, a self-employed shopkeeper, takes goods costing £30 from his trading stock for his own personal use. If he had sold the stock to a customer he would have charged £45. When computing his trading profit, what adjustment would need to be made to the net profit shown by his accounts if:

(a)   he pays nothing for the goods?

(b)   he puts £30 of his own money into the till so as to pay for the goods?

(c)   he puts £45 of his own money into the till?

9.5   (a)   As from 1 January 2023, a motor car with a retail price of £21,000 is leased for four years at a cost of £300 per month. The car is used only for trade purposes and has an emission rating of 62g/km. How much of the monthly charge should be disallowed when calculating trading profits?

(b)   A sole trader is granted a 15-year lease on premises which he uses for business purposes. He pays a premium of £15,000 and writes off £1,000 per year in his business accounts. How much of the £1,000 should be disallowed each year when calculating trading profits?

9.6   Linda's income statement for the year ended 31 March 2023 is as follows:

	£	£
Sales		82,500
Less: Cost of sales		37,200
Gross profit		45,300
Add: Rents receivable	1,200	
Bank interest receivable	80	
Profit on sale of non-current asset	310	1,590
		46,890
Less: Wages and salaries	22,620	
Business rates and insurance	1,750	
Heating and lighting	2,170	
Repairs and renewals	4,280	
Telephone	880	
Motor expenses	3,250	
Sundry expenses	1,650	
Bad and doubtful debts	640	
Credit card interest	120	
Loss on sale of non-current asset	70	
Depreciation	2,500	39,930
Net profit for the year		6,960

Notes:

(a)   Linda draws a salary of £200 per week from the business. This is included in the wages and salaries figure.

(b)   Repairs and renewals are as follows:

	£
Decoration of business premises	400
Installation of new improved heating system	3,800
Minor repair	80
	4,280

(c)   It has been agreed with HMRC that one-quarter of telephone costs and one-fifth of motor expenses relate to private use.

(d)   Sundry expenses include business entertaining of £520.

(e)   Trade debts written off in the year amount to £440 and £200 has been set aside as a general allowance (or provision) for bad and doubtful debts.

Compute Linda's trading profit (before deduction of any capital allowances) for the year ended 31 March 2023.

*9.7 Imran owns a business which operates from rented premises. He has a 10-year lease on the premises and he paid a premium of £7,000 on 1 January 2022 in order to renew this lease. His income statement for the year to 31 December 2022 is as follows:

	£	£
Gross profit for the year		52,618
Add: Interest receivable	212	
Surplus on sale of office equipment	300	512
		53,130
Less: Wages (see Note 1)	19,280	
Rent, rates and insurance (see Note 2)	7,915	
Electricity	4,328	
Telephone (see Note 3)	1,650	
Repairs (see Note 4)	2,286	
Printing and advertising	1,250	
Motor expenses (see Note 5)	5,712	
Legal and professional expenses (see Note 6)	3,000	
Sundry expenses (see Note 7)	4,777	
Bad and doubtful debts (see Note 8)	860	
Bank charges and interest	2,765	
Lease premium amortisation	700	
Depreciation	7,749	62,272
Net profit/(loss) for the year		(9,142)

Notes:

1. Wages include £5,800 for Imran's wife (who works part-time for the business) and £1,000 for his son (a student who does not work for the business at all). Also included in wages are Imran's personal income tax and personal National Insurance contributions totalling £3,524.

2. Insurance includes Imran's private medical insurance premium of £1,405.

3. It has been agreed that one-sixth of telephone costs relate to private use.

4. Repairs include £750 for the cost of essential repairs to a newly-acquired second-hand forklift truck which could not be used until the repairs had been carried out.

5. Motor expenses are as follows:

	£
Vehicle servicing and repairs	1,165
Fuel and oil	2,815
Loss on disposal of motor vehicle	422
Road fund licences and insurance	610
Fine for speeding by Imran	700
	5,712

It has been agreed that one-tenth of motor expenses relate to private use.

6. Legal and professional expenses comprise legal fees of £850 (on renewal of Imran's 10-year lease), debt collection fees of £1,250 and accountancy fees of £900.

7. Sundry expenses are:

	£
Business entertaining	3,320 /
Staff Christmas dinner	312 ♭
Subscription to trade association	350 ✓
Donation to political party	200 ✗
Miscellaneous small items (all allowable)	595
	4,777

8. Trade debts of £500 were written off during the year. The general allowance for doubtful debts was reduced by £100 and the specific allowance for doubtful debts was increased by £460.

9. During the year, Imran appropriated trading stock costing £220 from the business for personal use, paying £220 of his own money into the business bank account. His gross profit percentage on turnover is 20%.

Compute Imran's trading profit (before deduction of capital allowances) for the year to 31 December 2022.

*9.8 Ewan began trading on 1 April 2022. A brief summary of his income statement for the year to 31 March 2023 (prepared on the accruals basis) is as follows:

	£	£
Sales		68,750
Less: Cost of sales:		
Purchases	29,220	
Less: Inventory at 31 March 2023	6,190	23,030
Gross profit		45,720
Less: Expenses		18,760
Net profit for the year		26,960

Notes:

1. Trade receivables at 31 March 2023 were £5,840. Trade payables were £3,650. Accrued expenses were £830 and prepaid expenses were £310.

2. The expenses include motoring costs of £3,120 and loan interest of £600. There were no accruals or prepayments in relation to either of these expenses at the year end. Ewan drove 12,400 business miles during the year.

3. Equipment costing £4,500 (useful life five years) and a motor car costing £14,200 were bought in April 2022. Depreciation of £900 and £3,550 respectively on these items is included in expenses.

Calculate Ewan's trading profit for tax purposes, on the assumption that he decides to use the cash basis and claims a fixed rate deduction in relation to his motor expenses.

Chapter 10

Income from self-employment: Basis periods

Introduction

Income tax is charged for tax years. It would therefore be convenient if all self-employed people chose 5 April as their annual accounting date, so that the trading income for each tax year could easily be identified. However, self-employed people may choose any accounting date they wish. So it is necessary to devise a set of rules which can be used to link periods of account to tax years. ITTOIA 2005 states that the profits of a tax year are the profits of the "basis period" for that year. This chapter explains the basis period rules[†].

[†] *As from tax year 2024-25, the existing basis period rules will be abolished and will be replaced by a simpler system. Transitional rules will apply in tax year 2023-24. The new rules (introduced in Finance Act 2022) are outlined at the end of this chapter.*

The current year basis

The main principle of the self-employed basis period rules is that the basis period for a tax year is "*the period of 12 months ending with the accounting date in that tax year*". This is known as the "current year basis" (CYB). On this basis, the profits that are taxed in a tax year are normally the profits of the accounting year which ends in the tax year.

However, special rules apply when a business starts trading, ceases trading or changes its accounting date (see below).

EXAMPLE 1

(a) A trader prepares accounts to 31 December each year. Identify the basis period for tax year 2022-23.

(b) A trader prepares accounts to 30 September each year. For which tax year will the accounting year to 30 September 2021 be the basis period?

Assume in both cases that the special rules which are used on commencement, cessation or change of accounting date do not apply in any of the years concerned.

Solution

(a) The accounting year which ends during tax year 2022-23 is the year to 31 December 2022. Therefore this is the basis period for 2022-23. In other words, the profits of the year to 31 December 2022 are charged to income tax in tax year 2022-23.

(b) The accounting year to 30 September 2021 ends during tax year 2021-22 and is therefore the basis period for 2021-22. In other words, the profits of the year to 30 September 2021 are charged to income tax in tax year 2021-22.

Commencement of trade

Special rules are used to determine basis periods for the first two tax years when a new business starts trading. The first tax year in which trading profits are taxed is the tax year in which trade commences. When this tax year has been identified, basis periods for the opening tax years are determined in accordance with the following rules:

Tax year			*Basis period*
1			Date of commencement to the following 5 April (the "actual basis")
2	*either*	(a)	12 months to the accounting date in the second tax year (if possible)
	or	(b)	The first 12 months of trading (if the accounting date in the second tax year is less than 12 months after commencement)
	or	(c)	The actual tax year from 6 April to 5 April (if there is no accounting date in the second tax year)
3 etc.			Current year basis.

Note the following points:

(a) The basis period for the first tax year will often be less than 12 months long but the basis period for the second tax year will always be 12 months long.

(b) Basis periods for the opening tax years may overlap to some extent and therefore some of the profits made in the early years of trading may be the subject of more than one tax assessment (see below).

(c) If necessary, the trading profits for early periods of account are apportioned on a time basis in order to compute the amount of profit arising in each basis period.

(d) ITTOIA 2005 states that apportionments should be made by reference to the number of *days* in the period concerned, but adds that any other reasonable method of apportionment will be accepted so long as it is applied consistently. In practice, such calculations are usually made to the nearest month and this is the approach adopted in this book.

EXAMPLE 2

Identify basis periods for the first four tax years in each of the following situations:

(a) Vera starts trading on 1 January 2020, preparing accounts annually to 31 December.

(b) Wilbur starts trading on 1 October 2019. He chooses 30 June as his annual accounting date and prepares his first accounts for the nine months to 30 June 2020.

(c) Yasmin starts trading on 1 February 2020. Her annual accounting date is 30 April and she prepares her first accounts for the 15 months to 30 April 2021.

Solution

(a)
2019-20	Actual	1 January 2020 to 5 April 2020
2020-21	12 months to a/c date in year 2	year to 31 December 2020
2021-22	CYB	year to 31 December 2021
2022-23	CYB	year to 31 December 2022

(b)
2019-20	Actual	1 October 2019 to 5 April 2020
2020-21	First 12 months	1 October 2019 to 30 September 2020
2021-22	CYB	year to 30 June 2021
2022-23	CYB	year to 30 June 2022

(c)
2019-20	Actual	1 February 2020 to 5 April 2020
2020-21	Actual	6 April 2020 to 5 April 2021
2021-22	CYB	1 May 2020 to 30 April 2021
2022-23	CYB	year to 30 April 2022

Notes:

(i) For Wilbur, the accounting date which falls into the second tax year (30 June 2020) is less than 12 months after commencement, so it is not possible to tax the profits of the 12 months to that accounting date. Therefore the basis period for the second tax year is Wilbur's first 12 months of trading.

(ii) For Yasmin, no accounting date falls into the second tax year. So she is taxed on the actual profits made during that tax year. Note also that the accounting date which falls into the third tax year marks the end of a 15-month period of account, so the basis period for that year does not coincide with a period of account.

Overlap profits

If a business chooses 5 April as its annual accounting date, the basis periods used in the opening tax years will not overlap at all. Otherwise, the opening basis periods will overlap and some profits will form the basis of more than one tax assessment. Such profits are known as "overlap profits".

However, accounts prepared to 31 March or to the 1st, 2nd, 3rd or 4th of April are usually treated for this purpose as if they had been prepared to 5 April, thus avoiding very short overlap periods and very small amounts of overlap profits.

EXAMPLE 3

Albert begins trading on 1 May 2020 and has adjusted trading profits as follows:

	£
15 months to 31 July 2021	16,800
year to 31 July 2022	21,600

Compute Albert's trading income for each of the first three tax years and also calculate the amount of any overlap profits.

Solution

Albert's first period of account is fifteen months in length and his first basis period comprises the eleven months from 1 May 2020 to 5 April 2021. Trading income for the first three tax years is as follows:

Year	Basis	Basis period	Workings	Trading income £
2020-21	Actual	1/5/20 to 5/4/21	£16,800 x 11/15	12,320
2021-22	12 months to a/c date in year 2	1/8/20 to 31/7/21	£16,800 x 12/15	13,440
2022-23	CYB	y/e 31/7/22		21,600

The overlap period consists of the eight months from 1 August 2020 to 5 April 2021, which are common to the basis periods for 2020-21 and 2021-22. Overlap profits are therefore £8,960 (£16,800 x 8/15).

Overlap relief

In general, overlap profits which arise in the opening years of a business are relieved by deduction from the trading profits that are charged to tax in the final tax year when trade ceases. Note the following points regarding "overlap relief":

(a) Overlap relief ensures that, over the entire lifetime of a business, the total of the trading profits which are charged to tax is equal to the total of the adjusted trading profits for each period of account.

(b) Overlap profits are not index-linked. Therefore the real value of overlap relief is eroded by inflation, especially in the case of businesses which trade for many years.

(c) If overlap profits exceed the trading profits which are charged to tax in the final tax year, the resulting loss is eligible for tax relief (see Chapter 12).

However, if a business changes its accounting date at some point during its lifetime, it is possible that some of the overlap profits arising in the opening years may be relieved by deduction from the trading profits that are taxed in the year of the change. But it is also possible that further overlap profits might arise on a change of accounting date (see later in this chapter).

Cessation of trade

A cessation of trade occurs when the owner of a business retires or sells the business or dies. The final tax year in which trading profits are taxed is the tax year in which the cessation occurs. The basis period for this final tax year is determined as follows:

(a) If a business commences trading and ceases trading in the same tax year, the basis period for that year consists of the entire lifespan of the business.

(b) If a business ceases trading in its second tax year, the basis period for that year runs from 6 April at the start of the year up to the date of cessation. This rule overrides the usual commencement rules for the second tax year.

(c) Otherwise, the basis period for the final tax year runs from the end of the basis period for the previous tax year up to the date of the cessation. This basis period may be less than, equal to or more than 12 months in length.

If the final set of accounts prepared for a business covers a period which is of more than 12 months, it is possible that no accounting date at all falls into the penultimate tax year (the last year but one). This makes it impossible to apply the usual current year basis in that year. In these circumstances, the basis period for the penultimate tax year is the 12 months up to the normal accounting date falling in that year.

It is important to appreciate that income tax is charged on the owner of a business and not on the business itself. Therefore a change in the ownership of a business is treated for tax purposes as a cessation of one business followed by the commencement of another.

EXAMPLE 4

Carmen started trading on 1 July 2018 and chose 30 June as her annual accounting date. Identify the basis periods for her last two tax years if she ceases trading as follows:

	Date of cessation	Final set of accounts
(a)	31 March 2019	9 months to 31 March 2019
(b)	30 June 2019	year to 30 June 2019
(c)	30 June 2022	year to 30 June 2022
(d)	31 May 2022	11 months to 31 May 2022
(e)	30 April 2022	22 months to 30 April 2022

Solution

(a) Trade both commences and ceases in 2018-19. The basis period for this single tax year is the entire lifespan of the business i.e. 1 July 2018 to 31 March 2019.

(b) The cessation occurs in the second tax year. Basis periods are:

2018-19	Actual	1 July 2018 to 5 April 2019
2019-20	6 April to date of cessation	6 April 2019 to 30 June 2019

(c) 2021-22 CYB   y/e 30 June 2021
     2022-23 End of previous basis period up   y/e 30 June 2022
              to date of cessation

(d) 2021-22 CYB   y/e 30 June 2021
     2022-23 End of previous basis period up   1 July 2021 to 31 May 2022
              to date of cessation

(e) 2021-22 12 months to normal a/c date   1 July 2020 to 30 June 2021
     2022-23 End of previous basis period up   1 July 2021 to 30 April 2022
              to date of cessation

EXAMPLE 5

Damien starts trading on 1 July 2017 and chooses 31 December as his annual accounting date. He ceases trading on 30 September 2022 and has the following results:

	Adjusted trading profit
	£
6 months to 31 December 2017	8,400
year to 31 December 2018	9,200
year to 31 December 2019	10,500
year to 31 December 2020	7,500
year to 31 December 2021	6,400
9 months to 30 September 2022	5,800

Compute Damien's trading income for each tax year and show that the total of this income is equal to the total of the adjusted trading profits listed above.

Solution

Year	Basis period	Workings	Trading income
			£
2017-18	1/7/17 to 5/4/18	£8,400 + 3/12 x £9,200	10,700
2018-19	y/e 31/12/18		9,200
2019-20	y/e 31/12/19		10,500
2020-21	y/e 31/12/20		7,500
2021-22	y/e 31/12/21		6,400
2022-23	1/1/22 to 30/9/22	£5,800 – overlap relief £2,300	3,500
			47,800

The overlap period is from 1 January 2018 to 5 April 2018 (3 months) and the overlap profits are £2,300 (£9,200 x 3/12). The total of the trading income which is charged to tax is £47,800, the same as the total of the adjusted trading profits.

Change of accounting date

If a business changes its annual accounting date from one date (the "old date") to another date (the "new date"), special rules are used to determine the basis period for the year of change. The year of change is defined as the first tax year in which accounts are *not* made up to the old date or *are* made up to the new date (or both). There will be a change of basis period for a year of change so long as the following conditions are satisfied:

(a) The first set of accounts made up to the new date does not cover a period which exceeds 18 months in length.

(b) Notice of the change of accounting date is given to HMRC in a tax return and this return is not filed late.

(c) Either:

(i)   None of the previous five tax years has been a year of change resulting in a change of basis period, or

(ii) HMRC is satisfied that the change of accounting date has been made for genuine commercial reasons and not for tax avoidance purposes.

If all of these conditions are satisfied, the basis period for the year of change is determined as follows:

(a) The "relevant period" is identified as the period beginning immediately after the end of the basis period for the previous tax year and ending with the new date in the year of change.

(b) If the length of the relevant period is less than 12 months, the basis period for the year of change is the 12 months to the new date in the year of change.

(c) If the length of the relevant period is not less than 12 months, the basis period for the year of change is the relevant period itself.

(d) In consequence, the basis period for a year of change will always be of at least 12 months' duration.

If all of the required conditions are *not* satisfied, the basis period for the year of change is the 12 months to the old date in that year. However, the following tax year is then regarded as a year of change (the taxpayer being treated as though this were the first year in which the new date had been used) and a change of basis period will occur in that year if all of the conditions are satisfied in relation to that year. A change of accounting date can be carried forward indefinitely in this way until such time as the necessary conditions for a change of basis period are satisfied.

If a taxpayer regularly prepares accounts to a particular *day* in the year (e.g. the last Saturday in June) rather than a particular *date*, the fact that the accounting date will change slightly in each year does not trigger the change of accounting date rules.

EXAMPLE 6

(a) Gary began trading many years ago, preparing accounts to 30 September each year. He decided to change his accounting date to 30 June and the first accounts made up to the new date were for the period from 1 October 2020 to 30 June 2021. The conditions necessary for a change of basis period were all satisfied. Identify the basis periods for years 2019-20 to 2022-23 inclusive.

(b) Audrey began trading on 1 January 2018, preparing accounts to 31 December each year. She decided to change her accounting date to 31 March and the first accounts made up to the new date were for the period from 1 January 2020 to 31 March 2021. The conditions necessary for a change of basis period were all satisfied. Identify the basis periods for years 2017-18 to 2022-23 inclusive.

(c) Grant began trading many years ago, preparing accounts to 30 June each year. He decided to change his accounting date to 31 December and the first accounts made up to the new date were for the period from 1 July 2020 to 31 December 2020. The conditions necessary for a change of basis period were all satisfied. Identify the basis periods for years 2019-20 to 2022-23 inclusive.

(d) Clare began trading on 1 March 2017, preparing accounts to 31 January each year. Her first accounts were for the period to 31 January 2018. She decided to change her accounting date to 30 April and the first accounts made up to this new date were for the period from 1 February 2020 to 30 April 2021. The conditions necessary for a change of basis period were all satisfied. Identify the basis periods for years 2016-17 to 2022-23 inclusive.

Solution

(a) The year of change is 2021-22 (the first year in which the old date was not used and the new date was used). The basis period for 2020-21 ended on 30 September 2020, so the relevant period is from 1 October 2020 to 30 June 2021. This is less than 12 months long so the basis period for 2021-22 is the 12 months to 30 June 2021. Basis periods for 2019-20 to 2022-23 are:

2019-20	year to 30 September 2019
2020-21	year to 30 September 2020
2021-22	year to 30 June 2021
2022-23	year to 30 June 2022

Note that there is an overlap between the basis periods for 2020-21 and 2021-22. The treatment of overlap profits on a change of accounting date is explained below.

(b) The year of change is 2020-21 (the first year in which the old date was not used and the new date was used). The basis period for 2019-20 ended on 31 December 2019, so the relevant period is from 1 January 2020 to 31 March 2021. This period is not less than 12 months in length so the basis period for 2020-21 is the same as the relevant period. Basis periods for 2017-18 to 2022-23 are:

2017-18	1 January 2018 to 5 April 2018
2018-19	year to 31 December 2018
2019-20	year to 31 December 2019
2020-21	1 January 2020 to 31 March 2021
2021-22	year to 31 March 2022
2022-23	year to 31 March 2023

(c) The year of change is 2020-21 (the first year in which the new date was used). The basis period for 2019-20 ended on 30 June 2019, so the relevant period is from 1 July 2019 to 31 December 2020. This is not less than 12 months in length so the basis period for 2020-21 is the same as the relevant period. Basis periods are:

2019-20	year to 30 June 2019
2020-21	1 July 2019 to 31 December 2020
2021-22	year to 31 December 2021
2022-23	year to 31 December 2022

(d) The year of change is 2020-21 (the first year in which the old date was not used). The basis period for 2019-20 ended on 31 January 2020, so the relevant period is from 1 February 2020 to 30 April 2020. This is less than 12 months long so the basis period for 2020-21 is the 12 months to 30 April 2020, even though this accounting date was not used in 2020-21. Basis periods for 2016-17 to 2022-23 are:

2016-17	1 March 2017 to 5 April 2017
2017-18	1 March 2017 to 28 February 2018
2018-19	year to 31 January 2019
2019-20	year to 31 January 2020
2020-21	year to 30 April 2020
2021-22	year to 30 April 2021
2022-23	year to 30 April 2022

There is an overlap between the basis periods for 2019-20 and 2020-21 (as well as the usual overlaps arising on the commencement of trade).

Overlap profits on a change of accounting date

If a change of accounting date results in profits being taxed more than once, these overlap profits are added to any earlier overlap profits which arose in the opening years or on a previous change of accounting date. The total overlap profits are then carried forward for relief on cessation or on a subsequent change of accounting date.

On the other hand, if the basis period for a year of change exceeds 12 months, then a part of the overlap profits brought forward from previous years may be relieved in the year of change. The amount to be relieved is calculated according to the following formula:

$$\text{Amount relieved } = \text{ A} \times \frac{B - C}{D}$$

where: A = Total overlap profits brought forward and not yet relieved

B = Length of the relevant period

C = 12 (or 365 if daily apportionments are being used)

D = Total length of the overlap period(s) to which the total overlap profits brought forward relate.

EXAMPLE 7

(a) Byron began trading on 1 November 2017, preparing accounts to 31 October each year. He decided to change his accounting date to 31 August and the first accounts made up to the new date were for the period from 1 November 2019 to 31 August 2020. The conditions necessary for a change of basis period were all satisfied. The adjusted trading profits for Byron's first five periods of account were as follows:

	£
Year to 31 October 2018	24,000
Year to 31 October 2019	36,000
Period to 31 August 2020	32,000
Year to 31 August 2021	42,000
Year to 31 August 2022	48,000

Compute Byron's trading income for years 2017-18 to 2022-23.

(b) Michelle began trading on 1 January 2018, preparing accounts to 31 December each year. She decided to change her accounting date to 28/29 February and the first accounts made up to the new date were for the period from 1 January 2021 to 28 February 2022. The conditions necessary for a change of basis period were all satisfied. The adjusted trading profits for Michelle's first five periods of account were:

	£
Year to 31 December 2018	9,120
Year to 31 December 2019	10,500
Year to 31 December 2020	23,360
Period to 28 February 2022	28,780
Year to 28 February 2023	32,540

Compute Michelle's trading income for years 2017-18 to 2022-23.

Solution

(a) The year of change is 2020-21 (the first year in which the old date was not used and the new date was used). The basis period for 2019-20 ended on 31 October 2019, so the relevant period is from 1 November 2019 to 31 August 2020. This is less than 12 months in length so the basis period for 2020-21 is the 12 months to 31 August 2020. Trading income for 2017-18 to 2022-23 is:

Year	Basis period	Workings	Trading income £
2017-18	1/11/17 to 5/4/18	£24,000 x 5/12	10,000
2018-19	y/e 31/10/18		24,000
2019-20	y/e 31/10/19		36,000
2020-21	y/e 31/8/20	(£36,000 x 2/12) + £32,000	38,000
2021-22	y/e 31/8/21		42,000
2022-23	y/e 31/8/22		48,000

There are overlap profits of £10,000 (5 months) on the commencement of trade and a further £6,000 (2 months) on the change of accounting date. Total overlap profits carried forward are £16,000 (7 months).

(b) The year of change is 2021-22 (the first year in which the old date was not used and the new date was used). The basis period for 2020-21 ended on 31 December 2020, so the relevant period is from 1 January 2021 to 28 February 2022. This is not less than 12 months in length so the basis period for 2021-22 is the relevant period itself. Trading income for 2017-18 to 2022-23 is:

Year	Basis period	Workings	Trading income £
2017-18	1/1/18 to 5/4/18	£9,120 x 3/12	2,280
2018-19	y/e 31/12/18		9,120
2019-20	y/e 31/12/19		10,500
2020-21	y/e 31/12/20		23,360
2021-22	1/1/21 to 28/2/22	£28,780 – overlap relief £1,520	27,260
2022-23	y/e 28/2/23		32,540

There are overlap profits of £2,280 (3 months) on the commencement of trade. The relevant period is 14 months long, which exceeds 12 months by 2 months. Overlap relief in the year of change is calculated as £2,280 x 2/3 = £1,520. Overlap profits carried forward are £760 (1 month).

Transitional overlap relief

The basis period rules now in use were introduced by Finance Act 1994. Businesses which existed before 6 April 1994 used to be assessed on the *preceding year basis*, which meant that the basis period for a tax year was the accounting year ending in the *previous* tax year. The switch to the current year basis for these businesses occurred as from 1997-98.

One aspect of this transition which remains relevant today[†] is that these older businesses (which cannot claim overlap relief in the normal way) are eligible for *transitional overlap relief* on a change of accounting date or on the cessation of trade. An explanation of transitional overlap relief is provided on the website which accompanies this book. The website can be accessed at go.pearson.com/uk/he/resources.

[†] *Transitional overlap relief will cease to be relevant in tax year 2024-25 and subsequent years, when the current basis period rules are replaced by a new system (see later in this chapter).*

Averaging of trading profits for farmers and creative artists

Certain trades, professions and vocations are more likely than others to experience profits which fluctuate considerably from one period to the next, giving rise to corresponding fluctuations in the trading income which is charged to tax. In particular, this problem may affect farmers and market gardeners (who are at the mercy of the weather) and creative artists (with profits derived from literary works, musical works etc.).

ITTOIA 2005 allows farmers, market gardeners and creative artists to smooth out fluctuating profits by making a claim for *averaging*. The profits of farmers and market gardeners may be averaged over two consecutive years or over five consecutive years. The profits of creative artists may be averaged over two consecutive years only. Note the following points in relation to the averaging process:

(a) Trading profits may be averaged over two consecutive tax years if the trading profit for one of those years is less than 75% of the trading profit for the other year (or if the trading profit for one of the years is £nil).

(b) *For farmers and market gardeners only*, trading profits may be averaged over five consecutive tax years if one of the following is less than 75% of the other:

(i)   the average of the trading profits for the first four of those five years, and
(ii) the trading profit of the fifth year

or if the trading profit for at least one of the five years is £nil.

(c) If a loss has been incurred in any of the years which are involved in an averaging claim, this loss counts as a trading profit of £nil for averaging purposes. The loss is then eligible for tax relief (see Chapter 12).

(d) An averaging claim may not be made in relation to the tax year in which trade commences or the tax year in which trade ceases. Nor may such a claim be made if the business uses the cash basis (see Chapter 9).

(e) In the case of two-year claims, it is permissible for the earlier of those two years to be a year for which an averaging claim (either two-year or five-year) has previously been made. Similarly, in the case of five-year claims, it is permissible for any of the first four years to which the claim relates to be a year for which an averaging claim (either two-year or five-year) has previously been made. But overlapping claims of this nature must be made in chronological order.

(f) An averaging claim must be made by the first anniversary of the 31 January which follows the later of the tax years to which the claim relates. For example, a two-year averaging claim which relates to 2021-22 and 2022-23 (or a five-year claim which relates to 2018-19 through to 2022-23) must be made by 31 January 2025.

EXAMPLE 8

The recent adjusted trading profits of a self-employed farmer who began trading many years ago (and does not use the cash basis) are as follows:

	£
year to 30 November 2021	64,200
year to 30 November 2022	18,640

He has no other income. May an averaging claim be made for these two years and would the farmer benefit from such a claim? If so, what is the time limit for making this claim?

Solution

The tax years in question are 2021-22 and 2022-23. The lower of the two profit figures is £18,640 and this is less than 75% of £64,200 (i.e. £48,150) so an averaging claim may be made. If such a claim is made, the farmer's trading income for both 2021-22 and 2022-23 will be revised for tax purposes to £41,420 (the average of £64,200 and £18,640). The farmer would benefit from this claim in the following ways:

(a) the likelihood of paying higher rate tax in 2021-22 would be removed, so reducing the total income tax liability for the two years, and

(b) the farmer's cash flow situation would be improved, since the 2021-22 tax liability would be reduced and the 2022-23 tax liability would be increased.

The time limit for making the claim would be 31 January 2025.

EXAMPLE 9

A creative artist has been self-employed for many years. Adjusted trading profits/(losses) in recent years are as follows:

	£
year to 31 September 2018	43,000
year to 31 September 2019	28,440
year to 31 September 2020	(5,400)
year to 31 September 2021	13,800
year to 31 September 2022	21,600

Calculate the artist's trading income for 2018-19 to 2022-23 inclusive, assuming that the cash basis is not in use and that all possible averaging claims are made.

Solution

2018-19 and 2019-20

£28,440 is less than 75% of £43,000 (i.e. £32,250) so an averaging claim may be made. Averaging gives revised trading income of £35,720 in each year.

2019-20 and 2020-21

Revised trading income for 2019-20 is £35,720. Trading income for 2020-21 is £nil, so an averaging claim may be made. Revised trading income is £17,860 in each year.

2020-21 and 2021-22

Revised trading income for 2020-21 is £17,860. Trading income for 2021-22 is £13,800. This is not less than 75% of £17,860 (i.e. £13,395) so averaging is not possible.

2021-22 and 2022-23

£13,800 is less than 75% of £21,600 (i.e. £16,200) so an averaging claim may be made. Averaging gives revised trading income of £17,700 in each year. Trading income figures for tax years 2018-19 to 2022-23 are now:

	£
	£
2018-19	35,720
2019-20	17,860
2020-21	17,860
2021-22	17,700
2022-23	17,700 (which may perhaps be averaged with 2023-24).

EXAMPLE 10

A market gardener began trading many years ago and has been making good profits for many years. However, adverse weather conditions in 2022 caused his profits to fall very sharply in that year. Adjusted trading profits for the most recent five years are as follows:

	£
year to 30 December 2018	47,800
year to 30 December 2019	52,750
year to 30 December 2020	52,750
year to 30 December 2021	41,100
year to 30 December 2022	2,300

He has no other income and does not use the cash basis. The trading profits of 2019 and 2020 were averaged in a previous averaging claim. Identify any further averaging claims that might now be made.

Solution

A two-year averaging claim could be made in relation to 2021 and 2022. This would revise trading income for 2021-22 and 2022-23 to £21,700 per year and save basic rate tax in 2021-22 (*a Scottish taxpayer would save tax at basic rate and intermediate rate*). It would also avoid a waste of personal allowances in 2022-23.

But a better option might be to make a five-year claim. The average profit of the years 2018 to 2021 inclusive is £48,600 and the profit of £2,300 in 2022 is far less than 75% of this, so the claim may be made. A five-year claim would revise trading income to £39,340 per year and save higher rate tax in each of the first three years covered by the claim.

Basis period reform

As stated at the beginning of this chapter, FA 2022 abolishes the existing basis period rules and replaces them with a simpler system. The new rules will apply to tax year 2024-25 and subsequent years. Transitional rules will apply in tax year 2023-24. The essence of the new rules is that self-employed persons (sole traders or partners) will be charged to income tax on the profits actually arising in the tax year, with no special rules on commencement or cessation or on a change of accounting date. Overlap profits will no longer occur. The main features of the new system are as follows:

(a)   As from tax year 2024-25, self-employed persons will be charged to income tax on the actual profits arising during the tax year. If the annual accounting date of the person's business is 5 April, this is no different from the existing system. And there are rules to ensure that accounts drawn up to a date which lies between 31 March and 4 April inclusive will (in effect) be treated as if they had been drawn up to 5 April. But if the annual accounts are drawn up to some other date, if will be necessary to time-apportion profits (or losses) between tax years.

(b)   The legislation states that such apportionments should be performed "*by reference to the number of days in the periods concerned*". For instance, if a set of accounts covers the year to 31 December 2025 (of which the first 95 days fall into tax year 2024-25), 95/365ths of the profit for the period should be allocated to tax year 2024-25 and the remaining 270/365ths of the profit should be allocated to 2025-26.

   However, the legislation also states that the lengths of periods may be measured in a different way, as long as this way is reasonable and is used consistently. Presumably this will allow apportionments to be made on a monthly basis rather than a daily basis, so that 3/12ths of the profit for the year to 31 December 2025 may be allocated to tax year 2024-25, with the remaining 9/12ths being allocated to 2025-26.

(c)   It seems that time-apportionment (whether on a daily or monthly basis) will apply to all businesses without exception, including seasonal businesses whose profits are not in fact spread evenly over the accounting period.

(d)   In general, this system will bring forward the dates by which the profits of accounting periods must be ascertained and the necessary tax paid. For instance, under the existing basis period rules, the profit for the year to 31 December 2025 would normally form the basis for tax year 2025-26. A tax return (or end of period statement) for the year would have to be submitted by 31 January 2027 and a balancing payment would fall due on the same date. But under the new rules, part of the profit for the year to 31 December 2025 will fall into tax year 2024-25, for which the filing date and payment date is 31 January 2026 (i.e. only a month after the end of the accounting period).

   And if a business prepares annual accounts to 28/29 February, the deadline for filing a return and making a balancing payment in relation to the profit arising in the first month of each accounting period will fall a month *before* the end of the period.

(e)   In these circumstances, it is clear that businesses with annual accounting dates which fall near the end of the tax year (but before 31 March) will often have to estimate the profit for each accounting period, include the estimated figures in the tax return (or EOPS) and pay an estimated amount of tax. It will then be necessary to amend the return when the correct profit figure for the period is ascertained. Alternatively, such businesses might simply choose to change their annual accounting date (perhaps to 31 March or 5 April) so as to avoid this problem.

Transitional year 2023-24

(f)   Tax year 2023-24 will be a transitional year between the current rules and the new rules. In general (for existing businesses) the basis period for 2023-24 will begin immediately after the end of the basis period for 2022-23 and will end on 5 April 2024. Therefore, unless the business has an annual accounting date which falls between 31 March and 5 April, the basis period for 2023-24 will be more than 12 months long.

(g)   The first twelve months of the basis period for 2023-24 are referred to as the "standard part" and the remainder (if any) is referred to as the "transition part". For instance, the 2023-24 basis period for an established business with an accounting date of 30 June will comprise the 21 months to 5 April 2024, consisting of a standard part (year to 30 June 2023) and a transition part (1 July 2023 to 5 April 2024).

(h)   It is clear that businesses with accounting dates which fall early in the tax year will have exceptionally long basis periods for 2023-24, possibly resulting in exceptionally high tax liabilities. However, there are two mitigating factors:

   (i)   All outstanding overlap profits from previous years <u>must</u> be used in 2023-24, so reducing the tax liability for the year.

   (ii)   The profit arising during the transition part of the basis period for 2023-24 (after overlap relief has been deducted) will be automatically spread for tax purposes over the five tax years beginning with 2023-24. Though taxpayers may elect to accelerate the tax charge on these "transition profits" if they so wish.

(i)   FA 2022 explicitly excludes transition profits from the definition of "net income". This ensures that the taxation of such profits does not have undesirable side-effects such as causing a reduction in the taxpayer's personal allowance (see Chapter 3) or triggering a high income child benefit charge (see Chapter 7).

EXAMPLE 11

Raheem has been trading for many years, preparing accounts to 31 May each year. Recent adjusted trading profits are as follows:

	£
year to 31 May 2021	52,400
year to 31 May 2022	54,150
year to 31 May 2023	58,720
year to 31 May 2024	62,280
year to 31 May 2025	66,360
year to 31 May 2026	68,400

Compute Raheem's trading income for tax years 2021-22 to 2025-26 inclusive, assuming that he has unused overlap profits brought forward of £16,200 and makes no elections with regard to the transition profit (if any) that arises in tax year 2023-24.

Any necessary apportionments should be made on a monthly basis.

Solution

Basis periods for 2021-22 through to 2023-24 are as follows:

2021-22   year to 31 May 2021 (trading income £52,400)

2022-23   year to 31 May 2022 (trading income £54,150)

2023-24   1 June 2022 to 5 April 2024 (see below)

As from 2024-25, Raheem is assessed on the profits actually arising in each tax year.

The basis period for transitional year 2023-24 is twenty-two months long and is composed of a standard part (1 June 2022 to 31 May 2023) plus a transition part (1 June 2023 to 5 April 2024). Trading income during the standard part is £58,720. Trading income during the transition part is (10/12 × £62,280) = £51,900, less overlap relief £16,200. So the transition profit is £35,700 and this is spread evenly over tax years 2023-24 to 2027-28 inclusive (i.e. £7,140 in each year). Therefore trading income figures are as follows:

		£
2021-22		52,400
2022-23		54,150
2023-24	£58,720 + £7,140	65,860
2024-25	(2/12 × £62,280) + (10/12 × £66,360) + £7,140	72,820
2025-26	(2/12 × £66,360) + (10/12 × £68,400) + £7,140	75,200

Summary

Basis period rules which apply up to and including tax year 2022-23:

- Trading profits are charged to income tax on the current year basis. This means that the basis period for a tax year is normally the accounting year which ends in that tax year. However, special basis period rules apply in the opening and closing tax years of a business and on a change of accounting date.

- The first tax year in which trading profits are taxed is the tax year in which trade commences. The basis period for the first tax year runs from the date of commencement to the following 5th April.

- If there is an accounting date in the second tax year and this date is at least 12 months after commencement, the basis period for the second tax year is the 12 months to that accounting date. But if this accounting date is not at least 12 months after commencement, the basis period for the second tax year is the first 12 months of trading.

- If there is no accounting date in the second tax year, the basis period for that tax year is the actual tax year from 6th April to the following 5 April.

- Overlap profits arising in the opening years of a new business are relieved either on the cessation of trade or on a change of accounting date. However, further overlap profits may arise on a change of accounting date

- The final tax year in which trading profits are taxed is the tax year in which trade ceases. In general, the basis period for the final tax year runs from the end of the basis period for the previous tax year up to the date of cessation.

- Special rules are used in order to determine the basis period for the tax year in which a business changes its accounting date.

- Subject to conditions, farmers and market gardeners and creative artists may claim that the trading income of two consecutive tax years should be averaged. Farmers and market gardeners may also make a five-year averaging claim.

Basis period reform as from tax year 2024-25 (with transitional rules in 2023-24):

- The existing basis period rules will be abolished as from tax year 2024-25 and replaced by a system whereby self-employed persons are taxed according to the profits actually arising in the tax year. The profits of accounting periods which fall partly into one tax year and partly into another tax year will need to be apportioned on a time basis.

- Transitional rules will apply in 2023-24. Businesses which do not prepare accounts to 31 March or 5 April (or a date which falls between 31 March and 5 April) will be taxed on two profit elements in 2023-24 (the standard part and the transition part). Any available overlap relief will be deducted. Any transition profits that remain may be spread over a five-year period.

Exercises

A set of multiple choice questions for this chapter is available on the accompanying website.

10.1 Under the *current year basis*, for which tax years would the following accounting years form the basis period?

(a) year to 31 October 2021   (b) year to 31 March 2022

(c) year to 30 April 2022   (d) year to 5 April 2023

10.2 Frank began trading on 1 July 2019. Identify the basis periods for his first four tax years if he:

(a) chooses 30 June as his annual accounting date and prepares his first accounts for the year to 30 June 2020

(b) chooses 30 April as his annual accounting date and prepares his first accounts for the 22 months to 30 April 2021

(c) chooses 30 April as his annual accounting date and prepares his first accounts for the 10 months to 30 April 2020.

Also identify any overlap periods which arise in each case.

10.3 Greta commences trading on 1 January 2021 and chooses 30 June as her annual accounting date. Her first accounts are made up for the 18 months to 30 June 2022 and show an adjusted trading profit of £27,300. Compute Greta's trading income for the first three tax years and calculate the amount of any overlap profits.

10.4 Hitesh has been trading for many years, preparing accounts to 31 January each year. His last full year of trading is the year to 31 January 2021. Identify the basis periods for the last three tax years in each of the following cases:

	Date of cessation	Final set of accounts
(a)	31 May 2021	4 months to 31 May 2021
(b)	31 March 2022	14 months to 31 March 2022
(c)	30 April 2022	15 months to 30 April 2022

10.5 Phillip starts trading on 1 June 2017 and ceases trading on 31 July 2022. He has adjusted trading profits as follows

	£
1 June 2017 to 30 September 2018	28,800
year to 30 September 2019	19,900
year to 30 September 2020	14,300
year to 30 September 2021	13,800
1 October 2021 to 31 July 2022	11,100

Compute Phillip's trading income for all tax years.

*10.6   Ivy begins trading as a farmer on 1 January 2020, making up annual accounts to 31 December. Her adjusted trading profits/(losses) in the opening years are as follows:

	£
year to 31 December 2020	35,600
year to 31 December 2021	15,400
year to 31 December 2022	(12,900)

(a)   Compute Ivy's trading income for the first four tax years, assuming that no averaging claims are made.

(b)   Compute Ivy's revised trading income for the first four tax years, assuming that the cash basis is not used and all possible averaging claims are made.

*10.7   Ken starts trading on 1 October 2017 and chooses 30 April as his accounting date. He ceases trading on 31 January 2023 and has adjusted trading profits as follows:

	£
7 months to 30 April 2018	3,500
year to 30 April 2019	18,480
year to 30 April 2020	17,700
year to 30 April 2021	27,900
year to 30 April 2022	28,200
9 months to 31 January 2023	17,300

Compute Ken's trading income for all tax years.

*10.8   Belinda began trading on 1 March 2017 and chose 31 December as her accounting date. Her first accounts were for the period to 31 December 2017. She eventually decided to change her accounting date to 31 May and the first accounts made up to this new date were for the 17 months to 31 May 2021. The conditions necessary for a change of basis period were all satisfied. The adjusted trading profits for her first five periods of account were as follows:

	Adjusted trading profit
	£
1 March 2017 to 31 December 2017	43,700
year to 31 December 2018	52,590
year to 31 December 2019	54,300
1 January 2020 to 31 May 2021	71,060
year to 31 May 2022	68,200

Compute Belinda's trading income for 2016-17 to 2022-23 inclusive, showing the amounts of any overlap profits or overlap relief.

*10.9   Roger began trading on 1 January 2016, preparing accounts to 30 April each year. His first accounts were for the 16 months to 30 April 2017. In 2019 he decided to change his accounting date to 30 June. The first accounts made up to the new date were for the 14 months to 30 June 2019 and the conditions necessary for a change of basis period were all satisfied. Roger ceased trading on 31 May 2022. His adjusted trading profits were as follows:

	Adjusted trading profit
	£
1 January 2016 to 30 April 2017	33,920
year to 30 April 2018	29,700
1 May 2018 to 30 June 2019	33,300
year to 30 June 2020	41,600
year to 30 June 2021	37,900
1 July 2021 to 31 May 2022	23,500

Compute Roger's trading income for all tax years.

*10.10   Wesley began trading on 1 September 2019, preparing accounts to 31 August each year. His adjusted trading profits for the first eight accounting periods are as follows:

	Adjusted trading profit
	£
year to 31 August 2020	17,280
year to 31 August 2021	18,420
year to 31 August 2022	21,600
year to 31 August 2023	29,040
year to 31 August 2024	34,080
year to 31 August 2025	37,800
year to 31 August 2026	41,640
year to 31 August 2027	44,520

Compute Wesley's trading income for the first eight tax years in which his profits are charged to income tax, assuming that he makes no elections with regard to the transition profit (if any) which arises in tax year 2023-24. *Any necessary apportionments should be made a monthly basis.*

Also reconcile the total adjusted profits for the first eight accounting periods to the total trading income for the first eight tax years.

Chapter 11

Income from self-employment: Capital allowances

Introduction

Capital expenditure is generally not deductible when computing trading income but certain types of capital expenditure attract tax relief in the form of standardised depreciation allowances known as *capital allowances*. The purpose of this chapter is to define the categories of capital expenditure which are eligible for capital allowances and to explain how capital allowances are calculated for each of these categories.

Eligible expenditure

In order to be eligible for capital allowances, capital expenditure must usually fall into one of the following categories:

(a) plant and machinery
(b) structures and buildings
(c) patent rights
(d) know-how
(e) research and development.

This chapter is primarily concerned with the first two items on this list, which are the most important. However, the other categories are considered briefly at the end of the chapter.

Chargeable periods

Capital allowances are calculated in respect of *chargeable periods*. In the case of income tax, each period of account generally ranks as a chargeable period and so there is usually one capital allowances computation per period of account. Note that:

(a) The capital allowances for a period of account are treated as a trading expense and are deducted when computing the adjusted trading profit for that period. The basis period rules are applied to the trading profit *after* deduction of capital allowances.

(b)   A period of account lasting for more than 18 months is subdivided into one or more 12-month chargeable periods with (possibly) a short chargeable period at the end. Capital allowances are calculated separately for each of these chargeable periods and then aggregated to give the capital allowances due for the whole period of account.

(c)   The chargeable periods of *companies*, which pay corporation tax rather than income tax, are determined according to a different set of rules (see Chapter 23).

EXAMPLE 1

Lee begins trading on 1 January 2022 preparing accounts to 31 December each year. His adjusted trading profit for the year to 31 December 2022 (before capital allowances) is £21,000 and capital allowances of £1,200 are claimed for that year. Compute his trading income for 2021-22 and 2022-23.

Solution

The adjusted trading profit for the year to 31 December 2022 (after deduction of capital allowances) is £19,800. Therefore trading income for the first two tax years is as follows:

Year	Basis	Basis period	Workings	Trading income
				£
2021-22	Actual	1/1/22 to 5/4/22	£19,800 x 3/12	4,950
2022-23	12 months to a/c date in year 2	y/e 31/12/22		19,800

Plant and machinery

Capital Allowances Act 2001 (the main statute concerned with capital allowances) does not provide a definition of the term "plant and machinery". So it has been left mainly to case law to decide whether or not any given item should qualify as plant and machinery and therefore attract capital allowances. In *Yarmouth* v *France* (1887) it was stated that plant and machinery includes:

> "*whatever apparatus is used by a businessman for carrying on his business, not his stock in trade which he buys or makes for sale, but all his goods and chattels, fixed or movable, live or dead, which he keeps for permanent employment in his business*".

It is fairly clear that machinery of all types (including motor vehicles) and items such as office furniture and equipment should all qualify as plant and machinery. But difficulties arise in connection with expenditure on buildings and fixtures to buildings. Much case law has been concerned with the distinction between:

(a)   assets which perform an *active function* in the carrying on of the business (i.e. the apparatus *with which* the business is carried on), and

(b) assets which perform a *passive function* in the carrying on of the business (i.e. the setting *in which* the business is carried on).

Assets in the first of these categories qualify as plant and machinery whilst assets in the second category do not, but the distinction between the categories can be a very fine one. Some of the more important case law decisions are as follows:

Held to be plant and machinery:

(a) a dry dock built for the repair and the maintenance of ships, in *CIR* v *Barclay Curle & Co Ltd* (1969)

(b) a swimming and paddling pool, in *Cooke* v *Beach Station Caravans Ltd* (1974)

(c) a concrete grain silo, in *Schofield* v *R & H Hall Ltd* (1974)

(d) decorative display screens placed in the window of a building society's offices and incorporating the name of the building society, in *Leeds Permanent Building Society* v *Proctor* (1982)

(e) movable office partitions, in *Jarrold* v *John Good & Sons Ltd* (1962)

(f) display lighting in a store window, in *Cole Brothers Ltd* v *Phillips* (1982)

(g) light fittings and pictures on the walls of a hotel, in *CIR* v *Scottish and Newcastle Breweries Ltd* (1982)

(h) storage platforms built in a warehouse, in *Hunt* v *Henry Quick Ltd* (1992)

(i) a barrister's law books, in *Munby* v *Furlong* (1977)

(j) a synthetic football pitch, in *CIR* v *Anchor International Ltd* (2005).

Held *not* to be plant and machinery:

(a) prefabricated school buildings, in *St John's School* v *Ward* (1974)

(b) a moored ship used as a restaurant, in *Benson* v *The Yard Arm Club Ltd* (1979)

(c) a petrol station forecourt canopy, in *Dixon* v *Fitch's Garage Ltd* (1975)

(d) a football stand, in *Brown* v *Burnley Football and Athletic Co Ltd* (1980)

(e) a false ceiling built to hide electrical conduits, in *Hampton* v *Fortes Autogrill Ltd* (1979)

(f) a false ceiling, mezzanine floors, staircases, decorative floor and wall tiles all used to create ambience in a restaurant, in *Wimpey International Ltd* v *Warland* (1988)

(g) golf putting greens, in *Family Golf Centres Ltd* v *Thorne* (1998).

In an attempt to clarify the key distinction between buildings and plant, Capital Allowances Act 2001 provides a detailed list of types of expenditure on buildings or structures which are statutorily excluded from qualifying as plant. The Act also provides a detailed list of types of expenditure on buildings or structures which are not statutorily excluded from qualifying as plant and may therefore qualify if permitted by case law.

Expenditure statutorily deemed to be plant and machinery

By statute, expenditure of the following types always qualifies as plant and machinery:

(a) expenditure on the thermal insulation of a building

(b) expenditure on assets necessary to safeguard personal security

(c) expenditure after 5 April 2008 on "integral features" of a building (see below)

(d) expenditure on computer software

(e) expenditure on building alterations, incidental to installation of plant and machinery.

These types of expenditure all qualify as plant and machinery despite the fact that some of them would normally be disqualified by the rule excluding expenditure on buildings.

Capital allowances on plant and machinery

With some exceptions (see later), capital allowances are not calculated individually for each item of plant and machinery acquired by a business. Instead, expenditure on plant and machinery is pooled together and capital allowances are calculated with reference to the value of the pool. In fact, there are two pools to consider. These are:

(a) **Main pool**. This is the pool to which most general plant and machinery is allocated (e.g. factory machines, office equipment etc.). Motor vans, motor cycles and lorries are also allocated to this pool. The situation with regard to motor cars is as follows:

   (i) In general, cars with emissions which do not exceed 50g/km (*110g/km for cars acquired before 6 April 2021*) are allocated to the main pool. Cars with higher emissions than this are allocated to the special rate pool (see below).

   (ii) However, motor cars with emissions which do not exceed 0g/km (*50g/km for cars acquired before 1 April 2021*) are eligible for a 100% first year allowance and do not join any pool (see later in this chapter).

(b) **Special rate pool**. This is a pool of assets arising from any or all of the following:

   (i) the acquisition of motor cars with emissions which exceed 50g/km (*110g/km for cars acquired before 6 April 2021*)

   (ii) the acquisition of certain "integral features" of a building or structure; these are listed in CAA 2001 as electrical systems, water systems, heating and cooling systems, lifts, escalators/moving walkways and external solar shading

   (iii) expenditure on the thermal insulation of a building and on solar panels

   (iv) expenditure on assets with a working life of 25 years or more ("long-life" assets) but only if the business spends more than £100,000 a year on such assets.

The rate of capital allowances to which a business is entitled in relation to an item of plant and machinery depends upon the pool to which the item is allocated, as explained below.

Writing down allowance (WDA)

In general, a business may claim a *writing down allowance* for each one of its pools of plant and machinery in each chargeable period. The procedure for computing the amount of the writing down allowance for each pool is as follows:

(a)   The written down value (WDV) of the pool at the end of the preceding chargeable period is brought forward.

(b)   The cost of any plant and machinery which has been acquired during the chargeable period but which is not the subject of a claim for either first year allowance or annual investment allowance (see below) is added to the pool. Items of plant and machinery owned by the trader personally and then brought into the business at a later date are treated as if purchased at market value on that date. Plant and machinery acquired by hire purchase is treated as if bought for its cash price.

(c)   If any pool items have been disposed of during the chargeable period a disposal value is subtracted from the pool, equal to:

   (i)   sale proceeds, if the asset is sold in the open market

   (ii)   market value on the date of disposal, if the asset is given away or is sold for less than market value (but zero if given to charity)

   (iii)   scrap value or compensation received, if the asset is scrapped or destroyed.

   But if the disposal value exceeds the original cost of the item, only the original cost is subtracted from the pool. The profit on the disposal may give rise to a capital gains tax liability (see Chapter 19).

(d)   The available writing down allowance (WDA) is then calculated as a percentage of the pool balance. The applicable percentages are currently as follows:

Main pool   18% per annum
Special rate pool   6% per annum

   Note that WDA is calculated at a percentage rate *per annum*. This refers to the length of the chargeable period for which capital allowances are being claimed and WDA is scaled up or down accordingly if the length of this period is not 12 months. Note also that WDA is not restricted if an asset is acquired part of the way through the chargeable period and so has not been held for the whole of that period.

(e)   The WDA claimed for the chargeable period is subtracted from the pool, leaving a WDV which is carried forward to the next period. This WDV will then attract WDAs in future chargeable periods (even if all the plant and machinery has now been sold).

It is not mandatory to claim the maximum WDA available for a chargeable period and an individual with low profits (or a loss) may wish to claim less than the maximum, usually to avoid wasting personal allowances. The effect of such a claim is to increase the WDVs carried forward, thus increasing the allowances available in future chargeable periods.

EXAMPLE 2

Joanne started a business on 1 March 2021, preparing accounts to 31 December. Her first accounts were for the period to 31 December 2021. During this period and during the year to 31 December 2022 she bought and sold plant and machinery as follows:

		£
8 March 2021	Bought motor car (emissions 93g/km)	8,600
27 October 2021	Bought motor car (emissions 42g/km)	10,400
31 July 2022	Sold motor car bought in March 2021	6,650
31 July 2022	Bought motor car (emissions 85g/km)	14,200

Prepare her capital allowances computation for the first two chargeable periods.

Solution

	Main pool £	Special rate pool £	Allowances £
1/3/21 - 31/12/21			
Additions (£8,600 + £10,400)	19,000		
WDA @ 18% x 10/12	2,850		2,850
WDV c/f	16,150		
Total allowances			2,850
y/e 31/12/22			
WDV b/f	16,150		
Additions		14,200	
Disposals	(6,650)		
	9,500		
WDA @ 18%	1,710		1,710
WDA @ 6%		852	852
WDV c/f	7,790	13,348	
Total allowances			2,562

Notes:

(i) The motor car bought for £8,600 enters the main pool because it was acquired before 6 April 2021 and has emissions not exceeding 110g/km. The motor car bought for £10,400 enters the main pool because it has emissions not exceeding 50g/km.

(ii) WDA is scaled down by 10/12 for a ten-month period.

(iii) The motor car bought for £14,200 enters the special rate pool because it has emissions which exceed 50g/km.

(iv) Total capital allowances are £2,850 for the period to 31 December 2021 and £2,562 for the year to 31 December 2022.

Changes in the rate of WDA

When changes are made to the rates of WDA, the WDAs available for a chargeable period which spans the date of the change are calculated at "hybrid" rates. A change of this type most recently occurred on 6 April 2019, when the rate of WDA in the special rate pool fell from 8% per annum to 6% per annum.

Further details and worked examples may be found on the website which accompanies this textbook. The website address is go.pearson.com/uk/he/resources.

Small pools of plant and machinery

If the balance in the main pool or special rate pool before calculating WDA is £1,000 or less, the business may claim a WDA of any amount up to the amount of that balance. This rule means that it is not necessary for businesses to carry forward very small pool balances for many years, claiming ever diminishing WDAs in each chargeable period.

But businesses with a balance of £1,000 or less in the main pool or special rate pool can claim a WDA of less than the full balance if they so wish.

EXAMPLE 3

Patrick prepares accounts to 31 August each year. The written down value of his main pool of plant and machinery after deducting capital allowances for the year to 31 August 2021 was £1,900. There were no acquisitions during the year to 31 August 2022 but an item of plant that had been acquired for £3,000 in 2018 was sold in May 2022 for £1,250.

Prepare a capital allowances computation for the year to 31 August 2022, assuming that maximum allowances are claimed.

Solution

	Main pool £	Allowances £
y/e 31/8/22		
WDV b/f	1,900	
Disposals	(1,250)	
	650	
WDA	650	650
WDV c/f	0	
Total allowances		650

Note:

WDA for the year would normally have been 18% × £650 = £117, leaving a WDV carried forward of £533. However, since the WDV of the pool before calculating WDA is less than £1,000, a WDA of £650 may be claimed, leaving a WDV carried forward of £nil.

Annual investment allowance (AIA)

Expenditure on plant and machinery (other than motor cars) of up to a specified maximum amount each year is eligible for a 100% annual investment allowance (AIA). The amount of the "AIA maximum" has fluctuated considerably since April 2008, when AIA was introduced, but has been set at £200,000 per annum since 1 January 2016.

However, *for the period between 1 January 2019 and 31 March 2023*, the AIA maximum is increased five-fold to £1,000,000 per annum (reverting to £200,000 on 1 April 2023). The main features of the annual investment allowance are as follows:

(a) An AIA of 100% may be claimed in relation to qualifying expenditure that does not exceed the AIA maximum for the period. If expenditure exceeds the AIA maximum, the excess enters the appropriate pool and is eligible for WDAs in the usual way.

(b) A business may allocate the AIA between items of expenditure in any way that it chooses. For example, if a business spends £160,000 on main pool items and £80,000 on special rate pool items in a year in which the AIA maximum is £200,000, then £80,000 of the AIA might be allocated to the special rate pool and the remaining £120,000 to the main pool. This would maximise capital allowances for the period concerned, since the main pool attracts WDA at 18% whilst the special rate pool attracts WDA at only 6%.

A business which spends no more than the AIA maximum amount on special rate items each year might use this approach to avoid having a special rate pool at all. But a special rate pool is unavoidable if the business acquires motor cars with emissions exceeding 50g/km (*110g/km for cars acquired before 6 April 2021*) since motor cars are not eligible for AIA.

(c) The AIA maximum amount is increased or reduced proportionately for chargeable periods of more or less than 12 months in duration.

(d) Special rules apply if a chargeable period straddles a date on which the specified amount of the AIA maximum is increased or decreased (see below).

(e) A business is not required to claim the full AIA to which it is entitled. Any qualifying expenditure which is not the subject of a claim for AIA enters the appropriate pool and is eligible for WDAs.

(f) When an item of plant and machinery which has been the subject of an AIA claim is subsequently disposed of, the item's disposal value is subtracted from whichever pool the item would have joined if the AIA claim had not been made.

(g) If a person controls more than one business, these businesses are entitled to only one AIA between them if they are "related". Businesses are related if they are conducted from shared premises or if their activities are within the same industry classification.

Periods straddling a date on which the AIA maximum is increased

If a chargeable period straddles a date on which the AIA annual maximum is increased, special rules are used to calculate the maximum AIA available for that period. These rules were last applied in periods straddling 1 January 2019[†] (when the AIA annual maximum increased from £200,000 to £1,000,000). The maximum AIA for a chargeable period that straddles 1 January 2019 (working to the nearest month) is:

$$(£200,000 \times m/12) + (£1,000,000 \times n/12)$$

where "m" and "n" are the number of months in the period falling respectively before and after 1 January 2019. But the AIA that may be claimed in relation to expenditure incurred in the part of the period that falls before 1 January 2019 is restricted to £200,000 (scaled up or down pro rata if the chargeable period is not exactly 12 months long).

[†] *Similar rules applied to previous occasions on which the AIA maximum was increased.*

Periods straddling a date on which the AIA maximum is decreased

If a chargeable period straddles a date on which the AIA annual maximum is decreased, special rules are used to calculate the maximum AIA available for that period. These rules will apply to periods straddling 1 April 2023[†] (when the AIA annual maximum decreases from £1,000,000 to £200,000). The maximum AIA for a chargeable period that straddles 1 April 2023 (working to the nearest month) is:

$$(£1,000,000 \times m/12) + (£200,000 \times n/12)$$

where "m" and "n" are the number of months in the period falling respectively before and after 1 April 2023. But the AIA that may be claimed in relation to expenditure incurred in the part of the period falling after 31 March 2023 is restricted to $(£200,000 \times n/12)$.

[†] *Similar rules applied to previous occasions on which the AIA maximum was decreased.*

EXAMPLE 4

Samuel prepares accounts to 31 May each year. His expenditure on plant and machinery (other than motor cars) in the year to 31 May 2023 is £300,000, of which £225,000 is spent in December 2022 and the remaining £75,000 is spent in April 2023. Calculate the AIA that may be claimed for the period (working to the nearest month).

Solution

The AIA maximum for the year is £866,667 [(10/12 × £1,000,000) + (2/12 × £200,000)]. But no more than £33,333 (2/12 × £200,000) may be claimed in relation to expenditure incurred after 31 March 2023.

Therefore the AIA that may be claimed for the year is £258,333 (£225,000 + £33,333).

EXAMPLE 5

(a) Sharon started a business on 1 April 2021. She chose 31 December as her annual accounting date and her first accounts covered the period from 1 April 2021 to 31 December 2021. During this period she bought plant and machinery as follows:

		£
1 April 2021	Bought plant	6,000
19 May 2021	Bought motor car (emissions 47g/km)	8,400
17 October 2021	Bought motor van	13,000

She claims maximum capital allowances in all chargeable periods. Prepare a capital allowances computation for the nine months to 31 December 2021.

(b) Sharon's acquisitions and disposals of plant and machinery during the year to 31 December 2022 are as follows:

		£
8 January 2022	Bought plant	5,990
30 March 2022	Sold plant (original cost £3,500 on 1/4/21)	2,640

Prepare a capital allowances computation for the year to 31 December 2022.

Solution

(a)

	Main pool	Allowances
	£	£
1/4/21 - 31/12/21		
Additions not eligible for AIA	8,400	
WDA @ 18% x 9/12	1,134	1,134
	7,266	
Additions qualifying for AIA	19,000	
AIA @ 100%	19,000 —	19,000
WDV c/f	7,266	
Total allowances		20,134

Notes:

(i) The motor car is allocated to the main pool since it has emissions not exceeding 50g/km. Cars are not eligible for AIA.

(ii) WDA is scaled down by 9/12 for a nine-month chargeable period. The fact that the motor car was purchased part of the way through the period is irrelevant.

(iii) The AIA maximum for this nine-month period is (9/12 × £1,000,000) = £750,000. Sharon's expenditure of £19,000 is within this maximum.

(iv) A motor van is not a motor car and is therefore eligible for AIA.

(v) Total capital allowances for the period are £20,134.

(b)

	Main pool £	Allowances £
y/e 31/12/22		
WDV b/f	7,266	
Disposals	(2,640)	
	4,626	
WDA @ 18%	833	833
	3,793	
Additions eligible for AIA	5,990	
AIA @ 100%	5,990	5,990
	-	
WDV c/f	3,793	
Total allowances		6,823

Note:

AIA maximum for the year is £1,000,000. Qualifying expenditure (£5,990) is less than this, so AIA of £5,990 may be claimed. Total capital allowances for the year are £6,823.

First year allowance (FYA)

A first year allowance of 100% is available in relation to certain classes of expenditure on unused (not second hand) plant and machinery. Unlike WDAs and the AIA, FYAs are not scaled up or down for chargeable periods of more or less than 12 months in duration. The main first year allowances (FYAs) are currently as follows:

(a) Expenditure on a motor car with emissions not exceeding 0g/km (*50g/km for cars acquired before 1 April 2021*) is eligible for a 100% FYA as long as the expenditure is incurred on or before 31 March 2025.

(b) Expenditure on plant and machinery for use in the refuelling of vehicles with natural gas, biogas or hydrogen fuel is eligible for a 100% FYA as long as the expenditure is incurred on or before 31 March 2025.

(c) Expenditure on zero-emission goods vehicles is eligible for a 100% FYA as long as the expenditure is incurred on or before 5 April 2025.

(d) Expenditure on charging points for electric vehicles is eligible for a 100% FYA as long as the expenditure is incurred between 23 November 2016 and 5 April 2023.

When an item of plant and machinery which has been the subject of a claim for a 100% FYA is disposed of, the disposal value of the item is deducted from whichever pool the item would have entered if that claim had not been made.

EXAMPLE 6

Ian owns a large manufacturing business and he prepares accounts to 30 June each year. The written down value of his main pool of plant and machinery after deducting capital allowances for the year to 30 June 2022 was £116,250. There was no special rate pool on that date. Ian's purchases and sales of plant and machinery for the year to 30 June 2023 were as follows:

		£
9 July 2022	Bought car (emissions 0g/km)	12,700
17 July 2022	Sold plant bought for £11,000 in June 2022	12,500
30 November 2022	Bought car (emissions 53g/km)	14,000
5 April 2023	Bought factory electrical systems	38,300
25 June 2023	Bought plant	64,450

The electrical systems which were bought in April 2023 qualify as "integral features" of a building for capital allowances purposes. Prepare a capital allowances computation for the year to 30 June 2023, assuming that maximum allowances are claimed.

Solution

		Main pool £	Special rate pool £	Allowances £
y/e 30/6/23				
WDV b/f		116,250		
Additions not eligible for AIA		52,750	14,000	
Disposal		(11,000)		
		158,000		
WDA @ 18%		28,440		28,440
WDA @ 0%			840	840
		129,560	13,160	
Additions eligible for AIA	50,000			
AIA @ 100%	50,000	-		50,000
Additions eligible for 100% FYA	12,700			
FYA @ 100%	12,700	-		12,700
WDV c/f		129,560	13,160	
Total allowances				91,980

Notes:

(i) AIA maximum for the year is £800,000 [(9/12 × £1,000,000) + (3/12 × £200,000)]. But no more than £50,000 (3/12 × £200,000) may be claimed in relation to expenditure incurred on or after 1 April 2023. All of Ian's eligible expenditure is incurred on or after that date so the AIA maximum is £50,000.

(ii)   The AIA maximum of £50,000 could be allocated in any way between the expenditure of £38,300 on electrical systems and £64,450 on general plant. But capital allowances for the year are maximised if the AIA is allocated first to the expenditure of £38,300, since this expenditure would otherwise enter the special rate pool and be eligible for WDA at a lower rate than in the main pool.

(iii)   Setting the AIA first against the expenditure of £38,300 leaves £11,700 available to set against the general plant expenditure of £64,450. The balance of £52,750 is not eligible for AIA and therefore enters the main pool.

(iv)   The disposal value of the plant sold in July 2022 is restricted to original cost.

(v)   The car bought in July 2022 has zero emissions and is therefore eligible for a 100% FYA. The car bought in November 2022 has emissions exceeding 50g/km (and was acquired on or after 6 April 2021) so it is allocated to the special rate pool.

(vi)   Total capital allowances for the year are £91,980.

Balancing allowances and charges

If the disposal value of the plant and machinery disposed of during a chargeable period exceeds the balance of expenditure in the relevant pool before disposals are deducted, this indicates that the capital allowances claimed to date exceed the depreciation which has actually occurred. In these circumstances, the written down value of the pool is set to zero and a *balancing charge* is made, equal to the amount of the excess. A balancing charge is a negative capital allowance which is *added* to trading profits for tax purposes.

Balancing adjustments are also required when a business ceases trading (see later in this chapter) or when a non-pooled asset is disposed of. Non-pooled assets are assets which are treated individually for capital allowances purposes (see below). When a non-pooled asset is disposed of, a balancing adjustment is required so as to ensure that the total capital allowances granted in respect of the asset are exactly equal to its depreciation. If the asset's disposal value exceeds its WDV brought forward, a *balancing charge* is made, equal to the excess. If the asset's WDV brought forward exceeds disposal value, a *balancing allowance* is given, equal to the excess.

Non-pooled assets

Certain items of plant and machinery are not brought into the main pool or the special rate pool. Instead, these items are treated individually for capital allowances purposes, with each item having its own "single asset pool". The main items in question are:

(a)   assets with some private use

(b)   short-life assets.

The treatment of each of these items is explained below.

Assets with some private use

Any asset which is partly used for private purposes by the owner of a business is dealt with in a single asset pool. Capital allowances in relation to such an asset are calculated in the usual way and are deducted in full when calculating the WDV of the asset, but only the business proportion of these allowances may then be claimed. Note that:

(a) A balancing allowance or charge will arise on the disposal of an asset which is held in a single asset pool. The taxpayer may claim only the business proportion of any balancing allowance which arises in these circumstances and is taxed on only the business proportion of any balancing charge.

(b) Capital allowances are available in full on assets used for private purposes by an *employee* of the business, but the employee may then be assessed to income tax on a benefit in kind (see Chapter 8).

EXAMPLE 7

Allan prepares accounts to 5 April each year. His acquisitions and disposals of plant and machinery in the years to 5 April 2022 and 2023 include the following:

		£
8 April 2021	Bought Audi motor car (emissions 48g/km)	17,500
12 May 2021	Bought computer system	3,000
27 March 2023	Sold Audi motor car	14,950
27 March 2023	Bought BMW motor car (emissions 51g/km)	24,000

Private use of both cars is agreed to be 30%. There is 25% private use of the computer system. Compute the capital allowances available in relation to each of these items for the years to 5 April 2022 and 2023, assuming that Allan does not claim AIA in relation to the computer system.

Solution

	Audi (30% p.u.) £	Computer (25% p.u.) £		Allces £
y/e 5/4/22				
Additions	17,500	3,000		
WDA @ 18%	3,150		x 70%	2,205
WDA @ 18%		540	x 75%	405
WDV c/f	14,350	2,460		
Total allowances				2,610

	Audi (30% p.u.) £	Computer (25% p.u.) £	BMW (30% p.u.) £		Allces £
y/e 5/4/23					
WDV b/f	14,350	2,460			
Addition			24,000		
Disposal	(14,950)				
Balancing charge	(600)			x 70%	(420)
WDA @ 18%		443		x 75%	332
WDA @ 6%			1,440	x 70%	1,008
WDV c/f		2,017	22,560		
Total allowances					920

Note:

Both motor cars were bought on or after 6 April 2021. The Audi has emissions which do not exceed 50g/km, so WDAs on this car are calculated at 18% p.a. The BMW has emissions which do exceed 50g/km, so WDAs on this car are calculated at 6% p.a.

Short-life assets

A trader may elect that an asset (other than a car) which would normally join the main pool should instead be treated as a short-life asset. If this "de-pooling" election is made, the asset is treated on an individual basis, and then:

(a) if the asset is not disposed of within eight years of the end of the chargeable period in which it is acquired, it is transferred to the main pool at its written down value at the end of those eight years and the short-life election will have had no effect

(b) if the asset is disposed of within the eight-year period, a balancing allowance will be given (or a balancing charge will be made).

Making a short-life election in relation to an asset which is likely to be sold for less than its WDV within eight years will generate a balancing allowance on disposal, so ensuring that capital allowances are given as quickly as possible. There is (of course) no point in making such an election if a 100% AIA is available in relation to the asset. Note that:

(a) A short-life election relating to expenditure incurred during a chargeable period must be made by 31 January in the second tax year following the tax year in which the chargeable period ends.

(b) One effect of a short-life election is that the asset concerned is kept out of the main pool. This increases the likelihood that disposals from that pool will have a disposal value which exceeds the pool balance, so triggering a balancing charge (see earlier in this chapter). This factor should be borne in mind when making a short-life election.

EXAMPLE 8

Anita starts trading on 1 April 2023, preparing accounts to 31 March. Her only acquisitions and disposals of plant and machinery in the first three years of trading are as follows:

		£
1 April 2023	Bought general plant	205,000
1 April 2023	Bought office computer system	40,000
15 February 2026	Sold office computer system	15,000

Her AIA of £200,000 for the year to 31 March 2024 is set against the general plant. Compute capital allowances for the first three chargeable periods assuming that:

(a) she does not make any short-life elections

(b) she makes a short-life election with regard to the office computer.

Solution

(a) Without a short-life election, the computer joins the main pool. Expenditure of £5,000 on general plant also joins this pool and WDAs are as follows:

   – *y/e 31 March 2024*, WDA £8,100 (18% × £45,000), WDV c/f £36,900

   – *y/e 31 March 2025*, WDA £6,642 (18% × £36,900), WDV c/f £30,258

   – *y/e 31 March 2026*, WDA £2,746 (18% × (£30,258 – £15,000)), WDV c/f £12,512

   Total allowances over the three years are £217,488 (£200,000 + £8,100 + £6,642 + £2,746) and WDV carried forward is £12,512.

(b) If a short-life election is made with regard to the office computer, main pool WDAs are as follows:

   – *y/e 31 March 2024*, WDA £900 (18% × £5,000), WDV c/f £4,100

   – *y/e 31 March 2025*, WDA £738 (18% × £4,100), WDV c/f £3,362

   – *y/e 31 March 2026*, WDA £605 (18% × £3,362), WDV c/f £2,757

   Short-life asset allowances are as follows:

   – *y/e 31 March 2024*, WDA £7,200 (18% × £40,000), WDV c/f £32,800

   – *y/e 31 March 2025*, WDA £5,904 (18% × £32,800), WDV c/f £26,896

   – *y/e 31 March 2026*, balancing allowance £11,896 (£26,896 – £15,000)

   Total allowances over the three years are £227,243 (£200,000 + £900 + £738 + £605 + £7,200 + £5,904 + £11,896) and WDV carried forward is £2,757.

As expected, a short-life asset election has the effect of accelerating capital allowances in relation to the computer system. With such an election, total allowances over the first three years of trading are increased by £9,755 (£227,243 – £217,488). However, WDV carried forward at the end of the third year is correspondingly lower by £9,755 (£12,512 – £2,757) and this will reduce capital allowances in future years.

Allowances on cessation of trade

When a business ceases trading and all of the plant and machinery is disposed of, capital allowances for the final chargeable period are computed as follows:

(a) Any items acquired in the final period are added into the relevant pool.

(b) No WDA, AIA or FYA is given in the final chargeable period.

(c) The disposal value of each pool (including single asset pools) is subtracted from the balance of unrelieved expenditure, giving rise to balancing allowances or balancing charges. Assets which are taken over personally by the trader are treated as if sold for their market value on the date they are taken over.

However, the balancing adjustments normally made on a cessation can be avoided if the business is taken over by a connected person (e.g. the trader's spouse, civil partner or other relative) as long as an election to this effect is made by both parties. The plant and machinery concerned is then treated as if it had been sold to the connected person "*at a price which gives rise to neither a balancing allowance nor a balancing charge*". Effectively, the plant and machinery pools are transferred to the new owner at their WDVs for tax purposes.

EXAMPLE 9

Jake has been trading for many years, preparing accounts to 30 September each year. The written down value of his plant and machinery at 30 September 2021 was:

	£
Main pool	11,350
Motor car (20% private use by Jake)	13,200

Jake bought plant costing £1,150 in October 2021. This was his only transaction in plant and machinery until 31 July 2022, when he ceased trading and closed down his business. On that date, all of the items in his main pool were sold for a total of £12,850 (all items were sold for less than cost) and his car was sold for £12,000. Prepare Jake's capital allowances computation for the ten months to 31 July 2022.

Solution

	Main pool £	Car (20% p.u.) £	Allowances £
1/10/21 - 31/7/22			
WDV b/f	11,350	13,200	
Additions	1,150		
	12,500		
Disposals	(12,850)	(12,000)	
Balancing allowance/(charge)	(350)	1,200 x 80% = 960	610

Structures and buildings allowances (SBAs)

Capital allowances for the construction cost of new commercial structures and buildings were introduced by Finance Act 2019. Structures and buildings allowances (SBAs) may be claimed in relation to eligible costs incurred as from 29 October 2018 and are given at an annual rate of 3% (*2% prior to 6 April 2020*) on a straight-line basis. A brief summary of the main features of SBAs is as follows:

(a) SBAs are available in relation to expenditure on the construction of new structures and buildings as long as the construction work begins on or after 29 October 2018. For this purpose, construction costs include any demolition costs or site preparation costs necessary for construction. Eligible buildings include offices, retail premises and factories. Eligible structures include walls, tunnels and bridges.

(b) Dwellings (residential accommodation) do not qualify for SBAs, nor does any part of a commercial building that is used as a dwelling. SBAs are not available in relation to the construction of home offices within a dwelling.

(c) Land costs and the cost of obtaining planning permission are not eligible expenditure, but the claimant must have an interest in the land concerned. Expenditure on "integral features" of a structure or building (see earlier) continues to be dealt with by the plant and machinery capital allowances system and is not eligible for SBAs.

(d) SBAs are available only if the structures or buildings concerned are used for certain qualifying activities (e.g. trades, professions or vocations).

(e) SBAs begin when an eligible structure or building is first brought into qualifying use and are then given at a flat rate of 3% per annum over a period of 33 and one-third years (400 months). *Prior to 6 April 2020, the rate of SBAs was 2%. In a chargeable period which spanned 6 April 2020, the business could claim 2% p.a. for the part of the period falling before that date and 3% p.a. for the remainder of the period.*

(f) SBAs are reduced proportionately if the asset is first brought into qualifying use part-way through the chargeable period and are reduced or increased proportionately if the length of the period is not exactly 12 months. SBAs cease when a building or structure is demolished or is brought into residential use. However, SBAs remain available during a period of disuse if this immediately follows a period of qualifying use.

(g) Any SBAs that are available for a chargeable period but are not claimed are simply lost. It is not possible to carry forward unclaimed SBAs to a later period.

(h) The sale of a structure or building on which SBAs are being claimed does not result in a balancing adjustment. Instead, the buyer takes over the remaining SBAs to which the seller would have been entitled. The price paid by the buyer is not relevant.

Note that the cost of a structure or building for capital gains tax purposes is reduced by the amount of the SBAs that have been claimed by the owner. This will increase any capital gain arising on its disposal or decrease any capital loss (see Chapter 18).

EXAMPLE 10

Gurpreet (who prepares accounts to 31 December) paid £3m to acquire a piece of land and then paid a further £5m for the construction of a new purpose-built factory on this land. The construction contract was entered into on 1 February 2021 and the factory was first brought into use for trade purposes on 1 July 2022.

Gurpreet uses the factory in his manufacturing trade until 1 May 2037, when he sells it to another business for £11m (including £5m for land). Calculate the SBAs that may be claimed by Gurpreet and by the factory's new owner.

Solution

Eligible expenditure is £5m, so SBAs are (3% × £5m) = £150,000 p.a. Qualifying use begins halfway through the year to 31 December 2022, so the available SBAs for this year are £75,000 (£150,000 × 6/12). SBAs are then £150,000 for each of the fourteen years to 31 December 2036 with a final £50,000 (£150,000 × 4/12) in the year to 31 December 2037.

Assuming that the new owner does not demolish the building or start using it for residential purposes, SBAs of £150,000 per annum may be claimed for a further 18 years and six months (33 years and one-third years less the 14 years and ten months for which Gurpreet claims SBAs). The price paid by the new owner is not relevant to this calculation.

Miscellaneous capital allowances

Capital allowances are available in relation to some miscellaneous categories of capital expenditure. These include patent rights, "know-how" and research and development. Each of these categories is considered briefly below.

Patent rights

The treatment of purchased patent rights acquired for trade purposes is as follows:

(a)   Patent rights expenditure is pooled together. The patent rights pool is adjusted in each chargeable period for acquisitions and disposals and then WDA is calculated at 25% per annum on the reducing balance.

(b)   WDA is proportionately increased or decreased if the chargeable period is of more or less than 12 months.

(c)   As with plant and machinery, disposal value is restricted to original cost.

(d)   If the disposal value of a patent exceeds the balance of unrelieved expenditure in the pool, a balancing charge is made and the pool value is set to zero.

(e)   On cessation of trade, there will be a balancing allowance if the patents are sold for less than the balance of unrelieved expenditure in the pool. There will be a balancing charge if the patents are sold for more than the balance of unrelieved expenditure.

Know-how

"Know-how" is defined as industrial information and techniques of use in either:

(a)   the manufacturing or processing of goods or materials

(b)   the working of mineral deposits

(c)   agricultural, fishing or forestry operations.

All expenditure on know-how is pooled and capital allowances are calculated in much the same way as for patent rights. However, if know-how is sold for more than its original cost, the disposal value used in the capital allowances computation is the *full sale proceeds*. Depending upon the balance of unrelieved expenditure in the pool prior to the disposal, this will either create a balancing charge or restrict the value of subsequent WDAs. In either case, the profit made on the disposal is (in effect) treated as trading income.

Research and development

Capital expenditure on research and development related to the claimant's trade attracts a first year allowance of 100%. Any proceeds subsequently received on the disposal of a research and development asset are treated as a trading receipt.

Summary

▸   Capital allowances are granted for chargeable periods. For income tax purposes, each period of account usually ranks as a chargeable period, but periods of account lasting more than 18 months are divided into two or more chargeable periods.

▸   In order to qualify as plant and machinery, an asset must perform an active function in the trade, not merely provide the setting in which the trade is carried on. There is extensive case law in relation to this distinction.

▸   With some exceptions, expenditure on plant and machinery is pooled together for capital allowances purposes. Most general plant and machinery is allocated to the main pool but certain items are allocated to the special rate pool.

▸   Motor cars with emissions in excess of 50g/km are allocated to the special rate pool. Cars with lower emissions are generally allocated to the main pool but cars with emissions not exceeding 0g/km attract a 100% FYA.

▸   Writing down allowances (WDAs) on plant and machinery are calculated at 18% p.a. in the main pool and 6% p.a. in the special rate pool.

▸   Expenditure on plant and machinery of up to a specified maximum is eligible for a 100% annual investment allowance (AIA). The AIA maximum amount is normally £200,000 per annum. However, this is increased to £1m per annum *during the period between 1 January 2019 and 31 March 2023*. AIA is not available on motor cars.

- An item of plant and machinery which is used partly for private purposes is dealt with in a single asset pool. Capital allowances are calculated in the usual way but only the business proportion of these allowances may be claimed.

- Short-life assets are also allocated to single asset pools. A balancing allowance or charge will arise if a short-life asset is disposed of within eight years.

- Balancing allowances and charges will arise when plant and machinery is disposed of on a cessation of trade, unless the business is acquired by a connected person.

- Businesses which incur eligible capital expenditure on the construction of a qualifying structure or building may claim a structures and buildings allowance (SBA) calculated at 3% p.a. on the straight-line basis (*2% prior to 6 April 2020*).

- Capital allowances are also available in relation to qualifying expenditure incurred on patent rights, "know-how" and research and development.

Exercises

It should be assumed (unless stated otherwise) that maximum capital allowances are claimed in all cases. A set of multiple choice questions for this chapter is available on the accompanying website.

11.1   Maurice prepares accounts to 5 April each year. The written down value of his main pool at 5 April 2022 was £10,300. There was no special rate pool. His purchases and sales of plant and machinery during the year to 5 April 2023 were as follows:

		£
7 April 2022	Bought plant	600
11 April 2022	Sold machinery (original cost £4,000 in 2021)	4,200
11 July 2022	Bought motor car (emissions 44g/km)	8,000
1 November 2022	Bought machinery	400
12 January 2023	Sold equipment (original cost £7,000 in 2019)	3,000

Compute the capital allowances which may be claimed for the year to 5 April 2023, assuming no private use of any of the assets.

11.2   Laura started trading on 1 February 2022, preparing accounts to 30 April. Her adjusted trading profit for the 15 months to 30 April 2023 (before deduction of capital allowances) was £260,122. Her purchases of plant and machinery during the period were as follows:

		£
1 February 2022	Bought machinery	153,000
1 February 2022	Bought motor car (emissions 78g/km)	15,000
12 October 2022	Bought machinery	25,700
7 April 2023	Bought machinery	34,800

Compute her trading income for the first two tax years, assuming 40% private use of the car by Laura. Also compute the amount of any overlap profits.

11.3 Norma has prepared a set of accounts for the nine-month period to 31 December 2022. The written down value of her plant and machinery at 31 March 2022 was as follows:

	£
Main pool	178,400
Toyota motor car (50% private use by Norma)	18,200

Plant and machinery transactions during the period to 31 December 2022 were:

		£
17 April 2022	Bought plant	64,450
1 May 2022	Sold Toyota motor car	15,000
1 May 2022	Bought Saab motor car (emissions 42g/km)	29,600
4 June 2022	Bought motor van	14,500
12 October 2022	Bought Ford motor car (emissions 0g/km)	11,600
3 November 2022	Bought Peugeot motor car (emissions 66g/km)	15,400
1 December 2022	Sold plant (original cost £10,000 in 2018)	3,400

There was 50% private use (by Norma) of the Toyota and Saab motor cars. Prepare a capital allowances computation for the period to 31 December 2022.

*11.4 Raymond started trading on 1 October 2021. He chose 31 March as his accounting date and his first accounts were for the period from 1 October 2021 to 31 March 2022. His purchases and sales of plant and machinery during the first two accounting periods were as follows:

		£
1 October 2021	Bought machinery	130,000
1 October 2021	Bought motor van (emissions 212g/km)	16,200
12 November 2021	Bought motor car (emissions 153g/km)	18,800
18 December 2021	Bought office equipment	4,800
4 February 2022	Bought motor car (emissions 32g/km)	9,200
12 April 2022	Sold car bought in February 2022	9,600
12 April 2022	Bought motor car (emissions 37g/km)	25,500
25 November 2022	Sold machinery (cost £11,500 in October 2021)	8,300
3 February 2023	Bought machinery	50,000

There was 25% private use (by Raymond) of the motor car purchased in November 2021 but there was no private use of any of the other assets.

Required:

Prepare a capital allowances computation for the period to 31 March 2022 and for the year to 31 March 2023.

*11.5   Talat owns a large retail business and prepares accounts to 31 December each year. The written down value of his plant and machinery after deducting capital allowances for the year to 31 December 2021 was as follows:

	£
Main pool	113,210
Special rate pool	9,900
VW motor car (30% private use by Talat)	14,500

He had the following transactions during the year to 31 December 2022:

		£
6 January 2022	Sold VW motor car	17,200
6 January 2022	Bought BMW motor car (emissions 46g/km)	32,000
1 April 2022	Sold plant (original cost £1,000 in December 2021)	1,150
23 May 2022	Bought lifts and air conditioning systems	100,800
12 June 2022	Bought plant	112,550
5 October 2022	Sold main pool car (original cost £17,500 in 2019)	11,000
5 October 2022	Bought car (emissions 61g/km)	12,300
18 November 2022	Sold plant (original cost £4,200 in 2017)	1,310

The lifts and air conditioning systems bought in May 2022 qualify as "integral features" for capital allowances purposes. Private use by Talat of the VW and BMW motor cars has been agreed with HMRC to be 30%.

There were no capital transactions between 1 January 2023 and 31 March 2023, when Talat ceased trading and sold his business. The plant and machinery was disposed of (on 31 March 2023) as follows:

(i)   All of the plant and machinery other than motor cars was sold for £230,000. This consisted of £150,000 for main pool items and £80,000 for special rate items. All items were sold for less than original cost.

(ii)   Talat took over the BMW car. Its market value on 31 March 2023 was £25,000.

(iii)   The only other car remaining was the one acquired in October 2022 and Talat gave this to his brother, who will be using it for private purposes. The market value of the car on 31 March 2023 was £10,000.

Prepare the capital allowances computations for the year to 31 December 2022 and for the period from 1 January 2023 to 31 March 2023. *Assume that Talat decided to restrict his AIA claim for the year to 31 December 2022 to £60,000, to be split equally between the main pool and the special rate pool.*

Chapter 12

Income from self-employment: Trading losses

Introduction

If a self-employed person's adjusted trading profit for a period of account is negative, then a trading loss has been incurred. This has two main consequences:

(a) for tax purposes, the trading profit of that period is £nil

(b) tax relief may be claimed in respect of the loss.

Several forms of tax relief are available and each involves offsetting the loss against other income or gains of the person concerned, so reducing the amount of tax payable on that other income or on those gains. The purpose of this chapter is to explain the main tax reliefs available in relation to a trading loss.

This chapter also explains a restriction which applies to the total amount of certain tax reliefs (mainly loss reliefs) that may be claimed by an individual in a tax year.

Relief for trading losses

The rules which grant tax relief in relation to trading losses are located in the Income Tax Act 2007. This Act provides the following main reliefs:

(a) **Carry-forward trade loss relief**. A trading loss may be carried forward to future tax years and set against subsequent profits of the same trade.

(b) **Trade loss relief against total income**. A trading loss may be set against the trader's total income of the tax year in which the loss is incurred and/or the previous tax year.

(c) **Early trade losses relief**. A trading loss incurred in any of the first four tax years in which the trade is chargeable to income tax may be carried back and set against total income of the previous three tax years.

(d) **Terminal trade loss relief**. A trading loss incurred in the final 12 months of trading may be set against profits of the same trade in the year of cessation (if any) and the previous three tax years.

Each of these forms of loss relief is described below.

Carry-forward trade loss relief

On a claim under s83 ITA 2007, a trading loss may be carried forward and relieved against future trading profits. It is important to note the following points:

(a) Carry-forward relief is given against future *trading profits*.

(b) Furthermore, relief is given only against future trading profits arising from *the same trade* as that in which the loss was incurred. So if a trader ceases one trade and commences another, the losses of the old trade cannot be carried forward and relieved against the future profits of the new trade. Similarly, if a trader carries on two trades simultaneously, a loss incurred in one of the trades cannot be carried forward and relieved against the future profits of the other trade.

(c) Relief must be given against the *first available* trading profits arising in the future. The maximum possible relief must be taken in each year until the loss is fully relieved, even if this leaves insufficient income to absorb personal allowances.

(d) Strictly speaking, relief is given by deduction from the trader's total income when computing his or her net income (see Chapter 2). But the amount of relief given in any tax year cannot exceed the trading profits for that year.

(e) Any claim to carry forward a trading loss under s83 must be made within four years of the end of the tax year in which the loss arises.

EXAMPLE 1

Carla incurred a trading loss of £42,000 in the year to 30 June 2019 and claimed carry-forward relief. Her adjusted trading profits for the following three years are as follows:

	£
year to 30 June 2020	15,000
year to 30 June 2021	26,000
year to 30 June 2022	60,000

Carla's only other income consists of property income of £4,800 per annum. Calculate her net income (i.e. total income less reliefs) for tax years 2019-20 to 2022-23 inclusive.

Solution

	2019-20 £	2020-21 £	2021-22 £	2022-23 £
Trading income	nil	15,000	26,000	60,000
Income from property	4,800	4,800	4,800	4,800
Total income	4,800	19,800	30,800	64,800
Less: Trading losses b/f	-	15,000	26,000	1,000
Net income	4,800	4,800	4,800	63,800

Notes:

(a) Trading income for 2019-20 is £nil as there is a loss in the basis period for that year.

(b) The trading loss carried forward is relieved against future trading profits only and the maximum relief must be given in each year. There is a waste of personal allowances in 2020-21 and 2021-22 (*though 10% of the personal allowance might be transferred to a spouse or civil partner*). Carla would probably prefer to carry forward the whole loss to 2022-23 where it would save tax at higher rates, but this is not permissible.

Capital allowances

As explained in Chapter 11, any capital allowances that are claimed for a period of account are treated as a trading expense of the period. Therefore capital allowances are included automatically in the calculation of a trading loss.

It is important to remember that it is not mandatory to claim the maximum capital allowances available for a chargeable period. If a trading loss has been incurred it may be advisable to claim less than the maximum capital allowances (or even none at all) so as to avoid wasting personal allowances when the trading loss is relieved. Disclaimed capital allowances are not lost permanently, since higher WDVs are carried forward than would otherwise have been the case and this results in higher capital allowances in future years.

EXAMPLE 2

Colin's adjusted trading profits/(losses) for the years to 31 August 2021 and 2022 are:

	Before capital allowances £	Capital allowances available £	After capital allowances £
year to 31 August 2021	(7,900)	4,900	(12,800)
year to 31 August 2022	20,100	6,800	13,300

He is single and has no other income. If the trading loss is carried forward for relief against future trading profits, should Colin claim maximum capital allowances in these two years?

Solution

If Colin claims maximum capital allowances in both years, relief in 2022-23 for trading losses brought forward will be £12,800. This will almost entirely absorb the trading profit of £13,300 assessed in that year, leaving only £500 against which to set the personal allowance, most of which will therefore be wasted.

It would be better to claim no capital allowances at all for the two years. The trading loss brought forward from 2021-22 would then be £7,900 and this would be relieved against the trading profit of £20,100 in 2022-23, leaving income of £12,200 against which to set Colin's personal allowance. There would be minimal waste of personal allowances and the capital allowances available to Colin in future years would be increased.

Trade loss relief against total income

As illustrated earlier, carrying trading losses forward for relief against future profits of the same trade does not always provide the most satisfactory form of loss relief. Problems associated with carry-forward relief include:

(a) Loss relief is delayed until sufficient profits arise from the same trade in future years (if, indeed, they ever do).

(b) The trader has no control over the amount of relief given in each year and therefore personal allowances may be wasted.

(c) If tax rates are falling, relief may be given at a lower rate than the rates which were in force when the loss was incurred.

An alternative form of loss relief which overcomes some of these problems is "trade loss relief against total income". If claimed, this tax relief allows trading losses to be set against the trader's total income for the tax year in which the loss is incurred and/or the previous tax year (see below). It is important to note that:

(a) There is no obligation to make a claim to set a trading loss against total income. If no such claim is made, the loss may instead be carried forward against future trading profits. And any unrelieved losses remaining after a claim has been made to set trading losses against total income may be carried forward against future trading profits.

(b) *For losses incurred in 2020-21 and 2021-22*, a claim to set losses against total income may be extended by a further claim to carry back any remaining unrelieved losses and to set them against the trading income of earlier tax years (see later in this chapter for more details of this "temporary extension").

(c) Trading losses may be set against the trader's total income only if the business is being carried on "on a commercial basis" and "with a view to the realisation of profits". Furthermore, trading losses may not be set against total income if they arise in consequence of tax avoidance arrangements.

(d) If a claim is made to set trading losses against total income, relief is given by deducting the amount of the claim from the trader's total income when calculating his or her net income (see Chapter 2). Relief is given against non-savings income, savings income and dividends in the way which results in the lowest tax liability.

(e) ITA 2007 uses the term "sideways relief" to refer to the relief of trading losses against total income. This term is also used in connection with early trade losses relief. The amount of sideways relief which may be claimed by a "non-active" trader in relation to a trading loss is limited (see later in this chapter).

Note also that trade loss relief against total income is one of the tax reliefs that is subject to a restriction on the total amount of certain income tax reliefs that may be claimed by an individual in a tax year (see later in this chapter).

Relieving a trading loss against total income

ITA 2007 states that relief against total income may be claimed if a person who carries on a trade makes a trading loss "in the tax year". In most cases, the amount of the trading loss in a tax year is defined as the amount of the loss which was incurred in the basis period[†] for that tax year. However, in order to prevent double counting, a trading loss incurred in an overlap period is treated as a loss of the earlier tax year only.

On a claim under s64 ITA 2007, a trading loss incurred in a tax year may be set against the total income of:

either (i) the tax year in which the loss is incurred
  or (ii) the previous tax year
  or (iii) both of these years (if the loss is large enough for this).

A claim to set a trading loss against total income must be made by 31 January in the second tax year following the year in which the loss was made. For example, a claim in relation to a loss incurred in 2022-23 must be made by 31 January 2025. Note that:

(a) The trader can decide whether to make a claim for one of the available years, for both of these years, or for neither year. But partial claims are not allowed. A claim to set a trading loss against total income must be for as much of the loss as can be relieved, even if this sets the loss against income which would otherwise have been taxed at 0% or leaves insufficient income to absorb personal allowances.

  However, if a claim is made for both years, the trader can decide whether to claim maximum relief in the year of the loss (relieving the remainder of the loss in the previous year) or vice versa.

(b) A trading loss may be set against the total income of the previous tax year whether or not the loss-making trade was being carried on in that year.

(c) If a trader claims that two trading losses should be set against the total income of the same tax year (i.e. a loss incurred in that tax year and a loss incurred in the following tax year) then the claim in respect of the current year's trading loss takes priority.

[†] *As from 2024-25 (when basis periods are abolished) this will be the actual loss for the tax year.*

EXAMPLE 3

Ashok has been trading for many years. He is single and is not a Scottish taxpayer. Recent trading profits/(losses), adjusted for tax purposes, are as follows:

	£
year to 31 July 2020	32,400
year to 31 July 2021	13,900
year to 31 July 2022	(11,500)

Ashok's only other income comprises property income of £10,000 per annum. Identify the claims which he could make in relation to the trading loss incurred in the year to 31 July 2022. Which of these loss relief claims (if any) might be recommended?

Solution

Ashok's trading income is:

Year	Basis period	Trading income £
2020-21	y/e 31 July 2020	32,400
2021-22	y/e 31 July 2021	13,900
2022-23	y/e 31 July 2022	nil

He could make a claim to relieve the trading loss of £11,500 against his total income for 2022-23 only, 2021-22 only, both of these years, or neither year:

(a) A claim for 2022-23 only would relieve £10,000 of the loss against his other income, leaving no tax liability for the year and losses of £1,500 to carry forward against future trading profits. This would be a waste, since the other income of £10,000 would in any case have been covered by the personal allowance.

(b) A claim for 2021-22 only would relieve the entire loss against that year's total income of £23,900 (£13,900 + £10,000), leaving income of £12,400 (£23,900 − £11,500) from which to deduct the personal allowance. There would be some minor wastage of the personal allowance but the tax liability for 2021-22 would become zero. This seems to be a fairly efficient way of relieving the loss.

(c) A claim for both years is pointless, since:

  (i) a claim giving relief in 2021-22 first would leave no losses to relieve in 2022-23

  (ii) a claim giving relief in 2022-23 first results in a waste of the personal allowance for that year (see above).

(d) If a s64 claim is made for neither year, the loss could instead be carried forward and set against subsequent trading profits. This would mean that loss relief would be delayed until such time as sufficient profits of the same trade arose in future years.

On balance, a claim to set the trading loss against total income of 2021-22 might be recommended. This claim combines early relief of the loss with a very small wastage of the personal allowance. The claim would have to be made by 31 January 2025.

However, this claim would relieve the loss at only basic rate. If the first available future profits from the same trade are expected to be high, it might be better to carry the loss forward and possibly obtain relief at higher rate. *For a Scottish taxpayer, the claim against total income of 2021-22 would save tax at the starter rate and basic rate. Carrying the loss forward might save tax at intermediate rate or above.*

Relieving trading losses against capital gains

If a claim is made to set a trading loss against the total income of a tax year (or if no such claim is made because total income for that year is zero) the trader concerned may claim that any unrelieved part of the loss should be set against his or her capital gains. Such a claim must be made by 31 January in the second tax year following the tax year in which the trading loss was incurred. This relief is considered further in Chapter 17.

Temporary extension of s64 relief

In response to the increased trading losses caused by the coronavirus outbreak, Finance Act 2021 provides that trading losses incurred in 2020-21 and/or 2021-22 may be carried back for an extra two years and set against the trading profits of those years, so generating tax refunds for the taxpayers concerned. A summary of the rules is as follows:

(a) To qualify for this "extended relief", the taxpayer must normally make a claim first to set the trading loss against total income (a "s64 claim"). It does not matter whether the loss is set against total income of the loss-making year, the previous year, or both of those years. However, extended relief is also available if the taxpayer has no income in the loss-making year and the previous year, so that a s64 claim would be of no value.

(b) If a s64 claim is made to set the trading loss against total income of the previous year, then any unrelieved part of the loss may be carried back for two further tax years and set against trading income (of the same trade) of those two years (later years first).

(c) If a s64 claim in relation to the previous year is <u>not</u> made, then any unrelieved part of the loss may be carried back to that year and for two further tax years, and set against trading income (of the same trade) of those three years (later years first).

(d) A claim for this relief applies to *all* of the two or three tax years in which the loss is to be relieved. The taxpayer cannot specify the amount of relief to be given in each year.

(e) The amount of a trading loss that can be carried back in this way to the tax year immediately preceding the loss-making year is unlimited. But there is a cap of £2m (in total) on the amount of a trading loss that can be carried back to the two earlier years.

EXAMPLE 4

Luigi incurs a trading loss of £75,000 in tax year 2021-22. He had trading profits of £37,500 in 2020-21, £28,000 in 2019-20 and £18,000 in 2018-19. He also has property income of £6,000 per annum. Assuming that Luigi wishes to generate tax refunds in relation to his trading loss, explain the loss relief claims that he should make.

Solution

Luigi would not make a s64 claim to set his loss against total income for 2021-22, since this income (£6,000) is covered by the personal allowance. However, he would probably make such a claim for 2020-21. This would relieve £43,500 of the trading loss (£37,500 + £6,000) and generate a refund of all the income tax paid for 2020-21, though the personal allowance for that year would be wasted.

The s64 claim could then be extended by claiming that the remainder of the loss should be set against the trading income of 2019-20 and 2018-19 (in that order). Loss relief would be £28,000 in 2019-20 and £3,500 in 2018-19 (£75,000 – £43,500 – £28,000).

Early trade losses relief

Losses incurred in the early years of trading may (just like other trading losses) be carried forward against future trading profits or set against the trader's total income. But, in addition to these forms of tax relief, s72 ITA 2007 allows a trading loss incurred in *any of the first four tax years* to be set against the trader's total income of the three previous tax years. This is another form of "sideways relief" (see above). Note that:

(a) If this relief is claimed in relation to a trading loss, the loss is relieved against the trader's total income of the previous three tax years, *beginning with the earliest year*. For example, an early years trading loss incurred in 2022-23 could be set against the trader's total income of 2019-20, 2020-21 and 2021-22, in that order.

(b) A claim for early trade losses relief applies to *all* of the three years concerned. The trader cannot specify the years in which relief is to be given or the amount of relief to be given in each year. The maximum possible relief must be given in each year.

(c) Relief is given by deducting the amount of the trading loss from total income. Relief is given against non-savings income, savings income and dividends in the way which results in the lowest tax liability.

(d) A loss incurred in an overlap period is treated as *a loss of the earlier tax year only*. This rule ensures that a loss is relieved only once.

(e) Early trade losses relief is not available in relation to a trading loss unless the trade is carried on "on a commercial basis" with a reasonable expectation of profits.

(f) A claim for early trade losses relief must be made by 31 January in the second tax year following the loss-making tax year. The claim *cannot* be extended so as to set any unrelieved trading losses against capital gains.

Early trade losses relief is subject to a restriction on the total amount of income tax reliefs that may be claimed by an individual in a tax year (see later in this chapter).

Non-active traders

There is a limit of £25,000 on the amount of sideways relief which may be claimed by a "non-active" trader in relation to a trading loss. A non-active trader is a person who carries on a trade but is not personally engaged in the activities of that trade for at least 10 hours per week. The £25,000 limit applies to the *total* amount of the following reliefs:

(a) trade loss relief against total income
(b) early trade losses relief
(c) relief for trade losses against capital gains.

However, this limit does not affect the giving of sideways relief against profits of the same trade. So if (for example) a trade loss is carried back and set against total income of the previous year, the £25,000 limit does not apply to the amount of the loss (if any) which is set against profits of the same trade made in that previous year.

EXAMPLE 5

Carl begins trading on 1 July 2020 and chooses 30 June as his accounting date. His tax-adjusted trading profits/(losses) for the first two accounting years are as follows:

	£
year to 30 June 2021	(61,200)
year to 30 June 2022	(12,400)

Now that he is self-employed, Carl has no other income. Prior to becoming self-employed his only income was from employment, as follows:

	£
2017-18	23,900
2018-19	24,760
2019-20	35,920
2020-21 (to 30 June 2020)	9,180

Assuming that Carl makes all possible early trade losses claims, calculate his net income (i.e. total income less reliefs) for years 2017-18 to 2020-21 inclusive.

Solution

The losses which are eligible for early trade losses relief are:

Year	Basis period	Workings	Trading loss £	Early trade losses claim
2020-21	1/7/20 to 5/4/21	£(61,200) x 9/12	(45,900)	17-18 *to* 19-20
2021-22	y/e 30/6/21	£(61,200) – overlap £(45,900)	(15,300)	18-19 *to* 20-21
2022-23	y/e 30/6/22		(12,400)	19-20 *to* 21-22

Trading Income for 2020-21 through to 2022-23 is of course £nil. If all possible early trade loss claims are made, net income for years 2017-18 to 2020-21 is:

	2017-18 £	2018-19 £	2019-20 £	2020-21 £
Employment income	23,900	24,760	35,920	9,180
Trading income	-	-	-	0
Total income	23,900	24,760	35,920	9,180
Less: Early trade losses:				
2020-21 loss	(23,900)	(22,000)		
2021-22 loss		(2,760)	(12,540)	
2022-23 loss			(12,400)	
Net income	-	-	10,980	9,180

Terminal trade loss relief

In general, a trading loss may be carried forward against subsequent profits of the same trade or may be relieved against total income. But if a trading loss is incurred in the final year of trading, the first of these alternatives is not available since there can be no future profits against which to set the loss. In order to remedy this situation, s89 ITA 2007 provides a tax relief known as "terminal trade loss relief" which permits a trading loss incurred in the last 12 months of trading to be set against the profits of the same trade for the tax year in which cessation occurs and the previous three tax years. A claim for this relief must be made within four years of the end of the tax year in which the cessation occurs.

Calculating the terminal loss

The "terminal loss" eligible for terminal trade loss relief is the trading loss incurred in the final 12 months of trading, excluding any part of that loss which has already been relieved in other ways (i.e. by deduction from total income). The terminal loss is calculated by adding together the following components:

(a)   the actual trading loss incurred from 6 April to the date of the cessation

(b)   the actual trading loss incurred from a date 12 months before the date of the cessation to the following 5 April

(c)   any available overlap relief (see Chapter 10).

If either (a) or (b) is a profit, this counts as a zero in the calculation of the terminal loss.

EXAMPLE 6

Andrea ceases trading on 31 October 2022. Her adjusted trading profits/(losses) for the closing periods of account are as follows:

	£
year to 31 December 2020	6,600
year to 31 December 2021	2,400
10 months to 31 October 2022	(22,500)

Overlap profits of £3,200 arose when Andrea commenced trading. Calculate the terminal loss, assuming that no claims are made to set trading losses against total income.

Solution

		£
Trading loss 6/4/22 to 31/10/22	£(22,500) x 7/10	(15,750)
Trading loss 1/11/21 to 5/4/22	£2,400 x 2/12 + £(22,500) x 3/10	(6,350)
Overlap relief		(3,200)
Terminal loss		(25,300)

Relieving the terminal loss

As stated above, a terminal loss may be relieved against the profits of the same trade for the tax year in which cessation occurs and the previous three tax years. Note that:

(a) Relief is given in later years first. For example, a terminal loss which arises as a consequence of a business ceasing to trade during 2022-23 would be set against the trading profits of 2022-23, 2021-22, 2020-21 and 2019-20, in that order.

(b) The maximum possible relief must be given in each tax year.

(c) Strictly speaking, relief is given by deduction from the trader's total income. But the amount of relief given in any tax year cannot exceed the trading profits for that year.

EXAMPLE 7

Brendan ceases trading on 30 September 2022. His recent trading profits/(losses) are:

	£
year to 31 January 2020	44,700
year to 31 January 2021	6,500
year to 31 January 2022	2,100
8 months to 30 September 2022	(21,840)

He has no other income. Overlap profits of £4,700 arose when Brendan began trading and no claims are made to set Brendan's trading loss against his total income. Calculate the amount of the terminal loss and show how this may be relieved.

Solution

The calculation of the terminal loss is as follows:

		£
Trading loss 6/4/22 to 30/9/22	£(21,840) x 6/8	(16,380)
Trading loss 1/10/21 to 5/4/22	£2,100 x 4/12 + £(21,840) x 2/8	(4,760)
Overlap relief		(4,700)
Terminal loss		(25,840)

The terminal loss may be relieved as follows:

	2019-20 £	2020-21 £	2021-22 £	2022-23 £
Trading income	44,700	6,500	2,100	nil
Less: Terminal trade loss relief:				
(i) in 2021-22			(2,100)	
(ii) in 2020-21		(6,500)		
(iii) in 2019-20	(17,240)			
Net income	27,460	-	-	-

Post-cessation trade relief

Post-cessation expenses which were not provided for in the final accounts of a business are relieved first against any post-cessation receipts (taxed as trading income). Post-cessation expenses that cannot be relieved in this way and that fall into certain categories may be relieved against the taxpayer's total income for the tax year in which the expenses are incurred. The expenses concerned are:

(a) the costs of remedying defective work done whilst the business was operating

(b) bad debts which were not provided for in the accounts of the business, together with associated debt collection costs.

If the taxpayer's total income for a tax year is insufficient to absorb all of the post-cessation expenses eligible for relief in that year, the excess expenses may be set against the taxpayer's capital gains for the year. Expenses incurred more than seven years after cessation are not eligible for post-cessation trade relief.

Transfer of a business to a company

If the owner of a business transfers that business to a limited company, there is a change in the legal ownership of the business and the vendor is deemed to have ceased trading. In consequence, any trading losses sustained by the vendor before the date of the transfer cannot be carried forward and set against the company's trading profits.

Such trading losses might be relieved by deduction from the taxpayer's total income for the year of the loss and/or the previous year. Terminal loss relief might also be available. But a further tax relief is offered by ITA 2007, which provides that:

(a) if a business is transferred to a limited company wholly or mainly in exchange for shares in that company, and

(b) the vendor of the business continues to hold those shares, and

(c) the company continues to carry on the transferred business

then the vendor may set unrelieved trading losses against the first available income that he or she receives from the company (e.g. dividends or director's fees).

Losses on shares in unlisted trading companies

A person who subscribes for newly-issued shares in certain unlisted trading companies and then incurs a capital loss on the disposal of those shares may claim that this capital loss should be set against his or her total income as if it were a trading loss. This relief is generally available only if the company concerned is of a type which would qualify for the purposes of the Enterprise Investment Scheme (see Chapter 6).

Limit on income tax reliefs

Income Tax Act 2007 imposes a limit on the amount of tax relief that an individual may deduct from total income. This limit applies to the *aggregate* amount of certain specified reliefs. The main reliefs to which the limit applies are:

(a) Trade loss relief against total income
(b) Early trade losses relief
(c) Post-cessation trade relief
(d) Relief for losses on shares in unlisted trading companies
(e) Relief for eligible interest (see Chapter 4).

The total amount of the above reliefs which may be deducted from total income in a tax year is equal to the *greater* of £50,000 and 25% of the individual's "adjusted total income" for the year concerned. Note the following points:

(a) Adjusted total income is defined as the individual's total income for the year, less the gross amount of any pension contributions that are not relieved through a net pay arrangement (see Chapter 14). Any charitable donations made under a payroll giving scheme are added back when computing adjusted total income.

(b) An individual who claims more than one of the above reliefs may decide the order in which they are given. For instance, an individual with both trade losses and eligible interest might prioritise the interest, since relief for this will be lost if it cannot be given in the year concerned, whereas unrelieved trade losses are carried forward.

(c) The limit does not apply to trade losses caused by overlap relief. Nor does it restrict the extent to which trade losses can be deducted from profits of the same trade.

The limit on income tax reliefs does not affect the amount of relief for trading losses that may be set against an individual's capital gains.

Summary

▸ A trading loss may be carried forward and relieved against the first available profits of the same trade arising in the future.

▸ A trading loss may be relieved against total income for the year of the loss and/or the previous year. Any part of a trading loss which remains unrelieved after a claim has been made to set that loss against total income may be set against capital gains.

▸ A trading loss incurred in any of the first four tax years may be set against the trader's total income of the three previous tax years.

▸ A trading loss incurred during the final 12 months of trading may be set against the trading profits of the tax year in which trade ceases and the previous three tax years.

▶ If a business is transferred to a company, the unrelieved trading losses of the vendor may (subject to certain conditions) be set against the first available income which the vendor receives from the company.

▶ Capital losses incurred on the disposal of shares in certain unlisted trading companies may be treated as trading losses.

▶ The total amount of certain specified income tax reliefs (mainly loss reliefs) that may be claimed in a tax year is capped at the greater of £50,000 and 25% of the taxpayer's adjusted total income for the year.

Exercises

A set of multiple choice questions for this chapter is available on the accompanying website.

12.1 Sally (who began trading many years ago and has not ceased trading) incurs an adjusted trading loss of £40,000 in the year to 31 December 2022. She has no capital gains.

(a) What is her trading income for 2022-23?

(b) How could her trading loss be relieved?

12.2 Jane is self-employed. Her recent adjusted trading profits/(losses) are:

	£
year to 31 May 2019	(18,860)
year to 31 May 2020	4,710
year to 31 May 2021	6,210
year to 31 May 2022	14,810

Jane has other income of £10,000 per annum. Assuming that the trading loss is carried forward and set against future trading profits, calculate her net income (i.e. total income less reliefs) for tax years 2019-20 through to 2022-23.

12.3 Marcus begins trading on 1 January 2021 and has the following results:

	Adjusted trading profits/(losses) before capital allowances	Capital allowances claimed
	£	£
year to 31 December 2021	19,080	6,460
year to 31 December 2022	(7,480)	2,320

He is single and has no other income.

(a) Compute his trading income (before loss relief) for 2020-21 to 2022-23.

(b) Identify the claims that could be made in relation to the trading loss, assuming that early trade losses relief is <u>not</u> claimed. Which (if any) of these claims should be recommended?

12.4   Nathan begins trading on 1 October 2020, making up accounts to 31 December each year. His first two sets of accounts show the following adjusted trading losses:

	£
15 months to 31 December 2021	(56,850)
year to 31 December 2022	(32,660)

He has had no other income since becoming self-employed. Before this, his only income consisted of employment income, as follows:

	£
2017-18	25,100
2018-19	25,250
2019-20	26,400
2020-21 (to 30 September 2020)	13,450

Assuming that all possible early trade losses relief claims are made, calculate Nathan's net income (i.e. total income less reliefs) for years 2017-18 to 2020-21.

*12.5   Olive ceases trading on 31 May 2022. Her recent adjusted trading profits/(losses) are:

	£
year to 30 June 2018	37,450
year to 30 June 2019	39,190
year to 30 June 2020	16,120
year to 30 June 2021	(6,840)
11 months to 31 May 2022	(36,300)

Overlap relief of £7,140 is available. Calculate the terminal loss and show how this would be relieved, assuming that Olive has savings income of £10,000 per annum and that no claims are made to set trading losses against total income.

*12.6   Craig began trading on 1 August 2020 and has the following results:

	Adjusted trading profits/(losses) before capital allowances	Capital allowances claimed
	£	£
year to 31 July 2021	5,460	1,140
year to 31 July 2022	(27,400)	1,920

Before commencing to trade, Craig had only investment income. He sold all of his investments in May 2021 (realising a large capital gain) so as to raise extra working capital for his own business. His income from investments in recent years has been:

	£
2018-19	9,150
2019-20	9,940
2020-21	7,690
2021-22 (to May 2021)	510

(a)   Compute Craig's trading income for 2020-21 to 2022-23.

(b)   Explain the trading loss reliefs available to Craig. Which would you recommend?

Chapter 13

Income from self-employment: Partnerships

Introduction

The purpose of this chapter is to explain the taxation treatment of individuals who are members of a partnership. Most of the information given in the previous four chapters with regard to the computation of trading profits, basis periods, capital allowances and trading loss reliefs is applicable to partners as well as to sole traders. The main new factor which arises when dealing with a partnership is the problem of calculating each partner's share of the partnership profit or loss for taxation purposes and much of this chapter is devoted to that problem.

Note that a Limited Liability Partnership (LLP) which is regulated by the Limited Liability Partnership Act 2000 and which carries on a trade or profession is generally dealt with for tax purposes as a partnership rather than as a company.

Principles of partnership taxation

Under the partnership tax rules, a partnership is not regarded as a separate entity for taxation purposes and the partnership itself is not charged to tax. Instead, the profits of the partnership are allocated between the partners and then each partner is taxed as an individual. In detail, the procedure for each tax year is as follows:

(a)   The partnership submits a tax return to HMRC. This return provides information on the profit or loss for the period of account ending in the tax year and gives details of the profit-sharing agreement in force during that period. The return is also used to:

   (i)   claim capital allowances for the period of account, both on partnership assets and on individual partners' assets

   (ii)   claim relief for any business expenses incurred by partners personally.

(b)   The adjusted trading profit or loss of the partnership is calculated in the usual manner. Any drawings or other appropriations of profit made by the partners are disallowed. Capital allowances on partnership assets are treated as a trading expense.

(c) The adjusted trading profit or loss is then allocated between the partners according to the profit-sharing agreement in force during the period of account. If the agreement changes during the period of account, it is necessary to time-apportion the profit or loss, applying the old agreement to the pre-change profit or loss and the new agreement to the post-change profit or loss.

(d) Any capital allowances claimed on an individual partner's assets and any expenses incurred personally by a partner are deducted from the relevant partner's share of the adjusted trading profit or added to that partner's share of the adjusted trading loss.

(e) Partners are then assessed to tax individually, as if each partner's share of the partnership's trading profit or loss had arisen from a trade carried on by that partner alone. In effect, each partner is treated as a sole trader who:

(i) begins trading when joining the partnership

(ii) has the same periods of account as the partnership (except that a partner who joins or leaves the partnership part-way through a period of account will have an individual period of account which begins or ends part-way through a partnership period of account)

(iii) ceases trading when leaving the partnership.

(f) Each partner is solely responsible for the tax due on his or her share of the partnership profit. Partners must include their share of the partnership profit or loss in their own tax returns and in their self-assessment calculations.

EXAMPLE 1

Tom, Dick and Harry begin trading as a partnership on 1 January 2021, sharing profits in the ratio 3:2:1. With effect from 1 January 2022, they agree that Harry should receive a salary of £20,000 per annum, that partners should be entitled to 4% per annum interest on capital and that remaining profits should be shared in the ratio 5:3:2. The adjusted trading profits of the partnership are:

	£
y/e 31 December 2021	90,000
y/e 31 December 2022	110,000

Fixed capitals are Tom £50,000, Dick £60,000, Harry £80,000. Compute each partner's trading income for 2020-21, 2021-22 and 2022-23.

Solution

The allocation of trading profit for each period of account is:

	Tom £	Dick £	Harry £	Total £
y/e 31/12/21				
Profit (shared 3:2:1)	45,000	30,000	15,000	90,000
y/e 31/12/22				
Salary	-	-	20,000	20,000
Interest on capital	2,000	2,400	3,200	7,600
Remainder of profit (shared 5:3:2)	41,200	24,720	16,480	82,400
	43,200	27,120	39,680	110,000

Each partner is treated as a sole trader, commencing trade on 1 January 2021, making up accounts to 31 December and with trading profits for the first two accounting years as shown above. The trading income of each partner is:

Tom

Year	Basis period	Workings	Trading income £
2020-21	1/1/21 to 5/4/21	£45,000 x 3/12	11,250
2021-22	y/e 31/12/21		45,000
2022-23	y/e 31/12/22		43,200

Dick

Year	Basis period	Workings	Trading income £
2020-21	1/1/21 to 5/4/21	£30,000 x 3/12	7,500
2021-22	y/e 31/12/21		30,000
2022-23	y/e 31/12/22		27,120

Harry

Year	Basis period	Workings	Trading income £
2020-21	1/1/21 to 5/4/21	£15,000 x 3/12	3,750
2021-22	y/e 31/12/21		15,000
2022-23	y/e 31/12/22		39,680

Note:

In each case, the overlap period is from 1 January 2021 to 5 April 2021. Overlap profits are Tom £11,250, Dick £7,500 and Harry £3,750. These overlap profits will be relieved when the relevant partner leaves the partnership (or on a change of accounting date).

Notional profits and losses

If the effect of accounting for partners' salaries or interest on capital is to allocate a trading loss to an individual partner, even though the partnership as a whole has made a trading profit, that partner's share of the trading profit is set to £nil and his or her "notional loss" is allocated between the remaining partners in proportion to their original profit allocations.

A similar procedure is followed if a partner is allocated a "notional profit" in a year in which the partnership as a whole has sustained a trading loss.

EXAMPLE 2

(a) Lock, Stock and Barrel are in partnership, making up accounts to 30 June each year. Their profit-sharing agreement specifies that Lock and Barrel should receive annual salaries of £20,000 and £24,000 respectively and that remaining profits or losses should be divided equally. The partnership has an adjusted trading profit of £26,000 in the year to 30 June 2022. Show how this will be allocated between the partners.

(b) Rod, Pole and Perch are in partnership, also making up accounts to 30 June each year. Their profit-sharing agreement specifies that Perch should receive an annual salary of £25,000 and that remaining profits or losses should be shared in the ratio 3:2:1. The partnership has an adjusted trading loss of £5,000 in the year to 30 June 2022. Show how this will be allocated between the partners.

Solution

(a)

	Lock £	Stock £	Barrel £	Total £
Salaries	20,000	-	24,000	44,000
Remainder (£26,000 £44,000)	(6,000)	(6,000)	(6,000)	(18,000)
	14,000	(6,000)	18,000	26,000
Stock's notional loss divided in the ratio 14,000:18,000	(2,625)	6,000	(3,375)	-
Allocation of trading profit	11,375	-	14,625	26,000

(b)

	Rod £	Pole £	Perch £	Total £
Salaries	-	-	25,000	25,000
Remainder (£5,000 + £25,000)	(15,000)	(10,000)	(5,000)	(30,000)
	(15,000)	(10,000)	20,000	(5,000)
Perch's notional profit divided 15,000:10,000	12,000	8,000	(20,000)	-
Allocation of trading loss	(3,000)	(2,000)	-	(5,000)

Change in partnership composition

A change in partnership composition occurs if a new partner joins a partnership (or joins a sole trader to form a partnership) or if an existing partner dies or leaves the partnership. A change in composition has no tax effect on those persons who:

(a) were carrying on the trade beforehand (either alone or in partnership), and

(b) continue to carry on the trade after the change (either alone or in partnership).

Such persons are taxed on the current year basis as if the change had not taken place. But new partners have commenced trading and are subject to the commencement rules, whilst leaving partners have ceased trading and are subject to the cessation rules[†].

[†] *As from tax year 2024-25, basis periods are abolished for partnerships as well as for sole traders (see Chapter 10). Partners will thenceforth be taxed on the actual profits arising in the tax year.*

EXAMPLE 3

Red and White begin trading as a partnership on 1 October 2019, sharing profits equally. On 1 January 2021, they agree to admit Blue as a partner and to share profits in the ratio 3:2:1. The adjusted trading profits of the partnership are:

	£
y/e 30 September 2020	105,000
y/e 30 September 2021	120,000
y/e 30 September 2022	135,000

Compute each partner's trading income for the years 2019-20 through to 2022-23.

Solution

The allocation of trading profit for each period of account is:

	Red £	White £	Blue £	Total £
y/e 30/9/20 (shared equally)	52,500	52,500	-	105,000
y/e 30/9/21				
1/10/20 - 31/12/20				
£120,000 x 3/12 (shared equally)	15,000	15,000	-	30,000
1/1/21 - 30/9/21				
£120,000 x 9/12 (shared 3:2:1)	45,000	30,000	15,000	90,000
	60,000	45,000	15,000	120,000
y/e 30/9/22 (shared 3:2:1)	67,500	45,000	22,500	135,000

For tax purposes, each partner is now treated as a sole trader and is assessed on his or her share of the partnership trading profit. The position of each partner is as follows:

(a) Red began trading on 1 October 2019, preparing accounts to 30 September. Each period of account is of 12 months' duration. Profits are £52,500 for the year to 30 September 2020, £60,000 for the year to 30 September 2021 and £67,500 for the year to 30 September 2022.

(b) White began trading on 1 October 2019, preparing accounts to 30 September. Each period of account is of 12 months' duration. Profits are £52,500 for the year to 30 September 2020, £45,000 for the year to 30 September 2021 and £45,000 for the year to 30 September 2022.

(c) Blue began trading on 1 January 2021, preparing accounts to 30 September. The first accounts cover the nine-month period from 1 January 2021 to 30 September 2021 with profits of £15,000. Profits are £22,500 for the year to 30 September 2022.

Each partner's trading income is as follows:

Red

Year	Basis period	Workings	Trading income £
2019-20	1/10/19 to 5/4/20	£52,500 x 6/12	26,250
2020-21	y/e 30/9/20		52,500
2021-22	y/e 30/9/21		60,000
2022-23	y/e 30/9/22		67,500

White

Year	Basis period	Workings	Trading income £
2019-20	1/10/19 to 5/4/20	£52,500 x 6/12	26,250
2020-21	y/e 30/9/20		52,500
2021-22	y/e 30/9/21		45,000
2022-23	y/e 30/9/22		45,000

Blue

Year	Basis period	Workings	Trading income £
2020-21	1/1/21 to 5/4/21	£15,000 x 3/9	5,000
2021-22	1/1/21 to 31/12/21	£15,000 + 3/12 x £22,500	20,625
2022-23	y/e 30/9/22		22,500

Note:

In the case of Red and White, the overlap period is from 1 October 2019 to 5 April 2020 and each partner has overlap profits of £26,250. In the case of Blue, there is an overlap period from 1 January 2021 to 5 April 2021 and another overlap period from 1 October 2021 to 31 December 2021. Overlap profits are £5,000 + (£22,500 x 3/12) = £10,625.

Non-trading income

A partnership which has trading income may also have non-trading income. For partnership tax purposes, non-trading income falls into two categories:

(a) **Taxed income**

For this purpose, "taxed income" is defined as income from which tax has already been deducted at source (e.g. loan interest from a company) and dividends received. The amount of any taxed income arising in a period of account is divided between the partners in profit-sharing ratio and then each partner's share is apportioned between tax years and assessed to tax on the actual basis.

It is acceptable to allocate taxed income between tax years on the receipts basis if this would be more appropriate than time-apportionment.

(b) **Untaxed income**

For this purpose, "untaxed income" is defined as non-trading income which is not taxed income (e.g. income from property and bank or building society interest). The amount of any untaxed income arising in a period of account is allocated between the partners in profit-sharing ratio and is then assessed to tax using *the same basis periods as those used for the trading income*. If this treatment results in non-trading income being taxed twice when a partner starts trading, overlap relief is available[†].

If a partnership does not carry on a trade or profession, the treatment described at (a) above applies to *all* of the partnership's non-trading income.

[†] *As from tax year 2024-25, basis periods are abolished (see Chapter 10). The untaxed income of a partnership will then be taxed in the same way as taxed income.*

EXAMPLE 4

Hook, Line and Sinker begin trading as a partnership on 1 July 2020, sharing profits equally. The chosen accounting date is 30 June and the first accounts are made up for the year to 30 June 2021. In addition to its trading income, the partnership has non-trading income as follows:

	y/e 30/6/21 £	y/e 30/6/22 £
Income from property	7,500	9,000
Net loan interest received from a company	2,400	3,600

(a) Compute each partner's income from property for tax years 2020-21, 2021-22 and 2022-23.

(b) Compute the gross amount of loan interest on which each partner is taxed in tax years 2020-21 and 2021-22.

Solution

(a) Each partner is allocated property income of £2,500 in the year to 30 June 2021 and £3,000 in the year to 30 June 2022. Property income per partner for each tax year is as follows:

Year	Basis period	Workings	Property income £
2020-21	1/7/20 to 5/4/21	£2,500 x 9/12	1,875
2021-22	y/e 30/6/21		2,500
2022-23	y/e 30/6/22		3,000

Each partner is entitled to overlap relief of £1,875.

(b) Each partner is allocated net loan interest of £800 in the year to 30 June 2021 and £1,200 in the year to 30 June 2022. When grossed-up at 100/80, these figures become £1,000 and £1,500 respectively. Therefore the gross interest on which each partner is taxed in each tax year (assuming time-apportionment) is as follows:

Year	Workings	Savings income £
2020-21	£1,000 x 9/12	750
2021-22	(£1,000 x 3/12) + (£1,500 x 9/12)	1,375

The remaining 3/12ths of the interest received during the year to 30 June 2022 will be taxed in 2022-23, along with the first 9/12ths of any interest received net in the year to 30 June 2023.

Trading losses

As explained above, a trading loss is allocated between the partners in the same way as a trading profit. In general, each partner is then entitled to precisely the same loss reliefs as a sole trader (see Chapter 12) with regard to his or her share of the loss.

EXAMPLE 5

Game, Set and Match begin trading in partnership on 1 August 2020, preparing accounts to 31 January each year and sharing profits equally. With effect from 1 March 2021, they agree to share profits in the ratio 1:2:2. The adjusted trading profits/(losses) of the partnership are as follows:

	£
period to 31 January 2021	43,050
y/e 31 January 2022	21,600
y/e 31 January 2023	(7,420)

Compute each partner's trading income for tax years 2020-21, 2021-22 and 2022-23 and explain how the trading loss incurred in the year to 31 January 2023 will be treated.

Solution

The allocation of trading profit or loss for each period of account is:

	Game £	Set £	Match £	Total £
period to 31/1/21 (shared equally)	14,350	14,350	14,350	43,050
y/e 31/1/22				
1/2/21 - 28/2/21				
£21,600 x 1/12 (shared equally)	600	600	600	1,800
1/3/21 - 31/1/22				
£21,600 x 11/12 (shared 1:2:2)	3,960	7,920	7,920	19,800
	4,560	8,520	8,520	21,600
y/e 31/1/23 (shared 1:2:2)	(1,484)	(2,968)	(2,968)	(7,420)

Each partner's trading income is as follows:

Game

Year	Basis period	Workings	Trading income £
2020-21	1/8/20 to 5/4/21	£14,350 + 2/12 x £4,560	15,110
2021-22	y/e 31/1/22		4,560
2022-23	y/e 31/1/23		nil

Set

Year	Basis period	Workings	Trading income £
2020-21	1/8/20 to 5/4/21	£14,350 + 2/12 x £8,520	15,770
2021-22	y/e 31/1/22		8,520
2022-23	y/e 31/1/23		nil

Match

Year	Basis period	Workings	Trading income £
2020-21	1/8/20 to 5/4/21	£14,350 + 2/12 x £8,520	15,770
2021-22	y/e 31/1/22		8,520
2022-23	y/e 31/1/23		nil

Notes:

(i)   The basis period for 2020-21 for each partner includes two months out of the year to 31 January 2022. The profit for these two months is calculated by taking 2/12ths of the partner's profit for that year. In the case of Game (for example) it would be wrong to take £600 + (1/11 x £3,960) as the profit of the period from 1/2/21 to 5/4/21.

(ii) Each partner has overlap profits, calculated in the usual way.

(iii) Each partner may choose individually how to relieve his/her share of the trading loss incurred in the basis period for 2022-23. Possibilities include carry-forward against future trading profits, loss relief against total income or an early trade losses claim.

Treatment of certain interest as a loss

As explained in Chapter 4, certain types of loan interest are deductible from a partner's total income when computing his or her net income. The eligible loans are:

(a) a loan to purchase plant or machinery for use in the business of a partnership

(b) a loan to purchase an interest in a partnership.

If a partner's total income is insufficient to deduct such loan interest in full, the excess interest may be treated as a trading loss for the purposes of carry-forward trade loss relief and terminal trade loss relief (see Chapter 12).

Restrictions on trade loss relief for certain partners

Income Tax Act 2007 contains anti-avoidance rules which restrict the amount of tax relief that may be given for trading losses incurred by partners. These rules restrict the amount of sideways relief and capital gains relief that may be claimed by partners. As explained in Chapter 12, the term "sideways relief" refers to the relief of trading losses against total income, including early trade losses relief. The main restrictions are as follows:

(a) A limited partner or a member of an LLP is denied sideways relief or capital gains relief for a trading loss incurred in a tax year to the extent that the loss exceeds the partner's "contribution to the firm" as measured at the end of the basis period for that year. For this purpose, a partner's "contribution" is broadly equal to the amount of capital which the partner has contributed to the partnership, plus any share of profits that have not been withdrawn[†].

(b) Similarly, a "non-active" partner (one who is not personally engaged in the activities of the trade for at least ten hours per week) is denied sideways relief or capital gains relief for a trading loss incurred in an "early tax year", to the extent that it exceeds his or her contribution to the firm. For this purpose, an early tax year is defined as the tax year in which the partner began trading or one of the next three tax years[†].

(c) Furthermore, the total amount of sideways relief and capital gains relief given in relation to a trading loss incurred by a limited partner or non-active partner is capped at £25,000.

(d) Finally, trading losses incurred by any partner may not be set against total income or capital gains if the losses arise in consequence of tax avoidance arrangements.

[†] *When comparing a trading loss with a partner's contribution, the contribution is first reduced by any previous trading losses for which sideways relief or capital gains relief has been claimed.*

Note that the restrictions on sideways relief do *not* restrict the extent to which a trading loss may be relieved against the partner's profits from the loss-making trade. For example, if a trading loss is relieved against total income of the previous tax year, there is no restriction on the amount of the loss which may be set against the partner's trading profit from the partnership in that year. The aim of the anti-avoidance rules is to restrict the extent to which losses may be relieved against other forms of income.

Summary

▶ Each partner is taxed individually on his or her share of a partnership profit and each partner is solely responsible for his or her own tax liability.

▶ The adjusted trading profit of a partnership is allocated between the partners in accordance with the profit-sharing agreement for the period of account in which the profit arises. Notional profits and losses allocated to a partner are redistributed among the remaining partners.

▶ In effect, each partner is treated as a sole trader who begins trading when joining the partnership, has the same accounting dates as the partnership and ceases trading when leaving the partnership.

▶ The tax treatment of the non-trading income of a partnership depends upon whether the income ranks as taxed income or untaxed income and whether or not the partnership also has trading income.

▶ The trading losses of a partnership are allocated between the partners. Each partner may then choose individually how to relieve his or her share of the loss.

Exercises

A set of multiple choice questions for this chapter is available on the accompanying website.

13.1 Nickleby, Copperfield and Drood have traded as equal partners for many years, making up accounts to 31 December each year. As from 1 April 2022 they agree to share profits in the ratio 1:2:2. The adjusted trading profit for the year to 31 December 2022 is £183,000. Show how this profit is allocated between the partners.

13.2 Pickwick, Snodgrass and Tupman are in partnership, making up accounts to 31 March annually. Each partner receives 6% interest on fixed capital. Pickwick and Tupman are entitled to annual salaries of £40,000 and £30,000 respectively. Remaining profits or losses are divided equally. Fixed capitals are Pickwick £60,000, Snodgrass £100,000 and Tupman £50,000. The adjusted trading profit for the year to 31 March 2023 is £62,500. Show how this profit is allocated between the partners.

13.3 Dodson and Fogg began trading in equal partnership on 1 July 2019. On 1 July 2020, they admitted Jackson as a partner and agreed to share profits in the ratio 5:4:1. The adjusted trading profits of the partnership are:

	£
year to 30 June 2020	68,000
year to 30 June 2021	88,000
year to 30 June 2022	116,000

Compute each partner's trading income for 2019-20 through to 2022-23.

13.4   Wardle, Jingle and Trotter began trading on 1 October 2020, preparing accounts to 30 September each year and sharing profits in the ratio 7:2:1. Results for the first two years of trading are as follows:

	y/e 30/9/21	y/e 30/9/22
	£	£
Trading profit	117,460	136,540
Bank interest received	200	220
Loan interest received net (net amount)	992	1,088

(a)   Compute each partner's trading income for 2020-21, 2021-22 and 2022-23.

(b)   Compute each partner's bank interest for 2020-21, 2021-22 and 2022-23.

(c)   Compute the gross amount of loan interest on which each partner is charged to tax in 2021-22.

*13.5   Cluppins and Raddle form a partnership on 1 November 2018, preparing accounts to 31 May each year. Bardell is admitted as a partner on 1 January 2020. Cluppins leaves the partnership on 28 February 2021 and Winkle is admitted as a partner on 1 March 2021.

Profits and losses are shared as follows:

Cluppins and Raddle	1:2
Cluppins, Raddle and Bardell	7:8:5
Raddle, Bardell and Winkle	4:3:1

Adjusted trading profits are:

	£
1 November 2018 to 31 May 2019	60,000
year to 31 May 2020	120,000
year to 31 May 2021	30,000
year to 31 May 2022	80,000

Calculate each partner's trading income for 2018-19 through to 2022-23, identifying any overlap periods and profits.

Chapter 14

Pension contributions

Introduction

The most tax-efficient way of providing for a pension is to make contributions into a registered pension scheme. This might be an occupational pension scheme sponsored by an employer, a public service pension scheme established by the Government or a personal pension scheme taken out with a bank or insurance company. The main purpose of this chapter is to explain the tax reliefs which are available in relation to contributions made into registered pension schemes.

Registered pension schemes

The tax regime which now applies to pension schemes has been in effect since 6 April 2006 and was established by Finance Act 2004. This Act defines a pension scheme as "*a scheme ... to provide benefits to or in respect of persons -*

(a) on retirement,

(b) on death,

(c) on having reached a particular age,

(d) on the onset of serious ill-health or incapacity, or

(e) in similar circumstances."

A pension scheme may be either a "defined benefits" pension scheme or a "money purchase" pension scheme. In a defined benefits scheme, the benefits that are payable to a member are calculated by reference to earnings or length of service or some other such factor. An example of a defined benefits scheme is an occupational pension scheme in which an employee's pension rights are based upon his or her final salary. In a money purchase scheme, the benefits payable to a member are calculated by reference to the size of the pension fund built up during the member's working life.

Registration

A pension scheme which is registered with HMRC is known as a "registered pension scheme" and qualifies for various tax reliefs and exemptions. An application to register a pension scheme may be made if the scheme satisfies certain conditions and is either:

(a) an occupational pension scheme, or

(b) a public service pension scheme, or

(c) a pension scheme established by an insurance company, bank or similar institution.

An occupational pension scheme is one established by an employer or employers so as to provide benefits to employees. A public service pension scheme is (broadly) one established by the Government. The tax advantages of registration include:

(a) The scheme's investment income is exempt from income tax. Any capital gains made on the disposal of scheme investments are exempt from capital gains tax.

(b) Contributions made by scheme members attract tax relief (see below).

(c) Contributions made by employers attract tax relief (see below).

(d) Although pensions are chargeable to income tax, lump sums paid to scheme members on the commencement of a pension are generally exempt from income tax, subject to the operation of the "lifetime allowance" (see below).

Except on ill-health grounds, a registered pension scheme must not allow members to take any pension benefits until they reach normal minimum pension age. This rises from 55 to 57 as from 6 April 2028. However, there is no requirement that members should actually retire before benefits are taken. Therefore, a member of an occupational pension scheme could draw a pension from his or her employer's scheme whilst continuing to work for that employer. Pension benefits must normally begin by the age of 75.

Unregistered pension schemes

A registered pension scheme must comply with many regulations with regard to its investments, the payments it makes to its members and a number of other matters. A pension scheme which does not wish to register is under no compulsion to do so and therefore these regulations can be avoided. However, unregistered schemes do not qualify for any of the tax reliefs and exemptions enjoyed by registered schemes.

National Employment Savings Trust (NEST)

The National Employment Savings Trust (NEST) is a state-sponsored pension scheme which is intended to act as a default scheme for those employees whose employers do not offer an occupational scheme. For taxation purposes, NEST is treated as an occupational pension scheme and is registered with HMRC.

Tax relief for contributions by scheme members

An individual may belong to as many pension schemes as he or she wishes and may make unlimited pension contributions. However, there are limits on the amount of contributions which can attract tax relief.

To be eligible for tax relief, an individual's contributions must be "relievable pension contributions" made into a registered pension scheme and the individual concerned must be a "relevant UK individual" who is an "active member" of that scheme. Note that:

(a) Relievable pension contributions are contributions paid by the scheme member or by a third party on his or her behalf, excluding contributions made after the age of 75 and excluding employer contributions.

(b) An individual is a relevant UK individual for a tax year if *at least one* of a number of conditions is satisfied. The main conditions are that:

    (i) the individual has UK earnings that are chargeable to income tax for the year (i.e. income from employment or self-employment)

    (ii) the individual is resident in the UK at some time during the year.

    Income derived from the commercial letting of furnished holiday accommodation ranks as self-employment income for this purpose (see Chapter 5).

(c) An active member of a registered pension scheme is an individual who is accruing benefits under that scheme.

Tax relief can be claimed for a contribution only in the tax year in which payment is made. There are no provisions for carrying contributions back to previous tax years or forward to subsequent tax years.

Limit on tax relief

The maximum amount of pension contributions on which an individual can claim tax relief in any tax year is the *greater* of:

(a) 100% of the individual's UK earnings for the year that are chargeable to income tax

(b) the "basic amount", which is currently set at £3,600 (gross).

This means that individuals with earnings of less than £3,600 in a tax year (or even none at all) are nonetheless entitled to tax relief on pension contributions of up to £3,600. A self-employed person who incurs a trading loss (and therefore has no earned income) would benefit from this rule, as would a UK-resident individual whose entire income consists of unearned income (e.g. interest or dividends).

If an individual's earnings for a tax year are less than the basic amount, tax relief on the amount of any contributions beyond the level of earnings and up to the basic amount is available only if these contributions are made to a pension scheme which operates the tax relief at source method (see below).

EXAMPLE 1

Gordon is self-employed and he is a member of a registered pension scheme. His trading income for tax year 2021-22 is £27,800 but this falls to only £2,500 in 2022-23.

(a) How much may Gordon contribute to his pension scheme in each year ?

(b) How much of these contributions would attract tax relief?

Solution

(a) Gordon may make unlimited contributions to his pension scheme in both years.

(b) He may claim tax relief on contributions of up to £27,800 in 2021-22 and £3,600 in 2022-23 (assuming that his pension scheme operates tax relief at source).

Refund of excess contributions

If an individual makes pension contributions in a tax year which exceed the maximum amount on which tax relief can be claimed, then the excess contributions may be refunded (if the individual so wishes). Such a refund of pension contributions is known as a "refund of excess contributions lump sum".

A refund of excess contributions lump sum is not subject to income tax. This reflects the fact that the contributions which are being refunded by the pension scheme did not attract tax relief in the first place.

Methods of giving tax relief

There are three methods by means of which tax relief may be given on member's pension contributions. The method adopted depends upon the type of pension scheme and cannot be chosen by the member. The three methods of giving tax relief are as follows:

(a) **Relief at source**. If relief at source applies, a member's pension contributions are paid net of basic rate income tax (20%) and the pension scheme administrator recovers the tax deducted at source from HMRC. This basic rate relief is available even to scheme members who are non-taxpayers or whose marginal rate of income tax is lower than 20% (e.g. members whose highest rate of tax is the dividend ordinary rate[†]).

Also, the member's basic rate limit and higher rate limit[†] are both increased by the gross amount of the contributions, so giving relief at the higher rate or additional rate to higher rate and additional rate taxpayers. This is similar to the way in which higher and additional rate relief is given on Gift Aid donations (see Chapter 4). Another similarity with Gift Aid donations is that the member's "adjusted net income" (see Chapter 3) is reduced by the gross amount of the contributions.

[†] *In the case of Scottish taxpayers, basic rate relief is also available to scheme members whose marginal rate is the starter rate (19%). A Scottish member's basic rate limit, intermediate rate limit and higher rate limit are all increased by the gross amount of the contributions.*

If a scheme member makes pension contributions in excess of the maximum amount on which tax relief can be claimed (see above) and relief at source applies, the excess net contributions are treated as if they were actually gross contributions on which no tax relief is available.

(b) **Net pay arrangements**. The net pay arrangement applies if an employer deducts an employee's contributions to an occupational pension scheme from the employee's pay before operating the PAYE system. This automatically gives tax relief at the employee's marginal rate of income tax.

(c) **Relief on making a claim**. If (rarely) it is not possible to use relief at source or the net pay arrangement, tax relief on a member's pension contributions is given by deducting those contributions from total income when computing the member's income tax liability for the year. This might apply (for example) in the case of contributions to a retirement annuity contract which was taken out before 1 July 1988.

EXAMPLE 2

(a) Faisal has no earned income in 2022-23 but he does have substantial investment income. He belongs to a registered pension scheme which operates relief at source and he makes pension contributions during the year, all of which are eligible for tax relief. Compute the maximum amount of his net contributions in the year.

(b) Alana is self-employed. She has trading income of £62,000 in 2022-23 and no other income. She belongs to a registered pension scheme which operates relief at source and she makes contributions of £500 per month (gross) to this scheme in 2022-23. Explain how tax relief will be given in relation to these contributions.

(c) Bruce is self-employed and a member of a registered pension scheme which operates relief at source. He pays net contributions of £320 per month. His trading income for 2022-23 is £2,750 and he has no other income. Explain the tax treatment of his pension contributions for the year.

(d) Charlotte is employed at an annual salary of £24,000. She pays 7% of her salary each month into her employer's occupational pension scheme (which is a registered scheme). Explain how tax relief will be given in relation to her pension contributions.

Solution

(a) Gross contributions of up to £3,600 are eligible for tax relief in the year. Deducting basic rate (20%) tax relief at source gives maximum net contributions in the year of £2,880. Faisal is entitled to tax relief on gross contributions of £3,600 in 2022-23 even though he has no earned income in that year.

(b) Alana pays net contributions of £400 per month (80% of £500). Her basic rate limit is increased by £6,000 (12 x £500), so she pays higher rate tax on £6,000 less of her income than would otherwise have been the case. *If she is a Scottish taxpayer, her intermediate rate limit is also increased by £6,000.*

(c) Bruce is entitled to tax relief in 2022-23 on gross contributions of up to £3,600 (the greater of £2,750 and £3,600). The maximum net contributions are £2,880 (80% of £3,600). He has made payments totalling £3,840 (12 x £320) so excess contributions are £960. He will be treated as though he had made gross contributions of £4,560 (£3,600 + £960) with basic rate tax of £720 (20% of £3,600) deducted at source. This gives net contributions of £3,840. His pension scheme will recover £720 from HMRC.

(d) Charlotte earns £2,000 per month and makes monthly pension contributions of £140 (7% of £2,000). Her employer will deduct these contributions from her salary before operating the PAYE system, so she will pay income tax on only £1,860 per month.

Tax relief for contributions by employers

In general, contributions made by an employer into a registered pension scheme are deductible when computing the employer's trading profit for tax purposes. This is subject to the overriding condition that the contributions must be made wholly and exclusively for trade purposes. Note the following points:

(a) The amount of the contributions which may be deducted when computing the trading profit for a period of account is usually the amount of the contributions *actually paid* by the employer during that period. However, "spreading" provisions may apply to especially large contributions (see below).

(b) There is no upper limit on the amount of contributions which may be deducted when computing an employer's trading profits. This is in contrast to the situation with regard to an individual's own contributions, which are subject to a limit on the amount which may attract tax relief in each tax year (see above).

(c) Contributions made by an employer in respect of an employee are disregarded when computing the *employee's* income for tax purposes.

Spreading of relief

If there is an unusually large increase in an employer's pension contributions between one period of account and the next, tax relief on excess contributions may be spread over a number of periods. Assuming that the current period and the previous period are of equal length, the required procedure is as follows:

(a) The contributions made by the employer in the current period are compared with those for the previous period. Certain contributions made in the current period are disregarded when making this comparison (e.g. contributions paid into the scheme so as to fund cost-of-living increases in current pensions).

(b) If the amount of contributions in the current period is more than 210% of the amount for the previous period, then there is an excess and this may need to be spread.

(c)   The excess is equal to the contributions made in the current period less 110% of the contributions made in the previous period. Spreading does not apply if this is less than £500,000. Otherwise, tax relief on the excess contributions is spread as follows:

Amount of the excess	Tax relief spread equally over
£500,000 to £999,999	current period and next period
£1,000,000 to £1,999,999	current period and next two periods
£2,000,000 or more	current period and next three periods

A further adjustment is required if the current period and previous period are of unequal length. Spreading does not apply if the employer made no contributions at all in the previous period (e.g. if a new scheme has been established in the current period).

EXAMPLE 3

During the year to 31 May 2022, an employer made contributions of £400,000 into a registered pension scheme. Explain how tax relief will be given on the contributions made during the year to 31 May 2023 if the amount of these contributions is:

(a)   £800,000   (b)   £920,000   (c)   £1,000,000   (d)   £2,640,000

Solution

(a)   The current year contributions are 200% of those for the previous year. This does not exceed 210% so spreading does not apply. Tax relief on the contributions of £800,000 will be given in the year to 31 May 2023.

(b)   Current year contributions are 230% of those for the previous year but the excess of current year contributions over 110% of previous year contributions is only £480,000. This is less than £500,000 so spreading does not apply. Tax relief on the contributions of £920,000 will be given in the year to 31 May 2023.

(c)   Current year contributions are 250% of those for the previous year. The excess of current year contributions over 110% of previous year contributions is £560,000. This is between £500,000 and £999,999 so the excess must be spread equally over the current period and the next period.
      Tax relief on contributions of £720,000 (£440,000 + £280,000) will be given in the year to 31 May 2023 and tax relief on the remaining £280,000 of contributions will be given in the year to 31 May 2024.

(d)   Current year contributions are 660% of those for the previous year. The excess of current year contributions over 110% of the previous year's contributions is £2,200,000. This exceeds £1,999,999 so the excess must be spread equally over the current period and the next three periods.
      Tax relief on contributions of £990,000 (£440,000 + £550,000) will be given in the year to 31 May 2023. Relief on contributions of £550,000 will be given in each of the three years to 31 May 2024, 2025 and 2026.

Annual allowance charge

If an individual is a member of one or more registered pension schemes, an income tax charge (the "annual allowance charge") arises if the "total pension input amount" for the individual in a tax year exceeds the annual allowance for that year. The annual allowance for tax year 2022-23 is normally £40,000. However, this figure is reduced by £1 for every £2 by which the individual's "adjusted income" exceeds £240,000, subject to a minimum annual allowance of £4,000. Note the following points:

(a) For this purpose, "adjusted income" is broadly equal to the individual's net income for the tax year (see Chapter 2) after adding back any pension contributions which have been relieved through a net pay arrangement or by deduction from total income. Any employer pension contributions are also added.

(b) The maximum reduction of £36,000 (reducing the annual allowance from £40,000 to the minimum of £4,000) occurs when an individual's adjusted income for the year is £312,000 or greater, since (£312,000 – £240,000) ÷ 2 = £36,000.

(c) This process of reducing the annual allowance for "high-income individuals" is known as "tapering".

(d) The annual allowance is *not* tapered (even if adjusted income exceeds £240,000) if the individual's "threshold income" for the tax year does not exceed £200,000. For this purpose, "threshold income" is broadly equal to the individual's net income for the year *less* the gross amount of any pension contributions relieved at source.

If an individual's total pension input amount for a tax year exceeds the annual allowance for that year, the excess is charged to income tax at marginal rate (i.e. as if the amount of the excess were an additional slice of income on top of the individual's income from all other sources). This tax charge falls upon the individual, but may actually be paid by the pension scheme(s) concerned in return for a reduction in the individual's future pension benefits.

Pension input amount

An individual's total pension input amount for a tax year is found by calculating the pension input amount for each registered pension scheme to which the individual belongs and then aggregating these figures. Pension input amounts are calculated as follows:

(a) **Money purchase schemes**. The pension input amount for a tax year in relation to a money purchase scheme is equal to the total relievable contributions made by or in respect of the individual during that year, plus any employer contributions.

(b) **Defined benefits schemes**. The pension input amount for a tax year in relation to a defined benefits scheme is equal to the increase in value of the individual's pension rights under the scheme during that year. For this purpose, the value of an individual's pension rights on a specified date is equal to:

(i)   the amount of any lump sum which would be payable to the individual if he or she became entitled to payment of it on that date, *plus*

(ii)   16 times the amount of the annual pension which would be payable to the individual if he or she became entitled to payment of it on that date.

Before calculating the increase in value of an individual's pension rights under a defined benefits scheme, the value of those rights at the start of the year are adjusted for inflation. This adjustment reflects the annual increase in the Consumer Prices Index (CPI) up to the September prior to the start of the tax year concerned.

There is no pension input amount for a tax year in respect of a pension scheme if the individual (in consequence of severe ill health) becomes entitled before the end of that year to all of the benefits which may be provided under the scheme. Nor is there any pension input amount for a tax year if the individual dies before the tax year ends.

Carry forward of unused annual allowance

An individual whose pension input amount for a tax year is less than his or her annual allowance for that year (possibly tapered for a high-income individual) has "unused annual allowance" for the year concerned. However, this is not necessarily wasted, since unused annual allowance may be carried forward for up to three tax years, so making it less likely that an annual allowance charge will apply in those years. Note the following points:

(a)   The individual must have been a member of a registered pension scheme during a tax year in order to carry forward unused annual allowance from that year.

(b)   The current tax year's annual allowance must be set first against the individual's total pension input amount for the year. Unused annual allowance from the three previous tax years may then be taken into account, beginning with the earliest of those years. For instance, an individual whose pension input amount for tax year 2022-23 exceeds his or her annual allowance for the year may use unused annual allowance brought forward from 2019-20, 2020-21 and 2021-22, in that order.

(c)   The calculation of the amount of unused annual allowance from the previous three years (that may be carried forward to the current year) takes into account the fact that unused annual allowance in those years may already have been "used up" in an intervening tax year in which pension input amount has exceeded the annual allowance.

EXAMPLE 4

Calculate the annual allowance available in 2022-23 (including unused annual allowance brought forward) to an individual with total pension input amounts as follows:

2019-20   £25,000   2020-21   £62,000   2021-22   £31,000

Assume that the taxpayer is not a "high-income individual" in any of these years and that there is no unused annual allowance to bring forward from 2018-19 or earlier. The standard annual allowance is £40,000 in all years concerned.

Solution

Unused annual allowance is £15,000 in 2019-20 and £9,000 in 2021-22. But the pension input amount for 2020-21 exceeds the annual allowance for that year by £22,000 and this uses up all of the £15,000 brought forward from 2019-20. Therefore the annual allowance available in 2022-23 is £49,000 (£40,000 plus £9,000 b/f from 2021-22).

EXAMPLE 5

Diane (who is not a Scottish taxpayer) is self-employed and a member of three registered pension schemes. Her pension input amounts for 2022-23 are as follows:

Scheme A: £12,500
Scheme B: £4,400
Scheme C: £11,600

Diane's "adjusted income" for 2022-23 is £296,000 and her marginal rate of income tax for the year is 45%. Her "threshold income" for 2022-23 exceeds £200,000. Compute the annual allowance charge for the year, assuming that there is no unused annual allowance to bring forward from the previous three years.

Solution

Diane's adjusted income for 2022-23 exceeds £240,000 by £56,000. Therefore her annual allowance for the year is £12,000 (£40,000 − 1/2 × £56,000). Total pension input amount is £28,500. This exceeds the annual allowance by £16,500, so Diane's annual allowance charge for the year is £16,500 @ 45% = £7,425.

EXAMPLE 6

Compute the annual allowance charge payable by the following (non-Scottish) employees for tax year 2022-23, assuming in each case that "adjusted income" for the year does not exceed £240,000 and there is no unused annual allowance brought forward. Also assume that the Consumer Prices Index (CPI) rose by 3% in the year to September 2021.

(a) Jill belongs to a money purchase scheme. Her relievable contributions for 2022-23 are £15,000. Her employer's contributions for the year on her behalf are £30,000. Jill's taxable income for 2022-23 is £84,000.

(b) Eric's scheme is a defined benefit scheme. When he retires he will receive an annual pension equal to 1/80th of his final salary for each year of pensionable service. He will also receive a lump sum equal to 3/80ths of final salary for each year of pensionable service. Eric had completed 22 years of pensionable service by the start of 2022-23 and his salary was £72,000 per annum. His salary rose to £76,000 by the end of the tax year. His taxable income for 2022-23 is £67,500.

Both Jill's and Eric's pension contributions are relieved by means of the net pay arrangement. Neither of them made any Gift Aid donations during 2022-23.

Solution

(a)   Total pension input amount for the year is £45,000 and this exceeds the 2022-23 annual allowance by £5,000. With a taxable income of £84,000, Jill's marginal rate of income tax for the year is 40%. Therefore the annual allowance charge payable for 2022-23 is £2,000 (£5,000 × 40%).

(b)   If Eric became entitled to payment of his pension and lump sum at the start of the tax year, he would receive an annual pension of £19,800 (£72,000 x 22/80) and a lump sum of £59,400 (£72,000 x 66/80). The value of his pension rights at the start of the year is therefore £376,200 (£59,400 + (16 x £19,800)). Increasing this figure by 3% to reflect the change in CPI gives £387,486.

If Eric became entitled to payment of his pension and lump sum at the end of the tax year, he would receive an annual pension of £21,850 (£76,000 x 23/80) and a lump sum of £65,550 (£76,000 x 69/80). The value of his pension rights at the end of the year is therefore £415,150 (£65,550 + (16 x £21,850)).

Total pension input amount for the year is £27,664 (£415,150 − £387,486). This is less than the annual allowance of £40,000 for 2022-23 and therefore there is no annual allowance charge.

Lifetime allowance charge

There is no limit to the total amount of the benefits which an individual can receive from registered pension schemes during his or her lifetime. However, a charge to income tax known as the "lifetime allowance charge" will arise if total benefits exceed the lifetime allowance. Whenever pension benefits "crystallise" (e.g. when an individual starts taking a scheme pension) the value of the crystallised benefits is compared with the proportion of the lifetime allowance which remains unused. Any excess is chargeable to income tax. The lifetime allowance figures for tax years 2006-07 to 2022-23 are as follows:

2006-07	£1,500,000	2012-13	£1,500,000	2018-19	£1,030,000
2007-08	£1,600,000	2013-14	£1,500,000	2019-20	£1,055,000
2008-09	£1,650,000	2014-15	£1,250,000	2020-21	£1,073,100
2009-10	£1,750,000	2015-16	£1,250,000	2021-22	£1,073,100
2010-11	£1,800,000	2016-17	£1,000,000	2022-23[†]	£1,073,100
2011-12	£1,800,000	2017-18	£1,000,000		

Any excess of crystallised benefits over the available lifetime allowance is taxed at 55% if taken as a lump sum and at 25% otherwise. This tax charge falls jointly upon the individual and the pension scheme administrator. In practice, the tax will usually be paid by the scheme administrator and then deducted from the benefits paid to the individual.

[†] *Finance Act 2021 freezes the lifetime allowance at £1,073,100 until the end of tax year 2025-26.*

Operation of the lifetime allowance

Whenever a "benefit crystallisation event" occurs, it is necessary to compare the value of the benefits that have crystallised with the proportion of the individual's lifetime allowance which remains unused after any previous such events. The main examples of a benefit crystallisation event are the payment of a lump sum and the commencement of a pension. Note the following points:

(a) The value of a lump sum is the amount paid to the scheme member. The value of a pension is generally equal to 20 times the amount of the pension which will be paid to the member during the first twelve months.

(b) On the first occasion that a benefit crystallisation event occurs, the value of the benefits that have crystallised is compared with the lifetime allowance as it stands on the date of the event. On a subsequent event, the value of the crystallised benefits is compared with the *proportion* of the lifetime allowance (if any) that remains after previous such events. However, this proportion is applied to the lifetime allowance as it stands on the date of the subsequent event.

(c) If an individual becomes entitled to a scheme pension and a pension commencement lump sum from the same scheme on the same date, the payment of the lump sum is considered to be the earlier of the two events. This minimises the lifetime allowance charge, since the lifetime allowance is made available first to the lump sum (which would otherwise be taxed at 55%) rather than the pension.

EXAMPLE 7

Sharon is a member of two registered pension schemes. She receives no benefits from either scheme until 19 March 2015, when she takes a lump sum of £750,000 from one of her schemes. On 5 January 2023 she takes a lump sum of £500,000 from the other scheme. Calculate the lifetime allowance charge arising from these two events.

Solution

On 19 March 2015, crystallised benefits of £750,000 absorb 60% of the lifetime allowance (£1,250,000 for events occurring during 2014-15). There is no lifetime allowance charge and 40% of the lifetime allowance remains unused.

On 5 January 2023, crystallised benefits of £500,000 are compared with 40% of £1,073,100 (the lifetime allowance for events occurring during 2022-23). This is £429,240. Crystallised benefits exceed £429,240 by £70,760. Therefore there is a lifetime allowance charge of £38,918 (55% of £70,760).

The lifetime allowance has now been fully used, so the full value of any further pension benefits will be subject to the lifetime allowance charge.

EXAMPLE 8

Stuart is a member of a registered pension scheme. He took no benefits from this or any other scheme until February 2023, when he received a lump sum of £320,000 and began to receive a pension of £52,500 per annum. Calculate the lifetime allowance charge arising from these events.

Solution

The value of the pension is £1,050,000 (20 x £52,500) so the total value of the benefits received is £1,370,000. This exceeds the 2022-23 lifetime allowance of £1,073,100 by £296,900 and so there will be a lifetime allowance charge.

The lump sum is deemed to be the earlier of the two benefit crystallisation events, so it is the pension which has caused the lifetime allowance to be exceeded. Hence the excess is taxed at 25% and the lifetime allowance charge is £74,225 (25% of £296,900).

Summary

▸ In a defined benefits pension scheme, the benefits payable to members are usually based on final salary and length of service. In a money purchase scheme, the benefits payable to members are based upon the size of the pension fund built up during a member's working life.

▸ Registered pension schemes enjoy certain tax advantages when compared with unregistered schemes. A registered scheme's investment income is exempt from income tax. Any capital gains made on the disposal of scheme investments are exempt from capital gains tax. Tax relief is available in relation to contributions made by members and employers. Tax-free lump sums may be paid to members.

▸ The maximum amount of pension contributions on which an individual can claim tax relief in any tax year is equal to the greater of the individual's earnings for that year and £3,600. If earnings are less than £3,600, tax relief will be given on contributions beyond the level of earnings only if the pension scheme operates tax relief at source.

▸ Basic rate relief on an individual's pension contributions may be given by deduction at source. Relief at the higher rate and additional rate is then given by increasing the basic rate limit and higher rate limit by the gross amount of the contributions. *For Scottish taxpayers*, the intermediate rate limit is also increased by the gross amount of the individual's contributions.

▸ Alternatively, tax relief may be given by deducting an employee's contributions from his or her gross pay before operating the PAYE system. Exceptionally, relief may be given by deduction from the individual's total income.

> ▸ In general, employer contributions to an occupational pension scheme are deducted when computing the employer's trading profit for the period of account in which the contributions are paid. However, tax relief on contributions which are unusually large may be spread over two or more periods.
>
> ▸ A tax liability will arise if an individual's total pension inputs for a tax year exceed the annual allowance for that year (which is reduced for certain high-income individuals). The excess is charged to income tax at marginal rate and this tax charge falls upon the individual concerned.
>
> ▸ A tax liability may arise when a benefit crystallisation event occurs. The most common examples of such an event are the payment of a lump sum to a member and/or the commencement of a pension. The value of the crystallised benefits is compared with the unused proportion of the lifetime allowance and any excess is charged to income tax. The tax charge is calculated at either 55% or 25%, depending on whether the benefits are taken as a lump sum or a pension.

Exercises

A set of multiple choice questions for this chapter is available on the accompanying website.

14.1 State the maximum contribution to registered pension schemes on which an individual could obtain tax relief in 2022-23 if the individual's earnings for the year were:

(a) £120,000   (b) £1,200.

14.2 Freda is a member of a registered pension scheme which operates tax relief at source. She has income from self-employment of £60,000 in 2022-23 and makes pension contributions of £1,000 (gross) per month. Explain how tax relief will be given in relation to her pension contributions.

14.3 An employer's contributions into a registered pension scheme during the year to 30 June 2022 are £600,000. Explain how tax relief will be given on the contributions of £1,860,000 which the employer makes during the year to 30 June 2023.

14.4 Karen belongs to a number of registered pension schemes. Until tax year 2009-10 she had received no benefits from any of these schemes but in October 2009 she took a lump sum of £350,000 from one of her schemes. She received no further benefits until July 2022 when she took a lump sum of £1,120,000 from another of her schemes.

(a) Calculate the amount of any lifetime allowance charges arising in relation to either of Karen's lump sums.

(b) How would the situation change if the lump sum of £1,120,000 had been received in October 2009 and the lump sum of £350,000 had been received in July 2022?

14.5   Damon is a member of a defined benefit registered pension scheme. On retirement, he will receive an annual pension equal to 1/60th of final salary for each year of pensionable service. He will also receive a lump sum equal to 3/80ths of final salary for each year of pensionable service.

At the start of tax year 2022-23, Damon's annual salary was £360,000 and he had accumulated 20 years of pensionable service. By the end of the year his salary had risen to £390,000. He is not a Scottish taxpayer.

Damon's marginal rate of income tax for 2022-23 is 45% and he has no unused annual allowance brought forward from previous years. His "adjusted income" for the year is £427,500 and his "threshold income" exceeds £200,000. Calculate the annual allowance charge payable for 2022-23. (Ignore inflation).

*14.6   Edna's total pension input amounts for tax years 2019-20 to 2022-23 are as follows:

2019-20	£23,000
2020-21	£34,000
2021-22	£42,000
2022-23	£45,000

She has no unused annual allowance to bring forward from previous years. Her taxable income for 2022-23 (after deduction of the personal allowance) is £87,500 and she is not a "high-income individual" in any year. The standard annual allowance (before tapering) is £40,000 in all years concerned.

Calculate the annual allowance charge for 2022-23 and the amount of any unused annual allowance carried forward to 2023-24.

*14.7   Irma is self-employed. Her trading income for 2022-23 is £69,950 and during the year she makes net contributions to a registered pension scheme of £6,000. Her only other income in 2022-23 consists of property income of £7,400.

Assuming that Irma is not a Scottish taxpayer, calculate her income tax liability for the year. How would the liability differ for a Scottish taxpayer?

Chapter 15

Payment of income tax, interest and penalties

Introduction

Interest is charged on income tax which is paid late. Conversely, interest may be added to repayments of income tax. The main purpose of this chapter is to identify the dates on which income tax is payable and to explain how the interest due on underpaid or overpaid tax is calculated. This chapter also considers financial penalties to which a taxpayer may become liable as a consequence of non-compliance with tax law.

Payment of income tax

Under the Self Assessment system (see Chapter 1) income tax which is not deducted at source is payable† as follows:

(a) The taxpayer's income tax liability for the tax year in relation to all sources of income is aggregated. This tax liability is increased by the amount of any Class 4 National Insurance contributions (NICs) which are due for the year (see Chapter 16).

(b) Payments on account of the total liability (POAs) are due to be made on 31 January in the tax year and on the following 31 July. For example, the POAs for 2022-23 are due on 31 January 2023 and 31 July 2023. Each POA is equal to 50% of the taxpayer's liability to income tax and Class 4 NICs for the *previous* tax year, less any tax which was paid by deduction at source (including tax paid via PAYE). Note that:

   (i) POAs are not required if the taxpayer's total liability to income tax and Class 4 NICs for the preceding year (less tax deducted at source) was under £1,000.

   (ii) POAs are also not required if more than 80% of the taxpayer's liability for the previous year was satisfied by deduction of tax at source.

   (iii) A taxpayer who believes that his or her liability for the current year will be less than in the previous year may claim to make reduced POAs. There are penalties for making such a claim fraudulently or negligently (see below).

† *See the accompanying website for discretionary "Time to Pay" arrangements, whereby a taxpayer in financial difficulties may be able to settle the tax liability over an extended period of time.*

(c) A balancing payment (or repayment) is normally due on 31 January following the end of the tax year. For example, the 2022-23 balancing payment is due on 31 January 2024. But note that:

(i) If a tax return notice is issued late (i.e. after 31 October following the end of the tax year to which it relates) and this has not been caused by the taxpayer's failure to notify his or her chargeability to tax, then the balancing payment is due three months after the date of the notice.

(ii) If a self-assessment is amended by the taxpayer or by HMRC (or if a discovery assessment is raised) any additional amount payable is due 30 days after the date of its notification to the taxpayer or on 31 January following the end of the tax year concerned, whichever is the later. However, this rule does *not* defer the date from which interest accrues on the additional tax.

The amount of the balancing payment is equal to the income tax and Class 4 NICs liability for the year, less any tax deducted at source and less the POAs (if any). The taxpayer's liability to Class 2 NICs (see Chapter 16) is added to this payment, along with any capital gains tax payable for the year (see Chapter 17).

(d) Taxpayers with employment income may request that a balancing payment which is less than £3,000 should be collected by means of the PAYE system. For instance, a balancing payment for 2022-23 (normally due on 31 January 2024) could be collected via PAYE during tax year 2024-25. But this requires that the tax return for the year concerned is submitted by 30 December (see Chapter 1).

Interest is charged if any payment is made after the due date. Late payment penalties (see below) may also be imposed. Taxpayers receive regular statements from HMRC showing the amounts due, the amounts paid to date and the amounts of any interest and penalties.

EXAMPLE 1

(a) Warren's liability to income tax and Class 4 NICs for tax year 2021-22 was £17,200, of which £14,500 was paid via PAYE.

(i) Compute his POAs for 2022-23 and state the dates on which these fall due.

(ii) Compute the balancing payment for 2022-23 and state the due date of payment, assuming that Warren's liability to income tax and Class 4 NICs for 2022-23 is £19,300, of which £16,100 has been paid via PAYE.

(b) Diana's liability to income tax and Class 4 NICs for tax year 2021-22 was £3,400, of which £2,500 was deducted at source.

(i) Compute her POAs for 2022-23 and state the dates on which these fall due.

(ii) Compute the balancing payment for 2022-23 and state the due date of payment, assuming that Diana's liability to income tax and Class 4 NICs for 2022-23 is £11,400, of which none has been paid by deduction at source.

Ignore Class 2 NICs and capital gains tax.

Solution

(a) 84.3% of the liability for 2021-22 was paid via PAYE. This is over 80% and therefore no POAs are required for 2022-23. The remaining liability for 2022-23 of £3,200 (£19,300 – £16,100) is due for payment on 31 January 2024.

(b) 73.5% of the liability for 2021-22 was deducted at source. This does not exceed 80% but the remainder of the liability was only £900, which is under £1,000. Therefore no POAs are required for 2022-23. The liability of £11,400 for 2022-23 is due to be paid on 31 January 2024.

EXAMPLE 2

Barbara's liability to income tax and Class 4 NICs for tax year 2021-22 was £26,000, of which £4,000 was paid by deduction at source. Her liability for 2022-23 is £30,000, of which £1,000 has been deducted at source. State the dates on which Barbara is required to pay her 2022-23 liability and compute the amount payable on each date.

Ignore Class 2 NICs and capital gains tax.

Solution

Barbara paid 15.4% of her 2021-22 liability by deduction at source. This is not over 80% and the remainder of the liability (£22,000) was not less than £1,000. Therefore POAs are required for 2022-23. The required payments are as follows

(i) 31 January 2023, POA £11,000 (50% of (£26,000 – £4,000))

(ii) 31 July 2023, POA £11,000

(iii) 31 January 2024, balancing payment £7,000 (£30,000 – £1,000 – POAs £22,000).

Voluntary tax payments

When MTD is introduced for income tax (see Chapter 1), taxpayers will be able to make voluntary tax payments at any time. Such payments will appear as a credit on taxpayers' digital tax accounts and will be set against tax liabilities as they fall due. This will enable taxpayers to choose suitable payment patterns and so manage their cash flows better.

Direct recovery of tax debts

In certain circumstances, HMRC may recover tax debts[†] directly from a taxpayer's bank or building society accounts. Safeguards are in place to protect vulnerable taxpayers and to ensure that at least £5,000 remains in the taxpayer's accounts after a tax debt has been recovered. There is also a right of appeal against a direct recovery decision.

[†] *HMRC may also collect tax debts of up to £17,000 through the PAYE system (depending on the size of the taxpayer's employment income) with or without the taxpayer's consent. A debt paid in this way is treated as if paid on the first day of the tax year in which it is collected. For instance, a tax debt collected via PAYE during tax year 2022-23 is treated as if paid on 6 April 2022.*

Late payment penalties

In addition to the interest charged on tax which is paid late (see below), a taxpayer who makes a late balancing payment[†] may also incur a late payment penalty[‡]. Broadly, the late payment penalty system imposes a penalty equal to 5% of any tax not paid within 30 days of the due date, with two further 5% penalties for tax remaining unpaid six months and 12 months after the due date. The detailed rules are as follows:

(a) If all or part of a balancing payment remains unpaid more than 30 days after the due date, the penalty is 5% of the amount unpaid. The "penalty date" (the date on which this penalty is charged) is the date which falls 31 days after the due date of payment.

(b) If any of the balancing payment is not paid within the five-month period beginning on the penalty date, there is another penalty equal to 5% of the amount still unpaid.

(c) Finally, if any of the balancing payment is not paid within the eleven-month period beginning on the penalty date, there is a further 5% penalty.

(d) If a taxpayer is liable to a late payment penalty, HMRC must issue the taxpayer with a penalty notice. Late payment penalties are due for payment within the 30-day period beginning with the day on which the penalty notice is served.

Note that late payment penalties do *not* apply to POAs. Note also that a revised late payment penalties system is to be introduced as from April 2024 (see later in this chapter).

[†] *Late payment penalties also apply to discovery assessments and amendments to self-assessments.*
[‡] *See the accompanying website for a temporary Covid-19 waiver of late payment penalties.*

EXAMPLE 3

Barbara (see Example 2 above) makes the following payments for 2022-23:

	£
31 January 2023	11,000
8 September 2023	11,000
17 February 2024	4,000
11 August 2024	2,000
5 February 2025	1,000

Compute the late payment penalties (if any) which Barbara would incur (under the current late penalties system) and state the dates by which these penalties should be paid.

Solution

– The first POA is paid in full and on time. The second POA is also paid in full but is paid late. However, late payment penalties do not apply to late POAs so there is no penalty.

– The penalty date for the balancing payment is 2 March 2024 (i.e. 31 days after the due date of payment). £3,000 of the balancing payment is not paid before the penalty date. Therefore there is a late payment penalty of £150 (5% of £3,000).

- The five-month period beginning with the penalty date starts on 2 March 2024 and ends on 1 August 2024. £3,000 of the balancing payment remains unpaid at the end of this period and so there is another late payment penalty of £150 (5% of £3,000).

- The eleven-month period beginning with the penalty date starts on 2 March 2024 and ends on 1 February 2025. £1,000 of the balancing payment remains unpaid at the end of this period and so there is a late payment penalty of £50 (5% of £1,000).

Assuming that penalty notices are issued on 2 March 2024, 2 August 2024 and 2 February 2025 respectively, the first £150 penalty is payable by 31 March 2024, the second £150 penalty is payable by 31 August 2024 and the £50 penalty is payable by 3 March 2025.

Interest on overdue income tax

Interest on overdue POAs, balancing payments and penalties is calculated as follows:

(a) In the case of late POAs and balancing payments, interest runs from the due date of payment up to the date on which the tax is actually paid.

(b) In the case of discovery assessments and amendments to self-assessments, interest runs from the date on which the balancing payment is due for the year to which the assessment relates (normally the 31 January which follows the end of that year) even though the tax itself might not be due for payment until a later date.

(c) Interest on a penalty runs from the due date of payment for that penalty (generally 30 days from its imposition).

(d) Interest is calculated on a daily basis at the official Bank of England rate plus 2.5% (currently 0.75% + 2.5% = 3.25% per annum). Apparently it is HMRC practice to use a denominator of 366 in such calculations, whether or not a leap year is involved.

EXAMPLE 4

Barbara (see Examples 2 and 3 above) pays all of her late payment penalties on 3 March 2025. Calculate the total interest payable by Barbara in relation to her income tax and Class 4 NICs for 2022-23, assuming an interest rate of 3.25% throughout.

Solution

(i) Interest on the second POA (39 days late) is £38.09 (£11,000 x 3.25% x 39/366).

(ii) The first £4,000 of the balancing payment is paid 17 days late. The next £2,000 is 193 days late. The final £1,000 is 371 days late. Interest due is £73.26 ((£4,000 x 3.25% x 17/366) + (£2,000 x 3.25% x 193/366) + (£1,000 x 3.25% x 371/366)).

(iii) Interest on the first penalty (337 days late) is £4.49 (£150 x 3.25% x 337/366).

(iv) Interest on the second penalty (184 days late) is £2.45 (£150 x 3.25% x 184/366).

Total interest due is £118.29 (£38.09 + £73.26 + £4.49 + £2.45).

Interest on overpaid income tax

Repayments of overpaid POAs, balancing payments and penalties attract interest. This is calculated at the *greater* of 0.5% per annum and 1% less than the Bank of England rate. Such interest is referred to as *repayment interest* and is itself exempt from income tax.

Interest is calculated on a daily basis and runs from the "repayment interest start date" to the date on which repayment is made. The repayment interest start date is:

(a)   as regards POAs and balancing payments, the *later* of the actual date of payment and the date on which the tax was due to be paid

(b)   as regards income tax deducted at source (including PAYE), 31 January following the tax year for which the tax is deducted.

Repayments made by HMRC in relation to a tax year are attributed first to the balancing payment for that year, secondly in two equal parts to the POAs for that year and finally to tax deducted at source for the year. Note that:

(a)   If a repayment is triggered by a claim to carry back a loss or a payment from a later year to an earlier year (e.g. if a trading loss is carried back or if a Gift Aid donation is carried back) interest on this repayment runs from the 31 January following the later year, *not* the earlier year.

(b)   Penalties repaid to a taxpayer also attract interest, running from the date of payment of the penalty to the date of repayment.

(c)   Apparently it is HMRC practice to use a denominator of 365 when computing interest on a repayment, whether or not a leap year is involved.

(d)   HMRC does not pay repayment interest in relation to a repayment of income tax that has been deliberately overpaid by the taxpayer. This rule prevents taxpayers from using HMRC as a source of tax-free interest.

EXAMPLE 5

A taxpayer makes two POAs for 2022-23, each of £3,450. These payments are calculated correctly and paid on the due dates. It is eventually determined that the total liability for the year is in fact only £5,200, so that no balancing payment is required and a repayment of £1,700 should be made. HMRC makes this repayment on 12 October 2023. Calculate the repayment interest due, assuming an interest rate of 0.5% per annum.

Solution

The repayment comprises £850 in relation to the first POA (paid 31 January 2023) and £850 in relation to the second POA (paid 31 July 2023). Repayment is made 254 days after the first POA and 73 days after the second POA. Therefore, repayment interest is [(£850 x 0.5% x 254/365) + (£850 x 0.5% x 73/365)] = £3.81.

Penalties

A taxpayer who fails to comply with various statutory requirements may become liable to a number of financial penalties[†], the most important of which are listed below. Some of these penalties are fixed in amount but HMRC often has the power to "mitigate" (i.e. reduce) the amount charged if it sees fit to do so. Whether or not a penalty is mitigated will usually depend upon the seriousness of the taxpayer's offence and the degree to which the taxpayer has co-operated with HMRC. The main penalties are listed below.

[†] *The penalties charged in relation to a failure to notify chargeability (see below), late submission of a tax return and inaccuracies in a tax return or document are higher if offshore matters are involved. In some cases, the penalty could be as much as 200% of the amount of tax concerned.*

(a) **Failure to notify chargeability to tax**. An individual must notify HMRC if he or she is liable to income tax for a tax year, even if a notice requiring a return has not been issued for that year (see Chapter 1). Notification must be made within six months of the end of the tax year concerned.

   The penalty regime which applies to a "failure to notify" covers a range of taxes, including income tax, corporation tax and VAT. Under this regime, the penalty for a failure to notify liability to income tax for a tax year is expressed as a percentage of the tax which (because of the failure) remains unpaid on 31 January following the end of that year. But no penalty is charged if the taxpayer has a reasonable excuse for the failure to notify. The applicable percentage is determined as follows:

   (i) For a "deliberate and concealed" failure to notify, where the failure is deliberate and the taxpayer has attempted to conceal it, the percentage is 100%.

   (ii) For a failure which is "deliberate but not concealed" the percentage is 70%.

   (iii) Otherwise, the percentage is 30%.

   These penalties may be reduced if the taxpayer discloses the failure. There are greater reductions if the disclosure is "unprompted" than if it is "prompted". A disclosure is unprompted if it is made at a time when the taxpayer has no reason to believe that the irregularity has been discovered or is about to be discovered by HMRC.

(b) **Late submission of a tax return**. The penalty regime which applies to the late filing of a self assessment tax return is currently as follows:

   (i) A £100 penalty[†] is charged as soon as a tax return is late (by a single day). This applies whether or not the tax liability for the year has been paid and even if the taxpayer has no liability for that year or is owed a tax repayment for the year.

   (ii) If a return is more than 3 months late, HMRC may charge a penalty of £10 per day whilst the return remains outstanding (up to a maximum of £900).

   (iii) If a return is more than 6 months late, another penalty arises equal to the greater of £300 and 5% of the tax liability for the year.

   [†] *See the accompanying website for a temporary Covid-19 waiver of this late filing penalty.*

(iv) If a return is more than 12 months late, a further penalty arises, again equal to the greater of £300 and 5% of the tax liability for the year. But if the taxpayer has deliberately withheld information from HMRC, the percentage used in this penalty calculation becomes 70% (not 5%). This rises to 100% if the withholding of information is both deliberate and concealed. These higher penalties may be reduced if the taxpayer discloses the information which has been withheld.

The tax-geared penalties have to be estimated by HMRC in the first instance and then re-assessed when the taxpayer files the late return. Penalties are not charged if the taxpayer has a reasonable excuse for failing to submit on time (e.g. serious illness).

Note, however, that a revised late filing penalties system is to be introduced as from April 2024 (see later in this chapter).

(c) **Submission of an incorrect tax return**. A single penalty regime applies in relation to the submission of incorrect returns for the purposes of income tax and many other taxes. This common regime applies if an incorrect return leads to an understatement of the amount of tax due and the inaccuracy was either careless or deliberate. No penalty is charged if the taxpayer has taken reasonable care. The regime also applies if an assessment issued by HMRC understates the amount of tax due and the taxpayer fails to take reasonable steps to notify HMRC of this fact within 30 days.

The amount of any penalty under the regime is expressed as a percentage of the potential lost revenue. For a "deliberate and concealed" inaccuracy, the percentage is 100%. This percentage falls to 70% for an inaccuracy which is "deliberate but not concealed". Otherwise, the percentage is 30%. The percentage is also 30% in cases where the taxpayer has failed to notify HMRC of an under-assessment.

As with the "failure to notify chargeability" penalties (see above) these penalties may be reduced if the taxpayer discloses the infringement and there are greater reductions if the disclosure is unprompted than if it is prompted.

(d) **Fraud or negligence when claiming reduced POAs**. A taxpayer who makes a claim for reduced POAs and does so fraudulently or negligently may be subject to a maximum penalty equal to the difference between the POAs actually made and the POAs that should have been made.

(e) **Failure to keep records**. A taxpayer who fails to maintain or retain adequate records in support of the year's tax return may be subject to a penalty of up to £3,000.

(f) **GAAR penalty**. A penalty will generally be charged in cases where abusive tax arrangements have been successfully counteracted by means of the general anti-abuse rule (see Chapter 1). This penalty is equal to 60% of the additional tax payable as a result of the counteraction.

In every case, the penalty described above is charged *in addition* both to the tax itself and to any late payment penalties or interest charged in relation to that tax.

Reformed late filing and late payment penalties

Finance Act 2021 introduced reformed late filing and late payment penalty regimes. These regimes will apply to both income tax and VAT (see Chapter 30).

For income tax purposes, the reforms will take effect as from 6 April 2024 for taxpayers who have gross trading income or property income exceeding £10,000 a year and who are therefore mandated to join MTD for income tax (see Chapter 1). The reforms will apply as from 6 April 2025 for all other income tax self assessment taxpayers. A brief summary of the main features of the new penalties system is as follows:

Reformed late filing penalties

(a) Taxpayers will incur a "penalty point" each time that a submission deadline is missed, and will be notified of this fact by HMRC. However, a taxpayer who has a reasonable excuse for missing a deadline will not incur a penalty point.

(b) When a taxpayer's points total reaches a specified threshold, a fixed penalty of £200 will be charged and HMRC will notify the taxpayer accordingly.

(c) The applicable points threshold will depend upon the frequency with which the taxpayer is required to submit tax returns and other information to HMRC. For annual income tax returns, the threshold will be two points. For quarterly MTD updates, the threshold will be four points (see Chapter 1).

(d) When a taxpayer has reached the penalty points threshold, any subsequent failures to meet a submission deadline will not increase the points total any further. However, each such failure will result in another £200 penalty.

(e) In general, penalty points will expire after two years. But this will <u>not</u> be the case when the taxpayer is at the penalty points threshold. Once this threshold has been reached, the points total will be reset to zero only after a specified period of "good compliance", during which all submission deadlines are met on time.

(f) For annual tax returns, the length of the period of compliance will be 24 months. For quarterly MTD updates, the length of the period of compliance will be 12 months.

(g) Taxpayers will be able to appeal against the imposition of points or penalties (perhaps on the grounds that there was a reasonable excuse for missing a deadline).

It should be noted that penalty points will accrue separately for each tax concerned, so that (for example) late submission of a VAT return will not affect the taxpayer's points total in relation to income tax.

Reformed late payment penalties

(a) The reformed late payment penalty regime will apply to balancing payments and to most other payments required under the self assessment system, but (as with the current system) will not apply to POAs.

(b) No penalty will be charged if payment is made within 15 days after the due date. But a late payment penalty will be charged equal to 2% of any amount outstanding at the end of those 15 days. If any amount is still unpaid 30 days after the due date, a further penalty will be charged equal to 2% of the amount still outstanding.

(c) If payment has not been made in full within 30 days after the due date, there will then be a penalty calculated on a daily basis at 4% p.a. until payment is made.

(d) However, a taxpayer who makes a late payment but has a reasonable excuse will not incur a late payment penalty.

Summary

▸ Under the Self Assessment system, income tax and Class 4 NICs which are not collected at source (or via the PAYE system) are usually payable by means of two payments on account followed by a balancing payment. Any liability to Class 2 NICs or capital gains tax (CGT) is added to the balancing payment.

▸ Late payment penalties may be levied if a balancing payment is paid late and interest is charged on any tax paid late. Interest usually runs from the due date of payment up to the actual date of payment.

▸ Repayments of overpaid tax also attract interest, running from the date on which the tax was paid (or, if later, the due date of payment) up to the date of repayment.

▸ Financial penalties may be imposed for various breaches of the Self Assessment regulations. Penalties are most commonly imposed in connection with a failure to notify chargeability to tax, the late submission of a tax return or the submission of an incorrect tax return.

▸ The current penalty regime which applies to the late submission of a tax return is to be replaced in 2024 by a new "points-based" system. The late payment penalty regime is also to be reformed.

Exercises

Any liability to Class 2 NICs and capital gains tax may be ignored in these exercises. Also assume that the current late payment penalty system applies throughout. A set of multiple choice questions for this chapter is available on the accompanying website.

15.1 For each of the following taxpayers, state the dates on which the 2022-23 income tax is due to be paid and calculate the amount payable on each date. (Ignore Class 4 NICs).

(a) Guy's 2021-22 income tax liability was £1,600, of which £1,150 was paid via the PAYE system and a further £50 was deducted at source from savings income. His income tax liability for 2022-23 is £1,750, of which £1,310 is paid via PAYE and none is deducted at source.

(b) Marie's 2021-22 income tax liability was £6,730, of which £4,370 was paid via PAYE and £20 was deducted at source. Her 2022-23 liability is £6,580, of which £4,810 is paid via PAYE and £35 is deducted at source.

(c) Majid's 2021-22 income tax liability was £14,850, of which £11,990 was paid via PAYE and £110 was deducted at source. His 2022-23 liability is £16,110, of which £12,510 is paid via PAYE and none is deducted at source.

15.2 Dorothy's income tax and Class 4 NICs liability for 2021-22 was £24,600, of which £600 was deducted at source. Her liability for 2022-23 is £28,000, of which none is deducted at source. She made a first POA in respect of 2022-23 on 27 February 2023 and a second POA on 12 September 2023. She made a balancing payment for the year on 21 February 2024. All of her payments were for the correct amount.

(a) Calculate the late payment penalties payable by Dorothy in relation to 2022-23.

(b) Assuming an interest rate of 3.25% per annum, calculate the amount of any interest payable by Dorothy in relation to 2022-23.

15.3 Jabran did not receive a notice to file a tax return for 2021-22 but he was aware that he had income which had not been assessed to tax. He notified HMRC of this fact on 2 October 2022 and a return notice was issued to him on 15 November 2022. He completed the return and submitted it with the necessary payment on 7 April 2023.

Explain the penalties and interest which Jabran might be required to pay.

*15.4 Frances paid income tax and Class 4 NICs of £47,000 for tax year 2021-22, of which £19,000 was paid via the PAYE system. Her total liability for 2022-23 is £69,000, of which £21,000 is paid via PAYE. Her payments for 2022-23 are as follows:

	£
15 February 2023	14,000
14 September 2023	14,000
3 February 2024	16,000
15 December 2024	4,000

Calculate the late payment penalties and interest payable for the year, assuming that any penalties are paid on 15 December 2024 and that interest is charged at 3.25% p.a.

Chapter 16

National Insurance contributions

Introduction

National Insurance contributions (NICs) are payable by employees, by employers and by the self-employed. Contributions are collected by the National Insurance Contributions and Employer Office (NIC&EO) of HMRC and are paid into a National Insurance Fund. This fund, supplemented if necessary by a grant from the Treasury, is then used to provide contributory social security benefits such as the state retirement pension.

The purpose of this chapter is to explain the circumstances in which NICs are payable and the way in which NICs are calculated.

Class 1 National Insurance contributions

Class 1 NICs are payable in relation to employees who are at least 16 years old. The employees themselves pay *primary* Class 1 NICs whilst employers pay *secondary* Class 1 NICs on their employees' behalf. Employees who continue to work after reaching state pension age pay no further primary contributions but employers must still pay secondary contributions in relation to such employees.

The amount of the Class 1 NICs payable in relation to an employee depends upon the employee's earnings. For National Insurance purposes, an employee's earnings consist of his or her gross pay *before* deducting pension contributions, charitable donations made through a payroll giving scheme or any other expenses borne by the employee. However, certain payments are excluded from earnings when calculating the liability to Class 1 NICs. Some of the main exclusions are:

(a) tips received directly from customers

(b) any business expenses which are paid for (or reimbursed) by the employer, including reasonable travel and subsistence expenses and incidental overnight expenses

(c) mileage allowances received from the employer if these are calculated at a rate which does not exceed the AMAP rate for the first 10,000 miles, regardless of the number of miles actually driven by the employee (see Chapter 7); but any excess forms part of the employee's earnings chargeable to Class 1 NICs

(d) suggestion scheme awards

(e) purely personal gifts made by employer to employee (e.g. a birthday present)

(f) employer contributions to a registered pension scheme

(g) ex gratia compensation payments[†] for loss of employment (subject to conditions)

(h) pensions and redundancy pay.

Benefits in kind which are not convertible into cash are generally not subject to Class 1 NICs. However, the *employer* will incur a liability to Class 1A NICs in relation to such benefits if they are chargeable to income tax (see below). If an employee's remuneration is paid in the form of non-cash commodities such as gold bullion, gemstones or fine wines, a liability to Class 1 NICs arises if these assets are readily convertible into cash. Payments made in shares are generally liable to Class 1 NICs, unless they are "own company" shares provided under an approved share scheme or share option scheme (see Chapter 7).

[†] *However, an employer who makes an ex gratia compensation payment of more than £30,000 to an employee is liable to Class 1A NICs (see below) on the amount by which the payment exceeds £30,000. The employee does not incur a liability to NICs in relation to such a payment.*

Contribution periods

The main principles of the Class 1 National Insurance system are as follows:

(a) Primary and secondary Class 1 NICs are calculated according to the amount of an employee's earnings in a "contribution period". For those paid weekly or monthly, each week or month usually constitutes a contribution period. However, special rules apply to company directors (see later in this chapter).

(b) The liability to Class 1 NICs in a given contribution period is governed solely by the employee's earnings in that particular period and is totally unaffected by earnings in other periods. This is in contrast to the income tax PAYE system (see Chapter 7) which accumulates earnings over the year and calculates a tax liability each week or month based on the employee's total earnings for the tax year to date.

(c) If an employee has two or more employments in a contribution period, each of these employments is considered separately for the purpose of calculating the liability to Class 1 NICs. Earnings from two or more employments are aggregated only if the employments are with the same employer or with employers who "carry on business in association". The term "association" is not defined in the law relating to NICs but it is HMRC practice (when considering this question) to consider the interdependence of the employers concerned. Two or more employers are more likely to be associated for this purpose if they share facilities, personnel, customers etc.

Primary Class 1 NICs

The primary Class 1 NICs payable by an employee for a contribution period falling during tax year 2022-23 are calculated as follows:

(a) The employee's earnings in the period are compared with the *primary threshold*. The primary threshold for 2022-23[†] (*as from 6 July 2022*) is £242 per week or £1,048 per month. No primary Class 1 NICs are payable for a contribution period if the employee's earnings in the period do not exceed this threshold.

> [†] *The 2022-23 primary threshold for contribution periods falling before 6 July 2022 was £190 per week or £823 per month. The Spring Statement of March 2022 increased these figures to £242 and £1,048 respectively with effect from 6 July 2022.*

(b) If earnings in the contribution period exceed the primary threshold, primary Class 1 NICs are payable at 13.25% on earnings between the primary threshold and the upper earnings limit (UEL). The UEL for 2022-23 is £967 per week or £4,189 per month.

(c) Any earnings beyond the UEL attract primary Class 1 NICs at 3.25%.

(d) The primary threshold (as from 6 July 2022) is aligned with the income tax personal allowance for the tax year concerned. Therefore the weekly primary threshold is £242 (£12,570 ÷ 52) and the monthly primary threshold is £1,048 (£12,570 ÷ 12).

(e) Similarly, the UEL (for all UK taxpayers) is aligned with the point at which higher rate income tax becomes payable by non-Scottish taxpayers[‡]. This point is reached when total income exceeds the sum of the personal allowance and the basic rate band. In 2022-23 this sum is £50,270 (£12,570 + £37,700). Therefore the UEL for a week is £967 (£50,270 ÷ 52) and the UEL for a month is £4,189 (£50,270 ÷ 12).

It is worth noting that there is a lower earnings limit (LEL) as well as an upper earnings limit. The LEL for 2022-23 is £123 per week or £533 per month. The LEL has no effect on the amount of primary Class 1 NICs payable for a contribution period. But if an employee's earnings for a contribution period are less than the LEL, the employee is not credited with a contributions record for that period. This may have an impact on his or her entitlement to certain social security benefits in the future.

> [‡] *In 2022-23, the combined marginal rate of income tax plus NICs for non-Scottish employees rises from 33.25% (20% + 13.25%) to 43.25% (40% + 3.25%) when earnings go beyond the UEL. But Scottish employees are subject to a combined rate of 54.25% (41% + 13.25%) on earnings between £43,662 and £50,270, falling to 44.25% (41% + 3.25%) when earnings go beyond the UEL. This assumes that the employee's earnings are spread evenly over the year.*

Health and Social Care Levy (HSCL)

The rates of Class 1 primary contributions for 2022-23 (13.25% and 3.25%) are both 1.25% higher than in 2021-22 (when the rates were 12% and 2%). This is a temporary, one-year increase and is being used to provide extra funding for health and social care. Similar temporary increases of 1.25% also apply in 2022-23 to Class 1 secondary contributions, Class 1A contributions, Class 1B contributions and Class 4 contributions (see below).

As from 6 April 2023, an entirely separate "health and social care levy" (HSCL) will be introduced. This will be charged at 1.25% on employee earnings above the primary threshold and will be payable by the employee (even if over state pension age). The rates of Class 1 primary contributions will then revert to their previous levels of 12% and 2%.

EXAMPLE 1

(a) Compute the primary Class 1 NICs payable by the following weekly-paid employees for the week ending 26 August 2022:

   (i)   Employee A has earnings for the week of £110.

   (ii) Employee B has earnings for the week of £170.

   (iii) Employee C has earnings for the week of £405.

   (iv) Employee D has earnings for the week of £810.

   (v)   Employee E has earnings for the week of £1,000.

(b) Compute the primary Class 1 NICs payable by the following monthly-paid employees for the month of August 2022:

   (i)   Employee F has earnings for the month of £750.

   (ii) Employee G has earnings for the month of £2,215.

   (iii) Employee H has earnings for the month of £3,545.

   (iv) Employee I has earnings for the month of £5,800.

Solution

(a) (i)   Earnings do not exceed the primary threshold, so primary contributions for the week are £nil. *Earnings are also less than the LEL, so the employee is not credited with a contributions record for the week.*

   (ii) Earnings do not exceed the primary threshold, so primary contributions for the week are £nil.

   (iii) $13.25\% \times (£405 - £242) = £21.60$

   (iv) $13.25\% \times (£810 - £242) = £75.26$

   (v) $13.25\% \times (£967 - £242) + 3.25\% \times (£1,000 - £967) = £97.13$

(b) (i)   Earnings do not exceed the primary threshold, so primary contributions for the month are £nil.

   (ii) $13.25\% \times (£2,215 - £1,048) = £154.63$

   (iii) $13.25\% \times (£3,545 - £1,048) = £330.85$

   (iv) $13.25\% \times (£4,189 - £1,048) + 3.25\% \times (£5,800 - £4,189) = £468.54$

Secondary Class 1 NICs

The secondary Class 1 NICs payable by an employer in relation to an employee for a contribution period falling during 2022-23 are calculated as follows:

(a) The employee's earnings in the period are compared with the *secondary threshold*. The secondary threshold for 2022-23 is £175 per week or £758 per month. No secondary contributions are payable if earnings in the period do not exceed this threshold.

(b) If earnings in the period exceed the secondary threshold, secondary Class 1 NICs are normally payable at 15.05% on earnings above the threshold.

(c) However, employers are not required to pay secondary Class 1 NICs on earnings up to the "upper secondary threshold" (UST) for employees under the age of 21. The UST is currently set to the same figure as the UEL.

Furthermore, employers are not required to pay secondary Class 1 NICs on earnings up to the Apprentice UST (AUST) for employees who are apprentices and under the age of 25. The AUST is also currently set to the same figure as the UEL.

Note that the rate of Class 1 secondary contributions for 2022-23 (15.05%) is 1.25% higher than in 2021-22 (when the rate was 13.8%). As explained above, this is a temporary increase for just one year and the rate of Class 1 secondary contributions will revert to 13.8% on 6 April 2023. However, employers will then be required to pay the new health and social care levy (HSCL) at 1.25% on all employee earnings above the secondary threshold.

EXAMPLE 2

Compute the secondary Class 1 NICs payable in relation to each employee in Example 1. Assume in each case that the employee concerned is over 21 and is not an apprentice.

Solution

(a) (i)/(ii) Earnings do not exceed £175, so secondary contributions for the week are £nil.

(iii) 15.05% x (£405 – £175) = £34.61

(iv) 15.05% x (£810 – £175) = £95.57

(v) 15.05% x (£1,000 – £175) = £124.16

(b) (i) Earnings do not exceed £758, so secondary contributions for the month are £nil.

(ii) 15.05% x (£2,215 – £758) = £219.28

(iii) 15.05% x (£3,545 – £758) = £419.44

(iv) 15.05% x (£5,800 – £758) = £758.82

Employment allowance

In tax year 2022-23, most employers[†] may deduct an "employment allowance" (maximum £5,000) from their liability to secondary Class 1 NICs. So an employer with a liability that does not exceed £5,000 effectively pays no secondary contributions at all. As from 6 April 2003, the £5,000 employment allowance may be set against the employer's combined liability to secondary Class 1 NICs and the health and social care levy (HSCL).

[†] *The employment allowance is available only to those employers whose liability to secondary NICs for the previous tax year was less than £100,000. And the allowance is not available to companies with a single director and no other employees.*

Directors' Class 1 NICs

The fact that NICs are calculated separately for each contribution period means that the amount of the primary contributions payable on an employee's income for a tax year will depend upon the distribution of earnings over that year. Consider the following example:

EXAMPLE 3

During 2022-23, an employee earns £5,000 per month.

(a) Calculate the total primary Class 1 NICs payable for the year, taking into account that the primary threshold was £823 per month until 6 July 2022 and £1,048 thereafter.

(b) What would total primary contributions be if the employee received £60,000 on 6 April 2022 and nothing in the remaining 11 months of the year?

Solution

(a) For the first three months, primary contributions are 13.25% x (£4,189 – £823) + 3.25% x (£5,000 – £4,189) = £472.35 per month.

For the other nine months, primary contributions are 13.25% x (£4,189 – £1,048) + 3.25% x (£5,000 – £4,189) = £442.54 per month.

This gives a total of (3 × £472.35) + (9 × £442.54) = £5,399.91 for the year.

(b) Primary contributions for the month in which the employee was paid £60,000 would be equal to 13.25% x (£4,189 – £823) + 3.25% x (£60,000 – £4,189) = £2,259.85.

Therefore the employee would save £3,140.06 in primary contributions (£5,399.91 – £2,259.85) if the entire year's salary was received in April.

Employees are not normally able to arrange for all of their year's earnings to be paid in one contribution period. However, company directors may well have sufficient influence to make such an arrangement. To counter this, the Class 1 contributions of company directors are calculated on an *annual* basis, regardless of the distribution of their earnings over the tax year. In effect, the entire year becomes a single contribution period.

For 2022-23, the primary threshold is £11,908, the secondary threshold is £9,100, the upper earnings limit (UEL) is £50,270 and the lower earnings limit (LEL) is £6,396.

EXAMPLE 4

Rework the previous example, given that the employee in question is a company director.

Solution

Regardless of the distribution of earnings over the tax year, primary contributions would be equal to 13.25% x (£50,270 – £11,908) + 3.25% x (£60,000 – £50,270) = £5,399.19.

Class 1A National Insurance contributions

As stated above, benefits in kind which are not convertible into cash are generally exempt from Class 1 NICs. However, such benefits (if chargeable to income tax) give rise to a Class 1A contribution instead, *payable only by the employer*. For tax year 2022-23, a Class 1A contribution is calculated as 15.05% of the amount of the benefit in kind which is assessed on the employee for income tax purposes[†].

Note that the employment allowance of £5,000 (see earlier in this chapter) cannot be set against an employer's liability to either Class 1A NICs or Class 1B NICs (see below).

EXAMPLE 5

In 2022-23, George is provided with a petrol-engined motor car by his employer who pays for all fuel and other running costs. The car had a list price when new of £27,200 and has an emission rating of 114g/km. George's employer also pays his private medical insurance premium of £2,600 per annum.

Calculate the Class 1A contributions payable by George's employer for the year.

Solution

The benefits assessed on George for income tax purposes (see Chapter 8) are:

	£
Car (20% + 7% = 27% x £27,200)	7,344
Fuel (27% x £25,300)	6,831
Medical insurance premium	2,600
	16,775

Therefore the Class 1A contributions payable by George's employer for the year are equal to 15.05% x £16,775 = £2,524.64.

Class 1B National Insurance contributions

From time to time, an employer may enter into a PAYE Settlement Agreement (PSA) with HMRC. The effect of such an agreement is that the employer pays the income tax liability of employees in relation to certain benefits in kind. In these circumstances, the employer is liable to make a Class 1B contribution calculated (in 2022-23) as 15.05% of the sum of the benefits in kind and the associated tax which is payable under the terms of the PSA[†].

[†] *The rate of Class 1A and Class 1B contributions for 2022-23 is 1.25% higher than in 2021-22 (when the rate was 13.8%). This rate will revert to 13.8% on 6 April 2023 and employers will then be required to pay the HSCL at 1.25% on the amounts that are chargeable to Classes 1A and 1B.*

Class 2 National Insurance contributions

Class 2 NICs are payable by self-employed people who are over 16 years old and under pensionable age. These contributions are generally payable at a flat rate (for 2022-23) of £3.15 per week and are collected through the self assessment system. However:

(a) A self-employed person whose profit for the tax year is less than the "small profits threshold" (£6,725 for 2022-23) is not required to pay Class 2 NICs for that year but may do so voluntarily so as to maintain a full contributions record.

(b) A self-employed person whose profit for the tax year is not less than the small profits threshold but is less than the Class 4 "lower profits limit" (see later in this chapter) is not required to pay Class 2 NICs for that year. But such a person is nonetheless treated as if he or she had in fact paid Class 2 NICs for the year, thus maintaining a full contributions record. The lower profits limit for 2022-23 is £11,908.

For Class 2 NICs purposes, a self-employed person's profit for a tax year is equal to the amount of profit on which Class 4 NICs are payable (see later in this chapter). If this is not less than the lower profits limit, Class 2 NICs fall due for each week or part-week during the tax year in which the person is self-employed.

If a person has two or more businesses, the profits of all of them are aggregated when determining whether the person's earnings are less than the small profits threshold or less than the lower profits limit.

EXAMPLE 6

(a) Alison has been self-employed for many years and her profit for tax year 2022-23 is £6,700. Is she liable to pay Class 2 NICs for the year?

(b) Amanda starts a business on 23 May 2022 and she is self-employed throughout the remaining 45 weeks of tax year 2022-23. Her profit for 2022-23 is £15,300. Calculate the required Class 2 NICs for the year.

Solution

(a) Alison's profit for the year is less than the small profits threshold of £6,725. So she is not required to pay Class 2 NICs for 2022-23 (but may do so voluntarily).

(b) Amanda's profit for the year is not less than the lower profits limit of £11,908. She is required to pay Class 2 NICs for 2022-23 of £141.75 (45 × £3.15).

Class 3 National Insurance contributions

A person (employed or self-employed) whose earnings are too low in a contribution period to require payment of NICs may make a voluntary Class 3 contribution so as to maintain a full contributions record. For 2022-23, the Class 3 contribution is £15.85 per week.

Class 4 National Insurance contributions

In addition to the flat-rate Class 2 liability described above, self-employed people who are over the age of 16 and under pensionable age may also be liable to pay earnings-related Class 4 contributions. A self-employed person's Class 4 liability for a tax year is based on the amount of trading income which is charged to income tax for that year. Class 4 NICs are collected along with the income tax liability (see Chapter 15). Note that:

(a) The Class 4 liability is based on the person's trading income for the tax year *after* adjusting for capital allowances and trading losses.

Trading losses which are set against the non-trading income of a tax year for tax purposes (see Chapter 12) are set instead against the first available trading income of that year or subsequent years for Class 4 purposes.

(b) If a self-employed person has more than one business, the earnings from all businesses for the year are aggregated.

(c) There is no liability to Class 4 NICs if trading income does not exceed the *lower profits limit* (£11,908 for 2022-23). Otherwise, Class 4 NICs for 2022-23[†‡] are payable at 10.25% on profits between the lower profits limit and the upper profits limit (£50,270 for 2022-23) and at 3.25% on profits beyond the upper profits limit.

[†] *The rates of Class 4 contributions for 2022-23 are 1.25% higher than in 2021-22 (when the rates were 9% and 2%). Class 4 rates will revert to 9% and 2% on 6 April 2023. Self-employed people will then be required to pay the HSCL at 1.25% on trading income above the lower profits limit.*

[‡] *In 2022-23, the combined marginal rate of income tax plus NICs for non-Scottish self-employed taxpayers rises from 30.25% (20% + 10.25%) to 43.25% (40% + 3.25%) when profits go beyond the upper profits limit. But Scottish self-employed taxpayers are subject to a combined rate of 51.25% (41% + 10.25%) on profits between £43,662 and £50,270. This falls to 44.25% (41% + 3.25%) when earnings go beyond the upper profits limit.*

EXAMPLE 7

Calculate the Class 4 NICs payable in each of the following cases:

(a) Shawn has trading income for 2022-23 of £18,580.
(b) Catherine has trading income for 2022-23 of £55,000.
(c) Paul has trading income for 2022-23 of £11,400.

Solution

(a) 10.25% x (£18,580 – £11,908) = £683.88.
(b) 10.25% x (£50,270 – £11,908) + 3.25% x (£55,000 – £50,270) = £4,085.83.
(c) Paul's profits do not exceed the lower profits limit so Class 4 NICs for the year are nil.

Annual maximum contributions

An individual who has more than one source of employment will normally be required to make Class 1 contributions in respect of each employment. Similarly, an individual who is both employed and self-employed will normally be required to make Class 1 contributions in respect of the employment as well as Class 2 and Class 4 contributions in respect of the self-employment. In these circumstances, the total amount of NICs payable could become onerous. But relief is available in the form of limits on the amount of NICs payable by any one person in any one tax year. In practice, the calculation of these limits can be very complex but a simplified outline of the rules is as follows:

(a) **Maximum Class 1 and 2 contributions**. In any one tax year, the total of the Class 1 contributions payable by a person *at the main rate* (currently 13.25%) together with any Class 2 contributions is limited to the amount of the Class 1 contributions which would be payable by a weekly-paid employee who had 53 weeks of earnings equal to the UEL. For 2022-23, this calculation assumes a primary threshold of £229[†] per week and gives a maximum contribution of **£5,182.60** (53 × 13.25% × (£967 − £229)).

A refund is made if this limit is exceeded, but the refund calculation takes into account the fact that earnings above the primary threshold which do not attract contributions at 13.25% should attract contributions at 3.25% instead.

[†] *The 2022-23 primary threshold is £190 for the first 13 weeks of the year and £242 for the remaining 39 weeks. The average is ((13 × £190) + (39 × £242)) ÷ 52 = £229 per week.*

(b) **Maximum Class 1, 2 and 4 contributions**. A refund of *Class 4 contributions only* is made if the total of the main rate (13.25%) Class 1 contributions, Class 2 contributions and main rate (10.25%) Class 4 contributions paid by a person in a tax year exceeds the amount obtained by adding 53 Class 2 contributions to the maximum main rate Class 4 contribution for the year. For 2022-23 this limit is equal to **£4,099.05** (53 @ £3.15 + 10.25% × (£50,270 − £11,908)). The refund calculation takes into account the fact that profits above the lower profits limit which do not attract Class 4 contributions at 10.25% should attract Class 4 contributions at 3.25% instead.

EXAMPLE 8

(a) Sabrina has two employments throughout 2022-23. Calculate the refund of NICs due for the year if her regular monthly earnings from the two employments are:

(i) £1,200 and £1,500   (ii) £2,600 and £4,500.

(b) Stephanie is employed at a monthly salary of £4,750. She also has a small business and she pays 52 Class 2 NICs for 2022-23. She pays no Class 4 NICs. Calculate the refund of NICs due for the year.

(c) Stewart is self-employed and pays 52 Class 2 NICs for 2022-23. His trading income for 2022-23 is £43,050 and he also receives directors' fees of £18,500. Calculate the refund of NICs due for the year.

Solution

(a) Sabrina will have paid *main rate* Class 1 NICs as follows:

	(i) £	(ii) £
First employment:		
3 x 13.25% x (£1,200 − £823)	149.85	
9 x 13.25% x (£1,200 − £1,048)	181.26	
3 x 13.25% x (£2,600 − £823)		706.35
9 x 13.25% x (£2,600 − £1,048)		1,850.76
Second employment:		
3 x 13.25% x (£1,500 − £823)	269.10	
9 x 13.25% x (£1,500 − £1,048)	539.01	
3 x 13.25% x (£4,189 − £823)		1,337.97
9 x 13.25% x (£4,189 − £1,048)		3,745.64
	1,139.22	7,640.72

In case (i), total contributions do not exceed the maximum, so no refund is due.

In case (ii), contributions exceed the maximum by £2,458.12 (£7,640.72 − £5,182.60) so Sabrina is entitled to a refund. But the earnings which have given rise to the excess contributions are still subject to 3.25% contributions. Therefore the refund is reduced to (£2,458.12 × 10/13.25) = £1,855.18.

(b) Stephanie will have paid *main rate* Class 1 NICs and Class 2 NICs as follows:

	£
Class 1 (3 x 13.25% x (£4,189 − £823))	1,337.97
Class 1 (9 x 13.25% x (£4,189 − £1,048))	3,745.64
Class 2 (52 @ £3.15)	163.80
	5,247.41

This exceeds the maximum by £64.81 (£5,247.41 − £5,182.60). The required refund can be made entirely out of Class 2 contributions, so there is no need to collect 3.25% contributions on refunded main rate Class 1 contributions. The refund is £64.81.

(c) Stewart will have paid Class 1 primary contributions on his director's fees of (13.25% x (£18,500 − £11,908)) = £873.44. He will also have paid Class 2 contributions totalling £163.80 and Class 4 contributions of (10.25% x (£43,050 − £11,908)) = £3,192.05.

His total contributions are therefore £4,229.29.

Total main rate Class 1 and Class 2 contributions are within the maximum allowed. But the total of the main rate Class 1 contributions, Class 2 contributions and main rate Class 4 contributions exceeds the maximum of £4,099.05 by £130.24. So Stewart is entitled to a refund of Class 4 contributions. However, the profits which have given rise to the excess contributions are still subject to 3.25% contributions, so the refund is reduced to (£130.24 × 7/10.25) = £88.94.

Summary

▸ Primary Class 1 NICs are payable by employees. Secondary Class 1 NICs are payable by their employers. Class 1 NICs are calculated with respect to earnings in a contribution period and each contribution period is considered independently.

▸ In 2022-23, primary Class 1 NICs are payable at 13.25% on earnings that lie between the primary threshold and the upper earnings limit. Earnings that lie beyond the upper earnings limit attract primary Class 1 NICs at 3.25%. Secondary Class 1 NICs are payable at 15.05% on earnings that lie beyond the secondary threshold.

▸ The Class 1 NICs of company directors are assessed on an annual basis and are not affected by the distribution of the director's earnings over the year.

▸ Class 1A NICs are payable by employers in relation to benefits in kind which are not convertible into cash and which are chargeable to income tax. Class 1B NICs are payable by employers in relation to PAYE Settlement Agreements.

▸ Class 2 NICs are payable at a flat rate by self-employed people whose profits are not less than the lower profits limit. Class 2 NICs are collected by means of the Self Assessment system, along with the liability to income tax and Class 4 NICs.

▸ Class 3 NICs are paid voluntarily in order to maintain a full contributions record.

▸ Class 4 NICs are paid by self-employed people and are earnings-related. In tax year 2022-23, Class 4 NICs are payable at 10.25% on profits which lie between the lower and upper profit limits and at 3.25% on profits beyond the upper limit.

▸ There are annual maximum limits on the amount of NICs payable by an individual.

▸ The percentage rates at which Class 1 primary and secondary contributions, Class 1A contributions, Class 1B contributions and Class 4 contributions are calculated in tax year 2022-23 are all 1.25% higher than in 2021-22. This is a temporary increase and these percentage rates will revert to their previous levels as from 6 April 2023, when the new health and social care levy (HSCL) will be introduced.

▸ As from 6 April 2023, the health and social care levy will be charged on employees, employers and self-employed persons, even if the employee or self-employed person concerned is over state pension age.

Exercises

It should be assumed in these exercises that all employees are over 21 and not apprentices. A set of multiple choice questions for this chapter is available on the accompanying website.

16.1   Compute the primary and secondary Class 1 NICs payable in relation to the following employees:

(a)   A earns £256 for the week ending 25 November 2022.

(b)   B earns £861 for the week ending 25 November 2022.

(c)   C earns £1,006 for the week ending 25 November 2022.

(d)   D earns £750 for the month of September 2022.

(e)   E earns £3,300 for the month of September 2022.

(f)   F earns £6,000 for the month of September 2022.

16.2   Joan is a company director. Her salary is paid on the last day of each month. Her gross salary throughout 2022 was £8,400 per month but she was awarded a 4% pay increase as from 1 January 2023. She contributes 10% of her gross salary to the company pension scheme and the company makes a further 15% pension contribution on her behalf.

Calculate the NICs payable by Joan and by her employer for 2022-23.

She lives in accommodation provided by her employer and drives a company car. Her taxable benefits in kind during 2022-23 were £12,850.

Calculate the NICs payable by Joan and by her employer for 2022-23.

16.3   Mark starts his own business on 25 July 2022 and is self-employed for 36 weeks in tax year 2022-23. His trading profit which is assessed to income tax for 2022-23 is £12,590. Calculate the Class 2 NICs and Class 4 NICs payable by Mark for the year.

*16.4   Brenda is a company director and she earns a regular monthly salary of £8,000. In May 2022 she received a £20,000 bonus. She is provided with a diesel-engined company car which has an emission rating of 148g/km and had a list price when new of £26,000. The company pays all the running costs of the car, including fuel for private motoring. Her BUPA subscription of £2,750 per year is also paid by the company.

Calculate the NICs payable in respect of Brenda for 2022-23.

*16.5   Leonard is employed and received a gross salary of £3,500 per month during tax year 2022-23. He also has a small business and paid 52 Class 2 NICs for the year. His trading income for 2022-23 was £13,160.

Calculate the refund of NICs due to Leonard for the year (if any).

Review questions (Set A)

A1   Three brothers, Daniel, David and Derrick have been discussing their respective taxation affairs and how much they dislike paying tax. None of them are Scottish taxpayers.

Daniel's income for tax year 2022-23 consists of income from property of £52,770 and net debenture interest of £416.

David has an annual salary of £88,000. PAYE deducted from this salary was £27,800 for 2022-23. David paid 4% of his salary into an occupational pension scheme, with his employer contributing 6%. He also had the use of company car for the whole of the tax year. When new in March 2021, the car cost his employer £34,500 but it had a list price of £35,100. David contributed £6,000 towards the cost of the car. It has a diesel engine and CO_2 emissions of 102g/km. The employer pays all running costs of the car (including all fuel) and David pays his employer £100 per month as a contribution towards private fuel. During 2022-23, David also received £1,240 in dividends.

Derrick has an annual salary of £58,270. PAYE deducted from this salary was £10,830 for 2022-23. He was given an interest-free loan from his employer of £12,000 on 6 June 2022 to fund a luxury cruise for his sixtieth birthday. Derrick repaid £6,000 of this loan in January 2023 and intends to pay off the remaining £6,000 in October 2023.

All three brothers are delighted that their parents are still alive, although both were born in 1934. The parents were married in September 1955. Their father has a private pension which amounts to about £30,000 per year and they both receive the state pension.

Required:

(a)   Calculate the income tax payable by Daniel for 2022-23.

(b)   Calculate the income tax payable by (or repayable to) David for 2022-23.

(c)   Explain to David what changes he could make that would help him save tax.

(d)   Calculate the income tax payable by (or repayable to) Derrick for 2022-23. You do <u>not</u> need to compute the loan interest using the daily method. Assume that the official rate of interest is 2% per annum.

(e)   Explain to Derrick how he could have avoided paying tax on the interest-free loan.

(f)   Calculate the total National Insurance contributions payable by both David and his employer for 2022-23.

(g)   Explain how the married couple's allowance will operate in the circumstances of the father and mother. You are <u>not</u> required to complete any calculations.   *(CIPFA)*

A2   On 6 August 2022, Danh (who is not a Scottish taxpayer) commenced self-employment as a sole trader. In addition, on 6 September 2022, he joined an existing partnership run by Ebele and Fai. The following information is available for tax year 2022-23:

(a)   Danh's sole trader accounts for the eight months to 5 April 2023 showed a net profit of £70,200, after charging depreciation of £2,300, motor expenses of £3,300 and professional fees of £1,800. Other expenses were all allowable.

During the eight-month period, Danh drove a total of 12,000 miles, of which 4,000 were for private journeys. Professional fees comprised accountancy £340 and legal fees of £1,460 in connection with the grant of a new lease of business premises.

Danh uses one of the six rooms in his private house as an office. The total running costs of the house for the eight-month period were £4,200. No deduction has been made for the cost of using the office when calculating the net profit of £70,200.

The only item of plant and machinery owned by Danh is his motor car. This was purchased on 6 August 2022 for £14,800 and has emissions of 47g/km.

(b)   For the year to 5 April 2023, the partnership made a trading loss of £12,600. Until 6 September 2022, profits and losses were shared Ebele 60% and Fai 40%. As from that date, profits and losses are shared Danh 20%, Ebele 50% and Fai 30%.

Danh will claim to relieve his share of the partnership loss against his total income for 2022-23. During tax year 2022-23, he paid interest (gross) of £875 on a loan taken out to purchase his share in the partnership.

(c)   Danh received rental income of £14,400 in tax year 2022-23. His allowable property expenses were £1,480 and he also paid interest of £5,000 on a mortgage loan with which he had partly financed the purchase of the rented property.

Required:

Calculate Danh's income tax liability for 2022-23, assuming that he does not claim fixed rate deductions for any of his business expenses.   *(ACCA)*

A3   Dee commenced in self-employment on 6 April 2019. She initially prepared accounts to 5 April, but changed her accounting date to 31 July by preparing accounts for the four-month period to 31 July 2021. Dee's trading profits since she commenced trading have been as follows:

	£
Year ended 5 April 2020	35,160
Year ended 5 April 2021	32,880
Four months to 31 July 2021	16,240
Year ended 31 July 2022	54,120

Required:

(a)   Calculate the amount of trading profits that will have been assessed on Dee for each of the tax years 2019-20, 2020-21, 2021-22 and 2022-23.

(b)   State the amount of Dee's unrelieved overlap profits as at 5 April 2023.   *(ACCA)*

A4 In May 2022 Bernard, a self-employed plumber, and his son Gerald, a self-employed electrician, purchased 1,000 empty barrels from a Scottish whisky distillery. The barrels were over 100 years old and were of no further use to the distillery. Bernard and Gerald sawed the barrels into halves and sold them to several local garden centres for use as ornamental flower tubs. Bernard and Gerald paid £10 per barrel to the distillery and sold a half-barrel for £8. Three-quarters of the barrels were sold by Bernard and Gerald in the summer of 2022 and the remainder in the summer of 2023.

You are required:

To prepare a list of relevant points for consideration prior to writing a report to Bernard and Gerald on the liability to income tax on the profit generated by the venture. *(ACCA)*

A5 You are a trainee chartered certified accountant and your manager has asked you for your help with regard to a taxpayer who has made trading losses.

Sean has been in self-employment since 2011, but ceased trading on 31 December 2022. He has always prepared accounts to 31 December and he is not a Scottish taxpayer. His results for the final five years of trading were as follows:

	£
Year to 31 December 2018 - Trading profit	21,300
Year to 31 December 2019 - Trading profit	14,400
Year to 31 December 2020 - Trading profit	18,900
Year to 31 December 2021 - Trading profit	3,700
Year to 31 December 2022 - Trading loss	(23,100)

For each of tax years 2018-19 to 2022-23, Sean has property business profits of £13,000. Sean has unused overlap profits brought forward of £4,600.

Required:

Identify the loss relief claims that are available to Sean and explain which of these claims would be the most beneficial. You should clearly state the amount of any reliefs claimed and the rates of income tax saved. However, you are not expected to compute any income tax liabilities. *Assume for the sake of simplicity that income tax rates, bands and allowances for all years are the same as in 2022-23*. *(ACCA)*

*A6 Roseanne is a Scottish taxpayer. She starts trading on 1 July 2022 and prepares accounts for the 16 months to 31 October 2023. The adjusted trading profit for this period is £38,560. Her only other income is bank interest of £500 per annum. In April 2023 she receives a notice to submit a tax return for 2022-23 but does not submit this return until 16 March 2024. The return is submitted electronically. Also on 16 March 2024, she pays all of the income tax and Class 4 NICs which fall due for payment on 31 January 2024.

Required:

(a) Calculate Roseanne's liability to income tax and Class 4 NICs for tax year 2022-23 and state the amount (or amounts) that fall due for payment on 31 January 2024. *(Ignore Class 2 NICs)*.

(b) Calculate any possible interest and penalties payable by Roseanne, assuming an interest rate of 3.25% per annum.

*A7   Stephen is a UK resident taxpayer with two different sources of income. He works part-time as an IT consultant for a small number of clients, on a project management basis. A separate contract is drawn up for each project, specifying the deadline, expected output and the fee to be paid. Stephen uses his own laptop when necessary, and works from home most of the time.

Stephen also works two days a week (Thursdays and Fridays) for a nearby NHS Trust hospital where his wife (see below) works. He is given an office at the hospital, where he is required to be present between 8am and 6pm to work with the in-house IT team. In addition, the Trust provides 10 fully-paid days off in the year, and allows Stephen to invoice the Trust for the day even when he is sick.

Stephen's wife, Susan, is a pharmacist who works in an NHS Trust hospital. Susan was born in 1979 and joined the hospital on 6 July 2022. Her gross pay for 2022-23 was £59,080 and income tax of £17,950 was deducted via PAYE.

Susan is provided with a motor car for both business and private motoring. Details of the cars provided during 2022-23 were as follows:

	Make	List price £	Emissions g/km	Fuel
6 July 2022 to 5 October 2022	Ford	15,600	87	Petrol
6 October 2022 to 5 April 2023	BMW	31,700	94	Petrol

Her employer paid for all of the running costs of both these cars but Susan contributed £150 per month for private use of the BMW car. She also reimbursed her employer for all of the private fuel used by the Ford motor car (but not the BMW motor car).

On 6 August 2022, the NHS Trust lent Susan £27,000 at an interest rate of 0.25% per annum. Susan repaid £18,000 of the loan on 6 March 2023.

Susan is provided with a mobile telephone and is allowed to use this telephone for both business and private calls. The NHS Trust did not have to pay for the telephone itself but paid call charges of £391 during the year (of which £128 related to private calls).

Susan's other income for 2022-23 consisted of gross pay from her previous employer of £17,920 (PAYE £3,260), dividends received of £4,300 and ISA interest of £240. She is not a Scottish taxpayer.

Required:

(a)   Discuss and apply the criteria which may be used to determine whether Stephen should be regarded as employed or self-employed.

(b)   Prepare an income tax computation for Susan for tax year 2022-23. If any of her income is not taxable, explain why this is the case. (Assume that the official rate of interest is 2%).

(c)   Calculate both the Employer's and Employee's National Insurance Contributions (NICs) payable in relation to Susan for 2022-23.   *(CIPFA)*

*A8   Claud Chapperon is a self-employed distributor of wholesale clothing who began trading on 1 July 2014. His summarised accounts for the year to 30 June 2022 are shown below. The figures in brackets refer to the notes which follow.

	£	£
Sales (2)		400,000
Opening inventory (1)	40,000	
Purchases	224,000	
	264,000	
Closing inventory (1)	32,000	232,000
Gross profit		168,000
Wages and national insurance (3)	55,200	
Rent and rates	29,100	
Repairs and renewals (4)	3,490	
Miscellaneous expenses (5)	665	
Claud's own income tax and NICs	14,940	
Bad debts (6)	820	
Legal expenses (7)	1,060	
Depreciation	3,245	
Lease rental on Claud's car (8)	8,400	
Loss on sale of office furniture	60	
Gift Aid donations (9)	200	
Transport costs	3,870	
Interest (10)	990	
Running expenses of Claud's car (11)	2,000	
Premium on lease (12)	6,000	
Lighting and heating	1,250	
Sundry expenses (all allowable)	710	132,000
Net profit		36,000

Notes:

1.   The basis of both the opening and closing inventory valuations was "lower of cost or market value" less a general reserve of 50%.

2.   Sales include £500 reimbursed by Claud's family for clothing taken from stock. The reimbursement represented cost price.

3.   Included in wages are Claud's drawings of £200 per week and his wife's wages and secondary NICs totalling £16,750. His wife works full-time in the business.

4.   The charge for repairs and renewals includes £3,244 for fitting protective covers over the factory windows and doors to prevent burglary.

5. Miscellaneous expenses comprise:

	£
Theft of money by employee	65
Political donation to Green Party	100
Gifts of 100 "Chapperon" calendars	500
	665

6. Bad debts comprise:

	£
Trade debt written off	720
Loan to former employee written off (not made for trade purposes)	250
Reduction in general allowance	(150)
	820

7. Legal expenses comprise:

	£
Defending action re alleged faulty goods	330
Costs re lease of new larger premises	250
Unsuccessful appeal against previous year's income tax assessment	200
Defending Claud in connection with speeding offence	187
Debt collection	93
	1,060

8. Claud's leased car had a retail price of £20,000 and was leased from 1 July 2021 to 30 June 2022. The car has emissions of 89g/km.

9. Gift Aid donations consist of £120 paid to the local children's hospital and £80 paid to Oxfam. Both payments were made on 30 April 2022.

10. Interest is as follows:

	£
Bank overdraft interest (business account)	1,020
Interest on overdue tax	130
Interest credited on NS&I a/c (see note 13)	(160)
	990

11. HM Revenue and Customs has agreed that one-third of Claud's mileage is private. Included in the charge for motor running expenses is £65 for a speeding fine which was incurred by Claud whilst delivering goods to a customer.

12. The premium was for a lease of six years. The lease began on 1 July 2021.

13. Interest recently credited to the NS&I account is as follows:

	£
31 December 2021	160
31 December 2022	70

The following information is also provided:

(i) Capital allowances for the year to 30 June 2022 are £5,680.

(ii) Claud was born in 1966. He made net contributions of £11,800 to a registered pension scheme during 2022-23. His wife was also born in 1966.

(iii) Claud is a Scottish taxpayer.

You are required:

(a) To prepare a profit adjustment statement in respect of the period of account to 30 June 2022, showing the trading income for 2022-23.

(b) To calculate the Class 4 NICs payable by Claud for 2022-23.

(c) To prepare an estimate of Claud's income tax liability for 2022-23.   *(ACCA)*

*A9   Iris (who is single) starts a business on 6 July 2022, preparing accounts to 5 April. Her adjusted trading loss for the nine months to 5 April 2023 is £15,000. However, she is expecting a trading profit of approximately £55,000 in the year to 5 April 2024.

Before starting her own business, Iris was in employment. Her employment income in recent years has been as follows

2018-19	£37,630
2019-20	£22,660
2020-21	£26,150
2021-22	£35,830
2022-23 (up to 5 July 2022)	£23,260

She has no other income in any year between 2018-19 and 2022-23 inclusive. She is not a Scottish taxpayer.

Required:

(a) Assuming (for the sake of simplicity) that income tax rates, bands and allowances for all years are the same as those for 2022-23, calculate the effective percentage rate of tax relief that Iris would obtain if she claimed each of the following reliefs in relation to her trading loss:

- relief against total income for the year of the loss, *or*

- relief against total income for the previous year, *or*

- early trade losses relief, *or*

- carry-forward relief.

(b) Advise Iris as to the best course of action in relation to her loss.

*A10   Joseph Kent started business on 1 July 2020 as a joiner making conservatories. His tax-adjusted profits (before deduction of capital allowances) were as follows:

	£
Period to 31 December 2020	24,000
Year ended 31 December 2021	37,000
Year ended 31 December 2022	42,000

Capital additions and disposals were as follows:

£

Additions

1 July 2020	Plant and machinery	3,500
1 July 2020	Car (emissions 47g/km)	15,000
1 October 2020	Trailer	2,500
1 December 2021	Car (emissions 134g/km)	13,000
1 December 2022	Plant and machinery	2,400

Disposals

1 December 2021	Car acquired 1 July 2020	12,400
1 November 2022	Plant and machinery (at less than cost)	2,000

Private use of both cars has been agreed with HM Revenue and Customs at 20%. No claim is made to treat any of the assets as short-life assets.

Joseph's wife Sephora is a solicitor employed by a practising firm at a salary of £51,850 per annum. The following additional information is provided for 2022-23:

(i)   A new petrol-engined car was provided for Sephora's use in August 2021. The list price at that time was £22,800. Of this amount, £4,000 was contributed by Sephora so that a better car could be provided. She was required to pay £25 each month towards the private use of the car but not towards the private fuel, all of which was provided by her employers. The car has an emission rating of 103g/km.

(ii) Sephora has received a loan of £90,000 on the matrimonial home from her employers on which she pays interest at 0.25% per annum.

(iii) Sephora made a qualifying donation to the Oxfam charity on 1 July 2022 of £400 under the Gift Aid scheme.

(iv) Both Joseph and Sephora were born in 1983. They are not Scottish taxpayers.

You are required:

(a)   To calculate Joseph's trading income for 2020-21 to 2022-23 inclusive.

(b)   To calculate Sephora's income tax liability for 2022-23 (assuming an official rate of interest of 2% per annum).   *(ACCA)*

Part 2

CAPITAL GAINS TAX

Chapter 17

Introduction to capital gains tax

Introduction

The next six chapters of this book are concerned with capital gains tax (CGT), which was introduced in 1965 with the aim of taxing any gains which arise on the disposal of capital assets. Capital gains tax has undergone many changes since its inception and the changes that were made between 1965 and 1992 were consolidated into the Taxation of Chargeable Gains Act 1992. This Act has since been amended by subsequent Finance Acts.

Chargeable persons

A CGT liability may arise when a "chargeable person" makes a "chargeable disposal" of a "chargeable asset". The main categories of chargeable person are as follows:

(a) individuals who are resident in the UK

(b) business partners, who are each responsible for their share of the CGT due on the capital gains of a partnership

(c) the trustees of a trust or settlement

(d) the personal representatives of a deceased person.

Husbands and wives are assessed independently for CGT purposes, as are civil partners. The following are *not* chargeable persons for CGT purposes:

(a) companies and other corporate bodies, which pay corporation tax on their capital gains (not CGT) and so cannot incur a CGT liability

(b) various other organisations including registered charities, community amateur sports clubs, local authorities, health service bodies, registered pension schemes and approved scientific research associations, all of which are generally exempt from CGT (subject to certain restrictions).

Chargeable assets

All assets are regarded as chargeable assets except for those assets which are specifically exempted from CGT. The main exemptions are as follows:

(a) a taxpayer's principal private residence (see Chapter 21)

(b) motor cars, including vintage and veteran cars (but not personalised car registration plates); vehicles which are not covered by this exemption, such as vans, lorries and motor cycles, will generally fall within the scope of (d) below.

(c) items of tangible, movable property (referred to as "chattels") which are disposed of for £6,000 or less (see Chapter 19)

(d) chattels with a predictable useful life of 50 years or less ("wasting chattels") unless used in business and eligible for capital allowances (see Chapter 19)

(e) gilt-edged securities and qualifying corporate bonds (see Chapter 20)

(f) National Savings Certificates and Premium Bonds

(g) foreign currency† (if acquired for private use)

(h) winnings from pools, lotteries, betting etc.

(i) decorations for valour (unless acquired by purchase)

(j) damages or compensation received for personal or professional injury

(k) life assurance policies (unless purchased from a third party)

(l) Individual Savings Accounts (ISAs) and Child Trust Funds (see Chapter 6)

(m) subject to conditions, shares in a Venture Capital Trust (see Chapter 6)

(n) up to £50,000 worth of shares acquired by an employee as the result of adopting "employee shareholder" status‡ before 1 December 2016.

It is important to appreciate that neither a chargeable gain nor an allowable loss can arise on the disposal of an asset that is not a chargeable asset. This means that any gains made on the disposal of such assets are not taxable but it also means that any losses which arise will not usually attract tax relief.

However, losses arising on the disposal of Enterprise Investment Scheme (EIS) or SEIS investments, or on the disposal of investments which qualify for Social Investment Tax Relief (SITR) are eligible for tax relief even though gains arising on such disposals are not generally taxable (see Chapter 6).

† *In general, crypto-currencies (referred to as "crypto-assets") are not treated as money or currency and are regarded as chargeable assets for CGT purposes.*

‡ *Employee shareholders forfeit some of their employment rights (e.g. the right to claim unfair dismissal) in return for shares in the company for which they work. However, the Government intends to close employee shareholder status to new entrants at the next legislative opportunity.*

Chargeable disposals

The main and most obvious instance of a chargeable disposal occurs when a chargeable asset is sold. However, the sale of an asset in the course of a trade (i.e. the sale of trading stock or inventory) does *not* constitute a chargeable disposal since any gain arising on such a sale is taxed as a trading profit (see Chapter 9).

Before CGT was introduced in 1965 there was a great incentive for taxpayers to maintain that the gain arising on the sale of an asset was a capital gain (not taxable) rather than a trading profit (taxable). This incentive diminished with the introduction of CGT. But it is still important to distinguish between capital gains and trading profits since the rules of computation for capital gains and trading profits are different, as are the rates of CGT and income tax (see later in this chapter).

As well as the sale of a chargeable asset, the following are also chargeable disposals:

(a) the sale of *part* of a chargeable asset

(b) the gift of all or part of a chargeable asset

(c) the loss or destruction of a chargeable asset

(d) the receipt of a capital sum derived from a chargeable asset (e.g. compensation received from an insurance company if an asset is damaged).

With regard to gifts, it is important to realise that CGT is basically a tax on the increase in value of an asset whilst owned by the taxpayer. This increase in value is chargeable to tax even if the taxpayer gives the asset away and receives nothing in return.

In general terms, the date on which a chargeable disposal is deemed to occur is the date on which ownership of the asset changes hands, regardless of the date on which payment (if any) is made.

Non-chargeable disposals

The following types of disposal are *not* chargeable disposals and therefore any gains or losses arising on such disposals are exempt from CGT:

(a) gifts to charities and certain other bodies (e.g. art galleries and museums) and gifts of pre-eminent property to the nation (see Chapter 4)

(b) disposals caused by the death of the taxpayer.

Disposals between a husband and wife (or civil partners) who live together at any time during the tax year in which the disposal occurs *are* chargeable disposals. However, such disposals are deemed to occur at a disposal value such that neither a chargeable gain nor an allowable loss arises on the disposal (see Chapter 18). A similar treatment applies to:

(a) gifts of national heritage property, subject to certain undertakings being received by HMRC (e.g. with regard to reasonable public access)

(b) disposals of a company's shares which result in a controlling interest in that company being held by an employee ownership trust.

Basis of assessment

A person's CGT liability for a tax year is based upon the chargeable disposals made by that person during the tax year. For example, the liability for 2022-23 is based upon the chargeable disposals made between 6 April 2022 and 5 April 2023 inclusive. No liability to CGT arises until an asset is disposed of, so the mere fact that an asset has appreciated in value will not of itself trigger a CGT liability. The amount of a person's "taxable gains" for a tax year (i.e. the amount on which CGT is payable) is calculated as follows:

(a) The chargeable gain or allowable loss arising on each disposal made during the tax year is calculated separately (see subsequent chapters of this book).

(b) If total gains exceed total losses, the losses are subtracted from the gains to give the taxpayer's "net gains" for the year. If total losses exceed total gains, the gains are subtracted from the losses to give the "net losses" for the year.

(c) If there are net gains for the year, these are reduced first by any unrelieved losses brought forward from previous tax years or by any losses carried back on the death of the taxpayer (see later in this chapter).

(d) Net gains are then further reduced by the amount of the "annual exemption" for the year (£12,300 for 2022-23†). The amount of any net gains remaining after the annual exemption has been deducted is the "taxable gains" figure for the year. If net gains are too low to allow the whole of the annual exemption to be deducted, taxable gains for the year are £nil and the balance of the annual exemption is lost.

(e) If there are net losses for the year, taxable gains for that year are £nil and the whole of the annual exemption is lost. The net losses may then be carried forward for relief in future years, as described later in this chapter.

Husbands, wives and civil partners are each entitled to the full annual exemption. This exemption is also available to the trustees of a settlement established for the benefit of a disabled person. For trustees of other settlements the annual exemption is lower (£6,150 for 2022-23†). The personal representatives of a deceased person are entitled to the full annual exemption for the year of death and for the following two years.

† *Finance Act 2021 freezes these annual exempt amounts until the end of tax year 2025-26.*

EXAMPLE 1

Four taxpayers each make three chargeable disposals during 2022-23. Compute their taxable gains for the year (assuming that there are no unrelieved losses brought forward or carried back) if these disposals give rise to the following gains and losses:

(a) Taxpayer A has gains of £3,800, £4,100 and £6,650.

(b) Taxpayer B has gains of £5,700, £7,840 and a loss of £350.

(c) Taxpayer C has gains of £1,250 and £9,930 and a loss of £1,750.

(d) Taxpayer D has a gain of £8,950 and losses of £9,500 and £800.

Solution

(a) Total gains are £14,550 and there are no losses. Net gains are £14,550. Subtracting the annual exemption of £12,300 gives taxable gains for the year of £2,250.

(b) Total gains are £13,540. Total losses are £350 so net gains are £13,190. Subtracting the annual exemption of £12,300 gives taxable gains for the year of £890.

(c) Total gains are £11,180 and total losses are £1,750. Net gains are £9,430. This is less than the annual exemption of £12,300, so taxable gains for the year are £nil. The unused part of the annual exemption (£2,870) is lost.

(d) Total gains are £8,950 and total losses are £10,300. Net losses are £1,350. Taxable gains for the year are £nil and the whole of the annual exemption is lost.

Rates of CGT

For tax year 2022-23, there are two main rates of CGT. These are the *standard rate* of 10% and the *higher rate* of 20%. But the tax rates which apply to gains arising on the disposal of residential property (to the extent that these gains are not eligible for principal private residence relief) are 18% and 28% (see Chapter 21). Furthermore, a special rate of 10% applies to gains which qualify for "business asset disposal relief" (BADR). In general, gains may qualify for BADR if they arise on the disposal of a business (see Chapter 22).

These rates of tax are applied to the taxable gains which remain after capital losses and the annual exemption have been deducted. For individuals, the process is as follows:

(a) Gains which qualify for BADR are always taxed at the BADR rate of 10%.

(b) If the individual's taxable income for the year (see Chapter 2) exceeds the basic rate limit, gains which do not qualify for BADR are taxed at the higher rate of 20% (or 28% in the case of residential property gains).

(c) If taxable income does not exceed the basic rate limit, any unused part of the basic rate band is first absorbed by gains which qualify for BADR. Gains which do not qualify for BADR are then normally taxed at the lower rate of 10% to the extent that they do not exceed any remaining part of the basic rate band and at 20% otherwise. But these rates are increased to 18% and 28% in the case of residential property gains.

The basic rate limit[†] for 2022-23 is usually £37,700 (see Chapter 2) but this may be increased for Gift Aid donations (Chapter 4) or pension contributions (Chapter 14).

(d) In general, capital losses and the annual exemption may be deducted from capital gains in such a way that the CGT liability is minimised. Similarly, any unused part of the basic rate band (after BADR gains have been deducted) may be allocated between residential property gains and other gains in the most beneficial way.

The rate of CGT applicable to trustees and personal representatives is 10% for gains which qualify for BADR, 28% for residential property gains and 20% for all other gains.

[†] *For this purpose, a Scottish taxpayer is treated as if he or she were <u>not</u> a Scottish taxpayer, so the applicable basic rate limit is the basic rate limit which applies in the remainder of the UK.*

EXAMPLE 2

Calculate the amount of CGT payable for 2022-23 by each of the following individuals. In each case, "taxable income" comprises the individual's total income, less reliefs which may be deducted from total income and less the personal allowance (see Chapter 2).

	Name	Taxable income £	BADR gains £	Residential prop. gains £	Other gains £	Allowable losses £
(a)	A	71,000	nil	nil	13,500	nil
(b)	B	71,000	13,500	nil	nil	nil
(c)	C	47,500	32,800	16,700	nil	nil
(d)	D	52,700	27,600	nil	5,900	1,000
(e)	E	34,990	nil	12,700	nil	nil
(f)	F	35,900	nil	nil	21,300	400
(g)	G	27,300	4,000	18,000	8,500	2,200

Assume in each case that there are no Gift Aid donations or pension contributions.

Solution

(a) Taxable income exceeds the basic rate limit, so the "other" gains are taxed at 20%. CGT payable is (£13,500 – £12,300) x 20% = £240.

(b) Taxable income is not relevant since gains which qualify for BADR are always taxed at 10%. CGT payable is (£13,500 – £12,300) x 10% = £120.

(c) The tax liability is minimised if the annual exemption is set against the residential property gains, since these are taxed at higher rates than gains which qualify for BADR. Taxable income exceeds the basic rate limit, so CGT payable is (£32,800 x 10%) + ((£16,700 – £12,300) x 28%) = £4,512.

(d) To minimise the tax liability, the allowable losses of £1,000 are set against the "other" gains of £5,900. Similarly, the annual exemption is set first against these gains. The remaining £7,400 of the exemption must then be set against the gains which qualify for BADR. CGT payable is (£27,600 – £7,400) x 10% = £2,020.

(e) After deducting the annual exemption, taxable gains are £400 and these consist of residential property gains. The unused part of the basic rate band is £2,710 (£37,700 – £34,990). This exceeds the taxable gains so CGT payable is (£400 x 18%) = £72.

(f) Taxable gains are £8,600 (£21,300 – £400 – £12,300) and these consists of "other" gains. The unused part of the basic rate band is £1,800 (£37,700 – £35,900). So the CGT payable is (£1,800 x 10%) + (£6,800 x 20%) = £1,540.

(g) The tax liability is minimised if the losses of £2,200 and the annual exemption of £12,300 are both set against the residential property gains, leaving £3,500 of these gains remaining (£18,000 – £2,200 – £12,300). The unused part of the basic rate band is £10,400 (£37,700 – £27,300) and BADR gains absorb £4,000 of this.

If the basic rate band is allocated next to the residential property gains, CGT payable is (£4,000 x 10%) + (£3,500 x 18%) + (£2,900 x 10%) + (£5,600 x 20%) = £2,440.

If the basic rate band is allocated next to the "other" gains instead, CGT payable is (£4,000 x 10%) + (£6,400 x 10%) + (£2,100 x 20%) + (£3,500 x 28%) = £2,440.

The tax liability is unaffected by the allocation of the basic rate band and this will generally be the case in 2022-23, since the gap between the 10% and 20% rates is the same as the gap between the 18% and 28% rates.

Relief for capital losses

If a taxpayer has net losses for a year, the CGT liability for that year is £nil and the annual exemption is lost. The amount of the net losses may then be carried forward without time limit and set against the net gains of future years.

Losses carried forward must be offset against the first available net gains, but are offset only to the extent that those net gains exceed the annual exemption for the year in which they arise, so preventing the annual exemption from being wasted. Any losses remaining unrelieved are carried forward again to subsequent years. This method of preserving the annual exemption applies *only* to losses brought forward from a previous year. It is *not* possible to preserve the annual exemption by restricting the set-off of current year losses.

Since married couples and civil partners are taxed independently, the losses of one spouse (or partner) cannot be offset against the gains of the other spouse (or partner).

EXAMPLE 3

Three taxpayers each have £3,000 of capital losses brought forward. Calculate their taxable gains for 2022-23 if their total gains and losses for the year are as follows:

(a) Taxpayer A has gains of £8,300 and losses of £1,300.

(b) Taxpayer B has gains of £14,700 and losses of £700.

(c) Taxpayer C has gains of £18,400 and losses of £1,200.

Solution

(a) Net gains for the year are £7,000. This is less than the annual exemption of £12,300 so taxable gains for the year are £nil and the balance of the annual exemption is lost. There is no scope for relieving losses brought forward, so the entire £3,000 is carried forward to 2023-24.

(b) Net gains for the year are £14,000. This exceeds the annual exemption by £1,700 so £1,700 of the losses brought forward are relieved in 2022-23, giving taxable gains for the year of £nil. The remaining £1,300 of the losses are unrelieved and are therefore carried forward to 2023-24.

(c) Net gains for the year are £17,200. This exceeds the annual exemption by £4,900 so the entire £3,000 of losses brought forward are relieved in 2022-23, giving taxable gains for the year of £1,900. There are no unrelieved losses to carry forward.

Anti-avoidance rules relating to capital losses

TCGA 1992 contains the following anti-avoidance rules, designed to prevent taxpayers from taking unfair advantage of the reliefs available in relation to capital losses:

(a) Capital losses incurred on a disposal to a connected person can be offset only against gains made on disposals to the *same person*, in the same or subsequent tax years. A taxpayer is deemed to be connected with a number of persons for CGT purposes, mainly relatives and business associates (see Chapter 18).

(b) A capital loss is not an allowable loss if it arises as a result of arrangements made by the taxpayer and a main purpose of those arrangements is to gain a tax advantage by creating an artificial capital loss.

Losses in the year of death

As stated earlier, disposals caused by the death of a taxpayer are exempt from CGT, although such disposals may give rise to an inheritance tax liability. But disposals made in the year of death (i.e. from 6 April up to the date of death) are *not* exempt from CGT and are taxed in the usual way, with a full annual exemption given for the year.

If a taxpayer suffers net losses in the year of death, these losses cannot (for obvious reasons) be carried forward. However, net losses incurred in the year of death may instead be carried back and set off against the net gains of the previous three years (most recent years first). As is the case with losses carried forward, losses carried back are set against a year's net gains only to the extent that those net gains exceed the annual exemption for the year in which they arise.

EXAMPLE 4

Sarah dies on 16 December 2022. She had made net capital losses of £7,300 between 6 April 2022 and the date of her death. Her net gains in the previous three years (and the annual exemption for each of those years) were as follows:

	Net gains	Annual exemption
	£	£
2019-20	13,150	12,000
2020-21	4,000	12,300
2021-22	16,650	12,300

Calculate her taxable gains for 2019-20 to 2022-23 inclusive.

Solution

Since losses in the year of death are carried back to the most recent year first, it is easier to begin with the year of death and then work backwards.

(a) In 2022-23, Sarah has net losses. Her taxable gains for the year are therefore £nil and the annual exemption (available in full) is lost. The net losses of £7,300 may be carried back to 2021-22, 2020-21 and 2019-20, in that order.

(b) In 2021-22, Sarah's net gains of £16,650 exceed the annual exemption by £4,350 so £4,350 of the losses carried back are relieved in 2021-22, giving taxable gains for the year of £nil. The remaining £2,950 of the losses are carried back to 2020-21.

(c) In 2020-21, Sarah has net gains of £4,000 which are less than the annual exemption of £12,300. Therefore taxable gains for the year are £nil and the balance of the annual exemption is lost. There is no scope for relieving losses carried back, so the £2,950 is now carried back to 2019-20.

(d) In 2019-20, Sarah's net gains of £13,150 exceed the annual exemption by £1,150 so £1,150 of the losses carried back are relieved in 2019-20, giving taxable gains for the year of £nil. The remaining £1,800 of the losses incurred in the year of death cannot be carried back any further and therefore cannot be relieved in any way.

Assuming that self assessments have already been made for 2019-20 and 2021-22, it will be necessary to revise these assessments to take into account the relief for losses carried back and to refund any CGT already paid for those years.

Relief for trading losses

If a taxpayer has claimed that a trading loss should be set against his or her total income for a tax year (or if no such claim can be made because total income for that year is zero) the taxpayer may further claim that any unrelieved part of the trading loss should be set against the capital gains of that year (see Chapter 12). If such a claim is made, the amount of the claim must be for the *lower* of the following two amounts:

(a) the amount of the unrelieved trading loss which is available for relief

(b) the "maximum amount", which is the amount of the taxable gains, *disregarding the annual exemption*, that would have been charged to CGT for the year if the claim had not been made.

It is very important to appreciate that the "maximum amount" is calculated as if the annual exemption simply did not exist. Not only is the annual exemption itself ignored in this calculation but so is the fact that capital losses brought forward might be restricted so as to preserve the exemption.

A trading loss which is set against capital gains in this way is treated as a capital loss incurred in the year of the claim and is therefore relieved *before* giving relief for capital losses brought forward.

EXAMPLE 5

(a) Richard has net gains for 2022-23 of £18,500 and capital losses brought forward of £3,300. Calculate his taxable gains for 2022-23.

(b) Richard has unrelieved trading losses (eligible for relief against his capital gains in 2022-23) of £27,500. Re-calculate his taxable gains for 2022-23 if he claims that these losses should (as far as possible) be set against his capital gains.

(c) Now calculate the taxable gains for 2022-23 if the capital losses brought forward are £12,100 instead of £3,300.

Solution

(a) Without a trading losses claim for 2022-23, taxable gains for the year will be:

	£
Net gains	18,500
Less: Capital losses b/f	3,300
	15,200
Less: Annual exemption	12,300
Taxable gains	2,900

There will be no unrelieved capital losses to carry forward.

(b) A trading losses claim would have to be for the lower of:

(i) the unrelieved trading loss (£27,500)

(ii) the taxable gains, *disregarding the annual exemption*, that would be charged to tax if a trading losses claim were not made (£15,200).

Therefore the claim would be for £15,200. This would be relieved in priority to capital losses brought forward. Taxable gains for the year would be:

	£
Net gains	18,500
Less: Trading losses	15,200
	3,300
Less: Annual exemption (restricted)	3,300
Taxable gains	nil

The remainder of the annual exemption (£9,000) would be lost. There would be no scope for relieving any of the capital losses brought forward, so the entire £3,300 would be carried forward to 2023-24. This claim would seem to be wasteful, since trading losses of £15,200 are sacrificed in order to reduce taxable gains by £2,900 and preserve capital losses of £3,300 (a total of £6,200).

(c) Without a trading losses claim, taxable gains would be calculated as follows:

	£
Net gains	18,500
Less: Capital losses b/f (restricted)	6,200
	12,300
Less: Annual exemption	12,300
Taxable gains	nil

There would be unrelieved capital losses of £5,900 carried forward. The maximum amount of a trading loss claim is £6,400 (£18,500 – £12,100) so the claim would have to be for £6,400 and taxable gains would then be:

	£
Net gains	18,500
Less: Trading losses	6,400
	12,100
Less: Annual exemption (restricted)	12,100
Taxable gains	nil

The remainder of the annual exemption (£200) would be lost and the capital losses of £12,100 would be carried forward to 2023-24 in their entirety. The effect of the claim would be to preserve capital losses of £6,200 at the expense of sacrificing trading losses of £6,400. This might be worthwhile if Richard believes that he will have more chance of relieving capital losses than trading losses in future years.

Administration of CGT

The tax administration system which was described in Chapter 1 applies to CGT as well as to income tax. Note that:

(a) Taxpayers are normally not required to fill in the capital gains tax section of their tax returns if both of the following conditions are satisfied:

 (i) total disposal proceeds for the year do not exceed four times the amount of the annual exemption (£49,200 for 2022-23)

 (ii) total chargeable gains for the year do not exceed the amount of the annual exemption (£12,300 for 2022-23).

 For this purpose, the term "total chargeable gains" means the total chargeable gains for the year *before* deduction of either current year losses or losses brought forward from previous years.

(b) Acquisitions of chargeable assets do not need to be entered on the tax return.

(c) A capital loss is not an allowable loss unless its amount is quantified and notified to HMRC. If the taxpayer submits a tax return for the year in which a loss is incurred, then notification must be made in that return. Otherwise, notification may be made by sending a separate notice to HMRC. Capital losses are not allowed unless they are notified to HMRC within four years of the end of the tax year concerned.

Payment of CGT

CGT is normally payable on 31 January following the end of the tax year to which the tax relates[†]. For instance, the date on which the 2022-23 CGT liability is normally payable is 31 January 2024. Payments on account of the CGT liability are *not* required.

However, if the proceeds of a disposal are received in instalments over a period of more than 18 months (beginning no earlier than the date of the disposal), the taxpayer may make a claim for the CGT due in relation to that disposal to be payable over the period of the instalments or over an eight-year period, whichever is the shorter.

The regime of interest and penalties which was described in Chapter 15 applies to both CGT and income tax.

[†] *As from 27 October 2021, the estimated amount of any CGT becoming due on the disposal of a UK residential property is payable within 60 days of completion.*

Summary

‣ A liability to CGT may arise when a chargeable person makes a chargeable disposal of a chargeable asset. UK resident individuals are chargeable persons. Companies are not chargeable persons.

‣ All assets are chargeable assets unless specifically exempted.

‣ A chargeable disposal occurs when all or part of a chargeable asset is sold (other than in the course of trade) or is given away, lost or destroyed.

‣ An individual's CGT liability for a tax year is based upon the chargeable disposals made by that individual during the year. For tax year 2022-23, the first £12,300 of net gains are exempt from CGT.

‣ CGT for 2022-23 is generally payable at the standard rate of 10% or at the higher rate of 20%. But gains on the disposal of residential property are taxed at 18% or 28% and gains which qualify for business asset disposal relief are always taxed at 10%.

‣ Net capital losses are carried forward and set against the net gains of subsequent tax years. Net losses incurred in the year of death may be carried back for three years.

‣ In certain circumstances, trading losses may be set against capital gains.

‣ CGT is normally payable on 31 January following the end of the tax year.

Exercises

A set of multiple choice questions for this chapter is available on the accompanying website.

17.1   Which of the following disposals might give rise to a CGT liability?

   (a)   the sale of antique furniture by a UK company

   (b)   the gift of shares from husband to wife (assuming that the couple live together)

   (c)   the gift of an oil painting to a charity

   (d)   the sale of an oil painting by a charity

   (e)   the sale of an oil painting by an art dealer

   (f)   the sale of an office building by a partnership.

17.2   Which of the following are chargeable assets for CGT purposes?

   (a)   shares in a limited company   (b)   gilt-edged securities

   (c)   an antique table worth £20,000   (d)   an antique chair worth £5,000

   (e)   a taxpayer's home   (f)   a vintage Bentley motor car.

17.3   An individual has capital losses of £2,500 in tax year 2022-23. There are no unrelieved losses brought forward from previous years. Compute the individual's taxable gains for 2022-23 if capital gains for the year are as follows:

   either   (a)   £nil

       or   (b)   £1,500

       or   (c)   £9,950

       or   (d)   £16,250.

17.4   In 2022-23, an individual has capital gains of £263,000 and allowable losses of £11,400. He has no unrelieved capital losses brought forward from previous years. His taxable income for 2022-23 (after deduction of the personal allowance) is £30,600 and he has made no Gift Aid donations or pension contributions. Calculate his CGT liability for the year, assuming that the gains of £263,000 comprise *either*:

   (a)   a gain of £263,000 which qualifies for business asset disposal relief (BADR), *or*

   (b)   a non-BADR gain of £263,000 arising on a sale of shares, *or*

   (c)   a non-BADR gain of £263,000 arising on a sale of residential property, *or*

   (d)   a BADR gain of £205,700 and a non-BADR gain of £57,300 on a sale of shares, *or*

   (e)   a BADR gain of £205,700 and a non-BADR gain of £57,300 on residential property.

17.5   An individual has capital losses brought forward from previous years amounting to £4,800. Compute the individual's taxable gains for 2022-23 if total gains and losses for the year are as follows:

   either   (a)   gains £11,400, losses £1,000

       or   (b)   gains £13,200, losses £300

       or   (c)   gains £18,300, losses £nil.

17.6   John dies on 3 March 2023. Between 6 April 2022 and 3 March 2023, he has capital gains of £1,200 and capital losses of £15,400. His net gains in recent tax years (and the annual exemption for each year) have been as follows:

	Net gains	Annual exemption
	£	£
2018-19	52,800	11,700
2019-20	18,500	12,000
2020-21	15,100	12,300
2021-22	3,750	12,300

Explain how (and to what extent) John's net losses in 2022-23 will be relieved.

17.7   On what date is CGT for 2022-23 normally due for payment?

*17.8   Rosemary's capital gains and losses in recent years (and the annual exemption for each year) have been as follows:

	Gains	Losses	Annual exemption
	£	£	£
2019-20	6,500	12,700	12,000
2020-21	11,600	2,350	12,300
2021-22	15,100	nil	12,300
2022-23	21,200	7,300	12,300

There were no unrelieved losses to bring forward from 2018-19 or earlier. Compute her taxable gains for tax years 2019-20 to 2022-23 inclusive.

*17.9   In 2022-23, Ahmed has capital gains of £130,000 and allowable losses of £24,000. He also has capital losses brought forward of £3,700.

Ahmed's taxable income for 2022-23 (after deduction of the personal allowance) is £22,700. He makes Gift Aid donations of £8,000 during the year. Compute his CGT liability for the year assuming that his gains of £130,000 comprise *either*:

(a)   a gain of £120,000 which qualifies for business asset disposal relief (BADR) and a non-BADR gain of £10,000 on the disposal of chattels, *or*

(b)   a BADR gain of £10,000 and a non-BADR gain of £120,000 arising on the disposal of residential property, *or*

(c)   a BADR gain of £7,500, a non-BADR gain of £70,000 on the disposal of residential property and a non-BADR gain of £52,500 on the disposal of shares.

*17.10   Melissa is a sole trader. Her capital gains and capital losses for 2022-23 are £27,000 and £700 respectively. She has capital losses brought forward from 2021-22 of £12,900 and she also has unrelieved trading losses of £18,500 which are eligible for relief against capital gains in 2022-23.

Calculate Melissa's taxable gains for 2022-23, assuming that:

(a)   a claim to relieve trading losses against capital gains is not made

(b)   a claim to relieve trading losses against capital gains is made.

Chapter 18

Computation of gains and losses

Introduction

The computation of the gain which arises on the disposal of a chargeable asset is basically a matter of subtracting the acquisition cost of the asset from its disposal value. However, it may be necessary to adjust the gain to take account of a number of other costs incurred by the taxpayer and the calculation becomes more complex if only part of the asset has been disposed of. Also, a different method of computation applies if the asset was acquired on or before 31 March 1982.

The purpose of this short chapter is to explain the basic method of computation (including part disposals) and to summarise the treatment of assets held on 31 March 1982.

Layout of a CGT computation

The computation of the chargeable gain or allowable loss arising on a chargeable disposal occurring during tax year 2022-23 is laid out as follows:

	£	£
Disposal value		xxx
Less: Incidental costs of disposal		xxx
		xxx
Less: *Allowable expenditure*:		
Acquisition cost of asset	xxx	
Incidental costs of acquisition	xxx	
Enhancement expenditure	xxx	
Cost of defending the owner's title to the asset	xxx	
Valuation fees	xxx	xxx
Chargeable gain or allowable loss		xxx

Each of the terms used in this layout is explained below.

Disposal value

If a disposal consists of the sale of an asset, disposal value is generally taken to be the proceeds of the sale. But if a sale does not constitute "a bargain made at arm's length", the sale proceeds are ignored and disposal value is taken to be the market value of the asset on the date of the sale. This rule applies particularly to transactions between "connected persons". For CGT purposes, a taxpayer is connected to his or her:

(a) spouse (husband, wife or civil partner)

(b) relatives (brothers, sisters, ancestors, direct descendants) and their spouses

(c) spouse's relatives and their spouses

(d) business partners and their spouses and relatives.

Market value is also used as disposal value if the disposal takes the form of a gift. But disposals between spouses who live together are deemed to occur at a disposal value such that neither a gain nor a loss arises (see Chapter 17). This rule takes precedence over the usual rules concerning sales to connected persons and gifts.

In general, the market value of an asset is the amount it would fetch if sold on the open market. Listed ("quoted") shares and securities are valued for CGT purposes as follows:

(a) on a day that the Stock Exchange is open, the lower of the two closing prices quoted for the shares on that day, plus one-half of the difference between those two prices

(b) on a day that the Stock Exchange is closed, at the value calculated by rule (a) for the latest previous day on which it was open.

Incidental costs of disposal include legal fees, auctioneers' fees, advertising costs etc.

Allowable expenditure

The following expenditure may be set against disposal value when calculating the gain or loss arising on a disposal:

(a) the acquisition cost of the asset (or its market value on the date of acquisition if it was acquired by gift or otherwise than by way of a bargain made at arm's length)

(b) incidental costs of acquisition (e.g. legal fees)

(c) "enhancement expenditure", which is expenditure on making improvements to the asset, so long as that expenditure is still reflected in the state of the asset at the time of disposal (but the costs of mere repairs and maintenance are disallowed)

(d) costs incurred in defending the owner's title to the asset (generally legal costs)

(e) valuation fees necessarily incurred for CGT purposes.

If an asset is acquired as the result of a disposal between spouses who live together, the deemed acquisition cost for the spouse receiving the asset is equal to the deemed disposal value for the spouse who makes the disposal (see above).

EXAMPLE 1

(a) A chargeable asset was bought in June 2018 for £41,200 and sold in August 2022 for £73,350. Compute the chargeable gain.

(b) A chargeable asset was bought for £15,000 in August 2014. Legal costs of £500 were incurred when the asset was acquired. The owner of the asset incurred enhancement expenditure of £2,000 in May 2015 and £3,000 in June 2019. The asset was sold in July 2022 for £28,000. Legal costs of £700 were incurred on the sale. Compute the chargeable gain.

(c) A taxpayer bought a chargeable asset for £40,000 in February 2017. The asset was sold for £30,000 in October 2022. Compute the chargeable gain or allowable loss if:

(i)   the asset was sold in an arm's length transaction

(ii) the asset was sold to the taxpayer's brother and had a market value of £45,000 on the date of the sale

(iii) the asset was sold to the taxpayer's wife (who lives with him) and had a market value of £45,000 on the date of the sale.

Solution

(a) The chargeable gain is (£73,350 – £41,200) = £32,150.

(b)

	£	£
Sale proceeds		28,000
Less: Incidental costs of disposal		700
		27,300
Less: Acquisition cost	15,000	
Incidental costs of acquisition	500	
Enhancement expenditure (£2,000 + £3,000)	5,000	20,500
Chargeable gain		6,800

(c)

	(i) £	(ii) £	(iii) £
Disposal value	30,000	45,000	40,000
Less: Acquisition cost	40,000	40,000	40,000
Chargeable gain/(allowable loss)	(10,000)	5,000	-

In case (iii), disposal value is set to £40,000 so as to ensure that neither a gain nor a loss occurs on this disposal to the taxpayer's spouse.

Part disposals

If only *part* of a chargeable asset is disposed of, only part of its cost can be allowed when computing the gain or loss. The allowable part cost is the full cost of the asset multiplied by the following fraction:

$$\frac{A}{A+B}$$

where: A is the value of the part disposed of (i.e. the disposal value), and

            B is the value of the part remaining in the taxpayer's ownership.

This part disposal fraction applies not only to the acquisition cost of the asset but also to any other items of allowable expenditure which relate to the whole asset. But any item of expenditure which relates only to the part of the asset which has been disposed of should be allowed in full.

EXAMPLE 2

Peter buys a chargeable asset for £26,000 in May 2014. He sells a one-quarter interest in the asset for £12,000 in August 2022, incurring incidental costs of disposal of £500. The value of the other three-quarters interest in the asset in August 2022 is £40,000. Calculate the chargeable gain.

Solution

	£
Sale proceeds	12,000
Less: Incidental costs of disposal	500
	11,500
Less: Part cost:	
$\dfrac{£12,000}{£12,000 + £40,000}$ x £26,000	6,000
Chargeable gain	5,500

Notes:

(i)   The fact that Peter has sold a one-quarter interest in the asset is irrelevant. What is relevant is that he has sold £12,000 worth out of an asset currently worth £52,000, as indicated by the part disposal fraction.

(ii)   If Peter disposes of the remaining three-quarters of the asset at some future time, the remaining £20,000 of the cost (£26,000 − £6,000) will then be allowable.

(iii)   The incidental costs of disposal are allowed in full since these relate solely to the part of the asset which has been disposed of.

Small part disposals of land

An exception to the usual part disposal rules occurs when a taxpayer makes a small part disposal of land. A part disposal of land is "small" if the land is freehold, or held on a lease with more than 50 years left to run, and the following conditions are met:

(a) If the disposal is caused by a compulsory purchase order, the disposal proceeds must not exceed 5% of the value of the whole piece of land. However, it is the practice of HM Revenue and Customs to treat disposal proceeds of £3,000 or less as small for this purpose, regardless of whether or not the 5% test is satisfied.

(b) If the disposal is not caused by a compulsory purchase order, the disposal proceeds must not exceed 20% of the value of the whole piece of land and the total proceeds of all disposals of land in the year of assessment must not exceed £20,000[†].

A taxpayer who makes a small part disposal of land which satisfies these conditions may claim that the disposal should not be treated as a chargeable disposal but that the proceeds of the disposal should instead be subtracted from the acquisition cost of the land. This claim has the following consequences:

(a) No gain or loss arises on the small part disposal.

(b) Since the acquisition cost of the land is reduced, the gain arising on a subsequent disposal of the remainder of the land is automatically increased.

In effect, the gain arising on the small part disposal is deferred until the remainder of the land is disposed of. Fairly obviously, the taxpayer should not make such a claim if the gain arising on the small part disposal would be covered by the annual exemption for the year.

Note that these rules apply only to small part disposals of *land*, whereas the more general part disposal rules explained earlier in this chapter apply to all types of chargeable asset.

[†] *When calculating the total proceeds of all land disposals in the year for this purpose, small part disposals of land which are caused by compulsory purchase orders (if any) are ignored.*

EXAMPLE 3

In July 2011, Malcolm bought a piece of land for £40,000. In June 2018 he sold part of the land for £11,000. This disposal was not caused by a compulsory purchase and was his only disposal of land in 2018-19. The value of the remainder of the land in June 2018 was £50,000. Malcolm had substantial capital gains in 2018-19, sufficient to absorb his annual exemption for the year, and therefore decided to make a small part disposal claim.

Calculate the chargeable gain arising in January 2023 when Malcolm sells the remainder of the land for £60,000.

Solution

The small part disposal claim made in 2018-19 was valid since the total value of the land immediately prior to the June 2018 disposal was £61,000 and the disposal raised £11,000 which is less than 20% of £61,000. Furthermore, the proceeds of all land disposals in the year did not exceed £20,000.

No gain or loss arises on the June 2018 disposal but the sale proceeds of £11,000 are subtracted from the acquisition cost of the land. The gain on the January 2023 disposal is therefore as follows:

	£
Sale proceeds	60,000
<u>Less</u>: Reduced acquisition cost (£40,000 – £11,000)	29,000
Chargeable gain	31,000

The effect of Malcolm's part disposal claim is that the whole of the gain arising on the two disposals taken together (£11,000 + £60,000 – £40,000 = £31,000) is charged to tax in tax year 2022-23, even though the first disposal took place in 2018-19.

Assets with negligible value

If the value of a chargeable asset has become negligible (i.e. the asset has become virtually worthless) the owner of the asset may make a "negligible value" claim. If this claim is accepted by HMRC, the asset is treated as if it had been disposed of at its current value and then immediately re-acquired at that value. The usual effect of a negligible value claim is to trigger an allowable loss.

EXAMPLE 4

In September 2016, Gloria acquired 1,000 ordinary shares in a listed company for £7,000. Trading in the shares was suspended in December 2022 and Gloria claimed that the shares then had a negligible value of only 10p per share. This claim was accepted by HMRC. Compute the allowable loss.

Solution

	£
Deemed disposal value (1,000 x 10p)	100
<u>Less</u>: Cost	7,000
Allowable loss	(6,900)

If Gloria succeeds in selling the shares at some time in the future, their deemed acquisition cost for CGT purposes will be £100.

Assets held on 31 March 1982

CGT was introduced in 1965 and applied to disposals made on or after 6 April 1965, which was originally the "base date" for CGT. However, this base date has since been changed to 31 March 1982. This means that if a taxpayer now disposes of an asset which he or she held on 31 March 1982, only the part of the gain which has accrued since that date is chargeable to tax. The calculation of the taxable part of the gain is achieved by means of a technique known as "rebasing" whereby the market value of the asset at 31 March 1982 is substituted for its acquisition cost in the CGT calculation[†]. In summary:

(a) The gain or loss arising on the disposal of an asset held on 31 March 1982 is calculated by comparing the asset's disposal value with its market value at 31 March 1982. Any enhancement expenditure incurred after 31 March 1982 is taken into account in the usual way when computing the gain or loss.

(b) The original acquisition cost of such an asset is not relevant for CGT purposes and is entirely ignored. In fact, all costs incurred on or before 31 March 1982 (including any enhancement expenditure incurred up to that date) are ignored and are replaced in the CGT computation by the asset's market value at 31 March 1982.

(c) In effect, the owner of the asset is treated as if he or she had bought it on 31 March 1982 for its market value on that date.

(d) When a part disposal is made of an asset which was held on 31 March 1982, the part disposal fraction which would normally be applied to the cost of the asset when computing the chargeable gain arising (see earlier in this chapter) is applied instead to the asset's market value at 31 March 1982.

   If there has been any enhancement expenditure since 31 March 1982, the amount of that expenditure, multiplied by the part disposal fraction, is also taken into account when computing the gain or loss.

However, from the viewpoint of tax year 2022-23, it is now quite uncommon for a taxpayer to dispose of an asset held on 31 March 1982 and so trigger the rebasing rules. Therefore these rules are considered no further here. But further information and a number of worked examples are available on the website which accompanies this book. The website can be accessed at go.pearson.com/uk/he/resources.

[†] *The rebasing rules were introduced by Finance Act 2008, but these rules do not apply to disposals made by companies. The corporation tax rules which apply when a company makes a disposal of an asset held on 31 March 1982 are summarised later in this book (see Chapter 24).*

Summary

▶ The disposal value of an asset is normally equal to sale proceeds, but if an asset is given away or is sold other than by way of a bargain made at arm's length, disposal value is normally deemed to be the market value of the asset on the date of disposal.

▶ Disposals between spouses who live together (including civil partners) are deemed to occur at a disposal value such that neither a gain nor a loss arises on the disposal.

▶ Allowable costs include the asset's acquisition cost, incidental costs, enhancement expenditure, costs of defending the owner's title and valuation fees.

▶ On a part disposal, the allowable part cost is calculated by multiplying the full cost by the part disposal fraction. Special rules apply to small part disposals of land.

▶ A taxpayer may claim that an asset has negligible value, so triggering a disposal which gives rise to an allowable loss.

▶ Rebasing applies on the disposal of an asset which was held at 31 March 1982. The gain or loss on disposal is calculated by comparing the disposal value with the market value of the asset at 31 March 1982.

▶ The gain or loss arising on the part disposal of an asset held on 31 March 1982 is calculated by comparing disposal value with the appropriate part of the asset's market value at 31 March 1982.

Exercises

A set of multiple choice questions for this chapter is available on the accompanying website.

18.1 Carol purchased a holiday flat in December 2014 for £100,000. She spent £5,000 on installing central heating in February 2017 and a further £750 on repainting the interior of the flat in March 2021. The flat was never Carol's main residence.

She sold the flat at auction in February 2023 for £172,000, paying a 5% fee to the auctioneer. Legal costs were £400 in December 2014 and £500 in February 2023. Compute Carol's chargeable gain on the disposal of the flat.

18.2 Francis (who is not an art dealer) bought an oil painting in August 1990. He sold the painting for £87,500 in March 2023. Compute the chargeable gain or allowable loss arising on this disposal if the cost of the painting in August 1990 was:

(a)   £10,000   (b)   £35,000   (c)   £100,000.

How would the situation differ if Francis was an art dealer and the painting was acquired as trading stock for sale to a customer?

18.3   David was given a chargeable asset in November 2016 at which time the asset had a market value of £7,500. He sold the asset in January 2023. Compute the chargeable gain or the allowable loss if his sale proceeds were:

(a)   £14,950   (b)   £6,350   (c)   £25,780.

18.4   Edwina bought a chargeable asset in August 2011 for £240,000, paying acquisition costs of £12,000. In June 2018 she sold a one-quarter interest in the asset for £100,000 and incurred disposal costs of £5,000. The remaining three-quarters interest in the asset was valued at £500,000 in June 2018.

(a)   Compute the chargeable gain arising in June 2018.

(b)   Also compute the chargeable gain arising in January 2023, when Edwina sold her remaining three-quarters interest in the asset for £520,000. Assume that disposal costs in January 2023 were £nil.

18.5   In June 2014, Gillian was given shares with a market value at that time of £6,000. In November 2021 she made a successful claim to the effect that these shares now had a negligible value of only £80.

(a)   Compute the allowable loss.

(b)   Compute the chargeable gain arising in March 2023, when Gillian sold the shares for £120.

*18.6   Jon bought a chargeable asset for £58,500 in October 1990. He incurred enhancement expenditure of £10,000 in December 1993 and a further £4,000 in July 2009. The asset was sold for £185,000 in February 2023.

(a)   Compute the chargeable gain.

(b)   Now re-compute the gain, assuming that the person who bought the asset from Jon in February 2023 was his civil partner (who lives with him).

*18.7   Karen bought a house in 1995 for £42,000. In November 1996 she spent £18,000 on dividing the house into two self-contained flats. In September 2020 she sold one of the flats for £95,000, at which time the other flat was valued at £105,000. In March 2023 she sold the second flat for £110,000. Karen never lived in either of the flats.

Compute the chargeable gains arising on Karen's two disposals, ignoring incidental costs of acquisition and disposal.

Chapter 19

Chattels and wasting assets

Introduction

A "chattel" is an item of tangible, movable property. A "wasting asset" is an asset with a predictable useful life not exceeding 50 years. If an asset is both a chattel and a wasting asset (e.g. a TV set) it is referred to as a "wasting chattel". Special capital gains tax rules apply to disposals of chattels, wasting assets and wasting chattels. The purpose of this chapter is to explain these rules.

The chattels exemption

The disposal of a chattel for £6,000 or less is exempt from capital gains tax. This rule removes from charge a great many trivial disposals and ensures that CGT is levied only if the disposal is material. The following points relate to the chattels exemption:

(a) This exemption applies only to chattels, not to assets in general.

(b) The exemption means that gains arising on the disposal of a chattel for £6,000 or less are not chargeable to CGT. It also means that losses arising on such disposals are not generally allowable. However, special rules apply to chattels acquired for more than £6,000 and disposed of for £6,000 or less (see later in this chapter).

(c) The £6,000 figure relates to the *gross* disposal proceeds. These are the proceeds before deducting incidental costs of disposal.

(d) If the gross disposal proceeds of a chattel exceed £6,000, the chargeable gain cannot exceed five-thirds† of the amount by which disposal proceeds exceed £6,000. This "marginal relief" ensures that taxpayers who dispose of chattels for more than £6,000 are not unduly penalised by the tax system.

† *The effect of the five-thirds formula is that the disposal of a chattel for £15,000 or less may benefit from marginal relief (depending upon the amount of allowable expenditure). If disposal proceeds exceed £15,000, the marginal relief formula will always give a greater gain than the gain calculated in the normal way.*

EXAMPLE 1

In 2022-23, a taxpayer makes a number of disposals, as listed below. Which of these disposals would be exempt from CGT?

(a)   An antique table sold for £5,000.

(b)   A watercolour painting sold at auction. The auctioneer deducted his 10% commission from the selling price and sent the taxpayer a cheque for the remaining £5,670.

(c)   A holding of shares sold for £4,500.

Solution

(a)   The antique table is a chattel disposed of for £6,000 or less. Therefore the disposal is exempt from CGT.

(b)   A watercolour painting is a chattel. The gross disposal proceeds must have been £6,300, since £6,300 less 10% = £5,670. The chattels exemption will not apply but the chargeable gain cannot exceed five-thirds of £300 (i.e. £500).

(c)   A shareholding is not a chattel. Therefore the £6,000 exemption does not apply and the disposal will be chargeable to CGT.

EXAMPLE 2

In December 2022, Michael sells a piece of antique furniture for £6,360, paying incidental disposal costs of £320. He had acquired the furniture in January 2015 as a gift from his mother. Compute Michael's chargeable gain if the market value of the furniture in January 2015 was:

(a)   £5,500   (b)   £4,900

Solution

	(a)	(b)
	£	£
Sale proceeds	6,360	6,360
Less: Incidental costs of disposal	320	320
	6,040	6,040
Less: Deemed acquisition cost	5,500	4,900
Chargeable gain	540	1,140 (restricted to £600)

Notes:

(i)   The maximum gain is £360 x 5/3 = £600. The gain of £540 in case (a) is less than £600, so the chargeable gain is £540.

(ii)   In case (b), £1,140 exceeds £600, so the gain is restricted to £600.

Chattels disposed of at a loss

If a chattel is disposed of at a loss, there are two possibilities. Either:

(a) the disposal proceeds exceed £6,000, in which case the allowable loss is calculated in the usual way, or

(b) the disposal proceeds are £6,000 or less, in which case the chattels exemption applies and it appears that no allowable loss could arise.

However, if a chattel is acquired for more than £6,000 and then disposed of for less than £6,000, the normal chattels exemption is overruled and an allowable loss is available. But the amount of this loss is restricted to the amount that would arise if the disposal proceeds were exactly £6,000.

EXAMPLE 3

In March 2023, Naomi sells an oil painting which she had acquired many years previously for £10,000. Compute the allowable loss if she sells the painting for:

(a) £7,200   (b) £2,700

Solution

(a) Naomi has disposed of a chattel for more than £6,000, so the disposal is not exempt from capital gains tax. The allowable loss is calculated in the usual way as (£10,000 − £7,200) = £2,800.

(b) Naomi has disposed of a chattel for less than £6,000 and so normally this disposal would be exempt from capital gains tax. However, since the asset was acquired for more than £6,000, a loss is allowed. This is calculated by substituting £6,000 for the disposal proceeds. The allowable loss is (£10,000 − £6,000) = £4,000.

Part disposals of chattels

A part disposal of a chattel may be made in one of two ways. Either:

(a) a part interest in a chattel may be disposed of, or

(b) for chattels forming a set, one or more of the items in the set may be disposed of.

Each of these forms of part disposal is considered below.

Disposal of a part interest in a chattel

If a disposal is made of a part interest in a chattel, then this part disposal will be exempt from capital gains tax only if the value of the *whole* chattel immediately prior to the part disposal is £6,000 or less.

If the value of the whole chattel exceeds £6,000 the disposal is not exempt from CGT and the usual part disposal calculation is performed. However, the chargeable gain on the part disposal is limited to five-thirds of the amount by which the value of the whole chattel exceeds £6,000, multiplied by the usual part disposal fraction.

EXAMPLE 4

In October 2016, Jackie bought a chattel for £3,500. In October 2022 she sells a one-third interest in this chattel for £2,000. Compute the chargeable gain if the market value of the remaining two-thirds interest in October 2022 is:

(a) £4,000   (b) £5,000.

Solution

(a) The value of the whole chattel on the date of the part disposal is £6,000. Since this value does not exceed £6,000 the part disposal is exempt from CGT.

(b) The value of the whole chattel on the date of the part disposal is £7,000. Since this value exceeds £6,000 the part disposal is not exempt from CGT. The computation of the chargeable gain is as follows:

	£
Sale proceeds	2,000
Less: Part cost:	
$\dfrac{£2,000}{£2,000 + £5,000} \times £3,500$	1,000
Chargeable gain	1,000 (restricted to £476)

Notes:

(i)   The part disposal fraction is £2,000/(£2,000 + £5,000) which is 2/7ths.

(ii)   If the whole chattel had been sold (for £7,000) the chargeable gain would have been restricted to (£7,000 – £6,000) x 5/3 = £1,667.

(iii) However, only 2/7ths of the chattel has been sold. So the gain is restricted to £1,667 × 2/7 = £476.

Disposal of part of a set

If a taxpayer acquires a set of chattels (e.g. a set of dining chairs) and then disposes of them individually, each disposal is regarded as a part disposal and will in general be chargeable to CGT only if the disposal proceeds of an individual item exceed £6,000.

However, a taxpayer who wished to dispose of a set of chattels with a total value which exceeds £6,000 could use this rule to avoid capital gains tax by disposing of the items one by one (with each disposal raising no more than £6,000). In order to prevent such tax avoidance, a series of disposals of chattels which form part of a set *to the same person or to persons connected with each other or acting together* are treated as a single transaction for capital gains tax purposes. If the individual disposals occur in different tax years, any gain which results from this treatment is apportioned between tax years in proportion to the sale proceeds of each disposal.

EXAMPLE 5

Andrew acquired a set of six dining chairs in January 2015 for £1,300. In March 2022 he sold three of the chairs to a friend for £5,200 (the other three chairs also being valued at £5,200 at that time). In August 2022 he sold the remaining chairs to the friend's brother for £5,300. Compute the chargeable gains arising on these disposals.

Solution

If it were not for the rule introduced above, neither of these disposals would be chargeable to CGT since neither of them raises more than £6,000. However, the two disposals are made to connected persons and are therefore to be regarded as a single transaction for CGT purposes. The total disposal proceeds are £10,500 (£5,200 + £5,300). This exceeds £6,000 so the disposals are chargeable. The computation is as follows:

	£
Sale proceeds	10,500
Less: Cost	1,300
Chargeable gain	9,200 (restricted to £7,500)

The maximum gain is (£10,500 − £6,000) x 5/3 = £7,500. £9,200 is greater than this, so the chargeable gain is restricted to £7,500. The apportionment of this gain between the two disposals is as follows:

March 2022 disposal $\dfrac{£5,200}{£10,500} \times £7,500 = £3,714$ (taxed in 2021-22)

August 2022 disposal $\dfrac{£5,300}{£10,500} \times £7,500 = £3,786$ (taxed in 2022-23)

Wasting chattels

Chattels which (on acquisition) have a predictable useful life of 50 years or less are referred to as "wasting chattels" and are generally exempt from CGT. So the disposal of a wasting chattel will usually give rise to neither a chargeable gain nor an allowable loss.

An exception to this rule occurs in the case of movable plant and machinery used in business and eligible for capital allowances. Plant and machinery is always regarded as having a predictable useful life not exceeding 50 years and therefore movable plant and machinery is a wasting chattel. Unless the general chattels exemption applies, disposals of movable plant and machinery used in business and eligible for capital allowances are *not* exempt from CGT. One of two situations may arise on such a disposal:

(a) Disposal proceeds may be less than original cost. In this (the most likely) case, the allowable loss is reduced by the total capital allowances[†] which have been available on the asset. This will reduce the loss to zero.

(b) Disposal proceeds may be greater than original cost. In this case, the total of the available capital allowances on the asset is zero and therefore capital allowances have no effect on the computation, which will proceed in the usual way.

Note that certain collectors' items such as antique clocks and watches are regarded as plant and machinery. Consequently, these items are treated as wasting chattels, even though their useful lives may considerably exceed 50 years. By virtue of this treatment, such items are exempt from CGT unless used in business and eligible for capital allowances.

[†] *The total capital allowances which have been available in relation to an asset are calculated for this purpose as the difference between the cost of the asset and its disposal value.*

EXAMPLE 0

An item of movable plant and machinery is bought in February 2020 for £8,000 and used solely for trade purposes. Capital allowances are available. Compute the chargeable gain or allowable loss which arises if the item is sold in July 2022 and the sale proceeds are:

(a) £5,500   (b) £6,500   (c) £7,500   (d) £8,500.

Solution

In case (a), sale proceeds do not exceed £6,000 so the disposal would seem to be exempt from CGT. But the asset was acquired for more than £6,000 and sold for less than £6,000 so the chattels exemption is overruled and disposal value is set to exactly £6,000.

In cases (a), (b) and (c), available capital allowances are equal to the difference between the asset's acquisition cost and its disposal value. In case (d), capital allowances are zero because disposal value is greater than cost. Disposal value in this case exceeds £6,000 by £2,500 so the gain cannot exceed £4,167 (£2,500 x 5/3). However, the chargeable gain is only £500 (see below) so marginal relief does not apply. Computations are as follows:

	(a)	(b)	(c)	(d)
	£	£	£	£
Disposal value	6,000	6,500	7,500	8,500
Less: Acquisition cost	8,000	8,000	8,000	8,000
	(2,000)	(1,500)	(500)	500
Less: Available capital allowances	2,000	1,500	500	0
Chargeable gain/(allowable loss)	0	0	0	500

Wasting assets

A wasting asset which is not a chattel is *not* exempt from CGT. Typical examples of such wasting assets include:

(a) intangible assets such as copyrights or patents with lives not exceeding 50 years

(b) short leases

(c) fixed plant and machinery.

In general, the original cost of a wasting asset is deemed to waste away on a straight line basis over the asset's predictable life. The computation of the gain or loss arising on the disposal of such an asset is achieved by comparing the disposal value with the unexpired portion of the asset's cost at the time of disposal. But special rules apply to the disposal of a lease (see later in this chapter).

However, if a wasting asset which is not a chattel is used for business purposes and is eligible for capital allowances, the calculation of the gain or loss arising on disposal takes into account the full cost of the asset (not its unexpired portion). The required treatment is the same as that required for wasting chattels (see above).

EXAMPLE 7

In January 2013, Fiona acquired a 25-year copyright at a cost of £30,000. In January 2023 she sold the copyright for £35,500. Compute the chargeable gain.

Solution

When the copyright was bought it had a 25-year life. When it was sold there were 15 years remaining. Therefore the computation is as follows:

	£
Sale proceeds	35,500
Less: Unexpired portion of cost (£30,000 × 15/25)	18,000
Chargeable gain	17,500

Leases

For capital gains tax purposes, leases are classified into long leases (those of more than 50 years) and short leases (those of 50 years or less). A chargeable disposal may occur in connection with a lease in any of the following ways:

(a) A taxpayer who has a long lease on a property assigns that lease to someone else.

(b) A taxpayer who has a short lease on a property assigns that lease to someone else.

(c) A taxpayer who owns the freehold of a property (or who has a long head-lease) grants a long lease (or long sub-lease) to someone else, the property eventually reverting to the taxpayer concerned.

(d) A taxpayer who owns the freehold of a property (or who has a long head-lease) grants a short lease (or short sub-lease) to someone else, the property eventually reverting to the taxpayer concerned.

(e) A taxpayer who has a short head-lease on a property grants a shorter sub-lease to someone else, the property eventually reverting to the taxpayer concerned.

Each of these cases is considered below. If a property is (or has been) the taxpayer's main residence, the gain arising on the disposal of a lease on the property may be subject to the principal private residence exemption described in Chapter 21.

Assignment of a long lease

The assignment of a long lease is treated as a disposal of the whole asset and therefore causes no CGT difficulties at all. The computation proceeds in precisely the same way as the computation on the disposal of any other whole asset.

EXAMPLE 8

In August 2016, Jim acquired a 99-year lease on a flat for £170,000. In August 2022, he assigned the lease to Shirley for £212,000. The flat was never Jim's residence. Compute the chargeable gain.

Solution

The chargeable gain in this case is simply £42,000 (£212,000 – £170,000). The fact that the lease is six years shorter by the time that Jim assigns it is of no consequence, since it is still a long lease (more than 50 years) on the date of assignment.

If the flat had been Jim's main residence for all or part of the period of ownership, the gain may have been reduced or eliminated by the principal private residence exemption.

Assignment of a short lease

A short lease is, by definition, a wasting asset. Therefore the computation of the gain arising on the disposal of a short lease should be achieved by comparing disposal proceeds with the unexpired portion of the lease's cost at the time of disposal.

However, unlike other wasting assets, the cost of a short lease is not deemed to waste away on a straight line basis. Instead, the cost of a short lease is deemed to waste away according to a table of percentages which is given in Schedule 8 of TCGA 1992 and is reproduced at the end of this chapter. The effect of this table is to write off the cost of a short lease slowly in the early years and more quickly in the closing years. The proportion of the cost[†] of a short lease which is allowed in the CGT computation on its disposal is:

$$\frac{\text{\% relating to number of years lease has left to run on disposal}}{\text{\% relating to original length of lease}}$$

If the lease was originally a long lease but the taxpayer has owned it for some years so that the lease now being assigned is a short lease, the denominator in the above fraction is taken as 100%, corresponding to "50 or more" in the Schedule 8 table.

Schedule 8 gives percentages for whole numbers of years only. If the duration of a lease is not a whole number of years, then the appropriate percentage is calculated from the table on a pro rata basis.

[†] *If any enhancement expenditure has been incurred, the proportion of this expenditure which is allowed in the CGT computation on disposal is equal to the Sch. 8 percentage for the number of years left on the date of disposal divided by the Sch. 8 percentage for the number of years left on the date of the enhancement expenditure.*

EXAMPLE 9

Jean acquired a 30-year lease on a property in July 2012 for £132,000. In July 2022 she assigned the lease to Lawrence for £145,000. The property was never Jean's residence. Compute the chargeable gain.

Solution

When the lease was acquired it had a 30-year life (Sch. 8 percentage 87.330%). When it was assigned there were 20 years remaining (Sch. 8 percentage 72.770%). Therefore the computation is as follows:

	£
Sale proceeds	145,000
Less: Unexpired portion of cost	
$\frac{72.770}{87.330}$ x £132,000	109,992
Chargeable gain	35,008

EXAMPLE 10

A taxpayer assigns a lease of duration 12 years and 5 months. Calculate the appropriate percentage for use in the CGT computation on the disposal.

Solution

The percentage for 12 years is 53.191%. The percentage for 13 years is 56.167%. The difference between these percentages is 2.976%. Therefore the appropriate percentage for a lease of duration 12 years and 5 months is 53.191 + (2.976 x 5/12) = 54.431%.

EXAMPLE 11

On 31 May 1992, Joan acquired a 45-year lease on a property for £135,000. On 31 May 2002, she incurred enhancement expenditure of £42,500. On 30 November 2022, she assigned the lease to Giles for £225,000. The property was never Joan's principal private residence. Compute the chargeable gain.

Solution

The gain arising on the disposal is as follows:

	£
Sale proceeds	225,000
Less: Unexpired portion of acquisition cost	
$\dfrac{60.294}{98.059}$ x £135,000	(83,008)
Unexpired portion of enhancement expenditure	
$\dfrac{60.294}{91.981}$ x £42,500	(27,859)
Chargeable gain	114,133

Notes:

(i)   When the lease was acquired it had a 45-year life (Sch. 8 percentage 98.059%).

(ii) When the enhancement expenditure was incurred there were 35 years remaining. (Sch. 8 percentage 91.981%).

(ii) When the lease was assigned there were 14 years and 6 months remaining. The Sch. 8 percentage for 14 years and 6 months is 58.971 + (2.646 x 6/12) = 60.294%.

Grant of a long lease

The grant of a long lease (or a long sub-lease) out of a freehold (or a long head-lease) is treated as a part disposal for CGT purposes and the normal part disposal rules apply. The value of the part disposed of is usually equal to the proceeds of the disposal. The value of the part remaining takes into account both:

(a) the right of the taxpayer making the disposal to receive rents from the tenant, and

(b) the taxpayer's "reversionary interest", which is the right to take back the property when the lease (or sub-lease) finishes.

Grant of a short lease

The grant of a short lease (or a short sub-lease) out of a freehold (or a long head-lease) is also treated as a part disposal for CGT purposes and therefore the part disposal rules apply again. However, part of the premium received on the grant of a short lease is assessable to income tax as property income (see Chapter 5) and therefore, in order to avoid double taxation, the disposal proceeds in the part-disposal computation are reduced by the amount of the premium which is assessable as property income.

EXAMPLE 12

Jeffrey acquired a freehold property in October 2014 for £299,000. In July 2022 he granted Jill a lease on the property for £260,000. The market value of the freehold after the lease had been granted was £200,000. The property was never Jeffrey's residence. Compute the chargeable gain, given that the lease granted to Jill was of duration:

(a) 99 years   (b) 40 years.

Solution

(a) This is a part disposal with A = £260,000 and B = £200,000. The computation is as follows:

	£
Sale proceeds	260,000
Less: Part cost:	
$\dfrac{£260,000}{£260,000 + £200,000} \times £299,000$	169,000
Chargeable gain	91,000

(b) This is also a part disposal but £57,200 (£260,000 − (2% x £260,000 x 39)) of the disposal proceeds will be assessable as property income and this must be taken into account in the CGT computation. The computation is as follows:

	£
Sale proceeds (£260,000 – £57,200)	202,800
Less: Part cost:	
$\dfrac{£202,800}{£260,000 + £200,000} \times £299,000$	131,820
Chargeable gain	70,980

Note that the numerator of the part disposal fraction is taken as the disposal proceeds *after* deducting the property income assessment, whilst the denominator takes into account the disposal proceeds *before* deducting the property income assessment.

Grant of a short sub-lease out of a short head-lease

In essence, the grant of a short sub-lease out of a short head-lease is treated in a similar fashion to the assignment of a short lease, as discussed earlier in this chapter. As before, the TCGA 1992 Schedule 8 table of percentages (reproduced at the end of this chapter) is used to determine the part cost that should be deducted in the capital gains tax computation. But since the property will be returning to the original tenant when the sub-lease finishes, the proportion of the cost of the short head-lease which is allowed in the CGT computation on the granting of a sub-lease is equal to:

$$\frac{P1 - P2}{P3}$$

where:

P1 = the percentage relating to the number of years left of the short head-lease when the short sub-lease begins

P2 = the percentage relating to the number of years left of the short head-lease when the short sub-lease ends

P3 = the percentage relating to the original length of the short head-lease.

Since part of the premium received by the taxpayer on the grant of a short sub-lease will be assessable to income tax as property income (see Chapter 5) the capital gain arising is reduced by the amount of the property income assessment. However, this reduction cannot be used to convert a gain into a loss or to increase a loss.

EXAMPLE 13

In September 2016, Joanna acquired a 15-year lease on a property for £45,000. In September 2022 she granted a four-year sub-lease to Dean for £20,000. The property was never Joanna's residence. Compute the chargeable gain.

Solution

The computation of the chargeable gain is as follows:

	£
Sale proceeds	20,000
Less: Proportion of cost	
$\dfrac{43.154 - 26.722}{61.617} \times £45,000$	12,001
	7,999
Less: Property income assessment (£10,160)	7,999
Chargeable gain	nil

Notes:

(i) P1 = 43.154 (9 years), P2 = 26.722 (5 years) and P3 = 61.617 (15 years)

(ii) The property income assessment (see Chapter 5) is:

	£
Premium received	20,000
Less: £20,000 x (4 − 1) x 2%	1,200
	18,800
Less: Relief for premium paid:	
$\dfrac{4}{15} \times (£45,000 - (£45,000 \times (15 - 1) \times 2\%))$	8,640
	10,160

(iii) The relief given for the property income assessment is restricted to £7,999 so as not to turn a gain into a loss.

Summary

▶ A chattel is an item of tangible, movable property. A wasting asset is an asset with a predictable useful life of 50 years or less. A wasting asset that is also a chattel is a wasting chattel.

▶ Chattels disposed of for £6,000 or less are generally exempt from CGT.

▶ If a chattel is disposed of for more than £6,000, the chargeable gain cannot exceed five-thirds of the amount by which disposal proceeds exceed £6,000.

▶ The allowable loss on chattels acquired for more than £6,000 and disposed of for less than £6,000 is restricted by substituting £6,000 for the disposal proceeds.

▶ Disposals of a part interest in a chattel are exempt from CGT if the value of the whole chattel is £6,000 or less.

▶ A series of disposals of chattels forming a set will be treated as a single transaction for CGT purposes if the disposals are to connected persons.

▶ Wasting chattels are exempt from CGT apart from movable plant and machinery used in business on which capital allowances are available.

▶ Wasting assets other than chattels are not exempt from CGT. In general, the original cost of a wasting asset is written off over its predictable life using the straight line method. However, special rules apply to leases.

▶ An assignment of a long lease is regarded as the disposal of a whole asset.

▶ An assignment of a short lease is a disposal of a wasting asset. The original cost of a short lease is written off over its predictable life, using a table of percentages contained in Schedule 8, TCGA 1992.

▶ The grant of a long lease is treated as a part disposal.

▶ The grant of a short lease (or sub-lease) out of a freehold (or long head-lease) is treated as a part disposal. The part of the premium received which is taxable as property income is deducted from disposal proceeds in the CGT computation.

▶ The grant of a short sub-lease out of a short head-lease is a part disposal of a wasting asset. The Schedule 8 table is used to determine the allowable cost used in the CGT computation. The part of the premium received which is taxable as property income is deducted from the gain arising but cannot be used to convert a gain into a loss or to increase a loss.

Short lease amortisation table

(Schedule 8 of TCGA 1992)

Years	Percentage	Years	Percentage	Years	Percentage
50 or more	100	33	90.280	16	64.116
49	99.657	32	89.354	15	61.617
48	99.289	31	88.371	14	58.971
47	98.902	30	87.330	13	56.167
46	98.490	29	86.226	12	53.191
45	98.059	28	85.053	11	50.038
44	97.595	27	83.816	10	46.695
43	97.107	26	82.496	9	43.154
42	96.593	25	81.100	8	39.399
41	96.041	24	79.622	7	35.414
40	95.457	23	78.055	6	31.195
39	94.842	22	76.399	5	26.722
38	94.189	21	74.635	4	21.983
37	93.497	20	72.770	3	16.959
36	92.761	19	70.791	2	11.629
35	91.981	18	68.697	1	5.983
34	91.156	17	66.470	0	0

Exercises

A set of multiple choice questions for this chapter is available on the accompanying website.

19.1   Classify each of the following assets as either chattels, wasting assets or wasting chattels:

(a)   A domestic washing machine.

(b)   A gold ring.

(c)   A personal computer.

(d)   A 20-year lease on a building.

(e)   A suit of clothes.

(f)   An antique vase.

19.2   In October 2022 Keith sells an antique cabinet for £7,200. He incurs incidental costs of disposal amounting to £200. The cabinet cost Keith £2,300 in July 2014. Compute the chargeable gain.

19.3   In September 2022 Kevin sells a drawing for £2,000. He bought the drawing in February 2016 for £50,000 when it was thought (incorrectly) to be by a famous artist. Compute the allowable loss.

19.4 In January 2023 Karl sells a one-quarter interest in a chattel for £2,500. On the date of this sale, the remaining three-quarters interest is valued at £8,500. The chattel had cost Karl £3,850 in January 2014. Compute the chargeable gain.

19.5 In January 2020 Katrina buys an item of movable plant and machinery for use in her business. The plant costs her £50,000 and capital allowances are claimed. Compute the chargeable gain arising in March 2023 when she sells the plant, assuming that sale proceeds are:

(a) £65,000

(b) £38,000.

19.6 In June 2020 Katie acquired a 5-year option to buy a piece of land. The option cost her £10,000. In June 2022 she sold the option for £8,000. Compute the chargeable gain.

19.7 Katherine acquired a 40-year lease on a property on 31 August 2004 for £75,000. On 31 August 2022 she assigned the lease to Francesco for £97,500. The property was never Katherine's residence. Compute the chargeable gain.

*19.8 In March 2015, Sean acquired a pair of matching antique silver candlesticks at a cost of £4,000. In August 2022 he sold one of the candlesticks to James for £6,750. At that time the other candlestick was valued at £5,750. In September 2022 he sold the other candlestick to Julia for £5,800. Calculate the chargeable gain arising on these two disposals if:

(a) James and Julia are unconnected.

(b) James and Julia are a married couple.

*19.9 On 31 March 2000, Estelle acquired a patent with a 42-year life at a cost of £21,000. She sold the patent on 31 March 2023 for £73,000. Compute the chargeable gain.

*19.10 On 1 May 2014, Edward paid £350,000 to buy a 20-year lease on a flat. On 1 November 2022 he granted a 5-year sub-lease on the flat to Petronella for £150,000. The flat was never Edward's principal private residence. Compute the chargeable gain.

Chapter 20

Shares and securities

Introduction

A disposal of shares or securities causes no CGT problems unless a taxpayer disposes of part of a shareholding which was built up over a period of time in a number of separate acquisitions. If this happens, it is impossible to identify the shares that have been disposed of, because shares of the same class in the same company are "fungible assets" (i.e. assets that cannot be individually distinguished). But the calculation of the gain or loss arising on the disposal cannot proceed until the cost of the shares has been established. Therefore TCGA 1992 specifies a set of *share identification* or *share matching* rules which are used to match disposals against acquisitions in these circumstances. The main purpose of this chapter is to explain these rules and to show how they are applied when calculating the gain or loss arising on a disposal of shares.

This chapter also explains the CGT rules which apply to bonus issues, rights issues and capital distributions and outlines the CGT treatment of the share disposals which occur when one company is taken over by another company.

The share matching rules

For CGT purposes, disposals of shares or securities are matched against acquisitions of *the same class of shares in the same company* in the following order:

(a) First, against any acquisitions made on the same day as the day of the disposal.

(b) Next, against any acquisitions that are made during the following 30 days, matching with shares acquired earlier rather than later within that 30-day period. This rule is intended to counter the practice known as "bed and breakfasting", whereby shares are sold and then almost immediately re-acquired so as to trigger gains or losses for tax avoidance purposes.

(c) Finally, against shares forming the "Section 104 holding". This consists of a pool of all the shares of that class in that company that were acquired before the date of the disposal and which have not been matched against previous disposals.

It is important to note that the share matching rules which apply when a *company* makes a disposal of shares are different from those which apply for CGT purposes. The rules which have effect for corporation tax purposes are explained in Chapter 24.

EXAMPLE 1

Paul made the following acquisitions and disposals of ordinary shares in Crimmon plc:

Date		Number of shares
5 June 2013	acquisition	3,000
17 May 2014	acquisition	500
17 May 2014	disposal	800
9 June 2014	acquisition	200
13 March 2017	disposal	2,000
28 March 2017	acquisition	1,750
17 October 2022	disposal	1,000

No further shares were acquired during 2022. Against which acquisitions will each of the above disposals be matched?

Solution

(a)   The 800 shares which were disposed of on 17 May 2014 are matched as follows:

  (i)   first, against the 500 shares acquired on the same day

  (ii)   next, against the 200 shares acquired in the next 30 days (on 9 June 2014)

  (iii)   finally, against 100 of the shares that form the s104 holding; these are the 3,000 shares acquired on 5 June 2013 and there are 2,900 shares left in this holding after the 17 May 2014 disposal has been matched.

(b)   The 2,000 shares disposed of on 13 March 2017 are matched as follows:

  (i)   first, against the 1,750 shares acquired in the next 30 days (on 28 March 2017)

  (ii)   finally, against 250 of the 2,900 shares that remain in the s104 holding (so there are 2,650 shares left in this holding after the 13 March 2017 disposal has been matched).

(c)   The 1,000 shares disposed of on 17 October 2022 cannot be matched against shares acquired on the same day or during the following 30 days. Therefore these shares must be matched against 1,000 of the 2,650 shares that remain in the s104 holding.

The situation after these three disposals have been matched is that Paul is left with 1,650 shares in his s104 holding of ordinary shares in Crimmon plc.

The Section 104 holding

A taxpayer's "Section 104 holding" of shares of a certain class in a certain company is a pool containing any shares that were acquired before the date of the current disposal but which have not been matched against previous disposals. The name of this pool is derived from Section 104 of TCGA 1992, which provides the legal basis for its existence.

If it were not for the provisions of Section 104, it would be necessary to maintain detailed records of the date and the cost of each individual share acquisition. However, the pooling arrangement provided by Section 104 eliminates the need to keep such detailed records. Instead, all that is required is a record of:

(a) the total number of shares in the s104 holding, and
(b) the total allowable expenditure in relation to those shares.

The total allowable expenditure of the shares in the s104 holding is generally equal to the total cost (or CGT acquisition value) of the shares concerned†.

Note that share acquisitions which are matched against same-day disposals or against disposals occurring within the previous 30 days (by virtue of the first two matching rules explained above) do not enter the s104 holding.

† *But if any of the shares in the s104 holding were acquired before 31 March 1982, their cost is replaced by their market value at that date. This is because rebasing acquires to the disposal of assets held on 31 March 1982 (see Chapter 18).*

EXAMPLE 2

Pauline makes the following purchases of preference shares in Bassoon plc:

Date	Number of shares	Cost £
23 June 1990	1,000	2,000
14 May 2001	2,000	5,800
8 July 2022	3,000	8,700

There were no disposals of these shares on or before 8 July 2022. Show Pauline's s104 holding of preference shares in Bassoon plc as at 8 July 2022.

Solution

	Number of shares	Allowable expenditure £
Acquired 23 June 1990	1,000	2,000
Acquired 14 May 2001	2,000	5,800
Acquired 8 July 2022	3,000	8,700
s104 holding c/f at 8 July 2022	6,000	16,500

Notes:

(i)   The three acquisitions which form the s104 holding have been combined into a single pool of 6,000 shares with total allowable expenditure of £16,500. It is now necessary to carry forward only these two "bottom line" figures, rather than the details of each individual acquisition.

(ii) On average, the allowable expenditure per share is £2.75 (£16,500 ÷ 6,000). When there is a disposal from the pool, this is the expenditure that will be allowed for each share that is disposed of (see below).

Disposals from the s104 holding

When there is a disposal of shares from the s104 holding, the number of shares that have been disposed of is deducted from the number of shares in the pool. It is then necessary to deduct a proportion of the allowable expenditure in the pool.

Strictly speaking, this proportion should be calculated using the part disposal fraction (see Chapter 18) which takes into account the value of the shares disposed of and the value of the remaining shares. In most cases, however, the value per share of the shares that have been disposed of will be the same as the value per share of the shares which remain, so that the proportion of the allowable expenditure which should be deducted from the pool can be based upon the *number* of shares disposed of.

The gain or loss arising on a disposal from the s104 holding is calculated simply as the difference between the disposal value of those shares and the amount which has been subtracted from the allowable expenditure in the pool as a consequence of the disposal.

EXAMPLE 3

Paula makes the following acquisitions of ordinary shares in Indigent plc:

Date	Number of shares	Cost £
1 July 2012	5,000	6,300
2 August 2013	2,000	2,500
3 February 2017	1,200	2,300
4 January 2023	1,800	3,400

She sells 500 shares on 28 March 2023. No further shares in the company are acquired within the next 30 days.

(a)   Show the s104 holding on 28 March 2023, just prior to and just after the disposal on that date.

(b)   Compute the chargeable gain or allowable loss on the disposal if sale proceeds are:

   (i)   £1,300   (ii)   £1,000   (iii)   £700

Solution

(a) The s104 holding is as follows:

	Number of shares	Allowable expenditure £
Acquired 1 July 2012	5,000	6,300
Acquired 2 August 2013	2,000	2,500
Acquired 3 February 2017	1,200	2,300
Acquired 4 January 2023	1,800	3,400
	10,000	14,500
Sold 28 March 2023 (500/10,000ths)	(500)	(725)
s104 holding c/f	9,500	13,775

Notes:

1. The disposal in March 2023 must be from the s104 holding since it cannot be matched against shares acquired on the same day or within the next 30 days.

2. The disposal is 500 shares out of 10,000 shares. So 500 shares are deducted from the pool, along with 500/10,000ths (1/20th) of the allowable expenditure.

3. On average, the allowable expenditure in the pool is £1.45 per share and so the allowable expenditure deducted on the disposal (£725) is equal to 500 shares at £1.45 per share.

(b)

	(i) £	(ii) £	(iii) £
Sale proceeds	1,300	1,000	700
Less: Allowable expenditure	725	725	725
Chargeable gain/(allowable loss)	575	275	(25)

Bonus issues

A bonus issue occurs when a company issues free extra shares to its shareholders. The number of bonus shares received by a shareholder is generally in proportion to his or her existing shareholding. For instance, a "1 for 5" bonus issue would give each shareholder one free extra share for every five shares previously held.

For CGT purposes, a bonus issue is treated as a reorganisation of share capital and therefore bonus shares are deemed to have been acquired on the same date that the original shares were acquired. The required CGT treatment is to uplift the number of shares in each of the taxpayer's previous acquisitions so as to reflect the bonus issue. Since all of these previous acquisitions are generally held together in the s104 holding, the desired effect can usually be achieved by simply adding the bonus shares into the "number of shares" column of the s104 holding. The allowable expenditure associated with this holding is not affected, since bonus shares are issued free of charge.

EXAMPLE 4

Sherjeel made the following acquisitions of ordinary shares in Truculence plc:

Date	Number of shares	Cost £
27 September 2003	1,200	3,600
28 July 2005	800	2,800
3 February 2010	500	2,000
5 July 2014	300	1,500

On 1 September 2017, the company made a 1 for 10 bonus issue. Calculate the chargeable gain arising on 1 March 2023 when Sherjeel sold 1,400 shares for £6 each, assuming that he made no further acquisitions within the next 30 days.

Solution

The disposal cannot be matched against acquisitions on the same day or within the next 30 days, so it must come from the s104 holding. The s104 holding is as follows:

	Number of shares	Allowable expenditure £
Acquired 27 September 2003	1,200	3,600
Acquired 28 July 2005	800	2,800
Acquired 3 February 2010	500	2,000
Acquired 5 July 2014	300	1,500
	2,800	9,900
Bonus issue 1 September 2017	280	-
	3,080	9,900
Sold 1 March 2023 (1,400/3,080ths)	(1,400)	(4,500)
s104 holding c/f at 1 March 2023	1,680	5,400

The disposal proceeds are £8,400 (1,400 x £6). Therefore the chargeable gain is £3,900 (£8,400 − £4,500).

Note:

The 280 bonus shares increase the number of shares in the s104 holding but do not increase the allowable expenditure in that holding.

EXAMPLE 5

On 13 May 2016, Ruben acquired 400 shares in Xantan Ltd at a cost of £1,800. On 17 July 2022, the company made a 1 for 8 bonus issue and (on the same day) Ruben sold his bonus shares for £7 each. Compute the chargeable gain.

Solution

On 17 July 2022, Ruben acquired 50 shares in Xantan Ltd at zero cost. He also sold 50 shares in the company for £350. Under the "same day" rule, acquisitions and disposals made on the same day would normally be matched together. So (if this rule applied) the chargeable gain would be (£350 − £0) = £350.

However, the same day rule does not apply, because the 50 bonus shares are treated as if they had been acquired on 13 May 2016. This increases the number of shares in the s104 holding to 450 (with a cost of £1,800).

The allowable expenditure on the disposal of 50 shares from the s104 holding on 17 July 2022 is (£1,800 × 50/450) = £200 and the chargeable gain is (£350 − £200) = £150.

Rights issues

A rights issue occurs when a company offers its shareholders the right to buy extra shares. Rights issues are similar to bonus issues in that the number of shares offered to each shareholder is generally in proportion to his or her existing shareholding. But rights shares are not issued free of charge. Shareholders who are offered rights shares may either:

(a)   ignore the rights issue (in which case there is no CGT impact)

(b)   sell their "rights" (see later in this chapter)

(c)   buy the shares which they are offered.

For CGT purposes, a rights issue is treated in a very similar way to a bonus issue. If a taxpayer buys rights shares, the number of shares in each of the taxpayer's previous acquisitions is uplifted to reflect the rights issue. But since rights shares are not free, it is also necessary to increase the allowable expenditure for each of these acquisitions.

Since all of the previous acquisitions are generally held together in the s104 holding, the desired effect can usually be achieved by adding the number of rights shares that have been acquired into the s104 holding and increasing the allowable expenditure of this holding by the acquisition cost of these rights shares.

EXAMPLE 6

Tina made the following acquisitions of ordinary shares in Hombus plc:

Date	Number of shares	Cost £
15 August 1996	500	1,250
23 January 2006	700	2,800

On 1 June 2017, the company made a 1 for 20 rights issue at £8 per share and Tina decided to buy the shares to which she was entitled. Calculate the chargeable gain arising on 12 November 2022 when Tine sold 840 shares for £7 each, assuming that she made no further acquisitions within the next 30 days.

Solution

The disposal cannot be matched against acquisitions on the same day or within the next 30 days, so it must come from the s104 holding. The s104 holding is as follows:

	Number of shares	Allowable expenditure £
Acquired 15 August 1996	500	1,250
Acquired 23 January 2006	700	2,800
	1,200	4,050
Rights issue 1 June 2017	60	480
	1,260	4,530
Sold 12 November 2022 (840/1,260ths)	(840)	(3,020)
s104 holding c/f	120	1,510

The disposal proceeds are £5,880 (840 x £7). Therefore the chargeable gain is £2,860 (£5,880 – £3,020).

Note:

The 60 rights shares increase the number of shares in the s104 holding and also increase the allowable expenditure in that holding.

Capital distributions

A capital distribution occurs when shareholders are repaid part of their share capital, usually when a company goes into liquidation. Unless the amount of the distribution is small (see below) a capital distribution is regarded as a part disposal for CGT purposes.

EXAMPLE 7

In March 2016, Vincent bought 10,000 ordinary shares in Apezium plc for £44,000. In June 2022, the company went into liquidation and Vincent received a first distribution of £0.50 per share. The market value of an ordinary share in Apezium plc just after this distribution was £0.75. Compute the allowable loss arising in June 2022.

Solution

The value of the part disposed of is £5,000 (10,000 @ £0.50) and the value of the part remaining is £7,500 (10,000 @ £0.75). The part disposal fraction is 5,000/12,500 which is equivalent to 2/5ths. Therefore the allowable expenditure for this disposal is 2/5ths of the allowable expenditure on the acquisition of the shares. The s104 holding is as follows:

	Number of shares	Allowable expenditure £
Acquired March 2016	10,000	44,000
Distribution June 2022 (2/5ths)	-	(17,600)
s104 holding c/f	10,000	26,400

The computation of the allowable loss is as follows:

	£
Disposal proceeds	5,000
Less: Allowable expenditure	(17,600)
Allowable loss	(12,600)

Sale of rights nil paid

Another example of a capital distribution occurs when a company makes a rights issue and a shareholder decides not to buy the shares concerned but instead to sell his or her rights to someone else (a "sale of rights nil paid"). When shareholders sell their rights they are *not* selling shares. What they are selling is the right to buy shares, often at an attractive price. The proceeds of such a sale are treated as a capital distribution. If the amount of money involved is small (see below) the amount received will be treated as a small capital distribution.

Small capital distributions

If the amount of a capital distribution is small when compared with the value of the shares concerned, the distribution is not treated as a disposal. Instead, the proceeds of the distribution are subtracted from the allowable expenditure relating to those shares. The effect of this is that the gain which would have been chargeable on the distribution is deferred until a subsequent disposal takes place. This is very similar to the treatment of small part disposals of land (see Chapter 18). Note that:

(a) A capital distribution is generally regarded as small if it consists of no more than 5% of the value of the company's shares just before the distribution was made. It is also HMRC practice to regard an amount of £3,000 or less as small for this purpose, even if the 5% test is not satisfied.

(b) Apparently HMRC will allow a small capital distribution to be treated as a disposal if this is to the taxpayer's benefit (e.g. if any gain is covered by the annual exemption).

EXAMPLE 8

In April 2018, Vanessa bought 1,000 shares in Entagon plc at a cost of £5 per share. The company went into liquidation and Vanessa received a first distribution of 40p per share in July 2022. The shares had a market value of £9.75 per share just after this distribution.

(a) Show how the distribution will be dealt with for CGT purposes.

(b) Calculate the chargeable gain arising in March 2023, when Vanessa received a second and final distribution of £9.82 per share.

Solution

(a) The value of the shares immediately prior to the distribution must have been £10.15 per share (£9.75 + £0.40). 40p is approximately 3.9% of £10.15 so the distribution ranks as a small capital distribution. The £400 received by Vanessa may be deducted from the £5,000 that she paid for her shares. This reduces the allowable cost on a subsequent disposal to £4,600.

(b) Assuming that the small capital distribution is not treated as a disposal, the s104 holding is as follows:

	Number of shares	Allowable expenditure £
Acquired April 2018	1,000	5,000
Distribution July 2022	-	(400)
	1,000	4,600
Disposal March 2023	(1,000)	(4,600)
s104 holding c/f	nil	nil

The gain arising on the disposal is:

	£
Disposal proceeds (1,000 @ £9.82)	9,820
Less: Allowable expenditure	4,600
Chargeable gain	5,220

Takeovers

A takeover occurs when one company acquires the shares of another company. The shareholders of the "target" company exchange their shares in return for cash, or shares of the acquiring company, or a combination of both cash and shares. The CGT treatment of such disposals is as follows:

(a) If a takeover is entirely for cash, the shareholders of the target company have sold their shares and have therefore made chargeable disposals. The fact that the shares have been sold as a consequence of a takeover is irrelevant and the gain or loss is computed in the usual way.

(b) If a takeover is entirely for shares (a "paper for paper" takeover), no chargeable disposals have taken place. A shareholder's newly-acquired shares in the acquiring company simply replace the shares originally held in the target company and are deemed for all CGT purposes to have been acquired on the same date and at the same cost as the original holding.

(c) If a takeover is partly for cash and partly for shares, a part disposal has taken place and a part disposal calculation is usually required. The value of the part disposed of is the amount of cash received and the value of the part remaining is the value of the shares received. However, if the amount of cash received by a taxpayer is no more than 5% of the total consideration (or no more than £3,000) the cash received may be treated as a small capital distribution.

EXAMPLE 9

The following information is available:

(a) In August 2015, Winston bought 8,000 shares in Hexico plc for £24,000.

(b) In October 2022, Zandac plc made a takeover bid for Hexico plc, offering the Hexico shareholders three shares in Zandac plus £1 in cash for every two Hexico shares.

(c) This offer was accepted on 29 October 2022, when the market value of shares in Zandac plc was £5 per share.

Compute Winston's chargeable gain.

Solution

Winston received 12,000 shares in Zandac plc, worth £60,000, plus £4,000 in cash, a total of £64,000. The amount received in cash is 6.25% of the total and exceeds £3,000, so this cannot be treated as a small capital distribution. The s104 holding is as follows:

	Number of shares	Allowable expenditure £
Acquired August 2015	8,000	24,000
Distribution October 2022 (6.25%)	-	(1,500)
s104 holding after distribution	8,000	22,500
s104 holding (Zandac plc) c/f	12,000	22,500

The gain arising on the disposal is:

	£
Disposal proceeds	4,000
Less: Allowable expenditure	1,500
Chargeable gain	2,500

EXAMPLE 10

The following information is available:

(a) In June 2017, Darren bought 1,000 ordinary shares in Cubson plc for £8,400..

(b) In August 2022, Phere plc made a takeover bid for Cubson plc, offering two ordinary shares and one preference share in Phere for each ordinary share in Cubson.

(c) This offer was accepted on 21 August 2022, when the market value of ordinary shares in Phere plc was £4 per share and the market value of preference shares in Phere plc was £2 per share.

Indicate how Darren's cost of £8,400 should be allocated between the ordinary shares and the preference shares which he received by virtue of the takeover.

Solution

Darren received 2,000 ordinary shares worth £8,000 and 1,000 preference shares worth £2,000, giving a total consideration of £10,000. Since 80% of this total took the form of ordinary shares in Phere plc, these ordinary shares are deemed to have cost him 80% of £8,400 = £6,720. Similarly, the preference shares are deemed to have cost him 20% of £8,400 = £1,680. All of these shares are treated as if acquired in June 2017.

Gilts and qualifying corporate bonds

Gilt-edged securities and "qualifying corporate bonds" are not chargeable assets for CGT purposes. Therefore neither a chargeable gain nor an allowable loss can arise on their disposal. Note that:

(a) Gilt-edged securities ("gilts") are UK government securities such as Treasury Stock, Exchequer Stock etc.

(b) Qualifying corporate bonds consist of company debentures and other fixed-interest securities which are expressed in sterling and comprise a normal commercial loan.

(c) Gains and losses arising on the disposal of gilt-edged securities or corporate bonds by a *company* are assessed under the "loan relationships" rules for corporation tax purposes (see Chapter 23).

Summary

▸ Special matching rules are used to match disposals of shares and securities against acquisitions. Disposals are matched first against shares acquired on the same day as the disposal, then against shares acquired in the next 30 days and then against shares comprising the s104 holding.

▸ The s104 holding is a pool of shares of the same class in the same company that were acquired before the date of the current disposal but have not been matched against previous disposals. It is necessary to keep a record of the total number of shares in this pool and their total allowable expenditure.

▸ In general, the CGT effect of a bonus issue is to increase the number of shares in the s104 holding. Allowable expenditure is not affected. The CGT effect of a rights issue which is taken up by the shareholder is to increase both the number of shares and the allowable expenditure in the s104 holding.

▸ A sale of rights nil paid is treated as a capital distribution.

▸ A capital distribution is treated for CGT purposes as a part disposal unless it qualifies as a small capital distribution, in which case the amount of the distribution is deducted from the acquisition cost of the shares concerned.

▸ If a takeover is entirely for cash, the shareholders of the target company have made chargeable disposals. If a takeover is entirely for shares, no chargeable disposals have taken place. If a takeover is partly for cash and partly for shares, a part disposal has occurred unless the amount of cash can be treated as a small capital distribution.

▸ UK government securities ("gilt-edged securities") and qualifying corporate bonds are not chargeable assets for CGT purposes.

Exercises

A set of multiple choice questions for this chapter is available on the accompanying website.

20.1   A taxpayer makes the following acquisitions of preference shares in Muvex Ltd:

Date	No of shares purchased
10 August 2022	1,000
20 October 2022	200
1 December 2022	150

No further shares are acquired during 2022 or 2023. How will the following disposals be matched against these acquisitions?

(a)   250 shares sold on 20 October 2022

(b)   420 shares sold on 12 November 2022

(c)   300 shares sold on 1 April 2023.

20.2   Sandra acquired the following ordinary shares in Mincer plc:

Date	No of shares	Cost
		£
29 January 1999	1,000	4,000
13 August 2003	1,000	9,500
4 October 2015	2,000	22,500

On 26 June 2022, Sandra sold 700 of her shares in Mincer plc. Assuming that she acquired no further shares in the company during 2022, calculate the chargeable gain or allowable loss if her sale proceeds in June 2022 were:

(a)   £8,400

(b)   £6,300

(c)   £5,200.

20.3   Jeremy acquired the following ordinary shares in Scarlon plc:

Date	No of shares	Cost
		£
19 September 2013	4,000	16,000
20 October 2015	2,000	12,000
21 November 2017	1,000	7,000
22 December 2022	3,000	24,000
13 January 2023	5,000	55,000

He made no further acquisitions during 2023. On 22 December 2022, he sold 10,000 shares in the company for £10 per share. Calculate the chargeable gain or allowable loss arising on this disposal.

20.4   William made the following acquisitions of preference shares in Pangol plc:

Date	No of shares	Cost
		£
17 February 2011	600	900
13 November 2015	200	400
9 October 2019	100	300

In January 2022, the company made a 1 for 4 bonus issue. In February 2023, William sold 450 shares for £4 per share. Calculate the chargeable gain, assuming that he made no acquisitions in the following 30 days.

20.5   Yvonne made the following acquisitions of ordinary shares in Ranghi plc:

Date	No of shares	Cost
		£
30 September 2010	2,000	1,200
1 December 2014	3,000	3,600

In January 2022, the company made a 1 for 5 rights issue at £1 per share and Yvonne decided to buy the shares which she was offered. In March 2023, she sold one-half of her shares in the company for £1.80 per share. Calculate the chargeable gain arising in March 2023, given that no further shares were acquired within the following 30 days.

20.6   (a)   In November 2010, Yorick bought 6,000 ordinary shares in Togon plc for £30,000. In March 2023, the company went into liquidation and Yorick received a first distribution of £1 per share. The market value of an ordinary share in Togon plc just after this distribution was £2. Compute the allowable loss.

(b)   In January 2014, Yolande bought 300 ordinary shares in Lippex plc. These shares cost £1.20 each. In May 2020, when shares in Lippex plc had a market value of £2 each, the company made a rights issue. Yolande sold her rights, realising £25. Compute the chargeable gain arising in November 2022 when Yolande sold all of her shares for £780, assuming that no further shares were acquired within the following 30 days.

20.7   The following information is available:

(a)   In June 2021, Walter bought 10,000 shares in Ovod plc at a cost of £7 per share.

(b)   In August 2022, Rundico plc made a takeover bid for Ovod plc, offering the Ovod shareholders eight Rundico shares plus £4 in cash for every five Ovod shares.

(c)   This offer was accepted on 28 August 2022, when the market value of shares in Rundico plc was £4.50 per share.

Compute Walter's chargeable gain.

*20.8   Suzanne acquired the following ordinary shares in Quarine plc:

Date	No of shares	Cost
		£
2 October 1999	200	640
10 January 2001	150	480
5 December 2008	400	1,420
8 November 2016	250	1,160
24 July 2022	300	1,400
10 August 2022	400	2,500
20 August 2022	350	2,600
31 August 2022	500	2,400

She made no further acquisitions. On 24 July 2022, Suzanne sold 1,200 shares for £7 per share. Compute the chargeable gain or allowable loss arising on this disposal.

*20.9   Saeed made the following purchases of ordinary shares in Hyban plc:

Date	No of shares	Cost
		£
24 August 1991	800	960
25 November 1996	1,200	1,440
26 February 2002	1,600	2,400
11 October 2011	400	800

In June 2018, the company made a 1 for 20 rights issue at £1.50 per share and Saeed took up the shares which he was offered.

Calculate the chargeable gain arising in November 2022, when Saeed sold 1,260 shares at £3 each. Assume that no further shares were acquired within the following 30 days.

*20.10   Susan made the following purchases of ordinary shares in Semicycle plc:

Date	No of shares	Cost
		£
11 January 2013	1,500	4,800
20 January 2019	1,140	5,700

In January 2023, the company went into liquidation and Susan received a first distribution of £2 per share. The market value of an ordinary share in Semicycle plc just after this distribution was £1. Compute the allowable loss arising in January 2023.

*20.11   The following information is available:

(a)   On 9 May 2013, Steven bought 2,000 ordinary shares in Vexacon plc for £8,000. On 28 November 2017, he bought a further 500 of the shares for £2,500.

(b)   In March 2023, Danshore plc offered the shareholders of Vexacon plc two shares in Danshore plus £2 in cash for every Vexacon share. This offer was accepted on 21 March 2023, when the market value of shares in Danshore plc was £4 per share.

Compute Steven's chargeable gain or allowable loss.

Chapter 21

Principal private residence

Introduction

This chapter examines the CGT consequences of the disposal of a taxpayer's principal private residence. Although a principal private residence is not a chargeable asset for CGT purposes, a CGT liability may arise when a property is disposed of which has been used as a residence for only part of the period of ownership or which has been used partly as a residence and partly for other purposes.

Principal private residence

A "dwelling-house" which is a taxpayer's only or main residence is known as that taxpayer's principal private residence (PPR). A taxpayer's PPR is not a chargeable asset for CGT purposes. Therefore any gain which arises on the disposal of a PPR is not chargeable to tax and any loss which arises is not allowable. For a property to be regarded as a PPR, the taxpayer must actually occupy the property as a main residence. Mere ownership is not sufficient. Furthermore, the term "residence" implies a degree of permanency and it is unlikely that the PPR exemption will apply to a property which has been used only as temporary accommodation. In *Goodwin* v *Curtis* (1998), a property which had been occupied by the taxpayer for only 32 days did not qualify as a residence.

The large majority of taxpayers own (at most) a single property and reside in that property, so that it is obvious that the property is the taxpayer's PPR. However, the following points may be relevant in more complex cases:

(a) A taxpayer may have only one PPR at any given time.

(b) A taxpayer who owns and lives in two (or more) properties may make an election to determine which property is to be regarded as the PPR. Such an election must be made within two years after the date from which it is to take effect. If no election is made, then the matter is decided by the facts of the case.

(c) A married couple who live together may have only one PPR between them. This rule also applies to civil partners who live together.

(d) The PPR exemption covers the residence itself together with grounds or gardens of up to half a hectare (5,000 square metres) in area. Larger areas may be included in the exemption if they are warranted by the size of the residence.

(e) The requirement that there must be actual residence in the property is relaxed if the taxpayer is required to live in job-related accommodation (see Chapter 8). In these circumstances, the PPR exemption is extended to any property which the taxpayer owns, so long as he or she intends to occupy the property as a main residence at some time in the future.

Partial exemption

If a property has been occupied as a PPR for only a part of the period of ownership, only a part of the gain realised on disposal will be exempt from CGT. The exempt part of the gain is equal to:

$$\frac{\text{length of period of residence}}{\text{length of period of ownership}} \times \text{whole gain}$$

The lengths of the periods of residence and ownership are usually calculated to the nearest month[†]. Note the following important points:

(a) If a property has been the taxpayer's PPR at some time, the final nine months[‡] of ownership count as a period of residence, whether or not the taxpayer was actually resident during those nine months (so helping taxpayers who move house and have difficulty in selling their previous residence). This rule applies even if the taxpayer claims another property to be his or her PPR during the nine months.

(b) If only *part* of a property is used as a taxpayer's PPR, then only part of the gain arising on disposal will qualify for PPR relief and the gain will need to be apportioned accordingly.

[†] *If the property was acquired before 31 March 1982, the period of ownership prior to that date and any period of residence prior to that date are ignored. This is because the base date for CGT is now 31 March 1982 (see Chapter 18).*

[‡] *In the case of disabled persons or long-term residents in care homes, the final 36 months of ownership of a PPR is always treated as a period of residence.*

EXAMPLE 1

On 1 April 1991, Allan bought a house for £58,000. He lived in the house until 31 October 2020 when he bought another house and made this his principal private residence. The house he had bought in April 1991 was eventually sold on 31 January 2023 for £290,000. Compute the chargeable gain.

Solution

In examples of this type it is necessary first to calculate the gain arising (ignoring any PPR exemption) and then to consider the PPR exemption as a second stage. The gain arising in this case is as follows:

	£
Sale proceeds	290,000
Less: Cost of acquisition	58,000
Chargeable gain (before PPR exemption)	232,000

Allan owned the house for 31 years and 10 months (382 months). He was actually resident in the house for 29 years and 7 months (355 months) and the final nine months of ownership also count as a period of residence, making a total of 364 months during which the PPR exemption applies. The chargeable gain is therefore as follows:

	£
Total gain (as above)	232,000
Less: $\dfrac{364}{382}$ x £232,000	221,068
Chargeable gain	10,932

Deemed residence

The period of residence in a property is deemed to include certain periods when the taxpayer was not actually resident, so long as:

(a) there is a period of actual residence both at some time before the period of absence and at some time after the period of absence, and

(b) the taxpayer claims no other property to be a PPR during the period of absence.

These periods of "deemed residence" are as follows:

(a) any periods of absence during which the taxpayer is working in an employment, all of the duties of which are performed *outside the UK* (or is living with a spouse or civil partner who is working in such an employment)

(b) a total of up to four years of absence during which the taxpayer is prevented from living in the PPR because he or she is employed *elsewhere in the UK* (or is living with a spouse or civil partner who is employed elsewhere in the UK)

(c) a total of up to three years of absence *for any reason* (although annual holidays and similar brief absences are ignored).

The requirement that the taxpayer must reside in the property at some time after the period of absence does not apply if the absence is work-related and the terms of the employment prevent the taxpayer (or spouse or civil partner) from returning to the residence.

EXAMPLE 2

On 1 June 2000, Alice bought a house in Derby for £45,000.

- She occupied the house as her PPR until 1 May 2002 when she left to work in Exeter, living in rented accommodation.
- She returned to the house in Derby on 1 November 2003 and stayed until 1 July 2006 when she left to take up a post in the USA, again living in rented accommodation.
- She returned to Derby on 1 February 2009 and stayed until 1 June 2020 when she bought a house in Nottingham and made this her principal private residence.
- On 1 February 2023 she sold the house in Derby for £164,000.

Compute the chargeable gain.

Solution

	£
Sale proceeds	164,000
Less: Acquisition cost	45,000
Chargeable gain (before PPR exemption)	119,000

Alice's period of ownership of the house in Derby (a total of 272 months) can be broken down into the following periods:

(i)	1 June 2000 to 30 April 2002	23 months	Actual residence
(ii)	1 May 2002 to 31 October 2003	18 months	Working in UK
(iii)	1 November 2003 to 30 June 2006	32 months	Actual residence
(iv)	1 July 2006 to 31 January 2009	31 months	Working abroad
(v)	1 February 2009 to 31 May 2020	136 months	Actual residence
(vi)	1 June 2020 to 31 January 2023	32 months	Living in new PPR

Periods (i), (iii) and (v) are exempt since Alice was actually resident in the property during those periods. Period (ii) is exempt since Alice was working elsewhere in the UK, the four-year time limit has not been exceeded and she was resident in the property both before and after the absence. Similarly, period (iv) is also exempt. The final nine months of ownership are generally exempt, which leaves the first 23 months of period (vi) to consider. During these 23 months Alice was claiming another property to be her PPR, so the period cannot count as a period of deemed residence and the gain arising during these 23 months is chargeable. The remaining 249 months benefit from the PPR exemption. The chargeable gain is therefore as follows:

	£
Total gain (as above)	119,000
Less: $\frac{249}{272}$ x £119,000	108,938
Chargeable gain	10,062

Letting relief

An extension to the PPR exemption, known as "letting relief", may apply if the owner of a property which is his or her PPR has (at some time during the period of ownership) let out *part* of the property as residential accommodation, so that occupation of the property has been shared with a tenant[†]. For instance, the owner of a house that has previously been occupied entirely as a PPR might let a room (or rooms) to a tenant whilst continuing to occupy the rest of the house as a PPR. In such a case, the usual PPR exemption on disposal of the property will cover only:

(i)   the gain arising on the whole property whilst occupied solely by the owner,

(ii) the gain arising on the whole property in the final nine months of ownership, and

(iii) the remainder of the gain, but only to the extent that this is attributable to occupation by the owner.

The balance of the gain will be chargeable to CGT, but may then be reduced or eliminated by letting relief (see below). In general, letting relief will *not* be granted if there have been structural alterations to the property, so that the part that has been let is entirely separate from the accommodation which forms the owner's residence (e.g. if the rooms occupied by the tenant comprise a self-contained flat with its own access from the road).

[†] *For disposals made prior to 6 April 2020, letting relief was also available if the whole property was let during periods of absence by the owner, but this is no longer the case. Letting relief now applies only if the owner of the property has shared occupancy with a tenant.*

Letting relief is calculated as the *lowest* of:

(a)   the gain which arises by reason of the letting

(b)   the gain which is exempt because of the PPR exemption

(c)   £40,000.

EXAMPLE 3

In relation to the previous example in this chapter, assume now that Alice always let her Derby house when she was not resident there. Compute the chargeable gain.

Solution

The only chargeable period was a period of 23 months during which a gain of £10,062 arose and during which the property was let. However, the *whole* property was let during this time and Alice did not share occupancy with her tenant. Therefore letting relief is not available and the chargeable gain remains at £10,062.

EXAMPLE 4

Alistair bought a house on 1 April 2002 for £125,000 and occupied the entire house as his principal private residence until 1 November 2010. As from that date, he rented out two rooms (comprising one-third of the house) to tenants and retained the remainder of the house as his own residence. This arrangement continued until 1 October 2022 when he sold the house for £615,000. Compute the chargeable gain.

Solution

	£
Sale proceeds	615,000
Less: Original cost	125,000
Chargeable gain (before PPR exemption)	490,000

Alistair owned the house for a total of 20 years and 6 months (246 months). PPR exemption is available for the 103 months during which he occupied the whole property and for the final nine months (a total of 112 months). He was resident in two-thirds of the property for the remaining 134 months, so two-thirds of the gain arising during these 134 months is also exempt. The other one-third is chargeable to CGT but letting relief is available. The chargeable gain is as follows:

	£	£
Total gain (as above)		490,000
Less: PPR exemption:		
£490,000 x 112/246	223,090	
£490,000 x 134/246 x 2/3	177,940	401,030
		88,970
Less: Letting relief, lowest of:		
(a) £88,970		
(b) £401,030		
(c) £40,000		40,000
Chargeable gain		48,970

Business use

If a property is used partly as a residence and partly for business purposes, the gain which is attributable to the part used for business purposes[†] is chargeable to CGT. No reliefs are generally available in relation to this gain. However, the usual exemption for the final nine months of ownership of a PPR <u>does</u> apply to any part of a property which (at some time during the period of ownership) has been occupied as the taxpayer's main residence, even if that part of the property is used for business purposes during those nine months.

[†] *The entitlement to full PPR exemption is not restricted if an individual sets aside a part of their residence for the use of an adult for whom they are caring under a local authority adult placement scheme, regardless of the fact that the income derived from this activity is generally treated as trading income.*

EXAMPLE 5

Ava bought a house on 1 July 2002 for £62,000. She occupied the entire property as her PPR until 1 August 2009 when she began using one-quarter of the house for business purposes. This continued until 1 November 2022 when she sold the house for £207,000. Compute the chargeable gain.

Solution

	£
Sale proceeds	207,000
<u>Less</u>: Acquisition cost	62,000
Chargeable gain (before PPR exemption)	145,000

Ava owned the house for 20 years and 4 months (244 months). For the first 7 years and 1 month (85 months) she occupied the entire house as her main residence. The PPR exemption applies to these 85 months and to the final nine months of ownership (a total of 94 months). The PPR exemption also applies to three-quarters of the gain arising in the remaining 150 months. The chargeable gain is as follows:

	£	£
Total gain (as above)		145,000
<u>Less</u>: PPR exemption:		
£145,000 x 94/244	55,861	
£145,000 x 150/244 x 3/4	66,854	122,715
Chargeable gain		22,285

Summary

▸ A taxpayer's principal private residence (PPR) is exempt from CGT.

▸ A taxpayer with two or more residences may elect which property is to be regarded as his or her PPR. Such an election must be made within two years after the date from which it is to take effect.

▸ A married couple who live together may have only one PPR between them. This rule also applies to civil partners who live together.

▸ If a property has been occupied as a PPR for only a part of the period of ownership, only a part of the gain realised on disposal will be exempt from CGT.

▸ The final nine months of ownership of a PPR always count as a period of residence.

▸ Subject to conditions, certain periods of absence are treated as periods of residence for CGT purposes. These include any time spent working abroad, up to four years spent working elsewhere in the UK and up to three years for any reason whatsoever.

▸ Letting relief of up to £40,000 may be available if part of a PPR has been let to a tenant as residential accommodation and the owner has shared occupancy with the tenant.

▸ If a residence is used partly for business purposes, the gain relating to the part used for business purposes is generally chargeable to CGT.

Exercises

A set of multiple choice questions for this chapter is available on the accompanying website.

21.1 Mohammed owns two properties - a flat in Central London and a country cottage in Sussex. In general he lives in his London flat during the week and spends the weekends in his Sussex cottage. Which of his two properties will be regarded as his principal private residence for CGT purposes?

21.2 Melanie bought a house on 1 September 1991 for £31,000. The house was sold on 31 December 2022 for £173,000. Compute the chargeable gain arising in each of the following cases:

(a) Melanie occupied the house as her principal private residence throughout the entire period of ownership.

(b) Melanie occupied the house throughout her period of ownership with the exception of the period between 1 June 1998 and 31 May 2002 when she lived with a friend. During this time the house stood empty.

(c) As (b) except that the house was let as residential accommodation during Melanie's absence.

21.3   Rupert bought a house in Manchester on 1 November 2000 for £75,000. He occupied the house as his principal private residence until 1 November 2004 when he left to work abroad for a year, living in rented accommodation. He moved back into his house on 1 November 2005 and stayed until 1 August 2009 when he left to work in Aberdeen, again living in rented accommodation until his return on 1 November 2013. This time he stayed for three years, leaving on 1 November 2016 to go to live with a friend. He never returned to the house and it was sold on 1 March 2023 for £343,000.

During his absences, Rupert always let his house in Manchester and claimed no other property to be his principal private residence. He also let rooms (comprising one-sixth of the house) to a tenant between 1 November 2005 and 31 July 2009. Compute the chargeable gain arising on the March 2023 disposal.

21.4   Samantha bought a house for £47,500 on 1 August 2001 and occupied the house as her principal private residence. On 1 June 2003 she began to use one-fifth of the house for business purposes. Unfortunately her business eventually failed and on 1 June 2010 she ceased trading. From that date onwards she resided in the entire house until it was sold on 1 August 2022 for £165,000. Compute the chargeable gain.

*21.5   Terry bought a house for £65,000 on 1 October 2002 and occupied the house as his principal private residence. He lived in the house until 1 October 2008 when he went to stay with relatives in Australia, letting the house in his absence. He did not return until 1 October 2012, when he began using one-quarter of the house for business purposes and the other three-quarters as his residence. This arrangement continued until 1 October 2022 when he sold the house for £190,000. Compute the chargeable gain.

Chapter 22

CGT reliefs

Introduction

A taxpayer's capital gains tax liability may sometimes be reduced or deferred by taking advantage of various CGT reliefs. The most important reliefs are concerned with:

(a)   damaged or destroyed assets

(b)   replacement of business assets

(c)   gift of business assets

(d)   transfer of a business to a limited company

(e)   disposal of a business ("business asset disposal relief")

(f)   reinvestment into EIS shares

(g)   loans to traders.

The main purpose of this chapter is to explain, for each of these reliefs, the circumstances in which the relief is available and the way in which the amount of relief is calculated.

Damaged assets

If an asset has been damaged and insurance money or other compensation is received in consequence, the situation is generally treated as a part disposal. The value of the part disposed of (A) is the amount of money received and the value of the part remaining (B) is the value of the asset on the date that the money is received. Any money which is spent on restoration is treated as enhancement expenditure.

However, in certain circumstances, the taxpayer may elect that such a situation should *not* be treated as a part disposal and that the amount of money received should instead be deducted from the allowable expenditure relating to the asset. This has the effect of increasing the gain arising on a subsequent disposal and is very similar to the CGT treatment of small capital distributions (see Chapter 20). The circumstances in which a part disposal may be avoided in this way are as follows:

(a)   All of the money received is applied to restoring the asset, or

(b) The asset is not a wasting asset and all the money received is applied to restoring the asset except for an amount which is small in comparison with the amount received and which is not reasonably required for restoration purposes, or

(c) The asset is not a wasting asset and the amount of money that is received is small in comparison with the value of the asset.

For this purpose, a sum is regarded as "small" if it does not exceed £3,000 or 5% of the amount with which it is being compared, whichever is the higher.

A part disposal calculation is unavoidable if only part of the money received is spent on restoring the asset and neither of the "small" tests is satisfied. However, the taxpayer may elect that the calculation should relate only to the amount which is received but not spent on restoration. If this election is made, the remainder of the money received is deducted from the allowable expenditure relating to the asset.

EXAMPLE 1

In July 2016, Laura bought an oil painting for £120,000. In October 2022, the painting was damaged by fire. In February 2023, Laura received compensation from her insurance company of £30,000. Compute the chargeable gain or allowable loss arising in each of the following circumstances:

(a) Laura spent none of the insurance money on restoration and the damaged painting was valued at £170,000 in February 2023.

(b) Laura spent £30,000 on restoring the painting in November 2022 and elected that the situation should not be treated as a part disposal.

(c) Laura spent £29,000 on restoring the painting in November 2022 and elected that the situation should not be treated as a part disposal.

(d) Laura spent £20,000 on restoring the painting in November 2022 and elected that the part disposal should relate only to the retained £10,000. The restored painting was valued at £200,000 in February 2023.

Solution

(a) This is a part disposal, with A = £30,000 and B = £170,000. The computation is:

	£
Disposal proceeds	30,000
Less: Part cost:	
$\dfrac{£30,000}{£30,000 + £170,000} \times £120,000$	18,000
Chargeable gain	12,000

The balance of allowable expenditure carried forward and used in the calculation of the gain arising on a subsequent disposal is £102,000 (£120,000 − £18,000).

(b) The entire amount received is spent on restoration so the election to avoid a part disposal is valid. The balance of allowable expenditure is:

	£
Incurred July 2016	120,000
Incurred November 2022	30,000
	150,000
Less: Received February 2023 (and not treated as a disposal)	30,000
	120,000

(c) The £1,000 retained is small in comparison with the amount received and therefore the election to avoid a part disposal is valid (so long as the £1,000 is not required for restoration purposes). The balance of allowable expenditure is:

	£
Incurred July 2016	120,000
Incurred November 2022	29,000
	149,000
Less: Received February 2023 (and not treated as a disposal)	30,000
	119,000

(d) By virtue of the election, the part disposal relates only to the retained £10,000, not to the entire £30,000 received. The computation is:

	£	£
Disposal proceeds		10,000
Less: Part original expenditure:		
$\dfrac{£10,000}{£10,000 + £200,000}$ x £120,000	5,714	
Part restoration expenditure.		
$\dfrac{£10,000}{£10,000 + £200,000}$ x £20,000	952	6,666
Chargeable gain		3,334

The balance of allowable expenditure carried forward in this case is:

	£
Incurred July 2016 (£120,000 – £5,714)	114,286
Incurred November 2022 (£20,000 – £952)	19,048
	133,334
Less: Received February 2023 (and not treated as a disposal)	20,000
	113,334

Without the election, the chargeable gain would be £11,739 (£30,000 – 30/230ths of £140,000). The balance of expenditure would be £121,739 (200/230ths of £140,000).

Destroyed assets

The loss or destruction of an asset is a chargeable disposal and usually results in a CGT computation in which the disposal value is equal to the amount of any insurance money or other compensation received. However, if *all* of the money received is spent (within 12 months) on the purchase of a replacement asset, the taxpayer may claim that the disposal of the original asset should give rise to neither a gain nor a loss. The cost of the replacement asset for CGT purposes is then reduced by the gain which would have been chargeable on the disposal of the original asset if this claim had not been made.

If only *part* of the money received is spent on the purchase of a replacement asset, the taxpayer may claim that the chargeable gain on the disposal of the original asset should be restricted to the amount of money retained (so long as this is less than the gain). The cost of the replacement asset is then reduced by the balance of the gain that would have been chargeable if the claim had not been made.

EXAMPLE 2

Maurice bought an item of jewellery in November 2017 for £125,000. In 2022 the jewellery was stolen. As a result, Maurice's insurance company paid him £141,500 in May 2022. In June 2022 he spent £150,000 on the purchase of replacement jewellery and claimed that neither a gain nor a loss should arise on the disposal of the original jewellery.

(a)   Compute the chargeable gain arising in March 2025 when the replacement jewellery is sold for £180,000.

(b)   How would this computation differ if the jewellery bought in June 2022 had cost only £140,000 and Maurice had made an appropriate claim?

Solution

(a)   Without a claim, the gain arising on the disposal of the original jewellery would be £16,500 (£141,500 – £125,000). The entire proceeds were spent on a replacement asset within 12 months so Maurice is entitled to make the claim. This reduces the deemed acquisition cost of the new jewellery to £133,500 (£150,000 – £16,500). The gain arising on the subsequent sale of the new jewellery is as follows:

	£
Disposal proceeds	180,000
<u>Less</u>: Deemed acquisition cost	133,500
Chargeable gain	46,500

(b)   £1,500 (£141,500 – £140,000) of the gain on the original jewellery is immediately chargeable. The remaining £15,000 may be deducted from the acquisition cost of the new jewellery, reducing this cost to £125,000 (£140,000 – £15,000). The chargeable gain arising on the March 2025 disposal becomes £55,000 (£180,000 – £125,000).

Replacement of business assets

Subject to certain conditions, a taxpayer may claim that the gain arising on the disposal of a business asset (the "old asset") may be "rolled-over" against the cost of acquiring a replacement business asset (the "new asset"). The main effects of a claim for roll-over relief are as follows:

(a) The disposal of the old asset is deemed to give rise to neither a gain nor a loss.

(b) The cost of the new asset for CGT purposes (its "base cost") is reduced by the gain which would have been chargeable on the disposal of the old asset if the claim for roll-over relief had not been made.

Full relief is available only if the disposal proceeds of the old asset are *wholly* applied in acquiring the new asset. If only *part* of the disposal proceeds are used to acquire the new asset, the effect of a claim for roll-over relief is that the chargeable gain on the disposal of the old asset is restricted to the amount of money retained (so long as this is less than the gain). The base cost of the new asset is then reduced by the balance of the gain that would have been chargeable to tax if the claim had not been made. The conditions which must be satisfied if a roll-over claim is to be accepted are:

(a) Both the old asset and the new asset must be drawn from the following list (though they need not both be the same type of asset):

  (i) land, buildings and fixed plant and machinery

  (ii) goodwill

  (iii) ships, aircraft, hovercraft, satellites, space stations and spacecraft

  (iv) certain agricultural quotas (*now mostly abolished*) and fishing quotas

  (v) Lloyd's syndicate rights

(b) The old asset must have been used only for trade purposes throughout the period of ownership and the new asset must be taken into trading use immediately upon its acquisition. But where the taxpayer operates two (or more) trades, there is no requirement that the old and new asset should be used in the same trade.

(c) The new asset must be acquired during the period beginning one year before the date of disposal of the old asset and ending three years after that date.

(d) The taxpayer must claim the relief within four years of the end of the *later* of the tax year in which the old asset is disposed of and the tax year in which the new asset is acquired. It is not possible to restrict the amount of a roll-over claim so as to preserve the annual exemption.

Note that a similar relief is available to companies (which pay corporation tax on their chargeable gains). For companies, however, the list of assets which are eligible for this relief excludes intangible assets such as goodwill and quotas. These assets fall instead within the scope of the corporation tax intangible assets regime (see Chapter 23).

EXAMPLE 3

In May 2011, Janine bought a building for £187,525 for use in her business. In July 2022 she sold the building for £260,000 and, in the same month, bought another building for use in her business. Assuming that Janine claims roll-over relief, calculate the chargeable gain arising on the July 2022 disposal if the replacement building has a cost of:

(a) £270,000 (b) £240,000 (c) £185,000.

Solution

The gain on the disposal of the original building is computed as follows:

	£
Sale proceeds	260,000
Less: Acquisition cost	187,525
Chargeable gain	72,475

(a)   The entire sale proceeds have been spent on a replacement building. None of the gain is immediately chargeable and the entire gain is rolled-over against the cost of the new building, reducing its base cost to £197,525 (£270,000 – £72,475).

(b)   £20,000 of the sale proceeds have been retained. Therefore £20,000 of the gain is immediately chargeable. The remaining £52,475 may be rolled-over against the cost of the new building, reducing its base cost to £187,525 (£240,000 – £52,475).

(c)   £75,000 of the sale proceeds have been retained. This exceeds the amount of the gain. Therefore the whole gain is immediately chargeable and no part of the gain may be rolled-over. The base cost of the new building is the full £185,000.

Replacement with a depreciating asset

If the new asset is a "depreciating asset" (i.e. an asset which is a wasting asset[†] or which will become one within ten years) the gain arising on the disposal of the old asset cannot be rolled-over and is *not* deducted from the cost of the new asset. Instead, the gain is temporarily deferred or "held-over" until it crystallises (i.e. becomes chargeable) on the *earliest* of the following three dates:

(a)   the date on which the new asset is disposed of
(b)   the date on which the new asset ceases to be used for trade purposes
(c)   the 10th anniversary of the acquisition of the new asset.

However, if a suitable non-depreciating asset is acquired at any time before the earliest of the above three dates, the held-over gain may be transferred to this new asset, so converting a temporarily held-over gain into a permanently rolled-over gain.

† *TCGA 1992 states that freehold land and buildings cannot be a wasting asset, regardless of the nature of the buildings concerned. But leasehold land and buildings are a wasting asset if the lease has no more than 50 years to run.*

EXAMPLE 4

In June 2022, Ian sold a freehold building for £200,000, realising a chargeable gain of £25,000. The building had been used only for trade purposes. In July 2022, he acquired fixed plant and machinery costing £220,000 and he elected that the gain on the building should be held-over against the plant and machinery. Explain the way in which the held-over gain would be treated if:

(a) Ian sells the plant and machinery in October 2026.

(b) Ian sells the plant and machinery in March 2034.

Solution

Plant and machinery is always regarded as a wasting asset (see Chapter 19) so the plant and machinery acquired in July 2022 is a depreciating asset.

(a) The replacement asset is sold before the 10th anniversary of its acquisition and so the deferred gain becomes chargeable in 2026-27.

(b) The replacement asset is still in Ian's possession ten years after its acquisition, so the held-over gain of £25,000 crystallises in July 2032 and forms part of Ian's chargeable gains in 2032-33.

EXAMPLE 5

Imagine now that Ian (in the above example) buys another freehold building for business use in November 2025 and elects to transfer the held-over gain on the fixed plant and machinery to the new freehold building. Explain the treatment of the held-over gain if the new building costs:

(a) £250,000   (b) £100,000.

Solution

(a) The entire proceeds of the sale of the original building have been invested in a new building so the whole held-over gain of £25,000 can be converted into a rolled-over gain, reducing the base cost of the new building to £225,000.

(b) £10,000 of the sale proceeds of the original building have not been invested in the new building and so cannot be rolled-over against its cost. This £10,000 will continue to be held-over against the plant and machinery and will become chargeable no later than July 2032. However, the remaining £15,000 is converted into a rolled-over gain, reducing the base cost of the new building to (£190,000 − £15,000) = £175,000.

Gift of business assets

The gift of an asset is a chargeable disposal and this is the case whether or not the asset is used in business. However, subject to certain conditions, a claim may be made for the gain arising on a gift of business assets to be held-over until the transferee disposes of the assets concerned. If such a claim is made, the transferor's gain on the disposal is reduced to zero and the transferee's deemed acquisition cost is reduced by the amount of the gain that would have been chargeable on the transferor if the claim had not been made. The conditions which must be satisfied are as follows:

(a) Both the transferor and the transferee must elect for the gain arising on the gift to be held-over. This election must be made within four years of the end of the tax year in which the gift is made.

(b) The gifted assets must consist of either:

    (i) assets used in a trade, profession or vocation carried on by the transferor or by the transferor's *personal company* (a company of which at least 5% of the voting rights are held by the transferor), or

    (ii) shares or securities of a trading company which is unlisted or which is the transferor's personal company (so long as the *transferee* is not a company).

If the gift is of shares or securities, rather than of individual business assets, the gain arising on the disposal is apportioned between the amount which relates to chargeable business assets owned by the company on the date of the gift and the amount which relates to other chargeable assets (e.g. investments). Only the part of the gain which relates to chargeable business assets is eligible for hold-over relief.

Sale for less than market value

Gift relief is also available if a business asset is sold for less than its market value (typically to a connected person). But if the consideration actually received by the transferor exceeds the original cost of the asset (so that part of the gain has been realised) the amount of the gain which may be held-over is reduced by the excess of the actual consideration over the asset's cost.

EXAMPLE 6

In March 2023, Jonathan gives a business asset to his daughter. Jonathan acquired the asset for £25,000 in May 2017 and its market value on the date of the gift is £60,000. Both Jonathan and his daughter elect that the gain arising should be held-over.

(a) Compute the gain arising on the gift and the amount which may be held-over.

(b) How would the computation differ if Jonathan's daughter paid him £32,000 for the asset?

Solution

(a) The chargeable gain is £35,000 (£60,000 – £25,000). The whole of this gain may be held-over, thus reducing Jonathan's daughter's deemed acquisition cost to £25,000 (£60,000 – £35,000).

(b) The chargeable gain is still £35,000, since this is not a bargain made at arm's length and therefore disposal value is taken to be the market value of the asset on the date of disposal. However, £7,000 of the gain (£32,000 – £25,000) has been realised in cash, so the amount of the gain which may be held-over is reduced to £28,000. The remaining £7,000 of the gain is immediately chargeable. The daughter's deemed acquisition cost is £32,000 (£60,000 – £28,000).

EXAMPLE 7

In August 2012, Kathy paid £60,000 to acquire 90% of the ordinary shares of an unlisted trading company. In May 2020, she gave all of the shares to her son and both Kathy and her son elected that the gain arising on this gift should (as far as possible) be held-over. The net assets of the company on the date of the gift (at market value) were as follows:

	£
Goodwill	100,000
Freehold building (used only for business purposes)	150,000
Listed investments	50,000
Net current assets (none of which are chargeable)	40,000
Total net assets	340,000

(a) Compute the gain arising on the gift and the amount which may be held-over.

(b) Compute the gain arising in March 2023 when Kathy's son sells all the shares for £350,000.

Solution

(a) Presumably, the value of the shares on the date of the gift was 90% of £340,000 = £306,000. So the gain arising on the gift was £246,000 (£306,000 – £60,000).

The company's chargeable assets on the date of the gift were £300,000 of which £250,000 comprised chargeable business assets. So £246,000 x 250,000/300,000 = £205,000 of the gain was held-over whilst the remaining £41,000 was chargeable.

(b) The gain arising in March 2023 is as follows:

	£
Sale proceeds	350,000
Less: Deemed acquisition cost (£306,000 – £205,000)	101,000
Chargeable gain	249,000

Transfer of a business to a limited company

Subject to certain conditions, the gain arising on the transfer of a business to a limited company in return for shares in that company is held-over until the transferor disposes of the shares. If this relief applies, the gain arising on the disposal of the business is deducted from the deemed acquisition cost of the shares. The required conditions are:

(a) The business is transferred as a going concern.

(b) All of the assets of the business (other than cash) are transferred to the company.

(c) The consideration received by the transferor consists wholly or partly of shares in the company.

This relief (known as "incorporation relief") applies automatically, so there is no need for the transferor to make a claim. However, the transferor may elect that incorporation relief should *not* apply. One situation in which such an election might be made is when the gain concerned is covered by the transferor's annual exemption.

If incorporation relief applies and the consideration for a transfer consists only partly of shares, then only part of the chargeable gain is held-over. In these circumstances, the held-over gain is calculated as follows:

$$\frac{\text{value of the shares received}}{\text{total consideration received}} \times \text{whole gain}$$

EXAMPLE 8

In November 2022, Leroy transfers his business to a limited company in exchange for £50,000 in cash and shares which are valued at £600,000. The gain arising on the transfer is £260,000. Leroy does not elect to disapply incorporation relief. Calculate the amount of the gain which is immediately chargeable and the amount which is held-over.

Solution

The held-over gain is £260,000 x 600,000/650,000 = £240,000. The remaining £20,000 of the gain is immediately chargeable. The deemed acquisition cost of the shares is reduced to £360,000 (£600,000 − £240,000).

Business asset disposal relief

A relief known as "business asset disposal relief" (BADR) may apply to the gains made by an individual on a "material disposal" of business assets. Prior to 6 April 2020, this relief was known as "entrepreneurs' relief". The relief is available in relation to disposals of:

(a) all or part of a business (including a share in a partnership) which the individual has owned throughout the period of two years ending on the date of the disposal, or

(b) assets used by a business at the time at which it ceases trading, as long as the business was owned by the individual (or by a partnership in which the individual was a member) throughout the two years ending on the date of cessation and the assets are disposed of within three years of that date, or

(c) shares or securities in a trading company which, throughout the period of two years ending on the date of the disposal, has been the individual's personal company and of which the individual has been an officer or employee.

In case (a) above, it is important to realise that the disposal must be the disposal of either a whole business or a significant part of a business. Merely disposing of a business asset does not qualify for BADR. The following points should also be noted:

(a) In the first two cases above, relief is available only in respect of disposals of "relevant business assets". These include goodwill but exclude assets held as investments.

(b) A trading company is one "*whose activities do not include to a substantial extent activities other than trading activities*". HMRC will generally accept that a company is a trading company if no more than 20% of its activities are non-trading activities.

(c) A company qualifies as an individual's personal company for BADR purposes if the individual holds at least 5% of the company's ordinary shares, has at least 5% of its voting rights, is entitled to at least 5% of its distributable profits and would be entitled to at least 5% of its net assets on a winding up.

(d) BADR claims are subject to a "lifetime limit", currently £1 million (see below).

(e) The disposal of shares acquired through the exercise of an Enterprise Management Incentives (EMI) option is eligible for BADR, subject to conditions (see Chapter 7).

Claims for business asset disposal relief must be made by the first anniversary of the 31 January following the tax year in which the disposal is made. For example, if a disposal occurs during tax year 2022-23, a BADR claim must be made by 31 January 2025.

Associated disposals

If an individual qualifies for BADR on a disposal of shares or securities or on a disposal of a share in a partnership, relief may also be available in relation to "associated disposals". An associated disposal is the disposal of an asset which is owned by the individual but has been used in the business of the company or partnership concerned.

Business asset disposal relief rate (10%)

If a BADR claim is made in respect of a qualifying disposal, any losses arising in relation to that disposal must first be deducted from the gains arising in relation to the disposal. The resulting amount is then taxable at the "business asset disposal relief rate" of 10%.

The calculation of a taxpayer's CGT liability for a tax year may involve both gains which qualify for BADR and gains which do not qualify. The taxpayer may also have capital losses in the year which arise from non-BADR disposals or capital losses brought forward from previous years. In these circumstances (as explained in Chapter 17):

(a) Non-BADR capital losses, capital losses brought forward and the annual exemption may be set against gains in such a way that the CGT liability is minimised. This result is achieved if losses and the annual exemption are set first against non-BADR gains (taxable at 10%, 20%, 18% or 28%) and only then against BADR gains.

(b) The unused part of the taxpayer's basic rate band (if any) is reduced by the amount of BADR gains arising in the year. Any part of the basic rate band which still remains after this deduction is then available for non-BADR gains.

The worked examples given in Chapter 17 illustrate these points.

The lifetime limit

Business asset disposal relief is subject to a "lifetime limit". A taxpayer may claim BADR more than once but this limit restricts the total amount of gains that can benefit from the relief during the taxpayer's lifetime.

The relief was originally introduced on 6 April 2008 with a lifetime limit of £1 million. This limit was subsequently increased to £2 million as from 6 April 2010, to £5 million as from 23 June 2010 and to £10 million as from 6 April 2011. However, *for disposals which occur on or after 11 March 2020*, the lifetime limit is reduced to £1 million.

Note that if an individual makes qualifying gains in excess of the lifetime limit and that limit is subsequently increased, retrospective relief is <u>not</u> given for the excess of those gains over the previous limit. Similarly, relief previously given is not clawed back if the lifetime limit is subsequently reduced.

EXAMPLE 9

Three taxpayers each wish to make a BADR claim in relation to a qualifying disposal made during 2022-23. Their previous claims are as follows:

(a) Gemma made a BADR claim in relation to a gain of £600,000 arising in June 2014.

(b) Robin made a BADR claim in relation to a gain of £2,300,000 arising in May 2010.

(c) Joyce made a BADR claim relating to a gain of £750,000 arising in October 2008 and a further BADR claim relating to a gain of £6 million arising in September 2010.

For each of these taxpayers, calculate the remaining amount of the BADR lifetime limit which is available in relation to the qualifying disposal made in 2022-23.

Solution

(a) Gemma's claim in June 2014 did not exceed the lifetime limit (which was £10 million at that time) so BADR was available in relation to the whole of the gain. The remainder of the lifetime limit is now £400,000 (£1,000,000 – £600,000).

(b) Robin's gain in May 2010 exceeded the lifetime limit of £2 million, so BADR would have been available for only £2 million of that gain. Although the limit later increased to £5 million and then £10 million, there is no retrospective relief in relation to the remaining £300,000 of the May 2010 gain. The remainder of the lifetime limit is now £nil, since the limit has now fallen to £1 million and Robin has already had relief of £2 million.

(c) Joyce's October 2008 claim was within the lifetime limit of £1 million and so BADR was available for the whole of the gain. By September 2010, the lifetime limit had risen to £5 million, so BADR was available in relation to £4,250,000 of the September 2010 gain. Although the limit later increased to £10 million, there is no retrospective relief for the remaining £1,750,000 of this gain. The remainder of the lifetime limit is now £nil, as the limit has now fallen to £1 million and Joyce has already had relief of £5 million.

EXAMPLE 10

Calculate the CGT payable in respect of the following disposals, assuming in each case that the annual exemption is fully utilised against other gains, that there are no allowable losses other than those stated and that taxable income for 2022-23 exceeds the basic rate limit. Also assume that BADR is claimed wherever possible.

(a) Wendy (who has never claimed BADR before) sells her business in January 2023 and realises a chargeable gain of £720,000 in relation to relevant business assets. She has owned the business since 1996.

(b) Tom sells his business in March 2023. He realises a gain of £300,000 on the disposal of his business premises but incurs a loss of £120,000 on the disposal of his goodwill. He has owned the business for 15 years and has made no previous BADR claims.

(c) In August 2022, Henry sells residential accommodation which he has been letting unfurnished to the same tenant since 2015. The gain on this disposal is £150,000.

(d) Since 2005, Brenda has been a director of a trading company which qualifies as her personal company. She sells her shares in October 2022 and realises a gain of £750,000. In November 2014, she had claimed BADR in relation to a gain of £360,000 arising on the disposal of a business.

Solution

(a) £720,000 does not exceed £1 million, so the whole of the gain qualifies for BADR. The gain is taxed at 10%, giving CGT payable of £72,000.

(b) The loss on the goodwill must be deducted from the gain on the premises before computing BADR. Tom's net gains are £180,000. This figure is taxed at 10%, so CGT payable is £18,000.

(c)   Henry's use of this property does not qualify as a trade and therefore BADR is not available. Relief would have been available if the letting of the property had qualified as the commercial letting of furnished holiday accommodation (see Chapter 5). CGT payable is £42,000 (£150,000 x 28%).

(d)   The disposal in November 2014 used up £360,000 of the lifetime limit, so £640,000 of the gain arising in October 2022 is taxed at 10% and the remainder is taxed at 20%. CGT payable is £86,000 (£640,000 x 10% + £110,000 x 20%).

Investors' relief

Finance Act 2016 extended a form of BADR to gains arising on the disposal of ordinary shares in unlisted trading companies by individuals (other than employees or officers of the company concerned). The shares must have been newly issued to the individual on or after 17 March 2016 and held for at least three years after 5 April 2016.

The rate of tax applicable to such gains is 10%. The total amount of gains eligible for this "investors' relief" is subject to a lifetime limit of £10 million. This limit is in addition to the £1 million lifetime limit which applies to business asset disposal relief.

Interaction of business asset disposal relief with other reliefs

A disposal which is eligible for business asset disposal relief may also qualify for the relief relating to a gift of business assets. But if a gift relief claim is made, no chargeable gain arises at the time of the disposal. Therefore a BADR claim is inappropriate and cannot be made successfully. Similar comments apply to a disposal to which incorporation relief applies and a disposal which is the subject of a claim for rollover relief.

In all of these cases, the fact that no chargeable gain arises at the time of the disposal[†] means that the opportunity to benefit from business asset disposal relief in relation to that disposal is lost. Whether or not a subsequent disposal (e.g. a disposal of gifted assets by the transferee) will qualify for BADR will depend upon the circumstances of that disposal and whether the necessary conditions are satisfied at that time for the relief to be available.

[†] *However, a gain which is eligible for BADR but is deferred into EIS or SITR investments (see below) remains eligible for BADR when the gain becomes chargeable.*

Reinvestment into EIS shares

The gain arising on the disposal of any asset may be deferred if an amount of money *equal to the gain* is used to subscribe for shares which are eligible under the rules of the Enterprise Investment Scheme (see Chapter 6). Note the following points:

(a)   The shares must be subscribed for during the period starting one year before and finishing three years after the disposal concerned.

(b)   There is no requirement that income tax relief should be available in relation to the investment. It follows that the taxpayer does not have to be unconnected with the company concerned and that the amount of a deferred gain can exceed the maximum amount on which income tax relief is granted.

(c) The deferred gain usually becomes chargeable on the disposal of the EIS shares, but further deferral is possible if further EIS shares are then subscribed for.

(d) A similar deferral relief applies to gains that are reinvested into Social Investment Tax Relief (SITR) investments (see Chapter 6).

Furthermore, the gain arising on the disposal of any asset may be reduced for tax purposes if the individual concerned also makes Seed EIS investments (see Chapter 6) during the tax year in which the disposal takes place. Up to 50% of the amount so invested may be set against chargeable gains, thus reducing (or eliminating) the CGT liability for the year.

Loans to traders

If a taxpayer lends money to a trader (sole trader, partnership or company) and then finds that all or part of the loan is irrecoverable, the loss incurred may be treated as a capital loss and set against the taxpayer's capital gains. This is subject to the following conditions:

(a) the money must have been borrowed for the purposes of a trade, profession or vocation
(b) the debt must be unsecured.

Subject to these conditions, the amount lost is treated as a capital loss of the year in which the taxpayer claims relief, though a claim may be backdated for up to two years if the debt was irrecoverable then. If relief is given and then all or part of the loan is recovered, the amount recovered is treated as a capital gain of the year in which recovery takes place.

Summary

‣ If the compensation received on the loss or destruction of an asset is spent on the purchase of a replacement, the taxpayer may claim that the disposal should give rise to neither a gain nor a loss. The gain which would have been chargeable is then subtracted from the cost of the replacement asset.

‣ The gain arising on the disposal of a business asset may be rolled-over against the cost of acquiring a replacement.

‣ If a business asset is replaced by a depreciating asset, the gain arising cannot be permanently rolled-over but may be temporarily held-over instead. This gain will become chargeable no later than 10 years after the replacement asset was acquired (unless the gain is transferred to a non-depreciating asset in the meantime).

‣ The gain arising on the gift of a business asset may be held-over until the transferee disposes of the asset.

> ▸ The gain arising on the transfer of a business to a limited company is held-over until the transferor disposes of the shares which were received in exchange for the assets of the business. The transferor may elect that this relief should not apply.
>
> ▸ Subject to certain conditions, business asset disposal relief is available in respect of gains of up to £1 million arising on the disposal of the whole or part of a business. Gains which qualify for this relief are taxed at only 10%.
>
> ▸ The gain arising on the disposal of any asset may be deferred if the amount of the gain is used to subscribe for shares eligible under the rules of the EIS.
>
> ▸ Up to 50% of the amount invested by an individual through the Seed EIS during a tax year may be set against any chargeable gains arising during that year.

Exercises

A set of multiple choice questions for this chapter is available on the accompanying website.

22.1   In October 2011, Matthew bought a piece of rare porcelain for £10,000. The porcelain was damaged in early 2018 and in February of that year Matthew spent £3,850 on restoration work. In July 2018, Matthew's insurance company paid him £4,000 and Matthew successfully claimed that this should not be treated as a part disposal. He sold the porcelain in March 2023 for £23,500. Compute the chargeable gain.

22.2   In February 2013, Maria bought a diamond necklace for £13,500. In 2016 the necklace was stolen and, as a result, an insurance payment of £14,000 was received in February 2017. In the same month, Maria spent £14,750 on the purchase of a replacement necklace and claimed that the disposal of the original necklace should give rise to neither a gain nor a loss. Compute the chargeable gain arising in January 2023 when the replacement necklace was sold for £20,000.

22.3   In June 2014, Pamela bought a freehold building for business use costing £150,000. In July 2022 she sold this building for £261,400 and immediately bought another freehold building, again for business use. Assuming that roll-over relief is claimed, calculate the chargeable gain arising in July 2022 if the cost of the new building is:

(a)   £258,900   (b)   £149,800   (c)   £276,800.

22.4   In August 2022, Susannah (a sole trader) gave a business asset to her son. The asset had been bought by Susannah for £91,500 in July 2012 and enhanced in May 2014 at a cost of £34,500. The asset's market value in August 2022 was £215,000. Both Susannah and her son elected that the gain arising should be held-over.

Compute the amount of the held-over gain. Also explain how the situation would differ if Susannah's son had paid her £150,000 for the asset.

*22.5   The following information is available:

(a)   In January 1991, Norman bought a freehold building for use in his business at a cost of £125,000. In June 2015, he sold this building for £875,000.

(b)   In September 2015, he spent £720,000 on buying another freehold building, again for business use. This building was sold in December 2022 for £930,000.

Calculate the chargeable gains arising on the disposal of each building (assuming that Norman claims roll-over relief).

*22.6   In May 2017, Ruth sold a freehold building which she had used exclusively for business purposes. The building was sold for £350,000, realising a chargeable gain of £92,500.

In June 2017, she bought fixed plant for £400,000 and elected to hold-over the gain on the building against this plant. In August 2022, she bought another freehold building for £335,000 and elected to transfer the held-over gain to this new building.

Explain the treatment of the £92,500 gain.

*22.7   Calculate the CGT payable in relation to each of the following disposals, assuming in each case that the annual exemption is fully utilised against other gains, that there are no allowable losses and that BADR is claimed wherever possible. The taxpayers concerned have made no previous BADR claims.

(a)   On 31 May 2022, Roger sold all of his shares in a trading company, realising a gain of £351,000. He has owned 25% of the company's ordinary share capital since March 2017 and has been a director of the company since June 2018.

(b)   On 31 July 2022, Dennis sold his business (which he has owned since May 1995) and realised gains of £1,525,000 in relation to relevant business assets.

(c)   On 31 August 2022, Denise sold her interest in a trading partnership and realised gains of £140,000 in relation to relevant business assets. She had been a member of the partnership for five years. Also on 31 August 2022, she sold a building which was owned by her personally but had been used by the partnership for business purposes since 2019. She realised a gain of £31,000 in relation to this building.

*22.8   In 2015, Shaun bought 20% of the ordinary shares of an unlisted trading company. The shares cost £140,000. He owned the shares until January 2023 when he gave all the shares to a friend. On the date of the gift, the shares had a market value of £500,000 and the company's assets were valued as follows:

	£
Freehold land and buildings	1,700,000
Goodwill	500,000
Investments	100,000
Motor cars	40,000
Net current assets	160,000

Calculate the chargeable gain, assuming that both Shaun and his friend elect that the gain arising should (as far as possible) be held-over.

Review questions (Set B)

B1   Mick Stone disposed of the following assets during tax year 2022-23:

(1)   On 19 May 2022, Mick sold a freehold warehouse for £522,000. This warehouse was purchased on 6 August 2010 for £258,000, and was extended at a cost of £99,000 during April 2012. In January 2016, the floor of the warehouse was damaged by flooding and had to be replaced at a cost of £63,000. The warehouse was sold because it was surplus to requirements as a result of Mick purchasing a newly built warehouse during 2021. Both warehouses have always been used for business purposes in a wholesale business run by Mick as a sole trader.

(2)   On 12 August 2022, Mick sold an acre of land for £81,700. He had originally purchased five acres of land on 19 May 2007 for £167,400. The market value of the unsold four acres of land as at 12 August 2022 was £268,000. The land has never been used for business purposes.

(3)   On 24 September 2022, Mick sold 70,000 £1 ordinary shares in Rolling Ltd, an unquoted trading company, for £367,500. He had purchased 50,000 shares in the company on 2 June 2014 for £96,000. On 1 June 2019, Rolling Ltd made a 3 for 2 bonus issue. Mick has been a director of Rolling Ltd since 1 January 2014.

(4)   On 19 January 2023, Mick made a gift of his entire holding of 24,000 £1 ordinary shares in Sugar plc, a listed investment company, to his son, Keith. On that date the shares were quoted on the London Stock Exchange at 698p - 710p. The shares had been purchased on 8 May 2017 for £76,800. Mick's shareholding was less than 1% of Sugar plc's issued share capital, and he has never been an employee or a director of the company.

Required:

(a)   Assuming that no reliefs are available, calculate the chargeable gain arising from each of Mick Stone's asset disposals during the tax year 2022-23.

(b)   State which capital gains tax reliefs might be available to Mick Stone in respect of each of his disposals during the tax year 2022-23, and what further information you would require in order to establish if those reliefs are actually available and to establish any restrictions as regards the amount of relief.

(ACCA)

B2   Yvonne had the following transactions in the shares of Scotia plc:

			£
18 August 2009	Bought	3,000 shares	6,000
19 September 2016	Bought	2,000 shares	5,000
13 March 2023	Sold	5,000 shares	23,000
28 March 2023	Bought	1,000 shares	4,400

Sally's capital gains tax position in 2022-23 was as follows:

	£
Capital gains arising in the year	37,900
Capital losses arising in the year	6,000
Capital losses brought forward	11,200

You are required to:

(a)   Calculate Yvonne's chargeable gain.

(b)   Calculate Sally's CGT liability for 2022-23, assuming that her taxable income for the year (i.e. total income less reliefs and the personal allowance) was:

(i)   £20,000   (ii)   £35,200   (iii)   £45,000.

Also assume that none of Sally's gains relate to the disposal of residential property or qualify for business asset disposal relief. She made no Gift Aid donations or pension contributions during 2022-23.   *(ACCA)*

B3   Jerome made the following gifts to family members during tax year 2022-23:

(1)   On 28 May 2022, Jerome made a gift of a house valued at £187,000 to his wife. His uncle had originally purchased the house on 14 July 2003 for £45,900. The uncle died on 12 June 2012 and the house was inherited by Jerome. On that date, the house was valued at £112,800. Jerome never occupied the house as his main residence.

(2)   On 24 June 2022, Jerome made a gift of his entire 12% holding of 12,000 £1 ordinary shares in Reward Ltd, an unquoted trading company, to his son. The market value of the shares on that date was £98,400. The shares had been purchased on 15 March 2014 for £39,000. On 24 June 2022, the market value of Reward Ltd's chargeable assets was £540,000, of which £460,000 was in respect of chargeable business assets. Jerome and his son have elected to hold over the gain on this gift.

(3)   On 7 August 2022, Jerome made a gift of an antique bracelet valued at £12,200 to his granddaughter. The bracelet had been purchased in September 2009 for £2,100.

(4)   On 29 January 2023, Jerome made a gift of nine acres of land valued at £78,400 to his brother. He had originally purchased ten acres of land on 3 November 2013 for £37,800. The market value of the unsold acre on 29 January 2023 was £33,600. The land has never been used for business purposes.

Required:

Calculate Jerome's chargeable gains for tax year 2022-23 and, for each of the recipients of assets (1) to (4) above, state their respective base cost for CGT purposes.   *(ACCA)*

B4   In the year to 5 April 2023, Thomas More made the following disposals:

(i)   A flat in a house that he had purchased on 1 December 2012 for £80,000. It had never been occupied as the main residence and had been consistently let during his period of ownership. The property had been converted into two flats in September 2013 at a cost of £32,000. The flat was sold for £142,000 on 1 December 2022 and out of this legal fees of £3,700 were paid. It was agreed that the value of the other flat was £130,000 in December 2022.

(ii)   20,000 shares which cost £111,700 in December 2013 and were sold for £150,000 in December 2022. (No shares were acquired within the next 30 days).

Required:

(a)   Calculate the capital gains tax payable on the sale of the flat and the shares. There were no other chargeable disposals in the tax year and no capital losses brought forward from previous years. Assume that Mr More's taxable income for 2022-23 exceeds the basic rate limit.

(b)   If you were told at the start of 2022-23 that Mr More intended making the above disposals and that his wife had capital losses of £30,000 brought forward (and did not intend to make any disposals in 2022-23) would there be any advice that you would consider giving to Thomas?   *(Amended from AAT)*

*B5   You have been consulted by Mr Christopher Rodrigues on two matters relating to capital gains tax. Extracts from his letter to you are:

"On 31 January 2023, I sold my shares in Fledgeby plc, a listed company. I had acquired them as follows:

1 January 2012	1,000	shares cost £4,200
19 June 2013	700	shares cost £2,950
31 December 2019	1,200	shares cost £5,620
11 August 2022	400	shares cost £2,100

I also took up a 1 for 4 rights issue at £3.50 per share on 31 May 2021. The shares were all sold for £38,000 on 31 January 2023 and I do not intend to buy any shares in the company in the future.

Also on 31 January 2023, I sold for £200,000 a plot of land that I had acquired in January 1990 for £10,000. A friend has told me that the gain might be either a capital gain or a trading profit. But, as capital gains and trading profits are both taxed, it doesn't really matter which way it is dealt with."

Required:

(a)   Calculate the chargeable gain arising on the sale of the shares in Fledgeby plc.

(b)   Do you agree with the statement of the other taxation practitioner? Draft brief notes that will form the basis of the letter that you will write to Mr Rodrigues.

(Amended from AAT)

*B6   On 30 June 2022 Jorge sold a house for £308,000. The house had been purchased on 1 January 2005 for £98,000 and used by Jorge as follows:

Months

16	Occupied
18	Unoccupied – travelling overseas
24	Unoccupied – required to work overseas by his employer
11	Occupied
30	Unoccupied – required to work elsewhere in the UK by his employer
22	Unoccupied – travelling overseas
26	Unoccupied – required to work elsewhere in the UK by his employer
27	Occupied
7	Unoccupied – required to work overseas by his employer
23	Unoccupied – travelling overseas
6	Unoccupied – lived with sister

210

Jorge let the house during all of his periods of absence. Throughout the period 1 January 2005 to 30 June 2022 Jorge did not have any other main residence. He also made the following disposals in 2022-23:

(i)   On 30 September 2022 he sold a copyright for £8,200. The copyright had been purchased on 1 October 2020 for £7,000 when it had an unexpired life of 10 years.

(ii)   On 6 October 2022 he sold a painting for £5,400. The painting had been purchased on 18 May 2018 for £2,200.

(iii)   On 14 December 2022 Jorge sold two acres of land for £92,000. Jorge's father-in-law had originally purchased three acres on 4 August 2010 for £19,500 but died on 17 August 2017 and the land was inherited by Jorge's wife. On that date the three acres were valued at £28,600. Jorge's wife transferred the land to him on 14 November 2020. On that date the three acres were valued at £39,000. The market value of the unsold acre of land as at 14 December 2022 was £38,000.

Required:

Calculate Jorge's taxable gains for tax year 2022-23.   *(ACCA)*

*B7   Gillian purchased 10,000 ordinary shares in Downtown plc in January 2017 for £20,000. In October 2022, Upmarket plc acquired the whole of the share capital of Downtown plc following a take-over bid. The terms of the take-over offer were:

One ordinary share and two preference shares in Upmarket plc, plus £3 cash

for every five shares held in Downtown plc. The share prices of Upmarket plc immediately after the take-over were:

Ordinary shares £10 each and Preference shares £3 each.

You are required to:

Calculate Gillian's chargeable gain arising in 2022-23.   *(ACCA)*

*B8   On 1 May 2008, Nigel acquired a 30-year lease for £20,000. He assigned the lease on 1 November 2022 for £75,000.

Kay purchased land in February 2014 for £20,000. She sold one-third of the land for £18,000 in March 2023 when the value of the remaining two-thirds was £60,000.

Shirley had the following dealings in the shares of Wingfield plc, a listed company:

			£
January 1991	Bought	4,000 shares	32,000
March 1998	1 for 4 rights issue	1,000 shares	7,000
November 2001	Bought	3,000 shares	24,000
January 2012	1 for 2 bonus issue	4,000 shares	-
March 2023	Sold	7,000 shares	56,000

No further shares were acquired during 2023.

You are required to:

(i)   Calculate Nigel's chargeable gain.

(ii)   Calculate Kay's chargeable gain.

(iii) Calculate Shirley's chargeable gain.   *(ACCA)*

*B9   *Assume that today's date is 1 March 2023.*

On 27 August 2022, Ruby sold an investment residential property and this resulted in a chargeable gain of £47,100. For tax year 2022-23, Ruby has taxable income of £23,435.

In addition to the above disposal, Ruby intends to make one further disposal during tax year 2022-23. This disposal will be either her holding of £1 ordinary shares in Pola Ltd or her holding of 50p ordinary shares in Aplo Ltd.

Pola Ltd is an unquoted trading company, in which Ruby has a 10% shareholding. The shareholding was purchased on 14 July 2015 for £23,700 and could be sold for £61,000. Ruby has been an employee of Pola Ltd since 2013.

Aplo Ltd is a quoted trading company, in which Ruby has a shareholding of 40,000 50p ordinary shares. She received these shares as a gift from her father on 27 May 2018. On that date, the shares were quoted on the stock exchange at 212p - 218p. There were no recorded bargains on that date. The shareholding could be sold for £59,000.

The gift of the shares in Aplo Ltd from her father was not eligible for holdover relief and the sale of these shares would not be eligible for business asset disposal relief.

Required:

(a)   Calculate Ruby's CGT liability for tax year 2022-23, assuming that her only disposal in that tax year is the investment property disposed of on 27 August 2022.

(b)   Calculate Ruby's revised CGT liability for tax year 2022-23 if, during March 2023, she also disposes of *either* (i) her shareholding in Pola Ltd; *or alternatively* (ii) her shareholding in Aplo Ltd.   *(ACCA)*

Part 3

CORPORATION TAX

Chapter 23

Introduction to corporation tax

Introduction

The next six chapters of this textbook deal with corporation tax, which is the tax that companies pay on their profits. The main purpose of this first chapter is to provide an introduction to the basic principles of corporation tax. Most of the relevant legislation is to be found in the Corporation Tax Act 2009, the Corporation Tax Act 2010 and the Taxation of Chargeable Gains Act 1992, as amended by subsequent Finance Acts.

Scope of corporation tax

UK resident companies are liable to pay corporation tax on their "taxable total profits", no matter where in the world those profits arise. Companies which are not UK resident are within the charge to UK corporation tax only if they trade in the UK through a permanent establishment, carry on a UK property business or a trade of dealing in UK land, or have gains arising on the disposal of UK land (see Chapter 32). Note that:

(a) A company's taxable total profits include both its income and its chargeable gains. The term "chargeable gains" is normally used in preference to "capital gains".

(b) The main source of income for most companies is likely to be trading income. But a company may also have other sources of income. These could include bank interest, loan interest, property income etc.

(c) In general terms, a company's income is computed in a broadly similar way to that of an individual. The main differences between the assessment of a company's income and an individual's income are explained later in this chapter. The way in which a company's chargeable gains are calculated is considered in Chapter 24.

For corporation tax purposes, a "company" means any corporate body or unincorporated association (excluding partnerships). As well as limited companies, this definition includes clubs and societies, which are liable to corporation tax on income from non-members.

Organisations that are generally exempt from corporation tax (subject to various conditions and limits) include registered charities and registered pension schemes.

Accounting periods

Corporation tax is charged in respect of "accounting periods" and it is very important to distinguish between accounting periods and periods of account. An *accounting period* is a period for which corporation tax is charged. A *period of account* is a period for which a company prepares a set of accounts.

Although accounting periods and periods of account are often the same thing, this is not always the case. An accounting period *begins* when:

(a) the company comes within the charge to corporation tax, or

(b) when the previous accounting period ends, so long as the company remains within the charge to corporation tax.

An accounting period *ends* on the *earliest* occurrence of any of a number of events. The main events which cause the end of an accounting period are:

(a) the expiration of 12 months from the beginning of the accounting period

(b) the end of a period of account

(c) the company starting or ceasing to trade

(d) the company ceasing to be within the charge to corporation tax

(e) the company becoming, or ceasing to be, UK resident

(f) the company entering administration or ceasing to be in administration.

These rules have the following general consequences:

(a) The length of an accounting period can never exceed 12 months.

(b) If a set of accounts covers a period of 12 months or less, the period of account forms a single accounting period and a corporation tax assessment is raised for this period.

(c) If a set of accounts covers a period of more than 12 months, the period covered by the accounts is broken down into two or more accounting periods, each giving rise to a separate corporation tax assessment. The first accounting period consists of the first 12 months of the period of account. The second accounting period consists of the next 12 months (and so forth). If the period covered by the accounts is not an exact multiple of 12 months, the final accounting period will be of less than 12 months' duration.

EXAMPLE 1

Identify the accounting periods which relate to the following periods of account:

(a) Company A prepares accounts for the year to 31 December 2022.

(b) Company B prepares accounts for the six months to 31 October 2022.

(c) Company C prepares accounts for the sixteen months to 31 December 2022.

(d) Company D prepares accounts for the thirty months to 31 March 2023.

Solution

(a) The year to 31 December 2022 is a single accounting period.

(b) The six months to 31 October 2022 is a single accounting period.

(c) The sixteen months to 31 December 2022 is divided into two accounting periods - the 12 months to 31 August 2022 and the four months to 31 December 2022.

(d) The thirty months to 31 March 2023 is divided into three accounting periods. These are the 12 months to 30 September 2021, the 12 months to 30 September 2022 and the six months to 31 March 2023.

Taxable total profits

The main elements which are taken into account when computing a company's taxable total profits for an accounting period may be summarised as follows:

	£	£
Trading income	xxx	
Less: Trading losses brought forward (*from before 1 April 2017*)	xxx	xxx
Income from property		xxx
Income from non-trading loan relationships		xxx
Non-trading income from intangible fixed assets		xxx
Chargeable gains	xxx	
Less: Allowable capital losses	xxx	xxx
		xxx
Less: Property business losses	xxx	
Deficits on non-trading loan relationships	xxx	
Trading losses relieved against total profits	xxx	
Trading losses brought forward (*from on or after 1 April 2017*)	xxx	
Relief for qualifying charitable donations	xxx	xxx
Taxable total profits (TTP)		xxx

Most of the elements shown above are explained in this chapter but chargeable gains are dealt with in Chapter 24 and losses/deficits are considered in Chapter 26. The corporation tax treatment of foreign income is covered in Chapter 32. Note that:

(a) A company cannot be an employee and so cannot have employment income.

(b) There is no corporation tax equivalent of the personal allowances which are available to individuals who pay income tax.

(c) Corporation Tax Act 2010 uses the term "taxable total profits" to refer to a company's profits which are chargeable to corporation tax. But the terms "chargeable profits" or "profits chargeable to corporation tax" (PCTCT) are also sometimes used.

Trading income

A company's trading income for an accounting period consists of its trading profit for that period, as adjusted for tax purposes. The starting point for the calculation is the company's pre-tax profit for the relevant period of account. This figure is then adjusted by excluding non-trading income and adding back disallowed expenses. The adjusted trading profit of a period of account lasting for more than 12 months is apportioned between the accounting periods of which it is composed (see later in this chapter). Capital allowances claimed for each accounting period are then deducted.

This process is very similar to the equivalent process which applies to self-employed individuals (see Chapter 9)[†]. However, the following points should be noted:

(a) When calculating a company's trading income, there is no need to disallow the private proportion of expenses. This is because a company does not have a private existence. Any private use *by employees* is treated simply as a cost of employing staff (who may then be liable to income tax on a benefit in kind). A similar argument applies if a company provides an employee with any other goods or services.

(b) For a company, appropriations of profit (which are disallowed) consist principally of dividends payable to shareholders and transfers to reserves.

(c) A company's Gift Aid donations are disallowed when computing trading income but are then treated as qualifying charitable donations and are deducted when calculating the company's taxable total profits.

(d) Legal and other fees payable by a company in connection with the raising of loan finance are dealt with under the loan relationships regime (see later in this chapter).

(e) Losses caused by the dishonesty of a director are disallowed.

(f) Accounts drawn up in accordance with either UK GAAP or International Financial Reporting Standards (IFRS) are generally valid for corporation tax purposes.

(g) Unlike individuals, companies are entitled to a special tax relief in relation to their research and development expenditure. Furthermore, a special corporation tax regime applies to a company's income and expenditure in relation to intangible assets. Both of these matters are explained towards the end of this chapter.

Corporation tax assessments are raised for accounting periods (not for tax years) and so there is no need for any basis period rules. The basis period rules which apply to individuals (see Chapter 10) are completely irrelevant to companies. In particular, there are no special rules on commencement or cessation of trade or on a change of accounting date.

[†] *A corporation tax version of Chapter 9 is available on the website which accompanies this book. The website can be accessed at* go.pearson.com/uk/he/resources.

Capital allowances

A company's capital allowances are computed in much the same way as those of a self-employed individual (see Chapter 11)[†]. The only significant distinctions are as follows:

(a) Each accounting period ranks as a chargeable period when computing the capital allowances of a company. Therefore there is one capital allowances computation per accounting period. Since the duration of an accounting period cannot exceed 12 months, there is never any need to scale *up* writing down allowances, but these are scaled *down* for accounting periods of less than 12 months.

(b) A company may claim only one AIA, regardless of the number of businesses which it carries on. A group of companies (i.e. a parent and its subsidiaries) may claim only one AIA for the entire group. This AIA may then be shared between the members of the group in any way that the group sees fit.

(c) Companies which invest in unused (not second-hand) main rate plant and machinery between 1 April 2021 and 31 March 2023 may claim an enhanced FYA of 130% (the "super-deduction"). With a corporation tax rate of 19% (see Chapter 25) the company's tax liability for the accounting period concerned is reduced by $130\% \times 19\% = 24.7\%$ of acquisition cost. Furthermore, an enhanced FYA of 50% is available in relation to special rate expenditure incurred between the same two dates. Note that:

   (i)   If expenditure which qualifies for the super-deduction is made in an accounting period which straddles 1 April 2023, the FYA percentage is reduced. If there are n days in the accounting period, of which m days fall before 1 April 2023, then the FYA percentage is $100\% + (m/n \times 30\%)$.

   (ii) The disposal of an asset which has been the subject of a super-deduction claim gives rise to a balancing charge. If the disposal is made in an accounting period which ends before 1 April 2023, this charge is calculated by applying a factor of 1.3 to the disposal proceeds. The factor is reduced proportionately if disposal takes place in a period straddling 1 April 2023. The disposal of an asset which has been the subject of the 50% FYA also gives rise to a balancing charge.

   Motor cars are not eligible for either of the enhanced FYAs.

(d) 100% FYAs are available to trading companies which invest in plant and machinery for use in designated areas within Enterprise Zones. To qualify for this FYA, the expenditure must be incurred within eight years of the date of designation or by 31 March 2021 (whichever is the later). Until 30 September 2026, enhanced capital allowances are also available in relation to certain "Freeports".

(e) When computing a company's capital allowances, there is no need to make any private use restrictions. Any private use of assets by employees is treated as part of the cost of employing staff and capital allowances are available in full on such assets (though the employees concerned may then be liable to income tax on a benefit in kind).

[†] *A corporation tax version of Chapter 11 is available on the website which accompanies this book. The website can be accessed at* go.pearson.com/uk/he/resources.

EXAMPLE 2

A company's income statement for the year to 31 December 2022 is as follows:

	£	£
Turnover		1,640,430
Cost of sales		827,390
Gross profit		813,040
Other income		24,000
		837,040
Less: Distribution costs	187,770	
Administrative expenses	341,920	529,690
Profit for the year (before tax)		307,350

Notes:

1. The other income of £24,000 consists of rents receivable.

2. Distribution costs are as follows:

	£
Depreciation of distribution vans	18,530
Loss on disposal of distribution van	990
General distribution costs (all allowable)	168,250
	187,770

3. Administrative expenses are as follows:

	£
Depreciation of office equipment	12,680
Profit on disposal of office equipment	(3,710)
Loss on disposal of investments	27,000
Trade debts written off	10,600
Increase in general allowance for doubtful debts	8,400
Customer entertaining	2,760
Staff entertaining	5,550
Gift Aid donations	10,000
Legal fees re acquisition of new freehold offices	4,500
Motor expenses (one-half private motoring by employees)	59,060
Patent royalties payable for trade purposes	20,000
Embezzlement by director	50,000
General administrative expenses (all allowable)	135,080
	341,920

Compute the company's trading income (before deduction of capital allowances) for the year to 31 December 2022.

Solution

	£	£
Profit per accounts		307,350
Less: *Non-trading income*:		
Income from property	24,000	
Profit on disposal of office equipment	3,710	27,710
		279,640
Add: *Disallowed expenses*:		
Depreciation of distribution vans	18,530	
Loss on disposal of distribution van	990	
Depreciation of office equipment	12,680	
Loss on disposal of investments	27,000	
Increase in general allowance for doubtful debts	8,400	
Customer entertaining	2,760	
Gift Aid donations	10,000	
Legal fees re acquisition of new offices	4,500	
Embezzlement by director	50,000	134,860
Trading income (before capital allowances)		414,500

Notes:

(i)   The Gift Aid donations are disallowed when computing trading income.

(ii) Motor expenses incurred in relation to private motoring by employees are allowable when computing trading income, so long as the employees work in the trade.

(iii) Patent royalties payable for trade purposes are allowable (see later in this chapter).

EXAMPLE 3

After deducting capital allowances for the year to 31 December 2021, the tax written down values of a company's plant and machinery were as follows:

	£
General pool	112,500
Special rate pool	14,700 (BMW car bought May 2020, 152g/km)

The company's next set of accounts covered the 15-month period to 31 March 2023. Plant and machinery bought and sold during this period were:

		£
18 March 2022	Bought plant	40,000
31 August 2022	Sold plant (cost £20,000 in 2018)	8,500
6 November 2022	Sold BMW motor car	11,300
6 November 2022	Bought Audi motor car (emissions 93g/km)	25,600
29 January 2023	Bought electric motor car (zero emissions)	17,100
12 March 2023	Bought plant (new)	14,000
15 March 2023	Sold plant (cost £2,000 in November 2021)	2,200

Calculate the maximum capital allowances available for the 15 months to 31 March 2023, assuming 20% private use of the BMW and Audi cars by a director of the company.

Solution

The 15-month period of account must be broken down into two accounting periods, which are the year to 31 December 2022 and the three months to 31 March 2023. Each of these accounting periods requires a separate capital allowances computation.

		Main pool £	Special rate pool £	Allowances £
y/e 31/12/22				
WDV b/f		112,500	14,700	
Acquisition (no AIA)			25,600	
			40,300	
Disposals		8,500	11,300	
		104,000	29,000	
WDA @ 18%		18,720		18,720
WDA @ 6%			1,740	1,740
		85,280		
Acquisition	40,000			
AIA @ 100%	40,000	0		40,000
WDV c/f		85,280	27,260	
Total allowances				60,460
1/1/23 - 31/3/23				
WDV b/f		85,280	27,260	
Disposal		2,000		
		83,280		
WDA @ 18% x 3/12		3,748		3,748
WDA @ 6% x 3/12			409	409
		79,532		
Acquisition	14,000			
FYA @ 130%	18,200	0		18,200
Acquisition	17,100			
FYA @ 100%	17,100	0		17,100
WDV c/f		79,532	26,851	
Total allowances				39,457

Notes:

(i) Capital allowances are not restricted for private use by an employee.

(ii) Maximum AIA is £1m for the year to 31/12/22 and (3/12 × £1,000,000) = £250,000 for the three months to 31/3/23.

Income from property

In general, a company's income from property (or "property business profit") is calculated in much the same way as an individual's income from property (see Chapter 5)[†]. But the following important distinctions should be noted:

(a) Interest payable on a loan taken out by a company for the purpose of buying or improving let property is dealt with under the loan relationships rules and is therefore ignored when computing property income.

(b) The income tax rule that restricts tax relief for interest payable in relation to "buy-to-let" loans on residential property (see Chapter 5) does not apply to companies.

(c) The loss reliefs available to a company which suffers a loss in relation to a property business are different from those available to an individual (see Chapter 26).

(d) Rent-a-room relief does not apply to companies.

(e) A company's property business profit must be calculated on the accruals basis. The cash basis is not available.

[†] *A corporation tax version of Chapter 5 is available on the website which accompanies this book. The website can be accessed at* go.pearson.com/uk/he/resources.

UK-REITs

Subject to a number of conditions, a UK company with property income comprising at least 75% of its total profits and property business assets (plus cash) comprising at least 75% of its total assets may apply to become a UK Real Estate Investment Trust (UK-REIT).

The qualifying property income of a UK-REIT is exempt from corporation tax. Capital gains made on the disposal of investment property are also exempt from corporation tax. Such companies must distribute at least 90% of their tax-exempt profits to their shareholders, deducting basic rate tax at source (see Chapter 2).

Income from non-trading loan relationships

Income from non-trading loan relationships consists mainly of bank and building society interest and any other interest receivable by a company. Such interest is assessed on the *accruals* basis. Note that companies generally receive interest gross (i.e. without deduction of income tax at source). In particular:

(a) Companies receive bank and building society interest gross.

(b) Interest received by a UK company from an individual or from another UK company (e.g. loan interest, debenture interest etc.) is also received gross.

The loan relationships rules are explained in more detail later in this chapter.

EXAMPLE 4

A company prepares accounts to 31 December each year and lets two properties to tenants. The following information relates to the year to 31 December 2022:

(a) Property A is owned by the company. The property was let from 1 January 2022 to 30 June 2022 at an annual rent of £9,600, payable monthly in advance. However, the rent due on 1 May and 1 June 2022 was not paid and the tenant then absconded. The company has now written off this rent as a bad debt.

Having advertised for a new tenant (cost £200), the company re-let the property from 1 September 2022 at an annual rent of £10,200, payable monthly in advance. The rent due on 1 December 2022 was not received until 3 January 2023.

Apart from advertising, the only other expenses incurred by the company in relation to Property A during the year to 31 December 2022 were:

	£
Minor repairs	230
Interest on loan to acquire the property	8,400

(b) Property B is a leasehold property which was acquired by the company on 1 October 2022. The company paid a premium of £120,000 for the grant of a 25-year lease but is not required to pay rent. As from 1 October 2022, this property was let to a tenant at an annual rent of £12,000. The first year's rent was paid in advance. The tenant also paid a premium of £40,000 for the grant of a 10-year lease.

No expenses were incurred in relation to this property during the year.

Calculate the company's property business profit for the year to 31 December 2022.

Solution

	£	£
Rent receivable:		
Property A £9,600 x 6/12 + £10,200 x 4/12		8,200
Property B £12,000 x 3/12		3,000
Premium received £40,000 – (£40,000 x 2% x (10 – 1))	32,800	
Premium paid 10/25ths x (£120,000 – (£120,000 x 2% x (25 – 1)))	24,960	7,840
		19,040
Less: Bad debt £9,600 x 2/12	1,600	
Advertising	200	
Repairs	230	2,030
Property business profit		17,010

Note that the loan interest is not deductible when computing property income but will be dealt with under the loan relationships regime.

Dividends received

Dividends received from other UK companies are paid out of profits which have already been subject to corporation tax. Therefore, to avoid double taxation, such dividends are not included in the taxable total profits of the receiving company.

Furthermore, most foreign dividends received by UK companies are now exempt from corporation tax (see Chapter 32) and are treated exactly as if they were dividends received from other UK companies. Accordingly, an exempt foreign dividend is not included in the taxable total profits of the receiving company.

Relief for charitable donations

Certain charitable donations and gifts are referred to as "qualifying charitable donations" and are deducted when computing a company's taxable total profits. Qualifying charitable donations are as follows:

(a) donations made by a company under the Gift Aid scheme (see Chapter 4)

(b) gifts of listed shares or securities to a charity

(c) gifts of land and buildings to a charity.

The Gift Aid donations that are deducted when computing taxable total profits for an accounting period are the donations actually *paid* during that period. Accruals and pre-payments are ignored. Similarly, the amount deducted in relation to gifts of assets is the market value of the assets given in the period. Unlike Gift Aid donations made by individuals (see Chapter 4) a company's Gift Aid donations are *not* grossed-up.

Charitable donations incurred by a company for trade purposes (and not within the Gift Aid scheme) are deductible when computing the company's trading income.

Gifts of pre-eminent property to the nation

A company which makes a gift of "pre-eminent property" to be held for the benefit of the public or the nation (e.g. a work of art) is entitled (subject to conditions) to a corporation tax reduction equal to 20% of the value of that property. If this tax reduction exceeds the company's corporation tax liability, then the liability is reduced to zero and the balance of the tax reduction is lost.

Loan relationships

A company is a party to a "loan relationship" if it is a debtor or creditor with regard to any debt which is a loan under general law. The main classes of debt to which the term refers are bank and building society deposits, bank overdrafts, Government securities (i.e. "gilts" or "gilt-edged" securities), corporate bonds (e.g. debentures) and other corporate debt. The tax treatment of income and expenditure relating to a loan relationship depends upon whether the relationship has been entered into for trade purposes. The loan relationships rules may be summarised as follows:

(a) **Trading loan relationships**. When a company has entered into a loan relationship for trade purposes, then:

  (i) Any interest payable (and any other cost relating to the debt) is deductible as a trading expense.

  (ii) Any interest receivable (and any other income relating to the debt) is treated as trading income. This will usually apply only if the company's trade is that of lending money.

(b) **Non-trading loan relationships**. When a company has entered into one or more loan relationships for non-trading purposes, then all of the "debits" and "credits" (costs and income) relating to such relationships are aggregated. Then:

  (i) If total credits exceed total debits, the net credits form part of the company's taxable total profits and are charged to corporation tax.

  (ii) If total debits exceed total credits, the net debits may be relieved in a variety of ways (see Chapter 26).

  Interest payable on underpaid corporation tax is treated as a non-trading debit. Similarly, interest receivable on a repayment of overpaid corporation tax is treated as a non-trading credit (see Chapter 25).

It is important to appreciate that the above treatment of costs and income relating to loan relationships applies to all such costs and income, *whether of a revenue or capital nature*. This means that the profit (or loss) arising on a disposal of Government securities or corporate bonds by a company is taxable (or allowable) even though such assets would not be chargeable assets for CGT purposes if held by individuals.

Accounting for loan relationships

The amount of income and expenditure brought into account for a loan relationship is calculated on the *accruals basis*. Any payments made net[†] of income tax are grossed up before being included in the corporation tax computation. Income tax deducted at source from such payments must then be accounted for to HMRC (see Chapter 25).

[†] *It should be assumed in all of the worked examples below that any payments made net of income tax have already been grossed up, so that the figures shown are the gross amounts.*

EXAMPLE 5

A manufacturing company has the following results for the year to 31 March 2023:

	£
Trading income	883,000
Income from property	14,200
Bank interest (amount received)	3,200
Interest on Government securities (amount received)	28,000
Dividends from UK companies	18,450
Chargeable gains	123,000
Gift Aid donation paid	24,000

The following information is also relevant:

(a) Bank interest of £1,100 was owing to the company at the end of the year. The corresponding amount at the start of the year was zero.

(b) The Government securities were acquired on 1 July 2022. Interest of £28,000 is payable to the company on 30 June and 31 December each year.

Compute the company's taxable total profits for the year to 31 March 2023.

Solution

	£
Trading income	883,000
Income from property	14,200
Income from non-trading loan relationships (£4,300 + £42,000)	46,300
Chargeable gains	123,000
	1,066,500
Less: Qualifying charitable donations	24,000
Taxable total profits (TTP)	1,042,500

Notes:

(i) The bank interest is income from a non-trading loan relationship and is assessed on the accruals basis. The amount that is charged to corporation tax for the year is £4,300 (£3,200 received + £1,100 accrued).

(ii) The interest on Government securities is income from a non-trading loan relationship and is assessed on the accruals basis. The income accrued in the year of £42,000 (£28,000 + £14,000) forms part of the company's total profits.

(iii) The dividends received do not form part of the company's total profits for corporation tax purposes.

(iv) The Gift Aid donation of £24,000 is a qualifying charitable donation.

EXAMPLE 6

A company produces the following income statement for the year to 31 March 2023:

	£	£
Gross profit brought down from trading account		762,950
Add: Rental income (Note 1)	5,000	
Loan interest receivable (Note 2)	2,600	
Dividends received (Note 3)	18,750	
Bank interest receivable (Note 4)	789	
Patent royalties receivable (Note 5)	6,500	
Profit on sale of building (Note 6)	6,000	39,639
		802,589
Less: Operating expenses (Note 7)		568,912
Profit for the year before tax		233,677

Notes:

1. The property was let on 1 January 2023 at a rent of £20,000 per annum, payable annually in advance. The figure shown in the income statement represents the rent for the period 1 January 2023 to 31 March 2023. No allowable expenditure has been incurred in relation to the let property.

2. Loan interest of £1,950 was received during the year and a further £650 was owing to the company at the end of the year. None was owed to the company at the start of the year. The income statement shows the total of £2,600.

3. Dividends of £18,750 were received from other UK companies during the year.

4. Bank interest received in the year was £684. Of this, £100 was owed to the company at the start of the year. A further £205 was owing to the company at the end of the year but was not received until April 2023.

5. Gross patent royalties of £6,000 were received in the year and a further £500 was owing to the company at the end of the year. None was owed to the company at the start of the year. The income statement shows the total of £6,500. These patents are held for trade purposes.

6. The chargeable gain on the sale of the building is £2,350.

7. Operating expenses include:

	£
Directors' fees	100,000
Debenture interest (gross):	
Paid 1 January 2023	4,000
Accrued at 31 March 2023	2,000
Depreciation of tangible fixed assets	102,500
Customer entertaining expenses	2,400
Gift Aid donation paid in the year	750

All of the remaining operating expenses are allowable as trading expenses. The debentures were issued on 1 July 2022 for trade purposes. The company claims capital allowances for the year of £87,450.

Required:

(a) Compute the company's trading income for the year to 31 March 2023.

(b) Compute the company's taxable total profits for the year to 31 March 2023.

Solution

(a) The company's trading income is as follows:

	£	£
Profit per accounts		233,677
Less: *Non-trading income*:		
Income from property	5,000	
Loan interest receivable	2,600	
Dividends received	18,750	
Bank interest receivable	789	
Profit on sale of building	6,000	33,139
		200,538
Add: *Disallowed expenses*:		
Depreciation	102,500	
Customer entertaining	2,400	
Gift Aid donation	750	105,650
		306,188
Less: Capital allowances		87,450
Trading income		218,738

(b) The taxable total profits for the year are:

	£
Trading income	218,738
Income from property	5,000
Income from non-trading loan relationships (£2,600 + £789)	3,389
Chargeable gain	2,350
	229,477
Less: Qualifying charitable donations	750
Taxable total profits (TTP)	228,727

Notes:

(i) The computation of the company's trading income is performed in the same way as that of an individual. The starting point is the pre-tax profit shown by the accounts. Non-trading income included in this profit is subtracted and disallowed expenses are added back. The aim is to separate out the company's trading profit from the total net profit shown in the accounts. The debenture interest is an allowable expense since the debentures were issued for trade purposes. The patent royalties receivable are trading income since the patents are held for trade purposes.

It is important to classify the company's profits correctly and to arrive at a separate figure for each category of profit (e.g. trading income, property income, income from non-trading loans, chargeable gains etc.). This analysis is necessary because different rules of assessment apply to each category of profit and is especially important if the company has incurred any losses (see Chapter 26).

(ii)   Property income is computed on the accruals basis.

(iii) The accrued loan interest forms part of the company's income from non-trading loans (assuming that the loan was not made for trade purposes). The remainder of this figure is bank interest, which is also assessed on the accruals basis.

(iv)   Dividends received are not chargeable to corporation tax.

(v)   The chargeable gain on the sale of the building is fully chargeable to corporation tax since the company is not entitled to the annual exemption (see Chapter 24).

(vi)   The Gift Aid donation is a qualifying charitable donation.

(vii) It is assumed that the company has not elected into the "patent box" regime (see later in this chapter).

Long periods of account

As stated above, a period of account exceeding 12 months in length must be divided into two or more accounting periods, each of which will give rise to a separate corporation tax assessment. A company's income[†] and gains for a long period of account are allocated between accounting periods as follows:

(a)   Trading profits (before deduction of capital allowances) are usually time-apportioned. Capital allowances are then computed separately for each accounting period.

(b)   Property income is also usually time-apportioned.

(c)   A net credit on non-trading loan relationships is allocated between accounting periods on the accruals basis.

(d)   Chargeable gains are allocated to the accounting period in which the disposals occur.

(e)   Qualifying charitable donations are allocated to the accounting period in which they are made.

In practice, the time-apportionment method which is normally used for trading profits and for property income may be replaced by a more accurate method of allocation if one is available. For instance, if trading profits have been earned as a result of a small number of transactions and the profit arising on each such transaction can be calculated individually, trading profits may be allocated between accounting periods according to the transactions occurring in each period.

[†] *Dividends received are allocated on the receipts basis. Although dividends do not form part of a company's taxable profits, the dividends received in an accounting period may be significant when determining whether or not the company is liable to pay corporation tax by instalments and (as from 1 April 2023) the percentage rate at which corporation tax is payable (see Chapter 25).*

EXAMPLE 7

A company makes up accounts for the 21 months to 30 September 2022. The company's results for this period of account are as follows:

	£
Adjusted trading profits (before capital allowances)	630,000
Non-trade loan interest receivable:	
Received 31 October 2021	600
Received 30 April 2022	600
Accrued to 30 September 2022	500
Chargeable gains:	
Disposal on 25 May 2021	2,300
Disposal on 12 December 2021	700
Disposal on 15 February 2022	10,500
Gift Aid donations:	
Paid 31 December 2021	4,000
Accrued to 30 September 2022	3,000

The loan interest receivable relates to a £12,000 loan made on 1 May 2021 at 10%. The company makes a £4,000 Gift Aid donation on 31 December every year. Show how the period of account will be divided into accounting periods and calculate the company's taxable total profits for each accounting period. (Ignore capital allowances).

Solution

There are two accounting periods - the year to 31 December 2021 and the nine months to 30 September 2022. The taxable profits for each accounting period are as follows:

	12 mths to 31/12/21	9 mths to 30/9/22
	£	£
Trading income (12.9)	360,000	270,000
Income from non-trading loan relationship	800	900
Chargeable gains	3,000	10,500
	363,800	281,400
Less: Qualifying charitable donations	4,000	nil
Taxable total profits (TTP)	359,800	281,400

Notes:

(i)   The loan interest is allocated on the accruals basis. Interest on the loan accrues at £100 per month so the interest for the period from 1 May 2021 to 31 December 2021 (eight months) is £800 and the interest for the period from 1 January 2022 to 30 September 2022 (nine months) is £900.

(ii) The chargeable gains are allocated according to the date of disposal and the Gift Aid donations are allocated according to the date of payment. The accrued donations are not deductible until the accounting period in which they are paid.

Research and development tax relief

Small or medium-sized companies (SMEs) which incur research and development expenditure may claim tax relief on 230% of the amount of that expenditure. The expenditure must *not* be capital expenditure and must be relevant to the company's trade. Qualifying expenditure includes staffing costs, consumables etc. For this purpose, companies qualify as small or medium-sized if they have fewer than 500 employees and have either a turnover not exceeding €100 million[†] or total assets not exceeding €86 million[†]. Note that:

(a) In general, R&D tax relief for SMEs is given by deducting 230% of the qualifying R&D expenditure when computing the company's trading income. In other words, the expenditure itself is deductible, together with an additional 130%. If the effect of this is to create or increase a trading loss, the company may (if it so wishes) claim a payment from HMRC equal to 14.5% of the "surrenderable loss". This is the *lower* of:

   (i)   the amount of the trading loss

   (ii) 230% of the qualifying R&D expenditure.

   If such a claim is made, the surrendered loss is then ineligible for the loss reliefs that are normally available in relation to a company's trading losses (see Chapter 26).

(b) However, the amount of the SMEs R&D payment which a company may claim from HMRC in an accounting period is capped at £20,000 (scaled down for periods of less than 12 months) plus three times the company's liability to PAYE and NICs for the period. There is also a cap of €7,500,000[†] *per project* on the expenditure in respect of which a company may claim SMEs R&D tax relief.

[†] *Presumably these amounts will eventually be denominated in £ now that the UK has left the EU.*

"Above the line" tax credit for large companies

Large companies (i.e. non-SMEs) are allowed to deduct only 100% of their research and development expenditure when computing trading income. But such companies may then claim an "above the line" (ATL) 13% tax credit in relation to such expenditure. This tax credit operates as follows:

(a) The 13% tax credit is included as income when computing taxable total profits but is then deducted from the company's corporation tax liability for the period concerned. Assuming a corporation tax rate of 19% (see Chapter 25) the effect of the tax credit is to reduce the company's corporation tax liability by 10.53% of the R&D expenditure.

   For instance, if R&D expenditure is £1m, the ATL tax credit is £130,000 and taxable profits increase by £130,000. The tax liability increases by £24,700 (19% × £130,000) but is then reduced by £130,000, a tax saving of £105,300 (10.53% of £1m).

(b) If the 13% R&D tax credit exceeds the company's corporation tax liability for the period, the excess may (subject to conditions) be paid to the company by HMRC. Such payments are made net of corporation tax but the tax deducted may be set against the company's corporation tax liability in subsequent accounting periods.

Intangible fixed assets

A special tax regime applies to a company's income or expenditure in relation to intangible fixed assets (IFAs) such as patents, trademarks etc. In outline, the system is as follows:

(a) Subject to certain exclusions, tax relief is available for the cost of IFAs created or acquired by a company. The amount of relief is normally equal to the amortisation charged in the company's accounts. If an IFA is not amortised or is amortised over a very long period, the company may elect for a fixed rate tax allowance[†] of 4% p.a.

(b) Capital allowances are not available to companies in respect of patent rights or know-how. Computer software falls within the IFAs regime unless the company elects for capital allowances to apply.

(c) A loss on the disposal of an IFA is eligible for tax relief. Similarly, a profit on the disposal of such an asset is taxable income. But if an IFA is disposed of for more than original cost and the disposal proceeds are re-invested in newly-acquired IFAs, then the gain may be rolled-over against the cost of the new assets.

(d) Royalties payable or receivable for the use of IFAs (e.g. patent royalties) are within the scope of the IFAs regime and are dealt with on the accruals basis. Royalties which are paid or received net of basic rate income tax (see Chapter 25) are grossed up.

(e) If the IFAs are held or used for trade purposes, the related income and expenditure is taken into account when computing trading income. If IFAs are held or used for non-trade purposes, the income and expenditure is aggregated to produce an overall non-trading gain or loss. A loss may be relieved in a number of ways (see Chapter 26).

[†] *Goodwill acquired as part of the acquisition of a business is eligible for a fixed rate tax allowance of 6.5% p.a. This also applies to certain other goodwill-related assets.*

Patent box

A company which owns a patent (and has significantly contributed towards the creation or development of the patented innovation) may elect into the "patent box" regime and so benefit from paying a lower rate of corporation tax on the amount of the trading income which is derived from exploiting the patent. Such income includes patent royalties and income from the sale of patented products or the sale of patent rights.

If a company elects into the patent box regime, this income is taxed at an effective rate of only 10%. This is achieved by making an additional deduction from the company's trading profit and then taxing the profit at the normal rate. For instance, if the normal rate of corporation tax is 19%, deducting 9/19ths of the patent box income from the company's profit (leaving 10/19ths) will achieve the desired result (since $10/19 \times 19\% = 10\%$).

Summary

▸ Corporation tax is charged on the worldwide profits of UK resident companies. Non-resident companies are liable to UK corporation tax only if they trade in the UK through a permanent establishment, carry on a UK property business or a trade of dealing in UK land, or have gains arising on the disposal of UK land.

▸ Corporation tax is charged in respect of accounting periods. The length of an accounting period can never exceed 12 months. A period of account which is longer than this is divided into two or more accounting periods.

▸ A company's taxable total profits consist of its income and chargeable gains, less any qualifying charitable donations.

▸ A company's trading income is calculated in a similar way to the trading income of an individual. However, special corporation tax rules apply to research and development expenditure and to income and expenditure relating to intangible fixed assets.

▸ A company's property income is assessed in a similar way to the property income of an individual. However, interest payable on a loan for the purchase or improvement of property is dealt with under the loan relationships rules.

▸ A company's income and expenditure relating to loan relationships entered into for trade purposes is taken into account when computing the company's trading income. Net credits on non-trading loan relationships form part of taxable total profits.

▸ Dividends received from other UK companies are not part of the taxable profits of the receiving company. Most foreign dividends are also exempt from corporation tax.

▸ A company's qualifying charitable donations consist mainly of Gift Aid donations. These are relieved on the payments basis.

Exercises

A set of multiple choice questions for this chapter is available on the accompanying website.

23.1 Identify the accounting periods relating to the following periods of account:

(a) year to 30 November 2022

(b) 1 October 2021 to 31 July 2022

(c) 1 January 2023 to 31 January 2023

(d) 33 months to 31 August 2022

(e) 1 April 2021 to 30 September 2022.

23.2 On 1 January 2023, a company receives gross debenture interest of £1,600 from another UK company and pays net debenture interest of £8,640 to individuals. Explain the corporation tax treatment of each of these items.

23.3   During the year to 31 March 2023, a company which qualifies as medium-sized spends £180,000 on research and development. This is qualifying expenditure under the R&D tax relief scheme. Explain the corporation tax treatment of this expenditure.

23.4   A company's accounts for the 17 months to 30 June 2022 include:

	£
Trading income	425,000
Debenture interest receivable:	
Received 31 October 2021	2,400
Received 30 April 2022	2,400
Accrued to 30 June 2022	800
Income from property (let since 2018)	9,010
Chargeable gains:	
Disposal on 31 January 2022	28,700
Disposal on 1 February 2022	49,760
Dividend received from UK company	10,000
Gift Aid donations:	
Paid 31 July 2021	6,000
Paid 31 January 2022	6,000

The debentures were acquired (not for trade purposes) on 1 May 2021. Interest is payable half-yearly on 30 April and 31 October. Show how the company's period of account will be divided into accounting periods and compute the taxable total profits for each accounting period. Ignore capital allowances.

23.5   A company has the following results for the year to 31 March 2023:

	£	£
Trading profits, after capital allowances		1,561,400
Bank deposit interest (account opened 1 April 2022):		
Received 30 June 2022		1,820
Received 31 December 2022		3,670
Accrued to 31 March 2023		1,980
Chargeable gain on sale of factory		531,000
Dividends received from UK companies		132,000
Deed of covenant payable annually to a charity:		
Paid 1 October 2022 for year to 30 September 2023	9,000	
Less: Prepayment	4,500	4,500

The charitable covenant began on 1 October 2022 and falls within the Gift Aid scheme. Compute the taxable total profits for the year.

*23.6   A company's income statement for the year to 31 March 2023 is as follows:

	£	£
Gross trading profit		383,870
Receivable from other UK companies:		
Dividends		4,000
Debenture interest (Note 1)		6,000
Bank interest receivable (Note 2)		2,600
Income from property (Note 3)		4,000
Profit on sale of investments (Note 4)		22,490
		422,960
Less:		
Distribution costs (all allowable)	97,500	
Administrative expenses (all allowable)	101,150	
Directors' fees	50,000	
Interest on bank overdraft	23,780	
Debenture interest payable (Notes 5, 8)	50,000	
Patent royalties payable (Notes 6, 8)	7,500	
Depreciation of tangible fixed assets	108,300	438,230
Net loss for the year		(15,270)

Notes:

1. The company acquired £240,000 of 10% debentures (for non-trade purposes) on 1 January 2023. Interest is receivable half-yearly on 30 June and 31 December. No interest was received during the year to 31 March 2023.

2. Bank interest receivable includes interest of £450 which had accrued at 31 March 2023 but which was not received until April 2023. There was no accrued interest at 31 March 2022.

3. The property was let on 1 December 2022 at a rent of £1,000 per month payable quarterly in advance on 1 December, 1 March, 1 June and 1 September. There were no allowable expenses in the year to 31 March 2023.

4. The agreed chargeable gain on the sale of the investments was £8,450.

5. £500,000 of 10% debentures were issued (for trade purposes) on 1 April 2022. The interest is payable (net of income tax) on 1 January each year.

6. As from 1 July 2022, the company is required to pay patent royalties of £10,000 per annum, deducting basic rate income tax at source. The net amount paid in the year to 31 March 2023 was £4,000. The royalties are payable for trade purposes.

7. Capital allowances of £32,700 are claimed for the year.

8. All figures given in the income statement are gross.

Compute the taxable total profits for the year.

Chapter 24

Corporate chargeable gains

Introduction

A company's taxable total profits for an accounting period include any chargeable gains which arise from disposals made during that period. The chargeable gains of a company are computed in a similar way to the capital gains of an individual, but there are some important differences between the rules which apply to companies and the rules which apply to individuals. The purpose of this chapter is to explain how the chargeable gains of a company are determined for corporation tax purposes. The relevant legislation is in the Taxation of Chargeable Gains Act 1992, as amended by subsequent Finance Acts.

Chargeable disposals and chargeable assets

A chargeable gain or an allowable loss may arise if a company makes a chargeable disposal of a chargeable asset. A company's chargeable assets will usually consist of its tangible non-current assets (fixed assets) such as land and buildings, plant and machinery or investments, but certain assets are entirely exempt from the chargeable gains legislation. The main exemptions for a company are:

(a) motor cars

(b) items of tangible, movable property ("chattels") worth £6,000 or less

(c) chattels with a predictable useful life of up to 50 years ("wasting chattels") unless used in business and eligible for capital allowances

(d) gilt-edged securities and qualifying corporate bonds, which are dealt with by the loan relationships regime (see Chapter 23).

A chargeable disposal generally occurs when the whole or part of a chargeable asset is sold or given away. However, the gift of a chargeable asset to a charity is exempt.

Basis of assessment

The chargeable gains figure which is included in a company's taxable total profits for an accounting period is based upon the disposals made during that period. This figure is calculated as follows:

(a)   The chargeable gain or allowable loss arising on each disposal is calculated.

(b)   If total gains exceed total losses, the losses are subtracted from the gains to give net chargeable gains for the accounting period.

(c)   If total losses exceed total gains, the chargeable gains figure for the accounting period is £nil. The net losses are then carried forward for relief in subsequent accounting periods (see Chapter 26).

Companies are *not* entitled to the annual exemption which is available to individuals who pay capital gains tax (CGT).

Computation of gains and losses

A company's chargeable gains and allowable losses are computed in a similar way to those of an individual (see Chapters 18-22) but the following distinctions should be noted:

(a)   (i)   The gain arising on the disposal of a chargeable asset by a company may be reduced by "indexation allowance", which adjusts the gain to take account of inflation. Indexation allowance used to be available when calculating the capital gains of individuals for CGT purposes, but this is no longer the case.

     (ii)   Rebasing does not always apply when a company disposes of an asset acquired before 31 March 1982.

The way in which indexation allowance is calculated and the corporation tax treatment of assets acquired before 31 March 1982 are both explained below.

(b)   The share matching rules that are used when a company makes a disposal of shares or securities are different from the equivalent rules that apply when such a disposal is made by an individual. The share matching rules which are used for corporation tax purposes are explained later in this chapter.

(c)   The principal private residence exemption does not apply to companies.

(d)   When a company disposes of an intangible asset, any gain or loss which arises is dealt with by the intangible fixed assets regime (see Chapter 23). Such disposals fall outside the scope of the tax on chargeable gains.

(e)   Gift relief, incorporation relief, business asset disposal relief and EIS deferral relief do not apply to companies. But rollover relief is available on the replacement of tangible business assets (see Chapter 22).

Indexation allowance

Indexation allowance was introduced in 1982 with the intention of ensuring that capital gains caused by inflation should not be charged to tax.

Indexation allowance is calculated separately for each item of expenditure shown in a computation. In general, the indexation allowance available on an item of expenditure is equal to the amount of that expenditure multiplied by an *indexation factor*, which is computed according to the following formula (rounded to three decimal places):

$$\frac{RD - RI}{RI}$$

where: RD is the Retail Prices Index (RPI) for the month of disposal, and

RI is the RPI for the month in which the expenditure was incurred.

However, Finance Act 2018 "froze" indexation allowance at 31 December 2017, so that no relief is given for inflation occurring after that date. Indexation allowance on a disposal which occurs on or after 1 January 2018 is calculated as follows:

(a)   indexation allowance for any allowable expenditure incurred before 1 January 2018 is calculated as if the month of disposal were December 2017 (RPI 278.1)

(b)   no indexation allowance is available for any allowable expenditure which is incurred on or after 1 January 2018.

A table of RPIs is given at the end of this chapter.

EXAMPLE 1

A company bought a chargeable asset (not a chattel) in June 2003 (RPI 181.3) for £1,200. The asset was sold in August 2022 for £5,350. The RPI for December 2017 was 278.1. Compute the chargeable gain.

Solution

	£
Sale proceeds	5,350
Less: Acquisition cost	1,200
Unindexed gain	4,150
Less: Indexation allowance	
$\frac{278.1 - 181.3}{181.3} = 0.534 \times £1,200$	641
Chargeable gain	3,509

EXAMPLE 2

A company bought a chargeable asset in November 2000 for £15,000. Enhancement expenditure was £2,000 in January 2002, £3,000 in June 2006 and £4,500 in September 2018. The asset was sold in February 2023 for £48,000. RPIs are as follows:

November 2000	172.1	January 2002	173.3
June 2006	198.5	December 2017	278.1

Compute the chargeable gain.

Solution

	£	£
Sale proceeds		48,000
Less: Acquisition cost	15,000	
Enhancement expenditure (£2,000 + £3,000 + £4,500)	9,500	24,500
Unindexed gain		23,500
Less: Indexation allowance:		
(i) on acquisition cost		

$$\frac{278.1 - 172.1}{172.1} = 0.616 \times £15,000 \qquad 9,240$$

(ii) on enhancement January 2002

$$\frac{278.1 - 173.3}{173.3} = 0.605 \times £2,000 \qquad 1,210$$

(iii) on enhancement June 2006

$$\frac{278.1 - 198.5}{198.5} = 0.401 \times £3,000 \qquad 1,203 \qquad 11,653$$

Chargeable gain		11,847

Notes:

(i) The effect of indexation allowance is to convert each item of eligible expenditure to an equivalent amount as at 31 December 2017. This removes the element of inflation (up to that date) from the chargeable gain.

For instance, there was 61.6% inflation (indexation factor 0.616) between the date of acquisition of the asset and 31 December 2017. So the company needs to make a gain of £9,240 (61.6% × £15,000) merely to maintain its purchasing power up to 31 December 2017. A similar argument applies to the first two amounts of enhancement expenditure. In total, the company needs a gain of £11,653 to maintain its purchasing power up to 31 December 2017. Any gain beyond this figure is a chargeable gain.

(ii) The expenditure of £4,500 in September 2018 is not eligible for indexation allowance since it was incurred on or after 1 January 2018.

Restrictions on indexation allowance

Note the following points about the indexation allowance:

(a) If RPI goes <u>down</u> between the month in which expenditure is incurred and the month of disposal, the indexation allowance available for that expenditure is nil. *But this rule cannot apply unless the date of disposal is before 1 January 2018.*

(b) No indexation allowance is available in respect of any incidental costs of disposal, even if they were incurred prior to the month of disposal.

(c) Indexation allowance cannot be used to convert a gain into a loss. Therefore, if the available indexation allowance (calculated in the normal way) exceeds the unindexed gain, the indexation allowance is restricted so as to give neither a gain nor a loss.

(d) Indexation allowance cannot be used to increase an unindexed loss. If there is an unindexed loss on a disposal then the indexation allowance is nil.

EXAMPLE 3

A company acquired a chargeable asset for £5,000 in February 2004 (RPI 183.8). The asset (not a chattel) was sold in January 2023. The RPI for December 2017 was 278.1. Compute the chargeable gain or allowable loss if sale proceeds were:

(a) £9,000 (b) £5,500 (c) £4,800

Solution

	(a) £	(b) £	(c) £
Sale proceeds	0,000	5,500	4,800
Less: Acquisition cost	5,000	5,000	5,000
Unindexed gain or loss	4,000	500	(200)
Less: Indexation allowance			
$\dfrac{278.1 - 183.8}{183.8} = 0.513 \times £5,000 = £2,565$	2,565	500	nil
Chargeable gain or allowable loss	1,435	nil	(200)

Notes:

(i) In case (a), the indexation allowance can be given in full.

(ii) In case (b), the full indexation allowance would convert an unindexed gain of £500 into a loss of £2,065. Indexation allowance is restricted to £500 to prevent this.

(iii) In case (c) there is an unindexed loss, so indexation allowance is restricted to £nil.

Assets held on 31 March 1982

As explained in Chapter 18, the gain or loss arising on the disposal of an asset which was held on 31 March 1982 is usually calculated by means of the "rebasing" technique, whereby the market value of the asset at 31 March 1982 is substituted for its acquisition cost. The effect of this is that any increase or decrease in the asset's value before 31 March 1982 is ignored and only the gain (or loss) arising since 31 March 1982 is taxable (or allowable).

In the case of disposals made by individuals, rebasing is now mandatory. But this is not the case for companies. Under corporation tax rules, rebasing does *not* apply if the rebasing calculation results in a greater gain than the calculation based on original cost. A brief summary of the position is as follows:

(a) For corporation tax purposes, the chargeable gain arising on the disposal by a company of an asset held on 31 March 1982 is equal to the *lower* of the gain based on original cost and the gain based on market value at 31 March 1982. Furthermore:

   (i) When calculating the gain, indexation allowance is based on the change in RPI between March 1982 and the month of disposal (*or December 2017 if the disposal occurs on after 1 January 2018*). No further indexation allowance is available to compensate for the effects of pre-March 1982 inflation.

   (ii) In *both* the rebasing calculation and the calculation based on original cost, indexation allowance is calculated by reference to the *greater* of original cost and the asset's market value at 31 March 1982 (i.e. the same indexation allowance is given in both calculations).

(b) Similarly, if a company disposes of an asset held on 31 March 1982 and the disposal gives rise to a loss, then the allowable loss is the *lower* of the loss based on original cost and the loss based on market value at 31 March 1982.

   And if the calculation based on original cost gives a gain and the calculation based on market value at 31 March 1982 gives a loss (or vice versa) then there is neither a chargeable gain nor an allowable loss (the "no gain, no loss" situation).

(c) Finally, a company may elect *irrevocably* that gains and losses arising on disposals of assets held on 31 March 1982 should be calculated only by the rebasing method.

However, these rules are now falling into disuse as it becomes increasingly uncommon for a disposal to involve an asset held on 31 March 1982 (i.e. an asset which was acquired over 40 years ago). Therefore these rules are considered no further here. But further information and a number of worked examples are available on the website which accompanies this book. The website can be accessed at go.pearson.com/uk/he/resources.

Note also that additional special rules apply if a company disposes of an asset which was acquired before 6 April 1965. These rules are now used even less frequently than the rules that apply to assets held on 31 March 1982. But the additional rules are still applicable if they give a lower gain than the rebasing rules. Further information on this topic is available on the website which accompanies this book.

Disposals of shares or securities

The share matching rules which apply on a disposal of shares or securities by an individual were explained in Chapter 20 of this book. The main principle is that shares of the same class in the same company are pooled into the "Section 104 holding" and that disposals are generally matched against shares taken from this holding. Special rules apply if shares are bought and sold on the same day or if shares are sold and re-acquired within 30 days.

However, the share matching rules which are used when a *company* makes a disposal of shares or securities are not the same as the rules for individuals. A disposal of shares or securities by a company is matched against acquisitions in the following order:

(a) first, against acquisitions made on the same day

(b) next, against acquisitions made in the previous nine days (on a FIFO basis)

(c) next, against shares taken from the Section 104 holding, which (for companies) is the pool of shares acquired on or after 1 April 1982

(d) next, against the "1982 holding", which is a pool of shares acquired between 6 April 1965 and 31 March 1982 inclusive[†]

(e) finally, against shares acquired before 6 April 1965[†] (on a LIFO basis).

These rules have to be more complex than their CGT equivalents because companies are entitled to indexation allowance and because rebasing does not always apply when a company disposes of a pre-31 March 1982 asset.

[†] *The share matching rules which apply to shares held on 31 March 1982 and shares acquired before 6 April 1965 are explained on the website which accompanies this book.*

The Section 104 holding

A company's s104 holding of shares of a certain class in a certain company consists of the pool of shares which were acquired on or after 1 April 1982. Share acquisitions which are matched against disposals made on the same day or during the following nine days do not join the s104 holding.

The distinguishing characteristic of shares acquired on or after 1 April 1982 is that the indexation factor used on their disposal will differ according to the date of acquisition. If it were not for Section 104, it would be necessary to keep detailed records of the date and cost of each share acquisition made on or after 1 April 1982, so that indexation allowance could be calculated correctly on a disposal. However, the pooling system provided by Section 104 eliminates the need to keep these records. All that is required is a record of:

(a) the total number of shares in the pool

(b) their total cost

(c) their total *indexed cost*, which consists of total cost plus all indexation allowance due up to the date of the most recent "operative event". An operative event occurs whenever shares enter or leave the pool.

The indexed cost of the s104 holding is calculated as follows:

(a) The number of shares in the pool at 1 April 1985 (if any) is totalled and the cost of these shares is also totalled. The indexed cost of the pool at 1 April 1985 is calculated as total cost, plus an indexation allowance for each acquisition which forms part of the pool, based on the change in RPI between the date of the acquisition and April 1985.

(b) On the occurrence of a subsequent operative event, the indexed cost of the pool is increased by reference to the change in RPI since the previous operative event (if any) or since April 1985 (if the previous operative event was before April 1985). TCGA 1992 does not require the indexation factor used in this calculation to be rounded to 3 decimal places. Note that:

    (i) No indexation adjustment is required if the operative event in question is an acquisition of shares and the s104 holding was previously empty.

    (ii) No indexation adjustment is required if RPI has gone down since the previous operative event.

    (iii) No further indexation adjustments are required once the indexed cost of the s104 holding has been adjusted to reflect inflation up to 31 December 2017 (the date at which indexation allowance has now been frozen).

(c) The pool is then adjusted as follows:

    (i) If the event is an acquisition, the number of shares that have been acquired is added to the number of shares in the pool and their cost is added to both the cost and the indexed cost of the pool.

    (ii) If the event is a disposal, the number of shares disposed of is subtracted from the number of shares in the pool. It is then necessary to deduct a proportion of the cost and indexed cost of the pool. Strictly speaking, this proportion should be calculated using the part disposal fraction (see Chapter 18) which takes into account the value of the shares disposed of and the value of the shares remaining. In most cases, however, the value per share of the shares disposed of will be the same as the value per share of the shares remaining, so that the proportion to be deducted from the cost and indexed cost of the pool can be based upon the *number* of shares disposed of.

The unindexed gain (or loss) arising on a disposal from the pool is calculated as the difference between the disposal proceeds and the amount which has been subtracted from the cost of the pool as a consequence of the disposal. The indexation allowance due on the disposal is the difference between the amount subtracted from the cost of the pool and the amount subtracted from the indexed cost of the pool. As usual, indexation allowance cannot be used to create a loss or to increase a loss.

EXAMPLE 4

A company makes the following acquisitions of ordinary shares in JKL plc:

Date	No of shares	Cost £	RPI
1 July 1983	5,000	6,300	85.30
2 August 1984	2,000	2,500	89.94
3 February 1997	1,200	2,300	155.0
4 June 2003	1,800	3,400	181.3

The company sells 500 shares on 8 July 2022.

(a) Calculate the cost and indexed cost of the s104 holding on 8 July 2022, just prior to and just after the above disposal.

(RPI for April 1985 is 94.78 and RPI for December 2017 is 278.1).

(b) Compute the chargeable gain or allowable loss on the disposal if sale proceeds are:

(i)   £2,800   (ii)   £1,000   (iii)   £700

Solution

(a) The cost and the indexed cost of the s104 holding on 8 July 2022 are calculated as follows:

	No of shares	Cost £	Indexed cost £
Bought 1 July 1983	5,000	6,300	6,300
Bought 2 August 1984	2,000	2,500	2,500
Add: Indexation to April 1985			
(a) $\dfrac{94.78 - 85.30}{85.30} = 0.111$			
0.111 x £6,300			699
(b) $\dfrac{94.78 - 89.94}{89.94} = 0.054$			
0.054 x £2,500			135
s104 holding at 1 April 1985	7,000	8,800	9,634
Add: Indexation to February 1997			
$\dfrac{155.0 - 94.78}{94.78}$ x £9,634			6,121
			15,755
Bought 3 February 1997	1,200	2,300	2,300
s104 holding at 3 February 1997	8,200	11,100	18,055

	No of shares	Cost £	Indexed cost £
s104 holding at 3 February 1997	8,200	11,100	18,055
Add: Indexation to June 2003			
$\dfrac{181.3 - 155.0}{155.0}$ x £18,055			3,064
			21,119
Bought 4 June 2003	1,800	3,400	3,400
s104 holding at 4 June 2003	10,000	14,500	24,519
Add: Indexation to December 2017			
$\dfrac{278.1 - 181.3}{181.3}$ x £24,519			13,091
s104 holding b/f at 8 July 2022	10,000	14,500	37,610
Sold 8 July 2022 (500/10,000ths)	(500)	(725)	(1,881)
s104 holding c/f at 8 July 2022	9,500	13,775	35,729

Notes:

1. The indexation allowance calculated on operative events occurring after 5 April 1985 has not been rounded off to 3 decimal places.

2. The disposal in July 2022 must have come from the s104 holding since it cannot be matched against shares acquired on the same day or in the previous nine days.

3. The disposal is 500 shares out of a holding of 10,000. Therefore 500/10,000ths or 1/20th of the pool has been sold and so 1/20th of the cost and indexed cost are subtracted from the pool.

4. The cost of the shares disposed of is £725. Since the equivalent indexed cost is £1,881, the indexation allowance due on the disposal is £1,156 (£1,881 - £725).

(b)

	(i) £	(ii) £	(iii) £
Sale proceeds	2,800	1,000	700
Less: Cost	725	725	725
Unindexed gain or loss	2,075	275	(25)
Less: Indexation allowance (£1,156)	1,156	275	nil
Chargeable gain/(allowable loss)	919	nil	(25)

Bonus issues and rights issues

As explained in Chapter 20, bonus issues and rights issues are regarded as reorganisations of share capital and shares acquired as a consequence of such issues are not treated as acquisitions in the normal way. Instead, the required treatment of bonus shares and rights shares is to uplift the number of shares in each of the taxpayer's existing holdings. In the case of rights issues, it is also necessary to increase the cost of those holdings, since rights shares (unlike bonus shares) are not acquired free of charge[†].

[†] *A complication arises if a company which has both a s104 holding and a 1982 holding of shares in another company then acquires rights shares in that company. The required treatment is explained on the website that accompanies this book.*

EXAMPLE 5

A company made the following acquisitions of ordinary shares in Rujon plc:

Date	No of shares	Cost £	RPI
23 January 1997	600	2,400	154.4
18 June 2004	400	2,000	186.8

On 1 May 2012 (RPI 242.4), Rujon plc made a 1 for 5 rights issue at £8 per share and the company bought the shares it was offered. Calculate the chargeable gain arising in August 2022 when the company sold 750 shares for £20 each. (RPI December 2017 was 278.1).

Solution

The s104 holding:

	No of shares	Cost £	Indexed cost £
Bought 23 January 1997	600	2,400	2,400
Add: Indexation to June 2004			
$\dfrac{186.8 - 154.4}{154.4}$ x £2,400			504
			2,904
Bought 18 June 2004	400	2,000	2,000
	1,000	4,400	4,904
Add: Indexation to May 2012			
$\dfrac{242.4 - 186.8}{186.8}$ x £4,904			1,460
			6,364
Rights issue 1 May 2012 (1 for 5)	200	1,600	1,600
s104 holding at 1 May 2012	1,200	6,000	7,964

	No of shares	Cost £	Indexed cost £
s104 holding at 1 May 2012	1,200	6,000	7,964
Add: Indexation to December 2017			
$\dfrac{278.1 - 242.4}{242.4}$ x £7,964			1,173
			9,137
Sold August 2022 (750/1,200ths)	(750)	(3,750)	(5,711)
s104 holding c/f at August 2022	450	2,250	3,426

The gain arising on the disposal is:

	£
Sale proceeds (750 @ £20)	15,000
Less: Cost	3,750
Unindexed gain	11,250
Less: Indexation allowance	
(£5,711 - £3,750)	1,961
Chargeable gain	9,289

Disposal of a substantial shareholding

A gain arising on the disposal of all or part of a "substantial shareholding" by an investor company is (subject to conditions) exempt from corporation tax. Similarly, any loss arising on such a disposal is not an allowable loss. For this purpose, an investor company holds a substantial shareholding in an investee company if:

(a)   it holds at least 10% of that company's ordinary share capital, *and*

(b)   it is entitled to at least 10% of that company's profits, *and*

(c)   it would (on a winding up) be entitled to at least 10% of that company's assets.

This exemption applies only if the investor company has held a substantial shareholding in the investee company throughout a 12-month period beginning not more than six years before the disposal. Furthermore, the investee company must be a trading company.

Summary

▸ A company's chargeable assets usually consist of non-current assets such as land and buildings, plant and investments. Non-chargeable assets include motor cars, chattels worth up to £6,000, wasting chattels, gilts and qualifying corporate bonds.

▸ A chargeable disposal occurs when the whole or part of a chargeable asset is sold or given away (unless given to a charity).

▸ If allowable losses for an accounting period exceed chargeable gains, the net losses are carried forward and relieved against chargeable gains in subsequent periods.

▸ Companies may claim indexation allowance in relation to allowable expenditure incurred before 1 January 2018. The indexation allowance available depends upon the amount of the expenditure and the change in RPI between the month in which the expenditure was incurred and the month of disposal (or December 2017 if earlier).

▸ Indexation allowance cannot be used to convert a gain into a loss and cannot be used to increase an unindexed loss.

▸ Rebasing does not always apply when a company disposes of an asset acquired before 31 March 1982. In general, it is necessary to perform a calculation based on original cost as well as the rebasing calculation. The chargeable gain (allowable loss) is the lower of the two gains (losses) given by these calculations.

▸ But a company may elect that the rebasing method should always be used when calculating the gain or loss arising on disposals of assets held on 31 March 1982.

▸ When a company makes a disposal of shares or securities, the disposal is matched first against shares acquired on the same day, then against shares acquired in the previous nine days, then against the s104 holding and then against the 1982 holding.

▸ When calculating the indexed cost of the s104 holding, indexation factors are not rounded to three decimal places.

▸ Bonus shares and rights shares uplift the number of shares in the company's existing holdings. Rights shares also increase the cost of those holdings.

▸ A gain arising on the disposal of a substantial shareholding by an investor company is exempt from corporation tax, subject to certain conditions.

Retail Prices Index (RPI)

(*Source*: Office for National Statistics)

	Jan	Feb	Mar	Apr	May	Jun	Jul	Aug	Sep	Oct	Nov	Dec
1982			79.44	81.04	81.62	81.85	81.88	81.90	81.85	82.26	82.66	82.51
1983	82.61	82.97	83.12	84.28	84.64	84.84	85.30	85.68	86.06	86.36	86.67	86.89
1984	86.84	87.20	87.48	88.64	88.97	89.20	89.10	89.94	90.11	90.67	90.95	90.87
1985	91.20	91.94	92.80	94.78	95.21	95.41	95.23	95.49	95.44	95.59	95.92	96.05
1986	96.25	96.60	96.73	97.67	97.85	97.79	97.52	97.82	98.30	98.45	99.29	99.62
1987	100.0	100.4	100.6	101.8	101.9	101.9	101.8	102.1	102.4	102.9	103.4	103.3
1988	103.3	103.7	104.1	105.8	106.2	106.6	106.7	107.9	108.4	109.5	110.0	110.3
1989	111.0	111.8	112.3	114.3	115.0	115.4	115.5	115.8	116.6	117.5	118.5	118.8
1990	119.5	120.2	121.4	125.1	126.2	126.7	126.8	128.1	129.3	130.3	130.0	129.9
1991	130.2	130.9	131.4	133.1	133.5	134.1	133.8	134.1	134.6	135.1	135.6	135.7
1992	135.6	136.3	136.7	138.8	139.3	139.3	138.8	138.9	139.4	139.9	139.7	139.2
1993	137.9	138.8	139.3	140.6	141.1	141.0	140.7	141.3	141.9	141.8	141.6	141.9
1994	141.3	142.1	142.5	144.2	144.7	144.7	144.0	144.7	145.0	145.2	145.3	146.0
1995	146.0	146.9	147.5	149.0	149.6	149.8	149.1	149.9	150.6	149.8	149.8	150.7
1996	150.2	150.9	151.5	152.6	152.9	153.0	152.4	153.1	153.8	153.8	153.9	154.4
1997	154.4	155.0	155.4	156.3	156.9	157.5	157.5	158.5	159.3	159.5	159.6	160.0
1998	159.5	160.3	160.8	162.6	163.5	163.4	163.0	163.7	164.4	164.5	164.4	164.4
1999	163.4	163.7	164.1	165.2	165.6	165.6	165.1	165.5	166.2	166.5	166.7	167.3
2000	166.6	167.5	168.4	170.1	170.7	171.1	170.5	170.5	171.7	171.6	172.1	172.2
2001	171.1	172.0	172.2	173.1	174.2	174.4	173.3	174.0	174.6	174.3	173.6	173.4
2002	173.3	173.8	174.5	175.7	176.2	176.2	175.9	176.4	177.6	177.9	178.2	178.5
2003	178.4	179.3	179.9	181.2	181.5	181.3	181.3	181.6	182.5	182.6	182.7	183.5
2004	183.1	183.8	184.6	185.7	186.5	186.8	186.8	187.4	188.1	188.6	189.0	189.9
2005	188.9	189.6	190.5	191.6	192.0	192.2	192.2	192.6	193.1	193.3	193.6	194.1
2006	193.4	194.2	195.0	196.5	197.7	198.5	198.5	199.2	200.1	200.4	201.1	202.7
2007	201.6	203.1	204.4	205.4	206.2	207.3	206.1	207.3	208.0	208.9	209.7	210.9
2008	209.8	211.4	212.1	214.0	215.1	216.8	216.5	217.2	218.4	217.7	216.0	212.9
2009	210.1	211.4	211.3	211.5	212.8	213.4	213.4	214.4	215.3	216.0	216.6	218.0
2010	217.9	219.2	220.7	222.8	223.6	224.1	223.6	224.5	225.3	225.8	226.8	228.4
2011	229.0	231.3	232.5	234.4	235.2	235.2	234.7	236.1	237.9	238.0	238.5	239.4
2012	238.0	239.9	240.8	242.5	242.4	241.8	242.1	243.0	244.2	245.6	245.6	246.8
2013	245.8	247.6	248.7	249.5	250.0	249.7	249.7	251.0	251.9	251.9	252.1	253.4
2014	252.6	254.2	254.8	255.7	255.9	256.3	256.0	257.0	257.6	257.7	257.1	257.5
2015	255.4	256.7	257.1	258.0	258.5	258.9	258.6	259.8	259.6	259.5	259.8	260.6
2016	258.8	260.0	261.1	261.4	262.1	263.1	263.4	264.4	264.9	264.8	265.5	267.1
2017	265.5	268.4	269.3	270.6	271.7	272.3	272.9	274.7	275.1	275.3	275.8	278.1

Note: Finance Act 2018 froze indexation allowance at 31 December 2017.

Exercises

A set of multiple choice questions for this chapter is available on the accompanying website.

24.1 A company made the following disposals during the year to 31 March 2023:

(a) A factory building was sold for £650,000 on 13 June 2022. This building had cost £300,000 in August 2000 (RPI 170.5) and was extended in July 2002 (RPI 175.9) at a cost of £50,000.

(b) An office building was sold for £1,100,000 on 15 September 2022 and was then immediately replaced by another office building costing £1,050,000. The building sold in September 2022 had cost £600,000 in February 2003 (RPI 179.3). Rollover relief was claimed on the disposal of this building.

(c) A computer system was given to a charity on 14 July 2022. This computer system had cost £5,000 in September 2016 (RPI 264.9) and had a market value of £500 in July 2022. Capital allowances had been claimed in relation to the computer system.

(d) A motor car was sold for £80,000 on 12 June 2022. The car had cost £100,000 in June 2019. Capital allowances had been claimed.

(e) An item of movable plant and machinery was sold for £30,000 on 16 September 2022. This item had cost £70,000 in January 2015 (RPI 255.4). Capital allowances had been claimed in relation to the item.

(f) 8,000 ordinary shares in Exxak plc were sold for £80,000 on 18 December 2022. Shares in Exxak plc had been bought as follows:

Date	No. of shares	Cost	RPI
		£	
22 November 2002	4,000	16,000	178.2
14 December 2006	6,000	30,000	202.7
12 December 2022	3,000	36,000	-

(g) Government securities were sold for £40,000 on 17 October 2022. These securities had cost £45,000 in October 2015 (RPI 259.5).

The RPI for December 2017 was 278.1.

Required:

Compute the chargeable gain or allowable loss arising on each of the above disposals and outline any other corporation tax consequences of each disposal. Also compute the net chargeable gains figure which should be included in the company's taxable total profits for the year to 31 March 2023.

24.2   PCC Ltd is a manufacturing company which prepares accounts to 31 December each year. The company made the following disposals of chargeable assets in the year to 31 December 2022:

(i)   On 12 September 2022, 4,500 ordinary shares in Epsilon plc were sold for £7.50 each. PCC Ltd had bought ordinary shares in Epsilon plc as follows:

		£
14 January 1988	Bought 2,000 shares	4,000
27 June 1991	Bought 3,000 shares	15,000
10 March 2001	Bought 4,000 shares	28,000

(ii)   On 9 October 2022, two watercolour paintings (which do not form a set) were sold at auction. In each case, the auctioneer charged a 10% commission. The paintings had been acquired for £2,000 each in September 2002 and had been hanging in the company's reception area ever since. The net sale proceeds of the paintings (after deducting commission) were £5,175 and £5,805 respectively.

(iii)   On 1 June 2022, a short lease was assigned for £7,000. The lease was originally acquired as a 20-year lease on 1 January 2008 at a cost of £20,000.

(iv)   On 25 November 2022, a freehold property was sold for £115,000. The building had been acquired in August 2004 for £50,000. In February 2022 the company bought fixed plant for £100,000.

PCC Ltd intends to make any valid election which will reduce the amount of gains that are chargeable to corporation tax in the year to 31 December 2022.

On 1 January 2022, the company had capital losses brought forward of £6,689.

Required:

Compute the chargeable gain or allowable loss arising on each of the above disposals. Hence compute the net chargeable gains figure which should be charged to corporation tax for the year to 31 December 2022. Assume Retail Price Indices as follows:

January 1988	103.3	August 2004	187.4
June 1991	134.1	January 2008	209.8
March 2001	172.2	December 2017	278.1
September 2002	177.6		

Extracts from the short lease amortisation table given in Schedule 8 of the Taxation of Chargeable Gains Act 1992 are as follows:

5 years   26.722   6 years   31.195   20 years   72.770

(CIPFA)

*24.3   Timberlake Ltd prepares accounts to 31 March each year. The company made the following disposals of chargeable assets in the year to 31 March 2023:

(i)   In February 2023, a rare Bentley motor car used by the company's Managing Director was sold for £750,000. This car had cost £300,000 in November 2006.

(ii)   In October 2022, an office building was sold for £680,000. The building had been acquired in March 1987 for £170,000 and it was extended in September 1988 at a cost of £40,000.

(iii) In June 2022, a plot of land was sold for £120,000. This land had cost £42,000 in November 2004 and had been used for trade purposes.

In June 2005, the company had sold land for £50,000 and had made a claim for rollover relief in relation to this disposal. This land had cost £10,000 in October 1999 and had been used for trade purposes.

(iv)   In August 2022, gilt-edged stocks bought for £100,000 in January 2008 were sold for £110,500.

(v)   In June 2022, plant and machinery which was bought for £19,500 in August 2021 was sold for £22,500. In March 2023, plant and machinery bought for £16,000 in March 2017 was sold for £9,000. Capital allowances had been claimed in relation to both of these items.

(vi)   In February 2023, the company sold 500 ordinary shares in Theta plc for £10 per share. Timberlake Ltd had bought ordinary shares in Theta plc as follows:

		£
June 2001	Bought 2,500 shares	12,500
January 2008	Bought 3,000 shares	18,000

Timberlake Ltd had capital losses brought forward of £156,200 on 1 April 2022.

Required:

(a)   Compute the chargeable gain or allowable loss arising on each of the disposals made during the year to 31 March 2023. Assume Retail Price Indices as follows:

March 1987	100.6	June 2005	192.2
September 1988	108.4	November 2006	201.1
October 1999	166.5	January 2008	209.8
June 2001	174.4	March 2017	269.3
November 2004	189.0	December 2017	278.1

(b)   Compute the chargeable gains figure which should be included in the company's taxable total profits for the year to 31 March 2023.

(CIPFA)

Chapter 25

Computation and payment of the corporation tax liability

Introduction

Having ascertained a company's "taxable total profits" for an accounting period (including any chargeable gains), the next step is to compute the company's corporation tax liability for that period. The purpose of this chapter is to explain how the corporation tax liability is computed and to describe the system by means of which the tax is collected.

Corporation tax financial years

The rate of corporation tax is set for each *financial year*. For corporation tax purposes, a financial year (FY) runs from 1 April to 31 March inclusive and is identified by the year in which it begins. For example:

– FY2021 began on 1 April 2021 and ended on 31 March 2022
– FY2022 began on 1 April 2022 and ends on 31 March 2023

The fiscal year which applies to individuals (from 6 April to the following 5 April) is not relevant when dealing with corporation tax matters. Note that:

(a) If a company has an accounting period which coincides with a financial year (i.e. the year to 31 March) or which is entirely contained within a financial year, the rate of corporation tax for that financial year is applied to the company's taxable total profits for the accounting period, giving the corporation tax liability.

(b) If an accounting period straddles 31 March, the taxable total profits for the period are time-apportioned between the two financial years involved and then charged to tax at the rates applicable in those two years. A simple time-apportionment is always made in these circumstances. This is different from the way in which the profits of a long period of account are allocated between accounting periods (see Chapter 23).

It may seem obvious that the apportionment referred to in (b) above will be required only if the rate of corporation tax has changed from one financial year to the next. In practice, however, the amount of tax payable for each financial year has to be calculated separately in order to ascertain the figures required for the company's tax return.

EXAMPLE 1

A company has taxable total profits of £5,000,000 for an accounting period. Explain how the corporation tax liability for this period will be calculated if:

(a) the accounting period is the 12 months to 31 March 2023

(b) the accounting period is the nine months to 31 January 2023

(c) the accounting period is the ten months to 31 October 2022.

Solution

(a) The 12 months to 31 March 2023 coincide with FY2022, so the taxable total profits of £5,000,000 will be taxed at the FY2022 rate.

(b) The nine months to 31 January 2023 are entirely contained within FY2022, so the taxable total profits of £5,000,000 will be taxed at the FY2022 rate.

(c) The ten months to 31 October 2022 are contained partly within FY2021 (3 months) and partly within FY2022 (7 months). The taxable total profits of £5,000,000 will be time-apportioned between FYs as follows:

FY2021   1 Jan 2022 to 31 March 2022   £5,000,000 x 3/10 = £1,500,000
FY2022   1 April 2022 to 31 Oct 2022   £5,000,000 x 7/10 = £3,500,000

The profits of £1,500,000 falling into FY2021 will be taxed at the FY2021 rate and the profits of £3,500,000 falling into FY2022 will be taxed at the FY2022 rate.

Rates of corporation tax

At present, there is a single rate[†][‡] of corporation tax (the "main rate") for each financial year. The main rate has been 19% for several years and this remains the case for FY2022. But the main rate will rise to 25% in FY2023. In summary:

FY2018	**19%**	FY2019	**19%**	FY2020	**19%**
FY2021	**19%**	FY2022	**19%**	FY2023	**25%**

When the main rate rises to 25%, a "small profits rate" of 19% will be introduced and this will apply to companies with profits not exceeding £50,000. Further details of the rates structure which will apply as from FY2023 are given at the end of this chapter.

[†] *Different rates of corporation tax apply to "ring fence profits". However, these are profits arising from certain oil extraction activities and are outside the scope of this book.*

[‡] *Northern Ireland has been granted the power to set its own rate of corporation tax (subject to conditions) and it is expected that the main rate in Northern Ireland will eventually fall to 12.5% so as to match the rate in the Republic of Ireland. However, this is contingent upon the Northern Ireland Executive being able to demonstrate that its finances are on a sustainable footing.*

EXAMPLE 2

Calculate the corporation tax liability of each of the following companies for the accounting period concerned:

(a) A01 Ltd has taxable total profits of £800,000 for the year to 31 March 2023.

(b) A02 Ltd has taxable total profits of £250,000 for the six months to 31 October 2022.

(c) A03 Ltd has taxable total profits of £1,600,000 for the year to 31 December 2022.

In the case of A03 Ltd, what would the corporation tax liability be if the accounting period had been the year to 31 December 2023?

Solution

(a) The accounting period coincides with FY2022 so the applicable rate of corporation tax is the FY2022 main rate of 19%. The liability is £152,000 (£800,000 × 19%).

(b) The accounting period is entirely contained within FY2022 so the applicable rate of corporation tax is the FY2022 main rate of 19%. The corporation tax liability for the period is £47,500 (£250,000 × 19%).

(c) The first three months of the accounting period fall into FY2021 (main rate 19%) and the remaining nine months fall into FY2022 (main rate also 19%). The liability for the year is (3/12 × £1,600,000 × 19%) + (9/12 × £1,600,000 × 19%) = £304,000.

If the accounting period had been the year to 31 December 2023, the tax liability would be (3/12 × £1,600,000 × 19%) + (9/12 × £1,600,000 × 25%) = £376,000.

Due date of payment

For most companies, the corporation tax liability for an accounting period is payable by means of a single payment which falls due nine months and one day after the end of the period. However, certain large companies are required to pay their corporation tax by instalments (see below). Electronic payment of corporation tax is now compulsory.

EXAMPLE 3

(a) A company prepares a set of accounts for the year to 31 July 2022. When is the corporation tax liability for this period due for payment?

(b) A company prepares a set of accounts for the 18 months to 31 December 2022. When is the corporation tax liability for this period due for payment?

(c) A company has taxable total profits of £360,000 for the nine months to 30 November 2022. Calculate the corporation tax liability for this period and state the date on which this tax is due for payment.

Assume in all cases that the company is not required to pay by instalments.

Solution

(a) The year to 31 July 2022 is a single accounting period. Corporation tax for the period is payable nine months and one day after 31 July 2022, which is 1 May 2023.

(b) This period of account breaks down into two accounting periods. These are the year to 30 June 2022 and the six months to 31 December 2022. Corporation tax for these accounting periods is due as follows:

   (i) Corporation tax for the year to 30 June 2022 is payable nine months and one day after 30 June 2022, which is 1 April 2023.

   (ii) Corporation tax for the six months to 31 December 2022 is payable nine months and one day after 31 December 2022, which is 1 October 2023.

(c) The first month of the accounting period (March 2022) falls into FY2021 (main rate 19%). The remaining eight months fall into FY2022 (main rate also 19%). Therefore the tax liability is $(1/9 \times £360{,}000 \times 19\%) + (8/9 \times £360{,}000 \times 19\%) = £68{,}400$.

   The liability of £68,400 is payable nine months and one day after 30 November 2022, which is 1 September 2023.

Payment by instalments

As mentioned above, large companies are generally required to pay their corporation tax by instalments. The main features of the instalments system are as follows:

(a) In general, a company is defined as a "large company" for an accounting period if it has augmented profits for that period which exceed £1,500,000. For this purpose, a company's "augmented profits" are its taxable total profits for the period concerned *plus* exempt dividends received[†]. However, a large company is not required to pay tax by instalments for an accounting period if:

   (i) it has augmented profits of £10 million or less for the accounting period and was not a large company in the 12 months preceding that period, or

   (ii) its tax liability for the period does not exceed £10,000.

   The limits of £1,500,000, £10 million and £10,000 are all scaled down for accounting periods of less than 12 months. Furthermore, the £1,500,000 and £10 million limits are reduced if the company has one or more related companies (see Chapter 28).

(b) Instalment payments are based on the company's own estimate of its corporation tax liability for the accounting period. When the tax liability for the year is finalised, the company is charged interest on any underpaid instalments and is paid interest on any overpaid instalments.

[†] *If a company belongs to a group of companies, any "intra-group" dividends received from other companies in the group are ignored when calculating augmented profits. See Chapter 28 of this book for more information on groups of companies.*

(c)   In the case of a 12-month accounting period there are four equal instalments. The first instalment falls due six months and 14 days from the start of the accounting period. The remaining three instalments then fall due at quarterly intervals. For instance, if the accounting period is the year to 31 December 2022, instalments fall due on 14 July 2022, 14 October 2022, 14 January 2023 and 14 April 2023.

(d)   If an accounting period is less than 12 months in length, the final instalment is always due three months and 14 days after the end of the period, as would also be the case for a 12-month period. Earlier instalments fall due on the usual quarterly dates (beginning six months and 14 days from the start of the period) but only to the extent that those dates are before the date of the final instalment. For instance, if the accounting period is the eight months to 31 August 2022, corporation tax is due in three instalments on 14 July 2022, 14 October 2022 and 14 December 2022.

In order to calculate the amount of each instalment in these circumstances, it is first necessary to multiply the corporation tax liability by 3/n, where n is the number of months in the accounting period. Each instalment is then equal to this figure, except that the final instalment may be lower than this in order to bring the total of the instalments to the correct amount.

EXAMPLE 4

A large company has a corporation tax liability of £720,000 for an accounting period. The company was also large for the previous 12 months. State the dates on which instalments are payable and compute the amount of each instalment if the accounting period is:

(a)   the year to 31 March 2023   (b)   the five months to 31 May 2022.

Solution

(a)   Instalments are due on 14 October 2022, 14 January 2023, 14 April 2023 and 14 July 2023. Each instalment is equal to £720,000 x 3/12 = £180,000.

(b)   (i)   The date which is three months and 14 days after the end of the accounting period is 14 September 2022, so this is the date of the final instalment.

(ii)   The first instalment is due six months and 14 days from the start of the accounting period. The period began on 1 January 2022 so the first instalment is due on 14 July 2022.

(iii) The next instalment would normally be due three months later on 14 October 2022. However, this date falls after the date of the final instalment and so this instalment cannot be fitted in.

Therefore only two instalments are required and these are payable on 14 July 2022 and 14 September 2022. The first instalment is equal to £720,000 x 3/5 = £432,000. The second and final instalment is £288,000, bringing the total to £720,000.

Payment by instalments (very large companies)

A "very large" company is defined as one with augmented profits which exceed £20m[†] per annum. If a company is very large, the dates on which it is required to pay its instalments are all advanced by four months. So the instalments for a 12-month accounting period fall due on the 14th day of the third, sixth, ninth and twelfth months of that period.

[†] *The £20m limit is scaled down for accounting periods of less than 12 months and is also reduced if the company has one or more related companies (see Chapter 28).*

Income tax deducted at source

Certain payments made by companies are made net of basic rate income tax. These consist mainly of patent royalties and loan interest paid to individuals. A company which makes such payments must account to HMRC for the tax deducted at source. Similarly, a company which receives any income net of income tax may reclaim the tax suffered at source.

Further details are available on the website which accompanies this textbook. The website can be accessed at go.pearson.com/uk/he/resources.

Shadow ACT

Until 6 April 1999, companies were obliged to pay Advance Corporation Tax (ACT) when paying dividends. Subject to certain conditions, the ACT paid in respect of an accounting period was then offset against the company's corporation tax liability for the period.

ACT was abolished as from 6 April 1999 but some aspects of the ACT system are still relevant in a small number of cases. The present situation with regard to ACT (the "shadow ACT" system) is explained on the website which accompanies this textbook.

Interest on underpaid and overpaid corporation tax

Interest on underpaid corporation tax generally runs from the date on which the tax should have been paid until the date on which it is actually paid. Interest on overpaid corporation tax generally runs from the date on which the tax was paid or (if later) the date on which it was due to be paid, until the date of repayment. Interest on overpaid corporation tax is calculated at a lower rate than interest on underpaid tax. Note that:

(a) It is HMRC practice to use a denominator of 366 when calculating interest on underpaid tax and to use a denominator of 365 when calculating interest on overpaid tax, whether or not a leap year is involved.

(b) Interest receivable on a repayment of overpaid corporation tax is taxable as a credit arising from a non-trading loan relationship. Similarly, interest payable on underpaid corporation tax is deductible as a non-trading debit (see Chapter 23).

(c) The interest rate which applies to underpaid instalments is generally lower than the normal rate of interest during the period from the due date of the first instalment to the date which falls nine months and one day after the end of the accounting period.

Similarly, the interest rate applicable to overpaid instalments is generally higher than the normal rate during this period.

(d) If a company makes instalment payments on the assumption that it is a large company and this assumption later proves to be false, interest on any repaid instalments runs from the date on which a truly large company would have paid those instalments or (if later) the actual date of payment.

EXAMPLE 5

(a) A company calculates its corporation tax liability for the year to 30 September 2022 as £250,000 and pays this amount on the due date. The correct liability for the year eventually turns out to be £274,000 and the company pays a further £24,000 on 17 October 2023. Calculate the amount of interest payable by the company (assuming an interest rate of 3.25% per annum).

(b) A company calculates its corporation tax liability for the year to 30 November 2022 as £39,000 and pays this amount on the due date. The correct liability for the year eventually turns out to be only £33,300. The necessary repayment is made on 18 February 2024. Calculate the amount of interest payable to the company (assuming an interest rate of 0.5% per annum).

Neither company is a large company for the purposes of payment by instalments.

Solution

(a) The due date of payment for the year to 30 September 2022 is 1 July 2023 (i.e. nine months and one day from the end of the accounting period). Most of the corporation tax liability is settled on the due date but the final £24,000 is not paid until 17 October 2023, which is 108 days late. Interest payable by the company is:

$$£24,000 \times 3.25\% \times \frac{108}{366} = £230.16$$

(b) The due date for the year to 30 November 2022 is 1 September 2023. The overpaid tax of £5,700 is paid on this date but is not repaid until 18 February 2024, which is 170 days later. Interest payable to the company is:

$$£5,700 \times 0.5\% \times \frac{170}{365} = £13.27$$

Self Assessment

The system of "self assessment" for companies is similar in many ways to the equivalent system that applies for individuals (see Chapter 1). The main features of Corporation Tax Self Assessment (CTSA) are as follows:

(a) On the issue of an official notice by HM Revenue and Customs, a company must file a corporation tax return† for the accounting period specified in the notice, together with supporting accounts and computations. The return must normally be filed with HMRC by the *latest* of the following dates:

  (i) 12 months after the end of the accounting period specified in the notice

  (ii) 12 months after the end of the period of account in which the last day of the specified accounting period falls (but periods of account which last for more than 18 months are treated for this purpose as ending after 18 months)

  (iii) 3 months after issue of the notice.

  Most companies prepare their accounts to the same date each year and notices are usually issued within a few weeks of the end of each period of account, so that the required filing date is normally 12 months after the end of the period of account. There is nothing to prevent a company from submitting an early return. Online filing is now compulsory.

(b) The corporation tax return includes a formal self-assessment of the company's tax liability for the accounting period which is covered by the return. Unlike individuals, a company is *not* able to ask HMRC to calculate the tax liability.

(c) A company which is chargeable to corporation tax for an accounting period but has not received a notice requiring submission of a return must notify HMRC of its chargeability to tax within 12 months of the end of the period.

(d) HMRC has the right to amend a company's return (so as to correct obvious errors or omissions or anything else that is believed to be incorrect) within nine months of the date on which the return is filed. Similarly, the company has the right to amend its return and self-assessment within 12 months of the required filing date for that return.

  A company which believes that it has made an overpayment of corporation tax may make a claim for recovery of this overpaid tax (whether or not the purported overpayment was caused by an error in a tax return). Such a claim must be made within four years of the end of the accounting period to which it relates. Depending upon the circumstances of the case, HMRC may or may not accept the claim.

† *As part of the "Making Tax Digital" project (see Chapter 1) online "digital tax accounts" are to be introduced for companies and these will replace the corporation tax return. In general, companies will be required to update their digital tax accounts quarterly. However, quarterly reporting will probably not apply to "very large" companies with annual profits in excess of £20m, who already pay their tax at quarterly intervals during the accounting period (see earlier in this chapter). It is expected that MTD for corporation tax will not be introduced until at least April 2026.*

(e) If HMRC wishes to open an enquiry into a company's tax return which is filed on or before the required filing date, then the enquiry must usually begin within 12 months of the date on which the return is filed. This means that the "enquiry window" for returns which are submitted early will close correspondingly early.

However, if a company's tax return is filed late or if the company amends its tax return, the deadline for starting an enquiry is extended to the quarter date (31 January, 30 April, 31 July or 31 October) which follows the first anniversary of the date that the return is filed or the amendment is submitted.

(f) Unless an enquiry is opened, the tax liability for an accounting period may usually be regarded as finalised when the enquiry window closes. But HMRC may raise a later "discovery assessment" if it is discovered that insufficient tax has been assessed.

The time limit for making a discovery assessment is normally four years after the end of the accounting period concerned. However, this increases to six years if the loss of tax has been caused by negligence on the part of the company (or a related person) and 20 years in the case of dishonesty.

(g) If a company fails to file a return by the required date, HMRC may make a determination of the amount of tax due. A determination can be displaced only if the company delivers the required return.

(h) A company is required to keep and preserve adequate records to substantiate the information entered on its tax return. These records must be retained for at least six years after the end of the accounting period concerned.

(i) Corporation tax appeals are dealt with in much the same way as income tax appeals (see Chapter 1). The tax avoidance disclosure regime (DOTAS) which applies to income tax also applies to corporation tax.

Penalties

The main penalties which may be imposed in relation to corporation tax are as follows:

(a) **Late submission of tax return**. Penalties are charged if a company does not file its corporation tax return by the required date. These penalties are currently as follows:

    (i) If the return is up to three months late, a fixed penalty is charged of £100. This is increased to £500 for a third consecutive late return.

    (ii) If the return is over three months late, a fixed penalty is charged of £200. This is increased to £1,000 for a third consecutive late return.

    (iii) In addition to the above penalties, a further tax-geared penalty is charged if the return is submitted more than six months late. If the return is between six and 12 months late, the penalty is 10% of the tax unpaid six months after the return was due. If the return is more than 12 months late, the penalty rises to 20% of the tax unpaid six months after the return was due.

(b) **Failure to notify**. A penalty may be charged if a company which has not filed a tax return (and has not been issued with a notice requiring such a return) fails to notify HMRC of its chargeability to tax within 12 months of the end of the accounting period concerned. The penalty for a "failure to notify" is expressed as a percentage of the amount of tax which remains unpaid 12 months after the end of the period.

   As is the case for income tax (see Chapter 15) the applicable percentage varies from 30% to 100%, depending upon whether the failure to notify has been deliberate and/or concealed. The amount of any penalty is reduced if the failure is voluntarily disclosed and no penalty is charged if there is "reasonable excuse" for the failure.

(c) **Inaccurate tax returns**. A penalty may be charged if an inaccuracy in a tax return or other document leads to an understatement of the amount of corporation tax payable and the inaccuracy is either careless or deliberate. This penalty regime also applies if HMRC issues an assessment which understates the amount of tax payable and the company fails to take reasonable steps to notify HMRC of this fact within 30 days.

   As is the case for income tax (see Chapter 15) the amount of any penalty depends upon the company's degree of culpability and generally varies between 30% and 100% of the additional corporation tax which becomes payable as a result of correcting the inaccuracy or understatement.

(d) **Failure to keep records**. A company which fails to keep (and preserve) the records required to make a complete and correct tax return is liable to a penalty of up to £3,000 per accounting period.

As explained in Chapter 15, a unified "points-based" penalty system is being introduced across a range of taxes in relation to the late submission of a tax return. However, the implementation date for corporation tax is not yet known. A unified late payment penalty system is also being introduced and this will also apply to corporation tax in due course, despite the fact that late payment of corporation tax does not currently trigger a penalty (although interest is of course charged).

Rates of corporation tax as from FY2023

As stated earlier, the main rate of corporation tax will rise to 25% in FY2023 and a new "small profits rate" of 19% will be introduced. The rate of tax which applies to a company for a given accounting period will then depend upon the size of the company's augmented profits for that period, where augmented profits are the sum of taxable total profits and exempt dividends received. In outline, the system will work as follows:

(a) The small profits rate will apply if augmented profits for the period do not exceed the *lower limit* (£50,000). The main rate will apply if augmented profits are greater than or equal to the *upper limit* (£250,000). These limits will be scaled down proportionately for periods of less than 12 months and will also be scaled down if the company has associated companies (see Chapter 28).

(b) If augmented profits lie between the lower and upper limits, the main rate will apply but the liability will then be reduced by *marginal relief*, calculated in accordance with the following formula:

$$F \times (U - A) \times \frac{N}{A}$$

where: F   = the marginal relief fraction (3/200 for FY2023)
          U   = the upper limit (scaled down if necessary)
          A   = augmented profits
          N   = non-augmented profits (i.e. taxable total profits)

(c) It is important to note that the rate of tax as determined by the above rules is applied to the company's taxable total profits, *not* to its augmented profits.

(d) If an accounting period straddles 1 April 2023, the parts of the period which fall into FY2022 and FY2023 respectively are treated as two separate accounting periods.

EXAMPLE 6

Three companies each prepare a set of accounts for the year to 31 March 2024. Calculate the corporation tax liability of each company given the following information:

(a) A04 Ltd has taxable total profits of £525,000 and no dividends received.

(b) A05 Ltd has taxable total profits of £30,000 and no dividends received.

(c) A06 Ltd has taxable total profits of £42,000 and dividends received of £28,000.

Solution

(a) Augmented profits are £525,000. This figure exceeds the upper limit, so taxable total profits are taxed at the main rate. The liability is £131,250 (£525,000 × 25%).

(b) Augmented profits are £30,000. This figure does not exceed the lower limit, so taxable total profits are taxed at the small profits rate. The liability is £5,700 (£30,000 × 19%).

(c) Augmented profits are £70,000 (£42,000 + £28,000). This figure lies between the lower and upper limits, so taxable total profits are taxed at the main rate and marginal relief is then deducted. The computation is as follows:

	£
Corporation tax on £42,000 @ 25%	10,500.00
Less: Marginal relief:	
$\frac{3}{200}$ x (£250,000 – £70,000) x $\frac{£42,000}{£70,000}$	1,620.00
Corporation tax liability	8,880.00

On taxable total profits of £42,000, a tax liability of £8,880 gives an effective tax rate of 21.14%, which lies between the small profits rate and the main rate.

EXAMPLE 7

A company has taxable total profits of £100,000 for the year to 30 June 2023 and dividends received of £20,000. Calculate the corporation tax liability for the year.

Solution

The first nine months of the accounting period fall into FY2022 (in which all profits are taxed at the main rate of 19%). The remaining three months fall into FY2023.

(i)   For the nine months which fall into FY2022, taxable total profits are (9/12 × £100,000) = £75,000. Augmented profits are not relevant for this purpose in FY2022.

(ii) For the three months which fall into FY2023, taxable total profits are (3/12 × £100,000) = £25,000 and augmented profits are (3/12 × £120,000) = £30,000.

Scaled-down lower and upper limits for a three-month period are (3/12 × £50,000) = £12,500 and (3/12 × £250,000) = £62,500 respectively. Augmented profits of £30,000 lie between these limits.

The computation is as follows:

	£	£
FY2022		
Corporation tax on £75,000 at 19%		14,250.00
FY2023		
Corporation tax on £25,000 at 25%	6,250.00	
Less: Marginal relief:		
$\dfrac{3}{200}$ x (£62,500 − £30,000) x $\dfrac{£25,000}{£30,000}$	406.25	5,843.75
Corporation tax liability		20,093.75

Marginal rate

If augmented profits in FY2023 lie between the lower and upper limits, every £1 by which taxable total profits increase/decrease will generally cause an increase/decrease of 26.5p in the corporation tax liability, as long as augmented profits remain between the limits.

For instance, if a company had taxable total profits of £60,000 for the year to 31 March 2024 and received no dividends, its corporation tax liability would be £12,150. But a £100 increase in profit (to £60,100) would increase the tax liability by £26.50 to £12,176.50 (the calculations are left to the reader). In other words, the company is subject to a *marginal rate* of 26.5%. This is higher than the main rate of 25%, although the marginal rate would be somewhat reduced if the company also received dividends.

Marginal rates may be significant when a company is trying to determine the most tax-efficient way of relieving a loss (see Chapters 26 and 28).

Summary

▸   A corporation tax financial year runs from 1 April to the following 31 March. If a company has an accounting period which straddles 31 March, the taxable total profits for the period are time-apportioned between the two financial years involved and then charged to tax at the rates applicable in those two years.

▸   There is currently a single rate of corporation tax for each financial year (the "main rate"). This has been 19% for several years and will remain at 19% until FY2023.

▸   In FY2023, the main rate will rise to 25%. There will also be a small profits rate of 19%. Marginal relief will smooth the transition between these two rates.

▸   The due date of payment for corporation tax is normally nine months and one day after the end of the accounting period. Large companies are required to pay their tax by instalments (usually quarterly).

▸   Interest is charged on underpaid corporation tax but this interest is deductible under the loan relationships regime as a non-trading debit. Similarly, interest is paid on refunds of overpaid corporation tax but this interest is taxable under the loan relationships regime as a non-trading credit.

▸   The system of Self Assessment for companies is similar in many ways to the system for individuals. However, a company must compute its own corporation tax liability and cannot require HMRC to calculate the tax due.

▸   Companies are generally required to file a corporation tax return within 12 months of the end of each period of account. Online filing is now compulsory. Late submission results in a penalty fine and there are penalties for various other infringements of the law relating to corporation tax.

Exercises

A set of multiple choice questions for this chapter is available on the accompanying website.

25.1   A company's taxable total profits for an accounting period are £3,200,000. Compute the corporation tax liability if the accounting period is:

    (a)   the year to 31 March 2023   (b)   the year to 31 December 2022

    (c)   the ten months to 31 October 2022   (d)   the year to 31 March 2024

    (e)   the year to 30 June 2023   (f)   the eight months to 30 April 2023.

25.2 State the date (or dates) on which corporation tax is due for payment in relation to the following periods of account:

(a)   the year to 31 March 2023

(b)   the six months to 30 November 2022

(c)   the 21 months to 30 June 2022

(d)   the 27 months to 31 August 2022.

Assume in each case that the company concerned is not required to pay corporation tax by instalments.

25.3 (a)   ABC Ltd has taxable total profits of £1,800,000 for the year to 31 March 2023. Taxable total profits were £1,600,000 for the year to 31 March 2022.

Calculate the company's corporation tax liability for the year to 31 March 2023 and state the date (or dates) on which this tax is due to be paid

(b)   DEF Ltd has changed its accounting date from 31 December to 30 June. The first accounts to 30 June are for the six-month period to 30 June 2022. Taxable total profits for this six-month period are £960,000. Taxable total profits for the year to 31 December 2021 were £1,730,000.

Calculate the company's corporation tax liability for the six months to 30 June 2022 and state the date (or dates) on which this tax is due to be paid.

25.4 A company (which is not a member of a group) prepares a set of accounts for the year to 30 September 2022. Calculate the corporation tax liability for the year and state the date (or dates) on which this tax is due to be paid, in each of the following situations:

(a)   Taxable total profits for the year are £4,500,000 and dividends received are £nil.

(b)   Taxable total profits for the year are £1,250,000 and dividends received are £nil.

(c)   Taxable total profits for the year are £1,250,000 and dividends received in the year are £300,000.

Assume in each case that the company was "large" in the year to 30 September 2021.

25.5 A company calculates its corporation tax liability for the year to 31 August 2021 as £120,000 and pays this amount on 1 June 2022. The company's corporation tax return is submitted during August 2022 and the tax liability for the year is finalised at £124,650. The balance of £4,650 is paid on 3 October 2022. The company is not a large company for the purposes of payment by instalments. Calculate the interest payable, assuming an interest rate of 3.25% per annum.

25.6 State the date (or dates) on which a "large" company would be required to settle its corporation tax liability for each of the following accounting periods:

(a) the eleven months to 31 May 2022

(b) the eight months to 30 September 2021

(c) the four months to 30 April 2023

(d) the month to 31 January 2023.

Assume in each case that the company's tax liability for the period exceeds £10,000 and that the company was also large in the previous 12 months.

*25.7   A company (which is not a member of a group) has the following results for the year to
         31 March 2023:

	£
Adjusted trading profit, after deduction of capital allowances	360,284
Bank deposit interest (a/c opened 1 July 2022):	
Received 31 December 2022	9,957
Accrued to 31 March 2023	3,000
Dividend received in January 2023	24,300
Chargeable gains	295,327
Gift Aid donations:	
Paid 30 November 2022	30,000
Accrued to 31 March 2023	20,000

The company intends to make Gift Aid donations of £30,000 every six months, starting
on 30 November 2022.

(a)   Compute the company's corporation tax liability for the year.

(b)   State the date (or dates) on which this tax is due to be paid.

*25.8   A company (which is not a member of a group) has the following results for the 14 months
         to 31 December 2022:

	£
Adjusted trading profit, before deduction of capital allowances	1,413,510
Capital allowances claimed:	
Year to 31 October 2022	222,650
2 months to 31 December 2022	37,210
Chargeable gains:	
Disposal 12 May 2022	16,586
Disposal 6 November 2022	21,692
Building society interest:	
Received 31 December 2021	3,500
Received 31 December 2022	4,300
Dividend received on 25 September 2022	3,150

Accrued building society interest was £3,000 on 31 October 2021, £4,000 on 31 October
2022 and £nil on 31 December 2022.

Compute the company's total corporation tax liability for the 14-month period and state
the date (or dates) on which this tax is due to be paid.

*25.9   Compute the corporation tax liability of each of the following companies:

(a)   CompV Ltd has taxable total profits of £128,000 for the year to 31 March 2024 and
       receives no dividends.

(b)   CompW Ltd has taxable total profits of £48,000 and UK dividends of £6,000 for the
       year to 31 December 2023.

For CompV Ltd, recalculate the corporation tax liability if taxable total profits were lower
by £10,000 and demonstrate that the company's marginal rate is 26.5%.

Chapter 26

Corporation tax losses

Introduction

The tax reliefs available to a company which incurs a trading loss are similar in some ways to those available to individuals (see Chapter 12). In general, trading losses may be carried forward or may be set against the company's profits for the loss-making period and the previous 12 months. However, the corporation tax treatment of trading losses carried forward differs substantially from its income tax equivalent.

This chapter explains the tax reliefs that are currently available in relation to a company's trading losses. The corporation tax treatment of a company's non-trading losses is also considered towards the end of this chapter.

Relief for trading losses

The rules which grant tax relief in relation to a company's trading losses are located in the Corporation Tax Act 2010. The main reliefs provided by this Act are as follows:

(a) **Carry forward of trade loss relief**. A trading loss may be carried forward and set against the company's future profits. This is the relief which takes effect if no other tax relief is claimed in relation to a trading loss. Carried-forward losses incurred before 1 April 2017 may be relieved only against future profits of the same trade.

(b) **Trade loss relief against total profits**. If a claim is made to this effect, a trading loss may be set against the company's total profits of:

   (i) the accounting period in which the loss arises (the "loss-making period"), and

   (ii) if the claim so requires, the 12 months prior to the accounting period in which the loss arises (*extended to three years for losses incurred in accounting periods ending between 1 April 2020 and 31 March 2022*).

   Furthermore, a trading loss which is incurred in the 12 months before the company ceases to carry on that trade (a "terminal loss") may be set against the company's total profits of the preceding three years.

Each of these forms of loss relief is described below.

Carry forward of trade loss relief

The corporation tax treatment of trading losses carried forward depends upon when the losses were incurred. Trading losses incurred in accounting periods commencing on or after 1 April 2017 are treated differently from older losses. A trading loss incurred in a period which straddles that date is apportioned into a "pre-1 April 2017" loss and a "post-1 April 2017" loss and each part of the loss is treated differently. The rules are as follows:

(a) A trading loss which is incurred on or after 1 April 2017 may be carried forward and set against the *total profits* of later periods. The company may stipulate the amount of loss relief (if any) to be given in each later period and there is no obligation to relieve the loss at the earliest opportunity. However, this set-off is not available unless the loss-making trade is still being carried on in the later periods concerned. The trade must also be a "commercial" trade, carried on with a view to profit. Loss relief is given *before* deduction of qualifying charitable donations.

In the case of "uncommercial" trades (not carried on with a view to profit) trading losses incurred on or after 1 April 2017 are carried forward and automatically set against profits (if any) arising from the same trade in later periods. But the company may claim that only partial loss relief (or none) should be given in any later period.

(b) A trading loss incurred before 1 April 2017 may also be carried forward but is set against only *profits of the same trade* in later periods. For later periods starting on or after 1 April 2017, it is not necessary to relieve the loss at the earliest opportunity and the company may specify how much relief (if any) should be given in each period.

If a company ceases one trade and commences another, the losses of the old trade cannot be carried forward and relieved against future profits of the new trade. Nor, if a company carries on two trades simultaneously, can a loss incurred in one trade be carried forward and relieved against the future profits of the other trade.

(c) If a trading loss is carried forward to an accounting period in which the loss-making trade is terminated, relief for this loss may be claimed against total profits (for losses incurred on or after 1 April 2017) or the profits of the same trade (for losses incurred before 1 April 2017) of the three years up to the end of the terminal period.

The loss must be set against the profits of more recent accounting periods falling into the specified three years in priority to earlier periods. The maximum possible relief must be given in each period. A trading loss cannot be carried back to the period in which it arose (or earlier) or to periods before 1 April 2017.

(d) Restrictions apply if there is a change in the ownership of a company (see below).

(e) Finally, the total of the carried-forward losses that can be relieved in any accounting period which begins on or after 1 April 2017 is limited to £5m plus 50% of the company's profits beyond the first £5m (see later in this chapter).

Claims which specify the amount of loss relief to be given in a later period must be made within two years of the end of that period. Similarly, a claim with regard to losses carried forward to a terminal period must be made within two years of the end of that period.

EXAMPLE 1

In the year to 31 March 2021, a company incurred a trading loss of £270,000 which was carried forward. The company's results for the next two years are:

	y/e 31 March 2022	y/e 31 March 2023
	£	£
Trading profits (*the same trade as the loss*)	110,000	35,000
Income from property	375,000	432,000
Total profits	485,000	467,000

(a) Compute the company's taxable total profits (TTP) for the years to 31 March 2022 and 2023, assuming that maximum loss relief is taken as soon as possible.

(b) Would the company be wise to claim maximum relief as soon as possible, given that the main rate of corporation tax will rise to 25% in FY2023? What should the company do if the main rate of corporation tax was expected to *fall* in FY2023?

(c) How would the answer to part (a) of the question differ if the trading loss of £270,000 represented the unrelieved part of a larger loss that was originally incurred in the year to 31 March 2017 and was only partly relieved in the four years to 31 March 2021? Again assume that maximum loss relief is taken as soon as possible.

Solution

(a) The carried-forward trading loss was incurred on or after 1 April 2017 and is therefore relieved against the total profits of subsequent accounting periods. If the company takes maximum relief at the earliest opportunity, the loss is fully relieved in the year to 31 March 2022 and TTP for that year becomes £215,000 (£485,000 – £270,000). TTP for the year to 31 March 2023 is unchanged at £467,000.

(b) Since the main rate will rise to 25% in FY2023, the company might decide to delay loss relief until the year to 31 March 2024, so saving tax at 25% rather than 19% (assuming that the company pays main rate tax in that year). But this would depend upon there being sufficient profits in the year to 31 March 2024 to absorb the loss and would cause a delay in obtaining loss relief. Furthermore, relief would not be available in the year to 31 March 2024 unless the loss-making trade was still being carried on in that year.

If the main rate of corporation tax was expected to *fall* in FY2023, the company should claim maximum relief as soon as possible. Carrying forward any part of the loss beyond 31 March 2023 would save tax at a lower rate (and so save less tax).

(c) A carried-forward trading loss incurred in the year to 31 March 2017 can be relieved only against future profits of the same trade. If the company takes maximum relief at the earliest opportunity, relief is £110,000 in the year to 31 March 2022 and is £35,000 in the year to 31 March 2023. TTP for the years to 31 March 2022 and 31 March 2023 becomes £375,000 and £432,000 respectively.

The remaining £125,000 of the loss is carried forward to the year to 31 March 2024 and subsequent years.

Unrelieved qualifying charitable donations

In general, qualifying charitable donations (e.g. Gift Aid donations) made by a company in an accounting period are deducted when computing taxable total profits for that period and so reduce the company's corporation tax liability. But if a trading loss is incurred in an accounting period, the company's total income and gains may be insufficient to cover its donations, in which case some or all of those donations will be unrelieved. A similar situation might arise if trading losses are set against the profits of the period.

In these circumstances, the tax saving that the unrelieved donations would normally have provided is permanently lost. Unrelieved charitable donations cannot be carried forward for relief in subsequent periods or carried back for relief in previous periods.

EXAMPLE 2

A company has the following results for the three years to 31 March 2023:

	y/e 31/3/2021 £	y/e 31/3/2022 £	y/e 31/3/2023 £
Trading profits/(losses)	(78,900)	27,100	41,300
Chargeable gains	11,500	9,200	13,600
Gift Aid donations	5,000	5,000	5,000

Assuming that the trading loss of £78,900 is carried forward and that maximum loss relief is taken as soon as possible, calculate the company's taxable total profits for each of these three years. Should the company claim less than maximum loss relief in any year?

Solution

	y/e 31/3/2021 £	y/e 31/3/2022 £	y/e 31/3/2023 £
Trading profits	-	27,100	41,300
Chargeable gains	11,500	9,200	13,600
	11,500	36,300	54,900
Less: Trading losses b/f	-	36,300	42,600
	11,500	0	12,300
Less: Qualifying charitable donations	5,000	-	5,000
Taxable total profits (TTP)	6,500	0	7,300
Trading losses c/f	78,900	42,600	-
Unrelieved charitable donations	-	5,000	-

Note:

The company should claim loss relief of only £31,300 in the year to 31 March 2022, leaving sufficient income to cover the donations. Trading losses c/f would increase to £47,600 and this would reduce the tax liability for the year to 31 March 2023 by £950 (£5,000 × 19%).

Trade loss relief against total profits

CTA 2010 allows a trading loss to be relieved against total profits of the loss-making period and the previous 12 months. This relief applies only if claimed and is in two parts:

(a) A company may claim that a trading loss incurred during an accounting period should be relieved against the total profits of that accounting period (*before* deducting qualifying charitable donations).

(b) The company may then further claim that any part of the trading loss which remains unrelieved after a claim has been made under (a) above, should be relieved against the total profits of accounting periods falling wholly or partly within the 12 months prior to the loss-making period. Note the following points:

   (i) This relief is also given *before* deducting qualifying charitable donations.

   (ii) Relief is not available unless the loss-making trade was being carried on in the accounting periods to which the loss is carried back.

   (iii) If more than one accounting period falls wholly or partly into the 12 months preceding a loss-making period, relief is given in later accounting periods in priority to earlier accounting periods.

   (iv) If an accounting period falls only partly into the 12 months preceding a loss-making period, the profits of that period are time-apportioned and relief is available against only the profits which fall into the specified 12 months.

Trade loss relief against total profits is voluntary. A company wishing to relieve a trading loss in this way must make an appropriate claim within two years of the end of the loss-making accounting period. A claim may be made under (a) above without a further claim under (b). But a claim under (b) cannot be made without a prior claim under (a).

A company may not specify how much of its trading loss should be relieved against total profits. The effect of such a claim is to relieve trading losses to the fullest possible extent in each affected accounting period. Any part of the loss which remains unrelieved after relief has been given against total profits is eligible for carry-forward relief. If relief against total profits is not claimed, the entire loss is carried forward.

EXAMPLE 3

A company has the following results for the year to 31 December 2022:

	£
Trading loss	(112,500)
Income from property	14,000
Chargeable gains	103,000
Gift Aid donations	28,700

Assuming that a claim is made for the trading loss to be relieved against total profits, compute the company's taxable total profits for the year.

Solution

	£
Trading income	-
Income from property	14,000
Chargeable gains	103,000
	117,000
Less: Trade loss relief against total profits	112,500
	4,500
Less: Qualifying charitable donations	4,500
Taxable total profits (TTP)	0

Note:

Only £4,500 of the Gift Aid donations can be relieved. The remaining £24,200 is lost. The company cannot restrict the trading loss relief claim to as to avoid this outcome.

Temporary extension of trade loss relief against total profits

In response to the increased losses caused by the coronavirus outbreak, Finance Act 2021 provides that a company's trading losses may be carried back for an extra two years and set against the total profits of those years. A summary of the rules is as follows:

(a) This "extended loss relief" applies only to trading losses incurred in accounting periods which end between 1 April 2020 and 31 March 2022. As usual, the company must first claim that the trading loss should be set against current-year profits (if any) and may then further claim that any remaining part of the loss should be carried back and set against total profits of the previous three years (instead of 12 months).

(b) Relief is given in later periods in priority to earlier periods and the company cannot specify the amount of relief to be given in each period. Relief is not available in an accounting period unless the loss-making trade was being carried on in that period.

(c) The amount of a trading loss that may be carried back against profits of the previous 12 months is (as usual) unlimited. But there is a cap on the amount of a trading loss that can be carried back to the two earlier years, as follows:

(i) The total amount of the trading losses incurred in all accounting periods ending between 1 April 2020 and 31 March 2021 that may be carried back to the two earlier years is capped at £2m.

(ii) Similarly, the total amount of the trading losses incurred in all accounting periods ending between 1 April 2021 and 31 March 2022 that may be carried back to the two earlier years is also capped at £2m.

(d) In the case of a group of companies (see Chapter 28), the £2m caps relate to the whole group, not to each individual company.

EXAMPLE 4

A company has the following results for the three years to 31 March 2022:

	y/e 31/3/2020 £	y/e 31/3/2021 £	y/e 31/3/2022 £
Trading profits/(losses)	121,400	110,700	(141,500)
Loan interest receivable	3,300	8,400	8,800
Gift Aid donations	2,000	2,000	2,000

Assuming that all possible claims are made to relieve the trading loss against total profits, calculate the company's taxable total profits for each of the three years.

Solution

	y/e 31/3/2020 £	y/e 31/3/2021 £	y/e 31/3/2022 £
Trading income	121,400	110,700	-
Non-trading loan income	3,300	8,400	8,800
	124,700	119,100	8,800
Less: Relief against total profits (a)	-	-	8,800
	124,700	119,100	0
Less: Relief against total profits (b)	-	119,100	-
	124,700	0	0
Less: Extended relief	13,600	-	-
	111,100	0	0
Less: Qualifying charitable donations	2,000	-	-
Taxable total profits (TTP)	109,100	0	0
Trading loss c/f	-	-	-
Unrelieved charitable donations	-	2,000	2,000

Notes:

(i) In the year to 31 March 2022, the claim for relief against total profits must be for the maximum possible amount of £8,800. This leaves nothing against which to relieve the Gift Aid donations and therefore they are lost.

(ii) The remaining £132,700 of the trading loss is eligible for relief against total profits of the year to 31 March 2021. The claim must be for the maximum possible amount of £119,100. This leaves nothing against which to relieve the donations, which are lost.

(iii) £127,900 of the loss has now been relieved. Normally, the remaining £13,600 would have to be carried forward. However, the loss was incurred in an accounting period ending between 1 April 2020 and 31 March 2022 and so it is possible to carry back the loss for two more years. The final £13,600 is relieved in the year to 31 March 2020.

EXAMPLE 5

A company has the following results for the three accounting periods to 30 April 2023:

	y/e 31/7/2021	9 months to 30/4/2022	y/e 30/4/2023
	£	£	£
Trading profits/(losses)	13,400	69,900	(122,800)
Chargeable gains	1,200	3,500	38,600

Assuming that all possible claims are made to relieve the trading loss against total profits, calculate the company's taxable total profits for each of the three accounting periods.

Solution

		y/e 31/7/2021	9 months to 30/4/2022	y/e 30/4/2023
		£	£	£
Trading income		13,400	69,900	-
Chargeable gains		1,200	3,500	38,600
		14,600	73,400	38,600
Less: Relief against total profits (a)		-	-	38,600
		14,600	73,400	0
Less: Relief against total profits (b)	(1)		73,400	
	(2)	3,650		
Taxable total profits (TTP)		10,950	0	0
Trading losses c/f		-	-	7,150

Notes:

(i)   £38,600 of the trading losses incurred during the year to 30 April 2023 are relieved against total profits of that period. This leaves losses of £84,200 which are eligible for carry-back relief. The carry-back period is the previous 12 months.

(ii)   The nine-month accounting period to 30 April 2022 is entirely contained within the specified 12 months and so losses of £73,400 are relieved against total profits of that period. Losses relieved so far are now £112,000, leaving £10,800 still to be relieved.

(iii) Only three months of the year to 31 July 2021 fall into the specified 12 months. The maximum relief available is £3,650 (£14,600 x 3/12). The remaining £7,150 of the trading loss is carried forward.

(iv)   The loss-making accounting period did not end between 1 April 2020 and 31 March 2022. Therefore extended relief is not available.

Further points relating to relief against total profits

(a) Relief against total profits is available only if the loss-making trade is being carried on "on a commercial basis" with a view to profit.

(b) If a company claims that more than one trading loss should be relieved against the total profits of a single accounting period, earlier losses are relieved before later losses. For instance, trading losses incurred during the current period are relieved in priority to trading losses carried back from a later period.

(c) Trading losses incurred by a company in the 12 months before the loss-making trade ceases may be carried back and set against total profits of the preceding three years.

(d) In the case of *farming companies*, a loss is usually not eligible for relief against total profits if losses have also been incurred for the previous five years.

(e) There are restrictions on the carry-back of trading losses when there is a change in the ownership of a company (see below).

Repayments of corporation tax

If a claim to set a trading loss against total profits results in a repayment of corporation tax for an earlier accounting period, this repayment will attract interest. The amount of interest is calculated in the usual way (see Chapter 25) unless the accounting period for which repayment is being made began more than 12 months before the loss-making accounting period. In these circumstances, the interest is calculated as if the repayment were a repayment of tax for the loss-making accounting period itself.

EXAMPLE 6

A company which began trading on 1 April 2020 has no other income apart from its trading profits. Results for the first three accounting periods are as follows:

	y/e 31/3/2021	6 months to 30/9/2021	y/e 30/9/2022
	£	£	£
Trading profits/(losses)	180,000	120,000	(290,000)

All possible claims are made to set the trading loss of £290,000 against the company's total profits. All corporation tax payable is paid on the due date and the necessary repayment of corporation tax is made on 1 August 2023.

Calculate the amount of the repayment and the interest which will accompany this repayment, assuming an interest rate of 0.5% per annum.

Solution

The loss is relieved first against the profit of the six months to 30 September 2021, giving a refund of £22,800 (£120,000 × 19%). The loss is then relieved against the £90,000 profit of the six months to 31 March 2021, giving another refund of £17,100 (£90,000 × 19%). The remaining £80,000 of the loss is carried forward. This loss is not eligible for extended relief since the loss-making period did not end between 1 April 2020 and 31 March 2022.

Notes re interest:

(i)   The six months to 30 September 2021 did not begin more than 12 months before the loss-making period so interest on the refund of £22,800 will run from 1 July 2022 (the due date of payment for the six months to 30 September 2021).

(ii)   The year to 31 March 2021 did begin more than 12 months before the loss-making period so interest on the refund of £17,100 will run from 1 July 2023 (the due date of payment for the loss-making period itself).

(iii) The repayment takes place on 1 August 2023. This is 396 days after 1 July 2022 and 31 days after 1 July 2023. Therefore the interest due is:

$$(£22,800 \times 0.5\% \times \frac{396}{365}) + (£17,100 \times 0.5\% \times \frac{31}{365}) = £130.94.$$

Anti-avoidance legislation

Specific anti-avoidance legislation exists so as to prevent the following manoeuvre, which would otherwise be very tax-efficient:

(a)   Acquire a company with substantial amounts of unrelieved trading losses.

(b)   Revive the company's business.

(c)   Set the company's pre-acquisition trading losses against its post-acquisition profits, so avoiding corporation tax.

The legislation referred to above provides that if there is a change in the ownership of a company and certain conditions are satisfied, trading losses which arose before the change cannot be carried forward and set against trading profits (or total profits) arising after the change. Nor can trading losses arising after the change be carried back and set against total profits which arose before the change. The required conditions are that:

(a)   a change in ownership has occurred at a time when the company's business has become negligible and then (at any time after the change) there has been a significant revival of the company's business, or

(b)   a change in ownership and a major change in the nature or conduct of the company's business have both occurred within the same five-year period.

For this purpose, a change in ownership is deemed to occur if over half of the company's ordinary share capital is acquired either by one person or by a group of people, each acquiring at least a 5% shareholding.

Choice of loss relief

The main criteria which should be borne in mind when choosing the most effective way of relieving a trading loss are as follows:

(a) the expected amount (if any) of future profits from the same trade (for a loss incurred before 1 April 2017) or future total profits (for a loss incurred after that date)

(b) whether or not the company requires loss relief as soon as possible

(c) the rates of corporation tax[†] payable by the company in earlier accounting periods and the expected rates payable in future periods

(d) the possibility that qualifying charitable donations may be unrelieved

(e) in general, the desire to maximise the tax saved as a result of loss relief claims.

[†] *As from 1 April 2023, a company's profits might be subject to the main rate of 25%, the small profits rate of 19% or the marginal rate of 26.5% (see Chapter 25). If possible, it is preferable to set losses against profits that would otherwise be taxed at the marginal rate.*

Non-trading losses

The main reliefs available in relation to a company's non-trading losses are as follows:

(a) **Property business losses**. A property business loss is set first against total profits of the loss-making period. Any amount that cannot be relieved in this way is either:

   (i) carried forward and (to the extent claimed by the company) set against the total profits of subsequent accounting periods (as long as the property business is still being carried on in those periods), or

   (ii) relieved by means of group relief (see Chapter 28).

   There are "change in ownership" restrictions on the carry-forward of property losses which are similar to those relating to trading losses (see earlier in this chapter).

(b) **Net debits on non-trading loan relationships**. A deficit on a company's non-trading loan relationships (see Chapter 23) may be relieved in any of the following ways:

   (i) by set-off against total profits of the period in which the deficit occurs

   (ii) by group relief (see Chapter 28)

   (iii) by set-off against the company's income from non-trading loan relationships in the previous 12 months.

   Part of the deficit may be relieved in one way and part in another, if the company so wishes. Any part of the deficit for which relief is not claimed under (i), (ii) or (iii) above is carried forward and (to the extent claimed by the company) set against total profits of subsequent accounting periods. But carried-forward deficits incurred before 1 April 2017 may be set against only non-trading profits of subsequent periods.

(c) **Non-trading losses on intangible fixed assets**. All or part of a non-trading loss on intangible fixed assets (see Chapter 23) may be relieved against the company's total profits for the loss-making period. Any part of the loss which is not relieved in this manner and which is not relieved by means of group relief (see Chapter 28) is carried forward and treated as non-trading expenditure of the next accounting period.

(d) **Capital losses**. Capital losses are relieved first against chargeable gains of the same accounting period. Any unrelieved losses are carried forward and set against the first available chargeable gains of subsequent accounting periods. Capital losses cannot be relieved against any other form of income.

Restriction on deduction of carried-forward losses

As stated earlier in this chapter, there is now a limit on the total amount of carried-forward losses that can be relieved in an accounting period. The limit is broadly equal to £5m plus 50% of the company's total profits beyond the first £5m[†]. The detailed workings of this restriction are very complex but an outline of the main rules is as follows:

(a) A company's "deductions allowance" for a 12-month accounting period is normally £5m (reduced in proportion for periods of less than 12 months). However, in the case of a group of companies (see Chapter 28) the £5m deductions allowance relates to the whole group, not to each individual company.

(b) The company must specify how much (if any) of its deductions allowance for a period should be allocated to a "trading profits deductions allowance", a "chargeable gains deductions allowance" and a "non-trading profits deductions allowance".

(c) The amount of relief for carried-forward trading losses incurred before 1 April 2017 is limited to the company's trading profits deductions allowance plus 50% of the amount by which trading profits (of the same trade) for the period exceed that allowance.

(d) The amount of relief for carried-forward capital losses is limited to the company's chargeable gains deductions allowance plus 50% of the amount by which chargeable gains for the period exceed that allowance.

(e) The amount of relief for carried-forward non-trading loan relationship deficits incurred before 1 April 2017 is limited to the non-trading profits deductions allowance plus 50% of the amount by which non-trading profits for the period exceed that allowance.

(f) Finally, the amount of relief for carried-forward losses which may be set against total profits (e.g. trading losses incurred on or after 1 April 2017) is limited to the company's total deductions allowance plus 50% of the amount by which total profits for the period exceed that allowance, less any relief already taken under (c), (d) and (e) above.

[†] *Very few companies have profits which exceed £5m per annum and it is estimated that over 99% of all companies are unaffected by this restriction on relief for carried-forward losses.*

Summary

▸ Trading losses are carried forward for relief in later accounting periods, unless the company claims trading loss relief against total profits. Carried-forward losses that occur before 1 April 2017 are relieved only against future profits of the same trade.

▸ Qualifying charitable donations which cannot be relieved in the accounting period in which they are paid are lost and cannot be carried forwards or backwards.

▸ A company may claim that a trading loss should be relieved against total profits of the loss-making accounting period. Any part of the loss which remains unrelieved may then be set against total profits of the previous 12 months (*extended to three years for losses incurred in periods ending between 1 April 2020 and 31 March 2022*).

▸ If a claim to relieve a trading loss against total profits results in a repayment of corporation tax for an earlier accounting period, this repayment will attract interest.

▸ Corporation tax reliefs are also available in relation to property business losses, net debits on non-trading loan relationships, non-trading losses on intangible fixed assets and capital losses.

Exercises

A set of multiple choice questions for this chapter is available on the accompanying website.

26.1 A company has the following results for the three years to 31 March 2023:

	y/e 31/3/2021	y/e 31/3/2022	y/e 31/3/2023
	£	£	£
Trading profits/(losses)	(32,200)	23,800	40,300
Gift Aid donations	4,000	5,000	6,000

Assuming that the trading loss is carried forward and that maximum loss relief is taken as soon as possible, calculate the company's taxable total profits for each of the three years, showing the amount of losses carried forward at the end of each year. Also calculate the amount of tax saved as a result of trading loss relief.

26.2 A company has the following results for the year to 31 October 2022:

	£
Trading loss	(232,300)
Income from property	190,200
Chargeable gains	45,540
Gift Aid donations	24,000

Assuming that a claim is made to relieve the trading loss against total profits of the loss-making accounting period, calculate the taxable total profits for the year.

26.3 For companies, which of the following statements is true?

(a) Capital losses may be carried forward and relieved against future trading profits.

(b) Trading losses may be carried forward for relief against future chargeable gains.

(c) Trading losses may be relieved against chargeable gains of the same period.

(d) Capital losses may be relieved against trading profits of the same period.

26.4 A company has the following results for its three most recent accounting periods:

	y/e 31/10/2020	eight months to 30/6/2021	y/e 30/6/2022
	£	£	£
Trading profits/(losses)	59,700	73,600	(155,700)
Chargeable gains	8,400	-	48,700
Gift Aid donations	1,000	1,000	1,000

Assuming that all possible claims are made to relieve the trading loss against total profits, calculate the company's taxable total profits for each of the three periods.

26.5 The following information is available:

(a) A company's taxable total profits for the year to 31 March 2022 are £400,000.

(b) In the year to 31 March 2023, the company incurs a trading loss of £700,000 but has other taxable income and gains totalling £200,000.

(c) The company's taxable total profits for the year to 31 March 2024 are expected to be over £1,000,000.

Explain the trading loss reliefs available to the company. Which of these reliefs would be the most beneficial?

*26.6 A company has the following results for the four years to 31 March 2023:

	y/e 31/3/2020	y/e 31/3/2021	y/e 31/3/2022	y/e 31/3/2023
	£	£	£	£
Trading profits/(losses)	61,900	77,400	64,200	(172,500)
Chargeable gains/(capital losses)	(7,500)	4,300	2,700	5,700
Gift Aid donations	3,400	3,400	3,400	3,400

Calculate the total repayment of corporation tax (with interest) to which the company is entitled, assuming that:

(a) all possible claims are made to relieve the trading loss against total profits

(b) any repayment of corporation tax which is generated by these claims is made on 13 January 2024

(c) corporation tax for the three years to 31 March 2022 is all paid on the due dates

(d) the rate of interest paid on repayments of corporation tax is 0.5%.

Also explain how the situation would differ if the company were to cease trading on 31 March 2023 (computations are _not_ required).

Chapter 27

Close companies and investment companies

Introduction

In general terms, a "close company" is one which is controlled by a small number of people and a "company with investment business" is one whose business consists wholly or partly of making investments. Special corporation tax rules apply to each of these types of company and the main purpose of this chapter is to explain the nature of these rules.

This chapter also considers the taxation consequences which should be borne in mind when deciding whether to trade as an unincorporated business or as a close company.

Close companies

The essence of a close company is that its affairs can be controlled and manipulated by a small group of people, possibly for tax-avoidance purposes. In fact, most companies in the UK are close companies. Certain anti-avoidance legislation exists in relation to close companies and the main points of this legislation are explained later in this chapter. The first step, however, is to provide a precise definition of the term "close company".

Definition of a close company

A close company is a UK resident company which satisfies certain conditions. The main instance of a close company is a company which is under the *control* of:

(a) five or fewer *participators*, or

(b) any number of participators who are also *directors* of the company.

The rights of a participator's *associates* are aggregated with that participator's own rights for the purpose of determining whether a company is a close company. Some important terms used in this definition are explained below.

Control

Persons are deemed to have "control" over a company if, taken together, they:

(a) own over 50% of the company's issued share capital, or

(b) have over 50% of the company's voting power, or

(c) would receive over 50% of the company's income, if it were all distributed, or

(d) would receive over 50% of the company's assets, if the company were wound up.

Participators

A "participator" is defined as someone who has a share or interest in the capital or income of the company. In many cases, a company's only participators are its shareholders. But other persons (e.g. option holders, loan creditors) might also rank as participators.

Directors

A "director", for this purpose, is any person:

(a) who occupies the position of director (whether called a director or not), or

(b) whose directions or instructions are normally obeyed by the directors, or

(c) who is a manager of the company and (possibly together with associates) controls at least 20% of the company's ordinary share capital.

Associates

The main "associates" of a participator are:

(a) the participator's business partners

(b) the participator's relatives

(c) the trustees of a settlement established by the participator or by his/her relatives.

For this purpose, a participator's relatives comprise his or her spouse (or civil partner), parents and remoter ancestors, children and remoter issue, brothers and sisters.

EXAMPLE 1

A company's issued share capital consists of 1,000 £1 ordinary shares, held as follows:

	No of shares		No of shares
David	200	Helen	50
Emma	50	Ian	30
Frederick	100	Jacqueline	40
George	50	Others (1 share each)	480

None of the shareholders are associated in any way and no shareholder is also a director.

(a) Is the company a close company?

(b) Would the company be a close company:

    (i) if David were Jacqueline's brother, or

    (ii) if Emma married Ian, or

    (iii) if David were Jacqueline's brother and Emma also married Ian?

Solution

(a) The five largest shareholders own 45% of the share capital, so the company is not under the control of five or fewer participators. The company is also not under the control of its directors. Therefore the company is not a close company.

(b) (i) If David were Jacqueline's brother, her 4% holding would be aggregated with his and the five largest shareholders would control 49% (45% + 4%) of the share capital. The company would not be a close company.

    (ii) If Emma married Ian, his 3% holding would be aggregated with hers and the five largest shareholders would control 48% (45% + 3%) of the share capital. The company would still not be a close company.

    (iii) If David were Jacqueline's brother and Emma also married Ian, the five largest shareholders would control 52% (45% + 4% + 3%) of the share capital. The company would then be a close company.

EXAMPLE 2

A company's issued share capital consists entirely of ordinary shares, held as follows:

	% holding	Director
Keith	7	Yes
Leonora	7	Yes
Martin	7	Yes
Norma	7	Yes
Oliver	7	Yes
Penny	16	No
Richard	4	No
Others (all non-directors owning under 1%)	45	
Total	100	

None of the shareholders are associated in any way.

(a) Is the company a close company?

(b) Would the company be a close company:

    (i) if Penny were a manager, or

    (ii) if Penny were Richard's daughter, or

    (iii) if Penny were both a manager and Richard's daughter?

Solution

(a) The five largest shareholders own 44% of the share capital, so the company is not under the control of five or fewer participators. The company is also not under the control of its directors, who own 35% of the share capital. Therefore the company is not a close company.

(b) (i) If Penny were a manager, she would not rank as a director because her shareholding is less than 20%. The situation would be unaltered and the company would not be a close company.

(ii) If Penny were Richard's daughter, then his 4% holding would be aggregated with hers and the five largest shareholders would control 48% (44% + 4%) of the share capital. The company would still not be a close company.

(iii) If Penny were both a manager and Richard's daughter, then her deemed 20% holding (16% + 4%) would make her a director. The six directors would control 55% of the share capital and the company would then be a close company.

Exceptions

Certain types of company are statutorily excepted from close company status, even if they are controlled by five or fewer participators or by the participator-directors. The main exception consists of listed companies with a substantial public interest. In order for this exception to apply, a company must satisfy all of the following conditions:

(a) The company's voting shares must have been both dealt in and listed on a recognised stock exchange within the 12 months prior to the date on which the company's status is being determined.

(b) The total voting power possessed by the *principal members* of the company must not exceed 85% of the total voting power.

(c) At least 35% of the company's voting power must be in the hands of the public.

For this purpose, a "principal member" is a shareholder who (possibly with associates) has more than 5% of the voting power of the company and is also one of the top five shareholders. If two or more shareholders, each holding more than 5%, tie for fifth place, there will be more than five principal members.

The "public" excludes the company's directors, their associates, pension schemes for the company's own employees and most principal members. But principal members which are non-close companies or pension schemes (apart from pension schemes for the company's own employees) *are* included within the definition of the public.

EXAMPLE 3

A company's issued share capital consists entirely of ordinary shares. These shares have been listed on a recognised stock exchange for many years and there have been frequent dealings in them within the last 12 months. The company's shares are owned as follows:

	% holding	Director
QBBA Ltd (a non-close company)	13	-
DFFK Ltd (a close company)	7	-
Terry	8	Yes
Ursula	10	Yes
Vincent (a manager)	33	No
Wendy	4	No
Others (all non-directors owning under 1%)	25	
Total	100	

None of the shareholders are associated in any way. Is the company a close company?

Solution

At first sight, the company seems to be a close company. It is under the control of its directors (since Vincent ranks as a director) and it is also under the control of five or fewer participators. However, the company is listed on a recognised stock exchange and its shares have been dealt in within the past 12 months. Furthermore, its principal members (the top five shareholders, each owning more than 5% of the voting shares) hold only 71% of the company's voting power and the public (QBBA Ltd, Wendy and the others) hold 42%. Therefore the company is excepted from being a close company.

Consequences of close company status

The main tax consequences[†] of close company status are as follows:

(a) Benefits in kind provided by the company to its participators or their associates are generally treated as distributions.

(b) Loans made to participators or their associates are assessed to tax.

Each of these consequences is explained below. Note also that if a married couple (or civil partners) jointly own shares in a close company, dividends derived from those shares are always taxed in accordance with the actual proportions of ownership of the shares. This differs from the normal treatment of jointly owned assets (see Chapter 2).

[†] *Trivial benefits in kind provided to employees and costing no more than £50 each are exempt from income tax (see Chapter 8). However, an annual cap of £300 applies to the value of such benefits that can be received tax-free by a director of a close company.*

Benefits in kind provided to participators

Benefits in kind provided by a close company to its participators (or their associates) are generally regarded as distributions. The taxation effects of this are as follows:

(a) The cost to the company of providing the benefit is disallowed when computing its corporation tax liability.

(b) The company is deemed to have made a distribution equal to the amount of the benefit in kind which would have been assessed to income tax if the benefit had been received by an employee (see Chapter 8).

(c) The person receiving the benefit is taxed as if he or she had received a dividend of the same amount as the deemed distribution.

However, a benefit provided to a participator is *not* treated as a distribution if it is already assessable as employment income.

EXAMPLE 4

Throughout tax year 2022-23, a close company provides one of its shareholders (not a director or employee) with a motor car for private use. The company's accounts for the year to 31 March 2023 show an expense of £4,600 in relation to the running costs of this car. If the shareholder had been a director or employee, the taxable benefit for 2022-23 would have been £8,325. Explain the tax treatment of this item.

Solution

The £4,600 is disallowed when calculating the company's tax liability for the year to 31 March 2023. The company is deemed to have made a distribution of £8,325 and the shareholder is taxed as if he/she had received a dividend of £8,325 in tax year 2022-23.

Loans made to participators

If a close company makes a loan to a participator (or an associate of a participator), the tax consequences are as follows:

(a) The company is required to pay an amount of tax which is equal to the amount of the loan multiplied by the income tax dividend upper rate (currently 33.75%). This tax is payable nine months and one day after the end of the accounting period in which the loan is made. However, no tax is payable in relation to any part of a loan which is repaid to the company before the date on which the tax falls due.

(b) The tax paid when the loan was made is repaid to the company if the participator repays the loan or if the loan is written off. This tax repayment is made nine months and one day after the end of the accounting period in which the loan is repaid or written off.

(c) If a loan to a participator is wholly or partly written off, the amount written off is *not* treated as a debit arising under a loan relationship and therefore the company is denied tax relief in relation to this amount. Furthermore, the participator is deemed to have received dividend income equal to the amount written off.

In the case of a participator who is also an employee, this tax charge takes priority over the usual rules which apply to employee loans written off (see Chapter 8).

(d) Certain loans are excluded from the treatment described above. These include loans made to a participator in the normal course of the company's money-lending business and loans not exceeding £15,000 made to a participator who is a full-time employee or director of the company, so long as that participator (with associates) has no more than a 5% interest in the company.

EXAMPLE 5

On 1 May 2022, a close company which prepares accounts to 31 March each year lends £30,000 to Ravi, who is one of its directors. No interest is charged on this loan. Ravi owns 18% of the company's ordinary share capital. Explain the tax treatment of this loan if:

(a) Ravi repays the loan in full on 15 February 2024

(b) Ravi repays £10,000 of the loan on 15 February 2024 and the remaining £20,000 is written off by the company on the same day.

Solution

The loan is made during the year to 31 March 2023, so tax of £10,125 (33.75% of £30,000) is payable by the company on 1 January 2024. Since the loan is interest-free, it is treated as a beneficial loan and Ravi is subject to income tax on the related benefit in kind. As regards the eventual repayment or write-off of the loan:

(a) The loan is repaid during the year to 31 March 2024, so tax of £10,125 is repaid to the company on 1 January 2025.

(b) Tax of £10,125 is repaid to the company on 1 January 2025. But the company cannot claim tax relief in relation to the £20,000 of the loan which has been written off.

Ravi is treated as receiving dividend income of £20,000 in tax year 2023-24. If he has already used up his entire dividend allowance (see Chapter 2) this income will be taxed at the dividend ordinary rate (8.75%) to the extent that it falls within the basic rate band. Income tax at the dividend upper rate (33.75%) or the dividend additional rate (39.35%) might be payable if Ravi's total income is sufficiently high.

Companies with investment business

A "company with investment business" is defined by the Corporation Tax Act 2009 as "*a company whose business consists wholly or partly of making investments*". In order to qualify as such a company, the company must have a <u>business</u> of making investments. It is not sufficient merely to <u>hold</u> investments. The investment income of a company with investment business will normally consist of:

(a) income from property

(b) net credits on non-trading loan relationships

(c) chargeable gains.

The company may also receive dividend income. But dividends other than non-exempt foreign dividends (see Chapter 32) are not chargeable to corporation tax. The expenses incurred by a company in relation to its investment business fall into two categories:

(a) expenses which are directly related to one of the company's sources of income and which may be set against that income (e.g. property expenses offset against property income, debits on non-trading loan relationships set against credits)

(b) management expenses, which are not related to any particular source of income but which may be set against the company's total income.

Note that only genuine management expenses are allowed. For example, in *L G Berry Investments Ltd* v *Attwooll* (1964), excessive directors' remuneration included in management expenses was disallowed.

To the extent that management expenses cannot be relieved in the accounting period in which they are incurred they may be carried forward (without time limit) to future periods. There are some restrictions on the carry-forward of management expenses when there is a change in the ownership of a company. These restrictions are similar to those relating to the carry-forward of trading losses (see Chapter 26).

Close investment-holding companies (as from 1 April 2023)

As from 1 April 2023, a close company will be designated as a "close investment-holding company" (CIC) unless it exists wholly or mainly for one or more of a number of purposes defined by statute. The main purposes which will except a company from CIC status are:

(a) the carrying on of a trade on a commercial basis, or

(b) the letting of property (other than to connected persons).

A close investment-holding company will be subject to all the usual close company rules but will also be subject to further provisions. The most important of these is that (regardless of the size of its profits) a CIC will always be required to pay corporation tax at the main rate. The small profits rate and marginal relief (see Chapter 25) will not be available.

Choice of business medium

An individual who starts trading is faced with a choice between two alternatives:

(a) To trade as an unincorporated business, either as a sole trader or in partnership with others. In this case the individual is self-employed and the business profits are assessed to income tax as trading income.

(b) To trade as a limited company (probably a close company) with the individual concerned being a director and/or shareholder of the company. In this case, the company's profits are assessed to corporation tax and the individual's earnings and dividends from the company are assessed to income tax.

The choice between these two alternatives will be determined partly (though not solely) by taxation considerations. Some of the main factors which should be taken into account when deciding whether to trade as an unincorporated business or as a company include:

(a) the rates of income tax and corporation tax
(b) the NI contributions payable by the self-employed and by employees and employers
(c) the tax effects of distributing profits to the owner of the business
(d) the tax reliefs available on pension contributions
(e) the dates on which tax and NI contributions are due for payment
(f) the tax reliefs available in relation to trading losses
(g) the taxation of chargeable gains
(h) the tax treatment of loans made to the owner of the business.

Each of these factors is discussed below.

Rates of tax

The entire profits of an unincorporated business are charged to income tax, whether or not the profits are withdrawn from the business. Rates of tax for non-Scottish taxpayers[†] in 2022-23 are 20%, 40% or 45%, depending upon the owner's taxable income. A marginal rate of 40% applies if taxable income exceeds £37,700, which is a relatively small sum. The 45% rate applies if the owner's taxable income exceeds £150,000.

By contrast, a company's profits in FY2022 are charged to corporation tax at 19%, no matter how large those profits are. Furthermore, the owners of a company can determine the amount of profits to be paid out as directors' remuneration and can therefore control the extent to which profits are assessed to income tax rather than corporation tax.

However, retaining profits in a company to minimise the tax liability in the short term will increase the value of the company's shares. This will result in a higher capital gains tax liability in the longer term when shareholders dispose of their shares, though the gains concerned might be eligible for business asset disposal relief and/or other CGT reliefs.

[†] *For Scottish taxpayers, rates are 19%, 20%, 21%, 41% and 46%. A marginal rate of 41% applies if taxable income exceeds £31,092. Marginal rate is 46% if taxable income exceeds £150,000.*

National Insurance

In tax year 2022-23, self-employed persons pay flat-rate Class 2 NICs of £3.15 per week. Class 4 contributions are also payable. These are calculated at 10.25% on profits between £11,908 and £50,270 and at 3.25% on profits beyond £50,270.

The total amount of the Class 1 NICs payable in respect of directors' remuneration can be much higher. A director pays primary contributions at 13.25% on earnings between £11,908 and £50,270 and at 3.25% on any further earnings. In addition, the company pays 15.05% secondary contributions on earnings in excess of £9,100, although these contributions are deductible when calculating the company's profits for corporation tax purposes.

Distribution of profits

The amount of income tax payable on the profits of an unincorporated business is entirely unaffected by the level of the owner's drawings, if any. But the distribution of profits by a company (either as directors' remuneration or as dividends) has tax implications:

(a) The payment of directors' remuneration reduces the company's corporation tax liability at the expense of increasing the income tax liability of the directors concerned and creating a liability to both primary and secondary NICs.

(b) The payment of a dividend avoids the liability to NICs, but dividends are an appropriation of profit and are not deductible in the company's corporation tax computation. Furthermore, avoiding NICs will have an adverse impact on the shareholder's contributions record and this, in turn, may have an effect on his or her entitlement to certain social security benefits in the future.

The decision as to whether to pay out a company's profits as directors' remuneration or dividends (or a combination of both) is a complex one and should take into account all of the factors listed above. A constraint which may need to be borne in mind is the need to pay sufficient remuneration to comply with National Minimum Wage regulations.

EXAMPLE 6

A close company which prepares accounts to 31 March each year is owned and managed by a single shareholder/director who is not a Scottish taxpayer and who is paid a salary of £5,000 per month. In addition to this salary, the owner intends to withdraw £20,000 from the company on 31 March 2023. Two approaches are being considered:

(a) that the company should make an extra salary payment to the owner, such that the total of this payment and the related secondary NICs will equal £20,000

(b) that the company should instead pay a dividend to the owner, such that the total of this dividend and the company's extra corporation tax liability (when compared with the other approach) will equal £20,000.

The owner has no income apart from salary and dividends from the company. Consider the tax-effectiveness of each approach, performing all calculations to the nearest £.

Solution

	Extra salary £	Dividend £
Payments made by company:		
Salary	17,384	
Secondary Class 1 NICs @ 15.05%	2,616	
Corporation tax on an extra £20,000 @ 19%		3,800
Dividend		16,200
Total payments	20,000	20,000
Amount received by owner:		
Gross salary	17,384	
Dividend received		16,200
Primary Class 1 NICs @ 3.25%	(565)	
Income tax @ 40%	(6,954)	
Income tax at nil rate (£2,000 @ 0%)		0
Income tax at upper rate (£14,200 @ 33.75%)		(4,792)
Income remaining after tax	9,865	11,408

Notes:

(i) The owner's regular salary is sufficient to ensure that any extra salary attracts primary Class 1 NICs at 3.25% and that any further income is subject to income tax at the higher rate (or the dividend upper rate).

(ii) In this example, the payment of a dividend is more tax-effective than the payment of extra salary, mainly because of the fact that dividends do not attract NICs. The total liability to tax and NICs is reduced by £1,543 (£2,616 + £565 + £6,954 − £3,800 − £4,792) and therefore income remaining after tax increases by £1,543.

Pension contributions

In 2022-23, a self-employed individual may obtain tax relief on pension contributions of up to £3,600 or 100% of income from self-employment (whichever is the greater). Similarly, a company director may obtain tax relief on pension contributions of up to £3,600 or 100% of director's remuneration (whichever is the greater) whilst the company itself may make un-limited pension contributions on the director's behalf and deduct these contributions when computing taxable total profits. But this deduction is available only if the contributions are paid wholly and exclusively for trade purposes.

Dividends do not rank as earnings and therefore dividends received are ignored when computing the maximum pension contributions on which an individual may obtain tax relief. Furthermore, a shareholder in a company is not (per se) an employee of that company. So a company cannot make employer's pension contributions in relation to one of its shareholders unless that shareholder is also a director or other employee.

Dates of payment of tax and NICs

A self-employed person must make payments on account of the liability to income tax and Class 4 NICs. These fall due on 31 January in the tax year and on the following 31 July. A balancing payment (plus Class 2 NICs) is due on the following 31 January. Note that:

(a) At present, choosing an accounting date early in the tax year (e.g. 30 April) maximises the delay between earning profits and paying tax on them. For example, tax and Class 4 NICs on profits for the year to 30 April 2022 (basis period for 2022-23) are payable on 31 January 2023 and 31 July 2023 with a balancing payment on 31 January 2024.

(b) However, as from tax year 2024-25, self-employed people will be charged to income tax on the profits actually arising in the tax year (see Chapter 10) so that choosing an early accounting date will no longer be advantageous.

In general, close companies pay their corporation tax nine months and one day after the end of the accounting period. Income tax and Class 1 NICs in relation to directors' remuneration must be accounted for via the PAYE system.

Relief for trading losses

The main distinctions between trading loss reliefs for individuals and companies are:

(a) For individuals, trading losses which are carried forward must be set against the first available profits of the same trade. For companies, carried-forward trading losses incurred on or after 1 April 2017 are set against total profits in subsequent periods, and the company may determine the amount of relief to take in each such period.

(b) The trading losses of a self-employed individual may be set against that person's total income for the year of the loss, the previous year[†] or both of these years.

   In the case of a company, a claim to set a trading loss against total profits of the previous 12 months[†] cannot be made unless a claim has already been made to set that loss against total profits of the current accounting period.

(c) For individuals, terminal losses are carried back three years and set against profits of the same trade. For companies, terminal losses are set against total profits.

(d) In certain circumstances, the trading losses of an individual may be set against capital gains (see Chapter 12). A company receives a similar relief by virtue of the fact that a company's chargeable gains are automatically included in its total profits.

(e) Trading losses of an individual incurred in the opening years may be relieved against total income of the previous three years. There is no equivalent relief for companies.

Note that a company's losses can be relieved only against the company's own income and gains, not against the income and gains of individual shareholders.

[†] *For both individuals and companies, a "temporary extension" of trading loss reliefs allows trading losses to be carried back for three years. But there are significant differences between the way in which extended relief works for individuals and for companies (see Chapters 12 and 26).*

Chargeable gains

If an unincorporated business disposes of a chargeable asset, any capital gain that arises is assessed to CGT on the owner of the business. The rate of CGT for disposals occurring during tax year 2022-23 is usually 10% or 20%. The annual exemption is available.

The tax rules which apply when a company makes a chargeable disposal are somewhat different from those which apply for CGT purposes. In particular, indexation allowance (*frozen at 31 December 2017*) is available to companies but not individuals. Gains arising in FY2022 are charged to corporation tax at 19%. No annual exemption is available. Gains retained in the company increase the value of the company's shares, so resulting in an increased CGT liability when shareholders eventually dispose of their shares. In effect a chargeable gain may be taxed twice, first to corporation tax and then to CGT.

Close company loans to participators

As explained earlier in this chapter, close companies must pay tax when making loans to participators. A tax charge of this type can sometimes be triggered accidentally if a director who is also a shareholder overdraws his or her current account with the company. These provisions have no relevance to unincorporated businesses.

Incorporation

If the initial choice is to trade as an unincorporated business, the trader may still consider incorporation at some future time. Some of the main tax consequences of incorporation are as follows:

(a) The transfer of the assets of an unincorporated business to a company might give rise to a CGT liability. However, subject to certain conditions, the gains arising may be held-over until the shares which were acquired in exchange for the business assets are disposed of (see Chapter 22).

(b) If the company is under the control of the person who was previously the owner of the unincorporated business, assets which are eligible for capital allowances can be transferred at their written down values for capital allowances purposes, so avoiding the need for balancing adjustments (see Chapter 11).

(c) The transfer of assets to the company will not be treated as a supply for VAT purposes so long as the business is transferred as a going concern and the company is a taxable person at the time of the transfer (see Chapter 29).

(d) If the proprietor of the unincorporated business has unrelieved trade losses, these cannot be carried forward and used by the company. However, subject to certain conditions, such unrelieved losses may be relieved against the proprietor's income from the company (see Chapter 12).

Summary

▸ A close company is one which is under the control of five or fewer participators or any number of participator-directors. The rights of a participator's associates are taken into account when determining whether or not a company is a close company.

▸ Certain types of company (mainly listed companies with a substantial public interest) are excepted from close company status.

▸ Benefits in kind provided to the participators of a close company are treated as distributions. Loans to participators are charged to tax.

▸ A company with investment business is a company whose business consists wholly or partly of making investments. Management expenses incurred by such companies are set against total income. Excess management expenses may be carried forward.

▸ The choice of business medium (unincorporated business or close company) may be made for tax reasons. But this is a complex decision and involves many aspects of the income tax, capital gains tax, NICs and corporation tax systems.

Exercises

A set of multiple choice questions for this chapter is available on the accompanying website.

27.1 Andrew Pearson is a shareholder of APP Nottingham Ltd. Which of the following (if any) are his associates when deciding whether the company is a close company?

(a) his sister   (b) his brother-in-law   (c) his nephew

(d) his father   (e) his business partner in a firm of solicitors.

27.2 A private company's share capital consists of 5,000 ordinary shares, held as follows:

	Number of shares
Sejanus (a manager)	900
Claudius (a director)	400
Agrippa (a director)	300
Cleopatra (a director)	300
Tiberius (a director)	200
Gaius (a director)	200
Ptolemy	190
Livia (the grandmother of Claudius)	190
Apicata (the wife of Sejanus)	120
Others (all non-directors owning 10 shares or less)	2,200
Total	5,000

Is the company a close company?

27.3   On 31 October 2022, a close company which prepares accounts to 31 March each year provides one of its full-time working directors with:

(a)   an interest-free loan of £12,000 (the company does not provide loans in the ordinary course of its business)

(b)   a season ticket for the opera, costing the company £4,800.

Explain the tax treatment of these two items, assuming that the director in question owns 10% of the company's ordinary share capital.

*27.4   On 19 April 2022, a close company (which makes up accounts to 31 March annually) lends £100,000 to Siobhan, who is a director of the company and who owns 30% of its ordinary share capital. The company does not provide loans in the ordinary course of its business. Siobhan pays a commercial rate of interest on this loan until 1 October 2023, when she repays £60,000. She then continues to pay a commercial rate of interest on the remainder of the loan until it is written off by the company on 31 March 2024. Explain the tax implications of these transactions.

*27.5   Glenda has been self-employed for many years and prepares accounts to 31 March each year. Her adjusted profits (after deduction of capital allowances) are currently running at approximately £80,000 per annum. She has no other income for tax purposes and she is not a Scottish taxpayer.

Glenda is now considering incorporation and she would like to see a comparison of her current tax liability (including NICs) and the liability that would arise if she traded as a small company, with herself as the sole shareholder and director.

(a)   Assuming that Glenda continues to operate as a sole trader and that her adjusted trading profit for the year to 31 March 2023 is £80,000, calculate the total liability to income tax and NICs for tax year 2022-23.

(b)   Estimate the total liability to income tax, NICs and corporation tax that would arise for the year if Glenda formed a company and extracted £60,000 of the company's profit for the year either:

(i)   as a salary (so that her salary plus secondary NICs would total £60,000), or

(ii)   as a £60,000 dividend.

(c)   In case (b), how would the total liability be affected if Glenda took £9,100 in the form of a salary and the remainder of the £60,000 as a dividend?

Assume for the sake of simplicity that all director's remuneration and dividends are taken during tax year 2022-23. Perform all calculations to the nearest £.

Chapter 28

Groups of companies and reconstructions

Introduction

For corporation tax purposes, groups of companies are divided into a number of categories and each category enjoys certain tax advantages. These advantages may include:

(a) the transfer of trading losses and certain other deficits between group members

(b) the transfer of chargeable assets from one group member to another in such a way that no chargeable gain arises on the transfer.

However, group companies are more likely than non-group companies to be required to pay their corporation tax by instalments.

The main purpose of this chapter is to describe the categories of group which exist and the corporation tax rules which apply to each category. The tax implications of company reconstructions are also considered very briefly at the end of this chapter.

Related 51% group companies

Company A is a "related 51% group company" of Company B for an accounting period if, for any part of that period, either:

(a) Company A is a 51% subsidiary of Company B, or

(b) Company B is a 51% subsidiary of Company A, or

(c) Company A and Company B are both 51% subsidiaries of the same third company.

In general terms, one company is a 51% subsidiary of another company if more than 50% of its ordinary shares are owned (directly or indirectly) by that other company.

When a company has one or more related 51% group companies, the augmented profits[†] limits of £1,500,000[‡] and £10,000,000 that are used when determining whether or not the company must pay corporation tax by instalments (see Chapter 25) are divided by (N + 1), where N is the number of those related 51% group companies.

[†] *As stated in Chapter 25, intra-group dividends are excluded when calculating augmented profits.*

[‡] *The "very large company" limit of £20,000,000 is also divided by (N + 1).*

Counting related 51% group companies

The number of related 51% group companies (N) taken into account when determining whether or not a company should pay corporation tax by instalments for an accounting period is the number of such companies existing at the end of the <u>previous</u> period. If there was no previous accounting period, N is the number of such companies existing at the commencement of the current period. Note that:

(a)   A company is counted as another company's related 51% group company at the end of a period even if it became so only part-way through that period.

(b)   Related 51% group companies which are dormant are ignored.

(c)   Related 51% group companies are counted whether or not they are UK resident, even though overseas companies are generally outside the charge to UK corporation tax.

EXAMPLE 1

A Ltd owns 90% of the ordinary share capital of B Ltd and 70% of the ordinary share capital of C Ltd. C Ltd owns 70% of the ordinary share capital of D Ltd.

(a)   Which companies are related 51% group companies of A Ltd?

(b)   If B Ltd now acquired 60% of the ordinary share capital of an overseas company, would this overseas company also become a related 51% group company of A Ltd?

Solution

(a)   A Ltd directly owns more than 50% of the ordinary share capital of B Ltd and C Ltd. Therefore B Ltd and C Ltd are both related 51% group companies of A Ltd.

A Ltd does not directly own any shares in D Ltd but it indirectly owns 49% of that company's ordinary share capital (70% x 70%). However, this is not sufficient to make D Ltd a related 51% group company of A Ltd.

Therefore the related 51% group companies of A Ltd are B Ltd and C Ltd.

(b)   Indirectly (via B Ltd) A Ltd would own 54% (90% x 60%) of the overseas company's ordinary share capital, so this overseas company would also become a related 51% group company of A Ltd.

EXAMPLE 2

E Ltd has taxable total profits of £800,000 for the year to 31 March 2023 and receives no dividends. For many years, the company has owned 65% of the ordinary shares of F Ltd and 30% of the ordinary shares of G Ltd.

Calculate the corporation tax liability of E Ltd for the year to 31 March 2023 and state the date (or dates) on which this tax is due to be paid (assuming that the company was "large" for payment by instalments purposes in the year to 31 March 2022).

Solution

E Ltd had one related 51% group company (F Ltd) at 31 March 2022. Therefore the profit limit which is used when determining whether the company must pay tax by instalments for the year to 31 March 2023 is reduced to (£1,500,000 ÷ 2) = £750,000. Augmented profits for the year exceed this limit and so tax is payable by instalments.

The accounting period coincides with FY2022 and the applicable rate of tax is 19%. The liability is (£800,000 × 19%) = £152,000 and this is payable in four instalments of £38,000 each on 14 October 2022, 14 January 2023, 14 April 2023 and 14 July 2023.

EXAMPLE 3

S Ltd has taxable total profits of £120,000 for the six months to 30 September 2022 and receives no dividends. Until 1 June 2021, S Ltd had no related 51% group companies. However, on that date, its entire share capital was acquired by H Ltd. H Ltd has five other wholly-owned subsidiaries, two of which are dormant.

Determine whether or not S Ltd will be required to pay corporation tax by instalments for the six months to 30 September 2022.

Solution

S Ltd had four related 51% group companies (H Ltd and its three active subsidiaries) at the end of the previous accounting period. Therefore the profit limit which is used to determine whether or not the company must pay corporation tax by instalments for the six months to 30 September 2022 is reduced to ((£1,500,000 × 6/12) ÷ 5) = £150,000.

Augmented profits for the period are only £120,000. This does not exceed £150,000, so the company is not required to pay corporation tax by instalments for this period.

EXAMPLE 4

A company which has seven 51% subsidiaries has taxable total profits of £140,000 for the year to 31 May 2022. Dividends received in the year were £50,000. Calculate the corporation tax liability for the year and state the date (or dates) on which this tax is due to be paid, assuming that the company was "large" in the year to 31 May 2021 and *either*:

(a)   all of the dividends received were intra-group dividends, *or*

(b)   none of the dividends received were intra-group dividends.

Solution

(a)   The company has seven 51% related companies and so must pay tax by instalments if augmented profits exceed £187,500 (£1,500,000 ÷ 8). Intra-group dividends are ignored, so augmented profits are the same as TTP (£140,000) and instalments are not required. The liability of £26,600 (£140,000 × 19%) falls due on 1 March 2023.

(b)   Augmented profits (£190,000) exceed £187,500. Instalments of £6,650 each fall due on 14 December 2021, 14 March 2022, 14 June 2022 and 14 September 2022.

Associated companies (as from 1 April 2023)

As from 1 April 2023, the "related 51% group companies" rules will be repealed and replaced by "associated company" rules. In broad terms, one company is an associated company of another company if one of the companies controls the other, or if both companies are under the control of the same person (or persons).

The number of associated companies that a company has (N) will influence the rate at which corporation tax is payable (see Chapter 25) and will also be taken into account when determining whether the company is required to pay by instalments.

Group payment arrangements

If some or all of the companies in a group are liable to pay corporation tax by instalments, one of the group members (the "nominated company") may be nominated to make instalment payments on behalf of the entire group (or on behalf of those companies in the group that participate in the arrangement). This enables the instalment payments to be made on a group basis, based upon the estimated total tax liability of all of the companies covered by the arrangement (the "participating companies"). When the total liability of each group member is finally determined, the instalments already paid may be allocated between the participating members in such a way so as to minimise any interest payable.

For group payment purposes, a "group" is defined as a parent company together with its 51% subsidiaries. If any of these subsidiaries have 51% subsidiaries of their own, these are also included in the group, and so forth.

Note that it is not necessary for all of the companies in a group to participate in a group payment arrangement and that a number of separate arrangements may be established for a single group, each covering a subset of the members of the group.

Transfer pricing

For many years, the UK tax system has contained "transfer pricing" rules, the aim of which is to prevent UK companies from gaining a tax advantage by carrying out transactions at artificial prices with connected companies overseas (see Chapter 32). The transfer pricing rules require companies to calculate their profits for tax purposes as if such transactions had been carried out at the prices which would have applied between unconnected parties.

The original transfer pricing rules applied only to transactions with connected companies situated overseas, but these rules have now been extended to cover transactions between connected UK companies. Broadly, two companies are connected for this purpose if one of them controls the other or they are under common control. The rules require an adjustment for tax purposes to the profits of the company which gains a potential tax advantage from the transactions and a corresponding adjustment to the profits of the other company.

Small and medium-sized companies are exempt from the transfer pricing legislation.

75% groups

Company B is a 75% subsidiary of Company A if the following conditions are satisfied:

(a) Company A owns (directly or indirectly) at least 75% of the ordinary share capital of Company B, *and*

(b) Company A is entitled to at least 75% of the profits available to the ordinary shareholders of Company B, *and*

(c) Company A would be entitled to at least 75% of the assets available to the ordinary shareholders of Company B if Company B were to be wound-up.

Two companies are members of a 75% group if one company is a 75% subsidiary of the other or they are both 75% subsidiaries of a third company.

The UK resident members of a 75% group enjoy two main tax advantages[†]. These are the right to transfer certain losses and deficits between group members ("group relief") and the transfer of chargeable assets between group members in such a way that no chargeable gain arises on the transfer. These reliefs are described below.

Furthermore (subject to conditions) group relief may be available in relation to the losses of a non-UK resident company which is nonetheless within the charge to UK corporation tax and which is a member of a 75% group (see Chapter 32).

[†] *One disadvantage is that the £5m "deductions allowance" for carried-forward losses (see Chapter 26) pertains to the whole of a 75% group, not to each individual company. The same applies to the £2m caps involved in the temporary extended relief available for carried-back trading losses.*

EXAMPLE 5

P Ltd is the parent company of a small group. All companies are UK resident and all of the issued shares are ordinary shares. Shareholdings within the group are as follows:

(a) P Ltd owns 80% of Q Ltd, 100% of R Ltd and 60% of S Ltd.

(b) Q Ltd owns 90% of T Ltd.

(c) S Ltd owns 70% of V Ltd.

Identify 75% groups within this structure.

Solution

P Ltd owns (indirectly) 72% of T Ltd (80% x 90%) and 42% of V Ltd (60% x 70%). These shareholdings are less than 75% so T Ltd and V Ltd are not members of the 75% group headed by P Ltd. This 75% group comprises **P Ltd, Q Ltd and R Ltd**.

But there is also a second 75% group comprising **Q Ltd and T Ltd**.

Although Q Ltd belongs to both 75% groups, a loss transferred to Q Ltd from a member of one of the groups cannot be "passed on" by Q Ltd to a member of the other group.

Group relief

Group relief consists of the surrender of trading losses and/or certain other items by one member of a 75% group (the "surrendering company") to another member of the same group (the "claimant company"). The main items which may be surrendered are:

(a)   trading losses and deficits on non-trading loan relationships (NTLR)

(b)   property business losses, non-trading losses on intangible fixed assets and qualifying charitable donations.

Capital losses cannot be surrendered under the group relief rules, but a capital loss can in effect be transferred from one group company to another by a different means (see later in this chapter). Note the following points with regard to group relief:

(a)   The surrender may be in whole or in part as best meets the requirements of the surrendering company and the claimant company. Trading losses and deficits on non-trading loan relationships may be surrendered even if they could instead have been offset against the profits of the accounting period in which they are incurred. The other items are available for surrender only to the extent that (in aggregate) they exceed the surrendering company's gross profits for the period in which they are incurred.

   For this purpose, a company's "gross profits" are its profits *before* deducting any amounts which are eligible for group relief and *before* deducting losses or other amounts carried forward or back from any other period.

(b)   A surrender may be made from subsidiary to parent, from parent to subsidiary or from subsidiary to fellow subsidiary.

(c)   Surrendered losses (or other items) must be set against the claimant company's profits for an *overlapping* accounting period. If the accounting periods of the surrendering company and claimant company do not correspond exactly, group relief is available only for the period of overlap between the two periods. The losses of the surrendering company and profits of the claimant company are time-apportioned to determine the amounts which fall into the overlap period. A similar time-apportionment is required when a company joins or leaves a group part-way through an accounting period.

(d)   Until 1 April 2017, only current-period losses were eligible for group relief. But as from that date, *carried-forward losses* (see Chapter 26) may be group relieved to the extent that they cannot be deducted from the surrendering company's own profits. Carried-forward losses and deficits which are eligible for group relief (as long as incurred on or after 1 April 2017) are:

   - trading losses and NTLR deficits
   - property business losses and non-trading losses on intangible fixed assets.

However, the claimant company must use its own carried-forward losses to the fullest extent possible before claiming group relief for another company's carried-forward losses. And the "deductions allowance" (see Chapter 26) applies to group relief for carried-forward losses as well as to a company's own carried-forward losses.

(e) The amount of the losses and other items surrendered to a claimant company cannot exceed that company's "available profits" for the corresponding accounting period. Available profits are the company's total profits *before* deducting any reliefs derived from a subsequent period but *after* deducting reliefs derived from a prior period or the current period. For example, the following items must be deducted when computing a company's available profits for group relief purposes:

- carried-forward trading losses relieved in the current period
- current-period trading losses which are relieved against total profits of the period (or which could have been relieved in this way)
- qualifying charitable donations for the period.

Note that group relief is given *before* relief for trading losses carried back.

(f) A group relief claim must be made within two years of the end of the claimant company's accounting period. Any amount paid to the surrendering company by the claimant company in return for the surrendered items is ignored for tax purposes so long as the payment does not exceed the amount of the surrendered items.

EXAMPLE 6

Low1 Ltd is a wholly-owned subsidiary of High1 Ltd. Both companies are UK resident and prepare accounts to 30 April each year. Results for the year to 30 April 2023 are:

	High1 Ltd £	Low1 Ltd £
Trading profit/(loss)	100,000	(180,000)
Chargeable gains	5,000	75,000
Gift Aid donations	12,000	-

Show how the trading loss sustained by Low1 Ltd may be relieved.

Solution

High1 Ltd has taxable total profits of £93,000 (£100,000 + £5,000 − £12,000). This sets a ceiling on the amount of group relief which may be claimed. The trading loss sustained by Low1 Ltd may be relieved in a number of ways. For example:

(a) The entire loss could be carried forward for relief in subsequent accounting periods.

(b) £75,000 of the loss could be relieved against the company's chargeable gains and the balance of £105,000 could then be carried forward. Alternatively, the remaining £105,000 of the loss could be relieved (as far as possible) against the total profits of Low1 Ltd for the previous 12 months.

(c) Group relief of anything up to £93,000 could be claimed and the balance of the loss then dealt with as above.

EXAMPLE 7

Low2 Ltd is a 75% subsidiary of High2 Ltd and both companies are UK resident. Recent results are as follows:

	High2 Ltd £	Low2 Ltd £
Trading loss for year to 31 March 2022		(40,000)
Available profits:		
year to 31 December 2021	35,000	
year to 31 December 2022	56,000	

Compute the amount of group relief that may be claimed.

Solution

The accounting periods of High2 Ltd and Low2 Ltd do not correspond, so it is necessary to time-apportion profits and losses, as follows:

	1/4/2021 - 31/12/2021 (9 months) £	1/1/2022 - 31/3/2022 (3 months) £
(i) High2 Ltd profit	26,250	14,000
(ii) Low2 Ltd loss	(30,000)	(10,000)

The group relief available in each period is the lower of (i) and (ii). Therefore, High2 Ltd may claim that group relief of up to £26,250 should be set against its 2021 profits and that group relief of up to £10,000 should be set against its 2022 profits. The remaining £3,750 of the loss is not eligible for group relief in the year to 31 March 2022. But if this part of the loss is carried forward, it may be eligible for group relief in subsequent periods.

Using group relief effectively

Group relief should be used to ensure that trading losses (and other eligible items) are relieved as tax-effectively as possible, so that the group's total tax liability is minimised. Points to bear in mind are:

(a) Claimant companies could claim less than the maximum capital allowances available for an accounting period, so increasing the profits available for group relief set-off.

(b) A company which has incurred a trading loss might lose tax relief on qualifying charitable donations if the loss is set against the company's total profits. This loss of tax relief might be avoided if the loss is group-relieved instead.

(c) *As from FY2023*, losses etc. should be surrendered to claimant companies which pay corporation tax at higher rates (especially the marginal rate of 26.5%) rather than to claimant companies which pay corporation tax at lower rates (see Chapter 25).

Group relief could also be utilised to reduce the profits of selected group companies to the level where those companies would no longer be required to pay tax by instalments.

Transfer of chargeable assets within a group

If a chargeable asset is transferred from one member of a 75% group to another, the transfer is deemed to have occurred at a value giving rise to neither a gain nor a loss. When an asset which has been transferred between group members in this way is finally disposed of outside the group, the chargeable gain arising on the disposal is then (in effect) calculated with reference to the original cost of the asset to the group. Note that:

(a)   The definition of a 75% group for this purpose is less rigorous than the definition which is given above in relation to group relief. A *capital gains group* consists of a principal company plus its 75% subsidiaries (as previously defined) plus the subsidiaries' 75% subsidiaries and so forth, subject to the over-riding requirement that the principal company must have more than a 50% interest in each member of the group.

(b)   A 75% subsidiary which is part of a capital gains group cannot also be the principal company of another capital gains group.

EXAMPLE 8

J Ltd owns 80% of the ordinary share capital of K Ltd, which owns 80% of the ordinary share capital of L Ltd, which owns 80% of the ordinary share capital of M Ltd, which owns 80% of the ordinary share capital of N Ltd. All of these companies are UK resident. Which of the companies belongs to a capital gains group with J Ltd as the principal company?

Solution

At first sight, all five companies seem to belong to the capital gains group which has J Ltd at its head. However, J Ltd must have more than a 50% interest in each member of the group. J Ltd's actual interests in each member are as follows:

K Ltd	80%
L Ltd	80% x 80% = 64%
M Ltd	80% x 80% x 80% = 51.2%
N Ltd	80% x 80% x 80% x 80% = 40.96%

J Ltd's interest in N Ltd does not exceed 50%, therefore the capital gains group contains only J Ltd, K Ltd, L Ltd and M Ltd.

Since M Ltd is a member of this group it cannot also be the principal member of another capital gains group. So it is not possible for M Ltd and N Ltd to form a second capital gains group containing just those two companies.

Roll-over relief for capital gains groups

For the purposes of roll-over relief on the replacement of a business asset (see Chapter 22) all of the companies in a capital gains group are treated as a single company. So a gain arising on the disposal of a business asset by one member of a group can be rolled-over against the cost of a qualifying business asset acquired by another member of that group.

However, the asset against which a gain is rolled-over in these circumstances must be an asset which has been newly acquired *by the group as a whole*. It is not possible to roll-over a gain against an asset which has been acquired by one group member from another.

Degrouping charge

A chargeable gain or allowable loss may arise in connection with an intra-group transfer if a company has a chargeable asset transferred to it from another group member and then leaves the group (still owning the asset) within six years of the date of the transfer. In these circumstances, the transferee company is deemed to have sold the asset on the date of the intra-group transfer for its market value on that date (triggering a gain or loss) and then to have immediately re-acquired the asset on the same date and for the same amount.

The tax treatment of such a "degrouping" gain or loss depends upon the circumstances which have caused the transferee company to leave the group, as follows:

(a) If the transferee company has left the group because of a share disposal made by another group member, then any degrouping gain is added to disposal proceeds when computing the gain/loss arising on that share disposal. Any degrouping loss is treated as allowable expenditure when computing the gain/loss arising on the disposal.

The event that most frequently causes a company to leave a group is the disposal by a parent company of its shares in a subsidiary. Such a disposal necessitates the above treatment of degrouping gains or losses, so that (in effect) any such gains or losses arising when the subsidiary leaves the group are passed on to the parent.

However, it is important to note that the disposal by a parent company of shares in a subsidiary is likely to qualify as the disposal of a "substantial shareholding". Since gains arising on such disposals are exempt from tax (see Chapter 24), this means that any degrouping gains arising in these circumstances would also be exempt.

(b) If the transferee company has *not* left the group because of a disposal of shares by another group member, then any degrouping gain or loss is treated as if it had occurred in the accounting period in which the transferee company leaves the group and is taken into account when computing the transferee company's tax liability for that period.

These provisions would apply if (for example) a subsidiary company leaves a group because it has made a share issue and, as a result of that issue, its parent company no longer owns at least 75% of the subsidiary's shares.

EXAMPLE 9

S1 Ltd and S2 Ltd belong to the same capital gains group. In May 2019, S1 Ltd transferred a chargeable asset to S2 Ltd. The original cost of this asset to S1 Ltd was £10,000 and its market value in May 2019 was £25,000. Indexation allowance of £1,350 would have been available in May 2019 If the asset had been sold outside the group. S2 Ltd (which prepares accounts to 31 December) leaves the group in March 2023.

(a)   Calculate the degrouping gain arising on the departure of S2 Ltd.

(b)   Explain the tax treatment of this gain.

Solution

(a)   S2 Ltd is deemed to have sold the asset for £25,000 in May 2019 and then to have immediately re-acquired it for the same amount. The sale would have given rise to a chargeable gain of £13,650 (£25,000 − £10,000 − £1,350) so a degrouping gain of £13,650 arises when S2 Ltd leaves the group.

(b)   The treatment of this gain depends upon the circumstances in which S2 Ltd has left the group. If this departure has been caused by a share disposal made by another member of the group (probably S2's parent), then the £13,650 is added to disposal proceeds when calculating the gain or loss arising on that share disposal. Otherwise, the degrouping gain is treated as a chargeable gain of £13,650 accruing to S2 Ltd in the year to 31 December 2023.

Capital losses

Capital losses cannot be surrendered to another member of the group. This is in contrast to trading losses and certain other items which can be surrendered. At one time, the only way around this problem was to transfer assets between group members in such a way that chargeable gains and capital losses arose in the same company. Imagine that Company L and Company G were both members of a capital gains group, that Company L had capital losses and that Company G was about to dispose of an asset and realise a chargeable gain. Company L's capital losses could be set against this gain in the following way:

(a)   Company G could transfer its asset to Company L (on a no gain/no loss basis).

(b)   Company L could then dispose of the asset. The gain would be realised by Company L rather than Company G, so allowing Company L's losses to be set against it.

But a simpler procedure is now available. Two companies that are members of a capital gains group may jointly elect that all or part of the gain (or loss) arising on a disposal by one of the companies should be treated as if it had been realised (or incurred) by the other company. This allows gains and losses to be brought together in the same company without having to actually transfer assets between group members. The election must be made within two years of the end of the accounting period in which the disposal occurs.

Pre-entry capital losses

A group which anticipates making disposals which will give rise to substantial chargeable gains might try to shelter those gains from tax by acquiring a "capital loss company". This is a company which has capital losses brought forward and/or assets which would realise capital losses on disposal. The intention of the acquisition would be to offset these capital losses against the group's chargeable gains (by means of the procedure outlined above) and so reduce the group's overall corporation tax liability.

However, anti-avoidance legislation exists which prevents groups from gaining a tax advantage in this way. This legislation applies only if certain conditions are satisfied. The main conditions are as follows:

(a) There must be a "qualifying change of ownership" of the capital loss company. This condition is satisfied if the company joins a group.

(b) The change of ownership must occur in connection with "arrangements", of which one of the main purposes is to secure a tax advantage.

If these conditions are satisfied, the anti-avoidance legislation applies and it is not possible to set the acquired capital losses against the group's chargeable gains.

Even if these conditions are *not* satisfied, there is in any case a restriction on the relief available in relation to a company's *pre-entry capital losses*. Pre-entry capital losses are defined as capital losses incurred by the company before joining a group. Such losses may be set only against gains arising on disposals of:

(a) assets which the company owned before it joined the group ("pre-entry assets"), or

(b) assets acquired *from outside the group* since the company joined the group.

Consortia

A company is owned by a consortium (and is known as a *consortium company*) if at least 75% of its ordinary share capital is owned by other companies (which are known as *consortium members*) each of which <u>directly</u> owns:

(a) at least 5% of the consortium company's ordinary share capital, but

(b) less than 75% of that share capital.

A 90% subsidiary of a consortium company is also regarded as a consortium company. A company (B Ltd) is a "90% subsidiary" of another company (A Ltd) if A Ltd directly owns at least 90% of the ordinary share capital of B Ltd.

Group relief for a consortium

Group relief is available (in either direction) between a consortium member and a consortium company, so long as both companies are UK resident[†] and the consortium company is either a trading company or a company whose business consists wholly or mainly of holding shares in trading companies which are its 90% subsidiaries. Note the following points with regard to group relief for a consortium:

(a) The relief is restricted in proportion to the consortium member's shareholding in the consortium company. For instance, if CC Ltd is a consortium company and CM Ltd is a consortium member which owns p% of CC Ltd, then:

    (i) If CM Ltd is the claimant company, it may claim up to p% of CC Ltd's losses.

    (ii) If CM Ltd is the surrendering company, it may surrender to CC Ltd losses of up to p% of CC Ltd's profits.

(b) A group relief claim must be agreed by all the consortium members.

(c) The amount of a consortium company's trading loss which is available for group relief is the amount of that loss less any potential claim for relief against total profits of the loss-making period, whether or not such a claim is actually made.

[†] *See Chapter 32 for the situation with regard to non-UK resident companies.*

EXAMPLE 10

The ordinary share capital of W Ltd (which is a trading company) is owned 30% by X Ltd, 25% by Y Ltd and 45% by Z Ltd. All of these companies are UK resident and they prepare accounts to 31 March. Results for the year to 31 March 2023 are as follows:

	W Ltd	X Ltd	Y Ltd	Z Ltd
	£	£	£	£
Trading profit/(loss)	(62,000)	41,000	11,000	38,000
Chargeable gains	10,000	-	-	-

What are the maximum possible group relief claims which may be made?

Solution

W Ltd could claim (potentially) that £10,000 of its trading loss should be set against its total profits of the loss-making period. Therefore, whether or not such a claim is made, the loss available for group relief is £52,000 (£62,000 − £10,000). This amount is then shared between the consortium members in proportion to their shares in W Ltd, as follows:

	X Ltd	Y Ltd	Z Ltd
	£	£	£
Share of W Ltd available loss	15,600	13,000	23,400
Taxable total profits (before group relief)	41,000	11,000	38,000
Maximum group relief claim	15,600	11,000	23,400

Corporate interest restriction

The "corporate interest restriction" places a limit on the amount of the interest expense that may be deducted when calculating the corporation tax liability of a single UK company or the UK members of a "worldwide group". For this purpose, a "group" is a group as defined by international financial reporting standards (IFRS). A single company is referred to in the relevant legislation as a "single-company worldwide group".

In broad terms, the total deduction for interest payable (and other finance charges) which can be made when calculating the corporation tax liability of the UK members of a group is restricted to 30% of the total earnings before interest, tax, depreciation and amortisation ("EBITDA") of those companies. If this limit is exceeded, there is a "disallowed amount" and the parent company of the group is required to file a "statement of allocated interest restrictions" which sets out the amount of the interest restriction that will be applied to each company in the group when computing each company's corporation tax liability.

However, a group with an interest expense not exceeding a "de minimis" figure of £2m per annum is exempt from the corporate interest restriction.

Company reconstructions

If a company transfers a trade to another company, this ranks as a cessation of that trade and therefore unrelieved trading losses incurred before the date of the transfer cannot normally be carried forward and used by the successor company. However, if a trade is transferred between two companies (both within the charge to UK corporation tax in respect of that trade) and at least 75% of the trade is effectively owned by the same persons both:

(a) at some time within the year before the date of the transfer, and

(b) at some time within the two years after the date of the transfer

then any unrelieved trading losses of the transferred trade may be carried forward and set against subsequent profits of the same trade (for losses incurred before 1 April 2017) or total profits of the successor company (for losses incurred on or after that date).

For instance, this "succession of trade" relief would be available if a company created a 75% subsidiary and transferred a trade to that subsidiary. However, this relief does not extend to non-trading losses or capital losses, neither of which can be carried forward and used by the successor company. Subject to certain conditions, the following provisions also apply to such "company reconstructions":

(a) For capital allowances purposes, assets are transferred at their tax-written down values, with no balancing adjustments.

(b) Chargeable assets are transferred to the successor company on a no-gain, no-loss basis, as long as the transferor receives no consideration for the assets concerned and the assets remain within the scope of UK corporation tax.

443

Summary

▶ If a company has N "related 51% group companies", the profits limits which are used for payment by instalments purposes are divided by (N + 1).

▶ Transfer pricing rules apply to transactions carried out at artificial prices between group companies.

▶ Trading losses and certain other items may be surrendered between members of a 75% group. This is known as "group relief". Subject to certain conditions, group relief is also available between consortium members and consortium companies.

▶ Chargeable assets are transferred between members of a capital gains group on a "no-gain, no-loss" basis. However, a degrouping charge may arise if a chargeable asset is transferred from one group member to another and then the transferee company leaves the group within six years.

▶ Capital losses cannot be surrendered to another group member. However, two group members may elect that a gain or loss arising in one of the companies should be treated as if it had arisen in the other company.

▶ If a trade is transferred between two companies, the unrelieved trading losses of the transferor company may (subject to certain conditions) be carried forward and used by the successor company.

Exercises

A set of multiple choice questions for this chapter is available on the accompanying website.

28.1   Armco1 Ltd and Armco2 Ltd are 100% subsidiaries of Headco Ltd, which has no other subsidiaries. They are all UK resident and the group has existed for several years. How will the relationship of the three companies affect the way in which they are taxed?

28.2   U Ltd has three subsidiaries (one of which is dormant) and has the following results for the year to 31 December 2022:

	£
Trading profits	485,000
Income from property	12,000
Dividends received from subsidiaries	128,000
Dividends received from non-group companies	30,000
Gift Aid donations	17,000

Compute the corporation tax liability for the year and state the date (or dates) on which this tax is due to be paid. Assume that the group has existed for many years.

28.3 Basenote Ltd is a wholly-owned subsidiary of Apexine Ltd. Both companies are UK resident and prepare accounts to 31 March each year. Results for the year to 31 March 2023 are as follows:

	Apexine Ltd	Basenote Ltd
	£	£
Trading profit/(loss)	120,000	(90,000)
Income from property	7,000	3,000
Gift Aid donations	12,000	4,000

Calculate the maximum group relief that may be claimed for the year by Apexine Ltd. What difference would it make if Basenote Ltd also had carried-forward trading losses from the previous year of £20,000?

28.4 A1 Ltd owns 90% of the ordinary share capital of A2 Ltd. A2 Ltd owns 80% of the ordinary share capital of A3 Ltd and 70% of the ordinary share capital of A4 Ltd. All companies are UK resident.

(a) Identify any 75% groups within this group structure.

(b) Which of these companies form a capital gains group with A1 Ltd as its principal company?

28.5 The ordinary share capital of PP Ltd (a trading company) is owned 32% by QQ Ltd, 35% by RR Ltd and 23% by SS Ltd. The remaining 10% is owned by various individuals, none of whom own more than 1%. All companies are UK resident and prepare accounts to 31 July. Results for the year to 31 July 2022 are as follows:

	PP Ltd	QQ Ltd	RR Ltd	SS Ltd
	£	£	£	£
Trading profit/(loss)	(96,000)	41,000	38,000	11,000
Chargeable gains	-	15,000	-	-
Income from property	12,000	6,000	11,000	4,000
Gift Aid donations	-	(3,000)	(2,000)	(1,000)

Compute the maximum possible group relief claims.

*28.6 T Ltd has owned 90% of the ordinary share capital of B Ltd for many years. Both are UK resident. Recent results for the two companies are as follows:

	T Ltd y/e 31/3/2022	T Ltd y/e 31/3/2023	B Ltd y/e 30/11/2022
	£	£	£
Trading profit/(loss)	880,000	130,000	(174,000)
Chargeable gains	25,000	13,000	3,000
Gift Aid donations	5,000	5,000	-

No dividends have been received by either company in any of these years and maximum group relief is claimed. Calculate the corporation tax which is payable by each company for each accounting period and state the due date (or dates) of payment.

Review questions (Set C)

C1   Tolbooth Ltd is a manufacturing company. It commenced trading on 1 April 2021 and prepared its first set of accounts for the 18 month period to 30 September 2022. As the accounting technician responsible for preparing the tax computation, you have extracted the following information from the audit file:

		£
(i)	Trading profits (before capital allowances)	690,000

(ii) Rental income:
    £20,000 per year from property rented on 1 April 2021.
    Rent received annually in advance on 1 April.

(iii) Bank deposit interest:

Received 30 June 2021	200
Received 31 December 2021	200
Accrued to 31 March 2022	100
Received 30 June 2022	1,200
Accrued to 30 September 2022	445

(iv) Plant and machinery purchased on 1 April 2021:

Factory machinery	121,000
Motor car (45 g/km)	25,000

(v) Gift Aid donations:
    £5,000 every six months as from 31 December 2021

Paid 31 December 2021	5,000
Accrued to 31 March 2022	2,500
Paid 30 June 2022	5,000
Accrued to 30 September 2022	2,500

(vi) Chargeable gain on disposal 1 August 2022	8,300

Required:

(a)   State how the first period of account to 30 September 2022 will be divided into accounting periods.

(b)   Calculate the corporation tax liability for each accounting period.

(c)   State the due date (or dates) of payment of the company's corporation tax liability for the 18 months to 30 September 2022.

(d)   What difference would it make if the trading profit for the 18 months (before capital allowances) was £3,690,000 instead of £690,000?

(Amended from AAT)

C2   Quadrant Ltd has the following results for its three most recent accounting periods:

	y/e 31/7/2020	nine months to 30/4/2021	y/e 30/4/2022
	£	£	£
Trading profit/(loss)	2,050,000	260,000	(895,000)
Loan interest receivable	51,600	39,000	28,700
Chargeable gains/(losses)	32,000	(3,000)	47,000
Gift Aid donations	10,000	8,000	5,000

Notes:

1.   There were no trading losses brought forward on 1 August 2019.

2.   Capital losses brought forward on 1 August 2019 were £67,300.

3.   Following a bad trading result for the year to 30 April 2022, the company expects to return to making a sizeable trading profit in future years.

Required:

(a)   Compute the company's corporation tax liability for each of the three accounting periods, assuming that no claims are made in relation to the trading loss.

(b)   Compute the company's corporation tax liability for each of the three accounting periods, assuming that claims are made to relieve the £895,000 trading loss at the earliest possible opportunity. Also compute the amount of any trading losses which will be carried forward.

(c)   Calculate the amount of tax which would be saved in consequence of the claims referred to in (b) above. Would you recommend these claims?

(CIPFA)

C3   AA Ltd, BB Ltd and CC Ltd have the following results for the year to 31 March 2023:

	AA Ltd	BB Ltd	CC Ltd
	£	£	£
Trading profits	1,230,400	267,800	852,500
Interest receivable	16,300	-	15,000
Property income	-	5,000	-
Chargeable gains	46,400	13,600	37,300
Allowable capital losses	(2,900)	(77,400)	-
Dividends received	240,000	1,800	90,000
Gift Aid donations paid	5,200	1,000	4,800

None of these companies is a member of a group.

Required:

(a)   Compute each company's corporation tax liability for the year and state the due date (or dates) of payment in each case.

(b)   Explain how these liabilities and dates of payment would alter if the above figures were for the year to 30 September 2023 instead of the year to 31 March 2023.

C4   VFD Limited (which is not a group company) has prepared a set of accounts for the ten months to 31 March 2023. These accounts show a pre-tax profit of £1,429,530. Relevant information is:

(i)   Depreciation charged in the period was £156,945.

(ii)   UK dividends received were £137,260.

(iii)   The written down value of the company's plant and machinery as at 1 June 2022 for capital allowances purposes was as follows:

	£
Main pool	153,190
Special rate pool	40,880

The special rate pool contained only the managing director's Volvo motor car which had emissions of 118g/km.

(iv)   Additions and disposals were as follows:

July 2022	Sold machinery (original cost £75,000)	26,450
October 2022	Bought new plant and machinery	126,700
November 2022	Sold Volvo motor car	35,000
November 2022	Bought Audi motor car (emissions 107g/km)	52,000
February 2023	Bought second-hand motor lorry	50,000

Required:

Calculate the corporation tax liability for the period ended on 31 March 2023 and state the date (or dates) on which this is due for payment.   *(CIPFA)*

C5   Antietam Ltd makes up accounts to 30 September annually. Results for the 12 months to 30 September 2022 are as follows:

	£
Trading profits (before capital allowances)	173,000
Capital allowances	32,000
Rental income	46,000
Chargeable gains	6,400
Dividends received	14,400

The company has capital losses brought forward from previous accounting periods of £1,400 and made a Gift Aid donation of £20,000 during the year.

Required:

(a)   Calculate the corporation tax liability of Antietam Ltd for the year to 30 September 2022 and state the due date of payment.

(b)   What difference would it make if you were told that the company has nine subsidiary companies and that all of the dividends received of £14,400 were paid to Antietam Ltd by its subsidiaries?   *(Amended from AAT)*

*C6   The statement of profit or loss of Jump Ltd for the three-month period ended 31 March 2023 is as shown below. The figures in brackets refer to the notes which follow.

	£	£
Revenue		264,900
Operating expenses:		
Depreciation	8,100	
Employee costs (1)	189,700	
Lease of motor car (2)	1,200	
Professional fees (3)	7,800	
Other expenses (4)	202,800	(409,600)
Operating loss		(144,700)
Other income		0
Loss before taxation		(144,700)

Note 1: Employee costs

	£
Employee training courses	3,400
Employee pension contributions paid	11,600
Cost of annual staff party (for eight employees)	1,500
Balance of expenditure (all allowable)	173,200
	189,700

Note 2: Lease of motor car

The lease is in respect of a motor car with emissions of 119g/km.

Note 3: Professional fees

	£
Accountancy	2,200
Legal fees in connection with the issue of share capital	3,800
Legal fees in connection with the renewal of a 20-year property lease	1,800
	7,800

Note 4: Other expenses

	£
Entertaining UK customers	1,700
Entertaining overseas customers	790
Political donations	800
Balance of expenditure (all allowable)	199,510
	202,800

Plant and machinery

On 1 January 2023, the tax written down values of the plant and machinery of Jump Ltd were as follows:

	£
Main pool	12,100
Special rate pool	5,700

The following motor cars were sold during the three months to 31 March 2023:

	Date of sale	Proceeds	Original cost
		£	£
Motor car (1)	7 January 2023	9,700	9,300
Motor car (2)	29 March 2023	6,100	13,200

The original cost of motor car (1) was added to the special rate pool when it was purchased and the original cost of motor car (2) was added to the main pool.

Group companies

Jump Ltd owns 80% of the ordinary shares of Hop Ltd and 60% of the ordinary shares of Skip Ltd. Hop Ltd commenced trading on 1 August 2022 and has taxable total profits of £63,000 for the eight-month period to 31 March 2023. Skip Ltd has been trading for many years and has taxable total profits of £56,000 for the year to 31 March 2023.

Required:

(a) Calculate the tax adjusted trading loss of Jump Ltd for the three-month period to 31 March 2023.

(b) Advise Jump Ltd as to the maximum amount of this trading loss that could be surrendered as group relief. *(ACCA)*

*C7 Q Ltd prepares accounts to 31 March each year. The company made the following two disposals of chargeable assets during the year to 31 March 2023:

(1) 1,250 shares in Hentic Ltd were sold on 28 June 2022 for £25,000. The previous purchases and sales of shares in Hentic Ltd had been as follows:

		£	RPI
12 May 2001	Bought 2,000 shares	14,000	174.2
17 June 2004	Rights issue (1 for 10)	1,000	186.8
6 July 2008	Sold 1,000 shares	9,000	216.5
21 June 2022	Bought 600 shares	9,000	

(2) The company's factory was sold for £437,500 on 4 March 2023. This factory had been purchased on 11 April 2002 (RPI 175.7) for £285,000.

Note:

The factory purchased in April 2002 was a replacement for a previous factory which had been purchased for £200,000 on 3 January 1992 (RPI 135.6) and sold for £320,000 on 14 June 2002 (RPI 176.2). Rollover relief was claimed in relation to the June 2002 disposal.

The RPI for December 2017 was 278.1.

Required:

(a) Calculate the chargeable gain arising on the sale of the shares on 28 June 2022.

(b) Calculate the chargeable gain arising on the sale of the factory on 4 March 2023, assuming that a further factory was purchased on 6 November 2022 for £360,000 and that rollover relief is claimed in relation to the March 2023 disposal.

*C8   For many years, W Ltd has owned 70% of the issued shares of X Ltd, 30% of the issued shares of Y Ltd and 80% of the issued shares of Z Ltd. All four companies are UK resident and all of the shares of each company are ordinary shares. Results for the year to 31 March 2023 for each company are as follows:

	W Ltd £	X Ltd £	Y Ltd £	Z Ltd £
Trading profit/(loss)	210,000	(65,000)	35,000	(45,000)
Dividends paid in the year	-	30,000	18,000	27,000

Required:

(a)   State (with reasons) which of X Ltd, Y Ltd and Z Ltd are "related 51% group companies" of W Ltd. Also explain how W Ltd might be affected by the fact that it has one or more related 51% group companies.

(b)   Explain how the corporation tax computation of W Ltd for the year to 31 March 2023 is affected by the fact that it has received dividends from the other three companies.

(c)   Calculate the maximum group relief that can be claimed by W Ltd for the year to 31 March 2023.

(d)   Assuming that maximum group relief is claimed, calculate the corporation tax liability of W Ltd for the year to 31 March 2023 and state the date upon which this tax is due for payment.

*C9   Neil has been in business for many years preparing accounts to 5 April each year. His profits in a typical year (adjusted for tax purposes) are approximately £50,000 and his drawings are £3,000 per month (i.e. £36,000 per year). He has no other income and he is not a Scottish taxpayer.

Neil is now thinking of forming a company (wholly owned by himself) to run his business. If this happens, he would extract £36,000 per year from the company, either as a director's salary or as a dividend.

Required:

(a)   Calculate the total amount of income tax and National Insurance contributions payable each year at present, with Neil operating as a sole trader.

(b)   Calculate the total amount of corporation tax, income tax and National Insurance contributions that would be payable each year if Neil decides to incorporate and takes a monthly director's salary of £3,000.

(c)   Calculate the total amount of corporation tax, income tax and National Insurance contributions that would be payable each year if Neil incorporates and takes a dividend of £36,000 per year.

Assume that the annual profits of the business continue to be £50,000. Use tax rates and allowances for tax year 2022-23 and corporation tax year FY2022 in your calculations and work to the nearest £.

*C10   The following information is available for Online Ltd for the year to 31 March 2023:

Operating profit

Online Ltd's operating profit for the year to 31 March 2023 is £896,700. Depreciation of £21,660 and amortisation of leasehold property of £9,000 (see leasehold property note below) have been deducted in arriving at this figure.

Leasehold property

On 1 April 2022, Online Ltd acquired a leasehold office building, paying a premium of £90,000 for the grant of a ten-year lease. This building was used for business purposes by Online Ltd throughout the year to 31 March 2023.

Plant and machinery

On 1 April 2022, the tax written down values of plant and machinery were as follows:

	£
Main pool	56,700
Special rate pool	12,400

The following transactions took place during the year to 31 March 2023:

		Costs/(proceeds) £
14 May 2022	Sold a motor car	(18,100)
18 July 2022	Sold all items in the special rate pool	(9,300)
27 January 2023	Purchased a motor car	13,700

The motor car sold on 14 May 2022 for £18,100 was originally purchased during the year to 31 March 2022 for £17,200. This expenditure was added to the main pool. The motor car purchased on 27 January 2023 for £13,700 has emissions of 48g/km.

Qualifying charitable donations

During the year to 31 March 2023, Online Ltd made qualifying charitable donations of £6,800. These were not included in arriving at the operating profit above.

Disposal of shareholding in Network plc

On 20 March 2023, Online Ltd sold its entire holding of £1 ordinary shares in Network plc for £90,600. Online Ltd had originally purchased 40,000 shares (less than a 1% shareholding) in Network plc on 24 June 2010 for £49,300. On 7 October 2013, Online Ltd sold 22,000 of the shares for £62,200. Indexation factors are as follows:

June 2010 to October 2013	0.124
June 2010 to December 2017	0.241
October 2013 to December 2017	0.104

Brought forward losses

As at 1 April 2022, Online Ltd had capital losses brought forward of £4,700 and trading losses brought forward of £12,500. The trading losses were incurred in the year to 31 March 2022 and the company wishes to relieve them as soon as possible.

You are required to:

Calculate Online Ltd's taxable total profits for the year to 31 March 2023.   *(ACCA)*

Part 4

MISCELLANEOUS

Chapter 29

Value added tax (1)

Introduction

This is the first of two chapters on value added tax (VAT). Value added tax is an indirect tax which was introduced in 1973 (when the UK joined the EU) and which is charged on the supply of a wide variety of goods and services. Current legislation is to be found in the Value Added Tax Act 1994 (VATA 1994), as amended by subsequent Finance Acts.

Until 1 January 2021, the underlying legislation on VAT was laid down in EU Directives, which are binding on all EU member states. But now that the UK has left the EU, these Directives no longer apply in the UK. Therefore the UK is now at liberty to amend its own VAT legislation as it sees fit.

The principle of VAT

The basic principle of the VAT system is that tax should be charged at each stage of the production and distribution process but that the total tax due should be borne by the final consumer of the product. This is achieved as follows:

(a) Traders who are registered for VAT (see below) are required to charge VAT on their sales and must account for this *output tax* to HMRC, but

(b) such traders are allowed to recover from HMRC the *input tax* which they pay to their own suppliers, so that

(c) in effect, registered traders suffer no VAT and the total VAT is borne by the consumer at the end of the distribution chain.

EXAMPLE 1

A Ltd owns a quarry. It extracts stone from this quarry and sells it to B Ltd for £10,000 plus VAT. B Ltd converts all of the stone into paving slabs and sells these slabs to C Ltd for £18,000, plus VAT. C Ltd owns a garden centre, where the paving slabs are sold to the general public for a total of £32,000, plus VAT. Show how VAT is charged and collected at each stage of this process, assuming that VAT is to be calculated at 20% throughout.

Solution

	Cost price before VAT	Input tax	Selling price before VAT	Output tax	Paid to HMRC
	£	£	£	£	£
A Ltd	-	-	10,000	2,000	2,000
B Ltd	10,000	2,000	18,000	3,600	1,600
C Ltd	18,000	3,600	32,000	6,400	2,800
Total VAT charged					6,400

Note:

None of the three companies involved suffers any net VAT. In each case, the total of input tax paid to suppliers and the amount paid to HMRC is precisely equal to the output tax charged to customers. The final consumers, who are unable to reclaim the VAT which they pay, bear the total VAT of £6,400.

Taxable persons

Formally, a charge to UK VAT arises when a *taxable supply* of goods or services is made in the UK by a *taxable person* in the course of business. The term "person" can refer to an individual, partnership or company, as well as to any other body which supplies goods or services in the course of business. There is no need for a profit motive to exist, just that goods or services are supplied for a consideration, so the term "person" can also refer to a charity, a club etc. A *taxable person* is a person making taxable supplies who is, or should be, registered for VAT. Persons must register if their turnover of taxable items exceeds a prescribed registration threshold and might register voluntarily even if turnover is beneath this threshold (see later in this chapter).

A taxable person should charge VAT to customers when making taxable supplies, must account for this output tax to HMRC and may reclaim the tax suffered on inputs. A person who is not a taxable person can neither charge VAT to customers nor reclaim input tax[†].

[†] *The main national museums and art galleries are an exception to this general rule, in that they are allowed to reclaim input tax even though they provide free admission to the public and so do not operate a business. A similar rule applies to the non-business activities of certain charities (e.g. palliative care charities, search and rescue charities and air ambulance charities).*

Taxable supplies

A *taxable supply* is any supply of goods or services in the UK other than a supply which is specifically exempted from VAT. VAT is charged on a taxable supply at the standard rate of 20%, unless the supply attracts tax at the reduced rate (5%) or at the zero rate (0%).

The types of supply which are exempt from VAT and the types of supply which are taxable at the reduced rate or the zero rate are listed later in this chapter.

Supply of goods

A supply of goods is deemed to occur when the ownership of goods is transferred from one person to another. In general, a supply of goods will fall within the scope of VAT only if it is made for a consideration (i.e. in return for money or payment in kind) but the following are also deemed to be supplies of goods for VAT purposes:

(a) gifts of business assets on which input tax has been reclaimed, other than:

    (i) gifts made to any one person in any rolling 12-month period costing in total no more than £50

    (ii) gifts consisting of samples (where a "sample" is a specimen of a product which is intended to promote sales of that product)

(b) goods permanently taken out of a business for private use by the owner or an employee of the business, in respect of which input tax has been reclaimed.

The sale of goods on hire purchase terms is deemed to be a supply of goods but VAT is charged on the cash price of the goods, not the HP price.

Supply of services

Any supply which is made for a consideration but which is not a supply of goods is deemed to be a supply of services. However, a gift of services is not a taxable supply. The hiring of goods to a customer is a supply of services, not a supply of goods, since the ownership of the goods does not pass to the customer. A supply of services is also deemed to occur if the owner or an employee of a business:

(a) temporarily makes private use of goods owned by the business, in respect of which input tax has been reclaimed, or

(b) makes private use of services which have been supplied to the business, in respect of which input tax has been reclaimed.

However, the private use of a business motor car is generally not a taxable supply.

Self-supply

A "self-supply" occurs when a taxable person makes a supply to himself or herself. For example, a self-supply of a motor car occurs if a motor manufacturer produces a car and then uses it instead of supplying it to a customer. The Treasury is empowered to order that, for VAT purposes, self-supplied goods or services are regarded as both:

(a) a taxable supply made *by* the business, and

(b) a taxable supply made *to* the business.

The effect of such an order is that output tax must be accounted for in relation to the supply but that an equal amount of input tax is deemed to have been suffered. This input tax may then be irrecoverable in whole or part (see Chapter 30).

Exempt supplies

A supply of goods or services is an exempt supply if it falls within one of sixteen exemption groups. In summary, these exemption groups are as follows:

Group 1 The sale or lease of land and buildings, *other than*:

   (i) the sale (or lease for more than 21 years) of new and certain second-hand buildings for residential or charitable use (zero-rated)

   (ii) the sale of new or uncompleted commercial buildings or land to be used for their construction (standard-rated)

   (iii) the grant of gaming rights, fishing rights or timber rights; the provision of hotel and holiday accommodation, caravan and camping pitches, boxes and seats at a theatre or sports ground, parking facilities and facilities for the storage or mooring of aircraft, ships etc; the letting of sports facilities, self-storage facilities or hairdressing facilities (all standard-rated)

   (iv) any supply which would otherwise be exempt, but in respect of which an election has been made to waive exemption (the "option to tax")

Group 2 Insurance

Group 3 Public postal services provided by the Royal Mail

Group 4 Betting, gaming and lotteries

Group 5 Financial services (e.g. bank charges, stockbroking, underwriting)

Group 6 Education provided by schools, universities and further education colleges

Group 7 Health and welfare services

Group 8 Burial and cremation services

Group 9 Subscriptions to trade unions and professional bodies

Group 10 Sports services provided by non-profit making bodies

Group 11 Disposals of works of art to approved bodies (e.g. the National Gallery)

Group 12 Certain fund-raising events organised by charities

Group 13 Cultural services

Group 14 Supplies of goods where input tax cannot be recovered

Group 15 Investment gold

Group 16 Supplies of services by groups involving cost sharing

The tax implications of a supply of goods or services being exempt are as follows:

(a) VAT cannot be charged on an exempt supply.

(b) A person who makes only exempt supplies cannot register for VAT, charges no output tax, is not a taxable person and cannot reclaim input tax.

(c) In effect, a person making only exempt supplies is in an identical position with regard to VAT as the final consumer at the end of a distribution chain.

Option to tax (land and buildings)

The fact that input tax cannot be reclaimed when making exempt supplies of land and buildings might lead the supplier to elect for the "option to tax". If such an election is made, the supplier charges output tax on the supply at the standard rate but may then reclaim input tax. The customer will of course have to pay VAT on the supply. But if the customer is also a taxable person, he or she will be able to reclaim the tax paid and so may not object.

Reduced rate supplies

A supply of goods or services is charged to VAT at the reduced rate of 5% if it falls within one of thirteen reduced-rate groups. These groups are as follows:

Group 1	Fuel and power supplied for domestic or charity use
Group 2	Installation of energy-saving materials (*zero-rated 1 April 2022 to 31 March 2027*)
Group 3	Grant-funded installation of heating or security equipment
Group 5	Children's car seats and car seat bases
Group 6	Certain residential conversions
Group 7	Certain residential renovations and alterations
Group 8	Contraceptive products (unless exempt from VAT)
Group 9	Certain welfare advice or information (unless exempt from VAT)
Group 10	Installation of mobility aids for the elderly
Group 11	Smoking cessation products
Group 12	Static holiday caravans
Group 13	Passenger transport in small cable-suspended transport systems

Group 4 is no longer in use.

Zero rate supplies

A supply of goods or services is charged to VAT at the zero rate (0%) if it falls within one of twenty-three zero-rate groups. These groups are as follows:

Group 1	Food (other than luxury foods and food supplied in the course of catering)
Group 2	Water and sewerage services unless supplied for industrial use
Group 3	Books, newspapers and journals (including electronic publications)
Group 4	Talking books and wireless sets for the blind and handicapped
Group 5	The sale (or lease for more than 21 years) of new buildings for residential or charitable use and second-hand buildings converted for residential use
Group 6	The sale (or lease for more than 21 years) of protected buildings that have been substantially reconstructed for residential or charitable use

Group 7   Certain categories of international services

Group 8   Passenger transport (but transport in vehicles seating less than 10 people and certain types of pleasure transport are standard-rated)

Group 9   Houseboats and static residential caravans

Group 10   Gold supplied by a central bank to another central bank

Group 11   Bank notes

Group 12   The dispensing of drugs and certain aids for disabled persons

Group 13   Exports

Group 15   The sale *by* a charity of donated goods and certain supplies made *to* a charity

Group 16   Children's clothing and footwear and protective boots and helmets

Group 18   Supplies made to a European Research Infrastructure Consortium (ERIC)

Group 19   Women's sanitary products

Group 21   Certain deemed supplies made in connection with online marketplaces

Group 22   Supplies made within designated "Freeports"

Group 23   Installation of energy-saving materials (*1 April 2022 to 31 March 2027*)

Groups 14, 17 and 20 are no longer in use.

If goods or services fall within one of the above zero-rate groups but also fall within one of the exempt groups, zero-rating takes priority. The tax implications of a supply of goods or services being zero-rated are as follows:

(a)   The supply is a taxable supply but the VAT due is calculated at 0%.

(b)   A person who makes only zero-rated supplies is nonetheless making taxable supplies and must usually register as a taxable person if taxable turnover exceeds the prescribed threshold. Having registered (and this may be done voluntarily if taxable turnover is less than the threshold) the person will then be able to reclaim input tax.

The value of a supply

The *value* of a taxable supply is the amount on which the VAT charge is based and this is normally equal to the price (before VAT) charged for the supply. For instance, if a standard-rated supply is made at a price of £100 plus VAT at 20%, the value of this supply is £100 and the "consideration" given for the supply is £120.

For standard-rated supplies, the VAT charge is equal to the consideration multiplied by the "VAT fraction". With a standard rate of 20%, this is 20/120 = 1/6th. Note that:

(a)   If a supply consists of a gift of business assets, the value of the supply is deemed to be the price (excluding VAT) which the person receiving the gift would have to pay to purchase goods identical in every respect to the goods concerned. This rule also applies if assets are taken permanently out of a business for private use by the owner of the business or by an employee.

(b) If the owner or an employee temporarily makes private use of business assets, the value of the resulting supply of services is generally based on the amount by which the assets have depreciated whilst being used for private purposes.

(c) If private use is made of services which have been supplied to the business, the value of the resulting supply of services is equal to an appropriate proportion of the value of the supply which was made to the business.

(d) If the consideration for a supply is paid in kind or if the supply is made to a connected person for less than market value, the value of the supply is taken to be the market value of the goods or services supplied.

EXAMPLE 2

(a) On 1 August 2022, a standard-rated supply is made with a value of £180. Calculate the VAT charged and the consideration for the supply.

(b) On 2 January 2023, a standard-rated supply is made for a consideration of £1,776. Calculate the VAT element and the value of the supply.

Solution

(a) The VAT charged is £36.00 (£180 x 20%) and the total consideration is £216.00.

(b) The VAT element is £296 (£1,776 x 1/6) and the value of the supply is £1,480.

Prompt payment discounts ("cash discounts")

If a customer is offered a discount in return for prompt payment (a "cash discount"), then the value of the supply is the VAT-exclusive price charged by the supplier, less any cash discount which is *actually taken* by the customer.

EXAMPLE 3

In June 2022, a standard-rated supply is made at a price of £4,000, plus VAT. The customer is offered a 3% discount if payment is made within 30 days. Calculate the value of the supply and the VAT charged on the supply if the customer:

(a) pays within 30 days   (b) does not pay within 30 days.

Solution

(a) If the customer pays within 30 days, the value of the supply is £3,880 (£4,000, less 3%) and the VAT charged is £776 (£3,880 x 20%). The consideration is £4,656.

(b) If the customer does not pay within 30 days, the value of the supply is £4,000 and the VAT charged is £800 (£4,000 × 20%). The consideration is £4,800.

Mixed supplies

A "mixed supply" occurs if a mixture of goods and/or services is invoiced together at a single inclusive price. If all of the items in the mixture are chargeable to VAT at the same rate, the value of the supply and the related output tax can be calculated in the usual way. Otherwise, it is necessary to apportion the price charged between the various elements of the mixture in order to calculate the output tax due.

There is no standard way of achieving this apportionment but the method used must be fair and justifiable.

EXAMPLE 4

A VAT-exclusive price of £320 is charged for a mixed supply of goods. The goods supplied consist of standard-rated goods which cost the supplier £141 (excluding VAT) and zero-rated goods which cost the supplier £19. Calculate the output tax due, assuming a standard rate of VAT of 20%.

Solution

From the information given, the only way of apportioning the price of the mixed supply into the standard-rated element and the zero-rated element is to split the price according to the cost of each element to the supplier. On this basis, the value of the supply represented by standard-rated goods is £320 x 141/160 = £282. VAT at 20% of this figure gives £56.40. Therefore the total price charged should be £376.40.

Composite supplies

A "composite supply" occurs if a mixture of goods and/or services is supplied together for a single price, but in such a way that it is not possible to split the supply into its component parts. In this case, the rate of VAT due (if any) is determined by considering the nature of the supply as a whole. For example, in the case of *Mander Laundries Ltd* (1973) it was held that the services of a launderette consist of a single, standard-rated supply of services, not a mixed supply of water, heat, hire of washing machines etc.

Imports and exports

Whilst the UK was a member state of the EU, the VAT treatment of imports and exports depended upon whether the transactions in question were between the UK and another EU member state or between the UK and a country which was not a member of the EU.

Now that the UK has left the EU, this distinction is no longer necessary and transactions between the UK and the EU are treated in much the same way as transactions between the UK and countries outside the EU, although there are some important exceptions.

The detailed rules are very complex but a summary of the situation which applies as from 1 January 2021 is given below. It is important to note that different rules apply to Great Britain (i.e. England, Scotland and Wales) and to Northern Ireland.

Imports of goods to Great Britain from outside the UK

VAT is charged on the import of goods into Great Britain from outside the UK at the same rate as if those goods had been supplied within the UK. The arrangements for collecting this VAT depend upon the value of the goods concerned and whether the goods are purchased by a UK business or by a UK consumer.

(a) If the value of a consignment of goods does not exceed £135, VAT must normally be charged at the point of sale and included in the price charged to the customer.

   – If the goods are sold directly to the UK customer by an overseas business, then that overseas business must register for UK VAT (see later) and must also account to HMRC for the output tax concerned.

   – If the goods are sold via an "online marketplace" (OMP) then the OMP must register and account for output tax. An OMP is "*a business which uses a website or mobile phone app to handle the sale of goods to customers*" and which is involved in the delivery of goods and the facilitation of customer payments.

(b) If the value of a consignment exceeds £135, VAT is not charged at the point of sale and so is not shown on the customer invoice. Instead, import VAT is payable at the point of entry to the UK or when the goods are delivered to the customer.

(c) However, if the customer is a UK business which is registered for UK VAT and which provides its registration number to the overseas supplier, then (regardless of the value of the consignment) the required amount of VAT is collected by means of a "reverse charge" procedure, as follows:

   – The overseas seller does not charge VAT on the sale, does not account for output tax to HMRC and does not need to register for UK VAT.

   – The UK business customer is responsible for the import tax[†] on the sale and uses a system known as "postponed accounting" to declare this tax on its next VAT return (see Chapter 30). However, from the point of view of the UK business concerned, this tax is also input tax and (if deductible) is declared as such on the same VAT return. However, some input tax is non-deductible (see Chapter 30).

   [†] *Import VAT is not payable on goods entering the UK through designated "Freeports".*

(d) These rules also apply to imports to Northern Ireland from outside the UK or the EU.

Exports of goods from Great Britain to outside the UK

Exports of goods from Great Britain to a destination outside the UK (or from Northern Ireland to a destination outside the UK or the EU) are zero-rated.

Northern Ireland

Under the Northern Ireland Protocol, the VAT treatment of movements of goods between Northern Ireland and the EU is aligned with EU VAT rules (as if Northern Ireland was a member state of the EU). In summary:

(a) When a registered person in one EU country supplies goods to a registered person in another EU country, the supply is zero-rated in the country of origin. The customer then accounts for VAT on the "acquisition" (the term "import" is not used) at whatever rate is applicable to those goods in the destination country.

   So NI businesses must zero-rate goods supplied to registered businesses in the EU and must account for UK VAT on goods acquired from such businesses.

(b) If the customer is not a registered person (and the supplier's total sales to non-taxable persons elsewhere in the EU do not exceed €10,000 p.a.) then the supplier charges VAT at the rate applicable in the country of origin. But if the €10,000 threshold is exceeded, VAT must be charged in the destination countries concerned.

   So NI businesses which sell goods to non-taxable persons in the EU must charge UK VAT if the threshold is not exceeded. Otherwise it is necessary to charge EU VAT at the appropriate rate in the destination country.

Note that sales of goods between Great Britain and Northern Ireland (in either direction) are sales within the UK and are therefore dealt with for VAT purposes in much the same way as any other sales of goods within the UK. However, special rules apply to goods which are sold from Great Britain to Northern Ireland for onward supply to an EU member state.

International services

International services are services which are supplied in the UK by an overseas supplier or supplied overseas by a UK supplier. The VAT treatment of international services depends upon the "place of supply" of those services. The general rules are as follows:

(a) Business to business (B2B) supplies are taxed at the place where the *customer* is established and it is the responsibility of the customer (not the supplier) to account for any output tax relating to such supplies. This is another "reverse charge" procedure.

(b) Business to consumer (B2C) supplies are taxed at the place where the *supplier* is established. For this purpose, a "consumer" is either a person who receives a supply of services for private purposes, or a charity etc. that has no business activities.

Therefore, if a UK business supplies services to an overseas business customer, the supply is outside the scope of UK VAT. If the services are supplied to an overseas consumer, the supply is subject to the normal UK rules (as if the customer had been in the UK).

   If a UK business *receives* services from overseas, the UK business must operate the reverse charge procedure and account for output tax at the appropriate rate. The VAT suffered by taxable persons as a result of this procedure is then treated as input tax. But, as stated earlier, certain classes of input tax are irrecoverable (see Chapter 30).

Domestic reverse charge procedure

A "domestic reverse charge" procedure applies to certain supplies made within the UK. This procedure applies when a supply of *mobile telephones or computer chips* with a value of at least £5,000 is made within the UK to a VAT-registered person. It is then the responsibility of the purchaser (not the seller) to account for the output tax on the supply. The aim of this procedure is to counter so-called "missing trader" fraud, whereby VAT is charged on a supply but the supplier fails to account for this tax to HMRC and cannot be traced.

Reverse charge arrangements also apply to emissions allowances, wholesale supplies of telecommunications services, wholesale supplies of gas and electricity and certain building and construction services.

Registration

The total value of the taxable supplies made by a person is known as that person's *taxable turnover*. A person whose taxable turnover in a 12-month period exceeds the registration threshold (£85,000[†] from 1 April 2017) must register with HMRC. Online registration is now available. A person who registers is issued a VAT registration number which must then be quoted on that person's tax invoices (see next chapter). Note that:

(a) The registration threshold does not apply to businesses which do not have a UK establishment. Such businesses are required to register for UK VAT as soon as they make their first supply of goods or services in the UK, regardless of value.

(b) A person who is liable to register but who fails to do so is still a taxable person and is held personally responsible for the output tax due in relation to supplies made since the date on which registration should have occurred.

When deciding whether or not the registration threshold has been exceeded, it is necessary to aggregate the taxable turnover from all of a person's business activities. The registration relates to the person, *not* to an individual business. It is important to bear in mind the definition of the word "person" for VAT purposes (see above) and to aggregate taxable supplies only if they are made by the same person.

[†] *This threshold will remain unaltered until April 2024.*

EXAMPLE 5

(a) Jim is a sole trader with a taxable turnover of £75,000 per annum. Is he required to register with HMRC?

(b) Pearl and Dean are in partnership, operating a business with a taxable turnover of £100,000 per annum. Is anyone required to register?

(c) Julia is a sole trader with a taxable turnover of £60,000 per annum. She is also in partnership with Julie, operating a business with a taxable turnover of £70,000 per annum and sharing profits equally. Is anyone required to register?

Solution

(a) No. Jim's taxable turnover does not exceed the registration threshold.

(b) Yes. The partnership is one "person" for VAT purposes and has a taxable turnover exceeding the registration threshold. Therefore the partnership must register.

(c) No. Julia as a sole trader is one person, whilst the partnership of Julia and Julie is another, quite separate, "person". Neither of these persons has a taxable turnover exceeding the registration threshold so neither of them is required to register.

Business splitting

"Business splitting" or "disaggregation" occurs when a business is divided into two or more smaller businesses, each operated by a different person and each with a taxable turnover not exceeding the registration threshold, in the hope of avoiding registration.

If this were successful, supplies could be made without charging VAT and the costs associated with making VAT returns and maintaining VAT records (see next chapter) could be avoided. One disadvantage would be that input tax could not be reclaimed. But for a business with mainly exempt or zero-rated inputs this disadvantage would be slight.

However, if a business has been split artificially, HMRC may direct that the persons conducting the split businesses should be treated as a single taxable person for VAT purposes. In fact, this direction may be made even if the split businesses have never been operated as a single unit, so long as HMRC is satisfied that only one business really exists.

When to register

A person is required to register for VAT if, at the end of any calendar month, the value of that person's taxable supplies for the year ended on the last day of the month exceeds the registration threshold (£85,000[†] as from 1 April 2017). If the person has been making taxable supplies for less than twelve months, registration is required if the value of taxable supplies made to date is greater than the registration threshold. HMRC must be notified within 30 days of the end of the relevant month. Registration will then usually take effect after the end of the month following the relevant month. However, registration is not required if HMRC is satisfied that the person's taxable turnover for the following twelve months will not exceed the deregistration threshold (£83,000[†] as from 1 April 2017).

Registration is also required if there are reasonable grounds for believing that taxable turnover during the next 30 days alone will exceed the registration threshold. In this case, HMRC must be notified by the end of the 30-day period and registration will take effect from the beginning of that period.

For the purpose of deciding whether the registration threshold is exceeded, any supplies consisting of the capital assets of the business are excluded from taxable turnover. However, such supplies normally receive no special treatment, so that the sale of a non-current asset will be a taxable supply unless the asset falls into one of the exemption groups.

[†] *Both of these thresholds will remain unaltered until April 2024.*

EXAMPLE 6

Kevin begins trading on 1 January 2021. Taxable turnover during the first two years of trading is as follows:

2021	£	2022	£
January	1,800	January	6,800
February	2,100	February	5,400
March	2,800	March	6,100
April	2,600	April	7,600
May	2,400	May	8,100
June	2,900	June	7,900
July	3,300	July	8,200
August	3,500	August	7,900
September	4,200	September	8,800
October	5,500	October	8,100
November	6,900	November	8,300
December	8,200	December	9,700

The turnover in January 2022 includes £2,000 relating to the sale of machinery previously used in the trade. State the date by which Kevin must notify HMRC that he has exceeded the registration threshold. When will registration take effect?

Solution

At the end of each month, cumulative taxable turnover during the previous 12 months (or since the start of trade, if less) are as follows:

2021	£	2022	£
January	1,800	January	49,200
February	3,000	February	52,500
March	6,700	March	55,800
April	9,300	April	60,800
May	11,700	May	66,500
June	14,600	June	71,500
July	17,900	July	76,400
August	21,400	August	80,800
September	25,600	September	85,400
October	31,100	October	88,000
November	38,000	November	89,400
December	46,200	December	90,900

The cumulative figure at the end of January 2022 is turnover for the months of February 2021 to January 2022 inclusive, less the £2,000 relating to the sale of a capital asset.

The registration threshold is passed at the end of September 2022. Kevin must notify HMRC by 30 October 2022. Registration will probably take effect from 1 November 2022.

Transfer of a business to an unregistered person

If a taxable person transfers a business as a going concern to a person who is not registered for VAT, the supplies made by the business before the transfer date are deemed (for the purpose of deciding whether or not the transferee should register) to have been made by the transferee. So if the transferred business, together with any other business operated by the transferee, had a taxable turnover exceeding the registration threshold in the 12 months prior to the transfer, the transferee must register for VAT immediately.

Voluntary registration

A person making taxable supplies which do not exceed the VAT registration threshold may nonetheless register for VAT voluntarily. This enables the person to recover input tax but also means that output tax must be charged when taxable supplies are made to customers. However, if these supplies are mainly zero-rated, or consist of standard-rate (or reduced-rate) supplies made wholly or mainly to customers who are themselves taxable persons, the fact that output tax must be charged will probably not deter customers.

Being registered for VAT will add to the administrative costs of running the business but this factor may be outweighed by the benefit of being able to recover input tax.

EXAMPLE 7

Lindsey is not registered for VAT. In the year to 31 March 2023, she has inputs costing £10,000 plus VAT at 20%. Her outputs total £35,000.

(a) How much profit does she make for the year?

(b) If she had registered for VAT voluntarily, how much profit would she have made?

(c) Does it matter whether the supplies that she makes are all:

  (i)   zero-rated?
  (ii) standard-rated supplies made to VAT-registered businesses?
  (iii) standard-rated supplies made to the general public?

Solution

(a) Her profit is £23,000 (£35,000 − £12,000).

(b) If she had registered for VAT and outputs had remained at £35,000, she would have been able to reclaim input tax, giving a profit of £25,000 (£35,000 − £10,000).

(c) (i)   If she makes only zero-rated supplies, voluntary registration has no effect on her selling prices and, therefore, no effect on her sales.

  (ii) If she makes only standard-rated supplies to VAT-registered businesses, her prices will increase by 20% but her customers will be able to reclaim the extra tax paid and so there should be no effect on her sales.

  (iii) If she makes only standard-rated supplies to the general public, increasing her prices may entail a loss of custom and she may prefer not to register.

Exemption from registration

HMRC may grant exemption from registration to a person making supplies which exceed the registration threshold, so long as these supplies are all zero-rated. An application for exemption might be sensible if the amount of input tax which could be reclaimed if the person were registered is small in comparison with the increased administrative costs associated with VAT registration.

Pre-registration input tax

Any VAT incurred before registration is not input tax. Nonetheless, it can be treated as input tax so long as certain conditions are satisfied. These conditions vary according to whether the VAT is incurred on a supply of goods or a supply of services:

(a) **Goods**. The VAT suffered on a pre-registration supply of goods may be treated as input tax so long as the goods were supplied to the taxable person for business purposes within the four years prior to the date of registration and were not sold or consumed before that date.

(b) **Services**. The VAT suffered on a pre-registration supply of services may be treated as input tax so long as the services were supplied to the taxable person for business purposes no more than six months before the date of registration.

Group registration

A group of companies may apply for the group to be registered as a single taxable person, rather than each company in the group being registered individually. Group registration has the following consequences:

(a) The input tax suffered by the group as a whole is set against the output tax charged by the group as a whole.

(b) One of the group companies is nominated as the "representative member" and takes responsibility for submitting VAT returns and accounting for VAT on behalf of the entire group. However, any other company in the group can be held liable if the representative member fails to pay the VAT which is due.

(c) Supplies between group members are not regarded as taxable supplies and are ignored for VAT purposes.

Individual group companies may register separately and choose not to join the VAT group. This may improve the cash flow position of a company with mainly zero-rated supplies which makes monthly VAT returns (see next chapter). It is also possible for a group of companies to form two (or more) VAT groups, with some of the companies belonging to one VAT group and some belonging to another.

Group registration offers tax avoidance opportunities in certain cases and HMRC may remove a company from a VAT group if avoidance is suspected.

Deregistration

Deregistration may be either voluntary or compulsory:

(a) A registered person may deregister voluntarily if HMRC is satisfied that taxable turnover, excluding supplies of capital assets, will not exceed the deregistration threshold (£83,000† from 1 April 2017) in the next 12 months.

(b) Compulsory deregistration is triggered when a registered person entirely ceases to make taxable supplies. The person must notify HMRC within 30 days that this has occurred and then deregistration will normally take effect as from the date on which taxable supplies ceased.

(c) Deregistration is also compulsory on a change of legal status (e.g. when a sole trader admits a partner or when the business of a partnership is taken over by a company).

On deregistration, the person concerned is deemed to make a supply of all the tangible assets of the business and output tax is charged accordingly. However, assets on which no input tax was reclaimed are excluded from this deemed supply and the output tax due is not collected if it does not exceed £1,000 in total. The deemed supply does *not* take place if the business is sold as a going concern to another taxable person.

† *This threshold will remain unaltered until April 2024.*

Summary

▸ VAT is chargeable when a taxable person makes a taxable supply of either goods or services in the course of business.

▸ A taxable supply is any supply of goods or services other than an exempt supply and may be charged to value added tax at either the standard rate, the reduced rate or the zero rate.

▸ A taxable person is a person who makes taxable supplies and who is (or should be) registered for VAT. A taxable person may be an individual, a partnership, a company, a charity, a club or an association.

▸ A person making taxable supplies which exceed the VAT registration threshold must register with HMRC. A person making taxable supplies which do not exceed the threshold may register voluntarily.

▸ A taxable person must account to HMRC for the output tax charged to customers but may (in general) recover the input tax charged by suppliers.

▸ A person making only exempt supplies cannot charge VAT to customers and is unable to recover input tax.

Exercises

A set of multiple choice questions for this chapter is available on the accompanying website.

29.1   Classify each of the following supplies as either taxable at the standard rate, taxable at the reduced rate, taxable at the zero rate or exempt:

(a)   a theatre ticket   (b)   a loaf of bread

(c)   bank charges   (d)   electricity supplied for business use

(e)   a taxi ride   (f)   a taxation textbook

(g)   gas supplied for domestic use   (h)   a subscription to a professional body

(i)   an insurance premium   (j)   a new commercial building

(k)   a meal in a restaurant   (l)   a train ticket

(m) exports   (n)   writing paper.

29.2   A standard-rated supply is made in May 2022 at a price of £340, plus VAT. Calculate the VAT chargeable and the consideration for the supply if:

(a)   no discount is offered

(b)   a 2% discount is offered for prompt payment and the customer takes advantage of this discount

(c)   a 2% discount is offered for prompt payment but the customer decides not to take advantage of this discount.

29.3   In each of the following cases, is anyone required to register with HM Revenue and Customs? If so, who?

(a)   Lorna is a sole trader, making taxable supplies of £100,000 per annum.

(b)   Mike owns two distinct businesses. One has a taxable turnover of £40,000 per annum and the other has a taxable turnover of £50,000 per annum.

(c)   Pat and Phil are in partnership. Their taxable turnover is £60,000 per annum. Phil also owns another business with a taxable turnover of £45,000 per annum.

(d)   JSmiCo Ltd has a taxable turnover of £250,000 per annum. The company's shares are owned entirely by John Smith and his wife.

29.4   Rosemary owns a business which has an annual turnover (excluding any VAT) of £90,000. Describe her VAT position if:

(a)   she makes wholly exempt supplies

(b)   she makes wholly standard-rated supplies

(c)   she makes wholly zero-rated supplies.

29.5   Explain the VAT consequences of a UK business (which is registered for VAT):

(a)   importing goods from outside the UK

(b)   exporting goods to a destination which is outside the UK.

Assume that the UK business concerned is situated in Great Britain.

*29.6 Smart Ltd began trading on 1 September 2022. Taxable turnover for the first four months of trading was as follows:

| September 2022 | £26,000 | October 2022 | £47,000 |
| November 2022 | £134,000 | December 2022 | £113,000 |

On 1 November 2022, the company signed a contract to supply standard-rated services valued at £96,000 (before VAT) for completion during November 2022.

Required:

State, giving reasons, the date from which Smart Ltd was required to register for VAT and the date by which it was required to notify HMRC of the registration. *(ACCA)*

*29.7 Answer the following questions:

(a) who should register for VAT?

(b) when should registration occur?

(c) what are the consequences of failing to register?

(d) when may a taxable person deregister?

(e) why might someone choose to register voluntarily?

*29.8 Sanjay began trading on 1 February 2022, selling standard-rated goods and services. He decided not to register for VAT voluntarily. His taxable turnover (excluding VAT) for the first 16 months of trading was as follows:

2022	£	2022	£	2023	£
February	2,550	August	5,430	January	10,080
March	3,660	September	6,320	February	7,920
April	3,880	October	7,410	March	6,780
May	4,240	November	11,050	April	5,100
June	4,860	December	12,270	May	4,890
July	5,290				

In January 2023, he sold some machinery (which had been used as a non-current asset) for £800. This is *not* included in the above turnover figures.

Sanjay is concerned that his monthly turnover has started to fall and he is considering offering customer discounts in an attempt to reverse this trend.

Required:

(a) Explain the term "taxable person" for VAT purposes.

(b) State the circumstances in which VAT registration is compulsory and explain why some persons may choose to register voluntarily.

(c) State the date by which Sanjay would be required to register for VAT. Would this be necessary if his monthly turnover for the remainder of 2023 seemed likely to continue on a downward trend?

(d) Explain the VAT consequences which would ensue if Sanjay began offering trade discounts or cash discounts to his customers. *(CIPFA)*

Chapter 30

Value added tax (2)

Introduction

The previous chapter outlined the main principles of value added tax and explained the processes of registration and deregistration. This chapter is concerned with the procedures used to account for VAT to HMRC and the way in which the tax is administered. Other matters considered in this chapter include non-recoverable input tax, the VAT position of persons who make both taxable and exempt supplies and a number of schemes which exist in order to simplify the workings of the VAT system.

Accounting for VAT

At regular intervals (usually quarterly) registered persons must submit a VAT return to HMRC, showing input tax and output tax† for the period covered by the return. Any excess of output tax over input tax is payable to HMRC. Any excess of input tax over output tax is repayable by HMRC. Note that.

(a) A VAT return must usually be submitted within one month and seven days of the end of the "tax period" to which it relates, together with any tax due. Online filing and electronic payment are now mandatory (subject to some minor exceptions).

(b) A registered person making supplies which are wholly or mainly zero-rated will be entitled to a VAT repayment in most tax periods. Such a person may opt to submit VAT returns monthly rather than quarterly, so speeding up tax repayments at the expense of making twelve returns per year rather than four.

† *Including import VAT accounted for by means of postponed accounting (see Chapter 29).*

Payments on account

A registered person who makes quarterly returns and whose annual VAT liability exceeds £2.3 million is obliged to make two payments on account to HMRC. The first payment is due one month before the end of the quarter and a second payment is due at the end of the quarter. A balancing payment is made when the VAT return is submitted.

Each of the two payments on account is usually calculated as 1/24th of the total VAT liability for the previous year. However, the business may choose to pay its actual VAT liability for each month rather than the set POAs.

The tax point

The date on which a supply is deemed to occur is known as the "tax point" of that supply. The tax point of a supply determines:

(a) for outputs, the tax period in which the tax on that supply must be accounted for

(b) for inputs, the tax period in which the tax on that supply may be reclaimed

(c) the rate of VAT applicable to the supply (if VAT rates change).

For a supply of goods the "basic tax point" is the date on which the goods are removed or made available to the customer. For a supply of services the basic tax point is the date on which the services are performed. However, the "actual tax point" of a supply will differ from the basic tax point in the following circumstances:

(a) If the supplier issues a tax invoice or receives payment on a date which is earlier than the basic tax point, the actual tax point for the supply (or part of the supply) to which that invoice or payment relates is the date on which the invoice is issued or on which the payment is received, whichever occurs first.

(b) Otherwise, if the supplier issues a tax invoice within 14 days after the basic tax point, then the invoice date becomes the actual tax point.

HMRC may extend the 14-day rule mentioned above if asked to do so by a registered person who is genuinely unable to issue invoices within 14 days of the basic tax point.

Tax invoices

If a taxable person makes a taxable supply to another taxable person, a "tax invoice" must be issued. The main purpose of this invoice is to provide documentary evidence of the transaction, so allowing the person receiving the supply to reclaim the input tax related to that supply. The required contents of a valid tax invoice are:

(a) the invoice number, date and tax point

(b) the name, address and VAT registration number of the supplier

(c) the name and address of the customer

(d) for each invoice item, a description of the goods or services supplied

(e) for each description, the quantity of the goods or the extent of the services, the unit price, the amount payable (before VAT) and the rate of VAT applicable.

(f) the total amount due, before VAT

(g) the rate of any cash discount available

(h) the total amount of VAT chargeable.

A less detailed tax invoice may be issued if the consideration for the supply does not exceed £250. A less detailed tax invoice need show only:

(a) the name, address and VAT registration number of the supplier

(b) the tax point

(c) a description of the goods or services supplied

(d) the total amount payable by the customer, including VAT

(e) for each rate of VAT chargeable, the gross amount payable (including VAT) and the rate of tax which is applicable.

The issue of a tax invoice is optional if a supply is made to a customer who is not a taxable person. Retailers are not required to issue a tax invoice unless the customer asks for an invoice. A VAT invoice may be issued electronically as long as the customer agrees to electronic invoicing.

Accounting records

Every taxable person must keep such records as are required by HMRC. The main records which must be kept[†] are as follows:

(a) business and accounting records (including orders, delivery notes, business correspondence, purchases and sales books, cashbooks and other account books, till rolls, bank statements, paying-in slips and annual accounts)

(b) a VAT account

(c) a copy of each tax invoice issued

(d) all tax invoices received (although tax invoices are not required for payments of £25 or less relating to telephone calls, car park charges, toll charges or purchases made through coin-operated machines)

(e) documentation relating to imports and exports.

HMRC may also specify additional record-keeping requirements for all businesses of a particular description and (in cases where additional records might assist in identifying supplies on which VAT might otherwise go unpaid) for individual businesses.

All records must be retained for a period of six years or for such lesser period as HMRC may allow. HMRC is empowered to require a taxable person to provide their VAT records for inspection and is also empowered to inspect these records at the business premises.

[†] *Since April 2019 (as part of the "Making Tax Digital" project - see Chapter 1) persons with taxable turnover which exceeds the registration threshold have been required to maintain digital records and to use approved software to provide HMRC with summary VAT data generated from these records. MTD for VAT was extended to all VAT-registered businesses as from April 2022.*

Special schemes

The VAT system offers a number of special schemes which are intended to simplify the workings of the VAT system, especially for smaller businesses. The main schemes are as follows:

(a)   the cash accounting scheme

(b)   the annual accounting scheme

(c)   the flat-rate scheme for small businesses

(d)   the flat-rate scheme for farmers

(e)   the margin scheme for second-hand goods.

Each of these schemes is explained below. There are also several special schemes for use only by retailers. The "retail schemes" are briefly considered later in this chapter.

Cash accounting scheme

A VAT-registered person whose taxable turnover is not expected to exceed £1,350,000 in the next 12 months may opt to join the cash accounting scheme. Those who join this scheme account for output tax in the tax period in which *payment is received* from the customer and reclaim input tax in the tax period in which *payment is made* to the supplier. The tax point is ignored when allocating inputs and outputs to tax periods.

   Joining this scheme allows a registered person to delay the payment of output tax to HMRC until the tax has actually been received from customers, which is beneficial if customers are given extended credit. The scheme also provides automatic relief for bad debts. On the other hand, input tax cannot be reclaimed until the tax has actually been paid to suppliers. A person may not join the cash accounting scheme unless:

(a)   the person's taxable turnover (excluding sales of capital items) is not expected to exceed £1,350,000 in the next 12 months

(b)   the person's VAT returns are up to date

(c)   all amounts due to be paid to HMRC have in fact been paid, or the person has come to an arrangement for such payments to be made

(d)   within the previous 12 months, the person has not been convicted of a VAT offence or assessed to a penalty for VAT evasion involving dishonest conduct.

A registered person who has joined the cash accounting scheme must withdraw from the scheme at the end of a tax period if taxable turnover for the 12 months to date exceeds £1,600,000. HMRC will allow such a person to remain in the scheme only if it can be demonstrated that the high turnover is not expected to recur and that taxable turnover for the next 12 months is expected to be no more than £1,350,000.

   The cash accounting scheme cannot be used for supplies of goods and services for which a VAT invoice is issued before the supply is made, or for supplies where a VAT invoice is issued and full payment is not due within six months of the invoice date.

Annual accounting scheme

A registered person with a taxable turnover which is not expected to exceed £1,350,000 in the next 12 months may apply to join the annual accounting scheme and submit only one VAT return per year. The scheme operates as follows:

(a) During the year the person concerned makes nine interim payments to HMRC, each equal to 10% of the VAT liability for the previous year. These payments must be made by direct debit or other electronic means and begin in the fourth month of the year.

(b) Optionally (and subject to HMRC approval) the taxable person may choose to make three interim payments in months four, seven and ten rather than the nine payments referred to above. In this case, each payment is equal to 25% of the VAT liability for the previous year.

(c) If a person joins the annual accounting scheme when first registering for VAT (or less than 12 months after registration), the interim payments are based initially upon the person's expected VAT liability for the year.

(d) At the end of the year the annual return is submitted together with a final payment consisting of the balance of the VAT liability. The return and payment must be made within two months of the end of the year.

(e) A person who operates the annual accounting scheme must withdraw from the scheme if taxable turnover exceeds £1,600,000 for the previous year.

The advantages of the scheme include a reduction in the number of VAT returns each year (from four to one) and more predictable cash flows. There is also more time at the end of the year in which to complete the required return and to pay any VAT which is due.

Flat-rate scheme for small businesses

An eligible business which is registered for VAT may opt to join the flat-rate scheme (FRS) for small businesses. This scheme enables a small business to calculate its VAT liability as a flat-rate percentage of total turnover and so avoids the need to keep detailed records of input tax and output tax. The FRS operates as follows:

(a) Output tax is charged to customers at the normal rate for the supply. Similarly, input tax is paid to suppliers at the normal rate. But the output tax charged to customers is not paid over to HMRC and (in general) input tax cannot be recovered.

(b) In each tax period, a flat-rate percentage is applied to the VAT-inclusive turnover for the period (including the value of any exempt supplies). The result of this calculation is the amount of VAT payable to HMRC for the period.

(c) The applicable flat-rate percentage depends upon the "category of business" to which the business belongs. With a standard rate of 20%, the flat-rate percentage currently ranges from 4% to 14.5%. However, a special rate of 16.5% applies to certain "limited cost" businesses (e.g. labour-only businesses).

(d) Input tax on the purchase of capital assets costing at least £2,000 (including VAT) can be reclaimed in the usual way, in which case output tax must be accounted for in the usual way on the eventual disposal of the asset.

(e) The FRS can be used in conjunction with the annual accounting scheme. It *cannot* be used in conjunction with the cash accounting scheme or a retail scheme (see later in this chapter). However, the FRS offers an optional cash-based turnover method and an optional retailer's turnover method.

The FRS is available to businesses with a taxable turnover which is not expected to exceed £150,000 in the next 12 months. A business must normally leave the FRS if its VAT-inclusive income exceeds £230,000 during any 12-month period ending on an anniversary of the date that it joined the scheme.

Flat-rate scheme for farmers (Agricultural flat-rate scheme)

In general, a farmer whose taxable supplies exceed the registration threshold is required to register for VAT in the normal way. Similarly, a farmer with taxable supplies beneath the threshold may register voluntarily. Farmers' supplies are mainly zero-rated, so a registered farmer will usually receive regular repayments of input tax, at the expense of maintaining the necessary records. However, an alternative to registration is the *flat-rate scheme for farmers*. This scheme is intended to reduce administrative costs and operates as follows:

(a) A farmer who joins the scheme does not register for VAT. This reduces administrative costs but deprives the farmer of the opportunity to reclaim input tax.

(b) In compensation, the farmer is allowed to add a flat-rate 4% to his or her selling prices and to retain this addition. The "flat-rate addition" may be charged only when selling designated goods or services to VAT-registered persons but applies even if the goods or services concerned would normally be zero-rated.

(c) When a taxable person buys goods from a flat-rate farmer, the flat-rate addition is treated as input tax and may be reclaimed, subject to the usual rules.

(d) Admission to the scheme is restricted to farmers with annual turnover not exceeding £150,000. Farmers must leave the scheme once annual turnover exceeds £230,000.

A farmer may not join this scheme if the total of the flat-rate additions which would be charged if the farmer were a member of the scheme exceeds the total amount of input tax which the farmer would otherwise be entitled to reclaim by £3,000 per annum or more.

Margin scheme for second-hand goods

In general, VAT is charged on the full value of goods sold, regardless of whether those goods are new or second-hand. However, subject to certain conditions, a taxable person selling second-hand goods may choose to sell them through the margin scheme and charge VAT only on his or her profit margin. The scheme operates as follows:

(a) Output tax is charged only on the seller's profit margin. This is the difference between the price at which the goods were obtained and their selling price. No output tax is charged to the customer unless the goods are sold at a profit.

(b) The seller's profit margin is deemed to be VAT-inclusive, so that the amount of VAT due is calculated by multiplying this margin by the VAT fraction. Expenses incurred by the seller (e.g. the costs of restoration, repairs etc.) are ignored when establishing the amount of the profit margin, but input tax on these expenses may be reclaimed.

(c) The buyer cannot reclaim the input tax suffered, even if he/she is a taxable person.

The main conditions which must be satisfied for the margin scheme to be used are that the goods concerned are second-hand and that they were acquired either on a supply on which no VAT was chargeable (e.g. from a member of the public) or from a taxable person who also sold the goods under the margin scheme. The sales invoice must include an indication that the margin scheme has been applied but does not show VAT as a separate figure.

EXAMPLE 1

An antiques dealer buys a table from a member of the public for £2,000. The dealer spends a further £750 (plus VAT) on restoration work and then sells the table to a customer for £5,000. Compute the amount of output tax which must be accounted for in relation to this sale, assuming that the table is sold through the margin scheme.

Solution

Ignoring restoration costs, the dealer's margin is £3,000. The output tax due is therefore £3,000 x 1/6 = £500. Input tax on the restoration costs may be reclaimed in the usual way.

Retail schemes

Retailers are those who supply goods and services directly to the public. A retailer's sales will often consist of a very large number of relatively small transactions and in these circumstances it would sometimes be difficult and expensive to keep detailed records of each transaction for VAT purposes. In response to this problem, retail schemes have been devised which enable retailers to calculate their output tax in a fairly straightforward way. The standard retail schemes are as follows:

(a) point of sale scheme
(b) apportionment scheme 1
(c) apportionment scheme 2
(d) direct calculation scheme 1
(e) direct calculation scheme 2.

Full information on the standard schemes is given on the website which accompanies this book. The website can be accessed at go.pearson.com/uk/he/resources.

Retailers with an annual taxable turnover exceeding £130 million cannot use any of these standard schemes. If such retailers wish to use a retail scheme they must negotiate an individual "bespoke retail scheme" with HMRC.

It should be noted that the growing use of information technology by large retailers and by many small retailers means that it is now much easier to record individual sales than it was when VAT was introduced in 1973. This means that the original rationale for the VAT retail schemes has been diminished over the years. Accordingly, retailers may not use any of these schemes unless permitted to do so. HMRC permission will be granted only if a retailer cannot reasonably be expected to account for VAT in the normal way, so that the use of a retail scheme is strictly necessary.

Bad debts

If a taxable person uses the cash accounting scheme, the output tax relating to a supply is not accounted for to HMRC until the consideration for that supply has been received from the customer concerned. So automatic relief is given for bad debts. But persons who do not use the cash accounting scheme might account for the output tax relating to a supply before the consideration for that supply is received and then find that a bad debt occurs. In these circumstances, a claim may be made for a refund of the VAT lost, so long as:

(a) goods or services have been supplied for a consideration and the related output tax has been accounted for to HMRC

(b) the value of the supply was no more than its open market value

(c) the debt has been written off in the books of account

(d) at least six months have elapsed since both the date of the supply and the date that payment was due

(e) the claim for bad debt relief is made within four years and six months from the later of the date of the supply and the date that payment was due.

A business that recovers input tax relating to a supply, but does not pay the supplier within six months of the date of supply or the date that payment was due (if later), must repay the input tax concerned to HMRC. This applies whether or not the supplier makes a claim for bad debt relief.

Non-deductible input tax

In general, a taxable person can reclaim the input tax relating to a supply so long as the supply is evidenced by a tax invoice and the goods or services involved are for use in the person's business. However, input tax is not reclaimable on certain types of supply, even though the supply is received in the course of business. The main examples of such non-deductible (or "blocked") input tax are:

(a)   VAT on business entertainment for customers (other than overseas customers).

(b)   VAT on the purchase of motor cars, apart from:

    (i)   cars acquired by a car dealer, as stock in trade

    (ii)   cars acquired for use by a driving school, car rental business or taxi business

    (iii)   cars acquired *wholly* for business use and not available for private use.

    If the input tax on the purchase of a car cannot be reclaimed, then the subsequent sale of that car is an exempt supply.

(c)   VAT on the purchase of second-hand goods that were sold under the margin scheme (see earlier in this chapter).

The VAT on goods or services which are not used at all for business purposes cannot be reclaimed. If goods or services are used partly for business purposes and partly for private purposes, then there are two possible treatments. Either:

(a)   the input tax on the supply is apportioned and the business element of the tax is then reclaimed, or

(b)   the whole of the input tax on the supply is reclaimed, but output tax is then accounted for in relation to the element of private use (the "Lennartz method").

The first treatment may be applied to supplies of either goods or services. The Lennartz method may be applied to supplies of goods (other than motor cars, land and property, ships, boats and aircraft) but cannot usually be applied to supplies of services. Special rules apply to the private use of car fuel (see below).

Fuel for private motoring

If an employee or the owner of a business is provided with car fuel† for private motoring, all of the input tax relating to fuel purchases by the business may be reclaimed but output tax must then be accounted for on the supply of fuel for private use. The amount of this output tax depends upon the car's level of carbon dioxide emissions (rounded down to the nearest 5g/km) and is determined by reference to a table of scale charges. As from 1 May 2022, the VAT-inclusive fuel scale charges are as follows:

Emission rating (g/km)	Fuel scale charge 12 month period £	Fuel scale charge 3 month period £	Fuel scale charge 1 month period £
120 or less	700	174	58
125	1,048	262	87
130	1,121	279	92
135	1,188	296	98
140	1,261	314	104
145	1,329	332	110
150	1,401	349	116
155	1,469	367	122
160	1,542	385	127
165	1,609	402	133
170	1,682	419	139
175	1,749	437	145
180	1,822	454	151
185	1,889	472	156
190	1,962	490	163
195	2,030	507	169
200	2,102	525	174
205	2,170	543	180
210	2,242	559	185
215	2,310	577	192
220	2,383	595	198
225 or more	2,450	612	203

† *For this purpose, "car fuel" does not include electricity for an electric or hybrid motor car.*

With a standard rate of 20%, output tax is 1/6th of the scale charge. Scale charges do not apply if *no input tax at all* is reclaimed in relation to road fuel, whether used for business or for private motoring and whether used in cars or in commercial vehicles. Scale charges may also be avoided if input tax is reclaimed only in relation to fuel used for business motoring and accurate records are kept from which this figure can be derived.

Note that the input tax suffered in relation to car repairs and maintenance is reclaimable in full (with no adjustment for private use) so long as the car is used for business purposes to some extent. However, only 50% of the input tax relating to car leasing charges is reclaimable if there is any private use of the car.

Partial exemption

As explained in the previous chapter, a taxable person who makes wholly taxable supplies may reclaim all input tax suffered (with the exceptions listed above). A person who makes wholly exempt supplies is not a taxable person and may reclaim no input tax at all.

A taxable person who makes partly taxable and partly exempt supplies is referred to as "partially exempt" and may reclaim part of the input tax suffered. The input tax which may be reclaimed for a tax period is the amount which is "attributed to taxable supplies". This amount is usually calculated as follows:

(a) Input tax suffered during the period on goods and services which are used exclusively for the purpose of making taxable supplies is attributed to taxable supplies and is reclaimable in full.

(b) Input tax suffered during the period on goods and services which are used exclusively for the purpose of making exempt supplies is attributed to exempt supplies and usually cannot be reclaimed at all (but see "de minimis" rule below).

(c) A proportion of any unattributed or "residual" input tax suffered during the period (on goods and services used for making both taxable and exempt supplies) is attributed to taxable supplies and may be reclaimed. This proportion is equal to:

$$\text{Residual input tax} \times \frac{\text{Value of taxable supplies}}{\text{Value of all supplies}}$$

The ratio of taxable supplies to all supplies is generally expressed as a percentage rounded up to the nearest whole number. But the percentage is rounded up to two decimal places if residual input tax is at least £400,000 per month (on average). When computing this ratio, certain supplies made by the person are omitted from the calculation, including self-supplies and supplies consisting of capital assets.

A taxable person may use the previous year's overall percentage to determine the provisional recovery of residual input tax in each tax period (see below) thereby avoiding the need to calculate a separate percentage for each period.

(d) If the total amount of input tax not attributed to taxable supplies for a tax period does not exceed a "de minimis" limit of £625 per month (on average) and is also no more than 50% of all the input tax for the period, then it is treated as being attributed to taxable supplies and is reclaimable in full.

Note that the calculation of reclaimable input tax for a tax period is only provisional. The calculation is performed again at the end of each year, taking into account input tax for the whole year and using a de minimis limit of £7,500 (12 × £625). Any difference between the amount of reclaimable input tax for the year and the amount calculated provisionally is an underpayment or overpayment of VAT and must be accounted for to HMRC.

The procedure described above is known as the "standard method" of computing reclaimable input tax for a partially exempt person. HMRC may approve or direct the use of an alternative method if this gives a more fair and reasonable result.

EXAMPLE 2

During the quarter to 31 December 2022, Nancy makes supplies as follows:

	£
Standard-rated supplies (excluding VAT)	120,000
Zero-rated supplies	80,000
Exempt supplies	50,000

She suffers input tax as follows:

	£
Attributed to taxable supplies	7,500
Attributed to exempt supplies	8,500
Unattributed	12,000

Compute the VAT provisionally payable to HMRC for the quarter.

Solution

	£	£
Output tax		
Standard-rated supplies £120,000 @ 20%		24,000
Zero-rated supplies £80,000 @ 0%		0
		24,000
Input tax		
Attributed to taxable supplies	7,500	
Unattributed:		
$\dfrac{£120,000 + £80,000}{£120,000 + £80,000 + £50,000}$ = 80% x £12,000	9,600	17,100
Payable to HMRC		6,900

The input tax not attributed to taxable supplies for the quarter is £10,900 (£8,500 + 20% x £12,000). This is more than £625 per month on average and so cannot be reclaimed.

Simplified de minimis tests

A business which passes either of two "simplified tests" for a VAT period is able to avoid a full partial exemption calculation and can provisionally reclaim input tax attributable to both taxable and exempt supplies. The two tests are as follows:

(a) **Test 1**. Total input tax incurred does not exceed £625 per month (on average) and the value of exempt supplies is no more than 50% of the value of all supplies.

(b) **Test 2**. Total input tax incurred less input tax directly attributable to taxable supplies does not exceed £625 per month (on average) and the value of exempt supplies is no more than 50% of the value of all supplies.

These two tests may also be applied at the end of each year to determine whether or not the business is "de minimis" for the entire year.

As a further simplification, a business which was de minimis for the previous year may treat itself as provisionally de minimis for each VAT period in the current year and review its de minimis status only at the end of the current year. This simplification does not apply to businesses which expect to incur more than £1 million of input tax in the current year.

EXAMPLE 3

(a) During the quarter to 31 August 2022, Justin makes taxable supplies of £30,000 and exempt supplies of £20,000. Input tax incurred is £1,500. Does he pass either of the two simplified de minimis tests for the quarter?

(b) During the year to 31 March 2023, Margaret makes taxable supplies of £140,000 and exempt supplies of £60,000. Input tax for the year is £27,600, of which £22,800 is directly attributable to taxable supplies. Does she pass either of the two simplified de minimis tests for the year?

Solution

(a) Input tax averages £500 per month and exempt supplies are 40% of total supplies. Therefore Justin passes the first test and may provisionally reclaim all of his input tax for the quarter.

(b) Input tax averages £2,300 per month, so Margaret fails the first test. But total input tax less input tax directly attributable to taxable supplies averages only £400 per month and exempt supplies are only 30% of total supplies. Therefore Margaret passes the second test and may reclaim all of her input tax for the year.

Administration of VAT

Overall responsibility for administration of the VAT system lies with the Commissioners for Revenue and Customs. HMRC has a number of dedicated specialist offices which deal with matters such as:

(a) VAT registration

(b) VAT accounting and debt management

(c) written enquiries relating to VAT.

HMRC officers may also enter business premises to inspect business records, check the accuracy of VAT returns and ensure compliance with VAT rules and regulations. HMRC will normally give 7 days' notice of such an inspection, but are empowered to visit without making an appointment if this is deemed necessary.

VAT assessments

VAT is largely a self-assessed tax and so it is not normally necessary to raise formal VAT assessments. But HMRC may issue such an assessment if a taxable person has failed to make a VAT return or has made a return which is incorrect or incomplete.

VAT assessments cannot usually be raised any later than four years after the end of the tax period to which they relate, but this time limit is extended to twenty years if the taxable person has behaved dishonestly or fraudulently. Any claim for a refund of overpaid VAT must also be made within four years in most cases.

Appeals

A person who disagrees with an "appealable" VAT decision made by HMRC may ask for the decision to be internally reviewed. The person concerned also has the right of appeal to a tribunal. Appeals are permissible in relation to most VAT matters, but certain matters cannot be the subject of an appeal.

The internal review process and the appeals system are very similar to their direct tax counterparts (see Chapter 1). In summary:

(a) A request that an appealable HMRC decision should be reviewed must normally be made in writing within 30 days of the date of the decision. A request may be accepted later than this if the person concerned has a reasonable excuse for failing to meet the 30-day time limit.

(b) An internal review is carried out by an HMRC officer who has not previously been involved with the decision in question. The review is normally completed within 45 days. The review officer then writes to the person concerned to inform him or her of the review's conclusions.

(c) If no internal review is requested, an appeal to a tribunal may be made within 30 days of the date of the original decision. Otherwise, an appeal to a tribunal may be made within 30 days of the date of the review conclusion letter.

(d) Most VAT appeals are dealt with by the Tax Chamber of the First-tier Tribunal. The Tax and Chancery Chamber of the Upper Tribunal hears appeals against decisions made by the First-tier Tribunal. A dispute on a point of law may then be referred to the Court of Appeal.

Disclosure of avoidance schemes for VAT (DASVOIT)

The DASVOIT rules (Disclosure of avoidance schemes for VAT and other indirect taxes) require those who promote and market VAT avoidance schemes to provide HMRC with details of each scheme. HMRC then allocates the scheme a reference number and this number must be passed on by the promoter to clients who use the scheme.

Taxable persons who rely upon such a scheme are required to notify HMRC that they are using the scheme and to quote its reference number.

Penalties, surcharges and interest

The main penalties which may be imposed in relation to VAT are as follows:

(a) **Criminal fraud**. A person who attempts to evade VAT in such a way that his or her conduct amounts to criminal fraud may, on a summary conviction obtained before a magistrate, be imprisoned for up to six months. The person may also be required to pay a fine of up to £20,000 or three times the amount of the tax evaded, whichever is the greater. If the conviction is on indictment, the term of imprisonment could be as much as seven years and there is no limit to the size of any fine.

Furthermore, a person who "participates" in a VAT fraud may be liable to a penalty equal to 30% of the potential lost revenue (i.e. the amount of VAT that would have been lost if the fraud had not been discovered). This participator penalty applies to businesses and company officers who have entered into a transaction, knowing that the transaction is connected with the fraudulent evasion of VAT.

(b) **Failure to notify**. A taxable person who fails to notify HMRC of his or her liability to register, or makes late notification, is liable to a penalty. This penalty is assessed in accordance with a penalty regime which applies to any failure to notify HMRC of a taxable activity. This penalty regime is not confined to VAT but covers a range of direct and indirect taxes (see Chapter 15).

Under this regime, the penalty for a failure to notify liability to register is calculated as a percentage of the "potential lost revenue". This is the amount of VAT for which the taxable person is liable between the date on which registration should have taken place and the date on which registration actually takes place. The percentage varies between 30% and 100%, depending upon the degree of culpability of the person in question but may be reduced if the person voluntarily discloses the failure to notify.

(c) **Incorrect VAT returns**. A taxable person who submits an incorrect VAT return is liable to pay a penalty. This penalty is assessed in accordance with a penalty regime which applies to the submission of incorrect tax returns generally and which covers a wide range of taxes (see Chapter 15). Under this regime, a penalty may be charged if an incorrect VAT return leads to an understatement of the amount of tax due and the inaccuracy was either careless or deliberate. A penalty may also be charged if a VAT assessment issued by HMRC understates the amount of tax payable and the taxable person fails to take reasonable steps to inform HMRC of this fact within 30 days.

The amount of any penalty imposed depends upon the person's degree of culpability and will usually vary between 30% and 100% of the additional tax which is payable as a result of correcting the inaccuracy or the understatement. But these penalties are substantially reduced if the taxable person voluntarily discloses the inaccuracy or the failure to report an under-assessment.

(d) **Default surcharge (prior to 1 January 2023)**[†]. A "default" occurs if a taxable person submits a late VAT return or makes a late payment of VAT (or both). In these circumstances, HMRC will usually issue a surcharge liability notice specifying a surcharge period running for 12 months from the last day of the tax period concerned. If a further default is made within this period, then:

- the surcharge period is extended to the first anniversary of the last day of the tax period to which the new default relates, and

- if the new default has resulted in any VAT not being paid on time, a default surcharge will be imposed, calculated as the greater of £30 and a percentage of the tax paid late. The surcharge percentage is 2% for the first default within the surcharge period, 5% for the second such default, 10% for the third default and 15% for the fourth and any subsequent default. However, surcharges are not imposed at the 2% or 5% rate for an amount of less than £400.

A surcharge period comes to an end only when no defaults have occurred for a continuous 12-month period. Note that special arrangements apply to businesses with a turnover not exceeding £150,000 per year. Such businesses are not issued with a surcharge liability notice on the first occasion that a default occurs but are offered help and support instead. However, a surcharge liability notice is issued if another default occurs within the following 12 months.

† *For tax periods beginning on or after 1 January 2023, the default surcharge will be replaced by a "points-based" regime for late submission of VAT returns and a system of late payment penalties (see Chapter 15 for further details). The points threshold for VAT will be two points for annual returns, four points for quarterly returns and five points for monthly returns. The good compliance period will be 24 months, 12 months and six months respectively.*

(e) **VAT wrongdoing**. A VAT "wrongdoing" penalty is charged if an "unauthorised person" issues a VAT invoice. This situation would arise if VAT invoices were issued by a person who is not registered for VAT.

The amount of the penalty varies from 30% to 100% of the amount shown as VAT on the unauthorised invoice, with substantial reductions if the person concerned voluntarily discloses the wrongdoing.

(f) **Breaches of regulations**. A taxable person who fails to comply with sundry VAT regulations will initially receive a written warning from HMRC. If non-compliance is continued, the person is liable on a first offence to a penalty of £5 per day until the breach is remedied. The penalty rises to £10 per day on a second offence (within a period of two years) and again to £15 per day on a third or subsequent offence. The maximum penalty which may be charged is equal to 100 times the daily rate and the minimum penalty is £50.

Certain penalties may be mitigated (i.e. reduced or not charged at all) if the taxable person has a reasonable excuse for his or her conduct. As mentioned above, some penalties may also be mitigated if the person concerned has voluntarily disclosed any non-compliance and has co-operated fully with HMRC.

Default interest and repayment supplement (prior to 1 January 2023)

Until 1 January 2023, the circumstances in which interest is payable to HMRC on underpaid VAT (or payable by HMRC on overpaid VAT) are summarised below.

(a) "Default interest" is usually charged on underpaid VAT which has been assessed by HMRC. This would apply if (for instance) a taxable person made an incorrect VAT return. However, interest is not charged if the error is corrected in a later return, which is permissible if the error does not exceed £10,000 or if the error is between £10,000 and £50,000 and does not exceed 1% of taxable turnover for the return period.

Conversely, if a taxable person makes an overpayment of VAT and this has been caused by HMRC error, the taxable person is paid interest on the tax that is refunded.

(b) If a taxable person is entitled to a repayment of VAT for a tax period, this repayment is increased by a "repayment supplement" of 5% (or £50, if greater) so long as:

– the return for the relevant tax period is submitted on time, and

– the amount stated to be repayable in the return is either correct or does not exceed the correct figure by more than 5% or £250 (whichever is greater), and

– HMRC fails to issue instructions for the repayment to be made within 30 days.

However, as from 1 January 2023, the interest rules for VAT will be aligned with the interest rules which apply for the income tax self assessment system (see Chapter 15).

Summary

▸ VAT is normally accounted for to HMRC on a quarterly basis, although a person who is entitled to a VAT repayment in most tax periods may submit monthly returns.

▸ The date on which a supply is deemed to occur is known as the "tax point".

▸ A tax invoice must normally be issued if a taxable person makes a taxable supply to another taxable person.

▸ There are several special schemes which aim to simplify the workings of the VAT system. These include the cash accounting scheme, the annual accounting scheme, the flat-rate scheme for small businesses, the flat-rate scheme for farmers and the margin scheme. There are also several special schemes for retailers.

▸ Input tax suffered in relation to certain types of supply is not recoverable. Special rules apply to car fuel bought by a business and then used for private motoring.

▸ A person making a mixture of taxable supplies and exempt supplies is "partially exempt" and may reclaim only part of the input tax suffered.

▸ The VAT system is administered by HMRC. Financial penalties are imposed for non-compliance with VAT regulations.

Exercises

A set of multiple choice questions for this chapter is available on the accompanying website.

30.1 The following information relates to the VAT return of Toucan Ltd for the three months to 30 November 2022. All figures are VAT-exclusive unless stated otherwise.

(i) Standard-rated supplies made to customers were £28,800. A cash discount of 2.5% was offered to customers who paid within 28 days and this discount was taken by customers who bought 50% of the supplies made during the quarter.

The figure of £28,800 includes a £1,600 sale which was made to a customer in September 2022. This customer went bankrupt in November 2022 and a bad debt of £1,600 was written off in the company's books on 30 November 2022.

On 15 November 2022, a customer was invoiced for £4,800 in relation to a sale of standard-rated goods. These goods were paid for on 4 December 2022 and were made available to the customer on 10 December 2022. This sale is NOT included in the above figure of £28,800 and was NOT eligible for the cash discount.

(ii) Standard-rated goods bought for resale or consumption cost £9,280. Standard-rated services cost £5,200.

(iii) On 1 September 2022, the company was charged VAT of £1,960 on the purchase of a motor car with emissions of 167g/km. Private use of this car by one of the company's employees accounts for 50% of its mileage. Maintenance charges in relation to the car were £280 for the quarter and fuel costs were £520. The company reclaims input tax on all car fuel.

(iv) In October 2022, the company bought a new non-current asset for a VAT-inclusive price of £14,100.

The company is now considering an application to join the flat-rate scheme for small businesses. Standard-rated sales are expected to run at £11,500 per month from now on and purchases of standard-rated items (other than non-current assets) on which VAT may be reclaimed are expected to be £5,500 per month. The company also anticipates the acquisition of a single non-current asset at a cost of £5,000 during 2023. All of these figures exclude VAT. The flat-rate percentage applicable to Toucan Ltd is 9.5%.

Required:

(a) Compute the VAT payable to (or repayable by) HMRC for the three months to 30 November 2022.

(b) Explain the flat-rate scheme for small businesses. Would Toucan Ltd be eligible to join this scheme? If so, would it be beneficial for the company to join the scheme?

(CIPFA)

30.2 Sebastian is self-employed. He drives a car with an emission rating of 198 g/km and he charges the cost of all the petrol used to his business bank account. In the quarter to 31 July 2022, he uses his car for both business and private journeys but he does not keep detailed mileage records. The VAT-inclusive cost of all the petrol bought in the quarter is £798. How should Sebastian deal with petrol in his VAT return for the quarter?

30.3　With regard to the VAT default surcharge, complete the following table:

Quarter to	VAT return late	VAT paid late	Surcharge period ends	Penalty
31 March 2021	Yes	Yes	31 March 2022	None
30 June 2021	No	No	?	?
30 September 2021	Yes	No	?	?
31 December 2021	Yes	Yes	?	?
31 March 2022	Yes	Yes	?	?
30 June 2022	No	No	?	?
30 September 2022	No	No	?	?
31 December 2022	Yes	Yes	?	?

Assume that any surcharge periods already in existence on 1 January 2023 will continue until they come to an end in accordance with the usual default surcharge rules.

*30.4　During the quarter to 31 December 2022, a taxable person makes the following supplies:

	£
Standard-rated supplies (including VAT)	326,400
Zero-rated supplies	88,000
Exempt supplies	440,000

Input tax for the quarter is £118,000. Of this input tax, 35% is attributed to taxable supplies, 40% is attributed to exempt supplies and 25% is unattributed. Compute the VAT provisionally payable to or reclaimable from HMRC for the quarter.

*30.5　Tracey is a sole trader. She has the following transactions during the quarter to 31 December 2022 (all amounts shown are VAT-exclusive):

	£
Sales to UK customers:	
Standard-rated	34,475
Zero-rated	12,600
Exports of goods:	
From Great Britain to customers situated outside the UK	25,900
Purchases:	
Standard-rated	25,800
Zero-rated	6,200
Expenses:	
Wages and salaries	22,450
Car repairs	120
Insurances	260
Entertaining UK customers	420
Other expenses (all standard-rated)	9,700
Capital transactions:	
Purchase of new plant and machinery	8,000
Purchase of motor van	12,000

Tracey drives a car with an emission rating of 118 g/km and reclaims input tax on all of the fuel used by this car, whether for business or private motoring. She does not keep detailed mileage records. Calculate the amount of VAT due for the quarter.

Chapter 31

Inheritance tax

Introduction

This chapter provides a basic introduction to inheritance tax (IHT). An IHT liability can arise in a number of ways but the events which most commonly trigger such a liability are the transfer of assets on the death of their owner and the gifting of assets during the lifetime of their owner.

IHT was introduced in 1986 to replace capital transfer tax. Current IHT legislation is to be found in the Inheritance Tax Act 1984 (originally the Capital Transfer Tax Act 1984) as amended by subsequent Finance Acts.

Transfers of value

The main situation in which a charge to IHT may arise is when a *transfer of value* of *chargeable property* is made by a *chargeable person*.

A transfer of value occurs when a transferor makes a "disposition" such that his or her estate is lower in value than it was before the disposition occurred. The value of a transfer for IHT purposes is equal to the reduction in the value of the transferor's estate. If the transferor also pays the IHT in relation to the transfer, this further reduces the value of the estate, so that the total value of the transfer is then equal to the amount of the disposition plus the associated IHT.

A disposition is a disposal of property or an interest in property. This includes disposals made during the lifetime of the transferor ("lifetime transfers") as well as disposals caused by the death of the transferor. However, certain dispositions are not regarded as transfers of value for IHT purposes and so cannot give rise to an IHT liability. The most significant of these dispositions are:

(a) dispositions without gratuitous intent (i.e. genuine commercial transactions which give rise to a loss and so cause a reduction in the value of the transferor's estate)

(b) dispositions made during the transferor's lifetime which are allowable expenditure for income tax or corporation tax purposes or which consist of pension contributions made by an employer for the benefit of employees

(c) dispositions made during the transferor's lifetime for the maintenance of his or her family (including spouses, civil partners, children and dependent relatives)

(d) dispositions caused by the fact that the transferor has died whilst on active service†.

† *This IHT exemption also applies to emergency services personnel and humanitarian aid workers. The exemption covers not only the estate of the deceased person but also any IHT that would normally be due on death in relation to transfers made during the person's lifetime (see below).*

Chargeable property

For IHT purposes, the word "property" refers to assets of any type and all property is chargeable property unless specifically excluded from charge. The main exclusions are:

(a) property situated outside the UK and owned by a person who is domiciled outside the UK (i.e. a person whose permanent home is situated outside the UK).

(b) government securities which give tax exemption to persons who are not resident in the UK and which are held by someone who is not UK resident

(c) "heritage property" designated as such by the Treasury, so long as undertakings are given with regard to maintenance of the property and the provision of public access

(d) certain decorations and other awards (e.g. medals for valour or gallant conduct) as long as these have never been disposed of in exchange for money or money's worth

(e) a reversionary interest in a trust or settlement, unless acquired by purchase (see later in this chapter for more information on trusts and types of trust).

Chargeable persons

An individual who is domiciled† in the UK (i.e. whose permanent home is in the UK) is a chargeable person and is liable to IHT in relation to all of his or her chargeable property situated throughout the world. An individual who is not domiciled in the UK is liable to IHT only in relation to property situated in the UK. Note that:

(a) Husbands and wives (and civil partners) are assessed to IHT independently.

(b) A partnership is not a chargeable person. Each partner is individually liable to IHT in relation to his or her share of the partnership assets.

(c) A company is not a chargeable person. But the participators of a close company (see Chapter 27) may incur IHT in relation to transfers made by that company.

(d) A person who is entitled to an "interest in possession" in property which is held in a trust (see later in this chapter) is regarded for IHT purposes as owning the property concerned, as long as this interest existed prior to 22 March 2006.

† *An individual who is not domiciled in the UK on the date of a transfer may nonetheless be deemed to be domiciled in the UK on that date for IHT purposes. This applies if the individual has been domiciled in the UK at any time within the previous three years. It also applies (in most cases) if the individual has been resident in the UK for at least 15 of the 20 tax years preceding the tax year in which the transfer takes place (see Chapter 32 for more details).*

Exempt transfers

Certain transfers are wholly exempt from IHT. In other cases, an exemption or relief may reduce the value of a transfer for IHT purposes. The main exemptions and reliefs are:

(a)   business and agricultural property reliefs (see later in this chapter)

(b)   exemptions for transfers made to certain transferees (see below)

(c)   exemptions available to the transferor (see below).

These exemptions and reliefs are applied to a transfer in the order given above.

Exemptions for transfers made to certain transferees

The following transfers are wholly exempt from IHT whether made on death or during the lifetime of the transferor:

(a)   transfers to the transferor's spouse (husband or wife) or civil partner

(b)   gifts to charities, community amateur sports clubs or qualifying political parties

(c)   gifts made for national purposes to designated bodies (e.g. museums) and gifts of pre-eminent property to the nation (see Chapter 4)

(d)   subject to conditions, transfers into a trust established for the maintenance, repair or preservation of designated heritage property or into an employee ownership trust.

Note that the spouse exemption is restricted if transfers are made by a UK domiciled transferor to a spouse or civil partner who is not UK domiciled (see Chapter 32). Note also that a transfer to a political party is exempt if *either* at least two members of that party were elected to the House of Commons at the last general election *or* one member of the party was elected and the party's candidates gained at least 150,000 votes at the election[†].

[†] *The Government intends that this relief should be extended to parties with representatives in the devolved assemblies and to parties that have gained representatives through by-elections.*

Exemptions available to the transferor

The following exemptions are available in relation to lifetime transfers only:

(a)   **Normal expenditure out of income**. Transfers consisting of "normal expenditure out of income" are wholly exempt from IHT. In order for a transfer to benefit from this exemption, HMRC must believe that the transfer is part of the normal expenditure of the transferor, is made out of the transferor's income (rather than capital) and leaves sufficient income to maintain his or her usual standard of living.

(b)   **Small gifts**. Gifts to individuals with a value of up to £250 per transferee per tax year (from 6 April to 5 April) are wholly exempt from IHT. This exemption cannot be used to exempt part of a gift which has a value exceeding £250 and applies only if the value of all the gifts made to the transferee in a tax year does not exceed £250.

(c) **Gifts in consideration of marriage**. Wedding presents given to either of the "parties" to a marriage (e.g. bride or groom) are exempt from IHT up to the following limits:

  (i) £5,000 if made by a parent of one of the parties

  (ii) £2,500 if made by a grandparent or remoter ancestor of one of the parties

  (iii) £2,500 if made by one of the parties to the other

  (iv) £1,000 in any other case.

  The above exemptions are per transferor per marriage and can be used to exempt part of the value of larger gifts. Similar rules also apply to gifts made on the registration of a civil partnership.

(d) **Annual exemption**. The first £3,000 of lifetime transfers made in any tax year (from 6 April to 5 April) is exempt from IHT. Note that:

  (i) If the total of the lifetime transfers made in a tax year exceeds £3,000, the exemption is set against the year's transfers in chronological order.

  (ii) Any unused part of the £3,000 annual exemption may be carried forward to the following tax year (but no further) and then set against the excess of that year's lifetime transfers over that year's annual exemption.

  (iii) Apparently it is HMRC practice to set the annual exemption against potentially exempt transfers (see below) as well as against chargeable lifetime transfers, even though potentially exempt transfers may never become chargeable to inheritance tax. There is some doubt as to whether this practice is statutorily correct but it has been followed in this book.

EXAMPLE 1

Tania made no transfers during 2020-21. Her only transfers during 2021-22 and 2022-23 are as follows:

		£
2021-22		
June 2021	Gift to her son on his marriage	6,000
October 2021	Gift to her granddaughter	4,500
January 2022	Gift to Oxfam (a charity)	10,000
March 2022	Gift to a friend	100
2022-23		
July 2022	Gift to her nephew	1,000
August 2022	Gift to her cousin	3,500

Calculate the value of each of the above transfers after deduction of all the relevant exemptions. None of the gifts are regarded as normal expenditure out of income.

Solution

(AE = Annual exemption)

	Value before AE £	AE for current year £	AE for previous year £	Value after AE £
2021-22				
Gift to son on marriage (£6,000 – £5,000)	1,000	1,000	-	-
Gift to granddaughter	4,500	2,000	2,500	-
Gift to charity (exempt)	-	-	-	-
Gift to friend (exempt as a small gift)	-	-	-	-
	5,500	3,000	2,500	-
2022-23				
Gift to nephew	1,000	1,000		-
Gift to cousin	3,500	2,000		1,500
	4,500	3,000		1,500

Note:

£500 of the 2020-21 annual exemption remains unused but cannot be carried forward beyond 2021-22. The 2021-22 and 2022-23 annual exemptions are fully utilised.

Potentially exempt transfers (PETs)

If a lifetime transfer is not exempt from IHT as a result of the various exemptions listed above, the transfer will be either a "chargeable lifetime transfer" or a "potentially exempt transfer". Chargeable lifetime transfers are charged to IHT immediately. But potentially exempt transfers (PETs) are charged to IHT only if the transferor dies within seven years of the date of the transfer[†].

A potentially exempt transfer is a lifetime transfer made by an individual to any of the following:

(a) another individual

(b) a trust for the benefit of a disabled person

(c) a trust for the benefit of a bereaved minor (in certain cases).

Most lifetime transfers are in fact PETs. But lifetime transfers made to trusts other than those mentioned above are chargeable lifetime transfers.

[†] *In other words, a PET becomes chargeable to IHT only if the transferor dies before the seventh anniversary of the date of the transfer.*

Types of trust

The above definition of a PET makes reference to various types of trust. Trusts were introduced briefly in Chapter 6 but are explained again below:

(a) A trust (or settlement) is an arrangement whereby property is held by persons known as trustees for the benefit of other persons known as beneficiaries.

(b) If one or more persons are entitled to the lifetime use of the trust property or to the income generated by the trust property, those persons are "life tenants" and the trust is a trust with an "interest in possession" (IIP). A person whose interest in the trust property will not take effect until some future event occurs (e.g. the death of a life tenant) is said to have a "reversionary interest".

(c) A trust with no interest in possession is sometimes referred to as a "discretionary trust". The trustees of such a trust have the discretion to distribute as much or as little of the trust income to the beneficiaries as they see fit.

For IHT purposes, most trusts are classified as "relevant property trusts" and are subject to a special IHT regime. This involves a "periodic" tax charge on the trust property every ten years and an "exit" charge when property leaves the trust. Furthermore, lifetime transfers into a relevant property trust are chargeable lifetime transfers (not PETs).

However, trusts for the disabled and trusts for bereaved minors are generally not relevant property trusts. Such trusts are not liable to the periodic or exit charges and any lifetime transfers into such a trust are PETs.

EXAMPLE 2

Consider each of the following lifetime transfers and classify each one as either an exempt transfer, a PET or a chargeable lifetime transfer. Assume in each case that the transfer was made during 2022-23 and that the annual exemption for both the current year and the previous year have been set against earlier transfers.

(a) a gift of £10,000 made by a husband to his wife

(b) a gift of £20,000 made by a mother to her son on his marriage

(c) a gift of £50,000 made to a trust for the benefit of a disabled person

(d) a gift of £100,000 made to a relevant property trust.

Solution

(a) wholly exempt   (b) exempt £5,000; PET £15,000

(c) PET   (d) chargeable lifetime transfer.

IHT payable on chargeable lifetime transfers

The amount of IHT payable on a chargeable lifetime transfer depends upon:

(a) the value of the transfer (less any relevant exemptions), which must be grossed-up if the tax is paid by the transferor

(b) the rates of IHT in force on the date of the transfer

(c) the total (including the current transfer) of the gross chargeable lifetime transfers made during the seven years ending on the date of the current transfer.

Grossing-up

IHT is chargeable on the *gross* value of a transfer. This is the reduction in the value of the transferor's estate which the transfer has caused. If the transferee pays the tax due on a lifetime transfer, the gross value of the transfer is simply the amount received by the transferee (less any exemptions). However, if the tax due is paid by the transferor, the amount received by the transferee (less exemptions) is only the net value of the transfer and this must be grossed-up at the appropriate rates to find the gross value.

In general, any capital gains tax payable by the transferor in relation to the transfer is ignored when calculating the reduction in value of the transferor's estate.

Rates of IHT applicable to chargeable lifetime transfers

The rates of IHT applicable to chargeable lifetime transfers made during tax year 2022-23 are as follows:

Gross chargeable lifetime transfers for the seven years to date	Rate of tax	Grossing-up fraction
first £325,000 ("nil-rate band")	0%	nil
remainder after the first £325,000	20%	100/80

The rates of tax have been 0% and 20% for many years but the threshold beyond which 20% tax is payable would normally be increased in each tax year, so increasing the width of the nil-rate band. However, this threshold has been frozen at £325,000[†] since 6 April 2009. Recent values of the IHT threshold have been:

Date of transfer	£
6 April 2006 to 5 April 2007	285,000
6 April 2007 to 5 April 2008	300,000
6 April 2008 to 5 April 2009	312,000
6 April 2009 to 5 April 2023	325,000

[†] *Finance Act 2021 provides that the IHT nil-rate band should remain unchanged at £325,000 until the end of tax year 2025-26.*

For each transfer, the calculation of the tax due involves the following steps:

(a) The total gross value of previous chargeable lifetime transfers made during the seven years to date is brought forward.

(b) If the total brought forward has utilised the whole of the nil-rate band, tax is due at 20% on the gross value of the current transfer.

(c) If the total brought forward has not utilised the whole of the nil-rate band, the balance of that band is set against the current transfer. If this does not absorb the whole of the transfer, tax is due at 20% on the gross value of the remainder.

EXAMPLE 3

On 1 July 2022, Violet makes a chargeable lifetime transfer (after deduction of relevant exemptions) of £48,000. Her only previous chargeable lifetime transfer was made in 2018 and had a gross value (after exemptions) of £283,000. Calculate the IHT due if:

(a) the transferee agrees to pay the tax due
(b) the tax due is paid by Violet.

Solution

The total of transfers in the previous seven years is £283,000, leaving £42,000 of the nil-rate band to set against the current transfer.

(a) If the transferee pays the tax, the gross value of the transfer is £48,000 and the IHT due is £42,000 @ 0% + £6,000 @ 20% = £1,200. The total of gross transfers for the seven years to 1 July 2022 is £331,000 (£283,000 + £48,000).

(b) If Violet pays the tax, the net value of the transfer is £48,000. The gross value and the tax due are calculated as follows:

	Net £	Gross £	Tax £
£42,000 grossed up @ 0%	42,000	42,000	0
£6,000 grossed up @ 20%	6,000	7,500	1,500
Totals	48,000	49,500	1,500

The gross value of the transfer is £49,500 and the tax due is £1,500. The total of gross transfers for the seven years to 1 July 2022 is £332,500 (£283,000 + £49,500).

Note:

Grossing up at 20% is equivalent to multiplying by 100/80. The transfer is treated as a gross transfer of £49,500, of which £42,000 is taxed at 0% and the remaining £7,500 is taxed at 20%. This gives a tax liability (payable by Violet) of £1,500. Therefore the amount by which Violet's estate decreases is (£48,000 + £1,500) = £49,500.

IHT payable on death

The IHT payable on death consists of:

(a) additional tax on any chargeable lifetime transfers which were made by the deceased person during the seven years ending on the date of death

(b) tax on any PETs made by the deceased person during those seven years

(c) tax on the estate of the deceased person as at the date of death, to the extent that the transfers made on death are not exempt from IHT.

Tax on chargeable lifetime transfers and PETs

The tax payable on death in respect of the chargeable lifetime transfers and PETs made in the seven years ending on the date of death is calculated as follows:

(a) The transfers are considered in chronological order with no distinction made between chargeable lifetime transfers and PETs.

(b) Tax is calculated on the gross value of each transfer using the IHT bands and rates in force *on the date of death* and taking into account any other chargeable transfers made *in the seven years ending on the date of the transfer* (including any PETs that have now become chargeable). Applicable rates of tax for deaths in 2022-23 are:

Gross chargeable transfers for the seven years to date	Rate of tax
first £325,000 ("nil-rate band")	0%
remainder after the first £325,000	40%

Note that the nil-rate band available on death in relation to a deceased person may be increased by a transfer of unused nil-rate band from a previously deceased spouse or civil partner (see later in this chapter).

(c) The tax calculated at (b) for each transfer may then be reduced by *taper relief*, depending upon the number of years which have elapsed between the date of the transfer and the date of death. Taper relief is given as follows:

Period between transfer and death	Percentage tax reduction
3 years or less	0%
Over 3 but not more than 4 years	20%
Over 4 but not more than 5 years	40%
Over 5 but not more than 6 years	60%
Over 6 but not more than 7 years	80%

(d) Finally, for each transfer, any tax already paid during the lifetime of the transferor is subtracted, leaving a balance of tax due on that transfer. This tax liability is usually the responsibility of the transferee. No repayment is given if the lifetime tax paid in relation to a transfer exceeds the liability on death.

EXAMPLE 4

Wilson dies on 20 December 2022, having made only the following transfers during his lifetime:

		£
6 June 2012	Gift to daughter	50,000
4 March 2016	Gift to relevant property trust	516,400
11 January 2017	Gift to son on marriage	50,000

Calculate the IHT payable during Wilson's lifetime (if any) in relation to each of the above transfers, assuming that Wilson paid this tax himself. Also calculate any further IHT payable in relation to these transfers on Wilson's death.

Solution

The value of each gift after deduction of exemptions is as follows:

		Value before AE	AE for current year	AE for previous year	Value after AE
		£	£	£	£
2012-13	Daughter	50,000	3,000	3,000	44,000
2015-16	Relevant property trust	516,400	3,000	3,000	510,400
2016-17	Son (£50,000 – £5,000)	45,000	3,000	-	42,000

Lifetime tax liability

The gifts to Wilson's son and daughter were PETs and gave rise to no immediate tax liability but the gift to the trust was a chargeable lifetime transfer. There were no other such transfers during the seven years to date so the whole of the nil-rate band (£325,000 at that time) was set against the gift. The tax due was £46,350, calculated as follows:

	Net	Gross	Tax
	£	£	£
£325,000 grossed up @ 0%	325,000	325,000	0
£185,400 grossed up @ 20%	185,400	231,750	46,350
Totals	510,400	556,750	46,350

Tax liability on death

The June 2012 PET is more than seven years old at the time of Wilson's death. This PET is exempt from tax and can be completely ignored for IHT purposes. The tax due on the other two transfers is calculated as follows:

(i) *Transfer made on 4 March 2016*

The gross value of this transfer is £556,750 and there were no other chargeable transfers in the seven years to date (5 March 2009 to 4 March 2016). The tax due at the death rates applicable on 20 December 2022 is:

	£
£325,000 @ 0%	0
£231,750 @ 40%	92,700
	92,700
<u>Less</u>: Taper relief (6-7 years) @ 80%	74,160
	18,540

The lifetime tax paid on the transfer (£46,350) exceeds the tax liability calculated on death (£18,540). Therefore there is no further tax to pay on Wilson's death in relation to this transfer. However, there is no repayment of the excess of £27,810.

(ii) *Transfer made on 11 January 2017*

The gross value of this transfer is £42,000. Previous gross chargeable transfers in the seven years to date (12 January 2010 to 11 January 2017) were £556,750, completely absorbing the nil-rate band. Therefore the tax liability on death is:

	£
£42,000 @ 40%	16,800
<u>Less</u>: Taper relief (5-6 years) @ 60%	10,080
	6,720
<u>Less</u>: Lifetime tax paid	0
IHT payable by Wilson's son	6,720

Tax on the deceased person's estate

IHT on the deceased person's estate (to the extent that the transfers made on death are not exempt from IHT) is calculated using the rates of tax applicable on death. The calculation normally proceeds as follows:

(a) First, the nil-rate band is reduced by the total of gross chargeable transfers (including any PETs) made in the seven years ending on the date of death. Note that a deceased person's nil-rate band may be higher than usual because of a transfer of unused nil-rate band from a previously deceased spouse or civil partner (see below).

(b) The remainder of the nil-rate band (if any) is then set against the value of the estate and tax at 40% is calculated on the balance.

(c) The tax due is divided by the value of the estate and the result (expressed as a percentage) is the "estate rate" i.e. the average rate of tax borne by the estate.

However, a lower rate of IHT (36%) applies to an estate if at least 10% of the estate is left to charity. The figure to which the 10% test is applied is the value of the net estate after deducting all IHT exemptions, reliefs and any available nil-rate band, but adding back the amount left to charity. Note that the 36% rate does <u>not</u> apply when calculating the tax charge arising on death in relation to transfers made in the previous seven years.

EXAMPLE 5

Toby dies on 2 March 2023, leaving an estate valued at £400,000. None of the transfers made on death are exempt from IHT. Calculate the IHT due on the estate if the total of the gross chargeable transfers made by Toby in the seven years up to his death was:

(a) Nil   (b) £125,000   (c) £370,000.

Solution

(a) £325,000 @ 0% + £75,000 @ 40% = £30,000. (Estate rate 7.5%)
(b) £200,000 @ 0% + £200,000 @ 40% = £80,000. (Estate rate 20%)
(c) £400,000 @ 40% = £160,000. (Estate rate 40%).

EXAMPLE 6

Rose dies on 10 July 2022, leaving an estate valued at £525,000. None of the transfers made on death are exempt from IHT apart from a bequest to the RSPCA (a charity). Rose made no chargeable transfers in the seven years prior to her death. Calculate the IHT due on the estate if the amount of the bequest to the RSPCA was:

(a) £10,000   (b) £30,000.

Solution

(a) The gift to charity is an exempt transfer and the nil-rate band is available in full. So IHT is due on £190,000 (£525,000 – £10,000 – £325,000). The total of this amount and the gift to charity is £200,000 and the gift is only 5% of this total. Therefore the lower rate does not apply and IHT due is £76,000 (£190,000 @ 40%).

(b) IHT is due on £170,000 (£525,000 – £30,000 – £325,000). The total of this amount and the gift to charity is £200,000 and the gift is 15% of this total. This is not less than 10% so the lower rate applies and IHT due is £61,200 (£170,000 @ 36%).

Transfer of unused part of nil-rate band

If one party to a marriage or a civil partnership dies and the amount that is chargeable to IHT on his or her death (including any transfers made in the previous seven years) does not use up all of the nil-rate band, the unused part of the nil-rate band may be transferred to the surviving spouse or civil partner for use on his or her death. Note that:

(a) The transferred part of the nil-rate band may be used only when the surviving spouse or civil partner dies. It is used when calculating any tax due on death in relation to transfers made in the seven years before the survivor dies and when calculating the tax due on the survivor's estate. It *cannot* be used to reduce the *lifetime* tax payable on any chargeable lifetime transfers made by the survivor.

(b)   The amount available for transfer is calculated by determining the proportion of the nil-rate band which was unused when the survivor's spouse or civil partner died. This proportion is then applied to the amount of the nil-rate band which is in force on the date of the survivor's death.

EXAMPLE 7

Harriet died on 21 October 2022. Her husband had died previously and his estate on death (including transfers made in the last seven years of his life) had absorbed £177,840 of the nil-rate band at that time. Calculate the nil-rate band which is available when calculating the IHT due on Harriet's death, assuming that her husband died in:

(a)   May 2006   (b)   February 2009.

Solution

(a)   When Harriet's husband died, the nil-rate band was £285,000. His estate absorbed £177,840 of this, leaving £107,160 (37.6% of the nil-rate band) unused. Therefore Harriet's nil-rate band on death is £325,000 + 37.6% of £325,000 = £447,200.

(b)   When Harriet's husband died, the nil-rate band was £312,000. His estate absorbed £177,840 of this, leaving £134,160 (43% of the nil-rate band) unused. Therefore Harriet's nil-rate band on death is £325,000 + 43% of £325,000 = £464,750.

Residence nil-rate band

With effect from 6 April 2017, an additional "residence nil-rate band" (RNRB) is available in relation to estates which include a residential property, as long as the property has been the deceased person's residence at some time and is "closely inherited". In general terms, this means that the property is left to the deceased person's direct descendants (children, grandchildren etc.). It is important to note that the RNRB is taken into account only when calculating the IHT payable on the estate. It is *not* available when calculating any tax payable in relation to transfers made in the seven years before death.

The amount of the RNRB is normally equal to the *lower* of the value of the property (net of mortgage debt) and the "maximum amount", which has been phased in as follows:

2017-18   £100,000   *2018-19*   £125,000   *2019-20*   £150,000
2020-21   £175,000 (*fixed until the end of 2025-26*)

However, the maximum amount is reduced by £1 for every £2 by which the value of the deceased person's estate (before reliefs and exemptions) exceeds £2 million: Note that:

(a)   Any unused proportion of the RNRB may be transferred to a surviving spouse or civil partner in the same way as the normal nil-rate band. A person will have unused RNRB if he or she dies not owning a residence, or owns a residence but does not leave it to direct descendants, or leaves a residence to direct descendants with a value of less than the maximum amount.

(b) If entitlement to the RNRB might be wholly or partly lost because an individual downsizes to a less valuable residence before death (or ceases to own a residence at all), any part of the RNRB which would otherwise be lost is still available if assets of an equivalent value are left to direct descendants.

EXAMPLE 8

Desmond died on 18 July 2018, having made no transfers in the previous seven years. He left his entire estate to his wife Emily, including the family home valued at £420,000. Emily died on 9 May 2022, having made no transfers in the previous seven years. She left her entire estate to her daughter, including the family home valued at £450,000. Calculate the total nil-rate band available in relation to Emily's estate, assuming that neither her estate nor her husband's had a value in excess of £2 million.

Solution

(a) Desmond's estate was exempt from IHT (spouse exemption) so 100% of his normal nil-rate band was unused. Emily's nil-rate band is increased by 100% to £650,000.

(b) Desmond did not leave a residence to his direct descendants, so 100% of his RNRB was also unused. By the time of Emily's death, the maximum RNRB was £175,000. So Emily's RNRB is increased by 100% to £350,000.

(c) The total nil-rate band available in relation to Emily's estate is therefore £1,000,000.

Quick succession relief

Quick succession relief (QSR) is available when property which is transferred on death was transferred to the deceased person within the previous five years and was charged to IHT at that time. The tax (if any) payable in relation to the transfer made on death is reduced by an amount which depends upon the gross value of the earlier transfer (G) and the amount of IHT paid on that transfer (T). The relief is calculated as:

$$\frac{G-T}{G} \times T \times QSR\%$$

The QSR percentage depends upon the length of the period between the earlier transfer and the date of death, as follows:

1 year or less	100%
Over 1 but not more than 2 years	80%
Over 2 but not more than 3 years	60%
Over 3 but not more than 4 years	40%
Over 4 but not more than 5 years	20%

Gifts with reservation

A "gift with reservation" is a gift of any property made in such a way that either:

(a) possession and enjoyment of the property is not *bona fide* (genuinely) assumed by the recipient of the gift at or before the start of the "relevant period", or

(b) the property is not enjoyed to the entire exclusion of the donor throughout the whole of the relevant period.

For this purpose, the "relevant period" is the period which ends on the date of the donor's death and which begins seven years before that date or (if later) on the date of the gift.

If there were no special rules relating to gifts with reservation, taxpayers would be able to divest themselves of property (so reducing the IHT charge on death) whilst continuing to benefit from that property. This is prevented by legislation which ensures that:

(a) property which is subject to a reservation at the date of the donor's death is treated as part of the donor's estate, and

(b) if any property ceases to be subject to a reservation before the donor's death, the donor is treated as having made a PET on the date that the reservation ceases to exist.

These rules are supplemented by regulations which deal with the possibility of a double tax charge arising if the gift is also a chargeable transfer.

Valuation

As stated at the beginning of this chapter, the value of a transfer for IHT purposes is equal to the reduction in value of the transferor's estate as a result of that transfer. In general, this is equivalent to the open market value of the transferred assets but this will not always be the case. For instance, if the transferor disposes of a small number of shares in a company, sufficient to convert a majority shareholding into a minority shareholding, it is likely that the true reduction in value of the transferor's estate will exceed the market value of the transferred assets. This aside, determining the market value of the transferred assets may in itself cause difficulty and special valuation rules are sometimes required.

Listed shares

For IHT purposes. shares which are listed on a recognised stock exchange (referred to as "listed shares" or "quoted shares") are valued at the *lower* of:

(a) the lower of the two closing prices quoted for those shares on the day of the transfer in the Stock Exchange Daily Official List, plus one-quarter of the difference between these two prices (the "quarter-up" rule)

(b) the average of the highest and lowest prices at which bargains relating to those shares (if any) were recorded on the day of the transfer.

If listed shares are transferred on a non-working day (for which prices are unavailable) the shares are valued as if transferred on the last working day before the date of the transfer or the first working day after it, whichever gives the lower figure.

EXAMPLE 9

On 1 June 2022, Shirley gives 5,000 shares in a listed company to her daughter. Shares in the company are quoted at 189p - 197p on that date, with recorded bargains at 190p, 192p and 196p. Calculate the market value of the shares for IHT purposes.

Solution

The quarter-up rule gives 189p + 1/4 x (197p − 189p) = 191p. The average of the highest and lowest recorded bargains is 193p, so the shares are valued at 191p and the transfer has a market value of 5,000 x £1.91 = £9,550.

Related property

When calculating the value of a transfer for IHT purposes, the existence of any "related property" may be taken into account. Related property consists of property which:

(a)   is owned by the transferor's spouse or civil partner, or

(b)   is owned (or has been owned within the previous five years) by a charity, political party etc. as a result of an exempt transfer made either by the transferor or by his or her spouse or civil partner.

Under the related property rules, the property being transferred and the related property are valued together (as a whole) and then part of that value is apportioned to the property being transferred. These rules are intended to prevent taxpayers from avoiding IHT by fragmenting the ownership of an asset and will only be used if the valuation given by the related property rules is greater than the valuation that would be calculated normally.

EXAMPLE 10

Roy owns 3,500 ordinary shares in an unlisted company which has an issued share capital of 10,000 ordinary shares. Roy's wife owns a further 1,600 shares. Shareholdings in the company are valued as follows:

	£		£		£
500 shares	5,000	3,000 shares	33,000	3,500 shares	43,750
4,600 shares	64,400	5,100 shares	96,900		

Roy now transfers 500 of his shares to a relevant property trust. Calculate the value of this transfer for IHT purposes.

Solution

Ignoring related property, Roy's estate has reduced in value by £10,750 (£43,750 − £33,000) and this would normally be the value of the transfer. But taking related property into account, the value of the transfer is calculated as follows:

	£
Value of Roy's holding before the transfer (£96,900 x 3,500/5,100)	66,500
Value of Roy's holding after the transfer (£64,400 x 3,000/4,600)	42,000
Value of the transfer	24,500

Since £24,500 exceeds £10,750, the value of the transfer is £24,500.

Overseas property

Property situated outside the UK is valued in the relevant foreign currency. This value is then converted into sterling, using the appropriate exchange rate for the day on which the transfer takes place.

Business property relief

Business property relief of either 100% or 50% is available in relation to a transfer (made in the transferor's lifetime or on death) which meets *all* of the following conditions:

(a) the property transferred consists of "relevant business property" (see below)

(b) the business is a "qualifying business" (investment businesses do not qualify)

(c) the property has been owned by the transferor for at least two years, or has replaced other relevant business property, such that the combined period of ownership of both the original and replacement property is at least two years out of the five years preceding the date of the transfer.

The main categories of relevant business property, together with the applicable rates of relief, are as follows:

		Rate of relief
(a)	Property consisting of a business or an interest in a business	100%
(b)	Securities in an unlisted company which gave the transferor control of the company immediately before the transfer	100%
(c)	Shares in an unlisted company	100%
(d)	Shares transferred from a controlling holding in a listed company	50%
(e)	Land, buildings, plant and machinery which, immediately before the transfer, were used for business purposes by a partnership in which the transferor was a partner or by a company of which he/she had control	50%

(f)   Land, buildings, plant and machinery which, immediately before   50%
the transfer, were used in the transferor's business and owned by
a trust of which the transferor was a life tenant.

No relief is given in relation to "excepted assets". These are assets which have not been used for business purposes throughout the two years prior to the transfer and which are not required for the future use of the business.

Agricultural property relief

Agricultural property relief of either 100% or 50% is available in relation to a transfer of agricultural property (in life or on death) so long as that property has been either:

(a)   occupied by the transferor and used for agricultural purposes throughout the two years preceding the date of the transfer, or

(b)   owned by the transferor throughout the seven years preceding the date of the transfer and occupied by the transferor or someone else for agricultural purposes throughout those seven years.

For this purpose, agricultural property consists mainly of agricultural land and pasture, woodlands and associated buildings. Land managed according to the terms of certain wildlife habitat schemes (together with any associated buildings) is also eligible for agricultural property relief. The rates of relief are:

(a)   100% if, immediately before the transfer, the transferor enjoys vacant possession of the property or the right to obtain it within the following 12 months

(b)   Otherwise, 100% if the property is let on a tenancy starting after 31 August 1995 and 50% if the property is let on a tenancy starting before 1 September 1995.

These rates apply only to the "agricultural value" of the property. This is the value that the property would have if it could only ever be used for agricultural purposes. If a property qualifies for both business property relief and agricultural property relief, agricultural property relief is given first.

Administration of IHT

Inheritance tax is administered by HMRC. For chargeable lifetime transfers and transfers caused by the death of the transferor, an "account" must be delivered to HMRC, giving details of the transfers made and their value. Details of this procedure are as follows:

(a) **Chargeable lifetime transfers**. The transferor must deliver an account to HMRC within 12 months of the end of the month in which the transfer occurred. There is no need to deliver an account if the transfer is exempt or potentially exempt, or if:

   (i) for chargeable lifetime transfers consisting wholly of cash or quoted stocks and securities, the total of all chargeable transfers made in the seven years to date does not exceed the IHT threshold (i.e. the amount of the nil-rate band)

   (ii) for chargeable lifetime transfers not consisting wholly of cash or quoted stocks and securities, the total of all chargeable transfers made in the seven years to date does not exceed 80% of the IHT threshold.

(b) **Death**. The personal representatives of a deceased person must deliver an account to HMRC within 12 months of the end of the month in which the death occurred. But there is no need to deliver an account if the person was UK-domiciled and:

   (i) the gross value of the estate, plus any transfers made during the seven years prior to death, does not exceed the IHT threshold (or double this threshold if 100% of the nil-rate band was transferred to the deceased person on the prior death of a spouse or civil partner), and

   (ii) no more than £100,000 of the estate is situated outside the UK, and

   (iii) any trust assets included in the estate of the deceased person are held in a single trust and do not exceed £150,000 in value, and

   (iv) there have been no chargeable lifetime transfers or PETs made within the seven years to date, other than transfers consisting of cash, listed securities or land and buildings (and contents) with a total gross value not exceeding £150,000.

If the deceased person was not UK-domiciled (and never had been) an account is not required so long as the value of UK assets transferred on death does not exceed £150,000 and these assets consist solely of cash, listed shares or listed securities.

When a transfer gives rise to an IHT liability, HMRC issues a notice which shows the value of the transfer for IHT purposes and the amount of tax payable. Appeals may be lodged within 30 days of the date of the notice.

Payment of IHT

The IHT relating to a transfer is usually payable six months after the end of the month in which the transfer (or the death) occurred. However, the tax on chargeable lifetime transfers made in roughly the first half of the tax year (6 April to 30 September) is not payable until 30 April in the following tax year.

It is notable that the tax on a transfer is usually due for payment before the end of the 12-month period within which an account of the transfer must be delivered to HMRC. Since interest is charged on tax paid late, there is an incentive to deliver the account (and pay the tax due) on or before the due date of payment.

Summary

▸ The main occasion on which IHT is charged is when a transfer of value of chargeable property is made by a chargeable person. A transfer may be a lifetime transfer or a transfer made on death.

▸ The value of a transfer is equal to the reduction in value of the transferor's estate as a result of the transfer. The value of a transfer for IHT purposes may be reduced by business property relief and/or agricultural property relief.

▸ Transfers made to certain transferees (e.g. spouses, civil partners, charities and certain political parties) are exempt from IHT.

▸ Lifetime transfers comprising small gifts, gifts made out of income and gifts made on marriage or civil partnership are wholly or partly exempt from IHT. The first £3,000 of lifetime transfers made in any tax year is exempt from IHT.

▸ A potentially exempt transfer (PET) is not chargeable to IHT unless the transferor dies within seven years. A chargeable lifetime transfer may be charged to IHT when the transfer is made (depending upon the total of the transfers made in the previous seven years) and may attract additional tax when the transferor dies.

▸ The amount of IHT charged on the estate of a deceased person depends upon the size of the estate and the total of any chargeable transfers made in the seven years before the person's death.

▸ The IHT on a transfer is normally payable six months after the end of the month in which the transfer takes place.

Exercises

A set of multiple choice questions for this chapter is available on the accompanying website.

31.1 Phoebe made the following transfers during 2022-23:

		£
12 April 2022	Gift to grandson	50
17 May 2022	Gift to her nephew on his marriage	3,000
3 August 2022	Gift to her husband	25,000
31 October 2022	Gift to a relevant property trust	10,000
1 January 2023	Gift to the Labour Party	5,000

None of the gifts are regarded as normal expenditure out of income. Phoebe made no transfers at all during 2021-22. Calculate the value of each of her 2022-23 transfers after deduction of all the available exemptions.

31.2   Classify each of the following lifetime transfers as either exempt, potentially exempt, or chargeable:

(a)   a gift to the transferor's favourite charity

(b)   a gift to a relevant property trust

(c)   a gift to the transferor's grandfather.

31.3   On 5 December 2022, Nicholas makes a gift of £80,000 (after deduction of all relevant exemptions) to a relevant property trust. His only previous chargeable lifetime transfers were in June 2013 (gross chargeable value after exemptions £200,000) and in July 2017 (gross chargeable value after exemptions £281,000). Calculate the lifetime IHT payable in relation to the £80,000 gift and state the due date of payment:

(a)   if the trustees pay the tax   (b) if Nicholas pays the tax.

31.4   On 31 March 2016, Martha gave £500,000 to her daughter as a wedding present. On 1 April 2017 she gave £497,000 to a relevant property trust. Martha died on 1 January 2023, having made only these two transfers during her life.

(a)   Calculate any lifetime tax due on each of the above transfers and state the due date of payment, assuming that Martha paid this tax herself.

(b)   Calculate any further tax due on Martha's death in relation to these transfers and state the due date of payment. (Assume that there is no unused nil-rate band to be transferred from a previously deceased spouse or civil partner).

31.5   On 29 September 2022, Hyacinth makes a transfer consisting of 1,000 shares in a listed company. The shares are quoted at 572p - 588p on that date, with recorded bargains at 572p, 577p and 578p. Calculate the market value of the transfer for IHT purposes.

*31.6   On 12 November 2012, Hazel made a gross chargeable transfer to a relevant property trust of £266,000 (after deduction of exemptions). On 1 April 2018 she gave £300,000 to her grandson. These were her only transfers. She died on 17 December 2022.

Calculate the inheritance tax payable by her grandson as a result of Hazel's death. (Assume that there is no unused nil-rate band to be transferred from a previously deceased spouse or civil partner).

*31.7   Tony died on 11 July 2022, leaving an estate which was valued at £900,000. None of the transfers made on his death were exempt from IHT. He had made the following transfers during his lifetime:

		£
3 May 2014	Gift to relevant property trust (tax paid by trustees)	113,000
1 July 2015	Gift to daughter	185,000
1 August 2015	Gift to son	250,000
10 November 2016	Gift to relevant property trust (tax paid by Tony)	447,000

Calculate the tax payable as a result of Tony's death. (Assume that there is no unused nil-rate band to be transferred from a previously deceased spouse or civil partner and that Tony's residence was not left to a direct descendant).

Chapter 32

Overseas aspects of taxation

Introduction

The main purpose of this final chapter is to consider the way in which the UK tax system deals with the overseas income and gains of UK resident individuals and companies. The treatment of non-resident individuals and companies with income or gains arising in the UK is also briefly considered.

The chapter begins by explaining the factors which affect an individual's UK tax status and then continues with a brief review of the overseas aspects of income tax, capital gains tax and inheritance tax. Overseas aspects of corporation tax are dealt with towards the end of the chapter.

Residence and domicile

The extent to which an individual is chargeable to UK tax depends upon that individual's *residence* and *domicile*. These key concepts are explained below.

Note that an individual's *nationality* is usually <u>not</u> an important factor when determining that individual's UK tax status.

Residence

A statutory definition of the term "residence" was introduced in Finance Act 2013 and took effect as from 6 April 2013. The rules which determine whether or not an individual is UK resident are complex and require over 60 pages of detailed legislation. However, a summary of the main rules is as follows:

(a) An individual is UK resident for a tax year if he or she meets either the "automatic residence test" or the "sufficient ties test" for that tax year. If neither test is satisfied the individual is not UK resident for the year.

(b) The automatic residence test is met if the individual meets any of the "automatic UK tests" and does not meet any of the "automatic overseas tests".

(c)   The most important <u>automatic UK tests</u> are as follows:

UK Test 1: the individual spends at least 183 days in the UK during the tax year

UK Test 2:

(i)   the individual has a home in the UK during all or part of the tax year, *and*

(ii)   spends at least 30 days in that UK home during the year, *and*

(iii) there is a period of at least 91 consecutive days (at least 30 of which fall within the tax year) in which the individual has that UK home and *either* has no home overseas *or* has one or more homes overseas but spends no more than 30 days in any of them during the tax year.

UK Test 3:

(i)   the individual works full-time in the UK for a period of 365 days, *and*

(ii)   all or part of that period falls within the tax year, *and*

(iii) more than 75% of the days in the 365-day period on which the individual does more than three hours of work are days on which he or she does more than three hours of work in the UK, *and*

(iv)   there is at least one day in the tax year in which the individual does more than three hours of work in the UK.

(d)   The most important <u>automatic overseas tests</u> are as follows:

Overseas Test 1:

(i)   the individual was UK resident for one or more of the previous three tax years,

(ii)   *but* spends less than 16 days in the UK during the tax year.

Overseas Test 2:

(i)   the individual was UK resident for none of the previous three tax years, *and*

(ii)   spends less than 46 days in the UK during the tax year.

Overseas Test 3:

(i)   the individual works full-time overseas during the tax year, *and*

(ii)   there are less than 31 days in the tax year on which the individual works for more than three hours in the UK, *and*

(iii) the individual spends less than 91 days in the UK during the tax year.

(e)   The <u>sufficient ties test</u> examines ties to the UK under various headings (e.g. family ties) and determines the individual's residence status by counting the number of such ties. The test also takes into account the number of days spent in the UK during the tax year and the individual's residence status for the previous three years.

It is important to appreciate that the concept of UK residence normally applies to *whole* tax years and it is not usually possible to apportion a tax year into periods of residence and non-residence. However, such apportionment (or "split-year treatment") is permitted in certain cases. These include:

(a) *the year of departure*, if an individual who was UK resident for the previous tax year leaves the UK in order to work full-time overseas (and will be non-UK resident in the following tax year because he or she will meet the third automatic overseas test)

(b) *the year of departure*, if an individual who was UK resident for the previous tax year (and will be non-UK resident in the following tax year) leaves the UK to live abroad, so long as he or she had a home in the UK at the start of the tax year but ceases to have a home in the UK by the end of the tax year

(c) *the year of arrival*, if an individual who was not UK resident in the previous tax year comes to live or work full-time in the UK (subject to conditions).

If a tax year is apportioned into periods of residence and non-residence, any personal allowances to which the individual is entitled are available in full for that year.

EXAMPLE 1

Peter has had a home in the UK for many years and has always been UK resident. He has worked in the UK throughout his adult life but he retired in December 2021.

During tax year 2022-23 he takes a long round-the-world holiday. He maintains his UK home and does not establish a home overseas, but he is present in the UK for only 43 days during the tax year. Is he UK resident for tax year 2022-23?

Solution

Peter does not meet either the first or the third automatic UK test. However, he does meet the second automatic UK test and he does not meet any of the automatic overseas tests. Therefore he meets the automatic residence test and is UK resident for tax year 2022-23.

Domicile

An individual's domicile[†] is the country or state which is considered to be the individual's permanent home. It is not possible to have more than one domicile at a time.

Individuals acquire a "domicile of origin" on birth. This is usually the domicile of the father or another person on whom the individual is dependent and is not necessarily the country of birth. Having reached the age of 16, an individual may then acquire a "domicile of choice", but such a domicile can only be acquired by settling in the chosen country.

If an individual acquires a domicile of choice, that domicile is also acquired by anyone under the age of 16 who is dependent on that individual. A domicile acquired in this way is known as a "domicile of dependency".

[†] *Individuals who are UK resident for a given tax year and have been UK resident for at least 15 of the previous 20 tax years are deemed to be domiciled in the UK for that tax year. Furthermore, individuals born in the UK with a UK domicile of origin are deemed to be domiciled in the UK for any tax year in which they are UK resident. Individuals who are deemed to be domiciled in the UK are not "non-doms" and cannot use the remittance basis (see below).*

Income tax - general rules

The general rules governing an individual's liability to UK income tax are as follows:

(a) Individuals who are *resident* in the UK for a tax year are liable to pay UK income tax on all of their income for that year, including any overseas income. Note that:

   (i) Overseas employment income is taxed in accordance with the rules of ITEPA 2003 (see later in this chapter). Overseas trading income, property income and investment income are taxed by ITTOIA 2005.

   (ii) ITTOIA 2005 provides that the "relevant foreign income" of a UK resident who is not domiciled in the UK may be taxed only to the extent that the income is remitted to the UK (the "remittance basis"). The term "relevant foreign income" covers most of the forms of overseas income to which ITTOIA 2005 applies.

   In general, an individual who wishes that the remittance basis should apply for a tax year must make a claim to that effect. However, the remittance basis is automatically assumed to apply to an individual whose unremitted income and gains are less than £2,000 in the year concerned (unless the individual notifies HMRC that he/she does not wish the remittance basis to apply).

   (iii) Individuals who claim the remittance basis and who have been UK resident for at least seven of the previous nine tax years are liable to an annual tax charge of £30,000. This increases to £60,000 for those who have been resident in the UK for at least 12 of the previous 14 years. Since this rule applies only to those who *claim* the remittance basis, it does not apply to individuals whose unremitted income and gains are less than £2,000 for the tax year.

   (iv) Personal allowances are generally available to UK residents. But individuals who claim the remittance basis are not entitled to personal allowances. Again, this rule applies only to those who *claim* the remittance basis.

   (v) Individuals who are taxed on the remittance basis may remit overseas income to the UK without incurring an income tax liability if this income is used to make a commercial investment in a qualifying business ("business investment relief").

(b) Individuals who are *not resident* in the UK are liable to pay UK income tax on their UK income only. Note that:

   (i) The UK property income of non-residents is usually payable after deduction of basic rate income tax by the letting agent or tenant.

   (ii) Personal allowances may be claimed by certain non-residents, principally those who are citizens of the UK or the European Economic Area (see Chapter 3).

(c) If a tax year is apportioned into periods of residence and non-residence, the above rules apply to the two periods as if they were separate tax years.

These general rules are subject to a number of exceptions, depending upon the type of income involved (see below).

Unremittable income

A UK resident who is liable to income tax on overseas income may make a claim to the effect that the income is "unremittable". Such a claim may be made if the income is not taxed on the remittance basis and cannot be remitted to the UK because of:

(a) the laws of the country in which the income arises, or

(b) the executive actions of the government of that country, or

(c) the impossibility of obtaining foreign currency in that country which could be transferred to the UK.

The effect of the claim is that the income is not taxed in the year in which it arises but is taxed instead in the year in which it ceases to be unremittable (if that occurs).

Double taxation relief (DTR)

The general rules given above are likely to lead to a number of situations in which income is taxed twice. For example, the overseas income of a UK resident will be taxed in the UK and might also be taxed in the country in which the income arises, depending upon that country's tax laws. Similarly, the UK income of a non-resident will be taxed in the UK and might also be taxed overseas. In order to avoid this situation, the UK has made "double taxation treaties" with many overseas countries. Typically, such a treaty might provide that certain forms of income should be exempt from income tax in the country of origin (or charged at a reduced rate) if receivable by a non-resident.

Unilateral double tax relief

Unless double tax relief is available (or prohibited) under the terms of a double taxation treaty with the country concerned, the UK taxation system provides "unilateral double tax relief" for foreign tax suffered by a UK resident who receives overseas income. Overseas income which is received net of foreign tax is grossed-up and charged to UK income tax in the usual way, but the taxpayer is then given tax relief equal to the *lower* of:

(a) the amount of foreign tax suffered (the "withholding tax") and

(b) the amount of UK tax due on the overseas income.

The amount of UK tax due on the overseas income is equal to the difference between the tax that is due on the taxpayer's total income (including overseas income) and the tax which would be due if the overseas income were ignored. If the foreign tax suffered exceeds the UK tax due, part of the foreign tax suffered will be unrelieved.

Unilateral relief is available only if the taxpayer has taken all reasonable steps to minimise the amount of the foreign tax liability.

EXAMPLE 2

Vicky's income for 2022-23 consists of her UK salary of £52,540 and rents from overseas property (net of 30% withholding tax) of £3,500. Vicky is UK resident in 2022-23 and she is not a Scottish taxpayer. Calculate her UK income tax liability for the year.

Solution

Property income is £5,000 (£3,500 x 100/70). Therefore total income is £57,540 (£52,540 + £5,000) and taxable income is £44,970 (£57,540 – £12,570). The income tax liability is:

		£
37,700	@ 20%	7,540.00
7,270	@ 40%	2,908.00
44,970		10,448.00

Less:	Double tax relief, *lower* of:	
	(a) foreign tax (£1,500)	1,500.00
	(b) UK tax on foreign income (40% x £5,000) = £2,000	
UK income tax liability		8,948.00

For a Scottish taxpayer, the tax liability would be (£2,162 × 19%) + (£10,956 × 20%) + (£17,974 × 21%) + (£13,878 × 41%) = £12,066.50, less DTR £1,500.00 = £10,566.50.

Income from employment

Income from employment is taxed according to detailed rules contained in the Income Tax (Earnings and Pensions) Act 2003. In general, the extent to which an individual's income from employment is taxable depends upon the individual's residence status and whether the duties of the employment are performed in the UK or overseas. The rules are briefly summarised as follows:

(a) **Employee resident in UK**[†]. Unless the remittance basis applies to the individual concerned (see below) the entire employment income of an individual who is UK resident is taxable on the receipts basis, regardless of whether the duties of the employment are performed in the UK or overseas.

   [†] *Special rules apply to UK resident "seafarers". These rules are explained on the companion website which can be accessed at* go.pearson.com/uk/he/resources.

(b) **Employee resident in UK (remittance basis)**. As explained earlier in this chapter, the remittance basis may apply to a UK resident individual who is not domiciled in the UK. If the remittance basis applies, then the extent to which employment income is taxable depends upon the individual's residence status in prior years. Broadly, the situation is as follows:

(i) If the tax year concerned is one which immediately follows three consecutive tax years in which the individual was not UK resident, employment income that is classified as "foreign earnings" may be taxed on the remittance basis. All other employment income is fully taxable (on the receipts basis). Foreign earnings are those which are in respect of duties performed wholly outside the UK.

(ii) Otherwise, the only employment income which may be taxed on the remittance basis is income that is classified as "chargeable overseas earnings". Chargeable overseas earnings are those obtained *from a foreign employer* in respect of duties performed wholly outside the UK.

(c) **Employee not resident in UK**. The employment income of an individual who is not resident in the UK is taxable (on the receipts basis) only to the extent that the income is in respect of duties performed in the UK.

Note that the income tax liability on any foreign pensions received by a UK resident is calculated on the full amount arising unless the remittance basis applies, in which case only the amount remitted to the UK is taxable.

Travelling and subsistence expenses

If the duties of an employment are performed abroad and the employee is resident in the UK, then certain travel and subsistence expenses that would not normally be deductible under the employment income rules (see Chapter 7) may be deducted when calculating the employee's earnings for tax purposes. These expenses are as follows:

(a) where duties are performed wholly abroad[†]:

(i) the costs of travelling abroad at the start of the employment and travelling back to the UK at the end of it

(ii) the costs of overseas board and lodging provided or reimbursed by the employer to enable the employee to perform the duties of the overseas employment

[†] *If the employer is a foreign employer, these expenses are deductible only if the employee is domiciled in the UK.*

(b) where duties are performed partly in the UK and partly abroad, travel expenses paid for or reimbursed by the employer (and assessable as earnings) relating to:

(i) travel by the employee between the UK and the overseas place of work

(ii) travel by the employee's spouse (or civil partner) and any minor children, if the employee is working abroad for a continuous period of 60 days or more, but limited to two return journeys per person per tax year.

Similar deductions to those described at (b) above are available to non-UK domiciled individuals who are working in the UK. However, these deductions are available for only five years, beginning with the date of arrival in the UK.

Trading income

The extent to which the profits of a trade, profession or vocation are charged to UK income tax depends upon whether or not the owner of the business is UK resident and whether the business is carried on in the UK or overseas. The rules are as follows:

(a) Trading profits arising to a UK resident are charged to income tax wherever in the world the trade is carried on. Therefore UK residents are taxed on the profits of businesses which are carried on wholly or partly overseas.

(b) If a business is carried on wholly overseas, then income arising from that business ranks as "relevant foreign income" (see earlier in this chapter). Therefore a UK resident who is not domiciled in the UK may claim that the income concerned should be taxed on the remittance basis.

(c) Trading losses arising from a business carried on wholly overseas may be carried forward in the usual way (see Chapter 12). Such losses are also eligible for terminal loss relief if incurred in the final year of trading. But "sideways relief" against total income is available only against overseas income which is not charged on the remittance basis and which consists of:

   (i)   trading profits arising from a business which is carried on wholly overseas

   (ii) employment income ranking as "chargeable overseas earnings" (see above)

   (iii) overseas pensions.

(d) Trading profits arising to a non-UK resident are chargeable to income tax only if the trade is carried on wholly or partly in the UK or is a trade of dealing in UK land. In the case of a trade which is carried on only partly in the UK, the profits which are charged to income tax are the profits arising from the UK part of the trade.

Travelling and subsistence expenses

If a trade is carried on wholly overseas and the proprietor of the business is absent from the UK wholly and exclusively for business purposes, then the expenses listed below are allowable deductions when computing trading profits (providing that those profits are not taxed on the remittance basis):

(a) expenses incurred by the trader in travelling between the UK and the location of the overseas business

(b) overseas board and lodging expenses

(c) expenses relating to travel by the proprietor's spouse (or civil partner) and any minor children if the proprietor is abroad for a continuous period of 60 days or more, but limited to two return journeys per person per tax year.

Income from property and investments

Income from property and income from savings and investments are charged to UK income tax according to the following rules:

(a) Income from property situated in the UK is taxable whether or not the person to whom the income arises is UK resident. Income from property situated overseas is taxable only if the person to whom the income arises is UK resident.

(b) Savings and investment income from a UK source is generally taxable whether or not the person to whom the income arises is UK resident. However, interest on UK Government securities is exempt from UK income tax if the recipient is not resident in the UK. Savings and investment income from an overseas source is taxable only if the person to whom the income arises is UK resident.

(c) Unless taxed on the remittance basis (see below), foreign savings income is eligible for the personal savings allowance and foreign dividends are eligible for the dividend allowance (see Chapter 2).

(d) Overseas property income and overseas savings and investment income generally rank as "relevant foreign income" (see above). Therefore a UK resident who is not domiciled in the UK may claim that these forms of income should be taxed on the remittance basis. However, overseas savings and investment income which is taxed on the remittance basis is taxed as if it were non-savings income and so cannot benefit from the starting rate for savings (0%), the savings nil rate, the dividend nil rate or the dividend lower, upper and additional rates (8.75%, 33.75% and 39.35%).

Capital gains tax - general rules

The general rules governing an individual's liability to UK capital gains tax (CGT) are:

(a) Individuals who are resident in the UK for a tax year are liable to CGT in relation to all the disposals of chargeable assets which occur in that year, no matter where in the world the assets are situated. Double tax relief may be available.

(b) Individuals who are not UK resident are generally not liable to CGT at all, even in relation to disposals of assets situated in the UK.

However, there are exceptions to these general rules. The main exceptions are as follows:

(a) An individual who is UK resident but not domiciled in the UK may claim that gains arising from disposals of overseas assets should be taxed on the remittance basis. No annual exemption is available for a tax year in which the remittance basis is claimed.

   Individuals who are taxed on this basis may remit overseas gains to the UK without incurring a CGT liability if the gains concerned are used to make a commercial investment in a qualifying business ("business investment relief").

(b) Individuals who acquire assets before temporarily leaving the UK (for up to five tax years) and then dispose of those assets whilst abroad remain chargeable to CGT in relation to these disposals. Gains are taxed in the year in which residence resumes.

(c) An individual who is not resident in the UK but who carries on a business in the UK is chargeable to CGT in relation to disposals of business assets situated in the UK.

(d) As from 6 April 2019, gains made by non-residents on the disposal of UK land and buildings are charged to CGT. For properties held on that date, the amount of such a gain is calculated by comparing disposal value with market value on 5 April 2019 or by time-apportioning the gain arising over the period of ownership. In the case of residential property, principal private residence relief may be available.

A claim may be made to defer a CGT assessment relating to a disposal of overseas assets if it can be shown that the gain in question cannot be remitted to the UK. The conditions which must be satisfied in order that such a claim should be successful are the same as the equivalent conditions for income tax (see above).

Inheritance tax - general rules

An individual who is domiciled in the UK is liable to inheritance tax (IHT) in relation to all of his or her chargeable property, wherever in the world that property is situated. An individual who is not domiciled in the UK is liable to IHT only in relation to property which is situated in the UK.

The IHT "deemed domicile" rules are different from the general rules given earlier in this chapter. For IHT purposes, an individual who is not actually domiciled in the UK on the date of a transfer (the "relevant date") is nonetheless deemed to be domiciled in the UK on that date if the individual:

(a) was domiciled in the UK at any time within the three years immediately preceding the relevant date, or

(b) is a "formerly domiciled resident" (see below) on the relevant date, or

(c) was UK resident for at least 15 of the 20 tax years immediately preceding the tax year in which the relevant date falls (the "relevant tax year") and also UK resident for at least one of the four tax years ending with the relevant tax year.

A "formerly domiciled resident" is a person who was born in the UK with a UK domicile of origin, is UK resident for the relevant tax year and was UK resident for at least one of the previous two tax years.

In general, transfers made between spouses (or civil partners) are exempt from IHT. But transfers made by a UK-domiciled spouse/partner to a spouse/partner who is not domiciled in the UK are exempt only up to the amount of the IHT nil-rate band (currently £325,000). However, a spouse or civil partner who is not domiciled in the UK may elect to be treated as domiciled in the UK for IHT purposes.

Corporation tax - general rules

A company's liability to UK corporation tax depends upon whether or not it is resident in the UK. A company is regarded as resident in the UK if it is incorporated in the UK or if its central management and control is situated in the UK. The general rules which govern a company's liability to UK corporation tax are as follows:

(a) A UK resident company is chargeable to UK corporation tax on all of its profits, no matter where in the world those profits are earned. Note the following points:

(i) The profits of a trade conducted through a permanent establishment situated overseas (e.g. an overseas branch) are treated as trading income. Trading losses are eligible for tax relief and group relief is generally available. But the losses of an overseas establishment may be surrendered only to the extent that those losses are not relievable in the overseas country.

However, a company may make an irrevocable election to the effect that the profits of *all* its overseas branches should be exempt from UK corporation tax. If this election is made, no relief will be available for foreign branch losses.

(ii) Most foreign dividends received by UK companies are exempt from corporation tax (with certain exceptions) and are treated as if they were UK dividends.

(iii) Gains arising on the disposal of overseas assets are generally chargeable gains and form part of the company's taxable profits.

(b) A non-UK resident company is chargeable to UK corporation tax[†] if it trades in the UK through a permanent establishment, carries on a UK property business or a trade of dealing in UK land, or has gains arising on the disposal of UK land. If a trade is carried on through a UK permanent establishment, the company is taxed on the trading profits, property income and chargeable gains of that UK establishment.

As regards trading losses:

(i) The trading losses of a UK permanent establishment of a non-UK resident company may generally be set against any other profits of the establishment or may be carried forward. Trading losses may also be surrendered to UK resident companies in the same 75% group, as long as those losses are not deductible or otherwise allowable against non-UK profits.

(ii) Similarly, a UK permanent establishment of a non-UK resident company may claim trading losses which are surrendered to it by UK resident companies in the same 75% group.

Assets transferred between a UK permanent establishment and a UK resident group company are transferred on a no-gain, no-loss basis, so long as the assets concerned remain within the charge to UK corporation tax.

[†] *Non-UK resident companies are not entitled to the small profits rate of corporation tax or marginal relief (as from 1 April 2023).*

Overseas subsidiaries

The profits of a non-UK resident subsidiary of a UK resident parent company might be subject to overseas tax but are not generally subject to UK tax unless the subsidiary ranks as a "controlled foreign company" (see later in this chapter). However:

(a) A subsidiary company which is not resident in the UK may nonetheless have profits which are chargeable to corporation tax, such as the trading profits of a UK permanent establishment (see above).

(b) The UK resident parent company will be liable to corporation tax on any non-exempt income received from the overseas subsidiary (e.g. royalties).

(c) A subsidiary company is counted as a "related 51% group company" when determining whether group companies must pay corporation tax by instalments, even if the subsidiary concerned is not resident in the UK (see Chapter 28).

Group relief is not available in relation to the trading losses of an overseas subsidiary unless these losses are attributable to the activities of the company in respect of which it is within the charge to corporation tax (see above).

Company migration

A UK resident company may wish to "migrate" overseas in order to escape paying UK corporation tax on its worldwide profits. This is only possible for companies which are incorporated outside the UK and involves moving the central management and control of the company to an overseas location. A company wishing to take this step must:

(a) notify HMRC, specifying the date on which it intends to become non-resident, and

(b) provide HMRC with a statement of all the tax payable up to that date, specifying the arrangements which will be made to ensure that this tax is paid.

On the date that a company becomes non-resident it is deemed to make a disposal of all its assets at their market value on that date. This deemed disposal may well result in a sizeable chargeable gain (referred to as the "exit charge"). However, if the company retains a permanent establishment in the UK, the deemed disposal does not include any assets which are situated in the UK and used for trade purposes by that establishment.

Controlled foreign companies (CFCs)

A UK resident company which wishes to operate overseas may choose to do so through a separate non-UK resident company which is under its control (an overseas subsidiary).

Since the profits of a non-UK company are generally not chargeable to UK corporation tax, this would seem to be beneficial (especially if the operation is carried on in a country with low tax rates). Furthermore, any dividends paid by the overseas subsidiary to its UK parent would usually be tax-exempt. However, some of these tax advantages are lost if the overseas subsidiary ranks as a *controlled foreign company* (CFC).

As an anti-avoidance measure, the profits of a CFC are apportioned between its shareholders and profits that are attributed to a UK resident company are charged to corporation tax (the "CFC charge"). The main features of the CFC regime are as follows:

(a) A CFC is a company which is resident overseas but is under UK control. The CFC regime also applies to the overseas branches of a UK company which has elected that the profits of all its overseas branches should be exempt from UK corporation tax.

(b) No CFC charge arises if the CFC qualifies for one or more exemptions. The main exemptions (broadly) are:

(i) **Exempt period**. The CFC regime does not apply to CFC accounting periods which end during the first 12 months in which a CFC is under UK control.

(ii) **Excluded territories**. A CFC is exempt if it is resident in one of a number of excluded countries and satisfies certain other conditions.

(iii) **Low profits**. A CFC is exempt if its accounting profits or its taxable total profits (calculated as if it were a UK company) do not exceed £50,000 or do not exceed £500,000, of which no more than £50,000 represents non-trading income.

(iv) **Low profit margin**. A CFC is exempt if its accounting profits do not exceed 10% of its operating expenditure.

(v) **Tax rate**. A CFC is exempt if it is subject to a level of overseas taxation which is equal to at least 75% of the corresponding UK tax (unless the CFC is resident in a country in which the local tax liability is determined under "designer rate" provisions which are intended to circumvent the CFC rules).

(c) If a UK company is required to pay a CFC charge in relation to its share of a CFC's taxable total profits, this charge is calculated at the average rate payable by the UK company for the accounting period in which the CFC's accounting period ends. But a UK company to which less than 25% of a CFC's profits are attributed is not required to pay a CFC charge at all.

The full CFC regime is extremely complex and involves many detailed rules. The basic aim of these rules is to ensure that the CFC charge applies only where necessary and should not apply in relation to genuine economic activities undertaken overseas, so long as there has been no artificial diversion of UK profits.

Transfer pricing

A UK resident company might attempt to reduce its corporation tax liability by transferring goods or services at an artificially low price to an overseas subsidiary. This would have the effect of lowering the UK company's profits (which are liable to UK tax) and increasing the subsidiary's profits (which are not liable to UK tax).

However, this tax avoidance manoeuvre is blocked by "transfer pricing" legislation which requires that a true market price should be substituted for the transfer price in these circumstances and that the UK company should make the necessary adjustment when completing its self-assessment tax return (see Chapter 28). Small and medium-sized companies are generally exempt from the transfer pricing legislation.

Double taxation relief for companies

Unless double tax relief is available (or prohibited) under the terms of a double taxation treaty with the country concerned, the UK tax system provides unilateral double tax relief for foreign tax suffered by a UK company which receives income from overseas.

Unilateral relief takes the form of a tax credit equal to the *lower* of the amount of foreign tax suffered and the amount of UK corporation tax payable on the foreign income. Any excess foreign tax is unrelieved (but see below).

EXAMPLE 3

In the year to 31 March 2023, a UK resident company had UK trading profits of £5,450,000 and overseas property income (net of 35% withholding tax) of £130,000. Compute the corporation tax liability for the year.

Solution

	UK	Overseas	Total
	£	£	£
Trading income	5,450,000		5,450,000
Property income £130,000 x 100/65		200,000	200,000
Taxable total profits (TTP)	5,450,000	200,000	5,650,000
Corporation tax @ 19%	1,035,500	38,000	1,073,500
Less: Unilateral DTR		(38,000)	(38,000)
Corporation tax due	1,035,500	-	1,035,500

The unilateral relief given is restricted to the UK tax due on the overseas income. The remaining £32,000 (£70,000 – £38,000) of foreign tax paid is unrelieved.

Unrelieved foreign tax

Unrelieved foreign tax arising in connection with trading income derived from an overseas permanent establishment (i.e. an overseas branch) may be carried back for up to three years or may be carried forward without time limit. Note that:

(a) When unrelieved foreign tax is carried back or carried forward, it is treated as if it were foreign tax paid in respect of the trading income of the same overseas branch in the accounting period to which it is carried. But if the rate of foreign tax suffered on such income is consistently higher than the UK tax rate, it is unlikely that there will be any scope for relieving unrelieved foreign tax from other accounting periods.

(b) These provisions are not relevant to a company which has elected that the profits of all its overseas branches should be exempt from UK tax (see earlier in this chapter).

Underlying DTR

If a UK resident company owns at least 10% of the voting power of an overseas company and receives a dividend from that company, an additional form of unilateral double taxation relief ("underlying relief") is available. The idea of underlying DTR is to give relief for the foreign tax suffered on the profits out of which the dividend has been paid.

However, most foreign dividends received by UK companies are now exempt from corporation tax, so underlying double tax relief applies only in the small minority of cases where a company receives a non-exempt foreign dividend.

A fuller explanation of underlying DTR is available on the website which accompanies this book. The website can be accessed at go.pearson.com/uk/he/resources.

Unilateral expense relief

A company may waive the right to claim unilateral "credit relief" (where DTR takes the form of a tax credit) and opt for unilateral "expense relief" instead. A company which opts for expense relief is assessed on the *net* foreign income, so that the foreign tax is treated as if it were an expense. Unilateral expense relief may be attractive if a company is making a claim to set a trading loss against its total profits, so that it has no corporation tax liability on the foreign income and cannot obtain any credit relief.

EXAMPLE 4

A UK company has a trading loss of £50,000 for the year to 31 March 2023. During the year, the company receives overseas property income (net of 40% withholding tax) of £12,000. Show the corporation tax computation for the year if:

(a) unilateral credit relief is claimed

(b) unilateral expense relief is claimed.

The company claims trading loss relief against total profits of the year to 31 March 2023.

Solution

	Credit relief	Expense relief
	£	£
Trading income	0	0
Property income (gross)	20,000	
Property income (net of foreign tax)		12,000
	20,000	12,000
Less: Trading loss	(20,000)	(12,000)
Taxable total profits (TTP)	0	0
Corporation tax liability	0	0
Unrelieved trading losses	30,000	38,000
Unrelieved foreign tax	8,000	nil

Notes:

(i)   No unilateral credit relief is available since the overseas income is absorbed by the trading loss, leaving a UK tax liability of £nil.

(ii)   Credit relief gives £8,000 of unrelieved foreign tax.

(iii) Expense relief eliminates the unrelieved foreign tax. The trading losses available for carry-back against total profits of the previous 12 months or carry-forward against future profits are increased by £8,000.

Interaction of charitable donations, loss reliefs and DTR

A company's taxable total profits are reduced by the qualifying charitable donations made in the accounting period (see Chapter 23) and by the amount of any trading losses relieved against the total profits of the period (see Chapter 26). Normally, it is sufficient simply to subtract donations and trading losses from the company's total income (and gains) without allocating these deductions to any particular source of income. But if unilateral double tax relief is claimed, such an allocation must be made so that the amount of UK tax payable on the foreign income can be calculated. This allocation may be made in any way that the company sees fit and should be done in such a way as to minimise the tax liability.

If any donations or trading losses are set against the foreign income, this will have the effect of reducing the UK tax due on that foreign income and so reducing the maximum unilateral DTR available. Therefore, donations and trading losses should be set first against UK income, then against foreign income.

EXAMPLE 5

In the year to 31 March 2023, a UK company has UK trading profits of £4,800,000 and overseas property income (net of 45% withholding tax) of £2,750,000. Gift Aid donations of £100,000 are made in the year. Compute the corporation tax liability for the year.

Solution

	UK £	Overseas £	Total £
Trading income	4,800,000		4,800,000
Income from property:			
£2,750,000 x 100/55		5,000,000	5,000,000
	4,800,000	5,000,000	9,800,000
Less: Charitable donations	100,000	-	100,000
Taxable total profits (TTP)	4,700,000	5,000,000	9,700,000
Corporation tax @ 19%	893,000	950,000	1,843,000
Less: Unilateral DTR		(950,000)	(950,000)
Corporation tax liability	893,000	-	893,000

Notes:

(i) The charitable donations are set against the UK income so as to maximise double tax relief on the overseas income.

(ii) DTR is limited to the UK tax due on the overseas income. Foreign tax paid is £2,250,000, of which £1,300,000 is unrelieved.

(iii) If the charitable donations had been set against the overseas income, DTR would have been only £931,000 (£4,900,000 x 19%). Unrelieved foreign tax would have been £1,319,000 and the corporation tax liability would have been £912,000.

Diverted profits tax

Large multinational companies which divert profits away from the UK so as to avoid UK corporation tax may incur a liability to the diverted profits tax (DPT) instead. The main objective of this tax is to counteract contrived tax avoidance "arrangements" which might be used by large groups to divert profits from the UK and so result in the erosion of the UK tax base. Broadly, a charge to DPT may arise if either:

(a) a company engages in artificial transactions which "lack economic substance" but have the effect of diverting profits away from the UK, or

(b) a non-UK resident company carries on a trade in the UK but enters into arrangements which are designed to avoid the existence of a UK taxable presence (i.e. a permanent establishment in the UK).

If HMRC determines that DPT should apply in a particular case, a preliminary notice must be issued to the company concerned, explaining the reasons for the charge. This notice should also state the amount of the charge and explain how it has been calculated. The company has 30 days in which to make representations to HMRC and HMRC then has a further 30 days in which to issue a charging notice or state that no charge will be made.

DPT is charged at 25%[†] of the amount of the diverted profits and is payable within 30 days of the issue of the charging notice. There are penalties for late payment.

[†] *The rate of DPT will rise to 31% as from 1 April 2023.*

Digital services tax

The digital services tax (DST) applies to large groups of companies which provide search engines, social media services or online marketplaces. Such a group is liable to DST if the group's worldwide revenue from these "digital services" exceeds £500m, of which more than £25m is derived from UK users. The amount of DST payable is calculated at 2% of the amount by which revenue from UK users exceeds £25m. The total DST liability is calculated at group level but is then allocated between the companies that make up the group.

The UK intends to disapply the digital services tax as soon as an international agreement is implemented which ensures that multinational companies pay a fair share of tax in the countries in which they do business. This is expected to occur in 2023.

Summary

▸   An individual's liability to UK income tax depends upon residence. Individuals who are UK resident for a tax year are liable to pay income tax on their worldwide income for that year. Non-residents are liable to income tax on their UK income only.

▸   Double taxation relief (DTR) may be available if some of the income of a UK resident is subject to overseas tax as well as UK income tax.

▸   The extent to which an individual's income from employment is taxable in the UK depends upon the individual's residence status and whether the duties of the employment are performed in the UK or overseas.

▸   Trading profits arising to a UK resident are charged to income tax wherever in the world the trade is carried on. Trading profits arising to a non-resident are charged to income tax if the trade is carried on in the UK or is a trade of dealing in UK land.

▸   Income from UK property and investments is generally taxable in the UK whether or not the person to whom the income arises is UK resident. Income from overseas property and investments is taxable in the UK only if the person is UK resident.

▶ Individuals who are resident in the UK for a tax year are liable to UK capital gains tax on their disposals throughout the world in that year.

▶ Individuals who are UK domiciled are liable to UK inheritance tax. The IHT rules on "deemed domicile" are different from the general rules.

▶ UK resident companies are liable to UK corporation tax on their worldwide profits. A non-UK resident company is liable to corporation tax if it carries on a trade through a UK permanent establishment (or a trade of dealing in UK land), has capital gains arising from the disposal of UK land or has UK property income.

▶ Most foreign dividends received by UK companies are exempt from corporation tax.

▶ The profits of a controlled foreign company may be apportioned between the controlling UK companies and assessed to corporation tax.

▶ Double tax relief for UK companies takes the form of credit relief or expense relief. Underlying relief may be available in relation to non-exempt foreign dividends.

▶ A diverted profits tax (DPT) charge may arise if a company makes contrived arrangements to divert profits away from the UK and so avoid UK tax.

Exercises

A set of multiple choice questions for this chapter is available on the accompanying website.

32.1   (a)   Jean-Paul is a Canadian citizen. He owns a house in Canada and regards Canada as his home but he lives in the UK for eight months during tax year 2022-23. During these eight months he tours the UK and visits friends and relatives but he does no work. Is he UK resident for tax year 2022-23? And is any of his income for the year liable to UK income tax?

           (b)   Pierre is a French citizen. He lives and works full-time in France but during tax year 2022-23 he spends three weeks in the UK on a holiday. Is he UK resident for tax year 2022-23? Is any of his income for the year liable to UK income tax?

           (c)   Carole has lived in the UK all her life and has a home in London. She retires in March 2022 and decides to spent the next 12 months travelling abroad. During tax year 2022-23 she takes several long holidays but she keeps her London home and does not acquire a home overseas. She spends 44 days in the UK during the tax year. Is she UK resident for 2022-23?

32.2   Amy is domiciled in the UK and has lived in the UK all her life. On 1 January 2022 she leaves to work in Australia for two years, returning on 31 December 2023. During her absence she makes no visits to the UK. Explain her UK income tax status for tax years 2021-22 to 2023-24 inclusive. (Ignore the sufficient ties test).

32.3 (a) Explain the concept of "domicile" for tax purposes.

(b) If an individual is UK resident, to what extent does the individual's domicile affect his or her liability to UK tax?

32.4 (a) How would a UK resident company proceed if it wished to "migrate" overseas? Why might this be a desirable step?

(b) A UK resident company may make an election to the effect that the profits of its permanent establishments situated overseas (i.e. its overseas branches) should be exempt from UK corporation tax. Why might a UK company decide not to make such an election?

32.5 Explain the term "controlled foreign company" (CFC). In what circumstances are the profits of a CFC chargeable to UK corporation tax?

32.6 Brist Ltd is a UK resident company which prepares annual accounts to 31 March. In the year to 31 March 2023, the company had a UK trading profit of £2,120,000 and received overseas property income of £98,000 (this figure is net of 30% withholding tax).

(a) Compute the company's corporation tax liability for the year and explain the treatment of any unrelieved foreign tax.

(b) Would the situation be any different if the overseas property income was replaced by trading income from an overseas branch?

*32.7 Donald is resident and domiciled in the UK. He is not a Scottish taxpayer. He has the following income in tax year 2022-23:

	£
UK trading profits	42,200
Income from UK property	5,000
Income from foreign property (net of 45% withholding tax)	2,200

Donald claims only the personal allowance. Compute the amount of income tax payable for 2022-23.

*32.8 A UK resident company has 19 subsidiaries, five of which are situated abroad. In the year to 31 March 2023, the company had the following results:

	£
UK trading profits	720,000
UK dividends received	40,000
UK chargeable gains	120,000
Overseas bank interest (net of 40% withholding tax)	10,800
Gift Aid donations paid	80,000

None of the dividends received were from any of the company's subsidiaries. Calculate the company's corporation tax liability for the year to 31 March 2023 and state the date (or dates) on which payment falls due.

Review questions (Set D)

D1　Garfield has been registered for VAT since 1 April 2016. His business is situated in Great Britain. His partly completed VAT computation for the quarter to 31 March 2023 is shown below. The figures in brackets refer to the notes which follow.

	£
Output VAT	
Sales (all standard rated)	22,500
Discounted sale (1)	?
Equipment (2)	?
Fuel scale charge	73
Input VAT	
Purchases (all standard rated)	(11,200)
Motor car purchased on 1 January 2023	0
Equipment (2)	?
Bad debts (3)	?
Entertaining UK customers	0
Entertaining overseas customers (4)	?
Motor expenses (5)	?
VAT payable	?

Note 1: Discounted sale

On 10 February 2023, a sales invoice for £4,300 (before VAT) was issued by Garfield in respect of a standard rated supply. Garfield offered the customer a 10% discount for payment within 14 days and the customer paid within the 14-day period. This invoice has not been taken into account in calculating the output VAT figure of £22,500, and this is the only sale for which Garfield has offered a prompt payment discount.

Note 2: Equipment

During the quarter to 31 March 2023, Garfield acquired some new equipment at a cost of £12,400 (before VAT). This equipment was imported from outside the UK and Garfield provided his VAT registration number to the overseas supplier.

Note 3: Bad debts

On 31 March 2023, Garfield wrote off three bad debts. Details are as follows:

Amount before VAT	Invoice date	Payment due date
£1,400	30 July 2022	29 August 2022
£2,700	12 September 2022	12 October 2022
£1,900	4 October 2022	3 November 2022

Note 4: Entertaining

During the quarter to 31 March 2023, Garfield spent £960 on entertaining his overseas customers. This figure is inclusive of VAT.

Note 5: Motor expenses

The motor car purchased on 1 January 2023 is used 60% for business mileage. During the quarter to 31 March 2023, Garfield spent £1,008 on repairs to the motor car and £660 on fuel for both business and private mileage. Both of these figures include VAT.

Additional information

Garfield does not use the cash accounting scheme, the annual accounting scheme or the flat rate scheme, but he has read that the use of these schemes can be beneficial for small businesses such as his. His VAT-exclusive annual turnover is currently £450,000. He pays for most of his purchases and expenses on a cash basis but allows many of his customers 30 days credit when paying for sales.

Required:

(a) Calculate the amount of VAT payable for the quarter to 31 March 2023.

(b) State which VAT schemes Garfield is currently permitted to use and explain which ONE of these schemes would be the most beneficial for him to use.   *(ACCA)*

D2   Larry died on 1 November 2022 leaving an estate valued at £300,000. He had never had a wife or civil partner and he left his estate to his best friend. On 1 October 2014 he had set up a discretionary trust and made a gross chargeable transfer to this trust of £275,000 (after deducting exemptions). His only other lifetime transfers were as follows:

12 March 2017	£60,000 to his mother
13 February 2018	£60,000 to his father
6 October 2019	£18,500 to his nephew (wedding present)
15 April 2021	£25,000 to a charity

Required:

Calculate the IHT payable (if any) on each of the four gifts and on the estate at death.

D3   A UK company has the following results for the year to 31 March 2023:

	£
Trading profits	175,000
Chargeable gains	23,000
Capital losses brought forward on 1 April 2022	18,000
Overseas property income (net of 15% foreign tax)	5,100
Overseas property income (net of 25% foreign tax)	6,375
Dividends received	nil
Gift Aid donations	7,500

Required:

Calculate the corporation tax payable for the year.

D4   A Ltd owns 85% of B Ltd and 60% of C Ltd. B Ltd owns 90% of D Ltd. The remaining 40% of C Ltd is owned by E Ltd. All these percentages represent holdings of ordinary shares and all companies are UK resident. Results for the year to 31 March 2023 are as follows:

	Trading profits (losses)	Loan interest receivable	Overseas property income	Gift Aid donations
	£	£	£	£
A Ltd	240,000	5,000	-	1,000
B Ltd	45,000	2,500	8,200	500
C Ltd	(30,000)	-	-	-
D Ltd	(25,000)	-	-	-
E Ltd	80,000	-	-	1,000

The overseas property income of B Ltd is the net figure after deduction of 18% foreign tax. A Ltd received a dividend of £17,000 from B Ltd on 31 December 2022.

Required:

Calculate the corporation tax payable for the year by all of these companies, assuming that maximum group relief is claimed for the trading losses and that double tax relief is given where appropriate.

*D5   Quiver Ltd is VAT-registered. During the quarter to 31 March 2023, the company made the following supplies of goods and services:

	£
Standard-rated supplies (including VAT)	75,840
Zero-rated supplies	16,800
Exempt supplies	12,500

The company also suffered the following input tax during the quarter:

	£
Attributed to taxable supplies	5,210
Attributed to exempt supplies	860
Unattributed	2,470

The input tax which is attributed to taxable supplies includes £1,710 in relation to the purchase of a motor car on 1 January 2023 and a further £180 in relation to the fuel used by this car during the quarter. The car has emissions of 168g/km and is used for both business (70%) and private (30%) motoring and the company pays all fuel costs.

Unattributed input tax includes £620 of input VAT on UK customer entertaining costs and £590 of VAT on staff entertaining costs.

Required:

Calculate the VAT liability of Quiver Ltd for the three months to 31 March 2023 and explain why this calculation is provisional.   *(CIPFA)*

*D6   Mrs Lammle, who is registered for VAT, has traded as a manufacturer of standard-rated items since 1 June 2006. She has decided to retire on 31 May 2022, her 65th birthday, and you are asked to finalise her tax position up to that date. You are provided with the following information:

(i)   Mrs Lammle has always prepared accounts to 31 May each year. Overlap profits of £37,500 arose on commencement.

(ii)   The last accounts will be for the year to 31 May 2022. Interim accounts have been prepared to 28 February 2022, revealing the following:

	£
Sales	100,200
Cost of sales	24,700
Gross profit	75,500
Expenses	29,000
Net profit	46,500

All of the above figures are net of VAT and contain no disallowable items.

(iii)   For the last three months to 31 May 2022 (which is also the last VAT quarter), you have extracted the following figures from the accounting records:

	£
Sales:	
To UK customers	30,654
To customers outside the UK	8,000
Materials purchased:	
Standard-rated	4,098
Zero-rated	2,000
Exempt	800
Expenses:	
General (all standard-rated)	6,120
Wages	7,000
Hire of machinery	612
Business bank charges	500
Entertaining UK clients	400

All of the above include VAT if appropriate. There was no stock at 1 March 2022 and there is no outstanding stock left at 31 May 2022. All of the general expenses are allowable for income tax purposes.

(iv)   The tax written down value of the plant and machinery carried forward after capital allowances had been calculated for the year to 31 May 2021 was:

	£
Plant and machinery main pool	12,375
Special rate pool (car with no private use)	5,250

No plant and machinery was acquired during the year to 31 May 2022.

(v) The business was sold as a going concern (to another taxable person) on 31 May 2022. The items sold were:

	£
Freehold shop	200,000
Freehold workshop	130,000
Goodwill	180,000
Plant (no item worth more than £6,000)	25,000
Car	6,000

The shop and the workshop were acquired on 1 June 2006 for £30,000 and £21,000 respectively. All of the items of plant were sold for less than original cost.

Required:

(a) Calculate the VAT due for the quarter to 31 May 2022.

(b) Calculate the final adjusted profit for the year to 31 May 2022, after deduction of capital allowances.

(c) Calculate Mrs Lammle's trading income for 2022-23.

(d) Calculate the capital gains tax due on the disposal of the business, assuming that business asset disposal relief is claimed. Mrs Lammle has made no previous claims for this relief. She has no other disposals in tax year 2022-23 and has no capital losses brought forward. *(Amended from AAT)*

*D7 Jimmy died on 14 February 2023. He had made the following gifts during his lifetime:

(1) On 2 August 2021, he made a cash gift of £50,000 to his grandson. This was a wedding present.

(2) On 14 November 2021, he made a cash gift of £800,000 to a trust. Jimmy paid the inheritance tax arising from this gift.

At the date of his death Jimmy owned the following assets:

(1) His main residence valued at £260,000.

(2) Building society deposits of £515,600.

(3) A life assurance policy on his own life. Proceeds of £210,000 were received from the insurance company following Jimmy's death.

Funeral costs amounted to £5,600. Under the terms of his will, Jimmy left £300,000 to his wife, with the residue of his estate to his nephew.

The nil rate band in tax years 2021-22 and 2022-23 was £325,000.

Required:

(a) Explain why it is important to differentiate between potentially exempt transfers and chargeable lifetime transfers for inheritance tax purposes.

(b) Calculate the inheritance tax payable as a result of Jimmy's death.

(ACCA)

*D8   P Ltd is the parent company of a small group. All of the companies in the group are UK resident apart from Q Corp., which is resident in the USA and trades only in that country. The following diagram represents holdings of ordinary shares:

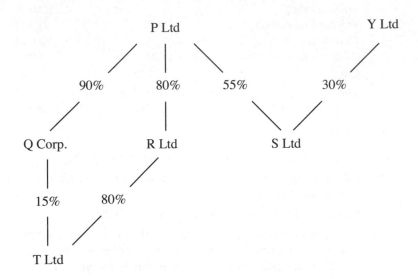

The trading profit or loss of each company for the year to 31 March 2023 is as follows:

		£				£
P Ltd	Profit	240,000		S Ltd	Profit	180,000
Q Corp.	Loss	(72,000)		T Ltd	Profit	56,000
R Ltd	Loss	(84,000)		Y Ltd	Loss	(95,000)

None of the companies had any other income or gains during the year or made any Gift Aid donations. No dividends were paid during the year.

Required:

(a) Identify the trading losses that may be surrendered to other companies in the group and the companies to which these losses may be surrendered.

(b) Calculate the corporation tax liability of each company for the year, assuming that group relief is claimed wherever possible.

(c) If any of the trading losses are not eligible for group relief, explain any alternative forms of relief that might be available.

Part 5

ANSWERS

Answers to exercises

Chapter 2

2.1

Non-Scottish taxpayers:

(a) £1,830 @ 20% = £366.00

(b) £32,300 @ 20% = £6,460.00

(c) £37,700 @ 20% + £34,333 @ 40% = £21,273.20

(d) £37,700 @ 20% + £112,300 @ 40% + £170,000 @ 45% = £128,960.00

Scottish taxpayers:

(a) £1,830 @ 19% = £347.70

(b) £2,162 @ 19% + £10,956 @ 20% + £17,974 @ 21% + £1,208 @ 41% = £6,871.80

(c) £2,162 @ 19% + £10,956 @ 20% + £17,974 @ 21% + £40,941 @ 41% = £23,162.33

(d) £2,162 @ 19% + £10,956 @ 20% + £17,974 @ 21% + £118,908 @ 41% + £170,000 @ 46% = £133,328.80

2.2

(a)

		Total £	Non-savings £	Savings £
Business profits		28,175	28,175	
Bank interest		720		720
Total income		28,895	28,175	720
<u>Less</u>: Personal allowance		12,570	12,570	
Taxable income		16,325	15,605	720

Income tax due

Non-savings income	: Basic rate	15,605	@ 20%	3,121.00	
Savings income	: Nil rate	720	@ 0%	0.00	
		16,325			
Tax liability				3,121.00	

Taxable income does not exceed £37,700, therefore the personal savings allowance is £1,000 and savings income of £720 is taxed at the nil rate. *For a Scottish taxpayer*, the income tax liability would be (£2,162 × 19%) + (£10,956 × 20%) + (£2,487 × 21%) = £3,124.25.

(b)

	Total £	Non-savings £	Savings £
Business profits	50,420	50,420	
Building society interest	930		930
Bank interest	570		570
Total income	51,920	50,420	1,500
Less: Personal allowance	12,570	12,570	
Taxable income	39,350	37,850	1,500

Income tax due

Non-savings income	: Basic rate	37,700	@ 20%	7,540.00
	: Higher rate	150	@ 40%	60.00
Savings income	: Nil rate	500	@ 0%	0.00
	: Higher rate	1,000	@ 40%	400.00
		39,350		
Tax liability				8,000.00

Taxable income exceeds £37,700 but does not exceed £150,000. Therefore the personal savings allowance is £500 and savings income of £500 is taxed at the nil rate. Non-savings income absorbs the whole of the basic rate band, so the remaining £1,000 of savings income is taxed at the higher rate of 40%.

For a Scottish taxpayer, the liability on non-savings income would be (£2,162 × 19%) + (£10,956 × 20%) + (£17,974 × 21%) + (£6,758 × 41%) = £9,147.30. This would increase the total liability by £1,547.30 to £9,547.30.

(c) Grossed-up loan interest is (£130,604 × 100/80) = £163,255. There is no non-savings income so the first £5,000 of savings income is taxed at the starting rate of 0%. However, taxable income exceeds the higher rate limit so the personal savings allowance is £nil.

The income tax liability is (£5,000 × 0%) + (£32,700 × 20%) + (£112,300 × 40%) + (£13,255 × 45%) which is a total of £57,424.75. Income tax deducted at source is £32,651 (£163,255 – £130,604) so income tax payable is (£57,424.75 – £32,651.00) = £24,773.75.

For a Scottish taxpayer, the computation would be unchanged.

2.3

	Total £	Non-savings £	Savings £	Dividends £
Self-employment income	29,950	29,950		
Income from property	15,730	15,730		
Bank interest	200		200	
Dividends	250			250
Total income	46,130	45,680	200	250
Less: Personal allowance	12,570	12,570		
Taxable income	33,560	33,110	200	250

Income tax due

Non-savings income	: Basic rate	33,110	@ 20%	6,622.00
Savings income	: Nil rate	200	@ 0%	0.00
Dividend income	: Nil rate	250	@ 0%	0.00
		33,560		
Tax liability				6,622.00

The personal savings allowance is £1,000 and the dividend allowance is £2,000. Therefore all of the savings income and dividend income is taxed at 0%.

For a Scottish taxpayer, the tax liability on non-savings income would be (£2,162 × 19%) + (£10,956 × 20%) + (£17,974 × 21%) + (£2,018 × 41%) = £7,203.90.

2.4

	Total	*Non-savings*	*Savings*
	£	£	£
Retirement pension	57,160	57,160	
Bank interest	620		620
Total income	57,780	57,160	620
Less: Personal allowance	12,570	12,570	
Taxable income	45,210	44,590	620

The personal savings allowance is £500, so £500 of the savings income is taxed at the nil rate. The tax liability is (£37,700 × 20%) + (£6,890 × 40%) + (£500 × 0%) + (£120 × 40%) = £10,344.00.

Dividends of £620 would have been covered by the dividend allowance of £2,000 and taxed at 0%. The tax liability would have been reduced by £48 (£120 × 40%) to £10,296.00.

Chapter 3

3.1

(a) £12,570   (b) (£12,570 – 1/2 × £8,000) = £8,570   (c) £nil

3.2

(a) PA is (£12,570 – 1/2 × £5,000) = £10,070. Taxable income is £94,930 (£105,000 – £10,070) so the income tax liability is (£37,700 × 20%) + (£57,230 × 40%) = **£30,432**.

(b) PA is £nil. The tax liability is now (£37,700 × 20%) + (£92,300 × 40%) = **£44,460**.

(c) The £20,140 increase in salary from £105,000 to £125,140 (where the PA becomes zero) is effectively taxed at 60% and the remaining £4,860 of the increase is taxed at 40%. Therefore the tax liability rises by (£20,140 × 60%) + (£4,860 × 40%) = **£14,028**.

For a Scottish taxpayer:

The liability in (a) would be (£2,162 × 19%) + (£10,956 × 20%) + (£17,974 × 21%) + (£63,838 × 41%) = **£32,550.10**. The liability in (b) would be (£2,162 × 19%) + (£10,956 × 20%) + (£17,974 × 21%) + (£98,908 × 41%) = **£46,928.80**. The liability rises by (£20,140 × 61.5%) + (£4,860 × 41%) which is equal to **£14,378.70**.

3.3

(a)   The husband is entitled to the MCA because he and his wife were born before 6 April 1935. The full MCA of £9,415 is available, since the husband's income does not exceed £31,400.

(b)   The husband is entitled to the MCA because he and his wife were born before 6 April 1935. His income exceeds the income limit by £40 so the MCA is reduced by £20 to £9,395.

(c)   The husband is entitled to the MCA because he was born before 6 April 1935. His income exceeds the limit by £6,400 (£37,800 − £31,400) so the MCA is reduced by £3,200 to £6,215.

(d)   The husband is entitled to the MCA because his wife was born before 6 April 1935. The full MCA of £9,415 is available, since the husband's income does not exceed the income limit of £31,400. His wife's income is disregarded for this purpose.

3.4

	(a) £	(b) £	(c) £
HUSBAND			
Net income	19,210	11,300	12,905
Less: Personal allowance	12,570	11,300†	12,570
Taxable income	6,640	0	335
Income tax			
£6,640 @ 20%	1,328.00		
£0 @ 20%		0.00	
£335 @ 20%			67.00
Less: MCA £9,415 @ 10%	941.50		
MCA £9,415 @ 10% = £941.50			67.00
(£874.50 transferred to wife)			
Tax liability	386.50	0.00	0.00
WIFE			
Net income	20,510	21,445	20,375
Less: Personal allowance	12,570	12,570	12,570
Taxable income	7,940	8,875	7,805
Income tax			
£7,940 @ 20%	1,588.00		
£8,875 @ 20%		1,775.00	
£7,805 @ 20%			1,561.00
Less: MCA £9,415 @ 10% (higher-income partner)		941.50	
MCA transferred from husband			874.50
Tax liability	1,588.00	833.50	686.50

†*In case (b), the husband cannot claim the marriage allowance because MCA is claimed for the year.*

For Scottish taxpayers, the liability of the husband in case (a) would be £21.62 lower. The amount of the tax reduction transferred to his wife in case (c) would be £3.35 higher. The tax liability of the wife would be £21.62 lower in cases (a) and (b) and £24.97 (£21.62 + £3.35) lower in case (c).

3.5

	Total £	Non-savings £	Savings £
Retirement pension	11,550	11,550	
Income from annuity £912 × 100/80	1,140		1,140
Total income	12,690	11,550	1,140
Less: Personal allowance	12,570	11,550	1,020
Taxable income	120	0	120

Savings income of £120 is taxed at the starting rate for savings (0%) giving an income tax liability of £nil. Therefore Toby is entitled to a refund of the tax deducted at source of £228.

Toby cannot claim the MCA because his wife died before the start of the tax year. Even if he could claim MCA it would be wasted, because his tax liability is already £nil. Taxable income does not include any non-savings income, so it does not matter whether or not Toby is a Scottish taxpayer.

3.6

(a) Brian's liability is (£30,000 – £12,570) × 20% = £3,486. Daniel's liability is £nil.

(b) Brian's liability is reduced by £252 (£1,260 × 20%) to £3,234. Daniel's PA becomes £11,310 (£12,570 – £1,260). This is still sufficient to cover his income so his liability remains at £nil.

(c) If Brian's total income were £60,000 he would be liable to income tax at the higher rate and so it would not be possible for Daniel to transfer part of his personal allowance to him.

If Brian were a Scottish taxpayer, his liability in (a) would be (£2,162 × 19%) + (£10,956 × 20%) + (£4,312 × 21%) = £3,507.50 and his liability in (b) would be (£3,507.50 – £252.00) = £3,255.50.

3.7

	Richard £	Patricia £
Business profits	35,410	
Dividends		3,600
Less: Personal allowance	12,570	3,600
Taxable income	22,840	0
Income tax		
£22,840 @ 20%	4,568.00	
Less: MCA £7,410 @ 10%	741.00	
Tax liability	3,827.00	0.00

Notes:

(i) Richard's income exceeds the limit of £31,400 by £4,010. Therefore the MCA is reduced by £2,005 (1/2 × £4,010) to £7,410 (£9,415 – £2,005).

(ii) Patricia cannot transfer any of her PA to Richard because MCA is claimed for the year.

If Richard were a Scottish taxpayer, his tax liability would be (£2,162 × 19%) + (£10,956 × 20%) + (£9,722 × 21%) = £4,643.60, less MCA £741.00 = £3,902.60.

Chapter 4

4.1

	£
Total income	24,275
Less: Payment £200 × 100/80	250
Net income	24,025
Less: Personal allowance	12,570
Taxable income	11,455

Income tax

Tax borne @ 20%	2,291.00
Add: Tax deducted from payment	50.00
Tax liability	2,341.00

For a Scottish taxpayer, the first £2,162 would be taxed at 19%, reducing the liability by £21.62.

4.2

	(a) £	(b) £
Total income	54,160	54,160
Less: Interest paid	1,600	
Net income	52,560	54,160
Less: Personal allowance	12,570	12,570
Taxable income	39,990	41,590

Income tax

(a)	(b)		(a)	(b)
37,700	37,700	@ 20%	7,540.00	7,540.00
2,290	3,890	@ 40%	916.00	1,556.00
39,990	41,590			
Tax liability			8,456.00	9,096.00

Paul's tax liability is reduced by £640 if he pays the interest. The cost of the interest to him is therefore only £960 (amount paid £1,600 less reduction in tax liability £640). In effect, the interest paid of £1,600 is reduced by tax relief at 40% (£640), leaving £960 as the cost to Paul.

For a Scottish taxpayer, the marginal rate of tax would be 41% so tax relief on the interest would be (£1,600 × 41%) = £656. The cost of paying the interest would be (£1,600 − £656) = £944.

4.3

Rose's net income is £12,275 (£12,300 − £25). This is less than her personal allowance, so taxable income is £nil and the tax liability is zero. In fact the tax liability would also have been zero if the £25 payment had not been made, since Rose's total income is also less than her personal allowance. The payment has had no effect on her tax liability and so tax relief on the payment is zero.

4.4

(a) marginal rate (b) marginal rate (c) 10% (d) 30%

4.5

(a) The donation is deemed to be made net of 20% income tax. The charity concerned recovers £240 (£960 × 20/80) from HMRC, making the donation worth £1,200 in total.

(b) If the taxpayer does not pay income tax for 2022-23 of at least £240, the income tax liability for the year will be increased to exactly £240.

(c) The taxpayer's basic rate and higher rate limits for 2022-23 are both increased by £1,200. This results in a tax saving of up to £240 (40% – 20% = 20% × £1,200) for a higher rate taxpayer and up to £300 (45% – 20% = 25% × £1,200) for an additional rate taxpayer.

For a Scottish taxpayer, the intermediate rate limit is also increased by £1,200. Tax savings for a taxpayer whose marginal rate is the intermediate rate, higher rate or top rate would be equal to 1%, 21% or 26% of £1,200 respectively.

4.6

	£
Dividends received	63,670
Less: Personal allowance	12,570
Taxable income	51,100

Income tax	
£2,000 @ 0%	0.00
£36,250 @ 8.75%	3,171.87
£12,850 @ 33.75%	4,336.88
Tax liability	7,508.75

Note:

The grossed-up Gift Aid donation is £550 (£440 × 100/80) so the basic rate limit is increased by £550 to £38,250 (£37,700 + £550). This saves tax of (£550 × (33.75% – 8.75%)) = £137.50. So the cost to Raj is (£440 – £137.50) = £302.50. Total tax relief is £247.50 (an effective rate of 45%).

4.7

	Matthew	*Widow*
	£	£
Non-savings income	31,930	21,965
Less: Gift of shares to charity		500
Net income	31,930	21,465
Less: Personal allowance	12,570	12,570
Taxable income	19,360	8,895
Income tax @ 20%	3,872.00	1,779.00
Less: MCA £9,275 @ 10%	927.50	
Tax liability	2,944.50	1,779.00

Notes:

(i)   The grossed-up Gift Aid donation is £250.00 (£200 × 100/80).

(ii)   MCA is given in full in the year of death. Adjusted net income is £31,680 (£31,930 – £250) which exceeds £31,400 by £280. So the available MCA is £9,275 (£9,415 – 1/2 × £280).

For Scottish taxpayers, the husband's income tax liability (before MCA) would be (£2,162 × 19%) + (£10,956 × 20%) + (£6,242 × 21%) = £3,912.80. The wife's liability would be lower by £21.62.

Chapter 5

5.1

Rents received during the year are £6,200. The mortgage interest is not deductible since the loan relates to residential property. Therefore property income for 2022-23 is £4,900 (£6,200 – £1,300). The interest paid of £4,100 is treated as a tax reducer and is relieved at basic rate (20%), as long as adjusted total income for the year is at least £4,100.

5.2

	£	£
Rents received		16,640
Less: Advertising costs	135	
Repairs and maintenance	590	
Insurance costs	730	
Replacement of refrigerator	335	1,790
Property income		14,850

Notes:

(a)   "Replacement domestic items relief" is available in relation to the whole cost of the new refrigerator since it is substantially the same as the item which it replaces. Relief is also available for the costs of disposing of the old refrigerator. Total relief is (£325 + £10) = £335.

(b)   Interest on a buy-to-let mortgage of residential property is not a deductible expense. Capital repayments are also not deductible.

(c)   The mortgage interest of £3,420 is treated as a tax reducer and is relieved at 20% (as long as adjusted total income for the year is at least £3,420).

(d)   If a superior refrigerator costing £575 had been purchased instead of the one costing £325, the full cost of £575 would not be allowable. The deductible amount would be an estimate of how much it would cost to buy a similar refrigerator to the one being replaced (i.e. £325), so the computation would be unaltered.

However, if the superior refrigerator was itself replaced at some time in the future, relief would then be given on the cost of acquiring a similar superior model.

5.3

(a)   Premiums received in relation to the granting of long leases (i.e. leases of more than 50 years) are not assessable to income tax.

(b)   £12,000 – (49 × 2% of £12,000) = £240.

(c)   £12,000 – (19 × 2% of £12,000) = £7,440.

5.4

The income tax assessment on the landlord is £12,300 (£15,000 − (9 × 2% of £15,000)). Therefore Rashid will be allowed an annual deduction from his trading profits of £1,230 for each of the ten years of the lease.

5.5

All three flats pass the 210-day test. However, Flat 1 does not pass the 105-day test and so will not be regarded as a furnished holiday let unless it can be averaged with one or more of the other flats. Possible averaging claims are:

(a) Flat 1 with Flat 2. This is no use since the average number of days let is only 103.

(b) Flat 1 with Flat 3. This is also no use since the average number of days let is only 104.

(c) Flat 1 with Flat 2 and Flat 3. This is beneficial since the average number of days let is 105.

Chapter 6

6.1

				Total £		Savings £	Dividends £
Bank interest				520		520	
Loan stock interest £17,720 × 100/80				22,150		22,150	
Dividends received				53,600			53,600
Total income				76,270		22,670	53,600
Less: Personal allowance				12,570		12,570	
Taxable income				63,700		10,100	53,600

Income tax due					
Savings income	: Starting rate	5,000	@ 0%	0.00	
	: Nil rate	500	@ 0%	0.00	
	: Basic rate	4,600	@ 20%	920.00	
Dividend income	: Nil rate	2,000	@ 0%	0.00	
	: Ordinary rate	26,600	@ 8.75%	2,327.50	
	: Upper rate	25,000	@ 33.75%	8,437.50	
		63,700			
Tax liability				11,685.00	
Less: Tax deducted at source (£22,150 − £17,720)				4,430.00	
Tax payable				7,255.00	

Notes:

(a) The basic rate band is extended to £38,700 (£37,700 + (£800 × 100/80)).

(b) There is no non-savings income so the first £5,000 of savings income is taxed at the starting rate. Since taxable income exceeds the extended basic rate limit, the PSA is £500 and the next £500 of savings income is taxed at the savings nil rate.

6.2

	Total £	Non-savings £	Savings £	Dividends £
Retirement pension	11,956	11,956		
Bank deposit interest	480		480	
Dividends received	650			650
Total income	13,086	11,956	480	650
Less: Personal allowance	12,570	11,956	480	134
Taxable income	516	0	0	516

Taxable income consists entirely of dividends of £516. Since the first £2,000 of dividends are taxed at the dividend nil rate, the tax liability is zero. In fact the liability would still have been zero, even if the remaining £614 of the personal allowance (after using £11,956 against non-savings income) had been set against savings income and dividends in some other way.

Note: The ISA interest is exempt from tax.

6.3/6.4

See text.

6.5

	Total £	Non-savings £	Savings £	Dividends £
Business profits	102,850	102,850		
Building society interest	410		410	
Dividends received	7,240			7,240
Total income	110,500	102,850	410	7,240
Less: Personal allowance	7,320	7,320		
Taxable income	103,180	95,530	410	7,240

Income tax due

Non-savings income	: Basic rate	37,700	@ 20%	7,540.00
	: Higher rate	57,830	@ 40%	23,132.00
Savings income	: Nil rate	410	@ 0%	0.00
Dividend income	: Nil rate	2,000	@ 0%	0.00
	: Upper rate	5,240	@ 33.75%	1,768.50
		103,180		
				32,440.50
Less: EIS relief (30% × £20,000)				6,000.00
Tax liability				26,440.50

Note: The personal allowance is (£12,570 − 1/2 × £10,500) = £7,320. The PSA is £500.

For a Scottish taxpayer, the liability on non-savings income would be (£2,162 × 19%) + (£10,956 × 20%) + (£17,974 × 21%) + (£64,438 × 41%) = £32,796.10, an increase of £2,124.10.

Chapter 7

7.1

See text.

7.2

The basis of assessment for employment income is the receipts basis. The assessable income for 2022-23 is therefore £65,850 (£57,500 + £8,350).

7.3

(a) Free meals in the company canteen are exempt if available to all employees.

(b) Removal expenses of up to £8,000 are exempt if reasonable and incurred on first taking up an appointment or transferring to a new location.

(c) Long-service awards made in cash are taxable.

(d) A gift made in a personal capacity (rather than for services rendered) is exempt so long as it is reasonable in amount.

(e) The mileage allowance is exempt since it is less than the standard figure of 45p per mile for the first 10,000 miles. The employee has a deductible expense of £250 (2,500 × 10p).

(f) Employer contributions towards the additional household costs incurred by a homeworker are exempt from tax if supporting evidence is supplied to demonstrate that these costs have been incurred. Evidence would not be required if the contributions did not exceed £6 per week.

7.4

(a) Not generally deductible since not incurred in performing the duties of the employment. But there are exceptions to this rule in the case of site-based employees, employees undertaking business journeys from home and employees who are seconded to a temporary place of work.

(b) Deductible so long as necessarily incurred.

(c) Deductible if relevant to the employment.

(d) Deductible.

(e) Not deductible, even if worn only at the office. A suit provides warmth and decency and is therefore not purchased exclusively for the purposes of the employment.

(f) Not deductible unless reimbursed or paid out of a specific entertaining allowance. The expenses must also be wholly, exclusively and necessarily incurred.

Chapter 8

8.1

Annual value is £4,200 and there is an additional benefit of 2% × (£246,500 + £28,500 - £75,000) = £4,000, bringing the total to £8,200. However, there is 12% business use, which reduces the benefit by £984 (12% × £8,200) and the benefit is also reduced by the rent paid by Kim to her employer of £4,800 per annum. So the taxable benefit is £2,416 (£8,200 – £984 – £4,800).

8.2

Assuming that the diesel supplement applies, the applicable percentage is 34% (20% + 10% + 4%) so the taxable car benefit is £18,428 (34% of £54,200). Fuel benefit is £8,602 (34% of £25,300).

8.3

(a) The amount outstanding at the end of the tax year is £12,000. Therefore the average amount of the loan between 1 July 2022 and 5 April 2023 is (£20,000 + £12,000)/2 = £16,000. The loan was in existence for nine months of the tax year, so the taxable benefit using the normal method is equal to (£16,000 × 2% × 9/12) = £240.

(b) The taxable benefit using the alternative method is equal to (£20,000 × 2% × 6/12) + (£15,000 × 2% × 2/12) + (£12,000 × 2% × 1/12) = £270.

Chapter 9

9.1

The badges of trade are:

(i) subject matter (ii) length of ownership
(iii) frequency of transactions (iv) supplementary work
(v) reason for sale (vi) motive

(see the chapter for an explanation of each of these).

9.2

(a) Expenditure must be incurred wholly and exclusively for the purposes of the trade.

(b) Expenditure fails the "remoteness test" if it has no connection with the trade. Such expenditure is disallowed. Expenditure fails the "duality test" if it serves both a business purpose and a private purpose. Such expenditure cannot be allowed in full. However, if the expenditure can be apportioned with reasonable accuracy, then only the private element is disallowed.

9.3

(a) allowable so long as the salary is commensurate with the work done
(b) not allowable when computing trading profits, but relieved under the Gift Aid rules
(c) not allowable (capital expenditure)
(d) allowable so long as the diaries carry a prominent advertisement for the business
(e) allowable
(f) not allowable (fails the duality test)
(g) not allowable (related to capital expenditure)
(h) probably allowable as a trade subscription
(i) not allowable (food, drink or tobacco)
(j) allowable (relates directly to trading).

9.4

(a) add £45 (b) add £15 (c) no adjustment required.

9.5

(a) Disallow 15% × £300 = £45.

(b) The amount assessed on the landlord is (£15,000 − (14 × 2% of £15,000)) = £10,800. So the amount allowable in each year is £720 (1/15th of £10,800) and the amount to be disallowed each year is £280 (£1,000 − £720).

9.6

	£	£
Net profit for the year		6,960
Add: *Disallowed expenditure*:		
Proprietor's salary	10,400	
Cost of new heating system	3,800	
Telephone (1/4th of £880)	220	
Motor expenses (1/5th of £3,250)	650	
Entertaining	520	
General allowance for bad debts	200	
Loss on sale of non-current asset	70	
Depreciation	2,500	18,360
		25,320
Less: *Non-trading income*:		
Rents receivable	1,200	
Bank interest receivable	80	
Profit on sale of non-current asset	310	1,590
Trading profit (before capital allowances)		23,730

Chapter 10

10.1

(a) 2021-22   (b) 2021-22   (c) 2022-23   (d) 2022-23

10.2

(a)

2019-20	Actual	1 July 2019 to 5 April 2020
2020-21	12 months to a/c date in year 2	y/e 30 June 2020
2021-22	CYB	y/e 30 June 2021
2022-23	CYB	y/e 30 June 2022

There is an overlap period between 1 July 2019 and 5 April 2020.

(b)

2019-20	Actual	1 July 2019 to 5 April 2020
2020-21	Actual	6 April 2020 to 5 April 2021
2021-22	CYB	1 May 2020 to 30 April 2021
2022-23	CYB	y/e 30 April 2022

There is an overlap period between 1 May 2020 and 5 April 2021.

(c)

2019-20	Actual	1 July 2019 to 5 April 2020
2020-21	First 12 months	1 July 2019 to 30 June 2020
2021-22	CYB	y/e 30 April 2021
2022-23	CYB	y/e 30 April 2022

There is an overlap period between 1 July 2019 and 5 April 2020. There is another overlap period between 1 May 2020 and 30 June 2020.

10.3

				£
2020-21	Actual	1/1/21 to 5/4/21	£27,300 × 3/18	4,550
2021-22	Actual	6/4/21 to 5/4/22	£27,300 × 12/18	18,200
2022-23	CYB	1/7/21 to 30/6/22	£27,300 × 12/18	18,200

There is an overlap period between 1 July 2021 and 5 April 2022 (9 months). The overlap profits are 9/18 × £27,300 = £13,650.

10.4

(a)	2019-20	CYB	y/e 31/1/20
	2020-21	CYB	y/e 31/1/21
	2021-22	End of previous basis period to date of cessation	1/2/21 to 31/5/21
(b)	2019-20	CYB	y/e 31/1/20
	2020-21	CYB	y/e 31/1/21
	2021-22	End of previous basis period to date of cessation	1/2/21 to 31/3/22
(c)	2020-21	CYB	y/e 31/1/21
	2021-22	12 months to normal a/c date	1/2/21 to 31/1/22
	2022-23	End of previous basis period to date of cessation	1/2/22 to 30/4/22

10.5

Year	Basis period	Workings	Trading income £
2017-18	1/6/17 to 5/4/18	£28,800 × 10/16	18,000
2018-19	1/10/17 to 30/9/18	£28,800 × 12/16	21,600
2019-20	y/e 30/9/19		19,900
2020-21	y/e 30/9/20		14,300
2021-22	y/e 30/9/21		13,800
2022-23	1/10/21 to 31/7/22	£11,100 – £10,800	300
			87,900

Notes:

(i)   There is an overlap period from 1 October 2017 to 5 April 2018 with profits of 6/16 × £28,800 = £10,800. Therefore overlap relief of £10,800 is given in the tax year in which trade ceases.

(ii)   The total of the trading income assessed to income tax is £87,900. This is equal to the total of the adjusted trading profits earned over the lifetime of the business.

Chapter 11

11.1

	Main pool £	Allowances £
y/e 5/4/23		
WDV b/f	10,300	
Additions (ineligible for AIA)	8,000	
	18,300	
Disposals (£4,000 + £3,000)	(7,000)	
	11,300	
WDA @ 18%	2,034	2,034
	9,266	
Additions qualifying for AIA (£600 + £400)	1,000	
AIA @ 100%	1,000 –	1,000
WDV c/f	9,266	
Total allowances		3,034

Notes:

(i)   Maximum AIA for the year (working to the nearest month) is £1,000,000.

(ii) The disposal value of the machinery sold in April 2022 is restricted to original cost.

11.2

	Main pool £	Motor car (40% p.u.) £	Allowances £
15 months to 30/4/23			
Additions (ineligible for AIA)	18,133	15,000	
WDA @ 18% × 15/12	4,080		4,080
WDA @ 6% × 15/12		1,125 × 60% =	675
	14,053	13,875	
Additions qualifying for AIA	195,367		
AIA @ 100%	195,367	–	195,367
WDV c/f	14,053	13,875	
Total allowances			200,122

Notes:

(i)   AIA maximum is £1,183,333 [(14/12 × £1,000,000) + (1/12 × £200,000)]. But no more than £16,667 (1/12 × £200,000) may be claimed for expenditure which is incurred after 31 March 2023. So the AIA that may be claimed for the period is £195,367 (£153,000 + £25,700 + £16,667). The remaining £18,133 (£34,800 – £16,667) enters the main pool.

(ii) The car (acquired on or after 6 April 2021) has emissions that exceed 50g/km and so attracts WDAs at 6% p.a. WDAs are scaled up by 15/12 for a 15-month chargeable period.

The adjusted trading profit for the 15-month period is now £60,000 (£260,122 – £200,122). Trading income for the first two tax years is as follows:

Year	Basis period	Workings	Trading income
			£
2021-22	1/2/22 to 5/4/22	£60,000 × 2/15	8,000
2022-23	6/4/22 to 5/4/23	£60,000 × 12/15	48,000

Notes:

(i) There is no accounting date in 2022-23 (the second tax year) so the basis period for that year is the actual tax year from 6 April 2022 to 5 April 2023. There are no overlap profits.

(ii) The basis period for 2023-24 (transitional year) will be 6 April 2023 to 5 April 2024. Trading income for this period will include 1/15th of the profit for the period to 30 April 2023.

11.3

	Main pool £	Special rate pool £	Allowances £
9 months to 31/12/22			
WDV b/f	178,400		
Additions (ineligible for AIA)		15,400	
Disposals	(3,400)		
	175,000		
WDA @ 18% × 9/12	23,625		23,625
WDA @ 6% × 9/12		693	693
	151,375		
Additions eligible for AIA	78,950		
AIA @ 100%	78,950	-	78,950
Additions eligible for 100% FYA	11,600		
FYA @ 100%	11,600	-	11,600
WDV c/f	151,375	14,707	
Total allowances			114,868

Notes:

(i) The Peugeot motor car (acquired on or after 6 April 2021) is allocated to the special rate pool because it has emissions exceeding 50g/km. The rate of WDA in the special rate pool is 6%.

(ii) The motor van is eligible for AIA. Total additions (other than cars) are £78,950 (£64,450 + £14,500). This is within the maximum AIA of £750,000 (9/12 × £1,000,000) which may be claimed for the period.

(iii) The zero-emission car attracts a 100% FYA.

(iv) WDAs are restricted because the chargeable period is only nine months long.

(v) Capital allowances on the two private use cars are £3,598 (see below).

(vi) Total capital allowances for the year are £118,466 (£114,868 + £3,598).

	Toyota (50% p.u.) £	Saab (50% p.u.) £	Allowances £
9 months to 31/12/22			
WDV b/f	18,200		
Additions (ineligible for AIA)		29,600	
Disposals	(15,000)		
Balancing allowance	3,200 × 50% =		1,600
WDA @ 18% × 9/12		3,996 × 50% =	1,998
WDV c/f		25,604	
Total allowances			3,598

Notes:

(i)   The Saab attracts WDA at 18% per annum because it has emissions that do not exceed 50g/km.

(ii)   WDA is restricted because the chargeable period is only nine months long.

(iii)   The emission rating of the Toyota motor car is irrelevant (for this chargeable period) since it has been disposed of and so does not attract WDA in the period.

Chapter 12

12.1

(a)   The year to 31 December 2022 is the basis period for tax year 2022-23. There is a trading loss in this basis period, so trading income for 2022-23 is £nil.

(b)   The loss could be carried forward and set against the first available profits of the same trade. Alternatively, the loss could be set against total income of 2022-23 and/or 2021-22.

12.2

	2019-20 £	2020-21 £	2021-22 £	2022-23 £
Trading income	-	4,710	6,210	14,810
Other income	10,000	10,000	10,000	10,000
Total income	10,000	14,710	16,210	24,810
Less: Trading losses b/f	-	(4,710)	(6,210)	(7,940)
Net income	10,000	10,000	10,000	16,870

12.3

(a)

Year	Basis period	Workings	Trading income £
2020-21	1/1/21 to 5/4/21	(£19,080 – £6,460) × 3/12	3,155
2021-22	y/e 31/12/21	£19,080 – £6,460	12,620
2022-23	y/e 31/12/22		nil

(b)   The trading loss of 2022-23 is £9,800 (£7,480 + £2,320). A claim could be made to set this loss against total income in 2022-23 or 2021-22 or in both of these years:

(i)   A claim for 2022-23 is pointless since there is no income in that year.

(ii)   A claim for 2021-22 would reduce total income for that year to (£12,620 – £9,800) = £2,820 and so eliminate the very small income tax liability for the year. But the personal allowance would be mostly wasted.

(iii) A claim for both years is pointless since a claim for 2022-23 is pointless.

The 2021-22 claim would be less wasteful if Marcus declined to claim any capital allowances in either of the first two years of trading. Trading income for 2021-22 would become £19,080 and the 2022-23 loss would become £7,480. Claiming relief against total income in 2021-22 would then leave income of £11,600 for the year, absorbing most of the personal allowance.

Alternatively, Marcus could claim that the loss should be carried forward and set against the first available profits of the same trade. This may be a better option if these trading profits are expected to be substantial, especially if there is a chance of saving tax at higher rates.

12.4

The losses eligible for early trade losses relief are:

Year	Basis period	Workings	Trading loss £	Early trade losses claim
2020-21	1/10/20 to 5/4/21	£(56,850) × 6/15	(22,740)	17-18 *to* 19-20
2021-22	1/1/21 to 31/12/21	£(56,850) × 12/15 – overlap £(56,850) × 3/15	(34,110)	18-19 *to* 20-21
2022-23	y/e 31/12/22		(32,660)	19-20 *to* 21-22

If all possible early trade losses relief claims are made, total income is:

	2017-18 £	2018-19 £	2019-20 £	2020-21 £
Trading income	-	-	-	nil
Other income	25,100	25,250	26,400	13,450
Total income	25,100	25,250	26,400	13,450
Less: Early trade losses: 2020-21 loss	(22,740)			
2021-22 loss		(25,250)	(8,860)	
2022-23 loss			(17,540)	(13,450)
Net income	2,360	-	-	-

Notes:

(a)   Personal allowances are totally wasted in 2018-19 to 2020-21.

(b)   The loss incurred in 2022-23 has been only partly relieved. The remaining £1,670 (£32,660 – £17,540 – £13,450) is eligible for early trade losses relief in 2021-22 but there is no income in that year against which to set the loss. A claim should be made for the remaining loss of £1,670 to be carried forward and set against future trading profits.

Chapter 13

13.1

	Nickleby	Copperfield	Drood	Total
	£	£	£	£
1/1/22 - 31/3/22				
(£183,000 × 3/12 = £45,750)	15,250	15,250	15,250	45,750
1/4/22 - 31/12/22				
(£183,000 × 9/12 = £137,250)	27,450	54,900	54,900	137,250
Allocation of profit for the year	42,700	70,150	70,150	183,000

13.2

	Pickwick	Snodgrass	Tupman	Total
	£	£	£	£
Interest on capital	3,600	6,000	3,000	12,600
Salaries	40,000	-	30,000	70,000
Remainder (shared equally)	(6,700)	(6,700)	(6,700)	(20,100)
	36,900	(700)	26,300	62,500
Notional loss divided 36,900:26,300	(409)	700	(291)	-
Allocation of profit for the year	36,491	-	26,009	62,500

13.3

The allocation of profit for each period of account is:

	Dodson	Fogg	Jackson	Total
	£	£	£	£
y/e 30/6/20 (shared equally)	34,000	34,000	-	68,000
y/e 30/6/21 (shared 5:4:1)	44,000	35,200	8,800	88,000
y/e 30/6/22 (shared 5:4:1)	58,000	46,400	11,600	116,000

Each partner's trading income is:

Dodson

Year	Basis period	Workings	Trading income
			£
2019-20	1/7/19 to 5/4/20	£34,000 × 9/12	25,500
2020-21	y/e 30/6/20		34,000
2021-22	y/e 30/6/21		44,000
2022-23	y/e 30/6/22		58,000

Fogg

Year	Basis period	Workings	Trading income
			£
2019-20	1/7/19 to 5/4/20	£34,000 × 9/12	25,500
2020-21	y/e 30/6/20		34,000
2021-22	y/e 30/6/21		35,200
2022-23	y/e 30/6/22		46,400

Jackson

Year	Basis period	Workings	Trading income £
2020-21	1/7/20 to 5/4/21	£8,800 × 9/12	6,600
2021-22	y/e 30/6/21		8,800
2022-23	y/e 30/6/22		11,600

Note:

Dodson and Fogg each have overlap profits of £25,500. Jackson has overlap profits of £6,600.

13.4

(a) Trading profit of £117,460 for the year to 30 September 2021 is allocated Wardle £82,222, Jingle £23,492, Trotter £11,746. Trading profit of £136,540 for the year to 30 September 2022 is allocated Wardle £95,578, Jingle £27,308 Trotter £13,654. The partners' trading income is:

	Wardle £	Jingle £	Trotter £
2020-21 (6/12 × y/e 30/9/21)	41,111	11,746	5,873
2021-22 (y/e 30/9/21)	82,222	23,492	11,746
2022-23 (y/e 30/9/22)	95,578	27,308	13,654

(b) The bank interest of £200 for the year to 30 September 2021 is allocated Wardle £140, Jingle £40, Trotter £20. The bank interest of £220 for the year to 30 September 2022 is allocated Wardle £154, Jingle £44, Trotter £22. Each partner's bank interest is:

	Wardle £	Jingle £	Trotter £
2020-21 (6/12 × y/e 30/9/21)	70	20	10
2021-22 (y/e 30/9/21)	140	40	20
2022-23 (y/e 30/9/22)	154	44	22

(c) The loan interest of £1,240 (gross) for the year to 30 September 2021 is allocated Wardle £868, Jingle £248, Trotter £124. The loan interest of £1,360 (gross) for the year to 30 September 2022 is allocated Wardle £952, Jingle £272, Trotter £136. The gross amount on which each partner is charged to tax in 2021-22 (assuming time-apportionment between tax years) is:

	£
Wardle (£868 × 6/12 + £952 × 6/12)	910
Jingle (£248 × 6/12 + £272 × 6/12)	260
Trotter (£124 × 6/12 + £136 × 6/12)	130

Chapter 14

14.1

(a) £120,000.

(b) £3,600 (so long as at least £2,400 is paid to a scheme which operates relief at source).

14.2

She will pay net contributions of £800 per month, so obtaining relief at the basic rate. Her basic rate limit and higher rate limit will both be increased by £12,000 (and if she is a Scottish taxpayer her intermediate rate limit will also be increased by £12,000).

14.3

Current year contributions are 310% of those in the previous year. This exceeds 210% so spreading may be required. The excess of current year contributions over 110% of previous year contributions is £1,200,000, which is between £1,000,000 and £1,999,999. Therefore this excess must be spread over the current period and the next two periods. Tax relief on contributions of £1,060,000 (£660,000 + £400,000) will be given in the year to 30 June 2023. Relief on contributions of £400,000 will be given in each of the years to 30 June 2024 and 2025.

14.4

(a) The first lump sum absorbs 20% of the 2009-10 lifetime allowance of £1,750,000. There is no lifetime allowance charge and 80% of the lifetime allowance remains unused. The second lump sum of £1,120,000 exceeds 80% of the 2022-23 lifetime allowance of £1,073,100 by £261,520. There is a lifetime allowance charge of £143,836 (55% of £261,520).

(b) The first lump sum now absorbs 64% of the 2009-10 lifetime allowance. The second lump sum is less than 36% of the 2022-23 lifetime allowance and therefore there is no lifetime allowance charge on either lump sum.

14.5

If Damon became entitled to payment of his pension and lump sum at the start of the tax year, he would receive an annual pension of £120,000 (£360,000 × 20/60) and a lump sum of £270,000 (£360,000 × 60/80). The value of his pension rights at the start of the year is therefore £2,190,000 (£270,000 + (16 × £120,000)).

If he became entitled to payment of his pension and lump sum at the end of the tax year, he would receive an annual pension of £136,500 (£390,000 × 21/60) and a lump sum of £307,125 (£390,000 × 63/80). The value of his pension rights at the end of the year is therefore £2,491,125 (£307,125 + (16 × £136,500)).

Total pension input amount for 2022-23 is £301,125 (£2,491,125 – £2,190,000). This exceeds the minimum annual allowance of £4,000 by £297,125. Therefore the annual allowance charge is £133,706.25 (45% of £297,125).

Chapter 15

15.1

(a) No POAs are required because the 2021-22 liability (less PAYE and tax deducted at source) was less than £1,000. A balancing payment of £440 (£1,750 – £1,310) is due on 31 January 2024. However, since this does not exceed £3,000, Guy may request that this payment should be collected via the PAYE system during tax year 2024-25.

(b) The amount paid via PAYE and by deduction at source in 2021-22 (£4,390) was not more than 80% of the total liability for the year and the remainder (£2,340) was not less than £1,000. Therefore POAs are required for 2022-23. A first POA of £1,170 (one-half of £2,340) is due on 31 January 2023 and a second POA of £1,170 is due on 31 July 2023.

A balancing *repayment* of £605 (£6,580 – £4,810 – £35 – £2,340) will be due by 31 January 2024. Marie could have made a claim to pay reduced POAs for 2022-23 if she had known that the POAs based on her 2021-22 liability were likely to be excessive.

(c) No POAs are required because more than 80% of the 2021-22 tax liability was satisfied by PAYE and deduction at source. A balancing payment of £3,600 (£16,110 – £12,510) is due on 31 January 2024.

15.2

(a) The balancing payment was not more than 30 days late so there are no late payment penalties.

(b) The first POA of £12,000 was paid 27 days late, the second POA of £12,000 was paid 43 days late and the balancing payment of £4,000 was paid 21 days late. The interest payable is:

	£
£12,000 × 3.25% × 27/366	28.77
£12,000 × 3.25% × 43/366	45.82
£4,000 × 3.25% × 21/366	7.46
	82.05

15.3

(a) Jabran notified HMRC of his chargeability to tax within the permitted six months and so incurs no penalty in relation to this notification.

(b) His tax return was due to be submitted to HMRC within three months of the date of the notice. He filed the return late (but not more than three months late) and so incurs a penalty of £100.

(c) The balancing payment was due three months after the date of the notice. His payment was more than 30 days late and therefore he incurs a 5% late payment penalty.

(d) Interest is payable on the tax paid late and interest is payable on the late payment penalty if it is not paid within 30 days of the date of its imposition.

Chapter 16

16.1

(a) Primary   : 13.25% × (£256 – £242) = £1.85
Secondary : 15.05% × (£256 – £175) = £12.19

(b) Primary   : 13.25% × (£861 – £242) = £82.02
Secondary : 15.05% × (£861 – £175) = £103.24

(c) Primary   : 13.25% × (£967 – £242) + 3.25% × (£1,006 – £967) = £97.33
Secondary : 15.05% × (£1,006 – £175) = £125.07

(d) Primary   : nil (earnings do not exceed the primary threshold)
Secondary : nil (earnings do not exceed the secondary threshold)

(e) Primary   : 13.25% × (£3,300 – £1,048) = £298.39
Secondary : 15.05% × (£3,300 – £758) = £382.57

(f) Primary   : 13.25% × (£4,189 – £1,048) + 3.25% × (£6,000 – £4,189) = £475.04
Secondary : 15.05% × (£6,000 – £758) = £788.92

16.2

Class 1 NICs for a director are calculated on an annual basis. Pension contributions made by an employee are not deductible when calculating Class 1 NICs. However, any pension contributions made by an employer on behalf of an employee are not regarded as earnings for NICs purposes.

Gross pay for the year is (9 × £8,400) + (3 × £8,736) = £101,808.

Primary Class 1 NICs: 13.25% × (£50,270 – £11,908) + 3.25% × (£101,808 – £50,270) = £6,757.95.

Secondary Class 1 NICs: 15.05% × (£101,808 – £9,100) = £13,952.55.

Class 1A NICs (payable only by Joan's employer) are 15.05% × £12,850 = £1,933.92.

16.3

Mark's trading profit for 2022-23 (£12,590) is not less than the lower profits limit (£11,908) so he is liable to make Class 2 NICs of £113.40 (36 × £3.15). He is also liable to make Class 4 contributions of £69.90 (10.25% × (£12,590 – £11,908)). Therefore his total NICs liability is £183.30.

Chapter 17

17.1

(a) Companies are not chargeable persons, so the sale will not give rise to a CGT liability.

(b) Disposals between husband and wife who are living together are deemed to occur at a disposal value such that neither a gain nor a loss arises. So there will be no CGT liability on the gift.

(c) Gifts to charities are exempt from CGT.

(d) In general, charities are not chargeable persons and therefore disposals by charities do not give rise to a CGT liability (subject to certain restrictions).

(e) The sale is made in the course of trade. Therefore the profit arising will be a trading profit and not a capital gain.

(f) The partnership is not a chargeable person but the partners are. Any CGT liability arising on the disposal of the office building will be divided between them.

17.2

(a) Shares in a limited company are chargeable assets.

(b) Gilt-edged securities are not chargeable assets.

(c) A table is a chattel. Chattels disposed of for more than £6,000 are chargeable assets.

(d) A chair is a chattel. Chattels disposed of for £6,000 or less are not chargeable assets.

(e) A taxpayer's principal private residence is not a chargeable asset.

(f) Motor cars are not chargeable assets.

17.3

(a) Net losses are £2,500. The annual exemption is lost and taxable gains are £nil.

(b) Net losses are £1,000. The annual exemption is lost and taxable gains are £nil.

(c) Net gains are £7,450. The unused part of the annual exemption (£4,850) is lost. Taxable gains are £nil.

(d) Net gains are £13,750. The annual exemption of £12,300 is fully used and taxable gains are £1,450.

17.4

(a) Taxable gains are £239,300 (£263,000 – £11,400 – £12,300). Therefore the CGT liability is (10% × £239,300) = £23,930.

(b) The unused part of the basic rate band is £7,100 (£37,700 − £30,600). Therefore the CGT liability is (10% × £7,100) + (20% × £232,200) = £47,150.

(c) (18% × £7,100) + (28% × £232,200) = £66,294.

(d) The losses and the annual exemption are set against the gain of £57,300, leaving £33,600. The gain which qualifies for BADR absorbs the whole of the unused part of the basic rate band so the CGT liability is (10% × £205,700) + (20% × £33,600) = £27,290.

(e) (10% × £205,700) + (28% × £33,600) = £29,978.

17.5

(a) Net gains are £10,400. £1,900 of the annual exemption is lost and taxable gains are £nil. The losses brought forward of £4,800 remain unrelieved and are carried forward to 2023-24.

(b) Net gains are £12,900. This exceeds the annual exemption by £600, so £600 of the losses brought forward are relieved and taxable gains are £nil. The remaining £4,200 of the losses brought forward are carried forward to 2023-24.

(c) Net gains are £18,300. This exceeds the annual exemption by £6,000, so all of the losses brought forward are relieved. Taxable gains are £1,200 (£18,300 − £4,800 − £12,300). There are no unrelieved losses to carry forward.

17.6

Net losses in 2022-23 are £14,200. The annual exemption is lost and taxable gains for the year are £nil. The net losses may be offset against the net gains of 2021-22, 2020-21 and 2019-20, in that order, to the extent that those net gains exceed the annual exemption. Relief is £nil in 2021-22, £2,800 (£15,100 − £12,300) in 2020-21 and £6,500 (£18,500 − £12,000) in 2019-20. Total relief is £9,300. The remaining £4,900 of net losses in 2022-23 cannot be relieved at all.

17.7

31 January 2024.

Chapter 18

18.1

		£
Sale proceeds		172,000
Less: Incidental costs of disposal:		
Auctioneer's fee (5%)	8,600	
Legal fees	500	9,100
		162,900
Less: Acquisition cost	100,000	
Incidental costs of acquisition:		
Legal fees	400	
Enhancement expenditure	5,000	105,400
Chargeable gain		57,500

(The repainting costs do not rank as enhancement expenditure).

18.2

	(a)	(b)	(c)
	£	£	£
Sale proceeds	87,500	87,500	87,500
Less: Acquisition cost	10,000	35,000	100,000
Chargeable gain/(allowable loss)	77,500	52,500	(12,500)

If Francis was an art dealer who acquired the oil painting as trading stock, then the disposal would not be a chargeable disposal for CGT purposes. Therefore, there would be neither a chargeable gain nor an allowable loss on the disposal.

The painting's cost and sale proceeds would be taken into account when calculating Francis' trading profit or loss for the period in which the sale took place A trading profit would be charged to income tax (not CGT). A trading loss would be eligible for various income tax reliefs (see Chapter 12). If unrelieved in this way, a trading loss might be set against capital gains (see Chapter 17).

18.3

	(a)	(b)	(c)
	£	£	£
Sale proceeds	14,950	6,350	25,780
Less: Deemed acquisition cost	7,500	7,500	7,500
Chargeable gain/(allowable loss)	7,450	(1,150)	18,280

18.4

(a)

	£
Sale proceeds (June 2018)	100,000
Less: Incidental costs of disposal	5,000
	95,000

Less: Part cost:

$$\frac{£100,000}{£100,000 + £500,000} \times £240,000 \qquad (40,000)$$

Part incidental costs of acquisition:

$$\frac{£100,000}{£100,000 + £500,000} \times £12,000 \qquad (2,000)$$

Chargeable gain	53,000

(b)

	£
Sale proceeds (January 2023)	520,000
Less: Remainder of cost (£240,000 – £40,000)	(200,000)
Remainder of costs of acquisition (£12,000 – £2,000)	(10,000)
Chargeable gain	310,000

18.5

(a)

	£
Deemed disposal proceeds	80
Less: Deemed acquisition cost	6,000
Allowable loss	(5,920)

(b)

	£
Disposal proceeds	120
Less: Deemed acquisition cost (November 2021)	80
Chargeable gain	40

Chapter 19

19.1

(a)	Wasting chattel.	(b)	Chattel.	(c)	Wasting chattel.
(d)	Wasting asset.	(e)	Wasting chattel.	(f)	Chattel.

19.2

	£	
Sale proceeds	7,200	
Less: Incidental disposal costs	200	
	7,000	
Less: Acquisition cost	2,300	
Chargeable gain	4,700	(restricted to £2,000)

The gain is restricted to (£7,200 – £6,000) × 5/3 = £2,000.

19.3

	£
Deemed sale proceeds	6,000
Less: Acquisition cost	50,000
Allowable loss	(44,000)

19.4

	£
Sale proceeds	2,500
Less: Part cost: $\dfrac{£2,500}{£2,500 + £8,500} \times 3,850$	875
Chargeable gain	1,625

The maximum gain is (£11,000 – £6,000) × 5/3 × (£2,500/£11,000) = £1,894. The actual gain is less than this so the chargeable gain is £1,625.

19.5

	(a)	(b)
	£	£
Sale proceeds	65,000	38,000
Less: Acquisition cost	50,000	50,000
	15,000	(12,000)
Less: Available capital allowances	0	12,000
Chargeable gain or allowable loss	15,000	0

19.6

Katie is <u>not</u> selling land. She is selling an option to buy land (i.e. an intangible asset which gives the holder of the option the right to buy a certain piece of land at any time in the next five years). This option is a wasting asset. The computation of the gain arising on the disposal is as follows:

	£
Sale proceeds	8,000
<u>Less</u>: Unexpired portion of cost $\frac{3}{5} \times £10,000$	6,000
Chargeable gain	2,000

19.7

When the lease was acquired it had a 40-year life (Sch. 8 percentage 95.457%). When the lease was assigned there were 22 years remaining (Sch. 8 percentage 76.399%). Therefore the computation is as follows:

	£
Sale proceeds	97,500
<u>Less</u>: Unexpired portion of cost	
$\dfrac{76.399}{95.457} \times £75,000$	60,026
Chargeable gain	37,474

Chapter 20

20.1

(a)	20 October 2022	200	(bought on same day)
	10 August 2022	50	(s104 holding)
(b)	1 December 2022	150	(next 30 days)
	10 August 2022	270	(s104 holding)
(c)	10 August 2022	300	(s104 holding)

20.2

There were no acquisitions on the same day as the disposal or within the following 30 days, so the disposal must have come from the s104 holding. The s104 holding is as follows:

	Number of shares	Allowable expenditure £
Acquired 29 January 1999	1,000	4,000
Acquired 13 August 2003	1,000	9,500
Acquired 4 October 2015	2,000	22,500
	4,000	36,000
Sold 26 June 2022 (700/4,000ths)	(700)	(6,300)
s104 holding c/f	3,300	29,700

Note:

On average, the allowable expenditure in the pool is £9 per share. The allowable expenditure which is deducted on the June 2022 disposal (£6,300) is equal to 700 shares at £9 per share.

The gain or loss arising on the disposal is as follows:

	(a) £	(b) £	(c) £
Sale proceeds	8,400	6,300	5,200
Less: Allowable expenditure	6,300	6,300	6,300
Chargeable gain/(allowable loss)	2,100	0	(1,100)

20.3

The 10,000 shares disposed of on 22 December 2022 are matched as follows:

(a) The first match is against the 3,000 shares acquired on the same day as the disposal. These 3,000 shares were acquired for £24,000 and sold for £30,000 (3,000 × £10), so the chargeable gain on these 3,000 shares is £6,000.

(b) The next match is against the 5,000 shares acquired within the next 30 days. These 5,000 shares were acquired for £55,000 and sold for £50,000 (5,000 × £10), so the allowable loss on these 5,000 shares is £5,000.

(c) The third and final match is against 2,000 of the shares in the s104 holding. The s104 holding is as follows:

	Number of shares	Allowable expenditure £
Acquired 19 September 2013	4,000	16,000
Acquired 20 October 2015	2,000	12,000
Acquired 21 November 2017	1,000	7,000
	7,000	35,000
Sold 22 December 2022 (2,000/7,000ths)	(2,000)	(10,000)
s104 holding c/f	5,000	25,000

These 2,000 shares were acquired for £10,000 (the allowable expenditure deducted from the s104 holding on their disposal) and sold for £20,000 (2,000 × £10). Therefore the chargeable gain is £10,000.

Overall, the chargeable gain on the 22 December 2022 disposal of 10,000 shares is £11,000 (£6,000 − £5,000 + £10,000).

20.4

There were no acquisitions on the same day as the disposal or within the following 30 days, so the disposal must have come from the s104 holding. The s104 holding is as follows:

	Number of shares	Allowable expenditure £
Acquired 17 February 2011	600	900
Acquired 13 November 2015	200	400
Acquired 9 October 2019	100	300
	900	1,600
Bonus issue January 2022	225	-
	1,125	1,600
Sold February 2023 (450/1,125ths)	(450)	(640)
s104 holding c/f	675	960

The 450 shares which were disposed of in February 2023 were acquired for £640 (i.e. the allowable expenditure deducted from the s104 holding) and were sold for (450 × £4) = £1,800. Therefore the chargeable gain is £1,160.

20.5

There were no acquisitions on the same day as the disposal or within the following 30 days, so the disposal must have come from the s104 holding. The s104 holding is as follows:

	Number of shares	Allowable expenditure £
Acquired 30 September 2010	2,000	1,200
Acquired 1 December 2014	3,000	3,600
	5,000	4,800
Rights issue January 2022	1,000	1,000
	6,000	5,800
Sold March 2023 (3,000/6,000ths)	(3,000)	(2,900)
s104 holding c/f	3,000	2,900

The 3,000 shares which were disposed of in March 2023 were acquired for £2,900 (i.e. the allowable expenditure deducted from the s104 holding) and were sold for (3,000 × £1.80) = £5,400. Therefore the chargeable gain is £2,500.

20.6

(a) The value of the part disposed of is £6,000 (6,000 × £1) and the value of the part remaining is £12,000 (6,000 × £2) so there has been a 6,000/18,000 (1/3rd) part disposal. One-third is more than 5% and the amount received is more than £3,000, so this cannot be treated as a small capital distribution. The s104 holding is as follows:

	Number of shares	Allowable expenditure £
Acquired November 2010	6,000	30,000
Distribution March 2023 (one-third)	-	(10,000)
s104 holding c/f	6,000	20,000

The allowable loss is £4,000 (£6,000 – £10,000).

(b) The value of Yolande's shares immediately prior to the sale of rights was £600. £25 is less than 5% of £600, so the sale of rights ranks as a small capital distribution. Assuming that this distribution is not treated as a disposal, the s104 holding is as follows:

	Number of shares	Allowable expenditure £
Acquired January 2014	300	360
Distribution May 2020	-	(25)
	300	335
Sold November 2022	(300)	(335)
s104 holding c/f	-	-

The chargeable gain is £445 (£780 – £335).

20.7

Walter received 16,000 shares worth £72,000, plus £8,000 in cash, a total of £80,000. The amount received in cash is 10% of the total. This exceeds 5% and the amount exceeds £3,000. Therefore this does not rank as a small capital distribution and the situation must be treated as a part disposal. The s104 holding is as follows:

	Number of shares	Allowable expenditure £
Acquired June 2021	10,000	70,000
Distribution August 2022 (10%)	-	(7,000)
s104 holding after distribution	10,000	63,000
s104 holding (Rundico plc) c/f	16,000	63,000

The chargeable gain is £1,000 (£8,000 – £7,000).

Chapter 21

21.1

So long as Mohammed actually resides in both properties he may choose which is to be regarded as his principal private residence (PPR). Whichever property he bought and lived in first was automatically regarded as his PPR. After he bought the second property (and began residing in it) he could, if he wished, elect that this property should become his PPR for CGT purposes. He would do this if he thought that the gain arising on the disposal of the second property would exceed the gain arising on the disposal of the first property. The election would have to be made within two years after the date from which it is to take effect.

21.2

	£
Sale proceeds	173,000
Less: Acquisition cost	31,000
Chargeable gain (before PPR exemption)	142,000

The chargeable gain (before considering the PPR exemption) is £142,000. Considering each of the three cases individually:

(a) The house is not a chargeable asset and so the disposal is exempt from CGT. The chargeable gain is £nil.

(b) Melanie owned the house for 31 years and 4 months (376 months) and was absent for 48 months. There is no indication that the absence was work-related and this absence exceeds the permissible maximum "absence for any reason" by 12 months. Therefore the PPR exemption is £142,000 × 364/376 = £137,468 and the chargeable gain is £142,000 × 12/376 = £4,532.

(c) Letting relief applies only if Melanie has been sharing occupation of her residence with a tenant. This is not the case, so letting relief is not available. Therefore the chargeable gain remains at £4,532.

21.3

	£
Sale proceeds	343,000
Less: Acquisition cost	75,000
Chargeable gain (before PPR exemption)	268,000

Rupert's period of ownership (a total of 268 months) is broken down as follows:

(i)	1 November 2000 to 31 October 2004	48 months	Actual residence
(ii)	1 November 2004 to 31 October 2005	12 months	Working abroad
(iii)	1 November 2005 to 31 July 2009	45 months	Actual residence
(iv)	1 August 2009 to 31 October 2013	51 months	Working in UK
(v)	1 November 2013 to 31 October 2016	36 months	Actual residence
(vi)	1 November 2016 to 1 March 2023	76 months	Living with friend

The gains arising during periods (i) and (v) are exempt (actual residence) and five-sixths of the gain arising during period (iii) is also exempt. Period (ii) is exempt (working abroad). Period (iv) exceeds the four-year maximum allowed for working elsewhere in the UK but the other three months of this period are exempted as part of the 36 months allowed for any reason. The last nine months of ownership are exempt but the remaining 67 months of period (vi) cannot be exempt since they are not followed by a period of actual residence. Therefore full PPR exemption is available for a total of $(48 + 12 + 51 + 36 + 9) = 156$ months and five-sixths exemption is available for 45 months.

The fact that the property was always let in Rupert's absence is not relevant, since letting relief now applies only if there is shared occupancy of the property. However, letting relief is available in relation to the gain that arose during the 45 months when one-sixth of the property was let to tenants and Rupert occupied the remaining five-sixths. The chargeable gain is as follows:

	£	£
Total gain (as above)		268,000
Less: PPR exemption:		
£268,000 × 156/268	156,000	
£268,000 × 45/268 × 5/6	37,500	193,500
		74,500
Less: Letting relief (lowest of £7,500, £193,500		
and £40,000)		7,500
Chargeable gain		67,000

Note:
The gain arising during the 45 months when one-sixth of the property was let is equal to £268,000 × 45/268 × 1/6 = £7,500.

21.4

	£
Sale proceeds	165,000
Less: Acquisition cost	47,500
Chargeable gain (before PPR exemption)	117,500

Samantha owned the house for a total of 21 years (252 months). For 7 years (84 months) the house was used partly for business purposes. The computation of the chargeable gain is as follows:

	£	£
Total gain (as above)		117,500
Less: PPR exemption:		
£117,500 × 168/252	78,333	
£117,500 × 84/252 × 4/5	31,333	109,666
Chargeable gain		7,834

Chapter 22

22.1

The allowable expenditure in relation to the porcelain is £9,850 (£10,000 in October 2011, plus £3,850 in February 2018, less £4,000 received July 2018). The computation of the gain arising in March 2023 is:

	£
Sale proceeds	23,500
Less: Allowable expenditure	9,850
Chargeable gain	13,650

22.2

The gain arising on the theft of the original necklace would have been:

	£
Disposal proceeds	14,000
Less: Acquisition cost	13,500
Chargeable gain	500

The allowable cost of the new necklace is reduced to £14,250 (£14,750 – £500). The gain arising on its disposal is as follows:

	£
Disposal proceeds	20,000
Less: Deemed acquisition cost	14,250
Chargeable gain	5,750

22.3

The gain on the disposal of the original building is computed as follows:

	£
Sale proceeds	261,400
Less: Acquisition cost	150,000
Chargeable gain	111,400

(a) £2,500 of the sale proceeds have been retained. Therefore £2,500 of the gain is immediately chargeable. The remaining £108,900 may be rolled-over against the cost of the new building, reducing its base cost to £150,000 (£258,900 – £108,900).

(b) £111,600 of the sale proceeds have been retained. This exceeds the gain. Therefore the whole gain is immediately chargeable and no part of the gain may be rolled-over. The base cost of the new building is the full £149,800.

(c) The entire sale proceeds have been spent on a replacement building. Therefore none of the gain is immediately chargeable and the entire gain may be rolled-over against the cost of the new building, reducing its base cost to £165,400 (£276,800 – £111,400).

22.4

The amount of the held-over gain is computed as follows:

	£	£
Disposal value		215,000
Less: Acquisition cost	91,500	
Enhancement expenditure	34,500	126,000
Held-over gain		89,000

The son's deemed acquisition cost is £126,000 (£215,000 – £89,000). However, if he paid his mother £150,000 for the asset, she would have a chargeable gain of £24,000 (£150,000 – £126,000) and the held-over gain would then be only £65,000 (£89,000 – £24,000). His deemed acquisition cost would become £150,000 (£215,000 – £65,000).

Chapter 23

23.1

(a) The year to 30 November 2022 is a single accounting period.

(b) The period from 1 October 2021 to 31 July 2022 does not exceed 12 months and is therefore a single accounting period.

(c) The period from 1 January 2023 to 31 January 2023 does not exceed 12 months and is therefore a single accounting period.

(d) The 33-month period to 31 August 2022 is divided into three accounting periods. These are the year to 30 November 2020, the year to 30 November 2021 and the nine months to 31 August 2022.

(e) The 18-month period to 30 September 2022 is divided into two accounting periods. These are the year to 31 March 2022 and the six months to 30 September 2022.

23.2

Assuming that the debentures on which the company is receiving interest were acquired for non-trading purposes, the interest receivable is a credit on a non-trading loan relationship. The amount of debenture interest for the accounting period (computed on the accruals basis) is aggregated with any other debits and credits arising on non-trading loan relationships. Net credits are chargeable to corporation tax. Net debits are eligible for tax relief (see Chapter 26).

The income tax of £2,160 (£8,640 × 20/80) deducted from the debenture interest paid to individuals must be accounted for to HMRC. But the gross amount of interest payable for the accounting period (computed on the accruals basis) is allowed either as an expense when computing the company's trading income or as a debit when computing the net credit or debit arising from non-trading loan relationships (depending on whether or not the debentures were issued for trade purposes).

23.3

The company may deduct £414,000 (£180,000 × 230%) in relation to this R&D expenditure when computing its trading income for the year to 31 March 2023. If the effect of this deduction is to create or increase a trading loss, the company may claim a payment from HMRC equal to the *lower* of 14.5% of the trading loss and 14.5% of £414,000 (i.e. £60,030). However, this payment is capped at £20,000 plus three times the company's liability to PAYE and NICs for the year.

23.4

The 17 months to 30 June 2022 will be divided into two accounting periods. These are the 12 months to 31 January 2022 and the five months to 30 June 2022. The taxable total profits for each accounting period are as follows:

	12 months to 31/1/22 £	5 months to 30/6/22 £
Trading income (time apportioned)	300,000	125,000
Debenture interest receivable	3,600	2,000
Income from property (time apportioned)	6,360	2,650
Chargeable gains	28,700	49,760
	338,660	179,410
Less: Qualifying charitable donations	12,000	-
Taxable total profits (TTP)	326,660	179,410

Notes:

(a) The debenture interest receivable is allocated on the accruals basis. Interest accrues at £400 per month. In the first accounting period, interest is due for the nine months from 1 May 2021 to 31 January 2022. In the second accounting period, interest is due for the five months from 1 February 2022 to 30 June 2022.

(b) The chargeable gains are allocated according to the dates of the disposals. Even though the two disposals are on consecutive days, they fall into different accounting periods.

(c) Dividends received do not form part of a company's taxable total profits.

(d) The Gift Aid donations are allocated according to the date of payment.

23.5

The taxable total profits for the year to 31 March 2023 are as follows:

	£
Trading income	1,561,400
Income from non-trading loan relationships (£1,820 + £3,670 + £1,980)	7,470
Chargeable gains	531,000
	2,099,870
Less: Qualifying charitable donations	9,000
Taxable total profits (TTP)	2,090,870

Notes:

(a) Interest receivable is taxed on the accruals basis.

(b) Dividends received do not form part of a company's taxable total profits.

(c) Gift Aid donations are relieved on the payments basis.

Chapter 24

24.1

(a) *Disposal of factory building*

	£	£
Sale proceeds		650,000
Less: Acquisition cost	300,000	
Enhancement expenditure	50,000	350,000
Unindexed gain		300,000
Less: Indexation allowance:		
(i) on acquisition cost		
$\frac{278.1 - 170.5}{170.5} = 0.631 \times £300,000$	189,300	
(ii) on enhancement expenditure		
$\frac{278.1 - 175.9}{175.9} = 0.581 \times £50,000$	29,050	218,350
Chargeable gain		81,650

(b) *Disposal of office building*

	£
Sale proceeds	1,100,000
Less: Acquisition cost	600,000
Unindexed gain	500,000
Less: Indexation allowance:	
$\frac{278.1 - 179.3}{179.3} = 0.551 \times £600,000$	330,600
	169,400
Less: Rolled-over gain (£169,400 − £50,000)	119,400
Chargeable gain	50,000

£50,000 of the sale proceeds have been retained and therefore £50,000 of the gain is immediately chargeable. The base cost of the replacement building is reduced to £930,600 (£1,050,000 − £119,400).

(c) *Disposal of computer system*

There is no chargeable gain or allowable loss in relation to this disposal, since gifts to charity are not chargeable disposals.

The disposal value for the computer in the company's plant and machinery capital allowances computation for the year to 31 March 2023 will be £nil, because the disposal takes the form of a charitable gift. This will generate a balancing allowance if the computer is being treated as a short-life asset (see Chapter 11).

(d) *Disposal of motor car*

There is no chargeable gain or allowable loss in relation to this disposal, since cars are not chargeable assets

When the car was acquired it entered either the main pool or the special rate pool, depending upon its emission rating. A disposal value of £80,000 is subtracted from the relevant pool in the year to 31 March 2023.

(e) *Disposal of plant and machinery*

This plant and machinery is a wasting chattel. Wasting chattels are normally exempt assets but this item has been used in business and capital allowances have been claimed, so the exemption does not apply. However, the loss of £40,000 is reduced to £nil by capital allowances of the same amount.

The company's plant and machinery capital allowances computation for the year to 31 March 2023 will show a disposal of £30,000.

(f) *Disposal of shares in Exxak plc*

The disposal is matched first against the 3,000 shares acquired within the previous nine days. These shares cost £36,000 and were sold for £30,000, so there is an allowable loss of £6,000.

The remaining 5,000 shares of the disposal are matched with shares taken from the s104 holding, as follows:

	No of shares	*Cost*	*Indexed cost*
		£	£
Bought 22 November 2002	4,000	16,000	16,000
Add: Indexation to December 2006			
$\dfrac{202.7 - 178.2}{178.2} \times £16,000$			2,200
			18,200
Bought 14 December 2006	6,000	30,000	30,000
s104 holding at 14 December 2006	10,000	46,000	48,200
Add: Indexation to December 2017			
$\dfrac{278.1 - 202.7}{202.7} \times £48,200$			17,929
			66,129
Sold 18 December 2022	(5,000)	(23,000)	(33,065)
s104 holding c/f at 18 December 2022	5,000	23,000	33,064

These 5,000 shares were sold for £50,000 so the chargeable gain arising on their disposal is £16,935 (£50,000 – £33,065).

(g)   *Disposal of Government securities*

There is no chargeable gain or allowable loss in relation to this disposal, since disposals of Government securities (or "gilt-edged" securities) by a company are dealt with by means of the loan relationships regime.

Assuming that the securities were not held for trade purposes, there will be a debit on non-trading loan relationships of £5,000.

Total chargeable gains are £148,585 (£81,650 + £50,000 + £16,935) and allowable losses are £6,000. Therefore net chargeable gains for the year to 31 March 2023 are £142,585.

24.2

(i)   *Disposal of shares in Epsilon plc*

The s104 holding is as follows:

	No of shares	*Cost* £	*Indexed cost* £
Bought January 1988	2,000	4,000	4,000
Add: Indexation to June 1991			
$\dfrac{134.1 - 103.3}{103.3} \times £4,000$			1,193
			5,193
Bought 27 June 1991	3,000	15,000	15,000
	5,000	19,000	20,193
Add: Indexation to March 2001			
$\dfrac{172.2 - 134.1}{134.1} \times £20,193$			5,737
			25,930
Bought 10 March 2001	4,000	28,000	28,000
	9,000	47,000	53,930
Add: Indexation to December 2017			
$\dfrac{278.1 - 172.2}{172.2} \times £53,930$			33,166
			87,096
Sold 12 September 2022	(4,500)	(23,500)	(43,548)
s104 holding c/f	4,500	23,500	43,548

These 4,500 shares were sold for £33,750 (4,500 × £7.50) so the unindexed gain arising on the disposal is £10,250 (£33,750 – £23,500). The available indexation allowance is £20,048 but this is restricted to £10,250 and the chargeable gain is zero.

(ii) *Disposal of watercolour paintings*

The gross disposal proceeds of the paintings are £5,750 (£5,175 × 100/90) and £6,450 (£5,805 × 100/90) respectively. The first painting is disposed of for less than £6,000 and is exempt. The gain arising on the disposal of the second painting is as follows:

	£
Sale proceeds	6,450
Less: Incidental costs of disposal	645
	5,805
Less: Acquisition cost	2,000
Unindexed gain	3,805
Less: Indexation allowance:	
$\frac{278.1 - 177.6}{177.6} = 0.566 \times £2,000$	1,132
Chargeable gain	2,673 (restricted to £450 × 5/3 = £750)

(iii) *Disposal of short lease*

When it was assigned, the lease had 5 years and 7 months left to run. The Sch. 8 percentage is 29.331 (26.722 + 7/12 × 4.473). The loss on the disposal is as follows:

	£
Sale proceeds	7,000
Less: Cost (29.331/72.770 × £20,000)	8,061
Allowable loss	(1,061)

(iv) *Disposal of freehold property*

Assuming that the building and the plant are used for business purposes, all except £15,000 of the gain on the disposal of the building may be held over. The computation is as follows:

	£
Sale proceeds	115,000
Less: Acquisition cost	50,000
Unindexed gain	65,000
Less: Indexation allowance:	
$\frac{278.1 - 187.4}{187.4} = 0.484 \times £50,000$	24,200
	40,800
Less: Held-over gain	25,800
Chargeable gain	15,000

Total gains are £15,750 (£750 + £15,000). Allowable losses are £1,061 so net gains are £14,689. These are reduced by capital losses brought forward of £6,689 to £8,000.

Chapter 25

25.1

(a) The accounting period coincides with FY2022 so the applicable rate of corporation tax is the FY2022 main rate of 19%. The liability is (£3,200,000 × 19%) = £608,000.

(b) The first three months of the accounting period fall into FY2021 (main rate 19%) and the remaining nine months fall into FY2022 (main rate also 19%). Therefore the corporation tax liability is (£3,200,000 × 3/12 × 19%) + (£3,200,000 × 9/12 × 19%) = £608,000.

(c) The first three months of the accounting period fall into FY2021 (main rate 19%) and the remaining seven months fall into FY2022 (main rate also 19%). Therefore the corporation tax liability is (£3,200,000 × 3/10 × 19%) + (£3,200,000 × 7/10 × 19%) = £608,000.

(d) The accounting period coincides with FY2023 so the applicable rate of corporation tax is the FY2023 main rate of 25%. The liability is (£3,200,000 × 25%) = £800,000.

(e) The first nine months of the accounting period fall into FY2022 (main rate 19%) and the remaining three months fall into FY2023 (main rate 25%). Therefore the corporation tax liability is (£3,200,000 × 9/12 × 19%) + (£3,200,000 × 3/12 × 25%) = £656,000

(f) The first seven months of the accounting period fall into FY2022 (main rate 19%) and the remaining month falls into FY2023 (main rate 25%). Therefore the corporation tax liability is (£3,200,000 × 7/8 × 19%) + (£3,200,000 × 1/8 × 25%) = £632,000.

25.2

(a) The year to 31 March 2023 is a single accounting period. Corporation tax is due nine months and one day after 31 March 2023, which is 1 January 2024.

(b) The six months to 30 November 2022 is a single accounting period. Corporation tax is due nine months and one day after 30 November 2022, which is 1 September 2023.

(c) The 21 months to 30 June 2022 breaks down into two accounting periods. These are the year to 30 September 2021 and the nine months to 30 June 2022. Corporation tax for the year to 30 September 2021 is payable on 1 July 2022. Corporation tax for the nine months to 30 June 2022 is payable on 1 April 2023.

(d) The 27 months to 31 August 2022 breaks down into three accounting periods. These are the year to 31 May 2021, the year to 31 May 2022 and the three months to 31 August 2022. Corporation tax for the year to 31 May 2021 is payable on 1 March 2022. Corporation tax for the year to 31 May 2022 is payable on 1 March 2023. Corporation tax for the three months to 31 August 2022 is payable on 1 June 2023.

25.3

(a) The accounting period coincides with FY2022 so the applicable rate of corporation tax is the FY2022 main rate of 19%. The corporation tax liability is (£1,800,000 × 19%) = £342,000.

The company is large for the accounting period (and was also large in the previous 12 months) so corporation tax is payable by instalments. There are four instalments of £85,500 each and they fall due on 14 October 2022, 14 January 2023, 14 April 2023 and 14 July 2023.

(b) The first three months of the accounting period fall into FY2021 (main rate 19%) and the remaining three months fall into FY2022 (main rate also 19%). Therefore the corporation tax liability is (£960,000 × 3/6 × 19%) + (£960,000 × 3/6 × 19%) = £182,400.

The company is large for the accounting period since it has profits which exceed $6/12 \times £1,500,000 = £750,000$. The company was also large in the previous 12 months, so tax is payable by instalments. There are two instalments of £91,200 each and they fall due on 14 July 2022 and 14 October 2022.

25.4

The first six months of the accounting period fall into FY2021 (main rate 19%) and the remaining six months fall into FY2022 (main rate also 19%).

(a) The company is large for the accounting period (and was also large in the previous 12 months) so corporation tax is payable by instalments. The tax liability is $(£4,500,000 \times 6/12 \times 19\%) + (£4,500,000 \times 6/12 \times 19\%) = £855,000$. There are four instalments of £213,750 each and they fall due on 14 April 2022, 14 July 2022, 14 October 2022 and 14 January 2023.

(b) The company is not large for the accounting period, since it has profits which do not exceed £1,500,000. The corporation tax liability is $(£1,250,000 \times 6/12 \times 19\%) + (£1,250,000 \times 6/12 \times 19\%) = £237,500$. This is payable as a single amount and falls due nine months and one day after 30 September 2022, which is 1 July 2023.

(c) The company's augmented profits are $(£1,250,000 + £300,000) = £1,550,000$. This exceeds £1,500,000 so the company is large for the accounting period. The corporation tax liability of £237,500 (see (b) above) is payable in four instalments of £59,375 each on 14 April 2022, 14 July 2022, 14 October 2022 and 14 January 2023.

25.5

The due date of payment is 1 June 2022 (nine months and one day after 31 August 2021). The final payment of £4,650 was made on 3 October 2022, which is 124 days late. The interest payable is:

$$£4,650 \times 3.25\% \times \frac{124}{366} = £51.20.$$

25.6

In each case, the company must pay corporation tax by instalments and the final instalment is due three months and 14 days after the end of the accounting period. Earlier instalments are payable on the usual quarterly dates if they occur before the date of the final instalment.

(a) Instalments are due on 14 January 2022, 14 April 2022, 14 July 2022 and 14 September 2022. The first three instalments are each equal to 3/11ths of the corporation tax liability for the period. The final instalment is equal to the remaining 2/11ths of the liability.

(b) Instalments are due on 14 August 2021, 14 November 2021 and 14 January 2022. The first two instalments are each equal to 3/8ths of the corporation tax liability for the period. The final instalment is equal to the remaining 2/8ths of the liability.

(c) Instalments are due on 14 July 2023 and 14 August 2023. The first instalment is equal to 3/4ths of the corporation tax liability for the period. The second (and final) instalment is equal to the remaining 1/4th of the liability.

(d) The final (and only) instalment falls due on 14 May 2023 and is equal to the whole of the corporation tax liability for the period. It is not possible to fit in any earlier instalments since the first such instalment would normally have been payable on 14 July 2023.

Chapter 26

26.1

	y/e 31/3/2021 £	y/e 31/3/2022 £	y/e 31/3/2023 £
Trading profits	-	23,800	40,300
Less: Trading losses b/f	-	23,800	8,400
Trading income	-	0	31,900
Less: Qualifying charitable donations	-	-	6,000
Taxable total profits (TTP)	0	0	25,900
Trading losses c/f	32,200	8,400	-
Unrelieved charitable donations	4,000	5,000	-

Notes:

(i) The tax liability for the year to 31 March 2022 is now £nil. Before trading loss relief, TTP for the year would have been £18,800 (£23,800 – £5,000). The accounting period coincides with FY2021 (main rate 19%) so tax saved is (£18,800 × 19%) = £3,572.

(ii) The year to 31 March 2023 coincides with FY2022 (main rate 19%) so the tax liability is now (£25,900 × 19%) = £4,921. Before deducting trading loss relief, TTP for the year would have been (£40,300 – £6,000) = £34,300. The liability would have been (£34,300 × 19%) = £6,517, so tax saved is (£6,517 – £4,921) = £1,596.

(iii) Total tax saved is (£3,572 + £1,596) = £5,168. This represents an effective rate of relief on the trading loss of £32,200 of 16.05%.

(iv) However, the company could claim (by 31 March 2024) that only £18,800 of the carried-forward loss should be relieved in the year to 31 March 2022. This would leave enough profit to cover the charitable donations (which would therefore not be wasted). Losses carried forward to the year to 31 March 2023 would become £13,400, reducing the tax liability for that year to (£20,900 × 19%) = £3,971. This would save additional tax of (£4,921 – £3,971) = £950 and so increase the total tax saving to (£5,168 + £950) = £6,118. The effective rate of relief on the trading loss of £32,200 would then be 19%.

26.2

	£
Trading income	-
Income from property	190,200
Chargeable gains	45,540
	235,740
Less: Trade loss relief against total profits	232,300
	3,440
Less: Qualifying charitable donations	3,440
Taxable total profits (TTP)	0
Unrelieved charitable donations	20,560

26.3

Statements (a) and (d) are false. Statement (c) is true. Statement (b) is false for trading losses incurred before 1 April 2017 but is true for trading losses incurred on or after that date. The relevant loss relief rules in TCGA 1992 and CTA 2010 are as follows:

(a) Capital losses which are carried forward may be relieved only against future chargeable gains, not against future trading profits.

(b) Carried-forward trading losses which were incurred before 1 April 2017 may be relieved only against future profits of the same trade, not against future chargeable gains. However, carried-forward trading losses incurred on or after that date may be set against the total profits of later accounting periods (including the chargeable gains of those periods).

(c) Trading losses may be relieved against total profits (including chargeable gains) of the accounting period in which the loss is incurred.

(d) Capital losses are relieved against chargeable gains of the same accounting period but not against trading profits of that period.

26.4

	y/e 31/10/2020	eight months to 30/6/2021	y/e 30/6/2022
	£	£	£
Trading income	59,700	73,600	-
Chargeable gains	8,400	-	48,700
	68,100	73,600	48,700
Less: Trade loss relief (a)	-	-	48,700
	68,100	73,600	0
Less: Trade loss relief (b)	22,700	73,600	-
	45,400	0	0
Less: Qualifying charitable donations	1,000	-	-
Taxable total profits (TTP)	44,400	0	0
Trading losses c/f	-	-	10,700
Unrelieved charitable donations	-	1,000	1,000

Notes:

(i) The loss-making period did not end between 1 April 2020 and 31 March 2022, so the trading loss may be carried back for only 12 months. The period to 30 June 2021 is wholly within these 12 months. But only four months out of the year to 31 October 2020 fall within the 12 months so maximum relief available in this year is £22,700 (£68,100 × 4/12).

(ii) Trading losses of £145,000 (£48,700 + £73,600 + £22,700) are relieved against total profits, leaving losses to carry forward of £10,700.

26.5

The company could claim that the trading loss should be relieved against the total profits of the loss-making period. This would absorb £200,000 of the loss. If it so wished, the company could then claim further that the loss should be carried back and relieved against the total profits of the previous 12 months. This would absorb another £400,000. The remaining £100,000 would be carried forward.

If both claims were made, £600,000 of the loss would be relieved at 19% (main rate for FY2021 and FY2022) and £100,000 would be relieved at 25% (main rate for FY2023). Total tax saved would be **£139,000** (£600,000 × 19% + £100,000 × 25%). Alternatively, the company could make only the first claim and then carry forward the remaining £500,000 of the loss. Total tax saved would be **£163,000** (£200,000 × 19% + £500,000 × 25%). Or the company could decide to make neither claim and simply carry forward the entire £700,000, which would save tax of **£175,000** (£700,000 × 25%).

It is clear that carrying forward the entire loss is the most beneficial option, but this assumes that the expected profit of £1,000,000 in the year to 31 March 2024 is actually achieved. This approach also involves a delay in obtaining the benefits of loss relief. If there is some doubt about the profit forecast or if the company needs more immediate loss relief, the other alternatives should be considered.

Chapter 27

27.1

(a), (d) and (e) are associates, (b) and (c) are not.

27.2

The top five shareholders are Sejanus (with Apicata) 1,020 shares, Claudius (with Livia) 590 shares, Agrippa 300 shares, Cleopatra 300 shares and Tiberius 200 shares, totalling 2,410 shares. So the company is not under the control of five or fewer shareholders.

Sejanus is ranked as a director since he is a manager and, with his wife, owns 20.4% of the share capital. So the directors are Sejanus (with Apicata) 1,020 shares, Claudius (with Livia) 590 shares, Agrippa 300 shares, Cleopatra 300 shares, Tiberius 200 shares and Gaius 200 shares, totalling 2,610 shares. The company is under the control of its participator-directors and is a close company.

27.3

(a)   The director owns more than 5% of the company's share capital so the loan is taxable. The company must pay tax of £4,050 (33.75% of £12,000) by 1 January 2024 (unless the loan is repaid before then). Once paid, this tax is not refundable until nine months and one day after the end of the accounting period in which the loan is repaid or written off. The director will be subject to income tax on loan interest calculated at the official rate. If the loan is eventually written off (wholly or partly) the director will be taxed on the amount written off and the company will be denied any tax relief in relation to this amount.

(b)   The director will be subject to income tax on a benefit in kind of £4,800. But if the ticket had been given to a shareholder who was not a director or other employee of the company, it would have been treated as a distribution. The cost of the ticket would have been disallowed in the company's accounts and the shareholder would have been charged to income tax as if he or she had received a dividend of £4,800.

Chapter 28

28.1

(a)   Each company has two "related 51% group companies", so the profits limits used to determine whether or not corporation tax is payable by instalments are divided by (2 + 1) = 3. Therefore payment by instalments will be required for any of these companies which has augmented profits exceeding £500,000 (£1,500,000 ÷ 3) per annum.

(b) When calculating the augmented profits of Headco Ltd for payment by instalments purposes, dividends received from Armco1 Ltd and Armco2 Ltd are ignored.

(c) Transfer pricing legislation may apply to transactions between the companies, though small and medium-sized companies are generally exempt from this legislation.

(d) The companies form a 75% group, so trading losses and other items may be surrendered by one of the companies to either of the other companies.

(e) Chargeable assets are transferred between the companies on a no-gain, no-loss basis. A gain or loss arising in one company may be treated as if it had arisen in one of the other companies.

28.2

Dividends received are not charged to corporation tax (other than non-exempt foreign dividends), so the taxable total profits of U Ltd for the year are (£485,000 + £12,000 – £17,000) = £480,000.

The first three months of the accounting period fall into FY2021 (main rate 19%). The remaining nine months fall into FY2022 (main rate also 19%). So the corporation tax liability for the year is (£480,000 × 3/12 × 19%) + (£480,000 × 9/12 × 19%) = £91,200.

U Ltd has two "related 51% group companies" (the two active subsidiaries). Therefore the usual £1,500,000 profits limit for payment by instalments purposes is divided by (2 + 1) = 3, giving a profits limit of £500,000.

Taxable total profits for the year plus dividends received (other than dividends from subsidiaries) are (£480,000 + £30,000) = £510,000. This augmented profits figure exceeds £500,000, therefore U Ltd is "large" for the year to 31 December 2022.

If the company was also large for the year to 31 December 2021, the corporation tax liability of £91,200 is payable in four instalments of £22,800 each. These fall due on 14 July 2022, 14 October 2022, 14 January 2023 and 14 April 2023.

However, if the company was not large in the year to 31 December 2021, the corporation tax liability of £91,200 for the year to 31 December 2022 is payable nine months and one day after 31 December 2022, which is 1 October 2023.

28.3

Basenote Ltd has current year trading losses of £90,000 and excess donations of £1,000, giving a total of £91,000. Apexine Ltd has available profits of £115,000 (£120,000 + £7,000 – £12,000) so the maximum group relief that may be claimed is £91,000.

If Basenote Ltd also had carried-forward trading losses of £20,000 from the previous year, £3,000 of these losses could be set against the income from property and the remaining £17,000 would then be eligible for group relief. Excess donations would now be £4,000, so maximum group relief would be (£90,000 + £4,000 + £17,000) = £111,000.

28.4

(a) A1 Ltd owns 90% of A2 Ltd and (indirectly) 72% of A3 Ltd and 63% of A4 Ltd. So A1 Ltd and A2 Ltd form a 75% group. A2 Ltd and A3 Ltd form another 75% group.

(b) A1 Ltd, A2 Ltd and A3 Ltd form a capital gains group. A2 Ltd does not own at least 75% of A4 Ltd, so A4 Ltd is not a member of the capital gains group.

28.5

The trading loss of PP Ltd which is available for group relief is £84,000 (i.e. £96,000 less potential relief against total profits of £12,000). This is shared between the consortium members as follows:

	QQ Ltd £	RR Ltd £	SS Ltd £
Share of PP Ltd available loss	26,880	29,400	19,320
Available profits	59,000	47,000	14,000
Maximum group relief claim	26,880	29,400	14,000

Chapter 29

29.1

(a)	standard rate	(b)	zero rate
(c)	exempt	(d)	standard rate
(e)	standard rate	(f)	zero rate
(g)	reduced rate	(h)	exempt
(i)	exempt	(j)	standard rate
(k)	standard rate	(l)	zero rate
(m)	zero rate	(n)	standard rate.

29.2

(a) The value of the supply is £340. VAT charged is 20% of £340 = £68 and the consideration for the supply is £408.

(b) The value of the supply is £333.20 (£340 less 2%). VAT charged is 20% of £333.20 = £66.64 and the consideration for the supply is £399.84.

(c) The value of the supply is £340. VAT charged is 20% of £340 = £68 and the consideration for the supply is £408.

29.3

(a) Lorna must register since her taxable turnover exceeds the registration threshold.

(b) Mike must register since his aggregate taxable turnover exceeds the registration threshold.

(c) No-one need register. The partnership of "Pat and Phil" is not the same person as "Phil" so the turnover of the two businesses is not aggregated.

(d) The taxable "person" in this case is the company (not the shareholders) and therefore the company must register.

29.4

(a) She is not a taxable person, cannot register for VAT and cannot reclaim input tax.

(b) She is a taxable person and must register for VAT. She must account for output tax and may reclaim input tax.

(c) She is a taxable person and must register for VAT unless granted an exemption by HMRC. If she registers she may reclaim input tax. If she is granted exemption she will not be able to reclaim input tax but she will avoid the administrative burden which is associated with VAT registration.

29.5

(a)   VAT is charged on the import of goods into Great Britain from outside the UK at the same rate as if those goods had been supplied within the UK. As long as the UK business provides its VAT registration number to the overseas supplier, this VAT is collected by means of a reverse charge. The UK business is responsible for the output VAT concerned and declares this output tax on its next VAT return. However, from the point of view of the UK business, this tax is also input tax and (if deductible) may be reclaimed on the same VAT return.

(b)   Exports of goods from Great Britain to a destination outside the UK are zero-rated.

See Chapter 29 for more details of the VAT treatment of imports and exports, including the special rules related to Northern Ireland.

Chapter 30

30.1

(a)

	£	£
Output tax:		
Standard-rated supplies ((£14,400 + (£14,400 × 97.5%)) × 20%)		5,688
Supply invoiced 15 November 2022 (£4,800 × 20%)		960
Fuel scale charge (1/6 × £402)		67
		6,715
Input tax:		
Standard-rated goods (£9,280 × 20%)	1,856	
Standard-rated services (£5,200 × 20%)	1,040	
Car maintenance (£280 × 20%)	56	
Car fuel (£520 × 20%)	104	
Non-current asset (1/6 × £14,100)	2,350	5,406
Payable to HMRC		1,309

Notes:

(i)   Output tax is calculated on the selling price less any cash discounts actually taken.

(ii)   Output tax is payable in relation to the sale to the bankrupt customer. Bad debt relief cannot be claimed until at least 6 months have elapsed.

(iii)   The tax point of the £4,800 supply is the invoice date (earlier than the date of payment or the date on which the goods were made available).

(iv)   Input tax cannot be reclaimed in relation to a car not used wholly for business purposes.

(b)   The flat-rate scheme for small businesses (FRS) is available to businesses with a taxable turnover which is not expected to exceed £150,000 in the next 12 months. Toucan Ltd seems likely to satisfy this requirement. Membership of the scheme would allow Toucan Ltd to calculate its VAT liability as a flat-rate percentage of its total turnover and so avoid the need to keep detailed records of input tax and output tax. The FRS operates as follows:

(i)   Output tax is charged to customers at the normal rate for the supply. Similarly, input tax is paid to suppliers at the normal rate. However, the output tax charged to customers is not paid over to HMRC and (in general) input tax is not recoverable.

(ii) In each tax period, a flat-rate percentage is applied to the VAT-inclusive turnover for the period. The result of this calculation is the amount of VAT payable to HMRC.

(iii) Input tax on the purchase of non-current assets costing at least £2,000 (including VAT) can be reclaimed in the usual way.

If Toucan Ltd joined the FRS, its average monthly VAT liability would be £1,311 (£11,500 × 120% × 9.5%). If the company did not join the scheme, the average liability would be £1,200 ((£11,500 - £5,500) × 20%). In both cases, input tax could be reclaimed on the expected non-current asset purchase of £5,000. It would appear, therefore, that Toucan Ltd would not benefit from joining the FRS unless administrative savings exceeded £111 per month.

30.2

Input tax reclaimed is £798 × 1/6 = £133.00. The scale figure for this motor car for a 3-month period is £507, so output tax of £507 × 1/6 = £84.50 must be accounted for. The only alternative would be for Sebastian to reclaim no input tax at all in relation to car fuel, but this would increase his VAT liability for the quarter by £48.50.

30.3

Quarter to	VAT return late	VAT paid late	Surcharge period ends	Penalty
31 March 2021	Yes	Yes	31 March 2022	None
30 June 2021	No	No	31 March 2022	None
30 September 2021	Yes	No	30 September 2022	None
31 December 2021	Yes	Yes	31 December 2022	2%
31 March 2022	Yes	Yes	31 March 2023	5%
30 June 2022	No	No	31 March 2023	None
30 September 2022	No	No	31 March 2023	None
31 December 2022	Yes	Yes	31 December 2023	10%

Note:

A surcharge period began on 1 April 2021. This would have ended on 31 March 2022 but has now been extended four times. The current end-date is 31 December 2023 but any further defaults before then will extend the period again. Any more penalties in this period will be charged at 15%.

Chapter 31

31.1

	Value before AE £	AE for 2022-23 £	AE for 2021-22 £	Value after AE £
Gift to grandson (exempt as a small gift)	-	-	-	-
Gift on marriage (£3,000 – £1,000)	2,000	2,000	-	-
Gift to husband (spouse exemption)	-	-	-	-
Gift to relevant property trust	10,000	1,000	3,000	6,000
Gift to Labour Party (exempt)	-	-	-	-
	12,000	3,000	3,000	6,000

31.2

(a) exempt   (b) chargeable   (c) PET.

31.3

The total of transfers brought forward in the seven years to date is £281,000, leaving £44,000 of the nil-rate band to set against the current transfer.

(a) If the trustees pay the tax, the gross value of the transfer is £80,000 and the IHT due is £44,000 @ 0% + £36,000 @ 20% = £7,200, payable on 30 June 2023.

(b) If Nicholas pays the tax, the net value of the transfer is £80,000. The gross value and the tax due are as follows:

	Net £	Gross £	Tax £
£44,000 grossed up @ 0%	44,000	44,000	0
£36,000 grossed up @ 20%	36,000	45,000	9,000
Totals	80,000	89,000	9,000

    The tax due is £9,000, payable on 30 June 2023.

31.4

The value of each gift after deduction of exemptions is as follows:

		Value before AE £	AE for current year £	AE for previous year £	Value after AE £
2015-16	Daughter (£500,000 – £5,000)	495,000	3,000	3,000	489,000
2016-17	Relevant property trust	497,000	3,000	-	494,000

Lifetime tax liability

The gift to Martha's daughter was a PET, so no lifetime tax was payable. The lifetime tax on the gift to the trust was £42,250, payable on 31 October 2017 and calculated as follows:

	Net £	Gross £	Tax £
£325,000 grossed up @ 0%	325,000	325,000	0
£169,000 grossed up @ 20%	169,000	211,250	42,250
Totals	494,000	536,250	42,250

Note that the nil-rate band used in the calculation of a lifetime tax liability is the nil-rate band on the date of the transfer, <u>not</u> the nil-rate band on the date of death. However, in this case, the nil-rate band was £325,000 on the date of the transfer and remained at £325,000 until the date of death.

Tax liability on death

(i) *Transfer made on 31 March 2016*

    The gross value of this transfer is £489,000 and there were no other chargeable transfers in the seven years ending on the date of the transfer. Tax due at death rates for 1 January 2023:

		£
£325,000 @ 0%		0
£164,000 @ 40%		65,600
		65,600
<u>Less</u>: Taper relief (6-7 years) @ 80%		52,480
		13,120
<u>Less</u>: Lifetime tax paid		0
IHT payable by daughter on 31 July 2023		13,120

(ii) *Transfer made on 1 April 2017*

The gross value of this transfer is £536,250 and previous gross chargeable transfers in the seven years ending on the date of the transfer (2 April 2010 to 1 April 2017) were £489,000, using the whole of the nil-rate band. Tax due at death rates applicable on 1 January 2023:

	£
£536,250 @ 40%	214,500
<u>Less</u>: Taper relief (5-6 years) @ 60%	128,700
	85,800
<u>Less</u>: Lifetime tax paid	42,250
IHT payable by trustees on 31 July 2023	43,550

31.5

The quarter-up rule gives 572p + 1/4 × (588p − 572p) = 576p. The average of the highest and lowest recorded bargains is 575p, so the shares are valued at 575p each (£5,750 for 1,000 shares).

Chapter 32

32.1

(a) Jean-Paul meets the first automatic UK test and does not meet any of the automatic overseas tests. Therefore he meets the automatic residence test and is UK resident for tax year 2022-23. He is liable to pay UK income tax on all of his income for the year, including overseas income. However, he is not domiciled in the UK and so he may claim the remittance basis. If he does this, his UK income (if any) will be fully liable to UK income tax but his overseas income will be liable only to the extent that it is remitted to the UK.

(b) Pierre does not meet any of the automatic UK tests. He meets the second and third automatic overseas tests. Therefore he does not meet the automatic residence test and he is not UK resident for the year unless he meets the sufficient ties test. Assuming this is not the case, he will be liable to pay UK income tax only on his UK income for the year (presumably £nil).

(c) Carole meets the second automatic UK test. She does not meet any of the automatic overseas tests. Therefore she is UK resident for tax year 2022-23. She will pay UK income tax on all of her income for the year (e.g. retirement pensions, investment income etc.). There appears not to be any overseas income but any such income would also be chargeable to UK income tax.

32.2

(a) *In tax year 2021-22*, Amy meets the first automatic UK test and does not meet any of the automatic overseas tests. Therefore she would normally be regarded as UK resident for the tax year. However, she is leaving the UK to work overseas (presumably full-time) and she will be non-UK resident in 2022-23 because she will meet the third automatic overseas test. In these circumstances, the split-year treatment applies. Amy will be treated as UK resident until 31 December 2021 and as non-UK resident for the remainder of the tax year.

   She will receive the full personal allowance for 2021-22. Her income for UK tax purposes after 31 December 2021 will consist only of any income arising in the UK (e.g. rents from letting her house whilst away). Her Australian earnings will not be subject to UK tax.

(b) *In tax year 2022-23*, Amy meets none of the automatic UK tests and therefore she is not UK resident. Her Australian salary will not be subject to UK tax and she will be taxed only on her UK income (if any). As a citizen of the UK, she is entitled to personal allowances.

(c) *In tax year 2023-24*, Amy is in the UK for 97 days. She meets none of the automatic overseas tests and presumably she meets at least the second automatic UK test. Therefore she would normally be regarded as UK resident for the year. However, she was not UK resident in the previous year and she is arriving to live and work full-time in the UK. The split-year treatment will apply and Amy will be treated as non-UK resident until 31 December 2023 but as UK resident for the remainder of the tax year.

   She will receive the full personal allowance for 2023-24. Her income for UK tax purposes up until 31 December 2023 will consist only of any income arising in the UK. Once again, her Australian earnings will not be subject to UK tax.

32.3

(a) The domicile of an individual is the country or state which is considered to be the individual's permanent home. It is not possible to have more than one domicile at a time. In some circumstances, an individual who is not domiciled in the UK on a certain date is nonetheless treated as UK domiciled on that date for tax purposes. The "deemed domicile" rules for inheritance tax are different than the rules for income tax and capital gains tax. (See text for further details).

(b) If a UK resident is not UK domiciled, the remittance basis may apply so that foreign income is taxed only to the extent that the income is remitted to the UK. Similarly, gains arising from disposals of assets situated overseas may be taxed on the remittance basis. Also, an individual who is not domiciled in the UK is liable to inheritance tax only in relation to property which is situated in the UK. (See text for further details).

32.4

(a) A UK resident company may wish to migrate overseas (to a low-tax regime) in order to avoid paying UK corporation tax on its worldwide profits. This is only possible if the company moves its central management and control to an overseas location. (See text for further details).

(b) If a UK resident company makes this election, it applies to all of the company's overseas branches and is irrevocable. Although the profits of the company's overseas branches will be exempt from UK corporation tax, no tax relief will be available for any foreign branch losses that occur. A further disadvantage is that the company's overseas branches will fall within the controlled foreign company (CFC) regime and this may result in a CFC charge.

32.5

See text.

32.6

(a)

	UK	Overseas	Total
	£	£	£
Trading income	2,120,000		2,120,000
Property income £98,000 × 100/70		140,000	140,000
Taxable total profits (TTP)	2,120,000	140,000	2,260,000
Corporation tax @ 19%	402,800	26,600	429,400
Less: Unilateral DTR		(26,600)	(26,600)
Corporation tax due	402,800	-	402,800

Double tax relief is restricted to the UK tax payable on the foreign income. The remaining £15,400 (£42,000 – £26,600) of foreign tax is unrelieved. This arises because the foreign tax rate exceeds the UK rate by 11% (11% × £140,000 = £15,400). The unrelieved foreign tax is lost.

(b)

If the overseas income consisted of trading income from an overseas branch, the unrelieved foreign tax of £15,400 could be carried back for up to three years or carried forward without time limit. The unrelieved tax would then be treated as foreign tax paid in respect of the overseas branch in the accounting period to which it was carried back or carried forward. If the UK rate of tax exceeded the foreign rate of tax in any such accounting period, this would offer an opportunity to relieve some or all of the unrelieved foreign tax.

However, the company may have elected that the profits of all of its overseas branches should be exempt from UK corporation tax. In this case, the overseas income would be totally ignored in the company's tax computation and there would be no relief for any foreign tax paid.

Answers to review questions

Set A

Question A1

(a)

	Total	Non-savings	Savings
	£	£	£
Income from property	52,770	52,770	
Debenture interest (£416 × 100/80)	520		520
Total income	53,290	52,770	520
Less: Personal allowance	12,570	12,570	
Taxable income	40,720	40,200	520

Tax due on non-savings income is (£37,700 × 20%) + (£2,500 × 40%) = £8,540.00. Daniel is a higher-rate taxpayer so the savings allowance is £500 and the tax due on savings income is (£500 × 0%) + (£20 × 40%) = £8.00. Tax borne is (£8,540.00 + £8.00) = £8,548.00, but tax deducted at source is £104.00 so tax payable is (£8,548.00 – £104.00) = £8,444.00.

(b) David's employment income is as follows:

	£
Salary	88,000
Less: Pension contributions (4%)	3,520
	84,480
Car (20% + 5% + 4%) = 29% × (£35,100 – £5,000)	8,729
Fuel 29% × £25,300	7,337
	100,546

Total income is £101,786 (£100,546 + £1,240) so the personal allowance is reduced by £893 to £11,677 (£12,570 – £893). Taxable non-savings income is £88,869 (£100,546 – £11,677) and the tax liability is (£37,700 × 20%) + (£51,169 × 40%) = £28,007.60. The dividends fall within the dividend allowance of £2,000 and are therefore taxed at the dividend nil rate. Tax payable is (£28,007.60 – £27,800.00) = £207.60.

(c) The £100 per month contributed towards private fuel is not deductible when calculating the taxable fuel benefit. It would be better if the £100 per month were payable for the private use of the car. It would then become deductible.

(d)   The taxable benefit in relation to the beneficial loan is (£12,000 + £6,000)/2 = £9,000 × 2% × 10/12 = £150. Therefore the total employment income is £58,420. The personal allowance of £12,570 reduces this to £45,850 and the income tax liability is (£37,700 × 20%) + (£8,150 × 40%) = £10,800.00. Tax repayable is (£10,830.00 − £10,800.00) = £30.00.

(e)   There would have been no tax liability on the interest-free loan if it had not exceeded £10,000.

(f)   Primary Class 1 NICs are ((£50,270 − £11,908) × 13.25%) + ((£88,000 − £50,270) × 3.25%) = £6,309.19. Secondary Class 1 NICs are ((£88,000 − £9,100) × 15.05%) = £11,874.45. The employer is also liable to Class 1A NICs of ((£8,729 + £7,337) × 15.05%) = £2,417.93.

(g)   MCA is available because at least one of the couple was born before 6 April 1935 and they are legally married. The MCA will be claimed by the husband because they were married before 5 December 2005. The MCA for 2022-23 is normally £9,415 and results in a tax reduction of £941.50. But his income (private pension and state pension) exceeds the limit of £31,400 so the MCA will be reduced by £1 for each £2 over the limit, down to a minimum of £3,640.

Question A2

	£	£
Trading income (working)		73,176
Property income (£14,400 − £1,480))		12,920
Total income		86,096
Less: Interest paid	875	
Partnership loss (£12,600 × 7/12 × 20%)	1,470	2,345
Net income		83,751
Less: Personal allowance		12,570
Taxable income		71,181

Income tax due	
37,700 @ 20%	7,540.00
33,481 @ 40%	13,392.40
71,181	20,932.40
Less: Mortgage interest relief (£5,000 × 20%)	1,000.00
Income tax liability	19,932.40

Working: Adjusted trading profit

	£
Net profit per accounts	70,200
Depreciation	2,300
Motor expenses (£3,300 × 4,000/12,000)	1,100
Legal fees	1,460
Office expenses (£4,200 × 1/6)	(700)
Capital allowances (£14,800 × 18% × 8/12 × 8,000/12,000)	(1,184)
	73,176

Question A3

(a)/(b)

		£
2019-20	year ended 5 April 2020	35,160
2020-21	year ended 5 April 2021	32,880
2021-22	1 August 2020 to 31 July 2021 (£32,880 × 8/12) + £16,240	38,160
2022-23	year ended 31 July 2022	54,120

Overlap profits of £21,920 arise in respect of the eight months from 1 August 2020 to 5 April 2021.

Question A4

The taxation treatment of these transactions depends upon whether they constitute a trade. If so, any trading profit will be charged to income tax and that profit will be calculated in accordance with ITTOIA 2005. If not, the sales of the barrels will be treated as chargeable disposals for capital gains tax purposes and any gains will be charged to CGT in accordance with TCGA 1992.

ITA 2007 states that a "trade" includes "*any venture in the nature of trade*". This definition has been interpreted in numerous tax cases over the years and a set of criteria has emerged which can be used to distinguish between trading and non-trading activities. These criteria are known as the "badges of trade". In this particular case:

(a) *Subject matter*. It appears that the subject matter of the transaction is of a type normally associated with a trading venture, rather than of a type more normally associated with investments or personal consumption.

(b) *Frequency of transactions*. There was only one purchase but there were several sales. The fact that sales were made to a number of different garden centres gives the impression of trading.

(c) *Length of ownership*. This was a fairly short-term venture. Most of the barrels had been sold within a few months and this again gives the impression of trading.

(d) *Supplementary work*. The barrels were sawn in half and Bernard and Gerald canvassed garden centres in the hope of finding customers. These activities constitute supplementary work and support the view that they were trading.

(e) *Motive*. It seems clear that the barrels were bought with only one view in mind - resale at a profit. This is a clear indicator of trading.

(f) *Acquisition*. The barrels were not inherited or gifted. They were purchased by Bernard and Gerald. This supports the view that they were trading.

It seems clear that this was an adventure in the nature of trade. Therefore Bernard and Gerald will be charged to income tax on their trading profits in tax years 2022-23 and 2023-24.

Question A5

(a)   The year to 31 December 2022 forms the basis for tax year 2022-23, which is the final year of assessment for Sean's business. The trading loss of £23,100 for the year is increased by overlap profits of £4,600 to £27,700.

(b)   The loss cannot be carried forward because the business has ceased trading. Therefore the only reliefs available are relief against total income and terminal loss relief.

(c)   Sean could claim to relieve the trading loss against his total income of tax year 2022-23, tax year 2021-22 or both of those years. However, these claims would waste personal allowances. Total income for 2022-23 is £13,000. A loss relief claim for that year only would have to be for £13,000, leaving nothing against which to set the personal allowance. Similarly, total income for 2021-22 is £16,700 (£3,700 + £13,000) so a loss relief claim for that year only would also waste the personal allowance. A claim for both years would waste the whole of the personal allowance in one year and most of the personal allowance in the other year.

(d)   The trading loss of £27,700 is eligible for terminal loss relief because it is incurred in the final 12 months of trading. The terminal loss would be set against the trading profits (if any) of tax years 2022-23, 2021-22, 2020-21 and 2019-20, in that order. Loss relief would be £3,700 in 2021-22, £18,900 in 2020-21 and £5,100 (£27,700 – £3,700 – £18,900) in 2019-20. Since Sean's property income absorbs the personal allowance in all of those years, there would be no waste of allowances and the loss would be relieved at basic rate (20%).

(e)   Therefore the most beneficial way to relieve the trading loss is to make a terminal loss claim.

Set B

Question B1

(a)/(b)

(1)   The £63,000 cost of replacing the damaged floor is a repair. This is revenue expenditure not enhancement expenditure and is therefore not allowable in the computation of the chargeable gain. The gain is calculated as follows:

	£
Sale proceeds	522,000
Less: Allowable expenditure (£258,000 + £99,000)	357,000
Chargeable gain	165,000

Rollover relief will be available if the replacement warehouse was acquired no more than 12 months before 19 May 2022 but will be restricted if it cost less than £522,000. We need to know the cost and the precise acquisition date of the replacement warehouse.

(2)   This is a part disposal. The fact that one-fifth of the land (in area terms) has been sold is not relevant and it is necessary to apply the A/(A + B) part disposal fraction. A is £81,700 and B is £268,000 so (A + B) is £349,700.

	£
Sale proceeds	81,700
Less: Cost (£167,400 × (£81,700/£349,700))	39,109
Chargeable gain	42,591

(3) The s104 holding is as follows:

	No of shares	Cost
		£
Bought 2 June 2014	50,000	96,000
Bonus issue 1 June 2019	75,000	-
	125,000	96,000
Sold 24 September 2022	(70,000)	(53,760)
s104 holding c/f	55,000	42,240

The chargeable gain is (£367,500 – £53,760) = £313,740. Business asset disposal relief might be available but this will depend on whether Rolling Ltd is the taxpayer's personal company. We need to know whether he has held at least 5% of the company's ordinary shares (and voting rights etc.) for the last two years. We also need to know whether he has made any previous BADR claims and (if so) how much of the BADR lifetime limit of £1m remains available.

(4) The shares are valued for CGT purposes at (698p + (710p – 698p)/2) = 704p. Therefore the market value of the shares on the date of disposal is (24,000 × £7.04) = £168,960 and the gain arising is (£168,960 – £76,800) = £92,160. There is no question of gift relief or business asset disposal relief because Sugar plc is not a trading company.

Question B2

(a) The disposal is matched first with the 1,000 shares bought in the following 30 days. These shares were sold for £4,600 (1,000/5,000 × £23,000) and they were bought for £4,400, which gives a gain of £200. The disposal is then matched with 4,000 of the shares in the Section 104 holding, as follows:

	No of shares	Cost
		£
Bought 18 August 2009	3,000	6,000
Bought 19 September 2016	2,000	5,000
	5,000	11,000
Sold 13 March 2023 (4/5ths)	(4,000)	(8,800)
s104 holding c/f	1,000	2,200

These 4,000 shares were sold for £18,400 (4,000/5,000 × £23,000) so the gain on their disposal is £9,600 (£18,400 – £8,800). The total chargeable gain is £9,800 (£200 + £9,600).

(b) Sally's net gains for 2022-23 are £31,900. Deducting losses brought forward of £11,200 leaves £20,700. Deducting the annual exemption of £12,300 leaves £8,400. The CGT payable is calculated as follows:

(i) Unused basic rate band is £17,700 (£37,700 – £20,000). This exceeds £8,400 so CGT payable is (10% × £8,400) = £840.

(ii) Unused basic rate band is £2,500 (£37,700 – £35,200). So the amount of CGT payable is (10% × £2,500) + (20% × £5,900) = £1,430.

(iii) There is no unused basic rate band. So CGT payable is (20% × £8,400) = £1,680.

Question B3

(1) Assuming that Jerome and his wife live together, this transfer between spouses is made at a disposal value which gives rise to neither a gain nor a loss (i.e. £112,800). The base cost of the house for Jerome's wife is therefore also £112,800.

(2) The gain arising on the gift of shares (before gift relief) is £59,400 (£98,400 – £39,000). Gift relief is restricted to £59,400 × (£460,000/£540,000) = £50,600. Therefore the chargeable gain is £8,800 (£59,400 – £50,600). The son's base cost is (£98,400 – £50,600) = £47,800.

(3) The bracelet is a chattel. The chargeable gain is £10,100 (£12,200 – £2,100). This is less than the gain given by the marginal relief formula i.e. 5/3 × (£12,200 – £6,000) = £10,333. The granddaughter's base cost is £12,200.

(4) The value of the entire ten acres on the date of the gift is (£78,400 + £33,600) = £112,000. So the cost of the nine acres which are being given to Jerome's brother is £26,460 (£37,800 × (£78,400/£112,000)) and the chargeable gain is £51,940 (£78,400 – £26,460). The brother's base cost is £78,400.

Question B4

(a) *Disposal of flat*

	£
Sale proceeds	142,000
Less: Incidental costs of disposal	3,700
	138,300
Less: Part cost: $\frac{£142,000}{£142,000 + £130,000} \times £80,000$	(41,765)
Part conversion costs: $\frac{£142,000}{£142,000 + £130,000} \times £32,000$	(16,706)
Chargeable gain	79,829

Disposal of shares

The chargeable gain is £38,300 (£150,000 – £111,700).

Total gains are £118,129 (£79,829 + £38,300). The CGT liability is minimised if the 2022-23 annual exemption is deducted from the gain arising on the disposal of the flat, leaving £67,529 (£79,829 - £12,300). CGT payable is [(28% × £67,529) + (20% × £38,300)] = £26,568.12.

(b) Mr More might contemplate the transfer of assets to Mrs More (at no gain, no loss). She could then dispose of them and any gain arising would be taxed in her name. For example, he could transfer the shares to her. If she then disposed of them and realised the gain of £38,300, this would be entirely covered by her losses brought forward and her annual exemption, so saving CGT of £7,660 (20% × £38,300).

Set C

Question C1

(a) The accounting periods concerned are the year to 31 March 2022 and the six months to 30 September 2022.

(b)

	y/e 31/3/2022 £	6 months to 30/9/2022 £
Trading profits (time apportioned)	460,000	230,000
Less: Capital allowances:		
AIA £121,000 + WDA 18% × £25,000	125,500	
WDA 18% × £20,500 × 6/12		1,845
Trading income	334,500	228,155
Income from property	20,000	10,000
Income from non-trading loan relationships:		
£200 + £200 + £100	500	
£1,200 – £100 + £445		1,545
Chargeable gains		8,300
	355,000	248,000
Less: Qualifying charitable donations	5,000	5,000
Taxable total profits (TTP)	350,000	243,000
Corporation tax @ 19%	66,500.00	46,170.00

Notes:

(i) The AIA maximum for the year to 31 March 2022 is £1m. The qualifying expenditure of £121,000 is within this figure. Cars do not qualify for AIA. It is assumed that the company claims maximum capital allowances for the year.

(ii) The year to 31 March 2022 coincides with FY2021. Therefore corporation tax is payable at the FY2021 main rate of 19%.

(iii) The six months to 30 September 2022 are wholly contained within FY2022. Therefore corporation tax is payable at the FY2022 main rate of 19%.

(c) The due date of payment for the year to 31 March 2022 is 1 January 2023. The due date of payment for the six months to 30 September 2022 is 1 July 2023. In each case, the payment date is nine months and one day after the end of the accounting period.

(d) If trading profits were £3,690,000 for the 18 months (i.e. £3m higher than originally stated) then TTP for the two accounting periods would be £2m higher and £1m higher respectively. The revised tax liabilities would be £446,500 and £236,170.

The company would be "large" for payment by instalments purposes in both accounting periods since augmented profits would exceed £1,500,000 in the year to 31 March 2022 and £750,000 (6/12 × £1,500,000) in the six months to 30 September 2022.

However, the company was not large in the 12 months before the year to 31 March 2022 so the corporation tax for this year would still fall due on 1 January 2023. Corporation tax for the six months to 30 September 2022 would be payable in two instalments of £118,085 each on 14 October 2022 and 14 January 2023.

Question C2

(a)

	y/e 31/7/20	9 mths to 30/4/21	y/e 30/4/22
	£	£	£
Trading income	2,050,000	260,000	-
Income from non-trading loans	51,600	39,000	28,700
Chargeable gains	-	-	8,700
	2,101,600	299,000	37,400
Less: Gift Aid donations	10,000	8,000	5,000
Taxable total profits (TTP)	2,091,600	291,000	32,400
Corporation tax liability (see note)	397,404	55,290	6,156

Notes:

(i) Capital losses carried forward at 31 July 2020 are £35,300 (£67,300 – £32,000). Therefore net chargeable gains for the year to 30 April 2022 are £8,700 (£47,000 – £35,300 – £3,000).

(ii) Corporation tax is at 19% throughout.

(b)

	y/e 31/7/20	9 mths to 30/4/21	y/e 30/4/22
	£	£	£
Trading income	2,050,000	260,000	-
Income from non-trading loans	51,600	39,000	28,700
Chargeable gains	-	-	8,700
	2,101,600	299,000	37,400
Less: Trading losses	525,400	299,000	37,400
	1,576,200	0	0
Less: Gift Aid donations	10,000	0	0
Taxable total profits (TTP)	1,566,200	0	0
Corporation tax liability (see note above)	297,578	0	0

Notes:

(i) Only three months of the year to 31 July 2020 fall into the 12 months prior to the loss-making period. Therefore loss relief in this year is restricted to £525,400 (£2,101,600 x 3/12).

(ii) Trading losses c/f are £33,200 (£895,000 – £37,400 – £299,000 – £525,400).

(c)

The reduction in the liability for the year to 31 July 2020 is £99,826 (£397,404 – £297,578) so the total tax saved as a result of the loss relief claims is £161,272 (£99,826 + £55,290 + £6,156). The amount of the loss relieved is £861,800 (£895,000 – £33,200). A tax saving of £161,272 on a loss of £861,800 represents an effective rate of relief of 18.71%.

Instead of claiming relief against total income, the company could have carried the entire loss forward to future years where "sizeable" profits are expected. This might generate relief at 25% (or even at the marginal rate of 26.5%) if the loss is carried forward beyond 1 April 2023. But if there are any doubts about the profits forecast, or if the company prefers to obtain loss relief as soon as possible, setting the trading loss against total income (as above) seems to be a reasonable approach.

Question C3

(a)	AA Ltd	BB Ltd	CC Ltd
	£	£	£
Trading profits	1,230,400	267,800	852,500
Income from non-trading loans	16,300	-	15,000
Property income	-	5,000	-
Chargeable gains	43,500	-	37,300
	1,290,200	272,800	904,800
Less: Gift Aid donations	5,200	1,000	4,800
Taxable total profits (TTP)	1,285,000	271,800	900,000
Corporation tax at 19%	244,150	51,642	171,000

The corporation tax liabilities of BB Ltd and CC Ltd are due for payment on 1 January 2024.

But AA Ltd has augmented profits of (£1,285,000 + £240,000) = £1,525,000 and this exceeds £1,500,000. So unless AA Ltd was not large in the previous 12 months, the company must pay tax by instalments. These instalments are due to be paid on 14 October 2022, 14 January 2023, 14 April 2023 and 14 July 2023. Each instalment is (£244,150 × 1/4) = £61,037.50.

But if AA Ltd was not large in the previous 12 months, instalments are not required and the corporation tax liability of £244,150 is payable on 1 January 2024.

(b) If the accounting period was the year to 30 September 2023, the first six months would fall into FY2022 and the remaining six months would fall into FY2023. The tax liability of AA Ltd would be (£1,285,000 × 6/12 × 19%) + (£1,285,000 × 6/12 × 25%) = £282,700. Similarly, the tax liabilities of BB Ltd and CC Ltd would have been £59,796 and £198,000.

Corporation tax for the year to 30 September 2023 is normally payable on 1 July 2024. But if instalments apply, the due dates are 14/Apr/23, 14/Jul/23, 14/Oct/23 and 14/Jan/24.

Question C4

	Main pool	SR pool	Allowances
	£	£	£
10 months to 31/3/23			
WDV b/f		153,190	40,880	
Additions ineligible for AIA			52,000	
Additions eligible for AIA	50,000		
AIA	50,000	-		50,000
FYA (£126,700 × 130%)				164,710
Disposals		(26,450)	(35,000)	
		126,740	57,880	
WDA @ 18%/6% × 10/12		19,011	2,894	21,905
WDV c/f		107,729	54,986	
Total allowances				236,615

Note: Maximum AIA for this ten-month period is (10/12 × £1,000,000) = £833,333.

TTP is (£1,429,530 + £156,945 – £137,260 – £236,615) = £1,212,600. The corporation tax liability is £1,212,600 × 19% = £230,394.

This would normally fall due on 1 January 2024 but augmented profits are (£1,212,600 + £137,260) = £1,349,860. This exceeds (10/12 × £1,500,000) = £1,250,000 so the company is "large" for the accounting period. If it was also large in the previous 12 months, instalments are required.

The first three instalments are each equal to (3/10 × £230,394) = £69,118.20 and these fall due on 14 December 2022, 14 March 2023 and 14 June 2023. The final instalment is the remaining £23,039.40 and this falls due on 14 July 2023.

Question C5

(a)

	£
Trading profits (£173,000 – £32,000)	141,000
Income from property	46,000
Chargeable gains (£6,400 – £1,400)	5,000
Qualifying charitable donations	(20,000)
Taxable total profits (TTP)	172,000

The tax liability is (6/12 × £172,000 × 19%) + (6/12 × £172,000 × 19%) = £32,680.00 and this is payable on 1 July 2023.

(b) The £1,500,000 profits limit which determines whether or not tax is payable by instalments is divided by (9 + 1) = 10, giving a limit of £150,000. Augmented profits (including dividends received but ignoring dividends from subsidiaries) are £172,000. This exceeds £150,000 so the company is "large" for the year.

Unless the company was not also large in the previous 12 months, the corporation tax liability is payable in four instalments of £8,170 (£32,680 × 1/4). These instalments fall due on 14 April 2022, 14 July 2022, 14 October 2022 and 14 January 2023.

Set D

Question D1

(a)

	£
Output VAT	
Sales	22,500
Discounted sale (£4,300 × 90% × 20%)	774
Import of equipment - reverse charge (£12,400 × 20%)	2,480
Fuel scale charge	73
Input VAT	
Purchases	(11,200)
Equipment input tax (£12,400 × 20%)	(2,480)
Bad debts (£1,400 × 20%)	(280)
Entertaining overseas customers (£960 × 1/6)	(160)
Motor expenses (£1,668 × 1/6)	(278)
VAT payable	11,429

Note: Bad debt relief is available only if six months have passed since payment was due.

(b)   Annual turnover is too high for the flat rate scheme (limit £150,000) but the cash accounting scheme and annual accounting scheme are both available. The cash accounting scheme would be most beneficial. Output tax would not be accounted for until payment was received from credit customers and bad debt relief would be automatic. There would be little impact on the recovery of input tax, since most purchases and expenses are paid for on a cash basis.

Question D2

The value of each lifetime gift after deduction of exemptions is as follows:

		Value before AE £	Current year AE £	Previous year AE £	Value after AE £
2016-17	Mother	60,000	3,000	3,000	54,000
2017-18	Father	60,000	3,000	-	57,000
2019-20	Nephew (£18,500 – £1,000)	17,500	3,000	3,000	11,500
2021-22	Gift to charity (exempt)	-	-	-	-

The first three gifts were PETs and the gift to the charity was an exempt transfer, so there was no lifetime tax liability in relation to any of these gifts. The tax liability on death is as follows:

(i)   **Gift to mother**. Chargeable transfers in the previous seven years were £275,000, so the nil-rate band available for this transfer is £50,000. IHT (before taper relief) is (£4,000 × 40%) = £1,600. Taper relief (5-6 years) at 60% is £960, so IHT due is £640.

(ii)   **Gift to father**. Chargeable transfers in the previous seven years were (£275,000 + £54,000) = £329,000, so the nil-rate band available is £nil. IHT (before taper relief) is (£57,000 × 40%) = £22,800. Taper relief (4-5 years) at 40% is £9,120, so IHT due is £13,680.

(iii)   **Gift to nephew**. Chargeable transfers in the previous seven years were (£275,000 + £54,000 + £57,000) = £386,000, so the nil-rate band available is £nil. IHT (before taper relief) is (£11,500 × 40%) = £4,600. Taper relief (3-4 years) at 20% is £920, so IHT due is £3,680.

(iv)   **Estate**. Chargeable transfers in the previous seven years were (£54,000 + £57,000 + £11,500) = £122,500, so nil-rate band available is £202,500. IHT due is (£97,500 × 40%) = £39,000.

Question D3

	UK income £	Income net of 15% tax £	Income net of 25% tax £	Total £
Trading income	175,000	-	-	175,000
Chargeable gains	5,000	-	-	5,000
Overseas property income	-	6,000	8,500	14,500
	180,000	6,000	8,500	194,500
Less: Gift Aid donations	7,500	-	-	7,500
Taxable total profits (TTP)	172,500	6,000	8,500	187,000
Corporation tax at 19%	32,775	1,140	1,615	35,530
Less: DTR	-	900	1,615	2,515
Corporation tax liability	32,775	240	0	33,015

Note: There is unrelieved foreign tax of [(£8,500 × 25%) – £1,615] = £510.

Question D4

A Ltd controls 75% or more of B Ltd (85%) and D Ltd (85% × 90% = 76.5%) so these three companies form a 75% group. C Ltd is a consortium company owned by A Ltd and E Ltd.

The trading loss incurred by C Ltd may be surrendered to A Ltd and E Ltd in proportion to their shareholdings in C Ltd. The trading loss incurred by D Ltd may be surrendered to A Ltd or B Ltd. The tax saving would be the same in both cases. It is assumed that the loss is surrendered to A Ltd. The corporation tax liability of each company is as follows:

	A Ltd	B Ltd	C Ltd	D Ltd	E Ltd
	£	£	£	£	£
Trading income	240,000	45,000	-	-	80,000
Loan interest	5,000	2,500	-	-	-
Overseas property income:					
£8,200 × 100/82	-	10,000	-	-	-
	245,000	57,500	-	-	80,000
Less: Gift Aid donations	1,000	500	-	-	1,000
	244,000	57,000	-	-	79,000
Less: Consortium relief:					
60% × £30,000	18,000	-	-	-	-
40% × £30,000	-	-	-	-	12,000
	226,000	57,000	-	-	67,000
Less: Group relief	25,000	-	-	-	-
Taxable total profits (TTP)	201,000	57,000	0	0	67,000
Tax @ 19%	38,190	10,830	0	0	12,730
Less: DTR	-	1,800	-	-	-
Corporation tax liability	38,190	9,030	0	0	12,730

Notes:

(i) UK dividends received do not form part of the receiving company's taxable profits.

(ii) DTR is the lower of the foreign tax suffered (£1,800) and the UK tax on the foreign income (£10,000 × 19% = £1,900), which is £1,800. In general, Gift Aid donations are set against UK income so as to maximise DTR. However, in this case, even if the Gift Aid donations were set against the foreign income, this would still leave a UK tax liability on that income of £1,805 (£9,500 × 19%) so DTR of £1,800 would still be available.

(iii) If the D Ltd trading loss of £25,000 were surrendered to B Ltd (instead of A Ltd) this would be set against the UK income. Otherwise, DTR of £1,800 would be lost.

Index